Averting 'The Final Failure'

Stanford Nuclear Age Series

General Editor, Martin Sherwin

Averting 'The Final Failure'

JOHN F. KENNEDY AND THE SECRET
CUBAN MISSILE CRISIS MEETINGS

Sheldon M. Stern

Stanford University Press, Stanford, California   2003

Acknowledgments

This book began, at least in my mind, some 22 years ago when I first listened to the ExComm tapes at the JFK Library. I came home one day especially intrigued by the October 26 morning discussion in which Adlai Stevenson, my hero in the 1950s, attempted with little success to overcome the hostility of his ExComm critics. I told my wife that a narrative account of these meetings would be a wonderful project. But, of course, the vast majority of the tapes from these historic thirteen days remained classified until late 1996 and early 1997. I decided, once the tapes were finally opened, to opt for early retirement as soon as I became eligible (late 1999) in order to write this book.

I am especially grateful for the support of friends who believed in the concept, read and criticized drafts and made many valuable suggestions. Special thanks go to Jim Cooke and Patricia Busacker, a great husband and wife team, and to Mary Beth Klee and Lawrence Leamer. Their advice at key points made the final version far more readable and interesting. Many others provided encouragement and ideas along the way, including Andrew Chaikin, Barton Bernstein, Robert Dallek, Stephanie Fawcett, Dan H. Fenn, Robert Gilbert, Fred Kaplan, Nick King, Sergei Khrushchev, Brian McGrory, Edwin Quattlebaum, Richard Norton Smith, John Wright—and the late Patty Farnsworth.

My friends and former colleagues at the Kennedy Library—Jim Cedrone, Allan Goodrich, James Hill, William Johnson, Sharon Kelly, Steven Plotkin, Maura Porter and Ronald Whealan—were invariably helpful, especially with my often impatient requests for information when they were coping with rooms full of researchers. Nicholas Graham at the Massachusetts Historical Society also provided welcome assistance.

I am particularly indebted to Muriel Bell, director of acquisitions at Stanford University Press, and Professor Martin Sherwin, general editor of the Stanford Nuclear Age Series, in which this book appears.

Finally, I can never adequately sum up the patience, endurance and love from my wife Helen, my daughter Jennifer and my son Jeremy, that sustained me throughout this project.

Jeremy, a historian in his own right, provided a perceptive eye and a particularly critical ear, which enriched the substance of the narrative at every stage and helped insure that the transcriptions would be as accurate as possible.

Sheldon M. Stern

Newton, Mass.

Contents

Foreword

Sheldon M. Stern, who served as the John F. Kennedy Library's historian for nearly two and a half decades and has studied the tapes of the Cuban missile crisis meetings for over twenty years, has given us the most accurate, complete and compelling account of the thirteen October days in 1962 that brought the world to the brink of a nuclear holocaust. There are no end of articles and books about this most dangerous crisis in human history. But Stern's *Averting 'The Final Failure': John F. Kennedy and the Secret Cuban Missile Crisis Meetings* is the best of these studies and will become the starting point for all future work on President Kennedy's response to the Soviet challenge in Cuba.

Stern's book is not simply another edition of the missile crisis tapes, though his transcriptions of the ExComm conversations are the most precise reconstruction of these often difficult to understand discussions. (As one who has listened to many of these tapes, I greatly admire those with the patience and skill to identify speakers and make sense of what they are saying.) Rather, as Stern persuasively argues, his book provides "a new avenue of access to . . . the secret ExComm meetings." His volume is "a comprehensive and interpretive narrative account of this gripping and unique primary source . . . [and] fills an important gap in the historical literature" by allowing us to reconsider "many conventional assumptions about the ExComm discussions." Most important, we gain a compelling portrait of JFK as impatient with "Cold War assumptions and convictions," and as a man, despite some "blind spots," with a healthy skepticism about military solutions to what he believed was mainly a political problem.

Stern also convincingly shows that it is not enough to either hear these complex conversations or study them from the printed page. Students of the missile crisis are better served by a narrative account constructed by someone intimately acquainted with the tapes and best able to "capture the flavor and mood . . . the depth and intensity" of the discussions. Stern's book fills this need. As important, it demonstrates that Kennedy's "often rough give-and-take with the ExComm played a decisive role in continuing to shape JFK's perceptions and decisions. . . . Even in the final days and hours of the crisis," Stern writes, "the Ex-Comm had an enormous . . . psychological impact on President Kennedy's commitment to averting nuclear war. Every major option was discussed, frequently in exhaustive and exhausting detail—providing both the context and indispensable sounding board for the President in making his final decisions."

No one reading Stern's book can doubt John Kennedy's well-justified reputation for good sense in the face of terrible dangers. Stern's narrative account will permanently secure JFK's reputation as an astute statesman in a time of unparalleled crisis. This volume will stand as essential reading for anyone who wants not only to understand the events of October 1962 but also how a president managed great international dangers in the service of long-term stability and peace.

Robert Dallek

Washington, D.C.
November 2002

Preface: The JFK Cuban Missile Crisis Tapes

In the summer of 1973, the nation was transfixed by the nationally televised "Watergate" hearings into charges of illegal activities by the Nixon White House. On July 16, in testimony before the Senate Watergate committee, presidential aide Alexander Butterfield dropped a Molotov cocktail into the highly combustible Watergate scandal by revealing that President Richard M. Nixon had installed a voice-activated taping system in the White House to secretly record his meetings and discussions. Congress then subpoenaed the tapes; the President refused to turn them over and instead released a set of strategically edited transcripts. Ultimately the Supreme Court ruled unanimously against Nixon—and the rest is history.

The day after Butterfield's revelation, in an announcement that attracted a great deal of media attention, the director of the Kennedy Library, Dan H. Fenn, Jr., revealed that audio recordings of meetings dealing with "highly sensitive national defense and foreign policy," as well as tapes of presidential telephone conversations, had also been made during the Kennedy administration.[1]

These tapes included most of the secret meetings of the Executive Committee of the National Security Council, convened by President Kennedy during the Cuban missile crisis in October 1962. The Ex-

---

[1]Arthur M. Schlesinger, Jr., special assistant to President Kennedy, had reflected the views of many of his former White House colleagues by dismissing the possibility of secret taping by JFK as "absolutely inconceivable. It was not the sort of thing Kennedy would have done. The people in the White House then would not have thought of doing something like that." (*Harvard Crimson*, July 27, 1973, 1, 6)

Comm recordings provide an incomparable chance to scrutinize history exactly as it unfolded during the most dangerous event in the four and a half decades of the Cold War. The purpose of this book is to tell the unique story of those meetings in narrative form for the first time, and particularly to document the substance and quality of JFK's leadership.

Most readers are familiar with the "heroic" version of the Cuban missile crisis—initially fashioned by journalists in the first years after the event, encouraged by JFK himself, popularized by the writings of Kennedy administration insiders like Arthur Schlesinger, Jr. and Theodore Sorensen, and given wide currency in dramatizations such as "The Missiles of October." In this version, the courageous young American president, always cool under fire, successfully resisted the aggressive designs of the Soviet Union and its puppet regime in Cuba to win a decisive victory over Communism. And, even more important, having learned sobering lessons on the nuclear brink, Kennedy reached out to the Soviet Union and Cuba (secretly) in his last year in office and began the process of détente—reflected in his June 1963 American University speech urging a rethinking of Cold War dogma, the establishment of the Moscow-Washington Hot Line and the negotiation and ratification of the Limited Nuclear Test Ban Treaty. This view, in far more sophisticated form, achieved academic legitimacy in 1971 with the publication of Graham Allison's *Essence of Decision*, which depicted JFK's handling of the missile crisis as a model for rational presidential crisis management in the nuclear age.

This heroic consensus did not last long. In the 1970s and the 1980s, in the wake of the Vietnam war and the expanding documentary record on national security issues, revisionist historians called attention to JFK's secret war against Cuba, particularly Operation Mongoose, which encompassed sabotage and subversion against the Cuban economy, plots to overthrow and/or assassinate Castro and "contingency plans" to blockade, bomb or invade Cuba. Kennedy's heroic management of the crisis, measured against a more complete historical record, appeared to be largely a myth.

In addition, especially after the fall of the Soviet Union, new evidence on the Soviet side of the story suggested that Khrushchev's original explanation for this dangerous gamble in Cuba had been fundamentally true: the Soviet leader had never intended the missiles in Cuba as an aggressive threat to the security of the United States, but rather as a defensive move to protect his Cuban allies from covert or overt

American attacks and as a desperate effort to give the U.S.S.R. relative parity in the nuclear balance of terror. And finally, these documents also demonstrated that the Kennedy administration, after October 1962, never backed away from plots to eliminate Castro.

Now, especially since the declassification of the tape recordings of JFK's secret meetings, scholars have had a rare opportunity to jump off the heroic vs. revisionist treadmill and forge a fresh, new and in-depth view of the most unique component of this historical event. In fact, until this book, virtually none of the crisis scholarship has systematically included or investigated the incomparable evidence found on these tapes. And, as it turns out, the ExComm meetings are far more interesting, complex and surprising than many of the heroic or revisionist protagonists ever imagined.

JFK, without question, bore a substantial share of the responsibility for the onset of the crisis,[2] but, when faced with the real probability of nuclear war, he used his formidable intellectual and political skill to prevent the outbreak of hostilities. The President helped steer American policy makers and ultimately the two superpowers away from an apocalyptic nuclear conflict. A hawk in public, he actually distrusted the military, was skeptical about military solutions to political problems and horrified by the prospect of nuclear war. The confrontational JFK sketched by revisionist historians is barely perceptible during the Cuban missile crisis meetings. With great deliberation and subtlety, the President measured each move and countermove with an eye toward averting a nuclear exchange—which he dramatically declared could be "the final failure."

Transcripts of these meeting tapes can be invaluable, but they must inevitably reflect the weakness and flaws of the tapes themselves: frequent interruptions, garbled and rambling exchanges, inexplicable noises, overlapping comments, conversational dead ends and a great deal of repetition. By their very nature, transcripts must endeavor to present *all* the words and are often dense, forbidding and impenetrable to the non-specialist. The interpretive narrative in this book, on the other hand, seeks to bring the discussions to life as a clear, coherent story for the first time, making the concentrated, distilled essence completely understandable to both the scholar and the general reader.

The narrative format also aims to transform this complex, often redundant primary source, the ExComm tapes, into a lucid, user-friendly

---

[2]This key question is discussed in detail in the Introduction.

secondary source by eliminating peripherals, concentrating on essentials and citing only the indispensable material. Readers can now follow consistent themes, ideas, issues and the role of specific individuals as never before possible. The key moments of stress, doubt, decision, resolution—and even humor—are, in effect, accentuated and underscored by separating them from the background chatter, repetition and substantive cul-de-sacs which characterize the unedited tapes. In addition, the author has chosen to transcribe many verbal false starts, to include colloquial speech and to highlight words emphasized or inflected by the speakers themselves to help the reader grasp as completely and accurately as possible the meaning, intent and human dimension of these impromptu discussions. The participants, obviously, did not know how this potential nuclear showdown would turn out, and their uncertainty, strikingly captured in narrative form, often gives the discussions the nerve-racking quality of a work of fiction. But, of course, this unique story—indelibly documented on audio tape—is history, not fiction.

Listening to the JFK Tapes

A quarter of a century after "Watergate" revealed the existence of presidential recordings, it is now widely acknowledged that some taping was done by every president from Franklin D. Roosevelt through Richard Nixon.[3] Hundreds of hours of tapes have been declassified, the vast majority from the Kennedy, Johnson and Nixon administrations. These White House recordings provide a distinctive glimpse into some of the most intimate moments of presidential history: FDR, during the 1940 presidential campaign, trying to persuade civil rights activist A. Philip Randolph to cancel a march on Washington against racial discrimination; JFK working to retain the support of former President and General Dwight Eisenhower during the Cuban missile crisis; Lyndon Johnson speculating with J. Edgar Hoover about the Kennedy assassination; and, of course, Richard Nixon discussing hush money for the Watergate burglars.

On the day of Jimmy Carter's inauguration, January 20, 1977, after more than a decade of teaching United States history on the college level, I was appointed Historian at the John F. Kennedy Library in Mas-

[3]Gerald Ford, on his first day as President, ordered the removal of all White House taping equipment. (Richard Norton Smith to Sheldon M. Stern, January 27, 2003)

sachusetts.[4] I spent the next few years researching classified materials as background preparation for conducting scores of taped oral history interviews; later I verified the accuracy of the transcripts. I also worked for several months editing JFK's recorded telephone conversations—my first in-depth experience listening to White House recordings.

Then, in 1981–82, as part of my preparatory research for a series of oral history interviews on foreign policy in the Kennedy administration, I began listening to the tapes of the Cuban missile crisis ExComm meetings. The Kennedy Library was also preparing for their eventual declassification and I was very likely the first non-member of the Ex-Comm to hear and evaluate precisely what happened at these meetings; I was definitely the first professional historian to review these tapes. In 1983, I received an award from the Archivist of the United States for "careful and perceptive editing" of the JFK tapes. This experience would prove to be the most important of my historical career.

It is difficult to capture the intellectual and physical demands of working on these tape recordings. I sat for many hours at a stretch, wearing headphones, in front of a Tandberg reel-to-reel tape deck, the state-of-the-art equipment of the period, my foot on a pedal that allowed me to fast-forward, reverse, play or stop the tape.[5] The clunky and heavy Tandberg unit was difficult to move and awkward to operate; and, since it lacked a real-time timer, locating a specific moment on a tape could be incredibly frustrating. The first time I put a tape on the deck and pressed the play button was unforgettable. The tape sounded like an FM radio station without frequency lock—the voices almost drowned out by intense background hiss. I was concerned at first that it might be impossible to ever understand these conversations. (Dolby noise reduction appeared later in the 1980s, but the Kennedy Library, as a matter of policy, never used any noise reduction technology in order to avoid adulterating the sound of the originals. I listened to copies made directly from the master tapes themselves.)

To complicate the task even further, the recordings are also marred by distracting and extraneous sounds: a smoker emptying his pipe into an ashtray on the table, water being poured from a pitcher into a glass, coughing, sneezing, nose-blowing and throat-clearing, a knock on the

[4]After an FBI investigation, I was granted the national security clearances required for access to Top Secret classified materials. This book, of course, does not refer to any portions of the tapes that remain closed

[5]Tandberg units may also have been used in the White House to make the Kennedy meeting recordings.

door, the ringing of a telephone, the siren of an emergency vehicle passing on the street, the shouts of children at play on the White House grounds, and, most frequently, secondary conversations and people talking at the same time. In addition, there were persistent clanking noises on many tapes which sounded remarkably like a venting steam radiator. I finally checked the weather page in the *Washington Post* and was able to rule out that possibility; it was too mild in Washington that week for White House radiators to have been overheating. To this day, I don't have a clue about the source of this irksome noise.

These auditory complications frequently required listening to the same words several dozen times (in some cases, unfortunately, to no avail). Some voices, it turned out, were much harder to pick up because the individuals were seated at the opposite end of the table from the microphones hidden in light fixtures on the wall behind the President's chair in the Cabinet Room. But, after a few very tense and exasperating days, I began to develop an ear for the task and patience for the work. To my great relief, I also discovered that the first tape I played had been unusually substandard. (Some tapes had likely deteriorated due to inadequate storage and preservation.) The project became progressively more fascinating and exhilarating, but always remained laborious. It required absolute and undivided concentration (for example, I routinely disconnected my telephone). I quickly learned that missing even a second or two could mean losing a key part of a conversation and that the misidentification of just one word could dramatically alter both the speaker's intent and the historical record. There is, after all, a world of difference between someone saying "ever" as opposed to "never," or "I think" as opposed to "I don't think."

The most important requirements for reviewing these tapes were a broad knowledge of the history of the period, familiarity with the background and views of the individuals involved, the ability to recognize voices (listening first to oral history interviews was often helpful) and the attentiveness to pick up even fragmentary details and remarks. Some voices were distinctive, such as the Boston twang of the Kennedy brothers or the soft southern drawl of Secretary of State Dean Rusk. However, the quality of the voices could vary from meeting to meeting depending on where an individual sat in relation to the microphone or even from slight imperfections in the speed at which the tape was recorded. The White House taping device, by our standards, was technically archaic and decidedly low fidelity. McGeorge Bundy, for example, a member of ExComm who obviously knew all the other participants, listened to a number of meeting tapes in the early 1980s and had trouble identifying the voices of several of his former colleagues.

The discussions did not move forward with the consistent momentum or progression of a board meeting with a written agenda; rather, they plodded back and forth, with a great deal of repetition and many dead ends. Many participants often spoke in grammatically awkward sentence fragments—no one more than JFK himself. They could be blindly self-righteous and cynical (discussing, for example, American covert actions against Cuba), but also remarkably idealistic (expressing moral qualms, for example, about a sneak attack on Cuba) . Often, the most important decisions, such as choosing the quarantine as the first step in the American response, happened without an explicit or overt statement at any recorded ExComm meeting. Everyone simply recognized that that the President had decided and adjusted their responses accordingly.

Likewise, on the issue that produced the most ExComm friction— JFK's support for Nikita Khrushchev's offer to trade the missiles in Turkey and Cuba—the tapes prove incontrovertibly that the President, surprisingly and ironically, found himself supported *at times* by advisers who were not his political or ideological allies or intimates, such as John McCone (a Republican with close ties to former President Eisenhower), George Ball (an Adlai Stevenson friend and loyalist) and the temperamental Lyndon Johnson. JFK's most trusted insiders, Robert Kennedy, McGeorge Bundy, Robert McNamara and Theodore Sorensen, as well as the second tier of advisers, Dean Rusk, Llewellyn Thompson, Maxwell Taylor and C. Douglas Dillon, generally opposed the trade.

Listening to these tapes, in any case, was the historian's ultimate fantasy—the unique chance to be the fly on the wall in one of the most perilous moments in human history—to know, within the technical limits of the recordings, *exactly what happened*. Even at the most frustrating moments, when, for example, I had to give up and accept that I could not understand a key remark or exchange, I realized how fortunate I was to have the privilege and responsibility of reviewing these one-of-a-kind historical records.

JFK's share of the culpability for the onset of the crisis does not diminish his cautious and thoughtful leadership once the crisis had reached a potentially fatal flashpoint. The ExComm tapes prove that John F. Kennedy played a decisive role in preventing the world from slipping into the nuclear abyss. If the ExComm decisions had been made by majority vote then war, very likely nuclear war, would almost certainly have been the result. Of course, as we now know, JFK did have some essential help from his counterpart in the U.S.S.R.; Khrushchev too, resisted pressure from his own military and his ally Fidel Castro to escalate the crisis.

There are, evidently, no Khrushchev tapes.[6] But, the Kennedy tapes present historians with a unique opportunity to accurately assess presidential leadership in the most perilous moment of the Cold War. Many presidents have faced extremely grave crises, but never before or since has the survival of human civilization been at stake in a few short weeks of extremely dangerous deliberations and never before or since have their unique and secret discussions been recorded and preserved. And, given the end of the Cold War and the breakup of the Soviet Union, the Cuban missile crisis will hopefully remain, for policy makers and scholars, the only "case study" of a full-scale nuclear showdown between military superpowers. The tapes clearly reveal that a peaceful resolution was far from inevitable; the crisis could easily have ended in catastrophe despite the best intentions of leaders in Washington and Moscow.

The national security clearances required to serve as Kennedy Library historian allowed me to listen to the tapes, but barred me from publishing anything or from speaking publicly about these classified materials. It was both exasperating and amusing, for example, when a prominent historian told me in the early 1980s that JFK had been the ultimate macho cold warrior in recklessly rejecting Khrushchev's offer to trade U.S. missiles in Turkey for Soviet missiles in Cuba. Of course, having already heard these tapes, I knew that JFK had pushed the missile trade despite strenuous opposition from nearly all his advisers. I could only say, "You may be in for some major surprises when these tapes are declassified." Some historians will resist these conclusions, but my response is to provide the most accurate citations and rest my case *on the evidence*.

Finally, many readers are undoubtedly aware that transcripts of the October 16–29 Cuban missile crisis tapes were published in 1997.[7] I

---

[6]"Unfortunately, Nikita Khrushchev did not bequeath a set of tapes of the crisis-era Presidium meetings to historians." (Aleksandr Fursenko and Timothy Naftali, "Soviet Intelligence and the Cuban Missile Crisis," in James G. Blight and David A. Welch, eds., *Intelligence and the Cuban Missile Crisis* (London, Frank Cass, 1998), 83)

[7]Ernest R. May and Philip D. Zelikow, eds., *The Kennedy Tapes: Inside the White House During the Cuban Missile Crisis* (Cambridge, Mass.: Harvard University Press, 1997).

discovered early in 2000, however, that these transcripts were marred by serious errors and wrote two articles documenting this indisputable fact.[8] The Miller Center at the University of Virginia has now prepared a revised and significantly improved set of missile crisis transcripts (through October 28).[9] Nonetheless, my examination of the new edition revealed that many troubling inaccuracies remain.[10]

Since there are so many examples in which our conflicting transcriptions affect the substance of the historical record, it would be impossible to identify and explain every case without overwhelming the flow and integrity of this ExComm narrative. Instead, this problem has been thoroughly addressed in the Appendix to this book.

Origins of the JFK Tapes

There is, regrettably, no definitive answer to the intriguing question of why President Kennedy installed the first effective White House taping system for recording discussions in the Oval Office and the Cabinet Room. Evelyn Lincoln, JFK's personal secretary in the Senate and later in the White House, recalled that the President was enraged after the April 1961 Bay of Pigs disaster when several advisers who had supported the invasion in closed meetings claimed later to have opposed it; she also maintained that the President simply wanted accurate records for writing his memoirs. These explanations of JFK's motives are more complementary than contradictory, but they fail to explain why he did not begin taping for more than a year after the 1961 Cuban fiasco.

Robert Bouck, the Secret Service agent who actually installed the recording devices, later claimed that the president personally asked him to set up the taping system but never mentioned a reason. Bouck speculated that JFK wanted a reliable record of conversations dealing with U.S.-Soviet relations. In any case, it seems reasonable to conclude that Kennedy's decision was triggered by a desire to create an accurate

---

[8]Sheldon M. Stern, "What JFK Really Said," *Atlantic Monthly* 285 (May 2000), 122–28 and "Source Material: The 1997 Published Transcripts of the JFK Cuban Missile Crisis Tapes: Too Good to be True?," *Presidential Studies Quarterly* 30 (September 2000), 586–93. In addition, see my exchange of letters with the editors, *Atlantic Monthly* 286 (August 2000), 13, and *Presidential Studies Quarterly* 30 (December 2000), 791–99.

[9]Philip Zelikow, Timothy Naftali, Ernest May, eds., *The Presidential Recordings: John F. Kennedy: Volumes 1–3, The Great Crises* (New York: W.W. Norton, 2001). This edition, however, verifies reliable starting times for most of the meetings.

[10]Sheldon M. Stern, "The JFK Tapes: Round Two," *Reviews in American History* 30 (2002), 680–88.

record of his administration for his personal use after he left the White House.[11]

In the early summer of 1962, Bouck installed taping systems in the Oval Office and the Cabinet Room. The actual recording device was confined to one of two rooms in the basement—either directly beneath the Oval Office or in Evelyn Lincoln's nearby private file room.[12] The President did not have access to the tape recorder itself; that is, he could not personally press the play, record, stop or rewind buttons. JFK could only turn the system on or off in the Oval Office by hitting a "very sensitive" switch concealed in a pen socket on his desk, in a bookend near his favorite chair or in a table in front of his desk. The Cabinet Room switch was installed on the underside of the conference table in front of JFK's chair. The Oval Office microphones were hidden in the desk knee well and in a table across the room; the Cabinet Room microphones were mounted on the outside wall directly behind JFK's chair in spaces that once held light fixtures.[13]

A separate Dictaphone taping system was installed in the Oval Office and possibly in the President's bedroom around September 1962, to record telephone conversations. When the President decided to record a call, he pressed a button on his desk to turn on a light on Evelyn Lincoln's desk; she then turned on the dictabelt recording system (which she could also activate on her own).

Bouck and another agent, Chester Miller, maintained the recording system in the Oval Office and Cabinet Room and changed the tapes. Since the reel-to-reel tapes could record for a maximum of about two hours, Bouck subsequently installed a second backup tape machine which was automatically activated if the first machine ran out of tape. "As a matter of fact," Bouck later added, "I seem to recall that for awhile I had a third stand-by machine." The agents put the tapes in a plain sealed envelope and turned them over to Mrs. Lincoln for storage in a locked cabinet near her White House desk. "It was my under-

[11]Robert Bouck Oral History Interview, 1976, Oral History Collection [hereafter OHC], John F. Kennedy Library [hereafter JFKL], 2.

[12]Bouck Oral History, 3; Bouck also installed a tape machine in a study in the Executive Mansion, but it was virtually never used.

[13]Robert Bouck Interview, 1995, cited in Seymour Hersh, *The Dark Side of Camelot* (New York: Little, Brown, 1998), 7–8; Stephanie Fawcett, "The JFK White House Recordings," Paper presented to the Society for Historians of American Foreign Relations, 1997, 2, 4–5. Bouck claimed in his Kennedy Library Interview that the Oval Office switch was "a little push button under the Oval Office desk." (5)

standing," Bouck recalled, "that from her appointment book she could pretty well tell what was on the tapes. She and the President had a very close liaison to when he was taping. I never really knew what he taped."[14]

On November 22, 1963, after receiving confirmation of the President's death in Texas, Robert Kennedy apparently instructed Bouck to disconnect the Oval Office–Cabinet Room taping system.[15] Some historians initially questioned whether the attorney general even knew about the secret tapes, but, given the intensely personal and intimate relationship between the Kennedy brothers, it is impossible to imagine that JFK would or could have kept such a secret from his most trusted adviser and confidant. In addition, new evidence, discussed below, has eliminated all doubts about RFK's knowledge of the tapes.[16]

The records of the Kennedy administration, including the tapes, were temporarily moved to the National Archives in Washington and later transferred to the Federal Records Center in Waltham, Massachusetts to await construction of the permanent John F. Kennedy Library in Boston. The Kennedy tapes, however, were not initially turned over with the materials covered by the deed of gift that donated President Kennedy's White House records to the federal government. Recordings of private family matters were permanently excluded from the deed.

Finally, in 1976, the tapes were legally deeded to the Kennedy Library and the National Archives. The Library listed its holdings of Presidential Recordings at 248 hours of meeting tapes and 12 hours of telephone dictabelts (about 4 additional hours were accessioned in 1998).[17]

[14]Bouck Oral History, 3–4. Unfortunately, "there appear to be no receipts, memoranda, letters, notes or other documents contemporary to the Kennedy administration that deal with the recordings systems and their installation." (Special Supplement to the Register of Presidential Recordings, April 15, 1985, JFKL, 53)

[15]This account, confirmed by Bundy, also claims that RFK was actually disconnecting the system when Lyndon Johnson entered the Oval Office. However, Robert Bouck denies that RFK was present. (Evan Thomas, Robert Kennedy: His Life (New York: Simon and Schuster, 2000), 276, 451)

[16]Bouck claims that JFK once asked Kenneth O'Donnell and David Powers to limit their use of profanity in the Oval Office. Former JFK Library director Dan Fenn, who also served in the Kennedy White House, believes JFK's tongue-in-cheek remark convinced these aides that a taping system existed. (Bouck Oral History, 13; telephone conversation with Dan H. Fenn, Jr., January 16, 2003) However, JFK had no reason to believe these recordings would ever be made public (see further discussion below).

[17]The meeting tapes, in addition to the Cuban missile crisis, cover a wide spectrum of domestic and foreign issues: such as civil rights, railroad work rules, the 1963 Nuclear Test Ban Treaty, the Soviet Union, Berlin, Latin America, India, Africa and Southeast Asia.

Since the original plan to build the Library on the campus of Harvard University was delayed and eventually abandoned, the tapes remained in the temporary Waltham site until the permanent Kennedy Library at Columbia Point in Boston opened in October, 1979.

Opening the JFK Tapes

Soon after President Kennedy's death, RFK appears to have asked Evelyn Lincoln to transcribe some tapes. She may have worked on them briefly, but Bouck does not believe that Lincoln did any transcribing. Eventually George Dalton, a junior naval officer detailed to the White House, with equipment supplied by Bouck, took over this task. Dalton, who "did not know most of the names and terms," produced some extremely inaccurate and fragmentary transcripts before abandoning the project sometime before the existence of the tapes was publicly confirmed in 1973.[18]

Bouck was clearly wrong, however, in suggesting that no transcripts were prepared before November 22, 1963.[19] A document recently found at the Kennedy Library by Timothy Naftali proves conclusively that RFK knew about the tapes and that some transcripts, possibly by Dalton, existed as early as August 9, 1963. On that date, Evelyn Lincoln apparently turned over 18 missile crisis transcripts to Robert Kennedy's secretary in the Justice Department—raising the intriguing possibility that RFK, and conceivably even JFK himself, might have seen some rough transcripts or even listened to some of the tapes in 1963.[20]

[18]Kenneth O'Donnell, JFK's White House appointments secretary, later claimed that his secretary transcribed some of the recorded meetings and provided copies for him and the President, but "he was not sure who else may have received copies." (*Harvard Crimson*, July 27, 1973, 6) However, O'Donnell's former secretary, Pauline Fluet, has denied transcribing or even knowing about the tapes. She also insisted that Evelyn Lincoln could not even take dictation and "could never have transcribed anything." On the other hand, she seemed certain that JFK would have told O'Donnell about the secret taping system. (Telephone conversation with Pauline Fluet, January 15, 2003); Bouck Oral History, 4, 14)

[19]Bouck Oral History, 5, 14.

[20]E. William Johnson, former Kennedy Library chief archivist, recalls that George Dalton was still working on transcripts in the early 1970s at the temporary Kennedy Library site in Waltham, Massachusetts. But, this newly discovered document indicates that Dalton, Lincoln or perhaps a Secret Service agent actually produced some transcripts during the Kennedy administration. However, the precise provenance of the still-classified "Dalton transcripts" may never be entirely unraveled. The attorney general's access to the tapes and these transcripts could explain the relatively accurate quotes from the ExComm meet-

In 1983, surviving members of the ExComm received letters advising them that the first recordings would soon be declassified. The first public opening of the missile crisis tapes took place soon after—just over 30 minutes of tape and sanitized transcripts of several hours from the first meeting on October 16—plus heavily edited transcripts from October 27, produced for the most part by McGeorge Bundy and donated to the Kennedy Library.[21] However, transcribing was soon abandoned entirely because of prohibitive costs (since about one hundred hours are required to accurately transcribe one hour of tape). In 1994, the Library released nearly six hours of tapes from the meetings of October 18–22. But, researchers were on their own with the raw tapes. In order to provide some guidance at each opening, I answered questions from historians and journalists purchasing the recordings on audio cassettes.

Finally, on October 24, 1996, the Library opened more than 15 additional hours of tapes, from the meetings of October 23–29, bringing the total to over 20 hours. This enormous technical task was coordinated by Stephanie Fawcett, senior archivist in charge of national security declassification. She and I listened to the tapes independently and spent many days trying to reconcile differences in transcriptions and interpretation. Given the magnitude of the release, and the lack of transcripts for researchers, I wrote a 20-page guide to the new tapes, including extensive quotes. The guide was distributed at a press conference at which I discussed the impact of the newly released tapes on the historiography of the crisis and again responded to questions from scholars and reporters.

Two hours of tapes from the October 16 meetings were then declassified in early 1997, completing the release of all tapes from the critical thirteen days. In 1999, the Library released three hours of tapes from the post-crisis meetings through November 6; in 2000, nine hours of tape were opened, covering the sessions through November 16; in mid-2001, seven additional hours of tape, from the meetings through November 19, were declassified; and finally, later in 2001, two hours of

---

ings in *Thirteen Days*. RFK may actually have originally intended to use the transcripts to prepare a book on the missile crisis for JFK's planned 1964 reelection campaign. (see Timothy Naftali, "The Origins of 'Thirteen Days,'" *Miller Center Report* 15 (Summer 1999), 23–24)

[21]Bundy was granted access to the tapes because of "his dual role in 1962 as national security advisor and Executive Committee meeting participant, and his current work as an historian." (Foreword, Cuban Missile Crisis Meetings Transcripts, JFKL, 1983)

tapes were released from the meetings on November 20, the day President Kennedy formally ended the missile crisis by lifting the naval quarantine around Cuba—bringing the total from October 16 to November 20 to about forty-three hours.

The Historical Value of the JFK Tapes

Since the Kennedy taping system was manually activated (not voice activated like Nixon's) it was easily derailed by human carelessness or error. JFK sometimes recorded trivial discussions but curiously failed to record critical meetings such as his Oval Office confrontation with Soviet Foreign Minister Andrei Gromyko during the first week of the missile crisis. He generally neglected to turn the machine on until after a meeting had begun and sometimes forgot to turn it off so that the tape ran out. In at least one case, the tape was left running after a meeting and recorded the chatter of the White House cleaning crew.

Inevitably, in our increasingly cynical era, analysts have questioned or even dismissed the historical value of the tapes made in both the Kennedy and Johnson administrations because the two presidents knew they were being recorded and presumably could have manipulated the outcome to enhance their historical reputations. This view has been repeated again and again: JFK seemed "open and straightforward" but the value of the tapes "can only be diminished by the fact that the two key players of the crisis [JFK and RFK] knew they were being recorded." The apparent neutrality of the tapes is doubtful because "we can never determine how much either man tailored what he said in order to control the historical record." The tapes are "selective and somewhat misleading because the president could turn his tape recorder on and off at will." Even the editors of the 1997 edition of published transcripts seemed concerned about "the President selectively choosing what to record for posterity."[22]

William Safire, columnist, author and one-time aide to President Nixon, pushed this argument much further in a specific response to the 1997 publication of transcripts of the missile crisis tapes. Safire declared that "the [JFK] tapes inherently lie. There pose the Kennedy

---

[22]Hersh, *Dark Side*, 7–8, 351; Zachary Karabell, "Roll tape . . . Inside the White House with JFK, LBJ—and Overhearing Everyone Else," *Boston Globe*, October 19, 1997, P 1,5; Gil Troy, "JFK: Celebrity-in-Chief or Commander-in-Chief?" *Reviews in American History* 26 (1998), 634; May and Zelikow, *The Kennedy Tapes*, 691.

brothers knowing they are being recorded, taking care to speak for history—while their unsuspecting colleagues think aloud and contradict themselves the way honest people do in a crisis." The ExComm tapes, Safire insisted, "do not present pure, raw history" since JFK knew the tape was rolling and could "turn the meetings into a charade of entrapment—half history-in-the-making, half-image-in-the-manipulating. And you can be sure of some outright deception . . . [by] the turning-off of the machine at key moments."[23]

This argument is plainly groundless:

First: perhaps, just perhaps, in a recorded phone conversation between two people, it might be possible to manipulate the discussion somewhat to shape the outcome (as in the case of Linda Tripp and Monica Lewinsky). But, in a large meeting of some 15 people, operating under enormous stress and tension, it would be tactically and physically impossible. JFK could turn the tape machine on and off in the Cabinet Room—the switch was under the table in front of his chair—but he did not have access to the fast-forward, rewind, play or record buttons that he would need for selective recording. And, even if he did have those controls, how would he have kept the participants from seeing what he was doing? Imagine, for example, that JFK wanted to edit out remarks made by Robert McNamara and said, "Wait a minute, Bob, my shoe is untied," and reached under the table to rewind the tape and erase McNamara's words. Of course he had no way of knowing when to stop since there was no visible counter and he could not have seen one anyway unless he stuck his head under the table.

Second: JFK would never in his wildest imagination have conceived of the possibility that we, the public, would ever hear these tapes. He thought of them, quite correctly, as private property and of course

[23]William Safire, *New York Times*, October 12, 1997, Section 4, 15. Philip Zelikow and Ernest May report that "Three tapes were received by the [Kennedy] library with reels containing 'separate tape segments.' It is possible that they had been cut and spliced," possibly to eliminate references to plots against Fidel Castro. (Zelikow and May, *The Presidential Recordings*, v. 3, xx) However, Allan Goodrich, the Kennedy Library's senior audiovisual archivist, now concludes after reviewing the original archival processing notes that these reels "had two different types of tape—*Scotch* and *Ampex*—wound on them, and were not spliced together. This was obvious to us . . . since they were of different color. We spliced the two together in order to make masters. When we did, we realized that the segments were different meetings. How they came to be wound that way is something that maybe George Dalton could explain. We don't have a clue." (Allan Goodrich to Sheldon M. Stern, April 12, 2002)

could not foresee the Freedom of Information Act, "Watergate" and the Presidential Records Act which ultimately facilitated the opening of these confidential materials. He could have picked and chosen freely from the tapes when he wrote his memoirs—ignoring the frequent references to classified national security material and the potentially compromising personal and political remarks (especially on the recorded telephone conversations). Why would he need to "control" the content of the tapes when he was certain that historians and the public would not hear them unless he or his estate granted access to this portion of his personal property?[24]

Third: Safire seems to have forgotten that the President he worked for, Richard Nixon, knew that he was being recorded and nevertheless did *not* try to tailor his remarks for the tapes. As we all know, he repeatedly incriminated himself. Why? Because even well into the "Watergate" investigation and hearings, he never thought that he would or could be compelled by the courts to release these personal and confidential recordings to the public. If he had believed it early enough, he could easily have destroyed the tapes and likely have saved his presidency.

Fourth: the most critical point, however, demonstrates that Safire's argument is fatally flawed by what historians call "presentism." JFK and the other missile crisis participants, we should never forget, *did not know the outcome of the crisis when they were in the middle of dealing with it.* Even if President Kennedy had tried, as Safire puts it, to "pose" for history, how could he have known which position taken during the discussions would ultimately be judged favorably by historians? What if, for example, the Russians had responded to the blockade, as the Joint Chiefs had warned, by carrying out low-level bombing raids in the southeastern U.S. or by launching the operational nuclear missiles in Cuba at the American mainland? Historians today would still be listening to the same tapes (assuming any tapes or historians had survived), but with a radically different outlook. It would then be the Chiefs who had turned out to be right: the blockade would have

[24]"All actions taken with respect to the recordings from November 22, 1963 to May 6, 1976 [the date of transfer to the National Archives] were taken under the assumption that the materials were private property and that the executors of the Kennedy estate were fully within their legal and customary rights to examine the material prior to deciding which, if any of it, to withhold from the materials delivered to the National Archives for deposit in the Kennedy Library under the deed of gift." (Special Supplement, JFKL, 56)

proven to be, as they had declared, a feeble and inadequate measure, and air strikes to neutralize the airfields and missile sites—which we laud Kennedy for resisting—would appear to have been the correct course after all. In other words, the same tapes could now be interpreted to make Kennedy look appallingly negligent rather than diplomatically reasonable, *if the outcome had been different.*[25]

Alternatively, what if Khrushchev had not agreed on October 28 to remove the missiles, and the bombing and invasion planned for later that week had gone forward? Even assuming that Kennedy and Khrushchev could have avoided using nuclear weapons, a shaky assumption at best, there would still have been substantial casualties on both sides before some kind of cease-fire was *perhaps* reached through a neutral third party like the United Nations. Today, some scholars would denounce JFK for not demonstrating American firmness and grit by immediately attacking the missiles and drawing a "line in the sand" which would have deterred the Soviets from risking any military response; others would condemn President Kennedy for bombing and invading Cuba instead of publicly or privately agreeing to Khrushchev's secret proposal to swap the Turkish and Cuban missiles. Again, the same tapes could then be interpreted to make Kennedy look weak and indecisive on the one hand, or irresponsible and reckless on the other, *if the outcome had been different.*

Robert Kennedy's words on the tapes further highlight the fact that the participants could not know what position would seem "right" in the 20/20 vision of hindsight. RFK clearly knew of the taping system; but, during the meetings he took a generally hawkish stance, pushing for a tough strategy that would remove Castro and demonstrate American resolve to the Soviets. Yet, when he decided to write a book on the missile crisis (published posthumously) and to run for president in 1968, he downplayed his aggressive posture, painting himself as a persistent dove and conciliator. RFK knew only *after* the crisis had been resolved that a dovish position was "better" politically, and that having

[25]The editors of the 1997 Harvard Press transcripts have revised their position, "Kennedy could not know how the crisis or discussions would come out, so he would not know what to say that would make him look good." (Ernest R. May and Philip D. Zelikow, "Camelot Confidential," *Diplomatic History* 22 (Fall 1998), 649) Similarly, in the 2001 Norton edition, the editors concluded that JFK had no way of knowing which 1962 viewpoint "would look good to posterity." (Zelikow, *et al.*, *The Presidential Recordings*, v. 3, xxiii)

pursued a peaceful solution in 1962 would later seem very appealing to a nation divided by the Vietnam War.[26] He could not manipulate his image on the tapes any more than his brother since neither of them knew what was going to happen the next day or even the next hour.[27]

JFK, of course, also understood that history is not a play. There is no script. As he told the ExComm when the perilous naval quarantine around Cuba was about to be implemented, "What *we* are doing is throwing down a card on the table in a game which we don't know the ending of." President Kennedy and the ExComm, notwithstanding their Cold War ideological convictions and blinders, had no choice but to deal with the stress and danger in the situation at hand to the best of their abilities—with no guarantee of success or even survival.[28]

[26]Thomas, *Robert Kennedy*, 232. Robert F. Kennedy, *Thirteen Days: A Memoir of the Cuban Missile Crisis* (New York: W.W. Norton, 1999), 26–84. Theodore Sorensen essentially constructed this extraordinarily influential book, which has never been out of print, from RFK's notes.

[27]When RFK met with Soviet ambassador Dobrynin late on the evening of October 23 and angrily defended the U.S. decision to stop Soviet ships heading to Cuba, he nonetheless grimly admitted "I don't know how all this will end, but we intend to stop your ships." (Alexander Fursenko and Timothy Naftali, *"One Hell of a Gamble": Khrushchev, Castro, and Kennedy, 1958–1964* (New York: W.W. Norton, 1997), 253)

[28]The film "Thirteen Days," released in 2000, purports to dramatize the very meetings considered here. The script concocts a crucial role in the ExComm meetings for JFK aide Kenneth O'Donnell; this claim is pure fiction. The film does not even reveal that President Kennedy was taping the discussions, ignores the covert actions against Castro as well as Khrushchev's motives for placing the missiles in Cuba and inaccurately casts Robert Kennedy as a consistent dove (in line with RFK's book, but *not* with the tapes). As this volume demonstrates, the real story of these meetings is infinitely more exciting, compelling and revealing than anything Hollywood could invent.

"Now the question *really* is what action we take which *lessens* the chances of a nuclear exchange, which obviously is the final failure."

President John F. Kennedy, October 18, 1962

Introduction: The Making of the Cuban Missile Crisis

The Cold War: JFK's Crucible

The Cold War is over. The Soviet Union no longer exists. Global nuclear war between the two superpowers never happened. Anyone who had dared to predict in 1962 that these three assertions would become historical fact just over a quarter century after the dangerous Cold War confrontations of the Kennedy administration would have seemed hopelessly naïve or just plain foolish.

For young Americans of the early twenty-first century, unlike their counterparts from the mid 1940s into the early 1990s, the Cold War is no longer a perilous fact of everyday life but an increasingly remote historical curiosity—much like World War II or the Great Depression. Students find it almost impossible to understand that many Americans were entirely serious when they put bumper stickers on their cars reading, "Better Dead Than Red," or that public opinion surveys taken in the early 1960s revealed that most Americans thought that war—that is, nuclear war—with the Soviet Union was inevitable. Indeed, black and white film footage of schoolchildren attempting to protect themselves from nuclear attack by crouching under their desks and covering their heads with their arms, often evokes not merely disbelief, but even laughter.

The United States and the Soviet Union had been allies only a generation before during the historic struggle against Nazi Germany in World War II. It had, of course, been an alliance of necessity, the ultimate example of the dictum that politics makes strange bedfellows. Both sides, despite mutual suspicion and distrust, recognized that the defeat of the common enemy came first. The alliance had begun to crumble well before the death of President Franklin D. Roosevelt in April 1945, and the surrender of Hitler's Germany less than a month later.

On April 23, for example, the new President, Harry S Truman, in office for only eleven days, chose to "get tough" with the U.S.S.R. and shocked even some of his own advisers by tongue-lashing Soviet foreign minister Vyacheslav Molotov in the White House about Stalin's failure to implement the February 1945 Yalta agreements on Poland.[1] Truman, almost at once, seemed hostile to the more cautious and flexible outlook of FDR. Tensions continued to escalate during the Potsdam Conference in July as well, where Truman learned secretly of the successful test of the atomic bomb and the increasingly suspicious Allies warily crafted the joint occupation of Germany.

Historians remain divided about whether the United States or the Soviet Union was more responsible for the onset of the Cold War. A debate has raged for decades about whether President Truman authorized the use of the atomic bomb against Japan to save American (and Japanese) lives by ending the war quickly or was instead engaging in "atomic diplomacy" to convince the communist world that America had used nuclear weapons once and would not be afraid to use them again to assure U.S. domination of the postwar world. The idealistic language of this new American internationalism clearly masked a determined drive for political and economic hegemony at the dawn of the nuclear era.

Evidence released from archives in the former Soviet Union, however, has further highlighted the role of Joseph Stalin, the Soviet dictator whose reign of terror consumed the lives of many millions of his own people even *before* World War II:

> For the more we learn, the less sense it makes to distinguish Stalin's foreign policies from his domestic policies or even his personal behavior. Scientists have shown the natural world to be filled with examples of what they call 'self-selection across scale': patterns that persist whether one views them microscopically, macroscopically, or anywhere in between. Stalin was like that: he functioned in much the same manner whether operating within the international system, within his alliances, within his country, within his party, within his personal entourage, or even within his family. The Soviet

[1] Charles E. Bohlen, *Witness to History, 1929–1969* (New York: W.W. Norton, 1973), 213.

leader waged Cold War on all these fronts. The Cold War *we* came to know was only one of many from *his* point of view. . . . [Stalin's] personal propensity for Cold Wars . . . [was] firmly rooted long before he had ever heard of Harry Truman.[2]

"Since the system Stalin founded could never be sufficiently secure either internally or externally," it would be a mistake to portray the Soviet dictator as a mere reactor to outside events. The Soviet worldview was the product of a historical experience "dramatically different from that of the West" and American revisionist historians have often failed to recognize that Stalin combined "imperial expansionism . . . [and] traditional Russian messianism" with Marxist "ideological proselytism." He believed absolutely in the "special mission of the Russians: to be a world power, second to none":[3]

A devout believer in ruthless state power, Stalin was a child of the Russian Revolution with its apocalyptic belief in the catastrophic destruction of the old world in purifying flames and the emergence of a new millennium. For Stalin there were always two worlds, not one: his empire, born in the Russian Revolution and representing the Kingdom of Light and the force of the future; and the dying—therefore desperate and aggressive—world outside, against which he wanted to protect it. Any opposition to him from within was perceived as a black threat; any opposition from beyond Soviet borders represented the decadent taint of a passing order.[4]

Stalin's suspicions and xenophobia dictated the need for a physical buffer between the borders of the Soviet Union and Western Europe (especially Germany) and he took full advantage of post-war chaos and exhaustion to prop up Soviet satellite governments in Albania, Bulgaria, Czechoslovakia, Hungary, Poland, Romania and the Eastern zone of divided and occupied Germany. "Stalin at the end of the war was a quiet, aged, but very dangerous man. . . . who was pushing the reluctant and tired country to defy the West."[5]

The U.S. and its European allies quickly concluded that it would be dangerous, and probably impossible, to force the Soviets out of Eastern

[2]John Lewis Gaddis, *We Now Know: Rethinking Cold War History* (New York: Oxford University Press, 1997), 293–94.

[3]Vojtech Mastny, *The Cold War and Soviet Insecurity* (New York: Oxford University Press, 1996), 6; Vladislav Zubok and Constantine Pleshakov, *Inside the Kremlin's Cold War: From Stalin to Khrushchev* (Cambridge, Mass.: Harvard University Press, 1996), 2–4, 17.

[4]Zubok and Pleshakov, *Inside the Kremlin's Cold War*, 12.

[5]*Ibid.*, 11.

Europe. The Truman administration, also concerned about potential Soviet footholds in Iran, Greece and Turkey, initiated a policy of "containment," a term popularized in a 1947 article by State Department Soviet specialist George F. Kennan.

These historic events and decisions defined the beginnings of the Cold War: a struggle between the communist nations, led by the U.S.S.R., and the capitalist democracies of the West, led by the U.S., a struggle fought with escalating military budgets, propaganda and covert operations, wars by proxy, and the use of military and economic aid to influence or win over uncommitted or neutral nations. By 1946, the term "Cold War" had entered the American vocabulary, along with phrases such as "the iron curtain" (coined in a speech that year in Missouri by Winston Churchill).

In February 1946, in his first speech since the end of the war, Stalin declared that it was impossible to achieve peaceful coexistence "'in the contemporary capitalist conditions of world economic development.' . . . From that moment many in the United States regarded Stalin's speech as the declaration of the Cold War."[6] The speech prompted George Kennan's renowned "Long Telegram" from Moscow, warning the Truman administration: "we have here a political force committed fanatically to the belief that with the U.S. there can be no permanent modus vivendi." However, he added, "Impervious to logic of reason, it is highly sensitive to logic of force. . . . Thus, if the adversary has sufficient force and makes clear his readiness to use it, he rarely has to do so."[7] John F. Kennedy, first elected to Congress later that year, would soon become an articulate representative of the new generation of World War II veterans and Cold War leaders determined to heed Kennan's advice to avoid repeating the appeasement of the 1930s and instead achieve victory in what they perceived as a life-and-death struggle against international communism.

During the second half of the 1940s, due largely to the surprisingly effective political leadership of President Truman, the United States reversed its traditional political and military isolationism and abandoned its reluctance to become directly involved in the internal affairs of Europe.[8] A series of ground-breaking policy decisions rapidly shaped

[6]*Ibid.*, 35.

[7]George Kennan, "Telegraphic Message from Moscow," February 22, 1946, *Foreign Relations of the United States* [hereafter *FRUS*] VI: *Eastern Europe and the Soviet Union* (Washington, D.C.: United States Government Printing Office, 1969), 696–709.

[8]Political and military isolationism had not included economic isolationism—as demon-

the new Cold War era: the Truman Doctrine, based on the premise that U.S. security interests were now international, received bipartisan support in Congress in 1947 for granting economic and military aid to governments threatened by "armed minorities or by outside pressures"—reflexively believed to be instigated by the Soviet Union. In the same year Congress approved the Marshall Plan which supplied 13 billion dollars between 1947 and 1951 to rebuild war-ravaged Europe, promote free-market economic and industrial growth and undermine political support for communist parties and movements. The U.S. offered assistance to all European nations—assuming that the U.S.S.R. would likely refuse. Indeed, Soviet intelligence operatives reported to Moscow that the U.S. was actually working behind the scenes "to bring the Western zones of Germany into the plan and keep the Soviet Union out of it" and Molotov detected a plot to construct "'a strategic circle around the U.S.S.R.'" In fact, although the offer "was deeply subversive of Stalin's hegemonial concept of international order," Soviet foreign ministry officials seriously considered and initially favored the program. Young Congressman John Kennedy vigorously supported the Marshall Plan.[9]

Berlin quickly became the focal point of Cold War tensions. The victorious allies had divided the defeated German Reich into four zones of occupation (American, British, French and Soviet). In June 1948, President Truman reached accords with Britain and France to merge their three zones of occupation into a new republic of West Germany. This agreement included West Berlin, the sector of the German capital occupied by the three Western allies, despite the fact that it was located deep within the Soviet (Eastern) zone. Understandably fearful of a strong new Germany and suspicious of Allied plans to print their own currency, Stalin almost impulsively decided to attempt to remove the Western powers from their Berlin outpost in the Soviet zone by incrementally imposing an economic blockade against the Western sectors of Berlin.[10]

Truman, to preserve allied rights without military force if possible, ordered a massive airlift (Stalin had not restricted or closed air access) to bypass the roads, rail lines and waterways blocked by the Soviets; he

strated by the hollowness of Woodrow Wilson's calls for neutrality "in thought as well as deed" from 1914 to 1917.

[9]Zubok and Pleshakov, *Inside the Kremlin's Cold War*, 105; Mastny, *The Cold War*, 27.

[10]Mastny, *The Cold War*, 47–48.

also sent sixty nuclear-capable bombers to England. Two million people were supplied with food, fuel and other necessities by a quarter of a million flights round the clock—demonstrating to Stalin and the world the "stunning superiority" of U.S. air power. The Soviet leader finally lifted the blockade in May 1949. The previous month, a dozen Western Europe nations, desperate for a nuclear umbrella against the U.S.S.R. and security against a resurgent Germany, had established the North Atlantic Treaty Organization to provide for collective defense—an attack on any member nation would be regarded as an attack on all member nations. The division of Germany, symbolized especially by the tenuous Allied access to West Berlin, became the emblem of an increasingly acrimonious Cold War which might become hot at a moment's notice.[11]

1949 was a decisive year in the evolution of the Cold War: the U.S.S.R. tested its first atomic bomb, shattering the American nuclear monopoly which had existed since the end of World War II; Mao Zedong's communist forces seized control of mainland China; the U.S. joined NATO—the first "peacetime" military/mutual security alliance with Europe in American history—creating a powerful deterrent to potential Soviet incursions into central and western Europe.[12]

Early the next year, President Truman asked the National Security Council (established in 1947) to undertake a comprehensive study of American foreign policy for the new Cold War era. The resulting report, NSC-68, first drafted in April 1950, argued that the United States had to assume world leadership in resisting the spread of communism and concluded that the future of mankind would be determined by the outcome of this struggle against "communist slavery." NSC-68 advocated a vastly expanded military, a nearly four-fold increase in the defense budget and a dedication to the Cold War as a real war for the survival of freedom itself. This commitment to a Manichean showdown between good and evil had a profound influence on the generation that had fought in World War II and would be powerfully echoed in JFK's Inaugural Address eleven years later.[13]

[11]Mastny, *The Cold War*, 47–49; Zubok and Pleshakov, *Inside the Kremlin's Cold War*, 51–52.

[12]The U.S.S.R. formalized the Warsaw Pact alliance of the communist states of Eastern Europe in 1955.

[13]This harsh Cold War rhetoric is often dismissed as nothing more than self-serving, hysterical paranoia. JFK, specifically, has been accused of "Arrogance, ignorance, and impatience combined with familiar exaggerations of the Communist threat." (Thomas G.

Just two months after approval of the NSC-68 Jeremiad, the Cold War suddenly turned hot when North Korea invaded South Korea in June 1950. President Truman and his key foreign policy advisers, convinced that the invasion was meant to test western resolve and determined to avoid repeating the fatal errors at Munich, sent American military forces to Korea under United Nations command.[14] The intervention of Communist Chinese ground forces led to several years of bloody fighting until the new Eisenhower administration negotiated a fragile truce in 1953.

Documents released from archives in the former Soviet Union have confirmed that the plan to invade South Korea originated with North Korea's dictator Kim Il-Sung. Stalin, after initial reluctance, did endorse the "reunification of Korea" and supplied North Korea with

Paterson, "John F. Kennedy's Quest for Victory and Global Crisis," in Thomas G. Paterson, ed., *Kennedy's Quest for Victory: America's Foreign Policy, 1961–1963* (New York: Oxford University Press, 1989), 23) However, recently declassified Soviet documents, many available on the Website of the Cold War International History Project, have demonstrated that the U.S.S.R. ran a massive espionage network which infiltrated the highest levels of the State Department, the secret atomic weapons program at Los Alamos, New Mexico and even included a special assistant to FDR. The American Communist Party, controlled and financed by the U.S.S.R., was irrevocably committed to undermine and destroy democratic institutions in the United States. Senator Joseph McCarthy was an unscrupulous demagogue and McCarthyism was tragic and unnecessary, but the threat was not imaginary. Indeed, many of the most dangerous spies were unknown to McCarthy and never prosecuted because intelligence officials were determined to conceal the VENONA Project which had decoded secret Soviet messages during World War II. McCarthy, ironically, had no knowledge of the VENONA Project. See, for example, Harvey Klehr, John Earl Haynes and Kyrill M. Anderson, *The Soviet World of American Communism* (New Haven: Yale University Press, 1998); John Earl Haynes and Harvey Klehr, *Venona: Decoding Soviet Espionage in America* (New Haven: Yale University Press, 1999); Allen Weinstein and Alexander Vassiliev, *The Haunted Wood: Soviet Espionage in America— The Stalin Era* (New York: Random House, 1999). The record of world communism, massively documented by these blood-soaked regimes themselves, incontrovertibly proves that it *did* make a difference, despite the many failings of Western capitalist democracies, which side won the Cold War. See Stephane Courtois, *et al.*, *The Black Book of Communism: Crimes, Terror, Repression* (Cambridge, Mass.: Harvard University Press, 1999).

[14]The symbolism of Munich and appeasement haunted the generation shaped by World War II and the Cold War. But, the lessons of Munich were more personal than abstract for the young John Kennedy: his Harvard honors thesis, "Appeasement at Munich," had been published as *Why England Slept* just after the fall of France in 1940. His father, Joseph P. Kennedy, had also been politically disgraced by supporting British isolationism and appeasement as ambassador to England from 1938 to 1940. Even by 1960, the elder Kennedy's public appearances were carefully curtailed because of the fear that the sins of the father would be visited upon the son. Former President Truman, for example, responding to questions about Kennedy's Catholicism, quipped, "It's not the Pope I'm afraid of, it's the pop." (David McCullough, *Truman* (New York: Simon and Schuster, 1992), 970)

money, arms, ammunition, training, fighter planes and Soviet pilots—but no ground troops. Mao Zedong, despite having concluded a formal alliance with the U.S.S.R. in February, was more skeptical—fearing that a war in Korea could give the West a pretext for attacking and overthrowing the new communist regime in China (exactly the policy soon advocated by General Douglas MacArthur). Some Cold War scholars now conclude that although the invasion of South Korea was not consciously intended to test Western firmness, Stalin would probably have interpreted the failure to respond as a green light for further military adventurism. Truman's instinctive interpretation of Stalin's motives was apparently closer to being right than wrong.[15]

In fall of 1956, a serious breach in western unity resulted when Britain and France joined Israel to prevent Egyptian nationalist Gamal Nasser, already friendly to the U.S.S.R., from controlling the Suez Canal. The Eisenhower administration denounced the invasion and eventually used tough diplomatic pressure to force its erstwhile allies to withdraw from Suez. Only days after the British-French invasion of Suez, however, the Soviets sent troops and tanks into Hungary to crush a popular democratic uprising and the United States refused to intervene. Europeans concluded, mistakenly as it turned out, that the Soviets had used force in Hungary because of the American failure to back their vital interests in Suez. Not surprisingly, European concerns that the United States would not risk war on their behalf surfaced repeatedly during the Cuban missile crisis ExComm discussions—particularly in relation to NATO suspicions that the U.S. would make a deal involving Turkey with the U.S.S.R.—to the detriment of European security.[16]

Exactly a year later, the Soviet Union stunned the West by successfully launching *Sputnik*, the first man-made satellite to orbit the earth. The Eisenhower administration, alarmed about the U.S.S.R.'s apparent technical superiority, created the manned space program in 1958. But, *Sputnik* also seemed to prove that the Soviets were capable of developing effective ICBM technology, and "called into question, to an un-

---

[15]See Kathryn Weathersby, "New Findings on the Korean War," *Cold War International History Project Bulletin 3* [hereafter *CWIHPB*] (Fall 1993), 1, 14–18 and "New Evidence on the Korean War," *CWIHPB* 6–7 (Winter 1995–96), 30–125; Zubok and Pleshakov, *Inside the Kremlin's Cold War*, 54–55, 62–64.

[16]See Csaba Békés, "New Findings on the 1956 Hungarian Revolution," *CWIHPB* 2 (Fall 1992), 1–3 and Mark Kramer, "New Evidence on Soviet Decision-Making and the 1956 Polish and Hungarian Crises," *CWIHPB* 8–9 (Winter, 1996–97), 358–84.

precedented degree . . . the credibility of the U.S. strategic guarantee, the foundation of Western defense in the Cold War." Despite pervasive doubts about the reliability and deterrent value of first-generation American IRBMs, the administration, largely for political and symbolic reasons, offered these weapons to the NATO allies to "offset the IRBMs that U.S. intelligence expected the Soviets to deploy in Europe in the near future." NATO members were slow to embrace the proposals, but agreements were ultimately reached to deploy Thor missiles in England and Jupiter missiles in Italy and Turkey.[17]

The Kremlin, in 1958 and again in 1959, worked vigorously but unsuccessfully, in public and in private, to head off the NATO IRBM deployment. "Within the Kremlin walls, however, the IRBMs would continue to rankle." President Eisenhower himself, at a June 1959 White House meeting, conceded that the Jupiter deployment could be very unsettling for the U.S.S.R., and acknowledged that if the Soviets made a comparable move in Mexico or Cuba, "it would be imperative for us to take positive action, even offensive military action."[18]

Nuclear Confrontation in Cuba

Eisenhower was indeed prescient. The most perilous crisis of the Cold War would occur thousands of miles from Europe or Berlin and just ninety miles off the coast of southern Florida.[19] In the first hours of 1959, the Cuban guerrilla movement led by Fidel Castro ousted the brutal and corrupt regime of Fulgencio Batista, a pro-American military dictator with ties to United States business interests and the Mafia. Initially, Castro seemed a heroic figure to many Americans. At the 1959 New Year's Eve celebration in Manhattan's Times Square, when word flashed across the electronic news line on the *New York Times* Building that Castro had entered Havana, a loud cheer erupted from the huge crowd. In April, Castro visited the U.S. as a guest of the American Society of Newspaper editors and aroused genuine interest

[17]Philip Nash, *The Other Missiles of October: Eisenhower, Kennedy and the Jupiters, 1957–1963* (Chapel Hill: University of North Carolina Press, 1997), 12–14, 28, 68–69.

[18]*Ibid.*, 38–41; Laurence Chang, "The View from Washington and the View from Nowhere: Cuban Missile Crisis Historiography and the Epistemology of Decision Making," in James A. Nathan, ed., *The Cuban Missile Crisis Revisited* (New York: St. Martin's, 1992), 140.

[19]"The crisis was, in fact, the most acute and dangerous confrontation in the Cold War. It was, and remains, the closest we ever came to a nuclear exchange." (Chang, "The View from Washington and Nowhere," 132)

and enthusiasm in Washington, New York and at Harvard University—where nearly 9,000 people turned out to hear him speak and a dinner in his honor was hosted by the dean of arts and sciences, McGeorge Bundy. Castro was even interviewed by Edward R. Murrow on American television.[20]

However, suspicions of Castro quickly escalated in the State Department, the Congress and the White House when he summarily executed hundreds of Batista supporters, waffled on setting a date for free elections, seized American property without compensation, suppressed freedom of expression and political opposition and challenged Latin American sympathizers to support political subversion. In September 1960, Castro openly announced his commitment to export the Cuban revolution and free all of Latin America from Yankee imperialism. Cuba became increasingly dependent on Soviet military and economic assistance. Decades later, declassified documents from the former Soviet Union revealed that Raúl Castro, without his older brother's knowledge, and while Fidel was visiting the U.S. in 1959, had already secured Khrushchev's agreement to help the Cuban communists gain control over the island nation's armed forces.[21]

Cold War issues inevitably dominated the 1960 presidential campaign. President Eisenhower had been particularly embarrassed by the shooting down of a U-2 spy plane over the Soviet Union in May. The pilot, Francis Gary Powers, was captured, tried and convicted of spying. The President, after an awkward attempt to lie about the facts, finally admitted the truth, but refused to apologize. Soviet premier Nikita Khrushchev bitterly denounced Eisenhower, cancelled an upcoming summit meeting in Paris and angrily withdrew an invitation to have Eisenhower visit the U.S.S.R.

Senator John F. Kennedy, the Democratic presidential nominee, was harshly critical of the Eisenhower administration for failing to prevent the creation of a communist outpost in Cuba. The Eisenhower administration, in fact, was already supporting covert CIA efforts to sabotage and destabilize the new Cuban regime and to assist Cuban dissidents in

---

[20]Fursenko and Naftali, *"One Hell of a Gamble,"* 5–12; *FRUS: Kennedy-Khrushchev Exchanges,* VI (Washington, D.C.: United States Government Printing Office, 1996), 355–56; 402.

[21]Fursenko and Naftali, *"One Hell of a Gamble,"* 11–12. Fidel Castro had been distrustful of the Cuban communists *before* 1959. See Julia Sweig, *Inside the Cuban Revolution: Fidel Castro and the Urban Underground* (Cambridge, Mass.: Harvard University Press, 2002).

creating a government in exile. The CIA had also initiated contacts with the Mafia about poisoning Castro.[22] Vice President Richard Nixon, the GOP candidate, like JFK, had been shaped by the escalating international conflict with the U.S.S.R. since they each entered politics in 1946. Both candidates promised to upgrade U.S. military forces and resist Soviet expansionism around the world, particularly in the American hemisphere. Kennedy also exploited fears of a "missile gap" despite the fact that the classified briefings he received as a presidential candidate provided no such evidence. Nixon was furious about JFK's dissembling but powerless to expose him without revealing classified material.[23] Kennedy narrowly won.

On January 6, 1961, in a speech first broadcast on Moscow Radio nearly two weeks later, Khrushchev praised the Cuban revolution and declared that armed efforts to achieve national liberation from colonialism and imperialism were "sacred wars" which deserved the support of the Soviet Union and the world socialist movement. The speech was eventually disseminated among Kennedy's inner circle and may have contributed to the strident tone of his Inaugural Address—which drew a razor-sharp line between the "free world" and the communist world. The new President offered assurances to Latin America, but also sent a firm message to Khrushchev and Castro: "To our sister republics south of the border, we offer a special pledge—to convert our good words into good deeds, in a new Alliance for Progress, to assist free men and free governments in casting off the chains of poverty. But this peaceful revolution of hope cannot become the prey of hostile powers. Let all our neighbors know that we shall join with them to oppose aggression or subversion anywhere in the Americas. And let every other power know that this hemisphere intends to remain the master of its own house."[24] President Kennedy forwarded copies of Khrushchev's January 6 speech to the new National Security Council, admonishing its members to "Read, mark, learn and inwardly digest. . . . Our actions, our steps should be tailored to meet these kinds of problems."[25]

[22]Lawrence Freedman, *Kennedy's Wars: Berlin, Cuba, Laos and Vietnam* (New York: Oxford University Press, 2000), 151.

[23]For Robert McNamara's recollection of discovering early in the Kennedy administration that "there *was* a missile gap, but that is was in the reverse direction," see James G. Blight, Bruce J. Allyn and David A. Welch, *Cuba On the Brink: Castro, The Missile Crisis and the Soviet Collapse* (New York: Pantheon, 1993), 135–36.

[24]Zubok and Pleshakov, *Inside the Kremlin's Cold War*, 240; John G. Hunt, editor, *The Inaugural Addresses of the Presidents* (New York: Gramercy Books, 1997), 429.

[25]Richard Reeves, *President Kennedy: Profile of Power* (New York: Simon and Schus-

President Eisenhower broke diplomatic relations with Cuba shortly before leaving office in January. Khrushchev, at the same time, eagerly embraced Castro as a symbol of what he believed was the dynamic, forward-looking and inevitable advance of world communism. A potentially explosive situation was rapidly developing in American-Soviet-Cuban relations which would make the next three years among the most hazardous and crisis-filled periods of the entire Cold War era.

In the months between the election and the inauguration, President-elect Kennedy was briefed about the Eisenhower administration plan to have the CIA secretly train and support about 1,500 anti-Castro exiles in Guatemala for an attack on Castro's Cuba. American intelligence specialists predicted that significant elements of the Cuban population and armed forces would support an attempt to oust Castro and install a non-communist, democratic government friendly to the United States. CIA enthusiasm for "Operation Zapata" was not shared by the Joint Chiefs or the State Department.[26] But, despite lingering doubts about concealing American participation, JFK finally approved a modified plan for a night landing near an airfield capable of supplying tactical air cover—in the hope that the invasion could plausibly be explained as an independent initiative by guerrillas supporting internal Cuban opposition to the Castro regime.

McGeorge Bundy, soon after, assured the President that the CIA "have done a remarkable job of reframing the landing plan so as to make it unspectacular and quiet, and plausibly Cuban in its essentials." But, Admiral Arleigh Burke, Chief of Naval Operations, dissented, warning the President that the success of the plan depended entirely on the dubious assumption that the attack would spark an anti-Castro up-

---

ter, 1993), 40–41; Fursenko and Naftali, "One Hell of a Gamble," 78. The full text of Khrushchev's speech was probably not available in Washington in time to impact the actual drafting of the Inaugural Address.

[26]General Lyman Lemnitzer, the chairman of the Joint Chiefs, concluded that the plan had only a "fair chance of ultimate success" unless the rebels secured and maintained complete control of the air over the beachhead. (FRUS: Cuba, 1961–1962, X (Washington, D.C.: United States Government Printing Office, 1997), 69) Dean Rusk later admitted that he had not served the President well by failing to make "my opposition clear," especially in private. But, he explained, they had just taken office and their relationship was still evolving. (Dean Rusk Oral History Interview, 1970, OHC, JFKL, 90) Days before the invasion, however, Rusk told JFK's special adviser on Latin American affairs, Chester Bowles, "'Don't worry about this. It isn't going to amount to anything.'" Bowles asked, "'Will it make the front page of the New York Times?'" and Rusk replied, "'I wouldn't think so.'" (Chester Bowles Oral History Interview, 1970, OHC, JFKL, 61–62)

rising in Cuba. JFK's decision, however, had unwittingly limited the invasion site to beaches nearly eighty miles away from possible escape into Cuba's Escambray mountains.[27]

The exiles of Brigade 2506 landed at the Bay of Pigs on April 17, 1961. Two days of air strikes had destroyed barely 15% of Castro's combat aircraft, leaving the invaders mercilessly exposed to air attacks. As the plan quickly unraveled, Kennedy cancelled a second round of planned air strikes.[28] The invasion was quickly crushed by Castro's military and all the exiles were either captured or killed. On the afternoon of April 18, Bundy was forced to acknowledge that Cuba's military response had been stronger than anticipated and the popular uprising had failed to materialize (Castro had also arrested thousands of suspected opponents).[29]

Kennedy was denounced throughout the communist world, and anti-American demonstrations broke out in the Third World and in Western Europe. The extreme Right, which had become more vocal and organized in response to the Cold War and the civil rights movement, branded Kennedy a coward and a tool of the communists. In addition, the increasingly influential Cuban exile community in Miami and New Orleans festered with anger over the President's refusal to commit American air power in a last-minute attempt to save the doomed invaders.[30] Kennedy assumed personal responsibility for the fiasco (and later joked that his public approval ratings actually went up). Castro, in the wake of his stunning triumph, publicly proclaimed Cuba's commitment to communism.

This humiliating setback would have profound consequences for the remainder of the Kennedy administration. The Bay of Pigs failure con-

[27]FRUS: Cuba, 1961–62, X, 158–60; Fursenko and Naftali, "One Hell of a Gamble," 84–85; Bundy later claimed that he and the President had been deceived by the CIA about the distance between the invasion site and the mountains.

[28]Nearly a decade later, Rusk still felt that "failure to follow up with American armed forces" in April 1961 may have convinced Khrushchev to gamble on deploying missiles in Cuba. (Rusk Oral History, 136) However, regardless of Khrushchev's beliefs, "It is now clear that [President] Kennedy never promised U.S. military support to anyone, under any circumstances, at the Bay of Pigs." (James G. Blight and Peter Kornbluh, eds., Politics of Illusion: The Bay of Pigs Invasion Reexamined (Boulder, Colorado: Lynne Rienner, 1998), 3)

[29]FRUS: Cuba, 1961–62, X, 272–73.

[30]In August 1961, conservatives again skewered Kennedy for failing to respond militarily when the Soviets constructed the Berlin Wall. Demonstrators later carried placards demanding that the President show "less profile and more courage."

firmed JFK's lifelong suspicions about the military and his increasing skepticism about the "experts" in the intelligence community. "How could I have been so far off base?" he told White House special counsel Theodore Sorensen. "All my life I've known better than to depend on the experts. How could I have been so stupid, to let them go ahead?"[31] However, the President also developed, passionately promoted and encouraged by his brother, Attorney General Robert Kennedy, a preoccupation, if not an obsession, with getting rid of Castro and erasing this blot on the Kennedy record.[32]

Evidence released over the last decade has substantiated this growing anti-Castro animus within the Kennedy administration. In August 1961, for example, Richard Goodwin, a member of JFK's Latin American Task Force, was personally approached by Castro's number two man, Ernesto "Che" Guevara, at a meeting in Uruguay. Guevara, according to Goodwin's now declassified memo, suggested that Castro, despite believing that a permanent settlement with the U.S. was unlikely, might be willing to discuss an interim arrangement for reducing tensions and reestablishing normal trade relations. The possibilities included using trade as compensation for confiscated American property, a Cuban willingness to eschew a formal alliance with the Soviets, a Cuban commitment not to attack the American naval base at Guantanamo, plus vague promises concerning free elections and limiting Cuban support for revolutionaries in Latin America—in return for an end to U.S. hostilities. JFK interpreted the apparent peace feeler as a

---

[31]Theodore C. Sorensen, *Kennedy* (New York: Harper and Row, 1965), 309.

[32]Scholars remain divided over whether the Kennedys were "obsessed" by Castro's Cuba. "I think Kennedy *was* obsessed with Cuba," Piero Gleijeses argued at a 1996 conference on the Bay of Pigs, "and that obsession led to Operation MONGOOSE—a kind of terrorist operation, but an inefficient one. But I think the obsession of Kennedy with Cuba came in the wake of the failure of the Bay of Pigs, not before." James Blight asked Sam Halpern, a former CIA Operation Mongoose planner, to confirm that "in fact everything relating to Cuba in those days, was coordinated by, and motivated from, the White House—from the Kennedys." Halpern replied, "As Dick Helms [CIA deputy director for operations] was fond of saying: 'If anybody wants to see the whiplashes across my back inflicted by Bobby Kennedy, I will take my shirt off in public.' That's how he felt about this stuff. It was unbelievable. I have never been in anything like that before or since and I don't ever want to go through it again." Arthur Schlesinger, Jr. countered that RFK was balanced and rational on Cuba: "These were not instructions, they were exhortations." (Blight and Kornbluh, *Politics of Illusion*, 53, 118, 124–25) Jorge I. Domínguez also defines JFK's policies as an "obsession " and as "terrorism." ("The @#$%& Missile Crisis: Or, What Was 'Cuban' about U.S. Decisions during the Cuban Missile Crisis?," *Diplomatic History* 24 (spring 2000), 310–12)

sign of Cuba's weakness and accepted Goodwin's advice to have the CIA instead turn up the pressure against Castro and the Cuban economy.[33] Cold War ideology, combined with a personal grudge over the Bay of Pigs, had created a powerful incentive for the Kennedys to support a "secret war" to get even in Cuba.

In the months following the Bay of Pigs debacle, Soviet intelligence agents discovered credible evidence of American-backed plots to assassinate the Castro brothers and Guevara. Khrushchev and the Presidium formally warned Fidel of an operation evidently scheduled for late June.[34] In November, JFK authorized the creation of Operation Mongoose to undermine the Cuban regime and economy with clandestine operations and sabotage—including blowing up port and oil storage facilities, burning crops (especially sugarcane) and even disabling or assassinating Castro himself.

The Mongoose operation was no fly-by-night scheme run by ultra-right-wing extremists, as depicted in Oliver Stone's film fantasy, *JFK*. It became the largest clandestine operation in CIA history, "involving some four hundred agents, an annual budget of over $50 million and a variety of covert, economic, and psychological operations—including assassination attempts against Fidel Castro."[35] Robert Kennedy, who insisted that the Bay of Pigs "insult had to be redressed," became the moving force behind the Special Group (Augmented) of the "Cuba Project," committed to eliminating Castro by any means necessary. Operation Mongoose, the enforcement instrument for the SG(A), was directed by counter-insurgency expert General Edward Lansdale, but

[33]Richard Goodwin, "Conversation with Commandante Ernesto Guevara of Cuba," August 22, 1961, President's Office Files [hereafter POF], Cuba, 1961, JFKL; for Goodwin's published account of his meeting with Guevara, see *Remembering America: A Voice from the Sixties* (Boston: Little Brown, 1988), 190–208; Fursenko and Naftali, *"One Hell of a Gamble,"* 142–43.

[34]Fursenko and Naftali, *"One Hell of a Gamble,"* 134–37.

[35]Laurence Chang and Peter Kornbluh, eds., *The Cuban Missile Crisis, 1962: A National Security Archive Documents Reader* (New York: The New Press, 1998), 5; Philip Brenner, "Thirteen Months: Cuba's Perspective on the Missile Crisis," in Nathan, ed., *Cuban Missile Crisis Revisited,* 189; Minutes of the First Operation Mongoose Meeting with Attorney General Robert Kennedy, December 1, 1961 and Brig. General Edward Lansdale, The Cuba Project, February 20, 1962, in Chang and Kornbluh, *Cuban Missile Crisis,* 20–37; Raymond L. Garthoff, *Reflections on the Cuban Missile Crisis,* Revised Edition (Washington, D.C.: Brookings, 1989), 32. The Cubans clearly knew about "at least some of the assassination attempts." (Raymond L. Garthoff, "The Cuban Missile Crisis: An Overview," in Nathan, ed., *Cuban Missile Crisis Revisited,* 42)

RFK kept very close tabs on its activities. He also established ties to several U.S.-backed "Autonomous Anti-Castro Groups" and invited their leaders to his home. Even Richard Bissell, CIA director of operations, and other covert action insiders who had been working on the Cuban "problem" since 1959 considered RFK "a wild man" on the subject of Castro. Bissell also helped launch a secret CIA program of "last resort" political assassinations called "ZR/Rifle," which RFK regularly prodded for results.[36]

Historians have argued for decades about whether President Kennedy specifically authorized plots to assassinate Fidel Castro. JFK definitely discussed the advisability of eliminating Castro with senior associates and journalists, but never overcame his concerns that killing the Cuban leader would only exacerbate tensions with the Soviet Union. In early 1961, nonetheless, he assured his old Senate buddy, George Smathers, that "he was almost certain that it [the assassination] could be accomplished—I remember that—it would be no problem." Later that year, however, the President told a top aide, "we can't get into that kind of thing, or we would all be targets." Nonetheless, CIA plots against Castro's life continued under Kennedy.[37]

In a very real sense, however, concern about finding a "smoking gun" directly linking JFK to these schemes misses the point. "All one can say is that the obsession with Castro, and Robert's constant goading of the CIA, created a climate in which CIA officials might have been forgiven for believing that the higher authorities would not be unhappy with the Cuban leader's demise." King Henry II did not "order" the murder of "that turbulent priest," but the knights that slaughtered Thomas Becket in Canterbury Cathedral surely believed they were carrying out the wishes of their monarch. Richard Nixon did not "order" the Watergate break-in, but the burglars certainly believed that their action reflected the President's priorities. Robert Kennedy's relentless pressure on the CIA to deal with Castro, given his unique alter-ego relationship with his older brother, sent an unmistakable signal to intelli-

---

[36]Taylor Branch and George Crile III, "The Kennedy Vendetta: How the CIA Waged a Silent War Against Cuba," *Harper's Magazine* 251 (August 1975), 50; Richard Bissell interview in Reeves, *President Kennedy*, 265; Freedman, *Kennedy's Wars*, 151; May and Zelikow, "Camelot Confidential," 644.

[37]George Smathers Oral History Interview, 1964, OHC, JFKL, 7; Freedman, *Kennedy's Wars*, 152. For a detailed account of Kennedy administration efforts to topple or assassinate Castro, see Blight and Kornbluh, *Politics of Illusion*, 59–132.

gence operatives—notwithstanding the President's lingering ambivalence. The unspoken need to provide "plausible deniability," in any case, made a written order unwise and unnecessary.[38]

In this hostile context, the President and the Secretary of Defense asked the Joint Chiefs of Staff, at least a year before the missile crisis, to prepare "contingency plans" for a second invasion of Cuba—intended this time to have different results. JFK, nonetheless, was determined to leave *all* options open: "The President also expressed skepticism that in so far as can now be foreseen circumstances will arise that would justify and make desirable the use of American forces for overt military action. It was clearly understood no decision was expressed or implied approving the use of such forces although contingency planning would proceed." Robert Kennedy, however, was far more direct. "'We are in a combat situation with Cuba,'" he admonished a group from the CIA and the Pentagon. Another failure in Cuba was simply unacceptable.[39]

The administration's anti-Castro efforts reached a crescendo in 1962 with a successful diplomatic initiative to exclude Cuba from the Organization of American States and the implementation of a full economic embargo.[40] In addition, the U.S. pressured 15 Latin American nations to break relations with Cuba. Operation Mongoose documents also confirm that "a program and timetable" was in place to provoke a popular revolt in Cuba as a justification for American military intervention.[41] Cuban and Soviet agents, however, had infiltrated Mongoose anti-Castro exile groups and were fully aware of U.S. sabotage and covert operations. It is also clear that the "contingency" plans for a blockade, air strikes, and/or an invasion (tentatively scheduled for October) were in place well before the discovery of Soviet nuclear missiles

[38]Freedman, *Kennedy's Wars*, 150–52. The death of Becket was "a political murder ... not sanctioned by the reigning king," yet clearly carried out "in the hope of gaining favour" with him. (Charles Ross, *Richard III* (Berkeley: University of California Press, 1981, 103) See also Graham Allison and Philip Zelikow, *Essence of Decision: Explaining the Cuban Missile Crisis* (New York: Addison Wesley Longman, 1999), 369.

[39]Guidelines for Operation Mongoose, *FRUS: Cuba, 1961–1962*, X, #314, March 14, 1962; Fursenko and Naftali, *"One Hell of a Gamble,"* 148.

[40]The Organization of American States administered the Rio Treaty, a mutual defense pact of the nations of the Americas signed in 1947—two years before the creation of NATO.

[41]Garthoff, *Reflections*, 7. For a discussion of the 1962 expulsion of Cuba from the OAS, see Blight, *et al.*, *Cuba on the Brink*, 16–20.

in Cuba—although it is uncertain whether JFK would have implemented these plans without Khrushchev's October gamble.[42] The Soviet
leader certainly believed that American "diplomatic isolation" of Cuba
from the OAS amounted to "preparation for an invasion." In addition,
40,000 American military personnel took part in provocative amphibious invasion exercises near Puerto Rico in April and May, "at precisely
the moment when the Soviet leaders is reported to have made up his
mind to send the nuclear missiles" to Cuba.[43]

Thirty years later, at the Russian-Cuban-American missile crisis conference in Havana, Robert McNamara conceded that "if I had been a
Cuban leader at that time, I might well have concluded that there was
a great risk of U.S. invasion. And I should say, as well, if I had been a
Soviet leader at the time, I might have come to the same conclusion."
He dramatically reiterated to his Cuban hosts, "I want to be very
frank. If I'd been a Cuban, I would have thought exactly what I think
you thought"—namely, that "the U.S. intended to mount an invasion."[44] But, in 1962, the three antagonists had very different perceptions: Americans called this event the "Cuban missile crisis"; the Soviets dubbed it the "Caribbean crisis"; but the Cubans labeled it the "October crisis," because it represented only one episode in more than a
year of unremitting crises for Cuba. "From the Cuban perspective, the
October crisis was just one of many."[45]

Nikita Khrushchev, before meeting Kennedy in Vienna in June 1961,
told the Politburo that he was planning to push hard for concessions in
Berlin and elsewhere. He believed that JFK was immature, untested
and especially vulnerable after the Bay of Pigs. "This young man thinks
that, backed by the might of the United States, he can lead us by the

---

[42]Brenner, "Thirteen Months," 189–91; James G. Hershberg, "Before 'The Missiles of
October': Did Kennedy Plan a Military Strike Against Cuba?," *Diplomatic History* 14
(1990), 163–98; Paul H. Nitze (with Ann M. Smith and Steven L. Reardon), *From Hiroshima to Glasnost: At the Center of Decision: A Memoir* (New York: Grove Weidenfeld,
1989), 216.

[43]James G. Blight and David A. Welch, *On the Brink: Americans and Soviets Reexam-
ine the Cuban Missile Crisis* (New York: Noonday Press, 1990), 238; Hershberg, "Before
'The Missiles of October,'" 181–82.

[44]Chang and Kornbluh, *Cuban Missile Crisis*, 7; Blight, *et al.*, *Cuba on the Brink*, 41;
Bruce J. Allyn, James G. Blight and David A. Welch, "Essence of Revision: Moscow, Havana and the Cuban Missile Crisis," *International Security* 14 (1989–90), 145. The six international missile crisis conferences were held in Hawk's Cay, Florida (March 1987);
Cambridge, Massachusetts (October 1987); Moscow (January 1989); Antigua (January
1991) and Havana (January 1992 and October 2002).

[45]Brenner, "Thirteen Months," 201, 206.

hand and make us dance to his tune." Khrushchev predicted that Kennedy would fail and be forced "to talk with us on equal terms." On the other hand, Khrushchev's calculated belligerence in Vienna shocked JFK; Dean Rusk described the conversations between the two leaders about possible nuclear war as "brutal." Khrushchev's ideological harangues about the inevitability of world communism and his threat to sign a separate peace treaty with East Germany convinced JFK, particularly in the wake of the Bay of Pigs failure, that the Soviets would only respect American toughness in Cuba and Berlin. Kennedy accepted a recommendation by Rusk and Paul Nitze (Assistant Secretary of Defense for International Security Affairs) to proceed with the deployment of Jupiter missiles in Turkey—hoping to boost American credibility and "restrain Khrushchev over Berlin."[46]

The construction of the Berlin Wall later that summer, to prevent East Germans from fleeing to the West, temporarily took some of the heat off the Berlin issue.[47] JFK and his advisers, nonetheless, never forgot that West Berlin, actually some 200 miles inside East Germany, was the Achilles Heel of the Western alliance. It would not be an exaggeration to say that for the Kennedy administration the Cuban missile crisis was as much about Berlin as Cuba. As Fred Kaplan has observed, "It is hard to imagine," in the post–Cold War world, "the fear and passion that once surrounded the very word, 'Berlin.'" Nonetheless, recent scholarship has suggested that "Despite the firm belief of an entire generation of American policy-makers and some prominent historians that Khrushchev's gamble in Cuba was actually aimed at West Berlin, there is little evidence of that on the Soviet side." President Kennedy, however, was absolutely convinced that Khrushchev's move in Cuba was directly linked to the festering issue of Berlin.[48]

[46]Zubok and Pleshakov, *Inside the Kremlin's Cold War*, 243; Sergei Khrushchev, *Nikita Khrushchev and the Creation of a Superpower* (University Park: Pennsylvania State University Press, 2000), 442; Sergei Khrushchev served as his father's personal aide during the missile crisis. He was not permitted to travel outside the Soviet bloc until 1989, but is now an American citizen and a senior fellow at the Brown University Watson Institute for International Studies; *FRUS: Soviet Union, 1961–1963*, V (Washington, D.C.: United States Government Printing Office, 1998), 172–78; Thomas J. Schoenbaum, *Waging Peace and War: Dean Rusk in the Truman, Kennedy and Johnson Years* (New York: Simon and Schuster, 1988), 335–36; Fursenko and Naftali, *"One Hell of a Gamble,"* 130–31; Nitze, *Hiroshima to Glasnost*, 233; Nash, *The Other Missiles*, 99–101, 115.

[47]In April 1961, the Soviet embassy in Berlin reported to Moscow that the population of the German Democratic Republic (East Germany) had declined by 1.2 million during the 1950s. (Zubok and Pleshakov, *Inside the Kremlin's Cold War*, 249)

[48]Fred Kaplan, "JFK's First-Strike Plan," *Atlantic Monthly 288* (October 2001), 81–86;

Khrushchev was not a passive observer in the escalating tensions between the nuclear superpowers and these events cannot be understood without considering his personal view of this historically "preordained" confrontation with the United States. By early 1962, the Soviet leader was deeply concerned about U.S. covert operations in Cuba and feared that Castro's overthrow would threaten his own hold on power. In short, he saw "Castro's possible defeat as his own defeat." Several years later, he recalled, "one thought kept hammering at my brain: what will happen if we lose Cuba?" Khrushchev also feared that a perceived lack of determination to protect the Cuban revolution would erode his standing as the leader of the communist bloc and push Castro into closer ties with the U.S.S.R.'s increasingly belligerent rival—Mao's China.[49]

The Kremlin leader was willing to gamble because he believed, especially after the Vienna summit, that Kennedy did not have the stomach for the ultimate conflict with the Soviet Union. Khrushchev's "combination of cynical manipulation and revolutionary readiness to stand up to the imperialists produced a very dangerous moment." He was committed to "the victorious march of communism around the globe and Soviet hegemony in the Communist camp" and the Cuban adventure grew out of "his revolutionary commitment and his sense of rivalry with the United States."[50]

At the same time, Khrushchev felt compelled to make a show of strength against a genuine threat to the credibility of his authority at home. On the last day of May, in a radio speech, he had announced a doubling of state-regulated prices on meat, sausages and butter. The KGB soon reported "widespread discontent" and demands for strikes throughout the country. In Novocherkassk (the former Cossack administrative center) anti-government demonstrations "by thousands of workers, women and children" toppled the communist administration. Negotiations failed to restore order and Red Army troops and tanks, with Khrushchev's authorization to use "Civil War methods to deal with the dissenters," opened fire killing more than 20 protesters (most

Zubok and Pleshakov, *Inside the Kremlin's Cold War*, 260; Philip Zelikow, "American Policy and Cuba, 1961–1963," *Diplomatic History* 24 (Spring 2000), 323–26.

[49]Sergei Khrushchev, *Nikita Khrushchev*, 482; Strobe Talbott, ed. and trans., *Khrushchev Remembers* (Boston: Little, Brown, 1970), 493; Fursenko and Naftali, *"One Hell of a Gamble,"* 73.

[50]Zubok and Pleshakov, *Inside the Kremlin's Cold War*, 255, 260–61.

under age 25), wounding nearly 90, arresting hundreds and later executing 12 "instigators."[51]

Khrushchev was also getting ready to mount a show of strength abroad. In the early spring, during a conversation with Defense Minister Rodion Malinovsky in the Crimea, Khrushchev had been struck by the fact that American missiles just across the Black Sea in Turkey could reach the U.S.S.R. in a mere ten minutes; Soviet missiles, however, required nearly half an hour to reach the U.S. The fifteen Jupiter missiles in Turkey were clearly on Khrushchev's mind since they had only become operational between November 1961 and March 1962.[52] Soon after returning to Moscow, Khrushchev discussed deploying nuclear missiles in Cuba with his closest advisers. The Soviet leader had already responded favorably, albeit slowly, to Castro's September 1961 request for defensive surface-to-air missiles.[53] Offensive missiles, of course, were infinitely more provocative, but Khrushchev was convinced that his credibility as a world leader, especially within the communist bloc, required a bold defense of his fledgling socialist ally in the Americas. "Khrushchev had already been severely challenged by the Chinese and by senior figures in his own government for reducing Soviet military preparedness and not taking a sufficiently revolutionary stance in foreign policy."[54]

The U.S.S.R. had learned to live with U.S. nuclear weapons in Turkey, Italy, Britain and West Germany, and Khrushchev felt that it was time for the Americans to have "a little of their own medicine."[55] In addition, the United States had about a 4–1 advantage in intercontinental ballistic missiles and "a 17–1 superiority in deliverable warheads

---

[51]Zubok and Pleshakov, *Inside the Kremlin's Cold War*, 262–64; also see Samuel H. Baron, *Bloody Sunday in the Soviet Union: Novocherkassk, 1962* (Stanford, CA: Stanford University Press, 2001).

[52]Nash, *The Other Missiles*, 102–3. Thirty Jupiters were also deployed in Italy.

[53]Fursenko and Naftali, *"One Hell of a Gamble,"* 139–41.

[54]Allison and Zelikow, *Essence of Decision*, 84. (Barton J. Bernstein, however, faults Allison and Zelikow for treating the Soviet Union as "an ordinary state" and "often minimizing (if not ignoring) the role of communist ideology and of centralized party control." ("Understanding Decisionmaking, U.S. Foreign Policy and the Cuban Missile Crisis," *International Security* 25 (Summer 2000), 136)

[55]Talbott, ed., *Khrushchev Remembers*, 492–94; Sergei Khrushchev, *Nikita Khrushchev*, 484; Barton J. Bernstein, "Reconsidering the Missile Crisis: Dealing with the Problems of the American Jupiters in Turkey," in Nathan, ed., *Cuban Missile Crisis Revisited*, 65–67. The Pershing I missiles in West Germany did not actually have sufficient range to threaten targets in the Soviet Union.

and bombs against the Soviet heartland." It would take perhaps a decade to close the gap. Soviet intermediate range missiles, and Moscow had many, would kill the proverbial two birds with one stone at very modest cost by protecting communist Cuba and earning respect for the U.S.S.R. by appearing to equalize the world balance of power.[56] "In Khrushchev's mind—and he made this decision alone—a Soviet nuclear base in Cuba was the only way to manage these two difficult problems at once." It was a calculated gamble: "With forty missiles staring at Florida, day and night, no general in the Pentagon would again dare consider a nuclear first strike against the Soviet Union or an attack on Cuba." The latest evidence is compelling: "the driving force was Nikita Khrushchev himself."[57]

Anti-communist ideology had clearly fueled Kennedy administration policy in Cuba, but expansionist communist ideology had also motivated leaders in the Kremlin. At the Vienna summit Khrushchev had confidently lectured JFK about the inexorable triumph of world communism: this was not hyperbole or propaganda, the Soviet leader argued, but a scientific analysis of social and historical development. Khrushchev was absolutely committed to the success of the three-year-old communist revolution in Cuba and refused to abandon Castro in the face of American threats because, he concluded, "Such treachery was contrary to the very essence of proletarian internationalism." Khrushchev later wrote that the loss of this socialist beachhead in Latin America "would have been a terrible blow to Marxism-Leninism." In presenting his plan to put Soviet nuclear missiles in Cuba to the Pre-

[56]The Soviet General Staff insisted that the R-12 and R-14 missiles (with a range of 1,000+ and 2,000+ miles respectively) and the nuclear warheads had to be protected and constructed more than 100 surface-to-air missile installations. The buildup also included 60 strategic nuclear warheads, 100 tactical nuclear warheads, MIG21 fighters and IL-28 nuclear bombers, and, to repel an American invasion, about 43,000 Red Army troops. The Soviets had planned to send nearly 50,000 troops but that number was never reached because of the American quarantine. This massive effort required nearly 200 trips by 85 ships from seven different ports over a period of nearly three months. (Blight, *et al.*, *Cuba on the Brink*, 58–61; Sergei Khrushchev, *Nikita Khrushchev*, 501–2, 510–12; Fursenko and Naftatli, *"One Hell of a Gamble,"* 171, 188–89; Garthoff, *Reflections*, 36–37; Barton J. Bernstein, "Commentary: Reconsidering Khrushchev's Gambit—Defending the Soviet Union and Cuba," *Diplomatic History* 14 (1990), 232)

[57]Fursenko and Naftali, *"One Hell of a Gamble,"* 183, 189; Anatoli I. Gribkov, "The View from Moscow and Havana," in Anatoli I. Gribkov, William Y. Smith, Alfred Friendly (editor), *Operation ANADYR: U.S. and Soviet Generals Recount the Cuban Missile Crisis* (Chicago: Edition Q, 1993), 12–14; Raymond L. Garthoff, "US Intelligence in the Cuban Missile Crisis," in Blight and Welch, eds., *Intelligence and the Cuban Missile Crisis*, 24.

sidium, Khrushchev made clear that he was not simply reacting to American power but acting to implement the Marxist view of history: "We have to make Cuba a torch, a magnet, attracting all the destitute peoples of Latin America. . . . The blazing flame of socialism in Cuba," he proclaimed, "will speed up the process of their struggle for independence."[58]

Khrushchev was unalterably committed to "the revolutionary transformation of the world and the path to socialism and communism. . . . His passionate view of history and the world was very different from the detached and slightly fatalistic outlook of the U.S. president." He believed that the historical moment for the triumph of Marxist-Leninism was at hand—even his later memoirs are peppered with reflex Marxist ideology about "the class blindness of the United States," "the dying capitalist system," and JFK's "goal of strengthening capitalism, while I sought to destroy capitalism and create a new world social system based on the teachings of Marx, Engels, and Lenin." There was little significant opposition to Khrushchev's plan in the Kremlin—although the Soviet ambassador to Cuba, Aleksandr Alekseev, summoned to Moscow for this critical discussion, predicted that Castro might actually be afraid to take the missiles.[59]

A delegation of senior Soviet military officials traveled to Cuba to propose the plan, code-named Operation Anadyr. Khrushchev wanted Castro to know that "'we are ready to take a risk' for the Cuban revolution."[60] In an effort to preserve secrecy, they wore civilian clothes, carried false passports, brought no documents and were forbidden to contact Moscow, even in code. At the time of their arrival, in late May, American covert operations appeared to be escalating and even the Soviet ambassador had requested armed guards to protect him; Castro was predicting that an invasion was imminent. The Cuban

[58]Arthur M. Schlesinger, Jr., *A Thousand Days: John F. Kennedy in the White House* (Boston: Houghton Mifflin, 1965), 359; Talbott, ed., *Khrushchev Remembers*, 493; Sergei Khrushchev, *Nikita Khrushchev*, 483, 486–87.

[59]Zubok and Pleshakov, *Inside the Kremlin's Cold War*, 244, 246; Strobe Talbott, ed. and trans., *Khrushchev Remembers: The Last Testament* (Boston: Little, Brown, 1974), 511–14; Fursenko and Naftali, *"One Hell of a Gamble,"* 179; Gribkov, "View from Moscow and Havana," 7–14. For Alekseev's recollections, Blight, *et al.*, *Cuba on the Brink*, 77–80.

[60]The planners chose this code name "to confuse Soviets and foreigners about the destination of the military equipment. Anadyr was the name of a river at the Pacific tip of Siberia and of a strategic airbase in the same area from which Soviet bombers could reach the U.S. mainland. The Anadyr planners promoted the Siberian illusion to conceal the mission." (Fursenko and Naftali, *"One Hell of a Gamble,"* 180, 191)

leader's response to Khrushchev's plan was enthusiastic, not merely because it promised to protect Cuba and frustrate the United States, but because "it would serve the interests of world socialism and oppressed peoples in their confrontation with insolent American imperialism, which was trying to dictate its will throughout the world."[61] A five year agreement for the defense of Cuba, including the deployment of nuclear missiles under exclusive Soviet control, was approved by both governments later that summer but was never formally signed.[62] The entire world was inexorably heading for an ideologically fueled confrontation between the nuclear superpowers with potentially deadly political and military consequences.

Khrushchev, as it turned out, had badly underestimated the symbolic political importance of historic American power in the Western Hemisphere—going back to the Monroe Doctrine; he was totally unprepared for the intensity of the American response.[63] He also failed to take Castro's shrewd advice to deploy the missiles openly as a legitimate act of bilateral diplomacy (as the U.S. had done in Turkey and Italy). Many scholars agree that if Khrushchev had formally announced the decision "it was much less likely that the U.S. government would have sought, or been able, to compel retraction of the Soviet decision and preclude deployment." Castro himself insisted thirty years later, "We were not violating international law. Why do it secretly—as if we had no right to do it?"[64] Soviet duplicity and secrecy virtually guaranteed that the U.S. would regard Khrushchev's move as militarily aggressive (although President Kennedy and Robert McNamara rejected that view during the ExComm meetings).[65]

Kennedy had naïvely accepted predictions by American intelligence

[61]Garthoff, *Reflections*, 11; Sergei Khrushchev, *Nikita Khrushchev*, 491–93, 513.

[62]Garthoff, *Reflections*, 17. Garthoff concludes that Khrushchev never signed the Soviet-Cuban draft defense pact because he feared that Castro would embarrass the U.S.S.R. by leaking it." (25)

[63]Nearly three decades later, Khrushchev's foreign minister, Andrei Gromyko, claimed to have warned the Soviet leader, "Putting our nuclear missiles in Cuba would cause a political explosion in the United States." (Andrei Gromyko, "The Caribbean Crisis: On Glasnost Now and Secrecy Then," *The Current Digest of the Soviet Press*, May 17, 1989)

[64]Garthoff, *Reflections*, 24–26; Nash, *The Other Missiles*, 107; Blight, *et al.*, *Cuba on the Brink*, 344–52.

[65]Khrushchev's "appreciation of the situation [seems] to have been cloudy at best, his judgments bereft of any attribute of high-quality deliberations. Relying on haphazard and often inaccurate information, and without any sustained analysis of the sort commonplace in the American process, he manages a sullen, sporadic group of advisers and rivals." (Allison and Zelikow, *Essence of Decision*, 382)

early in 1961 that the Cuban people would rise in support of an American-sponsored invasion of their homeland. Khrushchev, likewise, impetuously swallowed the assurances of Soviet "experts" that these huge missiles could be "disguised as coconut palms" and the mounted warheads "crowned with a cap of leaves," enabling the U.S.S.R. to present the U.S. with a *fait accompli* in November. The Soviets had relied on deception and secrecy to throw the Americans off the trail; incredibly, however, Khrushchev had failed to work out a plan of action in the event that the Americans discovered the missiles sites under construction. He would be forced to improvise in the pressure cooker of the most dangerous crisis of the Cold War.[66]

In the summer of 1962, Cuba continued to loom very large in American politics. The Bay of Pigs had been a calamity. Covert operations had thus far failed. Castro's grasp on power seemed undiminished, and behind him, always, lurked the potential threat from his Soviet backers. Kennedy had lambasted the Eisenhower administration in 1960 for allowing a Communist stronghold only ninety miles from Florida. Now, the proverbial shoe was on the other foot. JFK's political opponents were more than ready to hang the Cuban albatross around his neck. Republican Senators Homer Capehart and Barry Goldwater stridently accused Kennedy of weakness and negligence in addressing this new red menace so close to U.S. shores. There was, they insisted, strong evidence of a Soviet offensive buildup in Cuba, evidence they accused the President of ignoring or even suppressing. The CIA was receiving regular reports of missile sightings from informants in Cuba and from "the steady stream of Cubans emigrating to the United States," but nothing was ever confirmed.[67]

JFK, despite his instinctive skepticism about military and intelligence "experts," accepted assurances from the CIA and the Joint Chiefs that

[66]Sergei Khrushchev, *Nikita Khrushchev*, 502, 559–62; Sergei Khrushchev was shocked that his father fell for "such primitive reasoning." On November 3, Khrushchev's deputy Anastas Mikoyan personally admitted to Castro, "our military had advised us, that under the palm leaves of Cuba the strategic weapons would be safely hidden from overhead reconnaissance." (Fursenko and Naftali, *"One Hell of a Gamble,"* 294) Khrushchev also failed to instruct Gromyko "to prepare convenient explanations in case the whole plot became public." (Zubok and Pleshakov, *Inside the Kremlin's Cold War*, 265) Ambassador Alekseev recalled, "Khrushchev's conviction that the operation would not be discovered was very firm. He actually believed that." (Blight, *et al.*, *Cuba on the Brink*, 80)

[67]Rusk recalled, "We tried to check out every rumor, every piece of evidence, every piece of gossip that pointed toward missiles in Cuba." (Rusk Oral History, 113); Garthoff, *Reflections*, 28.

there was no evidence of the Soviet offensive buildup charged by the Republicans. Then, on August 31, Kennedy's critics gained an important and more credible voice. Senator Kenneth Keating of New York, a moderate Republican, charged in the Senate that the Soviets had begun a major buildup of military personal and weapons in Cuba—including offensive nuclear missile bases. He accused the Kennedy administration of a dangerous cover-up.

The administration *was* covering up escalating attacks against Cuba: on August 24, Alpha 66, a Cuban exile group based in Florida, strafed a seashore hotel near Havana from a speedboat killing some twenty Russians and Cubans. Indeed, only 24 hours before this secret attack, JFK, at a White House meeting, had pondered his options for dealing with the possibility of offensive Soviet missiles in Cuba, "Could we take them out by air or would a ground offensive be necessary or alternatively could they be destroyed by a substantial guerrilla effort."[68]

Kennedy was puzzled and appalled by Keating's charges.[69] Coming just before the mid-term Congressional elections, such claims were potentially disastrous for the Democratic party and might threaten the President's prospects for reelection in 1964.[70] Kennedy pressed the CIA for answers, but was again told that photographs from U-2 reconnaissance aircraft showed only defensive surface-to-air missile sites in Cu-

[68]Garthoff, *Reflections*, 31; *FRUS: Cuba, 1961–62*, X, 954.

[69]The source of Keating's "remarkably accurate" claims remains one of the great mysteries of the Cuban missile crisis. For a time, it appeared that Keating's intelligence may have come from the CIA, perhaps even from John McCone himself. (Mark J. White, *Missiles in Cuba: Kennedy, Khrushchev, Castro and the 1962 Crisis* (Chicago: Ivan R. Dee, 1997), 65) However, more recent information suggests (but does not conclusively prove) that Keating had been receiving information about the Soviet buildup from a bizarre alliance of student radicals in Cuba, who had broken with Castro over communism and had begun feeding eyewitness reports to two wealthy and influential private citizens, the bitterly anti-Castro former ambassadors Clare Boothe Luce and William Douglas Pawley. (Max Holland, "A Luce Connection: Senator Keating, William Pawley, and the Cuban Missile Crisis," *Journal of Cold War Studies* 1 (1999), 139–67); Theodore Sorensen Oral History Interview, 1964, OHC, JFKL, 46.

[70]Kennedy's domestic political fortunes seemed bleak. Unemployment remained between 5 and 6% and the stock market failed to recover after losing a quarter of its value early in the year. JFK ignored the advice of aides and endorsed efforts to enact medical care for workers over 65 under Social Security and risked his personal prestige by addressing a nationally televised "Medicare" rally in New York. By the time of the May 20 gathering, JFK knew the bill would fail and seemed testy and nervous. Medicare lost narrowly in the Senate after defections by key Democrats, leaving the President frustrated and furious. For the political context of JFK's decision to install a White House taping system, see Timothy Naftali, "Introduction: Five Hundred Days," in Timothy Naftali, ed., *John F. Kennedy: The Great Crises, v. 1*, xli–liv.

ba. On September 4, the Soviets "opened a deliberate campaign to counter any Americans suspicions." Soviet ambassador Anatoly Dobrynin assured Robert Kennedy that he had heard directly from Premier Khrushchev that offensive nuclear weapons would not be placed in Cuba.[71] The President clearly wanted to believe these assurances, but he also wanted his adversaries, both Soviet and Republican, to know that he was determined to defend American interests in the Caribbean. On the day of Dobrynin's reassuring message, JFK issued a statement warning that the introduction of "offensive ground-to-ground missiles" in Cuba would raise "the gravest issues."[72] His words were carefully chosen, but the meaning was plain. Just seventy-two hours later, CIA analysts abruptly shifted their position. There had, they told the President, been subtle changes in the aerial photographs. It was at least possible, they conceded, that ground-to-ground missile sites were being laid out in Cuba.[73]

That same day, Ambassador Dobrynin also assured American U.N. ambassador Adlai Stevenson that the Soviets would supply nothing but defensive weapons to their Cuban allies. On September 11, the Soviet government announced through the official TASS news agency that weapons for Cuba "are intended solely for defensive purposes" and boasted, "Our nuclear weapons are so powerful in their explosive force and the Soviet Union has such powerful rockets to carry these nuclear warheads, that there is no need to search for sites for them beyond the boundaries of the Soviet Union." But JFK, under constant political scrutiny, and unsure about the true situation on the island, again flexed America's muscle. If, he declared at a September 13 press conference, Cuba should "become an offensive military base of significant capacity for the Soviet Union, then this country will do whatever must be done

---

[71]Garthoff, *Reflections*, 29; President Kennedy concluded at the October 29 ExComm meeting that Dobrynin's credibility as ambassador had been fatally compromised because he had apparently been misled by his own government. JFK turned out to be wrong; Dobrynin remained as Soviet ambassador in Washington until 1986.

[72]*Department of State Bulletin*, 9/4/62, 450.

[73]It is "far from clear" that the U.S. could have located the missiles much before October 14: "Had a U-2 photographed the area even just a week earlier, crucial items necessary for a positive identification might not yet have been present." (James G. Blight and David A. Welch, "What Can Intelligence Tell Us About the Cuban Missile Crisis, and What Can the Cuban Missile Crisis Tell Us About Intelligence?" in Blight and Welch, eds., *Intelligence and the Cuban Missile Crisis*, 6–7) "Discovery a week or two earlier in October (when weather caused delay) would not have changed the situation faced by the President and his advisers." (Garthoff, "US Intelligence in the Cuban Missile Crisis," 24)

to protect its own security and that of its allies." But Kennedy also urged Americans to keep the situation in perspective—strong nerves and common sense, he declared, were essential requirements in the nuclear age.[74]

Two days later, on September 15, unbeknownst to anyone in Washington—including the Soviet ambassador—the first MRBMs arrived at the Cuban port of Mariel. On October 4, undetected by the Americans, a Soviet ship delivered ninety-nine nuclear warheads of four different types to Cuba. Together, they totaled "over twenty times the explosive power that was dropped by Allied bombers on Germany in all of the Second World War."[75] Even as the warheads were being secretly delivered, Kennedy's advisors continued to insist that the Soviets would never be so foolish as to put nuclear weapons in Cuba since such a move would have no real effect on the balance of power. No one in the West doubted that the Soviets could destroy the United States several times over with the ICBMs and nuclear bombers they had already deployed on their own territory. Why, then, should they risk so dangerously provoking the U.S. with missiles they did not need?

The fact that Khrushchev's vast array of ICBMs was largely a fantasy was a jealously guarded Soviet secret. When Kennedy and Khrushchev had met in Vienna in June 1961, the President had proposed that the two Cold War rivals work together on a joint lunar program. The Soviet leader, despite his bluster about producing ICBMs like sausages, turned down the offer and critics around the world wondered what the U.S.S.R. had to hide. Sergei Khrushchev pressed his father about the reason for the refusal: "If we cooperate with the Americans," the senior Khrushchev admitted, "it will mean opening up our rocket program to them. We have only two hundred missiles, but they think we have many more." Khrushchev was concerned that the Americans might launch a first-strike if they discovered this potentially fatal Soviet weakness—which had been concealed by Khrushchev's military boasting and Russian successes in space. "So when they say we have some-

---

[74]"Statement on U.S. Provocations," *New York Times*, September 12, 1962, 16; *Public Papers of the Presidents: John F. Kennedy*, 1962 (Washington, D.C.: U.S. Government Printing Office, 1963), 674.

[75]Fursenko and Naftali, *"One Hell of a Gamble,"* 217. Discussions in Washington took place without accurate intelligence on the Soviet buildup in Cuba. (Garthoff, "US Intelligence in the Cuban Missile Crisis," 29) U.S. intelligence estimated, for example, that 100,000 Cubans were under arms—the actual figure was closer to 275,000.

thing to hide...?" Sergei persisted. "It is just the opposite," his father said with a laugh. "We have nothing to hide. We have nothing. And we must hide it." Khrushchev had been personally responsible for the exaggeration of Soviet strategic strength; now, by restraining American military threats against Cuba, he hoped to buy time to build a more credible nuclear deterrent.[76]

Khrushchev's anxiety about an American nuclear first-strike was clearly justified. In 1961, in response to concerns that NATO could not protect West Berlin against a Soviet attack with conventional weapons, secret plans were formulated for a nuclear first-strike against the "long-range striking capacity of the Soviets, and avoiding, as much as possible, casualties and damage in Soviet civil society." The strategy, nonetheless, assumed at least 500,000 to 1,000,000 Soviet casualties in the initial attack. President Kennedy clearly read and discussed what amounted to a "plan to wage *rational* nuclear war." Although he seemed uneasy about "my ability to control our military effort once a war begins," JFK remained open to a possible first-strike strategy. In October, Deputy Secretary of Defense Roswell Gilpatric, in a crucial speech, dismissed fears of a missile gap by signaling the Soviets that the administration knew the U.S. held a commanding lead in nuclear missiles—a development which contributed to Khrushchev's decision to ship nuclear weapons to Cuba as a short-term fix for Soviet strategic weakness.[77]

The United States had developed—and used—atomic weapons in 1945 and then enjoyed a nuclear monopoly for the next four years. Stalin, whose paranoia had rarely required any connection to reality, had dreaded a preemptive American nuclear attack. Khrushchev ultimately gambled in Cuba, at least in part, because he worried that U.S. nuclear superiority, confirmed by 45 Jupiter missiles in Turkey and Italy that were all operational by early 1962, could make the U.S.S.R. almost as vulnerable to atomic blackmail as it had been before 1949.

On September 21, the Defense Intelligence Agency received reports of "a first-hand sighting on September 12 of a truck convoy of 20 objects 65 to 70 feet long which resembled large missiles."[78] Later in Sep-

[76]James Schefter, *The Race* (New York: Doubleday, 1999), 145; Chang, "The View from Washington and Nowhere," 140–41.

[77]Fred Kaplan, "JFK's First-Strike," 81–86; For McNamara's recollections on the nuclear first strike option, see Blight and Welch, *On the Brink*, 29–30; Michael R. Beschloss, *The Crisis Years: Kennedy and Khrushchev, 1960–1963* (New York: HarperCollins, 1991), 328–31.

[78]*FRUS: Cuba, 1961–1962*, X, 1083–84.

tember, analysts at the National Photographic Interpretation Center detected distinctive patterns carved into the Cuban landscape which seemed identical to those previously seen before the construction of missile sites in the Soviet Union. But the photos did not turn up hard evidence of offensive missiles on Cuban soil. Nonetheless, apprehension was rising in Washington and rumors, charges and counter-charges swirled through the corridors of power.

On October 4, Robert Kennedy chaired a meeting of Operation Mongoose's senior policy makers, demanding a massive expansion of sabotage and subversion in order to bring down Castro. He even suggested mining Cuba's harbors. Secretly, the administration intensified "contingency" planning for coordinated air-strikes, a blockade and an invasion of Cuba. Dobrynin, however, continued to insist that the U.S.S.R. had no plans to place offensive nuclear weapons in Cuba, which was, as far as he knew, the truth.[79] Senator Keating, on October 10, escalated his charges of administration duplicity or incompetence—claiming to have "fully confirmed" proof that six offensive intermediate range nuclear missile bases were already under construction in Cuba.[80]

On October 14, the first day after authority for U-2 flights had been transferred from the CIA to the Strategic Air Command, photos revealed solid evidence of MRBM sites in Cuba. That morning, McGeorge Bundy, the President's special assistant for national security, appeared on ABC TV's "Issues and Answers." "I know," he asserted, "that there is no present evidence, and I think that there is no present likelihood that the Cubans and the Cuban government and the Soviet government would, in combination, attempt to install a major offensive capability."[81] Bundy received the stunning news by telephone while

---

[79]Sergei Khrushchev acknowledges that Soviet "deception wounded Kennedy deeply" but nevertheless offers a curious explanation for his father's duplicity: "As a result of the squabble with Eisenhower over the U-2 [in 1960], Father understood that deceit was a customary tool in the arsenal of U.S. politics. He now decided to make use of the lesson he had been taught." (Sergei Khrushchev, *Nikita Khrushchev*, 544, 532) Despite the overall even-handedness of his book and entirely understandable feelings for his father, it is puzzling that Sergei Khrushchev could argue that Nikita Khrushchev learned deception from the Americans. When weighed against the lies and crimes of the Stalin era, in which the elder Khrushchev had been an active accomplice for decades, deceit seems almost innocuous.

[80]Holland, "A Luce Connection," 154.

[81]Many Cubans, "to this day," remain skeptical: "But it was and remains my deepest conviction, and the conviction of most Cuban analysts, that the US intelligence community had to know that such a deployment was taking place prior to 15 October." (Domingo

giving a dinner party on Monday evening but waited until early on Tuesday morning to brief the President, later insisting that JFK needed an undisturbed night of sleep. The President, still in his pajamas, saw the evidence in the White House living quarters early on October 16. His face and voice taut with anger at Soviet duplicity, he told Bundy, "He can't do that to me." JFK reeled off the names of key members of the National Security Council and told Bundy to organize a meeting later that morning. He then summoned his brother to the White House. "Oh shit!, Shit!, Shit! Those sons a bitches Russians," RFK exclaimed upon seeing the U-2 pictures. The Kennedys had tried over forty back channel contacts with Georgi Bolshakov, an official at the Soviet embassy who was also a colonel in Soviet Military Intelligence (the GRU), in an effort to "cajole, flatter, and deter Khrushchev." Their efforts, as a result of calculated Soviet deception, had come to nothing.[82]

Four decades after the fact it seems entirely plausible that deployment of nuclear missiles in Cuba was regarded by the Soviets as ideologically provocative but militarily defensive—to protect Castro's revolution by frustrating American plans to attack Cuba and to reduce U.S. nuclear superiority and the risk of a first-strike. Khrushchev apparently believed that Kennedy would accept the Cuban missiles as a reasonable counterweight to American missiles in Turkey and Italy. But, the Soviet leader simply did not understand the intensity of American fears of a communist military outpost in the Western Hemisphere, which could be utilized by Khrushchev for nuclear blackmail over Berlin and by Castro for political and economic subversion in Latin America.

In any case, President Kennedy's speech to the nation on October 22, 1962 was, at the very least, shrewdly misleading. "The purpose of these bases," he warned, "can be none other than to provide a nuclear strike capability against the Western Hemisphere." However, as we now know from the ExComm tapes, JFK believed that the missiles represented a political challenge and dismissed their significance as an of-

Amuchastegui, "Cuban Intelligence and the October Crisis," in Blight and Welch, *Intelligence and the Cuban Missile Crisis*, 111)

[82]Elie Abel, *The Missile Crisis* (Philadelphia: Lippincott, 1966), 13; Dino Brugioni, *Eyeball to Eyeball: The Inside Story of the Cuban Missile Crisis*, edited by Robert F. McCort (New York: Random House, 1991), 223; McGeorge Bundy, *Danger and Survival: Choices About the Bomb in the First Fifty Years* (New York: Random House, 1998), 684–85; Fursenko and Naftali, *"One Hell of a Gamble,"* 223.

fensive military threat. Kennedy could not, of course, mention the administration's massive covert war against Cuba and painted the conflict with Castro and his Soviet sponsors in simplistic, black and white, Cold War language that made sense to most Americans: "Our policy has been one of patience and restraint, as befits a peaceful and powerful nation. . . . Our goal is not the victory of might, but the vindication of right."[83]

The Kennedy Paradox

President Kennedy, a prominent historian has argued, was as an implacable, macho Cold Warrior, "more enamored with military than with diplomatic means." "In *all* cases, [italics added] Kennedy strove to win" and never abandoned his commitment to "'a strategy of annihilation.'" This worldview was clearly revealed in the Cuban missile crisis: "President Kennedy helped precipitate the missile crisis by harassing Cuba . . . Then he reacted to the crisis by suspending diplomacy in favor of public confrontation." In the end, the nuclear superpowers luckily "stumbled toward a settlement."[84]

The first part of the statement about the missile crisis is perfectly true—President Kennedy bears significant responsibility for provoking the missile crisis—because of the Bay of Pigs invasion, ongoing covert plots against Cuba and Castro, a massive nuclear arms buildup and "contingency" plans to invade Cuba again. The Kennedy administration had clearly contributed to polarizing the Cuban issue and ironically had become stuck on its own political tar baby.

The second part of the statement on the missile crisis, however, is demonstrably false. President Kennedy did *not* choose confrontation over diplomacy during the crisis, certainly not after deciding on the quarantine, and consistently led the ExComm discussions away from military conflict with remarkable steadiness of purpose; and, fortunately for all of us, he never stumbled. The irrefutable evidence on the ExComm tapes proves conclusively that JFK consistently rose above his own Cold War rhetoric and policies during these decisive meetings and subtly and even audaciously steered the ship of state away from

[83]John F. Kennedy, Radio-TV Address of the President to the Nation, October 22, 1962, in Chang and Kornbluh, *Cuban Missile Crisis*, 160–64.

[84]Paterson, "John F. Kennedy's Quest," in Paterson, ed., *Kennedy's Quest for Victory*, 5, 7, 20; Thomas G. Paterson, "When Fear Ruled: Rethinking the Cuban Missile Crisis," *New England Journal of History* 52 (Fall 1995), 26.

nuclear confrontation. President Kennedy became "the driver of the debate. We see a president as analyst-in-chief. On each issue, he presses his colleagues to probe deeper implications of each option; to explore ways of circumventing seemingly insurmountable obstacles; to face squarely unpalatable trade-offs; and to stretch their imagination."[85]

In September 1961, Kennedy had declared in a speech at the U.N. that "it is absurd to suppose that we would unleash a nuclear war. . . . we believe that a peaceful solution is possible." Khrushchev was so impressed by Kennedy's words that he allowed *Pravda* to publish an article from an American magazine which concluded that "Kennedy had no illusions with respect to nuclear war and he was therefore searching for ways to achieve an honorable peace—although, like any human being, he was not immune to mistakes."[86] In fact, only weeks later, Kennedy and Khrushchev used secret diplomacy to defuse a potentially explosive confrontation. In October, American and Soviet tanks challenged each other at the Berlin Wall's Checkpoint Charlie in a menacing game of nuclear chicken. President Kennedy moved to resolve the crisis by making a secret overture to Khrushchev. JFK utilized Robert Kennedy's private contacts with Georgi Bolshakov to urge Khrushchev to contain the crisis by taking the first step back from the brink. (RFK's discussions with Bolshakov had begun a month before the June 1961 Vienna summit and continued into the Cuban missile crisis.) Khrushchev ultimately agreed to "blink first" by pulling back Soviet tanks. The Americans quickly followed suit and the crisis subsided. "In the future," Sergei Khrushchev later observed, "there would be more than one problem that he [Khrushchev] and the U.S. president would have to solve together."[87]

Did President Kennedy, another scholar recently asked, "single-handedly" prevent World War III during the missile crisis? "Yes, it's pretty much true," he concluded. "John Kennedy behaved more heroically than the standard history books have told—certainly far more heroically than the experts and wise men around him." Another writer agreed that Kennedy "never looked taller" because "his triumph had

[85] Allison and Zelikow, *Essence of Decision*, 357.

[86] Sergei Khrushchev, *Nikita Khrushchev*, 460–61.

[87] Sergei Khrushchev, *Nikita Khrushchev*, 466; Freedman, *Kennedy's Wars*, 89–91; for a detailed account of the secret settlement of the October 1961 Berlin confrontation, see Raymond Garthoff, "Berlin, 1961: The Record Corrected," *Foreign Policy 84* (Fall 1991), 142–56; on the origins of the RFK-Bolshakov contacts, see Fursenko and Naftali, *"One Hell of a Gamble,"* 109–14.

required him both to be more clever and better informed than his generals and the hawks in his Cabinet and to have the nerve to face them down." Indeed, a leading Cold War historian, after examining newly available evidence from Soviet and American archives, has concluded that JFK's handling of the missile crisis was nothing less than "a new profile in courage—but it would be courage of a different kind from what many people presumed that term to mean throughout much of the Cold War."[88]

These encomiums, in sharp contrast to JFK's public manipulation of Cold War rhetoric both in Congress and in the White House, point to a dimension of his behavior and beliefs which has been all but lost in the surge of anti-Kennedy revisionism over the last few decades: namely, his lifelong distrust of military leaders and military solutions to political problems, and, most significantly, his horror at the prospect of total war, especially nuclear war. This paradoxical dimension of Kennedy's leadership was recently captured by a journalist who knew him well— Hugh Sidey of *Time Magazine*:

> I am dissatisfied with some of the modern assessments of him and his Presidency. This is not a denial of his flaws, personal or political, many of which were obscured or ignored in those simpler times. It is to say that there was at the core of his stewardship a continuing and serious effort to steady a difficult world. . . . Once in the Presidency there is virtually no time for re-education or the deep introspection that might show a President where he is right or wrong and bring about a true change of mind. Events move too fast. A President may pick up more knowledge about a subject or find an expert aide on whom he can rely, but in most instances when he is alone and faced with a crucial decision he must rely on his intuition, a mixture of natural intelligence, education, and experience.[89]

Sidey vividly recalled a meeting with JFK in the spring of 1960 when the young Massachusetts senator was struggling to capture his party's presidential nomination. "What do you remember about the Great Depression?" Sidey asked in an effort to gauge Kennedy's grasp of economics. JFK replied with "absolute candor [that] surprised us both. 'I have no first-hand knowledge of the depression,' he answered. 'My family had one of the great fortunes of the world and it was worth

[88]Fred Kaplan, "Kennedy Legacy Shines...," *Boston Globe*, 1/13/01, A1; Robert Kuttner, "Watching '13 Days'...," *Boston Globe*, 1/28/01, F7; Gaddis, *We Now Know*, 272.

[89]Hugh Sidey, Introduction, *Prelude to Leadership: The European Diary of John F. Kennedy—Summer 1945* (Washington, D.C.: Regnery, 1995), xix–xxi.

more than ever then. . . . I really did not learn about the depression until I read about it at Harvard.'" Then JFK leaned forward and added,
"'My experience was the war. I can tell you about that.'"[90] He then
lectured Sidey for much of an hour:

> He had read the books of great military strategists—Carl Von Clausewitz,
> Alfred Thayer Mahan, and Basil Henry Liddell Hart—and he wondered if
> their theories of total violence made sense in the nuclear age. He expressed
> his contempt for the old military minds . . . Kennedy chortled over the
> boasts of those who developed new military technology, claiming the new
> weapons rarely lived up to their billing—at first. But they were almost al-
> ways perfected and then stockpiled—and then used. War with all of its
> modern horror would be his biggest concern if he got to the White House,
> Kennedy said. . . . If I had to single out one element in Kennedy's life that
> more than anything else influenced his later leadership it would be a horror
> of war, a total revulsion over the terrible toll that modern war had taken
> on individuals, nations and societies, and the even worse prospects in the
> nuclear age. . . . It ran even deeper than his considerable public rhetoric on
> the issue.[91]

This "deep core of realism about the world," Sidey concluded, came
out of Kennedy's personal past—"a past . . . that was serious much of
the time and was focused on understanding the events and people that
drove nations, the preparation of a young man for what was still an ill-
defined and distant challenge. . . . Policy at the top comes out of the
heart and mind of the President, or at the very least is tempered by his
personality. And his convictions and passions are almost always linked
to early impressions gained from family and school and youthful experience." During the tense summer of 1961, Sidey recalled, JFK observed gloomily, "'Ever since the longbow,' he said, 'when man had
developed new weapons and stockpiled them, somebody has come
along and used them. I don't know how we escape it with nuclear
weapons.'" "Domestic policy," he sometimes mused, "can only defeat
us; foreign policy can kill us."[92]

"There are, I have found, many compartments within the souls of
men who rise to great power," Sidey concluded, an assessment that can
be vividly documented in the formative years of John Kennedy.[93] The

---

[90]*Ibid.*, xxiv.

[91]*Ibid.*, xxiv–xxv, xxix.

[92]*Ibid.*, xvi, xx, xxviii; Schlesinger, *A Thousand Days*, 426.

[93]Sidey, Introduction, *Prelude*, xx. JFK's medical records, examined by Robert Dallek,
add yet another "compartment" to his presidency. During the missile crisis, "Kennedy took

twenty-two-year-old undergraduate, writing a month after the out-break of World War II, warned his Harvard classmates that the new war would be "beyond comprehension in its savage intensity, and which could well presage a return to barbarism."[94] Four years later, the letters written by the twenty-six-year-old junior naval officer from the South Pacific confirm that he was an acute observer of events around him and more dubious than ever about the logic and results of war: "The day I arrived," Kennedy wrote to his school chum Lem Billings, the Japanese launched "a hell of an attack":

> During a lull in the battle—a Jap parachuted into the water—we went to pick him up as he floated along—and got within about 20 yds. of him. He suddenly threw aside his life-jacket + pulled out a revolver and fired two shots at our bridge. I had been praising the Lord + passing the ammunition right alongside—but that slowed me a bit—the thought of him sitting in the water—battling an entire ship. We returned the fire with everything we had—the water boiled around him—but everyone was too surprised to shoot straight. Finally an old soldier standing next to me—picked up his ri-fle—fired once—and blew the top of his head off. He threw his arms up—plunged forward + sank—and we hauled our ass out of there. That was the start of a very interesting month—and it brought home very strongly how long it is going to take to finish the war.[95]

His doubts only intensified in a letter to his Danish lover, Inga Ar-vad:

> I would like to write you a letter giving in a terse sharp style an outline of the war situation first hand... in which I would use the words global war, total effort and a battle of logistics no less than eight times each... I refrain from this for two reasons... the first being I know you don't give a damn,

---

his usual doses of anti-spasmodics to control his colitis, antibiotics for a flare-up of his uri-nary-tract problem and a bout of sinusitis, and increased amounts of hydrocortisone and testosterone, along with salt tablets, to control his Addison's disease and boost his energy." The tape recordings of the ExComm meetings, Dallek nonetheless concludes, indicate that "the medications were no impediment to lucid thought during these long days; on the con-trary, Kennedy would have been significantly less effective without them, and might even have been unable to function." ("The Medical Ordeals of JFK," *Atlantic Monthly* 290 (December 2002), 51, 61; Dallek's *An Unfinished Life: John F. Kennedy, 1917–1963*, will be published by Little, Brown in 2003)

[94]John F. Kennedy, Editorial, *Harvard Crimson*, October 9, 1939.

[95]John F. Kennedy to K. Lemoyne Billings, May 6, 1943, Billings Papers, JFKL; Kennedy related the same incident to his parents, concluding: "That I understand is the usual story with the [Japanese] officers. With the men, however, there would seem to be no such desire for the glorious death." (John F. Kennedy to Rose and Joseph Kennedy, May 10, 1943, John F. Kennedy, Personal Papers [hereafter PP], JFKL.

and the second being that frankly I don't know a god-damned thing, as my copy of the Washington Times Herald arrives two months late, due to logistical difficulties... and it is pretty hard to get the total picture of a global war unless you are sitting in New York or Washington, or even Casablanca...

I understand we are winning it, which is cheering, albeit somewhat hard to see, but I guess the view improves with distance... I know mine would... I wouldn't mind being back in the States picking up the daily paper, saying 'Why don't those bastards out there do something?' It's one of those interesting things about the war that everyone in the States...want[s] to be out here killing Japs, while everyone out here wants to be back . . . It seems to me that someone with enterprise could work out some sort of an exchange, but as I hear you saying, I asked for it, honey and I'm getting it...[96]

But, young Kennedy reserved special contempt for the senior brass supposedly in control of the massive war effort:

Dearest Inga Binga, In regard to the food, which I know you know I do regard, as lousy . . . I have finally found out where those steaks are going that—and I quote—'the boys in the service are getting' end of quote. . . . Well, anyway, a general came aboard and my exec. and I managed to look as weak from hunger as we possibly could which required no great effort, so he finally broke down and invited us for a meal. We went, and they kept bringing in the steaks and the potatoes and the peas and the asparagus and the pie and the beer, all of which I disposed of in a style to which you had become accustomed. . . . Well, when we had finally finished he came out with the statement that he understood we got the same food, only he figured his was probably cooked a little better. . . . Having had a bottle of beer and therefore being scarcely in a condition to carry on an intelligible conversation, and remembering article no. 252 in Naval Regulations, that Generals are seldom wrong and Admirals never, and figuring that the problem of food distribution was a problem that was occupying better minds than the generals or mine, I merely conceded the putt and went on to the next hole.

I'm certainly glad I came—I wouldn't miss it for the world, but I will be extremely glad to get back. . . . Well honey, I must go and get some of that delightful food, superbly prepared and cuisined, and served in pleasant and peaceful surroundings...[97]

Just had an inspection by an Admiral. He must have weighed over three hundred, and came bursting through our hut like a bull coming out of

---

[96]John F. Kennedy to Inga Arvad, no date, spring 1943, Nigel Hamilton Research Materials [hereafter NHRM], Massachusetts Historical Society [hereafter MHS]. Some of JFK's letters were typed; he often used three dots in place of commas or periods.

[97]John F. Kennedy to Inga Arvad, no date, NHRM, MHS.

chute three. A burst of speed when he got into the clear brought him against the machine shop. He harrumpped a couple of times, and then inquired, 'And what do we have here?'

'Well, General,' was the answer, 'this is our machine shop.'

'Harrumph, and what do you keep in it, harrumph ah... MACHINERY?'

After it was gently but firmly explained to him that machinery was kept in the machine shop and he had written that down on the special pad he carried for such special bits of information which can only be found 'if you get right up to the front and see for yourself' he harrumphed again, looked at a map, and wanted to know what we had *there*—there being a small bay some distance away. When we said nothing, he burst out with, 'well, by God, what we need is to build a dock.' Well, someone said it was almost lunch and it couldn't be built before lunch... After a moment of serious consideration and a hurried consultation with a staff of engineers he agreed and toddled off to stoke his furnace at the luncheon table... That, Bingo, is total war at its totalest.[98]

Don't let anyone sell the idea that everyone out here is hustling with the old American energy. They may be ready to give their blood but not their sweat, if they can help it, and usually they fix it so they can help it. They have brought back a lot of old Captains and Commanders from retirement . . . and they give the impression of their brains being in their tails.[99]

JFK's cynicism about the war erupted regularly: "I have an entirely new crew," he irreverently told his parents in the spring of 1943, "and when the showdown comes I'd like to be confident they know the difference between firing a gun and winding their watch." "When I read that we will fight the Japs for years if necessary," he cautioned them four months later, "and will sacrifice hundreds of thousands if we must—I always like to check from where he is talking—it's seldom out here." He poignantly told Inga Arvad that the "boys at the front" rarely discussed the war that threatened to engulf them every day, but instead talked endlessly about "when they are going to get home." These impressions never faded: "That whole story was fucked up," he told journalist Robert Donovan years later about the war in the Solomon Islands. "You know the military always screws up everything."[100]

[98]John F. Kennedy to Inga Arvad, no date, NHRM, MHS.

[99]John F. Kennedy to Rose and Joseph Kennedy, May 14, 1943, PP, JFKL.

[100]*Ibid.*, John F. Kennedy to Rose and Joseph Kennedy, September 12, 1943, PP, JFKL; John F. Kennedy to Inga Arvad, no date, spring 1943, NHRM, MHS; Herbert S. Parmet, *Jack: The Struggles of John F. Kennedy* (New York: Doubleday, 1980), 111–12.

The insights of this son of wealth and privilege in 1943 point directly to his "deep core of realism about the world" during the Cuban missile crisis meetings a generation later:

> The war goes slowly here, slower than you can ever imagine from reading the papers at home. The only way you can get the proper perspective on its progress is to put away the headlines for a month and watch us move on the map, it's deathly slow. The Japs have dug deep, and with the possible exception of a couple of Marine divisions are the greatest jungle fighters in the world. Their willingness to die for a place like Munda gives them a tremendous advantage over us, we, in aggregate, just don't have the willingness. Of course, at times, an individual will rise up to it, but in total, no... Munda or any of these spots are just God damned hot stinking corners of small islands in a part of the ocean we all hope never to see again.
>
> We are at a great disadvantage—the Russians could see their country invaded, the Chinese the same. The British were bombed, but we are fighting on some islands belonging to the Lever Company, a British concern making soap... I suppose if we were stockholders we would perhaps be doing better, but to see that by dying at Munda you are helping to insure peace in our time takes a larger imagination than most men possess... The Japs have this advantage: because of their feeling about Hirohito, they merely wish to kill. American energies are divided, he wants to kill but he is also trying desperately to prevent himself from being killed. . . .
>
> This war here is a dirty business. It's very easy to talk about the war and beating the Japs if it takes years and a million men, but anyone who talks like that should consider well his words. We get so used to talking about billions of dollars, and millions of soldiers, that thousands of casualties sound like drops in the bucket. But if those thousands want to live as much as the ten that I saw [his PT boat crew], the people deciding the whys and wherefores had better make mighty sure that all this effort is headed for some definite goal, and that when we reach that goal we may say it was worth it, for if it isn't, the whole thing will turn to ashes, and we will face great trouble in the years to come after the war. . . .
>
> There was a boy on my boat, only twenty-four, had three kids, one night two bombs straddles [sic] our boat, and two of the men were hit, one standing right next to him. He never got over it. He hardly ever spoke after that. He told me one night he thought he was going to be killed. I wanted to put him ashore to work, he wouldn't go. I wish I had... He was in the forward gun turret where the destroyer hit us... I don't know what this all adds up to, nothing I guess, but you said that you figured I'd . . . write my experiences—I wouldn't go near a book like that, this thing is so stupid, that while it has a sickening fascination for some of us, myself included, I want to leave it far behind me when I go...[101]

[101]John F. Kennedy to Inga Arvad, September 26, 1943, NHRM, MHS; JFK's thought-

John Kennedy's aversion to war, particularly large-scale or global war, would become even more pronounced during the first decades of the nuclear era. As early as 1947, the twenty-nine-year-old freshman congressman, gripped by the escalating suspicions of the Cold War, had publicly warned of the potential for nuclear apocalypse: "The greatest danger is a war which would be waged by the conscious decision of the leaders of Russia some 25 or 35 years from now. She will have the atomic bomb, the planes, the ports, and the ships to wage aggressive war outside her borders. Such a conflict would truly mean the end of the world, and all our diplomacy and prayers must be exerted to avoid it."[102]

JFK had written, as the 1960 presidential campaign moved into full gear, "We should bear in mind a few impressive lines of advice from [Sir Basil Liddell] Hart's book: 'Keep strong, if possible. In any case, keep cool. Have unlimited patience. Never corner an opponent, and always assist him to save his face. Put yourself in his shoes—so as to see things through his eyes. Avoid self-righteousness like the devil—nothing is so self-blinding.' "[103]

All his life JFK had a high regard for personal courage and toughness, but, at the same time, he loathed the brutality and carnage of war. He had also recognized a profound historical paradox: human beings had never been capable of building a stable and peaceful world, but, at the same time, war, especially between nations possessing nuclear weapons, was no longer a rational option. Kennedy was as passionately anti-communist as any of his missile crisis advisers, but he understood that once military conflict was unleashed between the nuclear superpowers, all bets were off. One colleague recalled a briefing by Soviet specialists at which JFK had revealed "a mentality extraordinarily free of preconceived prejudices, inherited or otherwise. . . . He saw Russia as a great and powerful country, and it seemed to him there must be some basis upon which the two countries could live without blowing each other up." Kennedy once remarked at a White House meeting, "It is insane that two men, sitting on opposite sides of the world, should be able to decide to bring an end civilization." He was

---

ful and worldly-wise observations belie the fact he was barely two years older than Andrew Kirksey, the twenty-four-year-old "boy on my boat" killed on PT 109.

[102]John F. Kennedy, "Aid for Greece and Turkey," *Record of the House of Representatives*, April 1, 1947.

[103]John F. Kennedy, Review of B.H. Liddell Hart, *Deterrent or Defense*, *Saturday Review*, September 3, 1960.

convinced "that there was nothing more important to a President than thinking hard about war."[104]

JFK was profoundly impressed by a reported exchange between a former German chancellor and his successor after the outbreak of World War I. "How did it all happen?" the ex-chancellor asked. "Ah, if only one knew," was the reply. "If this planet is ever ravaged by nuclear war—" President Kennedy remarked in 1963, "if the survivors of that devastation can then endure the fire, poison, chaos and catastrophe—I do not want one of those survivors to ask another, 'How did it all happen?' and to receive the incredible reply: 'Ah, if only one knew.' "[105]

Nonetheless, JFK never lost his detached and ironic sense of humor about such potentially fatal realities in human affairs. After nuclear scientist Edward Teller testified against the Nuclear Test Ban Treaty at 1963 Senate hearings, Senator J. William Fulbright told the President, in a recorded phone conversation, that Teller's arguments had been quite persuasive and may have changed some votes. Kennedy replied with a bemused tone of resignation reflecting that deep core of realism about the world, "There's no doubt that any man with complete conviction, particularly who's an expert, is bound to shake anybody who's got an open mind. That's the advantage of having a closed mind."[106] The Cuban missile crisis provided the supreme test of John Fitzgerald Kennedy's capacity to have an open mind and, at the same time, to hold fast to his core beliefs about war in the face of unyielding pressure from the "experts" around him.

Key Members of the Executive Committee of the National Security Council

George W. Ball (1909–94)
Under Secretary of State
    Ball worked on the Strategic Bombing Survey during World War II. In 1952 and 1956, he joined the presidential campaigns of his former law partner, Adlai Stevenson. Several foreign policy position papers he

---

[104]Charles Bohlen Oral History Interview, 1964, OHC, JFKL; Goodwin, *Remembering America*, 218; Geoffrey Perret, *Jack: A Life Like No Other* (New York: Random House, 2001), 326.

[105]Sorensen, *Kennedy*, 513.

[106]JFK and J. William Fulbright, Tape 26B.5, August 23, 1963, POF, Presidential Recordings Collection [hereafter PRC], JFKL.

had written for Stevenson's ill-fated attempt to win a third nomination in 1960, impressed JFK and led to Ball's appointment to the State Department. During the ExComm discussions, Ball supported a blockade and was among the first to condemn proposed surprise air attacks as an American "Pearl Harbor." However, he also advocated a declaration of war in the early meetings and during the crucial October 27 discussions initially opposed the Cuba-Turkey missile trade, but switched sides after the shooting down of an American U-2 spy plane over Cuba.

McGeorge Bundy (1919–96)
Special Assistant to the President for National Security

Bundy attended the Dexter School in Brookline, Massachusetts with classmate John F. Kennedy in the 1920s. He did foreign policy research for Republican presidential candidate Thomas Dewey in 1948, and later worked for the Council on Foreign Relations. In 1953, at the age of thirty-four and without a Ph.D., Bundy became dean of the faculty of arts and sciences at Harvard. A Republican, Bundy worked for the Kennedy campaign in 1960 and was appointed to the top White House national security position. His role in the ExComm meetings is difficult to categorize. Bundy initially urged military action against the missiles alone because of concern about Soviet reprisals in Berlin. However, he was always eager to stand up for his personal policy choices and sometimes irritated the President. Bundy eventually supported extensive air strikes in Cuba and, in the later meetings, forcefully resisted JFK's willingness to "trade" Soviet missiles in Cuba for U.S. missiles in Turkey because he believed this choice would divide the NATO alliance and undermine American credibility.

C. Douglas Dillon (1909–2003)
Secretary of the Treasury

Dillon, an investment banker and Republican activist, first served in the Eisenhower administration as ambassador to France. Later, as Under Secretary of State for Economic Affairs, he had some heated personal exchanges with Khrushchev. Even though Dillon had generously supported Richard Nixon in 1960, Kennedy chose him to lead the Treasury Department in an effort to soften GOP opposition to his economic policies. Dillon, deeply suspicious of communism and Khrushchev's motives, initially supported air strikes on the missile sites alone as the course of action least likely to provoke Soviet retaliation, but eventually went along with the blockade as the first step in isolating and eventually ousting Castro. He vigorously resisted the proposal to remove American missiles from Turkey in exchange for the withdrawal of Soviet missiles from Cuba.

Roswell Gilpatric (1906–96)
Deputy Secretary of Defense

Gilpatric, a successful Wall Street lawyer, served as Assistant Secretary of the Air Force in the Truman administration and during the 1950s helped draft a report for the Rockefeller Brothers' Fund calling for an extensive buildup of U.S. weapons and research. Unlike his boss, Robert McNamara, Gilpatric generally supported the JCS view that the missiles represented a military rather than a diplomatic threat and was sympathetic to their proposals to eliminate them by bombing and/or invasion.

Lyndon B. Johnson (1908–73)
Vice President of the United States

As Senate Majority leader during the Eisenhower administration, Johnson had regularly been described at the second most powerful man in Washington. He found the inevitable obscurity of the vice presidency hard to accept and always felt that he did not have the respect of the "best and the brightest" around the President. Despite his initial reluctance to speak at the ExComm meetings, especially when JFK was present, and his ambivalence about the use of force, he did eventually make some important contributions to the crucial discussions on October 27.

U. Alexis Johnson (1908–97)
Deputy Under Secretary of State for Political Affairs

A career foreign service officer, Johnson served as ambassador to Czechoslovakia during the Eisenhower administration before being appointed to the Kennedy State Department. Johnson, like most members of ExComm, first supported surprise air strikes against the missile sites but ultimately endorsed the blockade. He was not an active participant in the discussions but worked behind the scenes drafting policy papers for the meetings.

John Fitzgerald Kennedy (1917–63)
President of the United States

JFK, a World War II naval hero in the South Pacific, ran successfully for three terms in the House of Representatives (1946, 1948, 1950) and two terms in the Senate (1952, 1958) before he was narrowly elected President in 1960. Kennedy subtly guided and managed the ExComm discussions without ever appearing overbearing or aggressive. He patiently listened to all points of view and seemed remarkably tolerant of harsh criticism. His determination to seek a political rather than a military solution, in order to avert "the final failure" of nuclear war, stands in sharp contrast to the Cold War rhetoric and policies which had helped propel him into the White House and the covert actions against Cuba which he had eagerly pursued since early 1961 and would continue to vigorously support in his final year as President.

Robert F. Kennedy (1925–68)
Attorney General of the United States

Robert Kennedy managed JFK's presidential campaign in 1960 before becoming Attorney General at the age of thirty-five. RFK played a disproportionately significant role in the missile crisis not merely because he was JFK's brother, but because he was accurately perceived by the ExComm to be the President's most intimate adviser and confidant. Indeed, the loyalty and trust between the Kennedy brothers was unique in the history of the American presidency. The author can vividly recall, for example, first listening to their recorded telephone conversations and often finding it difficult to even understand what they were talking about. Typically, as soon as the phone was picked up, the brothers, without any personal greetings whatsoever, would burst into a staccato exchange of barely coherent sentence fragments and exclamations before abruptly concluding with "OK," "good" or "right" and hanging up. Their intuitive capacity to communicate transcended the limits of conventional verbal discourse. *They* always understood each other.

If JFK temporarily left the room or did not attend an ExComm meeting, the participants instinctively recognized that RFK served as the President's stand-in and alter-ego. In the final days and hours before the October 28 breakthrough, not surprisingly, President Kennedy trusted only his brother as a personal and secret emissary to Soviet ambassador Anatoly Dobrynin. Nonetheless, RFK's stance during the ExComm meetings turned out to be much more complicated than the rather idealized and romanticized view popularized in his 1969 book, *Thirteen Days*. Indeed, RFK, in sharp contrast to his brother, was one of the most consistently hawkish and confrontational members of the ExComm.

Edwin Martin (1908–2002)
Assistant Secretary of State for Inter-American Affairs

Martin held State Department posts in Japan, Korea and Europe before President Eisenhower named him assistant secretary of state for economic affairs in 1960. After moving to Latin American affairs in 1962, Martin played a key role in the OAS resolutions condemning the deployment of Soviet missiles in Cuba and endorsing the U.S. blockade. He was also involved in coordinating covert actions against Cuba and strongly supported the blockade and all necessary steps for removing the missiles.

John McCone (1902–91)
Director, Central Intelligence Agency

A tough anti-communist and conservative Republican, McCone served as chairman of the Atomic Energy Commission in the Eisenhower administration before JFK named him to head the CIA after the Bay of Pigs fiasco. He was the first senior administration official to warn that the Soviets were planning to install offensive nuclear weapons in Cuba. McCone regularly briefed the ExComm on Soviet moves in Cuba and updated former President Eisenhower on JFK's behalf. He advocated removal of the missiles by whatever means necessary—including the use of military force. He did, however, break with most of his ExComm colleagues in the final meetings on October 27 by supporting the President's determination to consider a Turkish missile trade.

Robert S. McNamara (1916–)
Secretary of Defense

McNamara, a statistician and business school graduate, became president of the Ford Motor Company at age 43, but only weeks later was offered the top Defense Department post by President-elect Kennedy. He quickly earned a reputation for hard-nosed realism and a detailed grasp of technical issues. Although he supported an invasion early in the ExComm meetings, McNamara became the President's most persuasive ally by openly breaking with the Joint Chiefs and arguing that the Soviet missiles in Cuba posed a political rather than a military threat to the United States. He ultimately resisted surprise air strikes, supported the blockade and proposed a plan to reduce the likelihood of a Soviet attack on Turkey by defusing U.S. Jupiter missiles and substituting submarine-launched Polaris missiles. Nonetheless, he continued to oppose the President's support for a direct trade of the Cuban and Turkish missiles. He was one of the most articulate and outspoken members of the ExComm.

Paul H. Nitze (1907–)
Assistant Secretary of Defense for International Security Affairs

The principal author of NSC-68 in 1950, Nitze was committed to victory over the U.S.S.R. and international communism. He was one of the ExComm's most consistent hawks and argued, contrary to his superior, Robert McNamara, that the Soviet missiles in Cuba had altered the world balance of power. His tense exchange with President Kennedy about tightening JCS procedures so that U.S. missiles in Turkey could not be fired at the U.S.S.R. without a presidential order is one of the most dramatic moments of the ExComm meetings. He was a resolute opponent of the Cuba-Turkey missile trade.

Dean Rusk (1909–94)
Secretary of State

Rusk, a former Rhodes Scholar, served as Deputy Under Secretary of State in the Truman administration before becoming president of the Rockefeller Foundation from 1951 to 1960. Kennedy offered Rusk the top State Department post on the recommendation of former defense secretary Robert Lovett. In the first wave of writing after the Cuban missile crisis, RFK and several historians criticized Rusk for lack of leadership in the ExComm discussions. The tapes have proved otherwise. Rusk contributed detailed and thoughtful analyses of diplomatic policy choices throughout the meetings, and, like most ExComm members, shifted positions several times; he generally resisted surprise air strikes, endorsed the blockade and advised against seizing Soviet ships that had turned away from Cuba. However, he opposed a deal involving U.S. missiles in Turkey and, after a U-2 was shot down on October 27, urged JFK to enforce surveillance over Cuba despite the likelihood of clashes with Russian personnel on the ground. Later that evening, Rusk and JFK collaborated on a secret diplomatic effort, through the U.N., to prevent the outbreak of war.

Theodore C. Sorensen (1928–)
Special Counsel to the President

Sorensen served as speechwriter and trusted political adviser to Senator John Kennedy from 1953 to 1960. Despite the fact that Sorensen was not a foreign policy specialist, Kennedy, who relied on Sorensen's judgment, invited him to participate in the ExComm discussions. Sorensen spoke rarely, but generally came down on the side of caution and diplomacy rather than military force. However, he did join the majority in resisting a Turkish missile swap. He also wrote several important policy option memos during the crisis and was the principal author of JFK's October 22 speech to the nation.

Maxwell D. Taylor (1901–87)
Chairman of the Joint Chiefs of Staff

Taylor served as Army Chief of Staff during the Eisenhower administration and was chosen as chairman of the JCS by President Kennedy in 1962. Taylor generally represented the hawkish views of the Chiefs during the ExComm discussions. However, even though he favored bombing over invasion in the early meetings, he eventually shifted ground, even suggesting the possible use of nuclear weapons in Cuba to safeguard American military supremacy in the Caribbean. Taylor reluctantly accepted the quarantine, but always displayed respect for the President and avoided the condescending tone adopted by several members of the JCS.

Llewellyn E. Thompson (1904–72)
United States Ambassador-at-Large

Thompson had served as U.S. Ambassador to the Soviet Union from 1957 to 1962 and was the only regular member of the ExComm who knew Khrushchev personally. As a result, the President listened with special interest to Thompson's assessments of Soviet thinking and Khrushchev's motives. Thompson's advice, however, was generally hawkish. Despite endorsing the blockade, he supported a declaration of war and the ouster of Castro, advised the President that Khrushchev would never back down and strenuously resisted a trade of U.S. missiles in Turkey for Soviet missiles in Cuba in order to preserve U.S. credibility in Europe and avoid dividing the NATO alliance.

A grim but focused President Kennedy just seconds before addressing the nation and revealing the discovery of Soviet nuclear missiles in Cuba.

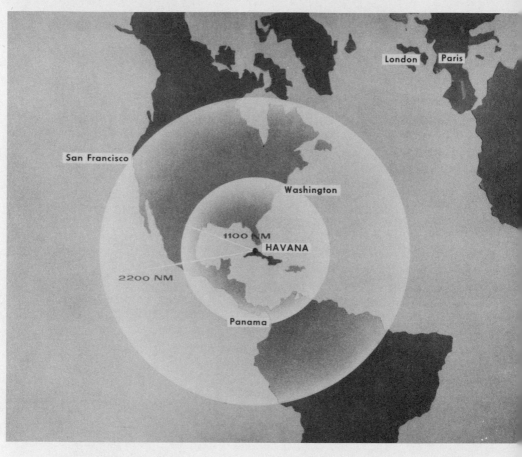

Department of Defense display board showing the range of Soviet MRBMs and IRBMs in Cuba.

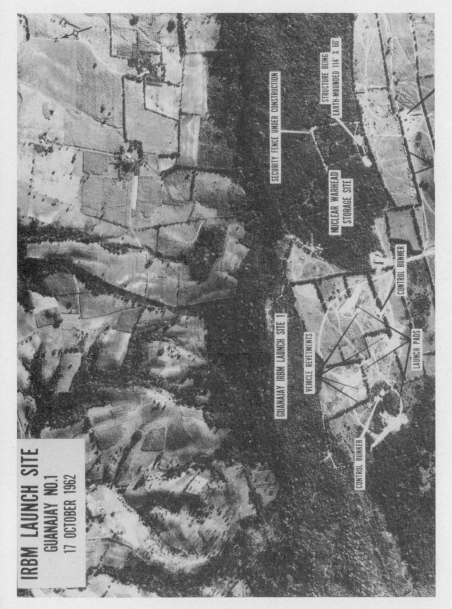

IRBM LAUNCH SITE
GUANAJAY NO.1
17 OCTOBER 1962

SECURITY FENCE UNDER CONSTRUCTION

STRUCTURE BEING
EARTH-MOUNDED 114' X 60'

NUCLEAR WARHEAD
STORAGE SITE

GUANAJAY IRBM LAUNCH SITE 1

VEHICLE REVETMENTS

CONTROL BUNKER

LAUNCH PADS

CONTROL BUNKER

October 17 high-level U-2 photo of an IRBM launch site at Guanajay

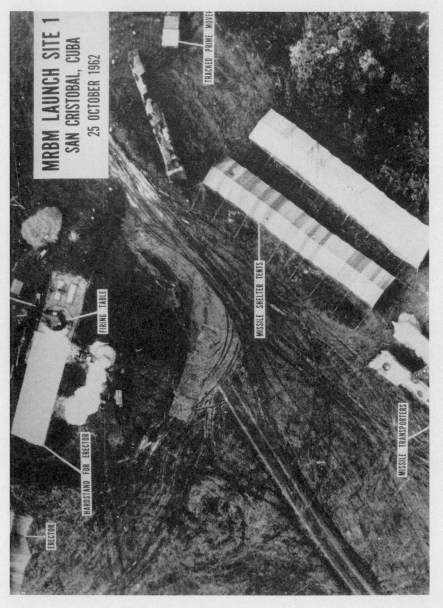

October 25 low-level surveillance photo of an MRBM launch site at San Cristobal

JFK and Ambassador Llewellyn Thompson (foreground) meet with Soviet Foreign Minister Andrei Gromyko (right) and Ambassador Anatoly Dobrynin in the Oval Office on October 18

President Kennedy signs the quarantine proclamation in the Oval Office on
October 23

The October 29 ExComm meeting (the only meeting photographed), view one. On the President's side of the table (Presidential Seal on the wall behind JFK)— *to JFK's left:* Robert McNamara, Roswell Gilpatric (pen in hand), Maxwell Taylor (not in uniform), Paul Nitze (right end of table); *to JFK's right:* Dean Rusk, George Ball (writing), John McCone's white hair just visible on the left end of the table in front of the fireplace.

The October 29 ExComm meeting, view two. Facing the bookcases on the side opposite the President—*from left to right:* Robert Kennedy (standing), Donald Wilson (partially obscured), Theodore Sorensen, McGeorge Bundy, Douglas Dillon, Lyndon Johnson, Llewellyn Thompson, U. Alexis Johnson.

The Secret Meetings
of the Executive Committee of
the National Security Council

Tuesday, October 16, 11:50 A.M., Cabinet Room

Identified Participants: John F. Kennedy, George Ball, McGeorge Bundy, Marshall Carter, Douglas Dillon, Roswell Gilpatric, Sidney Graybeal, Lyndon Johnson, U. Alexis Johnson, Robert Kennedy, Arthur Lundahl, Edwin Martin, Robert McNamara, Dean Rusk, Maxwell Taylor.[1]

"How do you know this is a medium-range ballistic missile?"
President John F. Kennedy

In the hectic early morning hours before the first ExComm meeting the President kept to his normal schedule in order to avoid the appearance of a crisis atmosphere at the White House.[2] At 9:30, he met with astronaut Walter Shirra and his family in the Oval Office and then escorted them around the White House grounds. An hour later, Kennedy participated in a meeting of the White House Panel on Mental Retardation, championed by his sister, Eunice Kennedy Shriver. He was genuinely and personally interested in the discussion and asked several questions. The panel members never suspected that he had far more pressing problems on his mind.[3]

[1]Tape 28, POF, PRC, JFKL.
[2]The formal term, "Executive Committee of the National Security Council," or "ExComm," was not created by Executive Order until October 22. The early discussions were technically meetings of the National Security Council. But, the term is now commonly used for all the meetings during the crisis.
[3]Only a month before, Mrs. Shriver had published an article, "Hope for Retarded Chil-

As the President's advisers gathered in the Cabinet Room just before noon, the human meaning of the situation they were facing was made poignantly plain when they found JFK talking with his daughter Caroline, just a month short of her fifth birthday. She quickly scurried from the room and the meeting began.

The fifteen men gathering that Tuesday morning, on very short notice, were stunned that the Soviets had embarked upon such a dangerous gambit just 90 miles off the Florida coast and infuriated that the United States had been deliberately and systematically deceived by high-ranking Soviet officials. Tension was unmistakable as the meeting got underway, but JFK and his advisers knew that nothing was to be gained from emotion and panic and that any effort to humiliate the Soviets would, very likely, only make the situation worse. This was one case where a favorite Kennedy family maxim, "Don't get mad, get even," did not apply.[4]

The tone of the discussions nearly always remained calm, deliberate and businesslike—at times making it difficult, when listening to the tapes, to grasp that the stakes were nothing less than world peace and human survival. The meetings were remarkably egalitarian and the participants spoke out freely with little or no regard for rank. Indeed, there were repeated disagreements with the President—sometimes bordering on rudeness if not disrespect. The discussions were often rambling and repetitious; many remarks were incomplete, obscure or grammatically fuzzy. Nonetheless, there were also frequent moments of laughter, even hilarity, clearly a cathartic necessity for people coping with such unrelenting anxiety and uncertainty. General Maxwell Taylor, chairman of the Joint Chiefs of Staff, later recalled that he tried to prepare in advance for the ExComm discussions but often found the impatient President pushing the discussion ahead too quickly: "The real problem was John F. Kennedy who wouldn't sit still for all this to take place. He very frequently precipitated these discussions before his advisers were ready to talk."[5]

---

dren," in the *Saturday Evening Post*, detailing for the first time the retardation of Rosemary, the first Kennedy daughter. "It was a historic moment in the history of mental retardation in America." (Laurence Leamer, *The Kennedy Women: The Saga of an American Family* (New York: Villard Books, 1994), 573)

[4]JFK selected the ExComm from those with official responsibilities in foreign relations and national security and from "those people in whose basic judgment he had some confidence. I don't mean to imply there was not a considerable overlap in those two groups." (Sorensen Oral History, 56)

[5]Maxwell Taylor Oral History Interview, 1964, 53, OHC, JFKL; U. Alexis Johnson ob-

From the outset, the overriding question was clear: could the United States eliminate this apparent Soviet provocation without initiating an armed clash which could easily spin out of control?[6] JFK and most of his ExComm advisers assumed that if the U.S. took military action against Cuba, the U.S.S.R. would move against West Berlin. The U.S. would then be forced to respond to that attack. The Soviets would respond in turn—and so on, step after step—escalating inexorably towards the unthinkable. As the meeting opened, President Kennedy and his counselors knew that a misguided, reckless or careless move might set in motion an irreversible and catastrophic chain of events.

But, before any American response could be discussed, on which the fate of millions might well hinge, the most basic question had to be answered first: what exactly were the Soviets building in Cuba? Aerial photography, difficult for the layman to interpret, provided the only evidence. Nothing in the photographs cried out "missiles!" To the untrained eye the strange objects in these high-level U-2 photos could easily be mistaken for trucks or farm equipment.

Few members of ExComm had any experience in photographic interpretation. Two intelligence experts, Arthur Lundahl, director of the National Photographic Interpretation Center (established in the final days of the Eisenhower administration under CIA direction) and missile expert Sydney Graybeal, were on hand to set up a display of U-2 photo boards and to provide much-needed technical expertise. Lundahl had been briefing, that is, educating, President Kennedy on photo interpretation for over a year and they had established an excellent working relationship. Nonetheless, JFK and most of his advisers were in largely uncharted territory and, at least at the outset, the President did more listening than talking. As the participants took their seats, JFK pored over the mounted photos, using a large magnifying glass supplied by Lundahl; he also unobtrusively hit the switch under the conference table, activating the tape recorder. Several participants later recalled that

---

served that the President's "confidence and coolness" concealed "the deep nervous and emotional energy that you knew was at work within him." (U. Alexis Johnson Oral History Interview, 1964, 28, OHC, JFKL)

[6]"Why did the president not try private negotiations first rather than a public confrontation?" Soviet sources themselves remain divided on this possibility—some believing Khrushchev would have responded to a private contact and others concluding that he "would not have backed down." (Bernstein, "Commentary: Reconsidering Khrushchev's Gambit," 231, 236; also see Bernstein, "Understanding Decisionmaking," 151) A private communication to Khrushchev was actively considered but rejected because "it would be undesirable to let the Soviets take the initiative." (Garthoff, *Reflections*, 49)

he muttered unintelligibly to himself and the look on his face seemed to suggest both deep concern and uncertainty.

Deputy CIA director General Marshall Carter began by explaining what the October 14 photographs of an MRBM site in San Cristobal revealed to his technically sophisticated eye.[7] "This is the result of the photography taken Sunday, sir." "Yeah," JFK murmured. "The President would like to see those," Carter remarked to Lundahl, as he began to elucidate the photos of "at least 14 canvas-covered missile trailers measuring 67 feet in length, 9 feet in width." Lundahl, pointing to the small, rectangular shapes in the photos told the President in a whispered aside: "These are the launchers here."

For several minutes, Carter and Lundahl continued to focus on the technical specifics revealed by the photographs.

"How far advanced is *this*?" the President finally asked in an almost clinical tone of voice.[8]

Lundahl hedged. "Sir, we've never seen this kind of an installation before."

"Not even in the Soviet Union?" Kennedy pressed.

"No sir," Lundahl admitted. The CIA had kept careful tabs on Soviet missile complexes with U-2 flights begun during the Eisenhower administration. But Lundahl reminded the President that U-2 coverage had been discontinued after Francis Gary Powers was shot down over the U.S.S.R. in May 1960. The NPIC director did not mention that ultra-secret *Discoverer* surveillance satellites had been photographing Soviet missile installations since the suspension of the U-2 flights.

JFK continued to pump the experts for details. The President, whose military experience was limited to his service as a junior naval officer in World War II, was not familiar with the technical jargon of missile-age weaponry, at least, not yet.

"How do you know this is a medium-range ballistic missile?" he asked bluntly.

"The length, sir," Lundahl responded patiently.

"The what? The length?" JFK repeated.

"Yes," Lundahl confirmed.

"The length of the missile?" Kennedy asked examining the photo. "Which part?"

[7]CIA director John McCone was attending a family funeral on the West coast.

[8]The author relied on the officially opened Kennedy Library analog cassettes for these transcriptions. These tapes were duplicated from the 1962 White House reel-to-reel master recordings, excluding still-classified material and later dubbed directly onto CD-ROMs.

"Mr. Graybeal," Lundahl continued, "our missile man, has some pictures of the equivalent Soviet equipment that has been dragged through the streets of Moscow that can give you some feel for it, sir."

Graybeal handed the President intelligence photographs from the Soviet Union's carefully orchestrated annual May Day display of military might. Kennedy perused them as Graybeal continued to describe missiles already photographed on Soviet territory; but, JFK quickly returned to the issue at hand: Cuba.

"It's ready to be fired?" the President asked grimly.

"No, sir," Graybeal replied.

"How long have... we can't tell that, can we, how long before they fire?"

"No, sir," Graybeal answered, even before the President had finished his question.

"What... what does it have to be fired from?" JFK persisted.

"It would have to be fired from a stable, hard surface," Graybeal replied. "This could be packed earth, it could be concrete or an asphalt."

The intelligence experts had indeed been caught off guard by what they had discovered. The sites were being assembled more quickly than previous surveillance inside the U.S.S.R. had led them to think possible. No one knew, therefore, when the missiles would become fully operational—when, that is, they would be capable of hurling their nuclear payloads at American military installations or major cities.

Secretary of Defense Robert McNamara asked Graybeal about the most critical issue implicit in the President's questions—whether Soviet nuclear warheads were also in Cuba. Graybeal could only confirm that U.S. spy planes had photographed and identified missiles but had been unable to locate nuclear warheads or sites for their storage. The photographic evidence, up to that morning, was inconclusive: "Sir, we've looked very hard. We can find nothing that would spell 'nuclear warhead' in terms of any isolated area or unique security in this particular area. The mating of the nuclear warhead to the missile . . . would take about a couple of hours to do this." McNamara observed that the sites were not fenced in, "It seems almost *impossible, to me*, that they would be ready to fire *with* nuclear warheads *on the site* without even a fence around it. It may not take long to place them there, to erect a fence. But at least at the moment there is *some* reason to believe the warheads aren't present and hence they are *not* ready to fire." Graybeal confirmed McNamara's assumption, "We do not believe they are ready to fire," providing at least some modestly good news. But, even if this assessment turned out to be correct, no one at the table knew how long it would remain correct.

General Taylor, sworn in by President Kennedy to chair the Joint Chiefs of Staff barely two weeks before, added ominously that there was no reason to assume that these sites could not be operational "very quickly, isn't that true?" Graybeal conceded that final preparation to fire would likely take only "in the order of two to three hours." But, of the eight missiles detected thus far, he added, only one appeared to be close to launch position near an erector. Lundahl, with a hint of professional pride in his voice, explained that the movement of Soviet missile–carrying vehicles, which had first been reported by ground observers in Cuba in August, was being monitored very carefully, "but this is the first time we have been able to *catch* them on photography—at a location." JFK and the ExComm must have wondered whether this additional critical information would be available soon enough.

"Am I correct," McNamara reiterated, still pushing his point, "in saying that we have *not* located any nuclear storage sites with certainty—as yet? And this is one of the most important problems we face," he insisted, "in properly interpreting the readiness of... of these missiles." McNamara prided himself on examining issues logically and dispassionately, and he could not bring himself to believe that the Soviets would risk a military confrontation with the United States over missiles that were not accompanied by nuclear warheads: "It's *inconceivable* to me that the Soviets would deploy nuclear warheads on an unfenced piece of ground. There *must* be *some* storage site there. It should be one of our important objectives to *find* that storage site." Lundahl offered the defense chief guarded assurance that two U-2 surveillance missions conducted the previous day could uncover this information. "Both of these missions go from one end of Cuba to the other, one along the north coast, one along the south, so additional data on activities or these storage sites, which we consider critical, may be in our grasp," he added cautiously, "*if* we can find them."[9] He was unable, however, "from photos alone," to confirm McNamara's speculation about a possible "hardened" warhead site just outside of Havana.

[9] At the October 2002 conference in Havana, newly declassified documents revealed that "US intelligence never located the nuclear warheads for the Soviet missiles in Cuba during the crisis, and only 33 of what photography later showed was a total of 42 medium-range ballistic missiles." (News Release, "The Cuban Missile Crisis, 1962: A Political Perspective After 40 Years," October 11, 2002), 2)

The ExComm in general seemed wary of delaying action against the missile bases simply because the warheads had not actually been located. General Carter saw eye to eye with McNamara—affirming that it would simply make no sense to put this class of missile in Cuba "unless it were associated with nuclear warheads." Secretary of State Dean Rusk affirmed, "Don't you have to assume these are nuclear?" and McNamara immediately replied: "Oh, I think there's no question about that. The question is one of readiness of the... to fire and... and this is *highly critical* in forming our plans."[10] The best face McNamara could put on the situation was, "it seems *extremely* unlikely that they are *now* ready to fire, or *may be* ready to fire within a matter of hours, or even a day or two." A presidential decision to order air strikes on the missile sites did not have to be made—at least not right away.

One decision quickly commanded a consensus: the President should immediately authorize further U-2 reconnaissance flights over Cuba, to be repeated as necessary in the event of bad weather, in order to determine precisely the number and location of Soviet missile sites (only the San Cristobal MRBM site had thus far been identified) and to find warheads and storage facilities that logically were assumed to be somewhere in Cuba. McNamara recommended deferring any decision on initiating low-level surveillance flights. All future military and diplomatic decisions, he suggested, would hinge on what the U-2 photographs revealed. JFK tried to clarify the situation, "In other words, the only missile base ("inter... intermediate-range missile," Carter interjected), missile base that we *now* know about is *this* one." "That's correct," Lundahl confirmed. "There are three that are associated," Bundy explained.

Rusk soon broke in. His placid, monotone voice and lengthy monologues would try the patience of some of his ExComm colleagues over the coming days, but he consistently raised issues at the heart of every move and countermove the President and his advisors would have to consider. The soft-spoken secretary of state, later written off by some ExComm colleagues and historians as a passive, lightweight southern gentleman, never in fact flinched from confronting the toughest ques-

[10]The MRBMs being installed in Cuba were provided with warheads more than 70 times as powerful as the primitive nuclear device which had obliterated Hiroshima in 1945. To Khrushchev, it seemed a stroke of military genius: without investing the research and rubles needed to improve his bombers and ICBMs, he had more than doubled the number of Soviet missiles capable of striking American cities. And he had done it practically overnight.

tion: how could the United States eliminate these missiles from Cuba without provoking Soviet retaliation, especially in Berlin, which could spark an all-out conventional war or even a nuclear exchange?[11]

"Mr. President," Rusk began gravely, as if delivering a professorial lecture, "this is a... there is an overwhelmingly serious problem. It's one that we, I think all of us, had not *really* believed the Soviets could carry this far." But, Rusk insisted, hard choices would have to be made, "Now I do think we have to set in motion a chain of events that will eliminate this base. I don't think we can sit still."[12] But, he predicted, sudden military action in Cuba would ultimately affect America's allies and likely involve U.S. forces and alliances all over the world. In short, from the perspective of America's highest ranking diplomat, there was no possibility that the U.S. could resolve the crisis alone: "there's no such thing, I think, as unilateral action by the United States." A confrontation with the U.S.S.R., fraught with international and even nuclear implications, would inevitably impact all of America's 42 allies around the world.

"So I think we... we have to think *very hard*," Rusk argued, "about *two major* courses of action as alternatives." The president could choose to "take all the risks that are involved" and authorize surprise air strikes to quickly eliminate the bases or "decide that this is the time to eliminate the Cuban problem by actually moving into the island." On the other hand, if the failure to locate the warheads did indeed provide a few days of military breathing space, Rusk recommended several diplomatic moves, such as seeking OAS support under the Rio Pact and initiating a direct contact with Castro, either through the Canadian ambassador in Cuba or through Castro's U.N. ambassador. The U.S., he believed, should privately warn the Cuban leader that his country was "being *victimized* here and that the Soviets are preparing Cuba for destruction *or betrayal*." The Soviet Union, he reported, had already floated hints in the press about "trading" Cuba for Berlin, that is, agreeing to abandon their foothold in the Western Hemisphere if the

---

[11]JFK allegedly felt that Rusk was an inflexible, cliché-bound organization man who confirmed his worst fears about the "bowl of jelly" called the State Department. (Schlesinger, *A Thousand Days,* 432–37) RFK even claimed that Rusk "had a virtually complete breakdown, mentally and physically" during the missile crisis. (Arthur M. Schlesinger, Jr., *Robert Kennedy and His Times* (Boston: Houghton Mifflin, 1978), 507) The ExComm tapes *do not* back up either of these harsh judgments.

[12]Implicit in Rusk's remarks was the belief that the presence of a Soviet military base in Cuba violated the Monroe Doctrine.

U.S. would abandon West Berlin. In fact, Rusk's proposal for a direct contact with Castro's government was not acted upon. The Kennedy administration treated Cuba as little more than "an afterthought" during the entire crisis and made no effort to deal directly with the Castro government.[13]

Rusk was certainly not displaying any concern for Castro's survival: he recommended calling up 150,000 military personnel or even declaring "a general national emergency so that we have complete freedom of action." He also urged further aerial surveillance of Cuba, a reinforcement of U.S. personnel at the Guantanamo naval base[14] and in the southeastern U.S., as well as a more vigorous and open commitment to the U.S.-backed guerrilla forces working to "create maximum confusion on the island. We won't be *too* squeamish at this point about the overt/covert character of what is being done," including planning with Cuban exiles in the U.S. for "a progressive junta that would pretty much combine all principal elements, other than the Batista group," to replace Castro.[15] Rusk, like his ExComm colleagues, was groping for a workable solution, *any* workable solution. If the United States could prevail by sowing distrust between Castro and the Soviet Union—well and good. If the U.S. could prevail by toppling Castro's regime, that too would be entirely acceptable.

Rusk's discourse concluded with a warning that the entire world might slip into war if the U.S. failed to communicate the gravity of the situation. He urged putting pressure on America's allies to cut off air and sea traffic with Cuba and advised the President to call in General Eisenhower for a complete briefing. In a particularly somber tone of voice, Rusk stressed the need for either choosing a quick strike or alerting "our allies *and Mr. Khrushchev* that there *is* an utterly serious

[13]"The lack of direct contact with the Cuban government may have delayed the settlement of the crisis. It almost certainly contributed to Castro's well-known decision to refuse to accept any on-site inspection." (Domínguez, "The @#$%& Missile Crisis," 305–7) Newly declassified documents discussed at the October 2002 Havana conference also revealed that the Canadian ambassador to the U.S. informed Rusk during the crisis that Cuba "was prepared at any time to negotiate its differences with the USA." Rusk dismissed the offer on the grounds that Castro was almost certainly "'a total instrument of Moscow.'" (*Boston Sunday Globe*, October 20, 2002)

[14]One of the most ironic elements in the missile crisis was the presence of an American naval installation at Guantanamo Bay, on the southeastern tip of Cuba, guaranteed by a 1934 treaty. Castro had been warned, after diplomatic relations were broken early in 1961, not to interfere with the operation of the base.

[15]Presumably, Rusk would not have agreed to include the Cuban communists in this "progressive junta."

crisis in the making here and that... because Mr. Khrushchev may not himself really understand that or believe that at this point. I think we'll be facing a situation that could *well* lead to general war. Now that we have an obligation to do what has to be done, but to do it *in a way* that gives everybody a chance to ah... pull away from it before it gets too hard."

No one sitting at the table could doubt that the usually imperturbable Rusk was alarmed: "Those are my reactions to this morning, Mr. President. I naturally need to think about this *very hard* in the next several hours." Rusk was wrestling with the dilemma the President and his advisers would repeatedly confront over the coming days: walking the fine line between an inadequate response that could, in their Cold War calculus, leave America and the Kennedy administration fatally weakened, or an overly aggressive response that could easily escalate into nuclear war.

McNamara echoed Rusk's concerns about the uncertainties and unknowns in the existing situation. Nevertheless, in a firm voice, he insisted that the tough but unavoidable military choices must be faced immediately. He urged the President to accept two essential "foundations for our further thinking." If the U.S. were to launch air strikes against the missile installations or any other Cuban target, he insisted, "we must agree *now* that we will schedule that prior to the time these missile sites become operational. I'm not prepared to say when that will be." McNamara's reasoning was grim and compelling: "*if* they become operational *before* the air strike," he warned, "I do not believe we can state we can knock them out before they can be launched, and *if* they're launched there is almost certain to be chaos in part of the East Coast or the area in a radius of 600 to 1,000 miles from Cuba." There was not much time for debate, he contended; the missiles must be neutralized before they could be fired, or the consequences of moving against them might be a rain of nuclear warheads on American soil. Less than half an hour into their first meeting, the President and his advisers were confronting the real possibility that millions of Americans might be only hours away from nuclear attack.[16]

McNamara's tough advice was technically detailed and well-informed; the President knew and respected its value. The defense sec-

---

[16]The air strike option remained on the table despite the fact that aerial photographs later indicated that several missiles sites had indeed become operational. (see Blight and Welch, *On the Brink*, 125–26)

retary maintained, in a cool and confident voice, that even though diplomatic negotiations with the U.S.S.R. should be explored, the U.S. must be prepared for an all-out attack on Cuba—contending that air strikes should be carried out not only on the missile sites, but also on the airfields, aircraft and potential nuclear storage sites. The air strikes would last several days and, he bleakly predicted, would result in hundreds or even two or three thousand Cuban casualties; he did not mention the likelihood of Soviet casualties. McNamara did not stop there: the bombing would be only a prelude to a full air and sea invasion about seven days after the start of the air campaign. Finally, he called for some degree of military mobilization and even a possible presidential declaration of national emergency. But, looming behind such plans was the unanswerable question: how would Khrushchev respond if the U.S. bombed Soviet missile sites, killed Russian and Cuban personnel and landed thousands of Marines on the beaches of Cuba?

General Taylor only deepened the uncertainties facing the President by challenging one of McNamara's key assumptions: that the missiles could be destroyed before they became operational. He cautioned that aerial intelligence could not provide precise knowledge of the operational status of the missiles and it would be impossible to determine whether the missiles were launch-ready before the U.S. attacked them; "we'll never have the," he admitted, "the exact, permanent... uh... the perfect timing." Nonetheless, Taylor did not want to give the Russians and Cubans a forewarning of American intentions and therefore urged that the missiles should be destroyed "without any warning whatsoever." He also added an additional step to McNamara's plan: "once we have destroyed as many of these offensive weapons as possible, we should indeed prevent any more coming in, which means a naval blockade."[17]

The JCS chairman, a veteran of the bloody invasion of Sicily and Italy in 1943, also cautioned the President against McNamara's argument that air attacks had to be followed by a land invasion. He recommended concurrent air strikes, a naval blockade, reinforcement of Guantanamo and evacuation of dependents plus continuous reconnaissance flights before making a decision "as to whether we invade or not. I think that's the *hardest* question militarily in the whole business and

[17]A blockade had clearly been included in the administration's military contingency planning even before the discovery of the Soviet missiles in Cuba. (Hershberg, "Before 'The Missiles of October,'" 171, 178)

one that we should look at very closely before we get our feet in that *deep mud* of Cuba."

The President and the ExComm, however, must have noticed a flaw in Taylor's own argument. The General's main point was that the U.S. could *never* be fully certain when the missiles would become operational. Even if an attack were launched immediately, he had carefully avoided saying that *all* the sites could be safely neutralized *before* at least some of the operational missiles could be fired at targets in the United States. Rusk clearly recognized this discrepancy and, while reminding the President of his upcoming meeting with Soviet foreign minister Gromyko in just 48 hours, cautioned, if the Russians "*shoot those* missiles," either before, during or after American air strikes, "we're in a general nuclear war."

McNamara nevertheless repeated his conviction that the missile bases could only be attacked before they became operational—evidently basing his judgment on the fact that nuclear warheads had yet to be located or photographed in Cuba. But, the usually confident Defense secretary added a sobering caveat: "If we saw a warhead on the site and we knew that that launcher was capable of launching that warhead, I would... frankly I would *strongly* urge against the air attack, to be quite frank about it, because I think the *danger* to this country in relation to the *gain* that would accrue would be *excessive*. This is why I suggest that *if* we're talking about an air attack, I believe we should consider it *only* on the assumption that we can carry it off *before* these become operational."

Several potential options, or combinations of options, had emerged by that point in the discussions on that first morning: political and diplomatic negotiations; air strikes against just the missile sites; air strikes against the missile sites *and* the SAM sites, Soviet aircraft, Cuban airfields and any nuclear storage sites; a full-scale invasion to remove Castro from power; a naval blockade—but only as a supplement to overt military action. At that moment, the consensus in the room was clearly hardening around some form of military response. But the risks in all these options were also becoming unsettlingly plain.

One central question remained unresolved—what was the Soviet motive for risking the shipment of nuclear missiles to Cuba? What, in short, was Khrushchev up to? Unraveling the Kremlin leader's motives for installing the missiles might, after all, help to predict his reaction to their possible destruction. JFK speculated, quite accurately as it later turned out, that the Soviets lacked confidence in the reliability of their own ICBMs: "What is the advantage? There must be some major reason for the Russians to set this up as a... must be that they're not satisfied with their ICBMs." Taylor observed that a Cuban base for launching short-range missiles against the U.S. did provide an important supplement to "their rather defective ICBM system . . . That's one reason." No one, however, seemed prepared to consider a second reason: Khrushchev's commitment to protect his Cuban allies. JFK and his advisers, more concerned about American responses, never systematically thought through the question of Khrushchev's motives at these meetings largely because their Cold War convictions had all but dictated the answer: Berlin and the nuclear balance of power. The possibility that the U.S.S.R. was committed to defend Cuba against an American attack "did not appear at all in the formal interagency or CIA intelligence assessments that went to the ExComm and the President."[18]

JFK, clearly uncertain about the efficacy of any military response, swung the discussion back to practicalities. He was especially worried that a blockade might be useless because additional missiles could be brought in by submarine. McNamara advised the President that in such an eventuality the only practical solution was to tell the Soviets frankly, "you'll take them out the moment they come in. You'll take them out and you'll carry on open surveillance." But, he also cautioned the President, in response to Bundy's concern about whether an attack on "the whole air complex" in Cuba was necessary, that several hundred air sorties would be needed to take out the missiles *and* the Soviet MiGs in Cuba. "If there are nuclear warheads associated with the launchers, you must assume there will be nuclear warheads associated with aircraft." In short, even taking out the missiles alone could be a costly error because coastal areas of the United States might be vulnerable to conventional or nuclear attack by Castro's air force flying Soviet MiGs low over the water to avoid radar: "It would be a *very* heavy price to pay in U.S. lives for the damage we did to Cuba."

The discussion returned to the problem of Soviet motives. Khrushchev's maneuver in Cuba might, as JFK had just suggested, be in part a reaction to the incontrovertible fact of overall American nuclear superiority. The deployment of missiles in Cuba, Rusk suggested, might

[18]Garthoff, "US Intelligence in the Cuban Missile Crisis," 26. "From a military point of view," Rusk later argued, "Soviet missiles in Cuba could get at our SAC bases with almost no advance warning and represented a very serious military change in the situation." (Rusk Oral History, 115)

even be an emotional response to the presence of American missiles in several NATO countries, reflecting Khrushchev's resentment that "we don't *really* live under fear of his nuclear weapons to the extent that he has to live under fear of ours. Also, we have nuclear weapons nearby, in Turkey and places like that."

America's top policy makers generally did not understand or take seriously that the Turkish missiles were deeply troubling to Khrushchev; nor did they seem to be very well informed about them. The President inquired, "How many weapons do we have in Turkey?" and General Taylor responded, "We have the... the Jupiter missiles." "We have how many?" Bundy asked and McNamara, also unsure of the specifics, answered uncertainly, "About *fifteen*, I believe to be the figure," leading Bundy to tentatively concur, "I think that's right. I think that's right."[19]

In the enveloping cloud of deeply held Cold War convictions and suspicions, it required genuine independence of mind for Rusk to cite CIA director John McCone's belief "that Khrushchev may feel that it's important for *us* to learn about living under medium-range missiles and he's doing that to sort of balance that uh... that political, psychological flank." Nonetheless, no one was quite ready to consider the possibility that Khrushchev and Castro, in the context of American covert activities in Cuba, might be committed to protecting the island nation against a second invasion by the Kennedy administration.

Rusk, who seemed to be consciously acting out his role as the nation's top diplomat by repeatedly emphasizing the impact of the Cuban crisis on international relations, also kept the diplomatic and military implications of the Berlin issue at the center of the discussion. "For the first time," he asserted, "I'm beginning *really* to wonder whether Mr. Khrushchev is entirely rational about Berlin. U Thant [U.N. acting secretary general] has talked about his obsession with it. And I think we have to keep our eye on that element." Perhaps, Rusk speculated, the Soviets "*grossly* misunderstand the importance of Cuba to this country" and were hoping to use American military action in Cuba, like the 1956 Suez-Hungary crises, as political/military cover for seizing West Berlin.

Bundy declared that Khrushchev's statements on the difference be-

[19]Evidently, neither JFK nor his advisers were up to snuff on the Turkish missiles and apparently did not realize that control of a Jupiter site would be handed over to the Turks in just six days—on October 22. (Nash, *The Other Missiles*, 103; Bernstein, "Reconsidering the Missile Crisis," 74–75)

tween offensive and defensive weapons "is all mixed up on this point," and he contemptuously quoted from and dismissed the Soviet leader's argument that the nuclear weapons deployed in Cuba would be purely defensive and no threat to the United States.[20] McNamara left open the possibility that the warheads "are not yet on Cuban soil," but reiterated the importance of making every effort to locate them. Bundy responded, "it's *perfectly* possible that this... that they are in that sense a bluff. That doesn't make them any less offensive to us, because we can't have proof about it." Treasury secretary C. Douglas Dillon, apparently leaning toward "quick [military] action" accompanied by a statement of assurance to the Soviets "saying this is all there is to it," expressed doubts about holding on to NATO and OAS support in the event of a major Russian reaction. Bundy agreed that U.S. allies might oppose military action in Cuba on the grounds that "if *they* can live with Soviet MRBMs, why can't *we*?" They would not be sympathetic if the U.S. risked losing Berlin or sparking an all-out war between the superpowers merely to avoid a threat Europe had faced stoically for years. "The prospect of that pattern," Bundy noted grimly, "is not an appetizing one." Rusk even expressed sympathy for NATO's jitters about being exposed to "all these great dangers without... without the slightest consultation, or warning, or preparation."

But, President Kennedy was dubious that NATO could be warned before unilateral air strikes were carried out: "warning them, it seems to me, is warning everybody. And obviously you can't sort of announce that in four days from now you're gonna take them out. They may announce within three days that they're gonna have [nuclear] warheads on 'em. If we come and attack, they're gonna fire them. Then what... whadda we do? Then we don't take 'em out. Of course, we then announce, 'Well, if they do that, then we're gonna attack with nuclear weapons.'"

JFK seemed increasingly doubtful that air strikes could really provide an immediate and relatively painless solution in Cuba. Indeed, Taylor acknowledged that even if air attacks took out the vast majority of missile sites in the first strike, "It'll never be a hundred percent, Mr. President," and would likely require continuous attacks over several days. Bundy pointed out the "*substantial* political advantage in limiting the strike, in surgical terms, to the thing that *is* in fact the cause of ac-

[20]Bundy also claimed that "we have other evidence" that Khrushchev "*honestly* believes or at least affects to believe, that we have nuclear weapons in Japan."

tion"—the missile sites alone, and U. Alexis Johnson, Deputy Under Secretary of State for Political Affairs, cautioned that several hundred air strikes against missiles, planes and airfields would make it "*very* difficult to convince anybody that this was *not* a preinvasion strike." Even if the air strikes succeeded in taking out the missiles, JFK reiterated glumly, the Soviets could continue to bring them in by submarine and it would be very difficult, militarily and politically, to indefinitely keep up a high level of air strikes. Taylor predicted that it might also be necessary to destroy the surface-to-air missiles simply to get at the offensive sites. And, given the general's doubts about whether bombing could destroy *all* the missiles *before* they were armed, an air attack could conceivably create catastrophic new dangers and the U.S. might end up far worse off than when the crisis started—under actual rather than merely potential nuclear attack. President Kennedy and his advisers were gradually coming to the conclusion that there might not be a quick, "surgical" fix for the Cuban dilemma.

President Kennedy raised the issue of keeping military intelligence secure from leaks. McNamara estimated that Congress could not be kept in the dark "for more than a week," but Bundy was confident that "a *new* security classification governing *precisely* the field of offensive capability in Cuba" would limit this information "to people who have an *immediate operational necessity* in intelligence terms to *work* on the data." Rusk suggested, however, that Senator Kenneth Keating had already revealed critical information about the missile sites on the floor of the Senate and JFK asked about the possible sources of Keating's information. Bundy recommended interviewing Keating to "check out his data."

JFK turned to Vice President Lyndon Johnson and asked if he had any thoughts. LBJ declared that the U.S. must take appropriate action to safeguard its security and warned that "the country's blood pressure *is* up, and they are *fearful*, and they're *insecure*, and we're gettin divided." But, the politically shrewd Texan admonished the President not to expect strong support from the OAS, the NATO allies—or the Congress. "I realize it's a breach of faith not to... *not* to confer with them," the once-powerful Senate Majority Leader admitted. "We're not gonna get much help out of them."

The President summed up the principal options on the table: attacking just the missile sites; broader air strikes against the missiles, the SAM's and the airfields; doing the first two *and* launching a naval blockade; some degree of consultation with the allies before the strikes.

Attorney General Robert Kennedy, increasingly worried by what he was hearing, spoke up for the first time. RFK was an unswerving hawk on the Cuban question; he was the administration's point-man on Operation Mongoose and an ardent supporter of plots to oust or assassinate Castro. Now, speaking directly to his brother, he defended the additional option raised earlier by McNamara—an invasion of Cuba. RFK voiced doubts about the effectiveness of any military action short of an all-out invasion: "you're droppin' bombs all over Cuba if you do the second [inclusive air strike] . . . You're covering *most* of Cuba. You're gonna kill an awful lot a people, and we're gonna take an *awful lot* a heat on it." In addition, he warned that the Russians would react to air strikes by declaring, "'Well, we're gonna send them [missiles] in again. And if you do it [bomb] again, we're gonna do... we're gonna do the same thing to Turkey.'" Only an invasion could provide finality, he implied, and justify the military and political risks involved in so much destruction and loss of life.[21]

The President, obviously impressed by his brother's reasoning, asked if it might take a month or two to mount such an invasion. McNamara repeated his earlier assertion that an invasion could be carried out within seven days of the air strikes. "You could get six divisions or seven divisions into Cuba," the President asked very skeptically, "in seven days?" Taylor outlined plans to send in 90,000 men, by ship and simultaneous air drop, in five to eleven days. "Do you think 90,000 are enough?" the President asked, always concerned about military overconfidence. "At least it's enough to start the thing going," Taylor replied somewhat evasively.

JFK wondered about how the Cuban people would react to an American invasion of their homeland and McNamara speculated that successful air strikes might lead to a national Cuban uprising requiring intervention "to prevent the slaughter of... of the free Cubans, we would have to invade to... to reintroduce order into the country. And we would be prepared to do that." If the air strikes were "highly successful" and triggered "a nationwide uprising," he added, it might be possible to introduce troops in less than seven days. But RFK did not seem satisfied, asking impatiently, "Is it *absolutely* essential that you wait seven days after you have an air strike?" Taylor explained that moving the ships and troops required for an invasion would sacrifice

<hr />

[21]Arthur Schlesinger, Jr's claim that "Robert Kennedy was a dove from the start" is *not* corroborated by the meeting tapes. (Schlesinger, *Robert Kennedy*, 507)

the element of surprise, but the attorney general reasoned that tension over Berlin could be used as a public cover for these military preparations. He also warned that it might be detrimental to wait even five days before invading, "the United States is gonna be under *such* pressure by everybody not to *do* anything. And there's gonna be also pressure... pressure on the Russians to do something against us. If you could get it in, get it started, so that there wasn't any turning back . . ."

The President also worried whether the administration could afford to wait nearly two weeks while the missiles reach "ready to go" status and Bundy added ominously that there might be other operational sites that had not even been discovered. McNamara, however, sided with Taylor, arguing that because of the extensive ship, transport aircraft and troop movements required to speed up an invasion, "we haven't been able to figure out a way to shorten that five- to seven-day period while maintaining surprise in the air attack." The defense secretary then described stocks of munitions and "POL" being quietly stockpiled in the southeastern U.S. for an invasion, and the President asked bluntly, "What's POL?" McNamara replied simply, "Petroleum, oil and lubricants."

As the meeting began to wrap up, despite all the serious concerns that had been raised about Soviet reprisals and possible military escalation, a consensus for direct action, at least against the missile sites, appeared to be gaining ground. President Kennedy also seemed ready to order attacks on Soviet aircraft in Cuba in order to prevent reprisals against the U.S. mainland—assuming, of course, that the MiGs were equipped with conventional rather than nuclear bombs. "I would think you'd have to presume they'd be using iron bombs and not nuclear weapons. Because, obviously," the President remarked with gallows humor, and also, perhaps, with a degree of wishful thinking, "why would the Soviets permit nuclear war to begin under that sort of half-assed way?" "I think that's reasonable," McNamara agreed.

After some discussion about informing key allies like French President Charles de Gaulle and West German Chancellor Konrad Adenauer, or warning the Cubans and the Soviets *before* starting the air strikes, JFK appeared to have made a decision, "I don't think we've got much *time* on these missiles. . . . We may just have to just *take them out* . . . We're *certainly* gonna do number one [the limited air strike]. We're gonna take out these missiles." He also agreed, despite delaying any final decisions, to move forward with planning for more inclusive air strikes (number two) and even for a general invasion (number three): "We ought to be making *those* preparations." Bundy asked whether the President had "*definitely* decided against a political track. I myself think we ought to work out a contingency on that." JFK certainly seemed skeptical about getting OAS support, "I think that's a waste of time," and likewise indicated that the prospects for backing from NATO were not much better. He did agree, however, to Bundy's very practical recommendation to conceal upcoming White House meetings "as intensive budget review sessions."

The President also specifically instructed that information about the presence of the missiles be kept "as tight as possible" in the State and Defense Departments, "but what we're gonna do about it really ought to be. . . . the tightest of all because otherwise we'll bitch it up." McNamara's suggested publicly announcing the U-2 reconnaissance flights and Bundy joked, "This is *covert* reconnaissance!"—and briefly laughed—alone. But, the defense chief also urged probing political channels for possible "contacts with... with Khrushchev" while concurrently planning for the air strikes and providing the President with specifics on their timing and potential effects. JFK stressed that it was necessary to know, "How many mornings from tomorrow morning would it take to get the... to take out *just* these missile sites (McNamara echoed, "missile sites"), which we need to know now." Moments later, after recommending "a general low-level photographic reconnaissance" over the missile bases before the air strikes, he stated definitively, "Then we would be prepared, almost any day, to take those out."

Robert Kennedy, however, again pressed the invasion option: "How long," he asked, "would it take to take over the island?" General Taylor explained that it was "very hard to estimate, Bobby," but suggested that the main resistance could be contained in five or six days, but months would be needed to clean up the loose ends. The President, despite the lessons he had supposedly learned from the Bay of Pigs experience about the reliability of intelligence agencies, wondered aloud if the CIA could provide accurate information "about our reception there"—that is, how the Cuban people would respond to American military intervention.

Bundy urged his colleagues to leave the White House by the East Gate in order to avoid being observed from the Press Room on the West Gate side. After some background discussion of when John McCone would return to Washington and when he might brief General Eisenhower, the meeting broke up with an agreement to reconvene at about 6:30 that evening.

The military planning endorsed by the ExComm continued at a rapid pace in the hours after the first meeting.[22] *A tense President Kennedy attempted to play diplomatic host at a previously scheduled luncheon for the Crown Prince of Libya, also attended by U.N. ambassador Adlai Stevenson; later he showed Stevenson the U-2 photos. During the afternoon, Dean Rusk met with senior State Department officials and Robert McNamara conferred with General Taylor and the Joint Chiefs on carrying out the military options discussed that morning.*

Robert Kennedy, later that afternoon, told CIA deputy director for planning, Richard Helms, of the President's "general dissatisfaction" with the forward movement of anti-Castro initiatives in Cuba. He also discussed possible ground attacks on the missile sites by anti-Castro guerrillas. RFK pledged to give more personal leadership to Mongoose—including daily morning meetings with the Special Group (Augmented) for the duration of the crisis. JFK himself, despite declining to sanction mining Cuban harbors, authorized risky "underwater demolition attacks on Soviet bloc shipping and a hit-and-run mortar and gunfire attack on three Soviet surface-to-air missile sites."[23] *These confrontational decisions reflected the assumptions that had emerged from the first ExComm session: military action, at least against the missile sites, was imminent and all but inevitable.*

Tuesday, October 16, 6:30 P.M., Cabinet Room

Identified Participants: John F. Kennedy, George Ball, McGeorge Bundy, Marshall Carter, Douglas Dillon, Roswell Gilpatric, Lyndon Johnson, U. Alexis Johnson, Robert Kennedy, Edwin Martin, Robert McNamara, Dean Rusk, Theodore Sorensen, Maxwell Taylor.[24]

"I don't know quite what kind of a world we live in after we've struck Cuba and we've... we've started it."

Secretary of Defense Robert McNamara

The ExComm reconvened in the early evening as planned. General Carter reviewed the latest intelligence on the missile sites, concluding

---

[22]Events between meetings and summaries of unrecorded meetings, based on written minutes and notes, appear in italics.

[23]Fursenko and Naftali, *"One Hell of a Gamble,"* 227–28.

[24]Tapes 28 & 28A, POF, PRC, JFKL.

that when completed they would be capable of launching 16–24 missiles with a range of about 1,100 miles; he also showed the President a map marked with the "circular range capability" of the MRBMs. JFK, like his brother, thinking about possible ground attacks on the missile sites by Operation Mongoose anti-Castro Cubans, asked "about the vulnerability of such a missile to atta—uh, bullets." "Highly vulnerable," McNamara declared, and Carter agreed that they were even "vulnerable to ordinary rifle fire." The deputy CIA director also reiterated that nuclear warheads or their storage facilities had yet to be located. JFK wasted no time in revisiting the central, looming unknown from the morning meeting: "General, how long would you say we had before these, at least to the best of your ability for the ones we now know, will be ready to fire?" Carter responded that the total complex could be operational in two weeks, *but* individual missiles "could be operational much sooner." He also revealed that photos from yesterday's flights would be available by midnight and McNamara estimated seven additional U-2 flights scheduled for the next day should provide coverage of the entire island. Carter did provide one piece of encouraging news, "It would *appear* that we have caught this in a very early stage of deployment."

The President, perhaps still hoping against hope that this predicament might be based on a technical misunderstanding, wistfully asked Carter if there was any question in his mind that these weapons were actually offensive ballistic missiles. The general's response was confident but somber: "There's no question in our minds, sir. And they are *genuine*. They are not a camouflage or a covert attempt to fool us." Bundy, however, refused to drop the President's point and urged Carter to consider that it could be "*really* catastrophic" to make "a bad guess" about the explosive power and range of these Soviet missiles, "We mustn't do that. How do we really know what these missiles are and what their range is? . . . That's really my question. How do we *know* what a given Soviet missile will do?" Carter and McNamara responded with additional technical data about identical missiles in the Soviet Union, but Bundy became rather quarrelsome, "I know that we've had these things in charts for years. But I don't know *how we know*." Finally, after McNamara and Rusk came to Carter's defense, Bundy reluctantly backed off: "I would apparently agree," he murmured rather timidly, "given the weight of it."

Rusk, however, supported by Edwin Martin, Assistant Secretary of State for Inter-American Affairs, again proposed a "one chance in a hundred" diplomatic effort to drive a wedge between Moscow and Havana by persuading Castro that the U.S.S.R. was prepared to bargain away Cuba's security for American concessions in Berlin. Martin proposed telling Castro that Khrushchev had exposed Cuba to an "attack from the United States and therefore the overthrow of his regime." Martin even suggested hinting to Castro that "we might have sympathy and help for him in case he ran into trouble trying to throw the old-line communists and the Soviets out." Rusk also warned that U.S. military action in Cuba would likely have profound diplomatic consequences, including a "maximum communist reaction in Latin America," which could lead to the overthrow of several governments, and intense anger in NATO, much like during the 1956 Suez crisis, "And we could find ourselves isolated and the alliance crumbling."

President Kennedy asked for the military's perspective and McNamara reported on discussions with the Joint Chiefs held between the ExComm meetings. To no one's surprise, the JCS, convinced that Castro would never abandon revolutionary communism in Latin America, opposed limiting air attacks to the missile sites alone because too much of Cuba's offensive capability would remain intact, inviting reprisals against American targets. Instead, speaking for the Chiefs, Taylor advised eliminating the missile sites and possible nuclear warhead storage facilities, as well as the Soviet fighters and bombers "with one hard crack." The general cautioned again that although American planes could destroy the great majority of these targets in a first strike, "We'll never get it all, Mr. President. But we then have to come back, day after day, for several days" to complete the job. That estimate of course left the morning's critical question dangling: would there be launch-ready nuclear missiles left in Cuba after the first air raids?

McNamara, always eager to rationalize and systematize the discussions, sought to summarize the options generated up to that point by the ExComm. He grouped the proposals into three possible courses of action, each progressively stronger than the last:

First, he outlined a political approach—including overtures to Khrushchev, Castro and the NATO and Rio Pact allies. But, he rejected this approach because it was "likely to lead to no satisfactory result"—especially because of the danger of starting military action "*after* they acquire a nuclear capability."

Second, he proposed a plan that "lies in between" military and political action: a declaration of open surveillance of Cuban air space and an indefinite naval blockade against offensive weapons entering Cuba.

These steps would be accompanied by an announcement that the U.S. would attack if Cuba initiated any offensive actions against the United States. "Attack who?" Bundy inquired. "The Soviet Union," McNamara replied matter-of-factly.

Third, the defense chief put forward the plan favored by the Joint Chiefs: extensive air strikes on the missile bases, the SAM sites, airfields, fighters and bombers ("700 to 1,000 sorties per day for five days"), and finally, an invasion by 90,000 to over 150,000 men. The defense secretary cautioned that any of these military steps was "*almost* certain" to lead to a Soviet military response somewhere in the world. Berlin, of course, was the most likely and worrisome target. "It may well be worth the price," he argued, and "Perhaps we should pay that." But, he suggested rather half-heartedly, that Khrushchev might be deterred from taking reprisals by a Strategic Air Command alert, "a *very* large-scale mobilization" and a declaration of national emergency. Finally, he warned that a Cuban uprising might "force an invasion to *support* the uprising."[25]

The political and military cards were now clearly and unambiguously on the table. Rusk nonetheless countered that any military action "involves heavy political involvement. . . . I don't think there's any such thing as a non-political course of action." JFK acknowledged that announcing the discovery of the MRBMs would deprive the military of a surprise strike since Castro and Khrushchev would obviously realize that "we're gonna probably do somethin' about it, I would *assume*." "He must know," the President concluded, "that we're gonna *find out*." Bundy reminded the commander-in-chief that Khrushchev had "been *very, very* explicit with us, in communications to us, about how dangerous this is"—especially in the official TASS statement of September 11. "That's right," JFK replied, typically overlooking American covert operations in Cuba: "He's initiated the danger, really, hasn't he? He's the one playing God, not us."

McNamara added that Soviets or Cubans "could drop one or two or ten high-explosive bombs some place along the East Coast, and that's the *minimum* risk we run to this country" from an advance warning. Taylor promptly agreed that the Florida area was particularly vulnerable—MiG fighters, armed with conventional bombs and flying at low

[25]Although the President and the ExComm repeatedly discussed possible Soviet military responses, particularly in Berlin or Turkey, they never worked out plans, at least at the meetings, to try to restrain or reverse armed conflict *after* the Pandora's Box of escalation had been opened. (Blight and Welch, *On the Brink*, 124–25)

level from Cuba to Florida, could inflict real damage on the United States. "Our whole air defense has been oriented in other directions," toward longer-range threats, he explained almost apologetically. "We've never had low-level defenses prepared for this country." President Kennedy did not initially seem alarmed, "We're not, talking overall, not *a great deal* of damage... if they get one strike," until Dillon asked, "What if they carry a nuclear weapon?" The President seemed genuinely startled by the suggestion, "Oh, if they carry a nuclear weapon... you assume they wouldn't do *that.*"

"I would *not* think," Rusk interjected, "that they would use a nuclear weapon unless they're prepared for general nuclear war. I just don't see that possibility." Bundy agreed, but the secretary of state conceded, "we could be just *utterly* wrong, but we've never *really* believed that... that Khrushchev would take on a general nuclear war over Cuba." JFK seemed almost to confess, "We certainly have been wrong about what he's tryin' to do in Cuba. There isn't any doubt about that." (Bundy simultaneously echoed, "doubt about that.") "Not many of us," JFK continued, "thought that he was gonna put MRBMs on Cuba." "Except John McCone," Bundy and Carter pointed out, and Kennedy muttered, "Yeah."[26]

President Kennedy was obviously not the only member of the Ex-Comm troubled by the dire possibilities and uncertainties in the situation. Bundy questioned whether the missiles were, in the end, as important as they seemed, "quite aside from what we've said and we're very hard-locked on to it, I know: What is the strategic impact on the position of the United States of MRBMs in Cuba? How gravely *does* this *change*," he rapped the table for emphasis, "the strategic balance?" Did the deployment of missiles in Cuba give the Soviets a military advantage which their own ICBMs could not provide?

McNamara had no illusions about the effect of the missiles on the world balance of power and boldly distanced himself from the military

[26]John McCone had persistently predicted since August that the Soviet deployment of surface-to-air missiles in Cuba was the first step toward placing offensive nuclear weapons on the island. The CIA director, "a rank amateur" with no intelligence expertise, "got it right while the professionals got it wrong." In fact, "McCone's instincts were good, but his reasons were bad" and his hunch "hardly seems worth the attention it has received." For example, the Soviets had deployed SAM missiles in several other countries without following up with strategic ground-to-ground missiles and had failed to use the SAMs in Cuba to prevent American U-2s from discovering their strategic missiles. (Blight and Welch, "What Can Intelligence Tell Us About the Cuban Missile Crisis?" 4–6)

under his authority: "Mac, I asked the Chiefs that this afternoon. In effect, they said 'substantially.' My own personal view is: not at all." General Taylor, not surprisingly, dissented, "I think from a cold-blooded point of view, Mr. President, you're quite right in saying that these are just a few more missiles targeted on the United States. However, they can become a... a very... a rather important adjunct and reinforcement to the strike capability of the Soviet Union," especially because "We have no idea how far they will go." In short, Taylor argued, it made a great deal of difference if these weapons were "in Cuba and not over in the Soviet Union." Bundy countered with a condescending laugh, "Oh, I asked the question with an awareness" of the political realities.

The President still seemed ambivalent: the Soviets could put so much nuclear warhead firepower into Cuba that knocking them out would become "too much of a gamble." And then, they would inevitably "squeeze us in Berlin." But, at the same time, he acknowledged, "You may say it doesn't make any difference if you get blown up by an ICBM flying from the Soviet Union or one that was 90 miles away. Geography doesn't mean that much." However, when Bundy declared that an attack on Cuba could quickly escalate to all-out war, the President made a startling admission, "That's why it shows the Bay of Pigs was really right," he added regretfully, "if we'd *done* it right." After hesitating for several seconds, the suddenly morose JFK muttered cryptically, "I would... better and better, worse and worse...," but trailed off indistinctly without finishing or clarifying his thoughts.

But regrets over past decisions did not make it any easier to ignore the missiles or make the warheads assumed to be in Cuba any less dangerous in the event of a U.S. attack. The strategic situation had been fundamentally altered, Taylor maintained; today, the administration was preparing "a quarter of a million American soldiers, marines and airmen to take an island we launched 1,800 Cubans against a year and a half ago"—an irony that prompted someone to laugh quietly in the background. RFK insisted that "a year from now" Cuba could try nuclear blackmail against other Latin American nations and JFK observed that failure to act would make Cuba appear "coequal with us," or, Dillon asserted, as if "We're scared of the Cubans." The United States had to respond, Edwin Martin insisted, because of "the psychological factor of our having taken it." The U.S. simply could not appear to "have sat back and let 'em do it to us, that is more important than the *direct* threat." Martin's view encapsulated classic Cold War doctrine: the mere appearance of weakness would encourage Soviet aggression.[27]

The President, however, essentially conceded that his administration's rhetoric had helped create a situation in which he *had* to act: "Last month," he began, in an almost jocular tone as several advisers chuckled in the background, "I said we weren't going to [accept offensive Soviet missiles in Cuba] and last month I should have said we're... well, that we don't care. But when we said we're *not* going to, and then they go ahead and do it, and then we do nothing," he suddenly became very somber, "then... I would think that our... risks *increase*." Bundy quietly interjected, "That's right." Of course, despite this frustrated appeal to hindsight, Kennedy surely knew that passively accepting the missiles at any point would have been politically untenable. JFK saw all too clearly that the United States had to *be seen* to act. "They've got enough to blow us up now anyway," he observed gloomily, "After all, this is a political struggle as much as military."

In that political context, JFK pondered again whether to make a public announcement about the discovery of the missiles 24 hours before initiating military action: "That would... that would be notification, in a sense, that a... of their existence and everybody could draw whatever conclusion they wanted to." Martin warned, however, that once an announcement is made, "you've got to move immediately, or the... you're going to have a ton of instability in *this* country." "Oh, I understand *that*," JFK retorted. RFK, however, asked whether planes could be put in the air over Cuba during the 24 hour warning period so that the missiles could be attacked if the Soviets or the Cubans tried to move them out of sight.

Taylor dismissed the idea, reminding RFK that "these are really mobile missiles" that could be concealed under trees after an announcement "and disappear almost at once, as I visualize it." McNamara agreed that the missiles present "a *very very* great danger to this... to this coast" because "it is *possible* that these are field missiles" which could be readied and fired between the announcement and the attack. "These *are* field missiles, sir," General Carter corrected the defense

---

[27]Since Khrushchev's missile forces were considerably smaller than the West knew, the Soviet nuclear deployment in Cuba, Raymond Garthoff wrote in 1962, did pose "'an appreciably heightened threat to the US strategic retaliatory forces' and hence to our deterrent capability." (*Reflections*, 207) By 1963, however, Khrushchev confided to his son Sergei that the U.S.S.R. had enough ICBMs to prevent an American attack. It was, he said, no longer necessary to hide the true extent of Soviet forces from the Americans.

chief somewhat irritably, "They're mobile support-type missiles." Taylor further estimated that they required only a 40-minute countdown. McNamara, Gilpatric, Dillon and Bundy, as a result, argued forcefully that a strike must precede or at least be made simultaneously with any statement, although Ball speculated that a few hours of warning was advisable, "more for the appearance than for the reality" since the Soviets would never accept an ultimatum. At least, Ball argued, some European allies should be given a few hours notice.

"I don't think," JFK contended, "we ought to abandon just knocking out these missile bases," as opposed to... that's a much more defensible, explicable, politically more satisfactory in every way action than the general strike which takes us into the city of Havana and plainly takes us into much more hazards of being shot down. Now I know the Chiefs say, 'Well, that means their bombers can take off against us.' But uh..." Bundy interposed firmly, arguing that if their bombers took off against us "then *they* have made a general war . . . which then becomes much more *their* decision. If we move this way, the political advantages are... are *very* strong, it seems to me, of the small strike. It corresponds to the, 'the punishment fits the crime,' in political terms. The... we are doing only what we warned repeatedly and publicly we would *have* to do. You know, we are *not* generalizing the attack."

JFK finally concluded that plans should move forward that night for option two, the general air strike, which would not preclude deciding later to do only number one, the limited air strike. Bundy promptly agreed, but RFK asked again, "Does that encompass an invasion?" "No," the President replied firmly, but added, "I'd say that's the third course." JFK quickly acceded, however, to Dillon and Taylor's insistence on including the SAM sites in any general air attack in order to clear access to the airfields. But, he repeated that preparations for both options must remain strictly covert in order to retain "the freedom to make the choice about number one depending on what information we have on it."

McNamara, perhaps picking up on the President's uneasiness about the unforeseen consequences of broader air action, cautioned that since some targets had yet to be located, especially additional missile launchers and nuclear storage facilities, it would be prudent to wait for new photography, which would be processed on Thursday and could be translated into target assignments by Friday, and hold off the air strikes until Saturday (October 20). Taylor noted that at least 24 hours would be needed just to brief the 400 pilots waiting for orders. "The President does not have to make any decision until 24 hours before the strike," the defense secretary maintained, "*except* the decision to be prepared." On the other hand, he pointed out that strikes against the known targets, the missiles, did not resolve the problem of the unknown targets, such as the still to be located nuclear warhead storage sites.

JFK inquired about what steps had to be taken in the next 24 hours to prepare for options one and two. McNamara urged the immediate preparation of "a *specific* strike plan *limited* to the missiles and the nuclear storage sites, which we have *not* done . . . but I think we ought to estimate the *minimum* number of sorties since you have indicated some interest in that possibility, we ought to provide you that option." "OK," the President replied.

But doubts had evidently been gnawing at the defense chief since the morning. McNamara turned from mechanics to an entirely different level of concern: "I *don't* believe," he admonished, "we have considered the consequences of *any* of these actions satisfactorily, and because we haven't considered the consequences, I'm not sure we're taking all the action we ought to take now to minimize those. I don't know quite what kind of a world we live in after we've struck Cuba and we've... we've started it." The usually confident McNamara even conceded, with prompting by General Taylor, that some of the targets would inevitably survive the strikes. "After we've launched 50 to 100 sorties, what kind of a world do we live in? How... how do we *stop* at that point? I don't *know* the answer to this," he grimly admitted. And, when Under Secretary of State George Ball added that deadly consequences could erupt "at any place in the world," McNamara emphatically agreed: "At any place in the world, George. That's right. I agree with you."

Taylor, nonetheless, made an audacious announcement: the Joint Chiefs "feel so strongly about the... the dangers inherent in the limited air strike that they would prefer taking *no* military action" rather than sacrifice the advantage of surprise and expose American civilians to retaliatory missiles launched from Cuba. JFK gently but firmly disagreed, insisting that "the chances of it becoming a much broader struggle are increased" with each step of military escalation. Once the airfields were attacked, JFK contended, "I mean you're right in a much more *major* operation, therefore the dangers of the worldwide effects, which are substantial to the United States, are increased."

The President, clearly maneuvering to resist JCS pressure for escalation in order "to get this thing under some degree of control," boldly and explicitly appealed to Taylor's earlier doubts about an invasion, "Let's not let the Chiefs knock us out on this one, General"—a striking thing to say to the chairman of the Joint Chiefs. "If you go into Cuba in the way we're talking about, and taking out all the planes and all the rest," JFK continued, "then you really haven't got much of an argument against invading." Taylor affirmed again "my... my inclination is all against... against the invasion, but nonetheless trying to eliminate as effectively as possible, every weapon that can strike the United States."

Kennedy then put the JCS chairman on the spot with a transparently leading question: "But you're not for the invasion?" and got exactly the answer he appeared to want: "I would not at this moment, no sir."[28] McNamara, however, again reminded his colleagues that "700 sorties a day for five days" could trigger an uprising in Cuba which would force a U.S. invasion. But Alexis Johnson argued that attacks on "military targets *primarily*, would *not* result in any substantial unrest. People would just stay home and try to keep out of trouble."

The pugnacious Robert Kennedy, however, had no interest in stopping with a limited air strike. Continuing to pound the hard-line strategy he had urged in the morning, RFK insisted there was every reason to assume that Khrushchev would reintroduce these weapons six months or a year or two after the air strikes. In that event, McNamara declared, a blockade would have to be established. "Then we're gonna have to sink Russian ships," RFK countered. "Then we're gonna have to sink Russian submarines." It was better, he insisted, to stand up to Khrushchev now and take the consequences—whatever they were. Perhaps "we should just get into it, and get it over with and say that, uh... take our losses," he exclaimed resolutely. "And if we're gonna... he wants to get into a war over *this*... Hell, if it's war that's gonna come on *this* thing, you know, he sticks those kinds of missiles in after the warning, then he's gonna... hey, he's gonna get into a war for... six months from now or a year from now on somethin'."[29]

[28]Taylor feared that if the U.S. got involved in a major invasion of Cuba, the Soviets would have an open road to seize Berlin. His concerns seem justified since at its height the plan for invading Cuba called for using 100,000 Army and 40,000 Marine combat troops, 579 Navy and Air Force combat aircraft, 175 Navy ships and 8 aircraft carriers. 14,500 paratroopers were to be used on the first day, "comparable to the force dropped during the invasion of Normandy. Potential casualties were estimated at some 18,500 in ten days of combat." (Garthoff, *Reflections*, 73–74)

[29]Sorensen later recalled that Robert Kennedy had been "particularly good" during the first week of ExComm meetings: "Never stating a position of his own, he was persistent in

McNamara, in sharp contrast to RFK, restated the need to put down on paper the possible consequences of any military action. JFK, repeating that the missiles did not really increase Soviet "strategic strength," effectively appealed for a "Russian expert" to explain Khrushchev's motives—"After all Khrushchev demonstrated a sense of caution over Laos. Berlin, he's been cautious." Ball, noting that Khrushchev was coming to the U.N. in November, suggested that he might be hoping to trade these missiles for concessions in Berlin. Bundy wished out loud, "one thing that I would *still* cling to is that he's not likely to give *Fidel Castro* nuclear warheads. I don't believe *that* has happened or is likely to happen." "Why does he put these in there, though?" JFK pondered, and Bundy explained that the warheads were Soviet controlled. "That's right. But what is the advantage of that?" JFK persisted. "It's just as if we suddenly began to put a *major* number of MRBMs in Turkey. Now that'd be *goddamn dangerous*, I would think." Bundy boldly pointed out, "Well we did it, Mr. President," and JFK replied rather lamely, "Yeah, that was five years ago. But that was during a different period then."[30]

Bundy speculated that Khrushchev's generals had probably been telling him for over a year "that he was missing a *golden* opportunity to add to his strategic capability." Ball conceded that Khrushchev was keenly aware of the deficiency of Soviet ICBMs and might be trying to enhance his strategic position; but, he also believed it might be a trading ploy. The missiles had to be regarded as Russian, he deduced, but Carter suggested that it might be clever to consider them "entirely Cu-

---

trying . . . to get people to agree" on alternatives and consequences. In point of fact, RFK frequently staked out his own very provocative positions during the first week. (Sorensen Oral History, 68)

[30]JFK may have been trying to hang the Turkish missile albatross around the neck of the Eisenhower administration by "forgetting" that he himself had chosen to proceed with the deployment and had never ordered the removal of the missiles. On April 11, 1988, at a Kennedy Library conference, McGeorge Bundy responded to a question about whether JFK had taken steps to pull the Jupiter missiles out of Turkey by raising his arms toward the heavens and in effect exclaiming: "Jack, you never ordered the removal of the Turkish missiles. You merely expressed an opinion about their lack of strategic value. A presidential opinion is not a presidential order." (also see Bernstein, "Reconsidering the Missile Crisis," 60–64)

Later in the ExComm deliberations, Dillon, who had served in the Eisenhower administration, admitted, "we didn't know what else to do with them, and we really made the Turks and Italians take them." JFK urged Sorensen to jot down that remark for the book they would later write—again ignoring his own role in their deployment. (Sorensen Oral History, 65) ban" if the U.S. should decide to invade.[31] "Ah, well," Bundy observed cynically, clearly relishing the use of power, "what we say for political purposes and what we think are *not* identical here." Ball, nevertheless, concluded hopefully, "I think Khrushchev *himself* would never... would never risk a major war on... on a fellow as obviously erratic and... and foolish as... as Castro." RFK, however, was not dissuaded, and even suggested using the American naval base at Guantanamo Bay to stage an incident that would justify military intervention: "You know, sink the *Maine* again or something."[32]

JFK, however, continued to display far more flexibility and caution than his younger brother: he knew he had to be prepared to act in any situation, yet he was unsure he wanted to act. Taylor urged the President not to firm up a military schedule until all the intelligence had been received. "No, I haven't," JFK replied. "I just think we ought to be *ready* to do something, even if we decide not to do it. I'm not saying we should do it." But he did, nonetheless, ask Taylor to outline "what do we have to be doing *now* so that ten days from now we're in a position to invade, if that was the need."

The President was obviously hedging his bets.

"Our principal problem," Bundy insisted, echoing McNamara's earlier concern, "is to try and imaginatively to think what the world would be like if we do this, and what it will be like if we don't." "That's *exactly* right," the defense chief interjected, "We ought to work on that tonight." After a brief discussion of possible steps to secure the release of the Bay of Pigs prisoners still held in Cuba,[33] Bundy, rather casually, raised a sensitive issue. "We have a list of the sabotage options, Mr. President. I... it's not a very loud noise to raise at a meeting of this sort, but I think it would need your approval. I take it

[31]When Khrushchev was informed about JFK's forthcoming speech on October 22, he did consider "another possibility . . . in case of attack," the U.S.S.R. could announce that "'all of the equipment belonged to the Cubans and the Cubans would announce that they will respond.' He assured his colleagues that he did not envision letting Castro threaten the use of the medium-range ballistic missiles against a U.S. invasion, but as a way of deterring the United States the Cubans could declare that they would 'use the tactical ones.'" (Fursenko and Naftali, *"One Hell of a Gamble,"* 241)

[32]In May 1961, after the assassination of the Dominican Republic's brutal strongman Rafael Trujillo, RFK, still smarting from the Bay of Pigs fiasco, pressed for American intervention to prevent a Castro-inspired communist takeover of the Dominican government. He even suggested blowing up the U.S. Consulate to create a pretext for sending in American troops. (*FRUS: American Republics, 1961–1963, XII* (Washington, D.C.: United States Government Printing Office, 1998), 634–41)

[33]Negotiations finally led to the release of the prisoners by Christmas, 1962.

you *are* in favor of sabotage." The President's national security adviser did not know, of course, that the meeting was being taped. Nonetheless, the circuitous language in his reference to JFK's support for sabotage suggests an instinctive inclination to offer the President some degree of "plausible deniability."

Bundy continued on this track—questioning whether it would be desirable to mine international waters, which could impact neutral or even friendly vessels, or whether it would be wiser to mine only Cuban waters since "mines are very indiscriminate." JFK, in a rather oblique reference to covert activities by the Special Group (Augmented) in Cuba, asked, "Is that what they're talking about, mining?" "That's one of the items," Bundy confirmed, "There are ah... there are... most of them relate to infiltration of raiders, and will simply be deniable internal Cuban activities." The President urged delaying any steps which could antagonize neutral or friendly nations. "I don't think we want to put *mines* out right now, do we?" Bundy suggested activating only "the internal ones" in Cuba, "not the other ones." The President evaded a direct reply, instead asking Vice President Johnson for his thoughts; LBJ, rather passively, replied that he had nothing essential to add.

JFK summed up the issues to be discussed the next day—providing a notification before bombing, deciding on the military alternatives, making a possible approach to Khrushchev—and rather unenthusiastically mentioned his planned October 17 political campaign trip. "I've gotta go to Connecticut . . . Why don't we meet at twelve. What time do I get back tomorrow night?" Bundy worried that "The cover will grow awfully thin" after repeated meetings at the White House and suggested convening the next day at the State Department.

The President soon turned to his scheduled Thursday (October 18) meeting with Soviet Foreign Minister Andrei Gromyko. He wondered about giving Gromyko an indirect ultimatum, but assumed the stone-faced diplomat would deny the Cuban buildup since Ambassador Dobrynin had already told RFK and former ambassador to the Soviet Union Charles Bohlen that the U.S.S.R. would not put offensive nuclear weapons in Cuba: "Now either he's lying, or he doesn't know." Perhaps, he mused, the Soviets might reconsider their decision if RFK hinted to Dobrynin, without actually revealing specific details, about the "far-reaching consequences" of such an action. "I can't understand their viewpoint," JFK admitted, recalling the warnings at his September 4 and 13 press conferences, "I don't think there's any record of the Soviets ever making this *direct* a challenge *ever*, really, since the Berlin blockade." Bundy argued, correctly as the evidence later proved, that the Soviet decision was likely made before the President had even made his statements, adding skeptically, "I wouldn't bet a *cookie* that Dobrynin doesn't know a *bean* about this." JFK, nervously and audibly slapping his knee, was clearly intrigued, "You think he *does* know." But RFK, who had personally spoken with the ambassador, concluded firmly "He didn't know . . . in my judgment."[34]

JFK was plainly baffled by Soviet behavior. He was trying, nonetheless, despite his Cold War mindset and instinctive distrust of communism and the U.S.S.R., to understand exactly what Khrushchev *thought* he was doing. The President agreed to the general consensus to press Gromyko on the September 11th Soviet assurance that offensive weapons would not be sent to Cuba, pointing out in evident frustration (again slapping his knee) that the Soviets had backed away in 1958 after China had shelled offshore islands controlled by Taiwan and had accepted a ceasefire in Laos in 1961. Bundy, too, admitted to being puzzled, like McNamara, by the absence of nuclear storage sites, "That's very queer."

President Kennedy had never pretended to be a Soviet "expert" during the meetings, but his irritation finally burst to the surface: "Well, it's a *goddamn* mystery to me. I don't know enough about the Soviet Union, but if anybody can tell me *any other time* since the Berlin blockade where the Russians have given us so clear a provocation, I don't know what it's been." The perplexed President seemed almost to defend the Soviets, "Because they've been awfully cautious, really. . . . Now maybe our mistake was in not saying sometime before this summer that if they do this we must act." Only minutes earlier, Kennedy had wondered aloud if his threats to take action against missiles in Cuba had helped push the superpowers into this predicament. Now he wondered if he had not been threatening *enough*.

JFK was concerned that because of his failure to act decisively enough earlier, he might be forced to act now in far more dangerous circumstances. He was groping for a third course, an uncertain path between two unacceptable alternatives: passive acquiescence and a decision to let slip the dogs of war. Despite the swirl of conflicting advice, President Kennedy's self-criticism and doubts about the military op-

---

[34]JFK frequently slapped his knee, or sometimes tapped his teeth, in stressful situations. The knee slapping is vividly captured in Robert Drew's 1963 cinéma vérité documentary, "Crisis: Behind a Presidential Commitment," about the struggle with Governor George Wallace over the desegregation of the University of Alabama.

tions had begun to subtly reshape the thrust of the ExComm's deliberations.

As the meeting slowly broke up, the U.S. course of action was still far from clear—although Ball recommended sending in low-flying reconnaissance planes "shortly before the strike, just to build the evidence. I mean... then you've got pictures that *really* show what you were... what was there." JFK wondered whether Ambassadors Bohlen and Thompson, the administration's top Soviet experts, could explain Russian behavior, nearly referring to these authorities as "these great demono... uh... uh... uh..." before barely catching himself. Perhaps JFK intended to say "Kremlinologists," but he almost said "demonologists," a rather less flattering term then in use to describe experts on the U.S.S.R.

Finally, the President, thinking about his political trip to New England and hoping to divert press attention from the meetings in the White House, prompted some laughter with a playful quip, "I wonder what we're gonna say up in Connecticut?" Kennedy can also be heard asking deputy CIA director Carter when his boss, John McCone, would be returning to Washington and might be available to brief General Eisenhower. JFK neglected, perhaps intentionally, to turn off the tape recorder as he left. Several advisors remained behind.

The tape machine, still secretly running, caught their remarks as they talked openly amongst themselves. To the listener, the change in the tone and character of the discussion after the departure of the President and Robert Kennedy is quite remarkable. The structure and formality of the meeting, and the inevitable personal and bureaucratic restraints on the conversation, all but evaporated. The ExComm members began to talk informally without the pressure to discern what the President thought and intended or whether he might consider their advice wise or foolish.

McNamara began the "post-meeting" by suggesting that they divide up potential targets in Cuba by the number of sorties required to knock them out, "starting *only* with the missiles and working up through the [still undiscovered] nuclear storage sites, the MiG's and the... and the SAM's and so on . . . Not," he forcefully added, "because I think that these are *reasonable* alternatives" but in order to give the President a clear idea of the military choices. "But, the most *important* thing we need to do is this appraisal of the world *after* any one of these situations, *in great* detail . . . and I would *strongly* urge we put it on paper." Bundy agreed emphatically: "What I would suggest is that someone be deputied to do a piece of paper which really is, 'What happens?' " after taking out just the missiles or the air bases as well. "I think any military action *does* change the world. And I think *not* taking action changes the world. And I think these are the two worlds that we need to look at." He suggested that they "spend the evening, really, to some advantage, separately, trying to have our own views of this," with the aim of trading written opinions before the next meeting.

Bundy also expressed great interest in getting Ambassador Llewellyn Thompson's "first sense of how *he* sees this" and McNamara, again the methodical organizer, suggested that "tonight we actually draft a paper" specifying exactly the weapons known to be in Cuba. Bundy also proposed a scheme for dropping paratroopers into Cuba after "a quite large-scale [air] strike" to determine which sites had actually been destroyed—thus hopefully confirming the success of taking out only "the thing *that gives the trouble* and *not* the thing that doesn't give the trouble." But, McNamara dismissed the idea as too risky and Bundy conceded, "it's probably a bad idea." The defense secretary asserted nonetheless "that there *are* some *major* [political and military] alternatives here though and I don't think we've discussed them fully enough today, and I'd like to see them laid out" on paper. "Once you start this political approach," McNamara warned, "I don't think you're going to *have* any opportunity for a military operation." Bundy contended that plans should be worked out to evaluate both "the chances of success" as well as "the pluses and minuses of nonsuccess."

"I completely agree with that," McNamara affirmed. Earlier in the meeting, the defense secretary had systematically laid out the military alternatives for the President, even though he had questioned whether they were worth the price of an almost certain Soviet response. Now, he asserted, with uncharacteristic passion, "It's not the chances of [military] success. It's the results . . . I'll be quite frank," he admitted, "I don't think there *is* a military problem there." "That's my honest [view] too," Bundy agreed. In a forceful and dominant tone hard to imagine if the President were still present, McNamara declared that the administration had simply pledged to act if Cuba acquired an offensive capacity against the U.S.: "This is a domestic *political* problem. In our announcement, we didn't say we'd go in and not that we'd kill them. We said we'd *act*. Well, how will we *act*? Well, we want to *act* to prevent their use." To act, McNamara argued, could mean three carefully orchestrated steps: 24 hour-a-day open surveillance; a blockade to stop further offensive weapons from coming in; and an ultimatum to Khrushchev warning that any sign of a launch from Cuba against the U.S.

would mean "a full nuclear strike" not only against Cuba but against the U.S.S.R. itself. The defense chief acknowledged, "Now this alternative doesn't seem to be a very *acceptable* one. But," he concluded in a rare display of sardonic humor, "wait until you work on the others!" "That's right," Bundy affirmed, as some strained laughter briefly broke out around the table. "This is the problem," McNamara teased, "but I've thought somethin' about the others this afternoon." The defense secretary explained that he was trying to work out "a little package that meets the action requirement" of the U.S. announcement "because as I suggested, I *don't* believe it's primarily a military problem. It's primarily a domestic *political* problem."

Ball raised the possibility that enforcing a blockade could actually mean "a greater involvement almost than a military action." But Carter, evidently leaning toward endorsing the blockade, which he characterized as "a series of single, unrelated acts, *not* by surprise," echoed McNamara's doubts about bombing the missiles in Cuba, "This comin' in there on Pearl Harbor [with a surprise attack] just frightens the *hell* out of me as to what goes *beyond*." Bundy, clearly puzzled, asked, "What goes... what goes beyond what?" and Carter replied, "What happens beyond that? You go in there with a surprise attack; you put out all the missiles. This isn't the *end*; this is the *beginning*, I think." It was the first time, but not the last, that comparing surprise air strikes in Cuba to the 1941 attack on Pearl Harbor would unsettle the Ex-Comm deliberations.

McNamara again asked his colleagues to continue to think about "what kind of a world do we live in" after attacking Cuba? "What do we expect *Castro* will be doing after you attack these missiles? Does he survive as a... as political leader? Is he overthrown? Is he stronger, weaker? How will *he* react? How will the Soviets react? What can... how can Khrushchev *afford* to accept this action without *some* kind of rebuttal? . . . Where? How do we react in relation to it? What happens if we do mobilize? How does this affect our allies' support of us in relation to Berlin?" No one, however, questioned McNamara's conclusion that all U.S. forces should be put on worldwide alert.

The morning meeting had ended with an apparently steadfast consensus for the use of force. But during the afternoon, reservations by the President and several ExComm members, especially McNamara, had contributed to a growing awareness of the potential dangers of any kind of military action. The participants, by the evening, seemed far less sure of themselves, and far less sure of any military course. The question that had been raised by General Carter could not be answered easily: if the United States attacked Cuba, particularly without warning, where would it end?

That evening the President was the guest of honor at a dinner party at the home of columnist Joseph Alsop, honoring Charles "Chip" Bohlen, who was preparing to leave for France to become U.S. ambassador. The President seemed distant and withdrawn and, entirely out of character, hardly mingled with the other guests. He later talked privately with Bohlen in the garden and even asked him to consider postponing his departure for Paris. Rusk went to the State Department for further discussions which lasted until nearly midnight. McNamara spent the night at the Pentagon.

The next morning, Wednesday, October 17, Adlai Stevenson sent a note to the President arguing that the Soviet missiles in Cuba would inevitably be regarded around the world as a quid pro quo for U.S. missiles in Turkey. He urged the President to remain open to negotiations on "the existence of nuclear missile bases anywhere . . . before we start anything." *The ambassador declared that "we can't negotiate with a gun at our head" and accused the Soviets of upsetting "the precarious balance in the world in arrogant disregard of your warnings—by threats against Berlin and now from Cuba—and that we have no choice except to restore that balance, i.e., blackmail and intimidation never, negotiation and sanity always."*[35]

President Kennedy remained determined to act normally, in an effort to keep the press and the Soviets from suspecting that a crisis was imminent. After an early morning briefing by CIA director John McCone, who had just returned to Washington, JFK authorized him to personally brief General Eisenhower. The President then left for Connecticut to campaign for Democrats in the upcoming mid-term elections. He was buoyed by large and enthusiastic crowds in Bridgeport, Waterbury and New Haven.

The ExComm met without the President at the State Department twice that day, eventually joined by Truman administration secretary of state Dean Acheson. The meeting, of course, was not taped but minutes and notes have survived. Although most participants remained uncertain and continued to vacillate, support seemed to be building

[35]Adlai Stevenson to John F. Kennedy, in Chang and Kornbluh, *Cuban Missile Crisis,* 129–30.

around three possibly concurrent courses of action: air strikes, a block-ade, and diplomatic efforts.

McNamara expressed concern that if air strikes proved necessary, any warning issued beforehand would sacrifice the key element of surprise. However, he also argued that air strikes on the missile sites alone were not likely to be fully effective. At the same time, he insisted that compre-hensive air strikes or an invasion were far too drastic—particularly as a first step. He seemed to be drifting toward the blockade option. Former Ambassador to Moscow, Llewellyn Thompson, supported by Taylor and McCone, argued that Khrushchev had engineered the confrontation over missiles in Cuba to gain leverage on Berlin. George Ball, on the other hand, urged restraint and renewed diplomatic efforts, insisting that Khrushchev simply did not understand the American perspective on his adventure in Cuba. The Joint Chiefs, however, with far fewer doubts, prepared plans for bombing the missiles, the SAMs and Soviet aircraft.[36]

Acheson epitomized the uncomplicated moral certainties of the "wise men" who had created the policy of containment in the early Cold War years. Invited to the meetings at JFK's request, Acheson took a hard line, insisting that a blockade would leave the missiles intact and make the U.S. vulnerable simultaneously to nuclear retaliation from Cuba and reprisals in Berlin. Surgical air strikes, on the other hand, would eliminate the nuclear threat and validate American power and resolve to Khrushchev. He did not address how the Soviets might respond in Berlin or Turkey, or what might happen if the U.S. failed to destroy all the missiles in the first assault.[37]

By the morning of October 18, new U-2 photography had turned up evidence of Intermediate-Range Ballistic Missile (IRBM) launch facili-ties in Cuba. These R-14 missiles had a range of over 2,000 miles, about twice that of the MRBMs, and carried far deadlier warheads.[38] Soviet IL-28 bombers were also discovered, aircraft capable of deliv-ering nuclear payloads.

Appalled by this sudden escalation of the danger, the ExComm re-convened with a renewed momentum for immediate military action.

[36]Memorandum of Meeting, October 17, 1962, FRUS: Cuban Missile Crisis and After-math, XI (Washington, D.C.: United States Government Printing Office, 1996), Documents #22 and #23.

[37]Ibid. For the historical context of Acheson's views, see Blight and Welch, On the Brink, 218–21.

[38]In fact, the R-14 missiles were never delivered to Cuba. (Fursenko and Naftali, "One Hell of a Gamble," 276, 311)

Thursday, October 18, 11:00 A.M., Cabinet Room

Identified Participants: John F. Kennedy, George Ball, McGeorge Bundy, Douglas Dillon, Roswell Gilpatric, U. Alexis Johnson, Robert Kennedy, Arthur Lundahl, Edwin Martin, John McCone, Robert McNamara, Dean Rusk, Theodore Sorensen, Maxwell Taylor, Llewellyn Thompson.[39]

"Now the question *really* is what action we take which *lessens* the chances of a nuclear exchange, which obviously is the final failure."

President John F. Kennedy

The meeting began with a heightened sense of urgency—even alarm. McCone, joining ExComm for the first time and perhaps trying to impress the President with technical wizardry, boasted as JFK turned on the recorder that six missions flown the previous day had produced "28,000 lineal feet of film and when this is enlarged it means the [National Photographic Interpretation] Center has to examine a strip of film 100 miles long, 20 feet wide." Someone on the President's side of the table, near the microphones, can be heard reacting to these numbers in a whispered, "Oh my God!" McCone noted somewhat smugly, "Quite a job!"[40]

Lundahl then reviewed the new photographic evidence in detail, especially the discovery of IRBM sites "like the things we have been seeing in the Soviet Union." His briefing, initially very dry and factual, became quite animated as he pointed out the extremely dangerous potential of the IRBMs: "The orientation of the axis of the pads," he emphasized, was "*three-one-five*, which will bring you into the central massif of the United States." He rose to near eloquence in explaining

---

[39]Tapes 30.2 and 30A.1, POF, PRC, JFKL.

[40]"In an era of satellites and space shuttles, it is almost impossible to appreciate how amazing U-2 photography was, as a technical feat, in 1962. By 1956, the United States had deployed an aircraft that could fly at 70,000 feet (beyond the altitude of the fighters or air defense missiles of that time), mount multiple cameras that could discern objects only a few feet long, and photograph steadily during hours of flight from a distance of nearly 14 miles. The cameras—synchronized—shot continuous panoramic photos over a swath of earth 100 miles wide. The thousands of feet of film that were used had to be stored in a small space aboard the plane." (Allison and Zelikow, *Essence of Decision*, 221) JFK sent former Secretary of State Dean Acheson to Paris to brief Charles de Gaulle on the photos: "He was obviously deeply impressed, said, 'From what height were these taken?'; I said, '65,000 feet.' He started to say, 'We don't have anything'—and then he caught himself and said, 'Well, I'm not very familiar with photography but this seems remarkable to me.'" (Dean Acheson Oral History Interview, 1964, OHC, JFKL, 28)

that although the evidence was not conclusive, "the elongation of the pads and the location of the control bunkers, between each pair of pads, has been the thing that has suggested to our hearts, if not our minds, the kind of thing that might accompany an IRBM"—a missile capable of reaching almost the entire United States mainland.

The President, clearly concerned, asked to see the photos. Lundahl, obviously pleased, replied with alacrity, "Yes, sir!" His footsteps can be heard as he brought the photos over to JFK, and for some 20 seconds the room remained eerily silent as President Kennedy examined the newest evidence. After resuming the briefing, Lundahl pointed out many construction details on the missile bases and tried to emphasize the importance of a specific picture by asking: "May I pass that one over to you, sir?" The tape captured the sound as Lundahl passed the picture to JFK; the President examined it for some ten seconds. Finally, Lundahl revealed photos of San Julian airfield in westernmost Cuba and identified twenty-two crates likely containing IL-28 bombers: "We've just caught them, apparently, at the start of the assembly operation."[41]

When Lundahl finished, JFK asked several questions about the extent of photographic coverage of Cuba and the number of missile sites, pads and erectors. Taylor asked if electronic emissions from the SAM sites had been detected and McCone, despite replying "No," estimated nonetheless that some of the SAMs would be operational within a week. President Kennedy, likely recalling the furor over doctored photographs designed to conceal U.S. involvement and shown at the U.N. during the Bay of Pigs debacle, inquired about releasing the U-2 photographs as political cover. He wanted to prove that the missiles were really there—that this was no political ploy or trick: "would it not be possible to demonstrate this to the satisfaction of an untrained observer, would it?" But Lundahl, citing eight years of experience in photo interpretation, downplayed the idea that the pictures could be made comprehensible to the layman: "I think it would be difficult, sir. . . . I think the uninitiated would like to see the missile in the... in the... in the tube that it fits in." But, the NPIC director agreed with suggestions by Bundy and McNamara that some of the photos of "mis-

[41]The Ilyushin IL-28 (NATO designation "BEAGLE") was a twin-engine turbo-jet strategic bomber introduced in 1948, with a maximum speed of 559 m.p.h., a 715-mile range and the capacity to deliver nuclear weapons.

siles lying on trailers in there, at lower level particularly, as Mr. Bundy says, could, I think, very clearly impact on people."

JFK thanked Lundahl, who cleared away his materials after assuring the President that the photos from new surveillance missions would be processed "on a 24-hour basis" and should be available by the weekend. Rusk, his voice partially drowned out by the clatter of Lundahl's clean-up, spoke up to explain that this new intelligence information "changes my thinking on the matter." He had become convinced that the Soviet buildup was not "just an *incidental* base for a few of these things" but "a *formidable* military problem," and failure to act "would undermine our alliances all over the world, very promptly." The secretary of state read from the President's explicit September 4 warning to the Soviets that "the gravest issues would arise" if offensive nuclear weapons were shipped to Cuba; and, virtually challenging JFK to live up to his words, Rusk warned of "the effect on the Soviets if we do nothing. I would suppose that they would consider this a *major* back down . . . [and] I think they would be *greatly* encouraged to go adventuring, to feel that they've got it made as far as intimidating the United States is concerned." Noting that "We've got a million men in uniform outside the United States," Rusk warned that inaction "would undermine and undercut the enormous support that we need for the kind of foreign policy that will eventually secure our survival."

On the other hand, Rusk counseled, military action against Cuba "involves *very* high risks indeed" of Soviet reprisals around the world—in Berlin, in Korea, or even "against the United States itself." "I don't think," he advised the President, "that you can make your decision under any assumption that this is a free ride" for the U.S. Rusk also warned that "an unannounced, unconsulted, quick [military] action on our part" could lead to disunity in NATO that "the Soviets could cap... capitalize upon very strongly." If the U.S. challenged the Soviet decision to embark "upon this *fantastically* dangerous course," he advised quite fervently, "no one can *surely* foresee the outcome."

The normally impassive Rusk counseled that war had a political as well as a military dimension: unless the United States was attacked, war had to be *seen* publicly as a last resort, not a first option. "I think the American people will *willingly* undertake great danger," Rusk confidently predicted, "if they have a *deep* feeling that we've done everything that was reasonably possible to determine whether this risk was necessary." Citing historical precedents from "the guns of August"[42] through World War II and the Korean War, he stressed the political need for further "consultation with Khrushchev" even though, he admitted, there was no reason to expect that the Soviet leader would back down in the face of diplomatic protests. "But at least it will take *that* point out of the way for the historical record, and just might have in it the uh... the seeds of prevention of a... of a great conflict."

Rusk also recommended seeking support from the Rio Pact nations, "our strongest legal basis for whatever action we need to take," and predicted that "there would be no real difficulty in getting a 2/3 vote in favor of necessary action. But if we made the effort and failed to get the 2/3 vote, which I *doubt* would be the result, then at least we will have tried and as far as the American people are concerned, we've done... we've done our very best on that." He likewise suggested the possibility of a declaration of national emergency or even a declaration of war on Cuba, bolstering his position by reading parts of a letter left by Bohlen before his departure for Paris. The ambassador had insisted that a tough but private appeal to Khrushchev must be attempted *before* attacking the missile sites in order to legitimize the American response and retain the support of the allies. He suggested that "the allied reaction would be dead against us" if the Soviets retaliated in Turkey, Italy or Berlin. Bohlen also recommended a new communication with Khrushchev and warned that the belief that limited air strikes would provide a quick solution "is an illusion"; rather, he argued, they would lead to "a total war with Cuba [and] . . . greatly increase the probability of general war." Instead, he endorsed a declaration of war, *after* consultation with our allies, to encompass all possible military options (air strikes, blockade or invasion). The President and the Ex-Comm must have noticed that Rusk had not personally or specifically endorsed any of these choices.

McNamara, in sharp contrast, abandoned his cautious October 16 position and boldly recommended an all-out air and land attack on Cuba. The defense secretary declared that, like the JCS, he could no longer support either limited or broad air strikes: "In other words, we consider nothing short of a full invasion as practicable military action,

[42]A reference to Barbara Tuchman's 1962 best seller, *The Guns of August*, about the outbreak of World War I.

and *this* only on the assumption that we're operating against a force that does not possess operational nuclear weapons."

President Kennedy, taken aback by the defense secretary's about-face, asked: "Why do you change... why has this information changed the recommendation?" McNamara declared that there were too many targets, including many that had not been located, to be realistically destroyed by air strikes. As a result, there was a heightened chance of the loss of Guantanamo and/or attacks on the civilian population on the eastern coast of the U.S. from the new IRBM bases or the IL-28 nuclear bombers. "I think we... we would find it hard to justify" these casualties, McNamara explained, "in relation to the very limited accomplishment of our limited number of [air] strikes."

But the President questioned this rationale, pointing out that even the more inclusive air strikes (against the airfields, SAM sites, etc.) could presumably be carried out in a day, but an invasion "would be seven, eight or nine days, with all the consequences [and] the increase in tension." Taylor stressed again that there could never be a guarantee of destroying 100% of the missile sites and airfields. But JFK persisted, "I would think you'd *have* to go on the assumption that they're not gonna permit nuclear weapons to be used against the United States from Cuba unless they're gonna be using them from everyplace." McNamara replied ominously, "I'm not sure they can stop it. . . . I don't believe the Soviets would authorize their use against the U.S., but they might nonetheless be used." He was obviously concerned about an accidental launch, a rogue action by Soviet or Cuban military personnel or a deliberate decision by Castro.[43]

The defense secretary momentarily fell back on his October 16 reply to Bundy's question about whether the missiles in Cuba altered the strategic balance, emphasizing again that his views were not shared by the Chiefs and other high officials in the defense department: "because it's not a *military* problem that we're facing; it's a *political* problem; it's a problem of holding the alliance together; it's a problem of... of *properly* conditioning Khrushchev for our future moves." These new

---

[43]At the 2002 Havana conference, General Anatoli I. Gribkov, who was in charge of the secret Soviet missile deployment to Cuba, revealed that security arrangements were so stringent that the warheads were stored at least 90 miles away from the missile sites. But, he also recalled that a nervous local commander ordered warheads shipped to a missile base on October 26 without authorization from Moscow. In retrospect, McNamara's apprehension appears to have been entirely justified. (*Boston Globe*, October 14, 2002, A8)

circumstances, including "the problem of dealing with our domestic public," rather than a real change in the military balance of power, he reasoned, justified an invasion of Cuba.

President Kennedy, coming as close to lecturing as he ever did at these meetings, soberly disagreed, suggesting that an American invasion of Cuba, on the contrary, would in fact severely strain the NATO alliance. Most of the allies, he reminded the defense secretary, regarded Cuba "as a fixation of the United States and not a serious military threat. . . . an awful lot of conditioning would have to go in before they would accept and support our action against Cuba because they think that we're... we're slightly demen... demented on this subject. So there isn't any doubt that whatever action we take against Cuba, no matter how good our films are . . . a lot of people would regard this as a *mad* act by the United States which is due to a loss of nerve because they will argue that *taken at its worst* the presence of these missiles really doesn't change" the nuclear balance of power. Away from the eyes and ears of journalists and the public, JFK could dispassionately acknowledge the validity of international perceptions of his administration's fixation with Castro and Cuba.

General Taylor pointed out that the latest photographs, especially those identifying IRBMs, proved that the Soviets "are moving very fast to make those... those weapons operational." Despite his earlier doubts about the wisdom of "the big showdown"—that is, invading Cuba—he concluded that it might already be too late to eliminate the entire missile threat without an invasion: "the targets that we're seeing" in the new photos suggest "that the kind of air attack we're talking about means nothing. We can't take *this* threat out by... by actions from the air." "You mean," Bundy interposed, "that for the long pull you're gonna have to take the island." "Yes, you can't destroy a hole in the ground," Taylor continued. Only diplomatic action or physical occupation of the sites "can prevent this kind of threat from building up." He seemed especially uneasy about alerting the Soviets before air attacks, but reluctantly conceded that a warning might be politically necessary. JFK, joined soon by Bundy, expressed concern that the Soviets might hide the mobile missiles in nearby woods if forewarned; but McNamara, seconded by Taylor, concluded that it was unlikely "we would lose them with a 24-hour discussion with Khrushchev." "How quick is our communications with Moscow," the President probed, obviously interested in this option: "say we sent somebody to see him, I mean he was *there* at the beginning of the 24-hour period to see Mr.

Khrushchev. How long would it be before Khrushchev's answer could get back to us, just by communication?" Ambassador Thompson speculated that a reply in code could be received in 5–6 hours, but suggested trying a contact by secure telephone. RFK asked if a phone call really had to go in code and Rusk observed that it might be faster to transmit a message directly through Ambassador Dobrynin.

McCone offered some presumably relevant intelligence, "so *far* as we know, there is no stated relationship that makes these *Soviet* missiles or *Soviet* bases." Raúl Castro and Che Guevara, he assured the President, had failed months before, according to the U.S. Intelligence Board, to conclude a bilateral defense pact with the U.S.S.R. or to join the Warsaw Pact. Therefore, it was difficult to predict the Soviet response, if any, to a U.S. attack on these bases.[44] JFK, nonetheless, wondered aloud "The question is *really* whether the Soviet reaction, and who knows this, could... would be measurably different if they were presented with an accomplished fact [or] ... whether their reaction would be different than it would be if they were given a chance to pull 'em out." The President then, quite casually, floated a trial balloon, echoing the suggestion made the previous day by Ambassador Stevenson, "If we said to Khrushchev that 'we have to take action against it, but if you're willing to pull them out, we'll take ours out of Turkey.'" JFK promptly shot down his own idea, speculating that Khrushchev might respond, "'If you take these out [with air strikes], we're gonna take Berlin or we're gonna do somethin' else.'" No one, as yet, responded explicitly to the President's first intimation that he might consider trading Soviet missiles in Cuba for American missiles in Turkey.

The advice from around the table continued to be generally hawkish. Llewellyn Thompson, ExComm's recognized Soviet specialist, who had established a personal "friendship" with Khrushchev when serving as ambassador to Moscow from 1957 to 1962, opposed first strikes from the air "because you'd have killed a lot of Russians" and the Soviets might threaten Turkey and Italy if given advance notice.[45] He instead endorsed the blockade, predicting that the U.S.S.R. would be deterred from running a blockade against offensive weapons, backed up

[44]U.S. intelligence did not know that a five-year renewable agreement to defend Cuba had in fact been negotiated in July during Raúl Castro's visit to Moscow. (Fursenko and Naftali, *"One Hell of a Gamble,"* 192; Blight, *et al., Cuba on the Brink,* 77–79; Garthoff, *Reflections,* 17, 25–26)

[45]Thompson's superior, Secretary of State Rusk, acknowledged the former ambassador's status as ExComm's "prime expert on the Soviet Union." (Rusk Oral History, 126)

by a formal declaration of war, "if that's the way we pitched it before the world." JFK inevitably asked about the status of weapons already in Cuba and Thompson recommended "Demand they're dismantled," but if surveillance proved they were armed, then take them out. He also tried to educate the President on the Russian view of the world: "The Russians have a curious faculty," he droned, "of wanting a legal basis despite all of the outrageous things they've done." The ambassador also suggested that Khrushchev would use "a lot of threatening language" about nuclear war, but JFK countered that he would "just grab Berlin." Thompson felt Khrushchev was more likely to react to air strikes in Cuba with a quid pro quo attack on a U.S. base in Turkey "and then say, 'Now I want to talk.'" Khrushchev's entire purpose, he insisted, was to "build up to talks with *you* in which we try to negotiate out the bases" in Cuba *and* Turkey.[46]

RFK, still passionately in favor of an invasion, took issue, cautioning that a blockade could become "a very slow death" over a period of months and would still require dangerous military steps such as "the examination of Russian ships, shooting down the Russian planes that try to land there. You have to do *all* those things." "Submarines," President Kennedy muttered in the background, reminding his advisers of another significant danger. Taylor suggested that the blockade could be implemented concurrently with other military actions and Bundy counseled the President, "simultaneously, it seems to me, you declare that a state of war exists and you call the Congress."

Thompson maintained that the Soviets would respond to a blockade and a declaration of war by denying "that these are Soviet bases. But naturally, we take exception to that. I think that what he'd say is that: 'What are you getting so excited about? The Cubans asked us for the missiles to deal with these émigré bases . . . they're much less offensive than your weapons in Turkey. You've got these armed with nuclear warheads. We haven't... we haven't given them... nuclear weapons to them. These are simply to deal with the threat to Cuba.'" "If we *act*," Bundy demanded, "they'd better be Cuban missiles, surely." But, despite scoffing at this defense of Cuba argument, Thompson admonished the President, "You want to make it, if you do any of these steps, make it as easy as possible for him to... to back down." If he replies, "'This is *so* serious, I'm prepared to *talk* to you about it.' We could scarcely

[46]For an account of JFK's relationship with Thompson, see David Mayers, "JFK's Ambassadors and the Cold War," *Diplomacy & Statecraft* 11 (November 2000), 186–92.

refuse then—that's if you have a world war being threatened." But, JFK again complained that a blockade would not stop the work on the missiles already in Cuba. Thompson noted, with a touch of irony, that the Soviet gamble in Cuba, at the very least, had finally satisfied his personal curiosity about why Khrushchev had promised to defer a confrontation over Berlin until after the American mid-term elections.

McCone interjected a potential political complication by reporting on the reaction of General Eisenhower to his recent briefing on the photography and other intelligence. The former President felt that an offensive Soviet base in Cuba was "*intolerable* from the standpoint of this country" but had dismissed bombing, limited or extensive, as unsatisfactory since the Soviets could easily retaliate in Turkey and elsewhere. He had also rejected a conventional invasion, moving slowly inland from the beaches, and instead insisted on "an all-out military action" going "*right* to the jugular first" with a "concentrated attack *right* on Havana first" to take out Castro's government "with a *minimum* loss of life and of time." Rusk pointed out that such a plan would require a declaration of national emergency or war in order to obtain the necessary manpower.

Perhaps emboldened by the report of Eisenhower's tough position, Thompson judged that "since Castro's gone this far in conniving" in the installation of the missiles, "it seems to me that in the end it *does* lead to the fact that... that Castro has to go"—particularly if he responds to U.S. actions by attacking Guantanamo. Dillon counseled that delaying military action to negotiate with the Soviets would achieve nothing: Khrushchev "might say, 'Sure, I'll take them out sometime,' and then do the opposite their old way." Despite his earlier forecast that Khrushchev might seek negotiations, Thompson reasoned that "the most he'd do in the way of concession would be to say that he will *not* take any *further* action while these talks go on. Meantime, we've said that we're going to keep an eye on 'em [the missiles] and crop 'em if they became operational. That might deter the Cubans." But, the former ambassador concluded gloomily, "I don't think he could ever just back down."

The discussion seemed to be going around in circles. McCone counseled against getting locked into open-ended negotiations with the Soviets while the work on the sites proceeded in Cuba, when the President probed again: "The only offer we would make, I... it would seem to me, that would have any sense, . . . giving him *some* out, would be our Turkey missiles." This time around JFK appeared to pick up some limited support: Bundy affirmed that such an offer would be equally valid as an adjunct to surprise air strikes. Despite "all the wicked things that have led to this," he advised that a message should be "in Khrushchev's hands" at the moment the air strikes begin stating "that we understand this base problem and that we *do* expect to dismantle our Turkish base. That has *one* small advantage," Bundy added, "which is that if he strikes back, we have at least given him a peaceful offer. I don't think we can keep that Turkish base . . ." But, when Rusk objected that a direct Cuba-Turkey missile exchange "would be quite serious," Bundy seemed to back off—indicating that a missile swap was only "one way" of minimizing the danger since "this is a political *not* a military problem."[47]

McNamara, always the hard-nosed realist, emphasized the substantial risks from unannounced air strikes: several hundred Soviet citizens would be killed—at a minimum. "Killed?" Bundy asked. "Killed. Absolutely!" the defense chief replied. "We're using napalm, 750-pound bombs. This is a... this is an *extensive* strike we're talking about." "Well, I hope it is!" Bundy eagerly avowed—in sharp contrast to the doubts he had expressed just two days earlier about an American military response in Cuba. McNamara predicted a strong response from Khrushchev: "I think the price is going to be high. It may still be worth paying to eliminate the missiles. . . . The very *least* it will be will be to remove the missiles in Italy and Turkey"—but he doubted that the Soviets would settle for that after their personnel had been killed in Cuba. "I think they'll take Berlin," Dillon predicted.

Ball, evidently alarmed by McNamara's casualty estimate, urged the President not to underestimate the "sense of affront" that would result from unannounced air strikes, even among America's allies, and pushed for the 24-hour warning explored earlier in the meeting. The U.S. had to offer "Khrushchev *some* way out. Even though it may be illusory, I think we *still* have to do it," he warned, because world opinion would turn against America. A strike without warning "is like Pearl Harbor," he declared, echoing General Carter's doubts on the first day of meetings. "It's... it's the kind of conduct that's such that one might expect of the Soviet Union. It is *not* conduct that one expects of the United States." A warning to Khrushchev, he asserted, "is *really* indispensable."

[47]By October 27, Bundy completely reversed his tentative early position on removing the Turkish missiles.

The mood of the meeting darkened as the President calculated that Khrushchev would "grab Berlin anyway." McNamara suggested that Khrushchev's price "will be about the same" regardless of any advance warning, but giving him the possibility of an out would cause "less friction with the rest of the world." On the other hand, he admonished the President, "once you start down that course" it's possible that Khrushchev "outmaneuvers you." Dillon too added that a warning would only be useful in placating world opinion.

JFK repeated that the allies would feel that the U.S. had "lost Berlin because of these missiles [in Cuba], which as I say, do not bother them."

Thompson disagreed, suggesting that Khrushchev would not attack Berlin immediately, but would instead "try to sap our morale."

"What do we do when really... I think he moves into Berlin?" RFK asked grimly.

"If we could trade off Berlin, and not have it our fault," Bundy quipped—but he was the only person to laugh.

"Well, when we're talking about taking Berlin," McNamara asked, "what do we *mean* exactly? Do they take it with Soviet troops?"

"That's what I would see, anyway," JFK responded.

"I think there's a real possibility of that," McNamara agreed. "We have U.S. troops there. What do they do?"

"They fight," Taylor asserted.

"They fight," McNamara agreed, "I think that's perfectly clear."

"And they get overrun," Kennedy predicted.

"Yes, they get overrun, exactly," McNamara concurred.

"Then what do we do?" RFK queried.

"Go to general war," Taylor pronounced, "assuming we have time for it."

"You mean nuclear exchange?" the President remarked grimly.

"Guess you have to," Taylor concluded.

The NATO alliance would deteriorate, JFK conceded, if the U.S. took military action in Cuba, but "if we don't take any action then of course there will be a more gradual deterioration." Rusk, Dillon and Bundy dissented in unison, warning that the deterioration would be "very rapid" if the U.S. failed to act. President Kennedy, in response to these increasingly bleak judgments about the military and diplomatic alternatives, reflected with stark eloquence, "Now the question *really* is what action we take which *lessens* the chances of a nuclear exchange, which obviously is the final failure."[48] "And, at the same time," he added pensively, "maintain some degree of solidarity with our allies."

JFK tried to focus on the practical political and diplomatic mechanics for averting nuclear doomsday: "Now, to get a blockade on Cuba," he asked, "would we have to declare war on Cuba?" A cacophony of responses followed, including Bundy, Ball and Alexis Johnson, with every voice declaring "yes" for diplomatic, legal and political reasons. But the President seized the initiative, "I think we *shouldn't* assume we have to declare war. The declaration of a state of war is a . . . Because it seems to me if you're gonna do that, you really... it doesn't make any sense not to invade. . . . We do the message to Khrushchev and tell him that if work continues, etc., etc. At the same time, launch the blockade. If work continues, then we go in and take them out. We *don't* declare war," he pronounced firmly. A declaration of war, in short, would increase pressure for an invasion and present an unnecessarily aggressive posture to the Soviets. Khrushchev might easily overreact—particularly in Berlin.

A blockade without a declaration of war, Ball nonetheless insisted, was illegal and Bundy called it "an act of aggression against everybody else." "Including our allies," Ball interjected. JFK retorted sharply, "I don't think anybody who gets excited because their ships are stopped under these conditions—they're not very much help to us anyway." RFK asked, "How many [OAS] votes are dead against it [the blockade]?" Edwin Martin speculated, "Probably four for sure." Despite his own admission that Khrushchev might simply refuse to stop work on the missile sites, the President maintained that a blockade without a declaration of war would not immediately raise the escalation stakes "as high as it would be under ordinary... other conditions."

Ball continued to defend the value of a formal declaration of war, asserting that if the President decided on the blockade alone, the U.S. must at least issue an ultimatum, demanding that "work *must* stop on the missile sites or you *take them out*." The American people "will not sit still while work goes on making these things operational." The blockade, he declared, using words much like RFK's, could become "rather a slow agony," increasing the "fears and doubts in the minds of people here." Thompson further contended that a declaration of war

---

[48]The fact that JFK thought of nuclear holocaust as "final" is entirely understandable. But, as the elected leader who might ultimately make the decision to use these weapons, nuclear war would be *his* failure, a fact that clearly weighed heavily on his mind.

could be justified as a necessary step to eliminate a threat to the U.S., which is "a little different from saying that we're going to war to destroy" Cuba. Bundy also bluntly lectured the President, "your whole posture" must reflect the fact that Khrushchev has done "unacceptable things from the point of view of the security of the hemisphere." He dismissed concerns about "the freedom of Cuba" and predicted, rather haughtily, that with or without a declaration of war, "You will, in fact, get into the invasion before you're through . . . either way."

McCone was equally pessimistic, forecasting that with Khrushchev's prestige in the balance, his ships "would go right through" the blockade. Thompson surmised that Khrushchev might observe the blockade, even without the declaration of war, simply because of the logistical difficulties in taking military action around Cuba: on the other hand, he could choose to risk "the *big* action in Berlin, which is this gamble which he's shown for four years he's reluctant to take." Rusk summed up the administration's perceived dilemma: Khrushchev may feel obligated to respond militarily, but could be deterred because he knows the U.S. would respond in kind. "Or maybe he's a little crazy," Rusk wondered, "and we can't trust him."

President Kennedy hypothesized about how the confrontation with the U.S.S.R. might have played out in reverse: if Khrushchev had warned the U.S. against putting missiles in Turkey and, after they were put in anyway, he had taken military action to destroy them. "To me," he mused, apparently wondering if such a limited assault could be contained without any further escalation, "there's some advantages to that if it's all over."

At this stage, however, the President clearly assumed that air strikes were still in the cards, at least against the missiles and Soviet planes in Cuba; but, he appeared to be gradually reconsidering his earlier objections to giving the Kremlin advance warning. JFK pondered announcing the presence of the missiles on Friday (October 19), without revealing what the administration planned to do, and calling the Congress back: "It isn't Pearl Harbor in that sense. We've told everybody. Then we go ahead Saturday and we take 'em out, and a... and announce that they've been taken out, and any more that are put in, we're gonna take those out." "And the air force," Bundy persisted, and the President repeated, "And the air force. And [we say] that we don't want any war." He emphasized that the air strikes would take place on Saturday, "Sunday has historic disadvantages," a sardonic reference to Sunday, December 7, 1941—the watershed date of their lives. Taylor, however, again expressed concern about the military disadvantages of an announcement, and the President conceded that there was no doubt that the Soviets would move their planes out of harm's way.

Robert Kennedy had evidently been rattled by the Pearl Harbor analogy.[49] Retreating from his belligerent posture for the first time in the meetings, he suddenly interjected, "I think George Ball has a hell of a good point . . . assuming that you do survive all this"—giving the Russians a warning would affirm "what kind of a country we are." Rusk, at ease with Biblical imagery, assured the President that a warning would be preferable to "carrying the mark of Cain on your brow for the rest of your lives." For 15 years, RFK avowed, the U.S. had worked to prevent a Russian first strike against us. "Now, in the interest of time, we do that to a *small* country. I think it's a hell of a burden to carry." The President acknowledged that the U.S. would lose the advantage of surprise, but a warning would give Khrushchev a chance to "get these Russians outa there in the next twelve hours," and, of course, the point was to "get these missiles," not to kill Russians.

JFK never lost sight of the fact that once military action started, there was no telling at what level of escalation it could be stopped—if at all. The Soviets might "get a couple of them [nuclear bombs] over on us anyway." He hoped that a measured American response would lead to a measured Soviet reaction. The Russian response to the attacking missiles, especially if they were warned beforehand, might be far less extreme than their reaction to an invasion. Likewise, he reasoned, their response to a blockade might be even more limited.

Thompson, however, was less hopeful and pointed out that Khrushchev had personally initiated this aggressive posture in Berlin. "I mean he's taken credit for it, time and time again." Even if he were warned before bombing Cuba, his behavior was difficult to predict. The former ambassador recalled that after the American U-2 was shot down over the U.S.S.R. in 1960, the Soviet military "who normally never talked to me, came over and tried to calm me down" because "*they* were concerned that Khrushchev was being impetuous and running risks." Thompson's concerns prompted the President to ask: "What is it we ask him to do under that notification? What is it we'd be trying to get out of him?" Rusk's answer was emphatic: the Presi-

---

[49]Two years later, Taylor accurately contended that until the Pearl Harbor argument against bombing Cuba, Robert Kennedy "had been a hawk constantly." (Taylor Oral History, 54)

dent would be taking political risks by giving advance warning and
Khrushchev would be expected, "in order to keep the fig leaf on for the
President," to cease work on the bases and withdraw Soviet missile
technicians. Sorensen stressed that on the key point, dismantling the
bases, any effort by the Soviets to delay or make counterproposals
would be unacceptable.

Thompson remained skeptical about dealing with Khrushchev at all,
but for the moment at least seemed to warm to the President's intima-
tions about making a deal on the Jupiter missiles, since, he observed,
the U.S. could simply substitute submarine-launched Polaris missiles to
protect Turkey. He even suggested that it would be advantageous for
the administration to propose the deal and invite Khrushchev to come
to the U.S. for talks, "'This won't wait for your trip in November,
come on over,'" he chuckled.[50] Otherwise, Thompson worried, "it
seems to me you're playing Russian roulette, you're really... you're
flipping a coin as to whether you have... end up with world war or
not."

President Kennedy continued to argue that there would likely be
some symmetry between U.S. action and a probable Soviet response,
"I... I feel that there's a difference in our action and therefore in their
response, between our knocking out these missiles and planes and
knocking out... and invading Cuba." He reasoned that it would be one
thing for Khrushchev to respond to the destruction of the Cuban missiles by attacking American missiles in Turkey; however, it would be
quite different if the Red Army responded to an American invasion of
Cuba by invading Turkey.[51] And, in addition, JFK cautioned, "nobody
knows what kind of a success we're gonna have with this invasion. In-
vasions are tough, hazardous. And they've got a lot of equipment. A lot
of... thousands of Americans get killed in Cuba and I think you're in
much more of a *mess* than you are if you take out these [missiles]." He
even raised the possibility that the Soviets might respond to a U.S. invasion of Cuba by invading Iran.

But, the President stressed that uncertainty remained regardless of

[50]"Khrushchev remained a prisoner of his own hopes and therefore unrealistic expectations that the secret could be maintained until he triumphantly disclosed it in late November on the trip he was planning then to take both to the United Nations in New York and
to Havana." (Garthoff, "US Intelligence in the Cuban Missile Crisis," 49)

[51]The President seemed to be suggesting that a limited Soviet bombing response against
the missiles in Turkey would be tactically acceptable to the United States. Of course, the
political fall out would have created very serious problems for the administration.

whether the U.S. bombed or invaded Cuba: "It may be that his [Khrushchev's] response would be the same," he observed rather gloomily, "nobody can guess that." And of course, there was always another wild card—Castro himself. If the Cubans tried to overrun Guantanamo after the air strikes, with or without a go-ahead from Moscow, Kennedy conceded, "we're gonna have to invade." Taylor assured the commander-in-chief, "He... he won't overrun Guantanamo, I can tell you. We may have a *big* fight around the place, but by the time we get the Marines in, with the... with the... with the carrier-based aviation, we can hold Guantanamo." The President urged General Taylor to make all necessary naval preparations over the next 3–4 days. Robert Kennedy, despite his earlier resistance to unannounced air strikes, continued to be drawn to an invasion: if you had the air attack on Monday (October 22), he asked, "How many days *after* that would you be prepared to invade?" "Seven to ten days," McNamara replied.

Before any of these grim possibilities had to be confronted, the practical details of the pre-strike notification to Khrushchev had to be arranged—whether to go through Ambassador Dobrynin or to send an emissary to the Kremlin. Thompson recommended a telegraph message to U.S. ambassador Foy Kohler in Moscow, RFK favored a personal presidential emissary and Rusk suggested a written message through Dobrynin. Thompson, backed by Dillon, agreed that a written message was preferable so that Khrushchev had to reply in writing, "Otherwise you get a fuzzy conversation." JFK instead suggested putting former defense secretary Robert Lovett on a plane to Moscow.

Bundy and Thompson predicted that Khrushchev would respond by calling for a summit meeting. Kennedy was not thrilled by the prospect: if we get a summit, "then he's gonna be talkin' about Berlin." Ball and Dillon argued that a summit would at least provide some political cover with NATO, world opinion and history. Bundy, still dubious about any warning at all, pounced on this point: "How much better are you off before history if you ask him 24 hours ahead of time, if he says, 'I want a summit,' and you say, 'Nuts'?"[52] He urged the President not to agree to a meeting unless they first secured an agreement on key issues—such as an immediate halt to construction of the missile sites.

Later that afternoon the President was preparing to meet with Soviet foreign minister Andrei Gromyko. The previously scheduled meeting

[52]Bundy was likely recalling the fabled response of General Anthony McAuliffe to the German demand for surrender during the Battle of the Bulge in late 1944.

had of course taken on enormous importance.[53] Taylor suggested that perhaps "we can get him to *lie*" and Rusk agreed, advising Kennedy to repeat the warning he had issued on September 4 about the grave issues raised by offensive nuclear weapons in Cuba: "See if he will lie about it," Rusk also proposed coyly, clearly hoping to catch his Russian counterpart in a brazen deception. Robert Kennedy also pressured the President to be wary that Gromyko might argue that the Soviet missiles in Cuba were no more offensive than the American missiles in Turkey, "Then what do you do?" Rusk rejected the comparison, insisting that the Jupiter decision was made in context of NATO, and the alliance "was itself built as a direct response to Soviet aggression [and] ... came into being as a result of Stalin's policies. It makes all the difference in the world."[54]

JFK mulled over the Turkish issue again: "How many missiles do we have in Turkey?" he asked. "Fifteen," Bundy answered, probably having checked since the nearly identical exchange on October 16, "plus nuclear-equipped aircraft?"—"Yes," McNamara and Gilpatric confirmed. RFK, always concerned about political damage to the President and still fuming about false Soviet promises not to do anything risky before the mid-term elections, was not interested in making any deals. The attorney general questioned whether the President himself should try to trap Gromyko "as blatantly as" suggested by Taylor and Rusk: "I suppose the other way is to do it rather subtly with me saying [to Gromyko], 'What are you doing in Cuba? This is embarrassing in this election. What are you sticking... what kind of missiles are you sticking in?'"[55] Taylor added that "If he denies it, you have something that you

[53]Unfortunately and inexplicably, JFK did not record this important Oval Office meeting.

[54]The launch of *Sputnik* in 1957, suggesting Soviet capability to produce ICBMs, had contributed to the decision to place U.S. Jupiter and Thor missiles in Europe. Khrushchev and Gromyko, in addition to resentment of the NATO deployment, justified the Soviet missiles in Cuba as a response to aggressive American policies toward Castro. In fact, several members of the Kennedy administration had warned in private about a dangerous American "double standard" toward missiles in Turkey vs. missiles in Cuba. (Nash, *The Other Missiles*, 95; Bernstein, "Reconsidering the Missile Crisis," 57–60)

[55]"You always had the feeling in dealing with Bobby," ExComm colleague U. Alexis Johnson later recalled, "that he was the fearless watchdog on behalf of the President. He had enormous possessive pride in the President, and he was looking after the President's interests in a way which, he felt, the President could not do." (Johnson Oral History, 36–37). RFK may have read the report on Khrushchev's assurance to U.S. ambassador Foy Kohler that morning in Moscow that the Soviet Union would not do anything to inflame U.S.-Soviet relations before the November mid-term elections. (May and Zelikow, *The Kennedy Tapes*, 88)

can confront Khrushchev with later." Bundy affirmed, "That's correct. Yeah. Yeah." Ted Sorensen also seconded RFK's suggestion—as "a pretty good gambit." Rusk mentioned that Khrushchev had not actually denied the presence of the missiles in Cuba during an October 16 discussion with Ambassador Kohler in Moscow and speculated that "They *must* know now that we know. They're working around the clock down there."

Taylor and several colleagues, however, urged the President to wait for additional intelligence photographs before they committed themselves: "I'm impressed," the general affirmed, "with how our mind has changed on this in 24 hours based upon this last intelligence." But McCone counseled, "I'm worried about this getting out. I think it's just remarkable that it's been held this week." McNamara countered that the intelligence already in hand was sufficient for developing a *"well thought-out* course of action" on the only two alternatives being discussed: a slow move to military action (a political statement followed or accompanied by a blockade) *or* a rapid move to military action (a brief warning to Khrushchev followed by an air attack). He suggested splitting up into a number of groups to make detailed plans for minimizing the military price which would have to be paid for each option. Early in the meeting, the defense secretary had passionately endorsed invading Cuba; but, by the end of the meeting, undoubtedly influenced by JFK's reservations, he did not even list invasion as an option.

President Kennedy, perhaps sensing an opportunity to nail down the historical record, confronted his advisers point blank: "Well, lemme ask... Is there anyone here who doesn't think that we ought to do something about this?" JFK's question was followed by about seven seconds of very loud silence, punctuated only by a murmured "no"— probably from McNamara—and captured dramatically by the tape machine turning secretly in the White House basement. Doing nothing was *not* an option.[56]

If inaction was not an option, some combination of diplomatic and military moves must follow. However, JFK countered that the military

[56]"In effect, Khrushchev thought that if the Americans were reasonable, they would tolerate the Soviet deployment. The Americans *were* reasonable; ergo, they would tolerate the deployment. This was clearly unreasonable. Even if Khrushchev's minor premise were correct, the major premise evinced an astonishing naiveté about American sensibilities." Khrushchev could have consulted many Soviet experts on the U.S., "But he asked none of them." (James G. Blight and David A. Welch, "The Cuban Missile Crisis and Intelligence Performance," in Blight and Welch, *Intelligence and the Cuban Missile Crisis*, 183)

options were more numerous and more complex than the two choices listed by McNamara: "As I say, you have the blockade without any declaration of war. You've got a blockade with a declaration of war. We've got strikes one, two and three [progressively escalating air strikes]. We've got invasion. We've got notification to Khrushchev and what that notification ought to consist of." Despite his obvious reluctance to formally declare war, Kennedy was fully aware that such a declaration by Congress remained an option in the event of unforeseen complications. However, ExComm members could not have failed to notice that the President had subtly listed the blockade *without* a declaration of war as the first choice among the available alternatives. RFK, however, tried to assure his brother, "it's not really that bad though," since a decision on whether to invade did not have to be made for at least three or four days.[57]

The meeting finally appeared to be winding down. A consensus quickly emerged to review the latest intelligence and especially the two principal military/diplomatic options "more definitively," RFK suggested, before getting back to the President that night. But questions remained about when to inform the press and the American public and how to prevent information about military preparations from leaking. The real issue, Bundy emphasized, was the "level of readiness" of the missiles. JFK replied that it didn't make "a hell of a difference" how many sites were ready if the Soviets really intended "to fire nuclear missiles at us." "If they were rational, Mr. President," Bundy pronounced.

McNamara concluded that preparations should be made for an air strike "at the *earliest* possible moment"—which would be Saturday morning—regardless of what decision the President ultimately made. But, for military reasons, RFK and Taylor advised waiting perhaps until Tuesday (October 23). "The more time we've got," the general as-

---

[57]In fact, several variations of the blockade option evolved over the next few days. The "hard" blockade, which Thompson argued should include a declaration of war and a demand for the removal of the missiles already in Cuba, would, in effect, be an opening military salvo; air strikes would clearly follow if Khrushchev remained adamant. The "soft" blockade, eventually enunciated by McNamara, aimed to demonstrate American naval superiority in its own "backyard" by halting the flow of missiles into Cuba, but, concurrently, buying time for diplomatic maneuvering about the bases already under construction. In the end, the "hard" blockade (which never included a declaration of war) metamorphosed pragmatically into a "pliable" blockade—with case-by-case decisions on whether to allow ships to pass and a stipulation that work on the missile sites must cease before negotiations on a final settlement could begin.

serted, "the better we can do it." McNamara agreed that a final decision could wait, but insisted, "we ought to be ready" because the Soviet missiles might become operational. "We ought to be ready in case"
by Saturday morning, JFK declared, and the defense secretary concurred.

The ExComm also concluded that JFK should make his second previously scheduled campaign trip; if he failed to go, the press would inevitably realize that something was up. Ball worried about how to
handle the possibility of leaks while the President was out campaigning
and a consensus emerged to simply be evasive—saying that all rumors
and reports about Cuba were being thoroughly investigated. "The
President," Rusk asked somewhat pontifically, "hopes to unify or not,
by going on this trip this weekend to hear about the country?" JFK,
politician to the core, replied dryly, "I don't unify the country, that's
not the purpose of the trip." Laughter rocked the table. The President
added that there was no choice: "the minute I call off [the campaign
trip] this thing's gonna break." "I don't think there's anything... any
problem about *unifying* the country," Dillon reasoned, "This action
will unify it just like that—no problem at all."

The conversation continued less formally for several minutes as
President Kennedy prepared to leave the room. Bundy joked about
press inquiries concerning the reasons for the White House meetings, "I
still believe that our best cover is 'intensive review of the defense
budget.' Now we haven't had to use it yet," he quipped amidst some
laughter. Rusk discussed calling off a scheduled dinner with Gromyko
that evening, but the President asked him to delay a decision. Mc-
Namara again urged the establishment of working groups to consider
implementing the blockade or air strike options and especially to "consider how the Soviets are going to respond. *This* is what we haven't
done." JFK, before leaving, asked to confer with Rusk and Thompson
at 4:30—just before his meeting with Gromyko.

The tape recorder was left running again after the President's departure and some fragmentary conversations, again more animated and
less structured, continued for several minutes about possible Soviet reactions and U.S. mobilization requirements. Edwin Martin speculated
on whether the blockade "has a chance of bringing down Castro" and
RFK asked doubtfully, "Has a blockade ever brought anybody down?"
Rusk argued that a blockade accompanied by limited air strikes
"would be a pretty good sized wallop [and] . . . a minimum in any
event, wouldn't it?" Taylor promptly agreed. Bundy asked if anyone

supported a blockade without a strike and several voices, including Thompson and McNamara, affirmed, "I am." "The great advantage of that, of course," Bundy pointed out, "is you don't kill any Russians." Alexis Johnson finally declared that a unilateral blockade, carried out without or before OAS backing and lacking a declaration of war, "is about the worst [choice] of all," and Bundy pronounced, rather surprisingly since RFK was still in the room, "You *must* declare, I think... I think the President did not fully grasp that."

McNamara emphasized again that the missiles would not be withdrawn from Cuba without a price: "Now the *minimum* price are missiles out of Turkey and Italy, it seems to me"—but considerable dissent continued about whether Castro should remain in power. Bundy argued that Castro had to go in any case, but McNamara cautioned, "He may or he may not. This is something to think about." The defense secretary, almost becoming a stand-in for the President, declared "Now it seems to me that's the... that's the *best* possible situation you could be in as a result of the military course. I can visualize many worse situations." If the alliance was not divided, and the missiles were removed from Cuba, Turkey and Italy, McNamara repeated, "that's the *best* possible solution. There are many *worse* solutions."

Taylor countered that the "collapse of Castro" should remain a top priority and Bundy avowed that Castro would not "sit still for a blockade and that's to our advantage. And... and I'm convinced *myself* that Castro has to go. . . . I just think his *demon* is self-destruction and we have to help him to that." But McNamara continued to hammer the theme of consequences: in that case, "the price is going to be larger. I really... I really think that we've *got* to think these problems through *more* than we have. At the moment I lean to the blockade because I think it *reduces the very serious risk* of large-scale military action from which this country *cannot* benefit"—especially as compared to the risks of a surprise strike. "Russian roulette and broken alliances," Bundy declared. "Russian roulette, exactly so, and broken alliances," McNamara repeated. The defense secretary's startling about-face since the start of the meeting must have been troubling to his more hawkish ExComm colleagues.

RFK, in particular, remained deeply troubled by the blockade because it did not force the Soviets to stop construction of the existing missile sites. "We tell them," RFK remarked skeptically, "they can build as many missiles as they want?" "Oh, no, no," McNamara countered. "What we say is, 'We are going to blockade you. This is a *dan-*

ger to us.' We insist that we talk this out and the danger be removed [from Cuba]." Thompson also pressed McNamara on the issue of the ongoing construction of the missile sites and Taylor brusquely asked the defense chief to explain his objection to air strikes against the missiles and bombers. "My real objection to it is that it kills several hundred Russians," McNamara replied bluntly. The discussion continued for several minutes and gradually ran down without a genuine meeting of the minds on the military and diplomatic choices.

After a bite to eat and a few laps across the White House swimming pool, President Kennedy met with Dean Acheson. The former secretary of state urged the President to destroy the missile sites immediately with surgical air strikes. He contemptuously dismissed the Pearl Harbor analogy as "silly" and told JFK it was "unworthy" of him to be taken in by such mush. The Russians, he insisted, understood only strength and the will to use it.[58] The President also kept his scheduled appointment with Eisaku Sato, Japan's minister for international trade. The discussion of bilateral commercial relations went smoothly and the Japanese official left without suspecting that JFK's attention was focused elsewhere.

At 5:00 P.M. President Kennedy met in the Oval Office with Soviet foreign minister Andrei Gromyko. Reading from a prepared foreign ministry script, Gromyko warned the President that Cuba did not belong to the United States and even tried to embarrass him by bringing up the Bay of Pigs. Kennedy, obviously irritated, replied that he had covered this ground with Khrushchev at Vienna, had acknowledged his mistake and pledged not to attempt another invasion. Gromyko also reiterated Khrushchev's commitment to ending the Western military presence in Berlin, but promised not to confront the administration before the November elections.

Kennedy later admitted that it had been difficult to resist pulling the U-2 photos out of his desk and exposing Gromyko's calculated lies. In contrast to Ambassador Dobrynin, Gromyko certainly did know about the missiles. But, the advantage of several more days of secret discussions far outweighed the momentary satisfaction of watching Gromyko's jaw drop. Kennedy repeated the warnings he had made in September that the U.S. would not tolerate Soviet offensive weapons in

[58]Walter Isaacson and Evan Thomas, *The Wise Men* (New York: Simon and Schuster, 1986), 622.

*Cuba, but was unable to detect any reaction from the poker-faced Gro-
myko. From that day on, JFK frequently referred to Gromyko as "that
lying bastard."*[59]

*After this frustrating meeting, JFK discussed military and diplomatic
alternatives with former defense secretary Robert Lovett and several
ExComm advisers in the Oval Office.*[60] *Lovett later recalled that Kennedy was furious but rather amused by Gromyko's "bare-faced lies."
Lovett endorsed the blockade and recalled, somewhat surprisingly, that
Robert Kennedy, in sharp contrast to his tough stance at the ExComm
meetings, also supported the blockade because it seemed reasonable to
start with "a less violent step." Lovett expressed delight that the attorney general "was apparently of the same opinion that I was." Finally,
the participants speculated about possible Soviet reprisals and Lovett
counseled the President that the risks could not be avoided.*[61]

*Late that evening the President and the ExComm met for further
discussions. Some participants used a relatively unknown tunnel from
the Treasury Department in order to enter the White House as unobtrusively as possible. It was feared that unusual activity in the Cabinet
Room during the evening would be noticed, so, to avoid alerting reporters to the unfolding crisis, the meeting was held in the Oval Room
on the second floor of the Mansion instead of in the Cabinet Room.
The Oval Room, unfortunately, had no taping system.*[62]

*At the outset of the meeting an agreement had seemed to be emerg-
ing in support of limited but direct action, most likely a blockade
rather than air strikes. But, as the discussions continued, the doubts
and uncertainties from the previous meetings resurfaced and this fragile
consensus began to unravel. The President finally directed the Ex-
Comm to go back to the drawing board before their next meeting, particularly to work out the details for implementing a blockade.*

*JFK returned to the Oval Office, apparently alone, at about mid-
night. To preserve details from his discussions with Acheson and
Lovett, as well as the unrecorded ExComm meeting in the Mansion, he*

[59]Brugioni, *Eyeball to Eyeball,* 287.

[60]Lovett, who had served as Truman's Secretary of Defense from 1951 to 1953, im-
pressed JFK during the transition. He was offered his choice of the top post in the State,
Defense or Treasury Departments but declined because of poor health. (Schlesinger, *A
Thousand Days,* 128–29)

[61]Robert Lovett Oral History Interview, 1964, OHC, JFKL.

[62]Minutes kept by Bromley Smith, executive secretary to the National Security Council,
provide the most reliable record of most of the unrecorded discussions.

dictated his still-fresh recollections directly into the microphones hidden in the knee well of his desk. This four-and-a half-minute recording, dubbed "the JFK monologue" when it was first heard at the Kennedy Library in the early 1980s, is surely the most intimate and personal of the missile crisis tapes. The President's dispassionate recall of details and coolly analytical tone in the face of these potentially catastrophic circumstances provides remarkable insight into the qualities of mind and temperament that allowed him to maintain his calm and deliberate posture throughout these stressful 13 days.

Thursday, October 18, near midnight, Oval Office

Identified Participant: John F. Kennedy.[63]

"The consensus was that we should go ahead with the blockade."

President John F. Kennedy

After naming each of the meeting participants, the President recalled, "During the course of the day, opinions had obviously switched from the advantages of a first strike on the missile sites and on Cuban aviation to a blockade."

JFK was clearly intrigued by the disagreement between the former secretaries of state and defense in the Truman administration: Acheson, Kennedy noted, had "favored the first strike" against the missile sites alone to remove the military threat and predicted that only a show of strength would deter an "extreme Soviet reaction." Lovett, on the other hand, believed that a first strike would undermine American alliances and lead to Soviet seizure of Berlin. The NATO allies would certainly blame the U.S., he warned the President, for "having seized... brought about the loss of Berlin with *inadequate* provocation, they having lived with these intermediate-range ballistic missiles for years." Lovett's words must have struck a chord with the President, given his own belief that the NATO members thought the Americans were "slightly demented" on the Cuban question.

Kennedy also noted that Bundy, consistent with the general reservations he had expressed at the recorded ExComm meetings, had argued against *any* military action on grounds very similar to those of Lovett. Instead he had urged the President "merely to take note of the exis-

[63]Tape 31.1, POF, PRC, JFKL.

tence of these missiles and to wait until the crunch comes in Berlin, and not play what he thought might be the Soviet game."

But everyone else, Kennedy seemed relieved to say, agreed that failure to respond would undermine the credibility of the U.S. commitment to defend Berlin, "would divide our allies and our country" and permit Khrushchev to set up a significant missile arsenal in the Western Hemisphere. The "crunch over Berlin," he concluded, would come in two or three months anyway. "The consensus was that we should go ahead with the blockade beginning on Sunday night. . . . against the shipment of additional offensive capacity, that we could tighten the blockade as the situation required."

Kennedy stressed for the record that he had insisted at this late evening meeting on a key point he had already raised at the morning meeting—that a declaration of war represented an unnecessary provocation. "I was most anxious that we not have to announce a state of war existing, because it would obviously be bad to have the word go out that we were having a war rather than it was a limited blockade for a limited purpose."

He concluded with a very practical political concern: "It was determined that I should go ahead with my speeches so that we don't take the cover off this and come back Saturday night."

John F. Kennedy then hit the off switch for the Oval Office tape recorder and presumably tried to get a decent night's sleep.

The urgency of these ongoing discussions and pending decisions had been highlighted even further by the October 18 release of a report by several intelligence committees concluding that the MRBMs in Cuba could be operational in as little as 18 hours. Also, the National Photographic Interpretation Center confirmed that at least two MRBM sites were already capable of launching their missiles and that at least two of the IRBM sites under construction could be operational within a month.

Early the next morning, Friday, October 19, General Taylor briefed the Joint Chiefs on the developing consensus for a blockade. The JCS, exasperated by what they regarded as civilian and presidential indecisiveness—or even spinelessness—again demanded sweeping surprise air strikes on the missile sites and airfields, followed by an invasion.

JFK's suspicions about the gap between military claims and performance had been significantly exacerbated by the Bay of Pigs deba-

cle. The President, with 20/20 hindsight, had concluded that JCS support for military action in Cuba had been incompetent and politically naïve. The Joint Chiefs, on the other hand, resented Kennedy's failure to order air support for the Cuban exiles on the beaches and suspected that he lacked the nerve to stand up to a direct challenge from Khrushchev and Castro.

The underlying tension between the JCS and the commander-in-chief was symbolized by the Single Integrated Operational Plan (SIOP), the master strategy for nuclear war, that included a first-strike option, and was redrafted annually by the JCS for the approval of the President. In September 1961, JFK had attended a briefing on the SIOP by JCS chairman General Lyman Lemnitzer. The President was appalled by the doctrinaire rigidity in the general's presentation and asked why so many sites in the People's Republic of China were targeted since the Chinese had no nuclear weapons. "It's in the plan, Mr. President," the general explained. Kennedy was livid when he left the meeting, telling Dean Rusk, "And we call ourselves the human race."[64]

"It's good to have men like Curt LeMay and Arleigh Burke commanding troops once you decide to go in," the President had once told Hugh Sidey. "But these men aren't the only ones you should listen to when you decide whether to go in or not." In short, he respected the military as soldiers, but not as policy-makers. LeMay, who considered SIOP his "bible" and regarded Cuba as a "sideshow" in the life-and-death struggle with the Soviet Union, once replied to a question about how he would deal with Cuba by scornfully retorting, "Fry it." These strains were bubbling close to the surface as the JCS joined the President and McNamara in the Cabinet Room for a Friday morning meeting that quickly escalated into a near confrontation.[65]

[64]Schoenbaum, *Waging Peace and War*, 330.
[65]Schlesinger, *A Thousand Days*, 912; Brugioni, *Eyeball to Eyeball*, 265.

Friday, October 19, 9:45 A.M., Cabinet Room

Identified Participants: John F. Kennedy, George Anderson, Curtis LeMay, Robert McNamara, David Shoup, Maxwell Taylor, Earle Wheeler.[66]

"This is almost as bad as the appeasement at Munich."
General Curtis LeMay, Air Force Chief of Staff

The tension in the room was palpable as the meeting got underway. General Taylor reported that the JCS was united on three military steps: eliminating the Cuban missile bases with surprise air attacks, continued surveillance to confirm the results of the strikes and a blockade to cut off the delivery of additional missiles. However, he acknowledged that the "political disabilities of this course of action" might require some sacrifice of the element of surprise in order to preserve the unity of America's alliances.

"I think the benefit at this point... this morning, Mr. President," Taylor began, "would be for you to hear the other Chiefs' comments" on the military options. Kennedy pointedly ignored Taylor's request. He began to speak immediately in an obvious effort to control the agenda of the meeting and demonstrate that the commander-in-chief was in charge and not required to submit to a tutorial by the military. Nevertheless, the President was initially hesitant and uneasy, repeatedly tripping over his words: "Let me just say a little a... first about a... what the problem is, a... from... at least from a... my point of view," he began. "I... ah... first, a... wh... er... I think we ought to think of why the Russians did this." He became progressively more confident and lucid, telling the Chiefs that if the U.S. did nothing in response to this "rather dangerous but rather useful play of theirs" the Soviets would end up with a significant military base in the Western Hemisphere from which to pressure the U.S. and damage American prestige in the world. Kennedy's Cold War logic was inescapable: a weak American response could upset, or at least appear to upset, the strategic balance of power.

But, he warned, if the U.S. attacked the missiles or Cuba it would give the Soviets "a clear line to take Berlin," much like their decision to send troops and tanks into Hungary in 1956 in the wake of the Suez

[66] Tape 31.2, POF, PRC, JFKL.

Crisis. The U.S. would then be regarded by the NATO allies, since "they think we've got this fixation about Cuba anyway," as "the Americans who lost Berlin. . . . [because] we didn't have the guts to take... *endure* a situation in Cuba." Lecturing the Chiefs on *realpolitik*, Kennedy reasoned, "After all, Cuba is 5 or 6 thousand miles from them. They don't give a damn about Cuba. But they do care about Berlin and about their own security. . . . I must say," he conceded, trying again to put himself in the other guy's shoes, "I think it's a *very* satisfactory position from their point of view."

If the U.S. did nothing, he added, the Soviets would have these missiles in position to threaten the U.S. should "we ever try to do anything about Cuba." The Cuba-Berlin connection, he stressed, is "what makes our problem so difficult." A quick air strike would remove the immediate military threat from these missiles. But, the "solution" might be worse than the problem since it would greatly increase the risk of the Soviets "taking Berlin by force at some point, which leaves me only one alternative, which is to fire nuclear weapons—which is a *hell* of an alternative, and begin a nuclear exchange." The President had by now become quite fluent and authoritative, and his use of the personal pronoun had sent a clear message to the Chiefs—he would listen to their advice, but the decisions were his, not theirs.

Even the limited blockade, he added, could provoke a new Berlin blockade by the Soviets, allowing them to undermine NATO by claiming "that we started it. . . . So I don't think we've got any satisfactory alternatives." If Cuba were the only issue, he argued again, "our answer would be quite easy," but in the Cold War calculus of power the real problem was Berlin. General LeMay tried to cut in, but the President brusquely cut him off, "On the other hand," he added, plainly emphasizing the fact that the buck stopped on his desk, "we've got to do something. Because if we do nothing we're going to have the problem of Berlin anyway."

The President then read from a recent intelligence report on the weapons already in Cuba, concluding "Communication targeted, integrated... integrated air defense system is now nearing operational status." He then asked openly, "What does that mean now—'integrated?'" "That... that means that we're... were hearing electronic emissions now," Taylor explained patiently, "suggesting that they have sectors for the air defense of Cuba." The general jumped on this opening to make plain that the Chiefs had unanimously agreed that American credibility in the world was ultimately at stake in both Cuba and

Berlin. Kennedy concurred: "That's right. That's right. So that's why we've gotta respond. Now the question is, what kind of response?"

The Air Force Chief of Staff finally jumped aggressively into the discussion, giving no indication that he had listened to or understood the grim contingencies raised by the President. LeMay declared, he admitted, "a little strongly perhaps," that the United States doesn't have "any choice except direct military action." The general warned that a blockade and political negotiations would only give the Soviets an opportunity to hide the missiles in the woods and prevent effective air attacks. LeMay turned Kennedy's Berlin argument on its head: "I don't share your view that if we knock off Cuba they're gonna knock off Berlin. We've got the Berlin problem staring us in the face anyway." On the contrary, the Soviets "are gonna push on Berlin and push *real hard*" only if the U.S. *failed* to take military action in Cuba, since they would then feel "they've got us *on the run.*"

A skeptical JFK interrupted to ask, "What do you think their reprisal would be" if the U.S. attacked Cuba? There would be no reprisal, LeMay asserted without missing a beat, as long as you tell Khrushchev again, "If they make a move [in Berlin], we're gonna fight. Now I don't think this changes the Berlin situation at all, except you've got to make one more *statement* on it."

The self-assured general moved in for the verbal kill: "So, I see no other solution. This uh... uh... blockade and... and political action I see leading into war. I don't see any other solution for it. It will lead right into war. This is almost as bad as the appeasement at Munich." The blockade, he declared after a dramatic pause, would not deter the Soviets from targeting the civilian population with their nuclear missiles or knocking out airfields in the southeastern U.S. with their MiGs or IL-28s. "So I... we just drift into... into a war under conditions that we don't like. I just don't see any other solution," LeMay concluded histrionically, "except direct military interv... intervention, *right now.*"

The JCS must have held their collective breath waiting for a reaction from the President. The general had gone well beyond merely giving advice or even disagreeing with his commander-in-chief. He had taken their generation's ultimate metaphor for shortsightedness and cowardice, the 1938 appeasement of Hitler at Munich, and flung it in the President's face. And, LeMay's words were far more than an abstract or metaphorical attack: everyone at the table knew that JFK's father, Joseph P. Kennedy, had been a supporter of Neville Chamberlain's policy of appeasement when he served as ambassador to England between 1938 and 1940. In fact, defeatism and isolationism had destroyed the elder Kennedy's credibility and political career and had even cast a long shadow over John Kennedy's political aspirations.

President Kennedy, in a remarkable display of *sang froid*, refused to take the bait; he said absolutely nothing. It is regrettable that the thoughts of the participants could not have been recorded as well as their words.[67]

After several seconds of awkward silence the discussion resumed. Admiral George Anderson, Chief of Naval Operations, asserted that the bombing-surveillance-blockade plan outlined by Taylor made sense militarily and politically. He assured the President, with evident professional pride, that the Navy could effectively enforce a complete blockade around Cuba. In that event, he noted, "we are *immediately* having a confrontation with the Soviet Union." But, he also endorsed LeMay's contention that the blockade would give the Soviets time to complete the installation of the missiles, the assembly of the IL-28 bombers and the readiness of the MiGs: "I agree with General LeMay that this *will* escalate and then we will be required to take other military action at greater disadvantage to the United States, to our military forces, and probably would suffer far greater casualties within the United States if these fanatics do indeed intend to... to fire any missiles." Anderson warned that the military could not prevent or even minimize loss of life in the U.S. unless they acted promptly. "I do not see that as long as the Soviet Union is supporting Cuba, that there is any solution to the Cuban problem except a military solution." The admiral warned that the communists had created a "master situation" which left the U.S. without any safe choices, "It's the same thing as Korea all over again, only on a grander scale." He acknowledged the danger to Berlin, but in-

---

[67]The first time I heard this tape, in 1981, I was astonished by LeMay's personal attack and expected President Kennedy to defend himself; instead, he chose to avoid a confrontation. Tension between JFK and LeMay was hardly new. Roswell Gilpatric recalled that whenever the President had to confer with LeMay, "he ended up in sort of a fit. I mean he just would be frantic at the end of a session with LeMay because, you know, LeMay couldn't listen or wouldn't take in, and he would make what Kennedy considered, and we all considered, perfectly, you know, outrageous proposals that bore no relation to the state of affairs in the 1960s. And the president never saw him unless at some ceremonial affair, or where he felt he had to make a record of having listened to LeMay, as he did on the whole question of an air strike against Cuba. And he had to sit there. I saw the President right afterwards. He was just choleric. He was just beside himself." (Roswell Gilpatric Oral History Interview, 1970, OHC, JFKL, 116) On the other hand, Kennedy admired candor, once remarking to Hugh Sidey, "I like having LeMay head the Air Force. Everybody knows how he feels. That's a good thing." (Schlesinger, *A Thousand Days*, 912)

sisted that only a strong U.S. response would deter the Soviets from aggression against that divided city.

JFK tried again to counter this military logic, "They can't let us just take out, after all their statements, take out their missiles, kill a lot of Russians and not do... not do anything." LeMay retorted disdainfully that history proved *his* point—citing the 1958 Lebanon crisis as proof that the Soviets would back off if the U.S. took a strong stand. Taylor expressed doubt that the Russians would actually seize Berlin, but the President warned that they might wait three months until the missiles were ready "and then squeeze us in Berlin." "That is true," Taylor conceded.

General Earle Wheeler, Army Chief of Staff, increased the pressure, going even further than the recommendations in the JCS chairman's opening remarks by insisting that only surprise bombing, a blockade *plus* an invasion could protect the people of the United States against a nuclear strike and "give us increasing assurance that we really *have* got the offe... offensive capability of the Cuban Soviets *cornered*. Now admittedly, we can never be *absolutely* sure until and unless we actually occupy the island." The general warned that Khrushchev might formally declare Cuba a Soviet base and a part of the Warsaw Pact during his November trip to the United Nations, which would mean that "Soviet prestige, world prestige, would be at stake." A Soviet base in Cuba "would immediately have a profound effect" in Latin America and around the world by raising questions about whether the U.S. was capable or willing to respond. In addition, because the Soviets had only limited numbers of ICBMs targeted at the U.S., "this short-range missile force gives them a sort of a quantum jump in their capability to inflict damage on the United States. And so as I say, from the military point of view, I feel that... that the lowest-risk cour... course of action is the full gamut of military action by us. That's it."

Finally, Marine Corps Commandant David Shoup told the President that Khrushchev might have deployed missiles so close to America so that Cuba could inflict damage on the U.S. while the Soviets "keep out of it." The longer the U.S. waited to eliminate this threat on its doorstep, he claimed, the greater the forces that would be required to do it—inevitably diminishing American power elsewhere in the world. "I can't conceive that they [Cuba] would attack us just for the fun of it. They might do it at the direction of Khrushchev. But I cannot see why they would attack us, because they couldn't invade and *take us*." But, despite dismissing Cuba as "that little *pipsqueak* of a place," Shoup argued that these missiles *"can* damage us *increasingly* every day," and the U.S. would inevitably have to use more and more substantial forces to invade Cuba and install a non-Communist government, making America even more vulnerable to communist aggression in Berlin, South Vietnam and Korea. To head off these developments, Shoup urged, "you'll have to invade the place," banging the table for emphasis, "and if that decision is made, we must go in with *plenty* of insurance of a *decisive success* and as quick as possible."

"Let's say, no matter what [missiles] they put in there," JFK countered, "we live *today* under" the Soviet nuclear threat. "If they don't have enough ICBMs *today*, they're gonna have 'em in a year." General LeMay, perhaps further emboldened by the unity of his colleagues, warned the President that the missiles in Cuba could expose the U.S. and Latin America to the threat of nuclear blackmail. As to the "political factor," the Air Force chief asserted, "that's not quite in our field . . . but you invited us to comment on this." Recalling the President's strong statements promising to take action against offensive weapons in Cuba, LeMay pronounced: "I think that a blockade and political talk would be considered by a lot of our friends and neutrals as bein' a pretty weak response to this. And I'm sure a lot of our own citizens would feel that way too."

"In other words, you're in a pretty bad fix at the present time," LeMay declared, almost taunting the President.

Kennedy had not heard, or perhaps thought he had heard incorrectly, "What'd you say?" he asked matter-of-factly.

"I say, you're in a pretty bad fix," LeMay repeated smugly.

"You're in with me," Kennedy replied, with an acerbic laugh, "personally."[68]

The President continued to hold his ground despite arguments by Taylor and Anderson that the threat to the U.S. base at Guantanamo would be increased during a blockade. "I think," the JCS chairman observed, "Guantanamo is going to resem... cease to be a useful naval base and become more of a fortress more or less in a permanent state of siege." JFK emphasized again that if military action was required, a limited air strike against the missiles was far less of an escalation than comprehensive bombing followed by a blockade and a 14–18 day inva-

---

[68]Robert Kennedy misattributed the "you're in a pretty bad fix" remark to General Shoup and inaccurately claimed that "Everyone laughed" after this tense exchange. (Robert Kennedy, *Thirteen Days*, 29)

sion; he insisted, "Well we have to assume that uh... I don't know what the... the Soviet response to each of these would have to be different"—that is, taking out just the missiles as opposed to invading and "fighting our way across the island."

LeMay stressed again that Cuban air power would have to be destroyed along with the missiles, but JFK reiterated that Cuba was not the real issue: "the problem is part of this worldwide struggle where we face the Communists, particularly, as I say, over Berlin." LeMay tried once more to personalize his differences with the President: "If you lose in Cuba, you're gonna get *more and more* pressure right on Berlin. I'm sure of that." Taylor declared that the Soviet base in Cuba was rapidly becoming more threatening than anyone had believed even earlier in the week. But, JFK again refused to be goaded, insisting that the Cuban missiles did not substantially alter the Soviet nuclear threat. He acknowledged that Soviet ICBMs might not be completely reliable, but they still had enough fire power to strike American cities, with or without Cuba, resulting in 80 to 100 million casualties, "you're talkin' about the destruction of a country!"

Taylor interjected that "we can never talk about invading again" with these missiles "pointed at our head." "Well, the argument... the logical argument," the President persisted, "is that we don't really have to invade Cuba. That's not really... that's just one of the difficulties that we live with in life, like you live with the Soviet Union and China.[69] And that's... the problem, however, is after uh... for us not to do *anything* and then wait 'til he brings up Berlin. And then we can't *do* anything about Cuba." The President grimly acknowledged that "the existence of these missiles does not... *adds* to the danger, but doesn't create it. There's a danger right there now." The Soviets already had enough missiles, planes and submarines, he reminded the JCS, "I mean, hell, they can kill, especially if they concentrate on the cities, and they've pretty well got us there anyway."

After several JCS officers reopened the question of the security of Guantanamo, the President asked when air strikes on the missiles and

[69]General LeMay had also attended a September 4 White House meeting to draft a presidential press statement about potential Soviet offensive missiles in Cuba. JFK had warned against a fixation on Cuba, "The fact of the matter is the major danger is the Soviet Union with missiles and nuclear warheads, not Cuba." An hour later, in a meeting with the leaders of Congress, he had reiterated that unless the Soviets place offensive nuclear weapons in Cuba, a major caveat, "we have to keep some [sense of] proportion." (Tape 19, POF, PRC, JFKL)

planes could be ready. LeMay replied that the optimum date was Tuesday, October 23, but the strikes could be ready by Sunday the 21st.[70] President Kennedy also expressed concern about news leaks on the preparations for the air strikes but Taylor insisted that "the danger is minimal." "How effective is an air strike of this kind, General, against a missile base?" JFK asked. LeMay replied intrepidly, "Well, I think we can guarantee hitting them."

As the President prepared to leave, General Wheeler observed, "There is no *acceptable* military solution to the Berlin problem, whereas there is in... in Cuba." A resolution in Berlin, he conceded, lies instead "in the diplomatic-economic-political field, if we put enough pressure on the Soviet bloc." He specifically predicted that the people of Berlin "can survive for a long time" if the Soviets responded to U.S. action in Cuba by signing a treaty with East Germany and cutting off Allied access to Berlin—assuming Russian troops didn't overrun the city.

"I appreciate your views," the President finally told the JCS, "as I said, I'm sure we all understand how rather unsatisfactory our alternatives are." But, he repeated that the potential advantage of the blockade "is to avoid, if we can, nuclear war by escalation or imbalance. . . . We've got to have some degree of control." General Shoup reminded the commander-in-chief that the Cuban missile bases were physically very close to the U.S., but JFK countered, "I don't think that it adds particularly to our danger. I think our danger is the use of nuclear weapons . . . particularly on urban sites." He reiterated that the Soviets already had enough nuclear missiles, along with planes and submarines, to attack American cities—or they surely would have enough within a year. "I don't think that's *probably* the major argument. The major argument is the political effect on the United States." McNamara, Taylor and the President also agreed to defer initiating low-level reconnaissance missions until a final decision had been made on the military course of action. "Thank you very much, Mr. President," Taylor concluded, and JFK soon left the meeting.

McNamara, who had been uncharacteristically quiet during most of this sporadic war of words, reiterated that only two courses of action were under active consideration, the air strikes and the blockade, and urged the Chiefs to recommend specific details and procedures for each

[70]For most of the remainder of the meeting, the sound quality of the tape is distorted by an intense and inexplicable background noise.

option. He also asked for details on "surveillance requirements for the blockade" and plans for the defense of Guantanamo. General Wheeler expressed confidence that with the help of the Joint Reconnaissance Group and the Defense Intelligence Agency "we can pull it together very quickly."

McNamara and Taylor departed, leaving LeMay, Shoup and Wheeler behind to talk as the door closed. Away, they believed, from prying ears, the remaining Chiefs voiced their disdain for civilian control of the military and left little doubt who they thought should be in charge of military decision-making. The hidden tape-recorder, of course, continued to turn.

Shoup lauded LeMay for challenging the President: "You were a... you pulled the rug right out from under him."

"Jesus Christ!" LeMay responded disingenuously, "What the hell do you mean?"

Shoup, repeating twice that he supported his Air Force colleague, "a hundred percent," mocked President Kennedy: "he's finally getting around to the word 'escalation.' . . . When *he* says 'escalation,' that's it. If somebody could keep 'em from doing the *goddamn thing* piece-meal, *that's* our problem You go in there and friggin' around with the missiles. You're screwed. You go in and friggin around with little else. You're screwed."

"That's right," LeMay exclaimed.

"You're screwed, screwed, screwed," Shoup protested, "He could say, 'either do the son of a bitch and do it right, and quit friggin around.'"

"That was my contention," LeMay huffed.

"Don't frig around and go take a missile out. . . . Goddamn it, if he wants you to do it, you can't fiddle around with takin' out missiles. You can't fiddle around with hittin' a missile site and then hittin' the SAM sites. You got to go in and take out the goddam thing that's gonna *stop you* from doin' your job."

"It's very apparent to me though," Wheeler contended, "from his earlier remarks that a... the political action of the blockade is *really* what he's. . . ."

"His speech about Berlin," Shoup interjected, "was the real . . ."

"He gave his speech about Berlin and he equates the two," Wheeler declared.

"That's right," Shoup and LeMay affirmed.

"If we sneer at Castro," Wheeler observed sarcastically, "Khrushchev sneers at [West Berlin Mayor] Willy Brandt."

The discussion soon trailed off and the tape ran out just as the last JCS participants left the Cabinet Room.

Friday, October 19, afternoon and evening
After the meeting, the President told his aide Dave Powers that he was stunned by LeMay's cocky certainty that Khrushchev would do nothing if the U.S. bombed the missile sites and killed a lot of Russians. "These brass hats have one great advantage in their favor," JFK fumed. "If we listen to them and do what they want us to do, none of us will be alive later to tell them that they were wrong."[71]

The President, still concerned about potential Democratic losses in the midterm congressional elections and determined to avoid tipping off the press about the crisis in Cuba, left Washington later that morning for a planned campaign trip to Ohio and Illinois. He was greeted by senior state officials and the obligatory high school bands and excited crowds. JFK normally enjoyed campaigning, but the trip seemed tedious until he received a spirited welcome at the Cook County Democratic Party dinner. However, on his visit to Lincoln's Tomb in Springfield, he seemed lost in thought.

Before departing, JFK told Bobby Kennedy and Ted Sorensen "this thing is falling apart" and urged them to forge a consensus for the blockade during his absence. But, if an agreement could not be reached, Kennedy insisted, "I'll make my own decision anyway."[72] *In the wake of his war of words with the JCS, Kennedy was far from convinced that a consensus could be achieved at all. The President knew, of course, that it would be far better to bring along a united ExComm rather than impose a decision on a divided ExComm. There would be carping enough regardless of his decision: Right-wing Republicans and southern Democrats would shriek that the President was not doing enough; Left-wing Europeans, Americans and Third World activists would denounce him for doing too much.*

Early that morning, as JFK was getting dressed to leave on his campaign tour, Bundy told him that after a sleepless night he had con-

[71]Kenneth O'Donnell and David Powers, *Johnny We Hardly Knew Ye* (Boston: Little, Brown, 1970), 318. Scholars have justifiably dismissed this book as Kennedy hagiography. However, this remark is strikingly similar to one JFK later made at the start of the 3:00 P.M. meeting on October 22. In addition, I worked with Dave Powers at the Kennedy Library for seventeen years and his personal recollection of the details of this incident seemed consistent with the evidence and entirely convincing.

[72]White, *Missiles in Cuba*, 95.

cluded that the quarantine was "dangerous and uncertain" because it did not deal with the missile sites already under construction in Cuba and could lead to a Soviet quarantine of Berlin. "'Well, I'm having some of those same worries,'" Kennedy admitted. "'Have another look at that [the air strike option] and keep it alive.'" The President evidently had not totally rejected possible air attacks against the Soviet installations. But, Bundy also recalled, "advocates of the air strike wanted to strike everything that could fly in Cuba, and that wasn't exactly what the President had in mind."[73]

Meetings at the State Department that afternoon and evening exposed the persistent divisions in the ExComm. Bundy put aside his earlier doubts about the military and diplomatic consequences of attacking the missile sites, which had been specifically cited in the President's midnight monologue, and dramatically reversed course. He told his colleagues that he had already spoken to JFK, and reiterated that after hours of sleepless uncertainty he now supported a surprise air strike since the blockade would not prevent completion of the missile bases already in Cuba—some of which could soon be operational. Acheson and Taylor, undoubtedly buoyed by Bundy's about-face, again called for immediate military action to destroy the missiles. McCone and Douglas Dillon agreed and even the cautious Ball seemed uncertain.[74]

McNamara, consistent with the position he had taken at the close of the morning meeting on October 18, endorsed contingency planning for air strikes but continued to support the blockade as a measured first step. He also admitted candidly, "we would at least have to give up our missile bases in Italy and Turkey and would probably have to pay more besides." RFK, substantively and symbolically standing in for his brother despite his own more aggressive posture at the earlier meetings, pointedly mentioned that he had spoken to the President only a few hours earlier and argued for the blockade because a sneak attack on a small country was not in the American tradition.[75] Just seventy-two hours before he had asserted that the U.S. should stand up to Khru-

[73]Bundy's private 1964 memo was first published in Kai Bird, *The Color of Truth: McGeorge Bundy and William Bundy: Brothers in Arms* (New York: Simon and Schuster, 1998), 234; see also Allison and Zelikow, *Essence of Decision*, 371.

[74]Leonard Meeker Minutes of the October 19, 1962 Meeting at the State Department, in Chang and Kornbluh, *Cuban Missile Crisis*, 133–37.

[75]Roswell Gilpatric later recalled that even if JFK was not present, RFK always attended "and in a passive but clearly recognized sense [was accepted by the ExComm as] the President's alternate." (Gilpatric Oral History, 50)

shchev and have the guts to go to war if necessary and "get it over with and take our losses"—a position that must have seemed appropriate for the administration's toughest enforcer of Operation Mongoose. However, he now reiterated his support for the President's position, which he had openly embraced the previous morning. A surprise attack would kill thousands of Cubans and Russians and was simply unacceptable given the historical memory of Pearl Harbor. A blockade, on the other hand, would demonstrate both American strength and restraint and give the Soviets a chance to reconsider their rash miscalculation in Cuba.[76]

RFK, nonetheless, quickly revealed that his own hard-hitting perspective lurked just beneath the surface, "it would be better for our children and grandchildren," he warned his colleagues, "if we decided to face the Soviet threat, stand up to it, and eliminate it, now. The circumstances for doing so at some future time were bound to be more unfavorable, the risks would be greater, the chances of success less good." The fragile morning consensus for a blockade was indeed coming apart. The ExComm seemed to be slipping toward deadlock. Rusk, grasping for a means to end the impasse, recommended that the advocates of bombing and blockade should each prepare a detailed paper defending their respective choices.[77]

Early the next morning, RFK, concerned about the divisive tone of the last ExComm meeting, phoned the President in Chicago and urged him to return to the White House at once. The President's physician was encouraged to diagnose that JFK had an upper respiratory infection and a slight fever. Press secretary Pierre Salinger announced that the President was ill and would cancel his remaining political appearances. JFK was photographed leaving Chicago wearing a hat and sporting a scarf around his throat; he immediately flew back to Washington. On the return flight, Salinger, who was still in the dark about Cuba, asked the President what was really going on. "The minute you get back in Washington," JFK promised, "you're going to find out what it is. And when you do, grab your balls."[78]

Saturday, October 20, 2:30 P.M.

Within an hour of his arrival, and after taking a brief swim in the White House pool, the President met again with the ExComm.

---

[76]Minutes October 19, 1962 Meeting at State Department, 133–37.
[77]Ibid.
[78]Pierre Salinger, *With Kennedy* (Garden City, New York: Doubleday, 1966), 252; Pierre Salinger, *John F. Kennedy: Commander in Chief* (New York: Penguin, 1997), 116.

"Gentlemen, today we're going to earn our pay," he remarked briskly as he entered the room. With grim humor reflecting the realization that any course of action might lead to disaster, he added pointedly, "You should all hope that your plan isn't the one that will be accepted."[79]

The meeting, unfortunately for the historical record, was again held in the Oval Room of the Mansion and was not taped; but, once again notes taken by Bromley Smith have preserved a reliable distillation of the discussion. The arguments were complex, sometimes contradictory and often overlapping, but it was clear at the outset that the ExComm was not united behind any policy choice; many participants were wavering back and forth among several options.

After an intelligence briefing by Lundahl and Ray Cline of the CIA, the President observed that "there is something to destroy in Cuba now, and, if it is destroyed, a strategic missile capability would be difficult to restore."[80] *These words must have given initial encouragement to the ExComm air strike proponents. Perhaps, especially given Bundy's dramatic about-face the previous day, JFK was backing away from the blockade.*

McNamara, with classic understatement, told the President that "there were differences among his advisers which had resulted in the drafting of alternative courses of action."[81] *He openly endorsed the "blockade route" as a first step toward the removal of the missiles and negotiations for "the withdrawal of United States strategic missiles from Turkey and Italy" and even suggested a possible "agreement to limit our use of Guantanamo to a specified limited time." The defense chief acknowledged that the blockade would probably create "political trouble" at home and might weaken the world position of the United States, but he acknowledged that a surprise strike was "contrary to our tradition" and a blockade was less likely to provoke a Soviet response "leading to general war."*[82]

JFK observed that additional missiles could become operational during a blockade and again asked General Taylor how many could be

---

[79]Brugioni, *Eyeball to Eyeball*, 314; Reeves, *President Kennedy*, 388; These claims seem credible since JFK later made a very similar remark at the October 22 meeting with the congressional leadership and Rusk specifically recalled and cited those words at the brief October 28 meeting.

[80]Minutes of the 505th Meeting of the National Security Council, October 20, 1962, NSF, JFKL, 1.

[81]*Ibid.*, 1–2.

[82]*Ibid.*, 3.

destroyed by air action. Taylor's hard-line response broke new ground by suggesting the possible use of nuclear weapons in attacking Cuba. Declining to explain his logic, the general boldly asserted that he did not share "McNamara's fear that if we used nuclear weapons in Cuba, nuclear weapons would be used against us." Attacking the missiles now, he insisted, was less dangerous than allowing them to remain there and this could be the last chance to take them out before they were camouflaged.[83]

Robert Kennedy, despite his belated support for a blockade, abruptly reversed himself again and returned to his tough stance of October 16, agreeing that "now is the last chance we will have to destroy Castro and the Soviet missiles deployed in Cuba."[84] *Bundy then handed the President a plan for air strikes also endorsed by Taylor and the JCS.*

The President reopened the question of giving advance warning before the air strikes. When Taylor, rather surprisingly, replied that the military would be "prepared to live with a twenty-four-hour advance notice" if it were politically helpful, JFK dismissed any notice of more than seven hours as of no political value; he added, however, that he was prepared to live with the Soviet bombers in Cuba since, unlike the missiles, they did not affect perceptions of the balance of power.[85]

RFK shifted ground yet again, arguing that a combination of a blockade and air strikes "was very attractive to him." If the Russians failed to halt missile construction once the blockade was in effect, air attacks could begin without the stigma of a Pearl Harbor-type attack.[86]

Suddenly, almost as if a dam had broken, most remaining participants took sides in rapid-fire statements: Rusk endorsed the blockade; McCone and Douglas Dillon agreed but insisted that air strikes should begin after 72 hours if the sites were not dismantled; Deputy Secretary of Defense Roswell Gilpatric also preferred limited force as a first step; McNamara warned that the 800 sortie air strikes proposed by the JCS would kill thousands of Russians and Cubans: "In such an event, the United States would lose control of the situation which could escalate to general war."[87] *Only General Taylor dissented: since the blockade*

[83] *Ibid.*, 3–4.
[84] *Ibid.*, 4.
[85] *Ibid.*, 6.
[86] *Ibid.*; RFK's claim that the ExComm "spent more time on this moral question during the first five days than on any other single matter" is flatly contradicted by the tapes. (Robert Kennedy, *Thirteen Days*, 30)
[87] *Ibid.*, 7–8.

would not eliminate the missiles, he argued, military force was inevitable and would be more costly if delayed.

At that point, JFK essentially ended the impasse by clearly articulating his position: "The President," Bromley Smith recorded, "agreed that a United States air strike would lead to a major Soviet response, such as blockading Berlin." Kennedy also raised once more the prospect of a missile trade, despite the standing objections of many skeptical advisers: "He agreed that at an appropriate time we would have to acknowledge that we were willing to take strategic missiles out of Turkey and Italy if this issue were raised by the Russians." The President asserted again that there were no safe choices: a blockade might also provoke a Russian move against Berlin. However, the blockade would at least buy time to monitor Soviet missile construction in Cuba and decide on any subsequent steps. If air strikes should become necessary, he concluded, he would favor attacking only the missiles and "repeated his view that we would have to live with the threat arising out of the stationing in Cuba of Soviet bombers."[88]

Rusk emphatically agreed, declaring that a surprise air strike "had no support in the law or morality, and, therefore, must be ruled out."[89] However, United Nations ambassador Adlai Stevenson, although endorsing the President's emerging position on the blockade, the air strikes and the withdrawal of U.S. missiles from Turkey, also urged the evacuation of the Guantanamo naval base. President Kennedy sharply rejected Stevenson's recommendation because it "would convey to the world that we had been frightened into abandoning our position."[90] As matters played out, Stevenson's advocacy of such a "soft" response had ironically made the President's willingness to consider a trade of the Turkish and Italian missiles—without yielding anything on Guantanamo—seem tougher and more palatable to the ExComm hawks. Stevenson's remarks also completely overshadowed McNamara's earlier hint about accepting a time limit on the American use of Guantanamo.

Kennedy then authorized setting up the blockade as soon as possible and "suggested that we inform the Turks and the Italians that they should not fire the strategic missiles they have even if attacked." He also urged alerting the JCS to clarify their orders and procedures so that

[88]*Ibid.*, 8.
[89]*Ibid.*
[90]*Ibid.*, 9.

American military personnel in Turkey would not launch the Jupiter missiles against the U.S.S.R. without a direct presidential order and also proposed that the warheads in Turkey and Italy be dismantled to make an unauthorized launch impossible. But he nonetheless agreed that preparations for a possible invasion of Cuba could move forward.[91]

The President "acknowledged that the domestic political heat following his television appearance [to inform the public of the crisis] would be terrific." Kennedy also urged reassurances to the Turks and Italians that Polaris-equipped submarines would guarantee their safety after the U.S. missiles were withdrawn. Finally, JFK asked Assistant Secretary of Defense Paul Nitze "to study the problems arising out of the withdrawal of missiles from Italy and Turkey, with particular reference to complications which would arise in NATO."

The tension between hawks and doves in this nearly three-hour discussion virtually jumps off the page despite the neutral and antiseptic language in Bromley Smith's notes. Sadly, we can only imagine what it would have been like to listen to this decisive meeting on audio tape. However, the turning point in the meeting was evident: the President, with key support from McNamara, had successfully resisted pressure for air strikes and an invasion and his cautious but practical responses had moved the decision-making process significantly forward.

Just after the meeting, eager for some fresh air and relief from the tension, JFK stood on the second-floor White House balcony chatting with RFK and Sorensen. "We are very, very close to war," he conceded bleakly; then summoning up his sardonic wit, he grinned and added, "I hope you realize there's not enough room for everybody in the White House bomb shelter," and they joked about who would make it onto the final list.[92] *Later, even though he had not made a final decision, JFK told Sorensen to prepare a quarantine speech. General Taylor, recognizing the turn of events at the meeting, returned to the Pentagon and told the JCS, "This was not one of our better days."*[93]

Nonetheless, JFK knew that it was far from clear whether any strategy could win this war of words without unleashing a war of missiles. The President's foreboding was confirmed that day by a new intelligence report on the Soviet military buildup in Cuba: sixteen MRBM launchers were now operational and capable of firing missiles in less

[91]*Ibid.*, 10.
[92]Sorensen Oral History, 64; Sorensen, *Kennedy*, 2–3.
[93]May and Zelikow, *The Kennedy Tapes*, 203.

than eight hours. The President also received an update on civil defense preparations and learned to his chagrin that emergency supplies of food, water and medicine had not been shipped to shelters across the nation; he ordered the distribution to begin immediately.

In addition, for the first time, a nuclear warhead storage bunker had been located and photographed in Cuba.[94]

Sunday, October 21, early A.M. through noon

On Sunday morning, after attending ten o'clock Mass with Mrs. Kennedy at St. Stephen's Church on Pennsylvania Avenue, the President met with Rusk and McNamara to finalize details on the quarantine decision. At around noon, Kennedy and several members of the ExComm were briefed in the Oval Room of the Mansion by General Walter C. Sweeney, head of the Tactical Air Command, on preparations for possible air strikes in Cuba. Again, in an effort to throw increasingly suspicious reporters off the trail, the Cabinet Room was not used and the meeting was not taped. Sweeney outlined specific plans to attack the missiles, aircraft and airfields over a period of days, building inexorably to an invasion. Although he assured the President that the raids would be effective, he admitted that the best possible outcome would be to destroy 90% of the sixteen known *MRBM launchers. And, he conceded, there were almost certainly many additional missiles yet to be discovered.*

JFK had raised this ominous possibility with General Taylor at the first ExComm meeting on October 16. Now, five days into the crisis, with construction continuing on the missile sites, this issue seemed more critical than ever: Soviet nuclear retaliation could easily be launched against the United States from Cuba even after the missiles had been bombed. The risk was unacceptable. The President's decision to start with the less provocative blockade (quarantine) was now firm and Sorensen worked energetically to draft a speech for October 22.

Meanwhile Cuban and Russian officials had learned of recent U-2 flights over San Cristobal. They likely suspected, even before Kennedy's speech, that the missiles had been discovered.

[94]The photograph of the storage bunker did not *prove* that nuclear warheads were in Cuba. "US intelligence was not able to identify the presence of nuclear warheads in Cuba at any time during the crisis. Although the question was raised in the ExComm on several occasions, no information was acquired that could positively answer it." Nonetheless, the ExComm assumed, correctly as it turned out, that nuclear warheads had been shipped to Cuba. (Garthoff, "US Intelligence in the Cuban Missile Crisis," 27)

Sunday, October 21, 2:30 P.M.

Since the President was not planning to address the nation until Monday evening, the ExComm met again in the Oval Room of the Mansion in a final effort to keep a lid on the crisis. Once the secret was out, all subsequent meetings would be held in the Cabinet Room or the Oval Office—and taped.

The ExComm deliberations had entered a new phase. The quarantine had been chosen and the meeting began with discussion of the upcoming presidential speech announcing the decision. Given the administration's strong reaction to Soviet missiles in Cuba, JFK expressed concern about how to justify the presence of U.S. missiles in Turkey and Italy. Rusk explained that these weapons had been deployed after the NATO allies had been threatened by Soviet missiles. Since the U.S. had not targeted Cuba with nuclear weapons, he argued, the two cases were not comparable. The President added another important distinction: the U.S. missiles had been deployed openly. He underscored "the clandestine manner in which the USSR had acted in Cuba." Rusk suggested that it would be politically beneficial to call the American naval action a quarantine rather than a blockade, even though "the legal meaning of the two words is identical . . . [because] it avoids comparison with the Berlin blockade."[95]

President Kennedy's decision, defined as a "quarantine of offensive missile equipment," would hopefully allow time to see if "the Soviets turn back their ships rather than submit to inspection."[96] General Taylor, making a last-ditch effort to keep open the military options he favored, urged the retention of the phrase "whatever steps are necessary." The President saw the logic in this point and agreed to retain this wording so that "he would not be hindered from taking additional measures [bombing and/or invasion] if we so decide at a later date."[97] JFK also argued, in a display of diplomatic realpolitik, that it was better for the U.S. "to frighten the United Nations representatives with the prospect of all kinds of actions and then, when a resolution calling for the withdrawal of missiles from Cuba, Turkey and Italy was proposed, we could consider supporting such a resolution."[98]

Despite the limited action he had endorsed, Kennedy was nevertheless

[95]Minutes of the 506th Meeting of the National Security Council, October 21, 1962, NSF, JFKL, 4.
[96]*Ibid.*
[97]*Ibid.*, 5.
[98]*Ibid.*

pessimistic about the Soviet response. He predicted that once he had given the speech, Khrushchev would speed up construction of the missile sites, announce that if the United States attacked Cuba, "Soviet rockets will fly," and perhaps even move to push us the U.S. out of Berlin.[99]

Admiral Anderson, Chief of Naval Operations, only heightened the President's long-standing doubts about military overconfidence by explaining that the Navy would fire a shot across the bow or disable the rudder of any ship which refused to stop for inspection. When the President expressed concern that a ship might be unintentionally sunk, the admiral assured him that it was not difficult to disable a ship without sinking it. But Kennedy, a veteran of naval combat, knew all too well the uncertainties of war at sea. At the same time, Anderson asked for authorization to shoot down any MiG taking hostile action or to attack any Soviet submarine en route to Havana.[100]

President Kennedy, somewhat surprisingly, expressed the belief that Khrushchev "knows that we know of his missile deployment" and would be ready with a planned response—which turned out to be incorrect. In that context, he again asked Nitze to study the problem of pulling U.S. missiles out of Turkey and Italy—just in case the situation later required a negotiated settlement involving the Jupiters. However, when the President insisted that the U.S. would accept nothing less than a permanent end to Soviet missile capability in Cuba, McNamara replied that only an invasion could insure that result.[101]

In a last-minute effort to prevent any possible failure of communication with the Soviets, the President also recommended that the word "miscalculate" be removed from his proposed draft letter to Khrushchev; he explained that "in Vienna Khrushchev had revealed a misunderstanding of this word when translated into Russian" and did not seem to grasp the possibility that miscalculation by either side could inadvertently unleash a nuclear war.[102]

As the meeting ended, the President approached the chief of naval operations, "Well, Admiral, it looks as though this is up to the Navy." Given his deep-seated distrust of military promises, it must have been an

---

[99]*Ibid.*, 8.

[100]*Ibid.*, 8–9.

[101]*Ibid.*, 9–10.

[102]*Ibid.*, 11. Khrushchev resented these warnings about war by miscalculation. He felt that the Americans were treating him like an irresponsible schoolboy and grumbled that no one had talked about war by mistake when the U.S. had enjoyed a nuclear monopoly. (Zubok and Pleshakov, *Inside the Kremlin's Cold War*, 245–46)

awkward statement for Kennedy to make. "Mr. President," Anderson assured his commander-in-chief, "the Navy will not let you down."[103]

A comprehensive effort was launched over the next few days to inform foreign leaders, embassies and consulates around the world of the imminent blockade. The President also sent personal representatives, carrying classified U-2 photos of the missile sites, to brief the heads of government of the key NATO allies—Britain, France and West Germany. His emissaries included former Secretary of State Dean Acheson, who briefed Charles de Gaulle, and who certainly could be relied upon not to minimize the threat posed by the missiles.

On the morning of October 22, with the President's speech to the nation only hours away, the Cubans and the Soviets received a clear signal that something was up when the evacuation of U.S. dependents began at the Guantanamo naval base. By 4 P.M., some 2,500 military family members, who had been given 15 minutes to pack one bag each, were on their way to Norfolk, Virginia aboard four Navy transport ships.

In a rather transparent and clumsy piece of psychological pressure leaked to the press from within the administration, the Soviet Union also learned that American forces were carrying out mock amphibious landings on the island of Vieques, near Puerto Rico. Their goal was to practice liberating the island from an imaginary dictator named "Ortsac" (Castro spelled backwards).[104]

Monday, October 22, 11:00 A.M., Oval Office

Identified Participants: John F. Kennedy, George Ball, McGeorge Bundy, Michael Forrestal, Roger Hilsman, U. Alexis Johnson, Robert Kennedy, Dean Rusk, Arthur Schlesinger, Jr.[105]

"I think maybe this is just a political problem. But I think we oughta be looking to the day when they're removed from Cuba, Italy and Turkey."

President John F. Kennedy

As preparations continued for the upcoming U.N. debate and for the President's speech to the nation that evening, several members of the ExComm, joined by a few additional officials, gathered in the Oval Of-

---

[103]See George W. Anderson, Jr., "The Cuban Missile Crisis," *Naval History* 6 (Winter 1992).

[104]Jack Raymond, "Navy and Marine Force Heads for Exercise Off Puerto Rico," *New York Times*, October 22, 1962.

[105]Tape 32.1, POF, PRC, JFKL. The President also updated General Eisenhower by phone minutes before this meeting (Dictabelt 30.2, Cassette J, POF, PRC, JFKL).

fice. The quality of this tape is *very poor*; much of the conversation is virtually inaudible and can be heard only in fragments. In any event, this gathering was less a formal meeting than an unstructured brainstorming session about finalizing the U.S. posture at the U.N. and the text of the President's speech. The following narrative, as a result, attempts only to capture some of the more audible high points as well as the general flavor of the discussion.

As the tape began, the President and Dean Rusk had been discussing a possible United Nations role in supervising the removal of nuclear missiles "from all countries other than those possessing [indigenous] nuclear weapons"—which in effect meant Cuba, Turkey and Italy. "This would be," Kennedy observed, "take them out of any country that is not a nuclear power." Rusk clarified that the proposal called for U.N. supervision, that is, halting construction and making certain that the missiles were not operational. Nevertheless, the President suggested that the U.S. should regard any such arrangement as "preparation for their removal, I would think," adding, "Why don't we go all the way?" He also observed shrewdly, "That gives us an excuse to get 'em out of Turkey and Italy? . . . We tried to get 'em out of there anyway," he recalled. "We're much better off" if they're removed.[106]

The President, however, opposed any third-party proposal to lift the quarantine until the missiles were physically removed from Cuban soil. "This isn't *our* proposal. . . . But I think we oughta always keep on this pressure about the removal," he argued, "because I don't think we're a hell of a lot better off if they're just sitting there, to be honest with you. We're not gonna be better off." The sound of writing can be heard in the background as JFK repeated his belief that the Soviets were probably not going to fire the missiles anyway; but he acknowledged that U.N. control would at least be a psychological improvement. "I think maybe this is just a political problem. But I think we oughta be looking to the day when they're removed from Cuba, Italy and Turkey." Bundy suggested that a "neutral-nation proposal for immediate inspection in-

[106]JFK had considered several recommendations early in 1961 for substituting Polaris missiles for the Jupiters in Turkey. But, the Turks "objected vigorously" and the Vienna summit and the resulting tensions over Berlin essentially settled the issue. "Kennedy at least theoretically had an opportunity to cancel the deployment, since construction had not yet begun when he entered office. He seriously considered doing so and yet deliberately decided to go ahead." The Jupiters were deployed to preserve American credibility despite widespread feelings in both the Eisenhower and Kennedy administrations that they were completely unreliable. (Nash, *The Other Missiles*, 95–102)

stead of sanitization [surgical air strikes]" might be acceptable. "Don't forget," he counseled, possibly backing away from his October 19 advocacy of surprise air attacks, "you can't have everything in one bite."

Rusk, Arthur Schlesinger, Jr., Bundy, JFK, RFK and several others then talked softly among themselves for more than fifteen minutes about points to be included in the draft statement for the U.N. debate, such as the mechanics for potential U.N. inspection of ships entering Cuban ports, a commitment to freedom and democracy in Cuba, the removal of "all missiles and offensive weapons" from Cuba and possible recognition of a Cuban government-in-exile. Schlesinger expressed concern that the label "offensive" could be interpreted to encompass American weapons at Guantanamo, but JFK, Rusk and Alexis Johnson argued that the U.S. had no offensive weapons at the naval base. The President can be plainly heard making handwritten entries and revisions and even crossing out or erasing some changes on his own copy. Finally, satisfied with the draft, JFK affirmed, "That's it! First class."[107]

The President raised the possibility of including warships from OAS nations on the quarantine patrol line. Alexis Johnson contended that the Navy was very cool to the idea and Rusk pointed out somewhat caustically, "Our armed forces think only *Americans* can fight!" The discussion then moved on to how to manage the public relations offensive surrounding the President's televised speech. Roger Hilsman, Assistant Secretary of State for Intelligence and Research, outlined plans to brief the OAS and NATO ambassadors an hour before the President spoke and proposed showing slides of the actual missile bases without revealing their number or showing a map identifying their locations. JFK, however, seemed uneasy about actually releasing the pictures for the ambassadors to take with them. Ball insisted that a decision also had to be made on whether to use the pictures at the U.N. debate and Hilsman claimed that the photos would "help me *enormously*" in briefing the ambassadors—although he acknowledged that they might also have to be made available to the press.

President Kennedy preferred confining reporters to "background briefings" and advised against press overexposure: "I don't think we have to have a formal press conference by the secretary [Rusk] tomor-

---

[107]The reference to "all missiles and offensive weapons" in Cuba would ultimately have a direct impact on the IL-28 bomber issue later in November. Schlesinger soon left to join Stevenson at the U.N.

row," he advised. "You'll get into a lot of things we don't want to discuss. So I think it's gotta be on background."[108] Kennedy, alert to the political potential of his own appearance on nationwide television, stressed, "Of course, their first story, I'd say, will be *my* speech." The President, always aware of the need to court the press, discussed how to inform key journalists like Walter Lippmann and James "Scotty" Reston and concluded, "The preliminary judgment is therefore, you show these pictures, perhaps on a background basis, to the uh... but we don't release them because of security." Ball cautioned, "I'd rather not have anything handed out, cause somebody will swipe one, just as sure as hell." Some sporadic laughter followed. "You just show it to them," JFK concluded, "let them look at it."

RFK raised the potentially embarrassing prospect that the press might ask about why the missiles had not been detected earlier. Hilsman, rather defensively, argued that "the first really suspicious refugee reports" had started coming in only about a week ago. Ball urged caution since Senator Kenneth Keating "claims he had 'em before *that*." RFK needled Hilsman as well, "Why didn't we detect them a month ago? What is your answer?" "My answer to this," Hilsman exclaimed, "is that Mr. Keating is *wrong*." He claimed that the New York senator's refugee informants had misidentified SAM sites as ballistic missiles. The President urged Hilsman to stress that point to the press and mused about the irony that "Keating just had it right, but he had it for the wrong reasons, which frequently happens."[109]

Hilsman obviously remained enthusiastic about the public relations potential of the photos, "Mr. President, there are some *lovely* photographs, one taken on Sunday, one on Monday [October 14–15], and the *enormous* change between Sunday and Monday, in twenty-four hours!" Robert Kennedy recommended showing photos of the same places "taken during this last week." "Yeah," JFK promptly agreed, "to show the kinds of changes." "But I do think," he reiterated to

---

[108]Information from a background briefing was not to be directly attributed to anyone in the administration.

[109]Keating's secret sources, as it turned out, were often correct. (Holland, "A Luce Connection," 139–67) Some of the late September and early October eyewitness refugee reports "probably were valid sightings of the medium-range missiles—but that could not be determined at the time." (Garthoff, "US Intelligence in the Cuban Missile Crisis," 22–23) Alexis Johnson later claimed, "I know of no proposal that was made by anybody that was turned down by anybody in the Department of State or elsewhere which could have led to earlier discovery of the missiles." (Johnson Oral History, 41)

Hilsman, "we ought to be thinking of all the unpleasant questions" that might come up at the press and diplomatic briefings.

The President, about to leave for a meeting in the Cabinet Room with the Berlin Planning Group (all but indistinguishable in this case from the ExComm) asked for specific details on the Soviet buildup—he was told that there were 100 MiG 15 and 21 fighters and about 8,000 to 10,000 Soviet military personnel in Cuba. He wondered about using less provocative wording in his speech, such as "technicians," but quickly agreed to Rusk and Hilsman's suggestions to simply say, "thousands" of Soviet "personnel."

Monday, October 22, around 12:00 noon, Cabinet Room

Identified Participants: John F. Kennedy, George Ball, McGeorge Bundy, Roswell Gilpatric, U. Alexis Johnson, Robert Kennedy, Paul Nitze, Dean Rusk, Theodore Sorensen, Llewellyn Thompson.[110]

"I don't think we ought to accept the Chiefs' word on that one, Paul."

President John F. Kennedy

Paul Nitze, assistant secretary of defense for international security affairs, began the meeting with a briefing on the Berlin situation before being interrupted by the President. JFK's top priority was to avert the unintended outbreak of nuclear war if the Soviets reacted to the blockade or air assaults in Cuba by attacking the American missile sites in Turkey. The President had first raised this issue at the October 20 afternoon meeting, recommending that the JCS issue new orders to American personnel on the Jupiter bases in Turkey not to fire their missiles at the U.S.S.R., even if attacked, without specific presidential authorization. Nitze reported that "McNamara and I wrote out a suggested instruction from him [the President] to the Chiefs and we took it up with the Chiefs. The Chiefs came back with a paper saying that those instructions are *already* out."[111]

[110]Tape 32.2, POF, PRC, JFKL.

[111]Barton J. Bernstein contends, "In simply strategic terms, these 'soft' IRBMs, vulnerable to a sniper's bullet and taking hours to fire, were useful only for a first strike. They never could have been used in retaliation, because they would have been easily wiped out in a first strike." ("Commentary: Reconsidering Khrushchev's Gambit," 232–33). How-

JFK was obviously not satisfied: "Well, why don't we reinforce 'em because, as I say, we may be attacking the Cubans and they may... a reprisal may come on these. We don't want them firing [the nuclear missiles] without our knowing about it." The tension in the room quickly surfaced when Rusk erroneously observed, "The ones in Turkey are not operational, are they?" and Nitze retorted very sharply, "Yes, they are!"[112]

Gilpatric confirmed that fifteen of the Turkish missiles were operational *and* on alert, and Kennedy softly pressed Nitze to be sure that his orders were fully understood, "Can we take care of that then, Paul? We need a new instruction out." Nitze, muttered a sullen and barely audible reply: "All right. I'll go back and tell them." "They object to sending a new one out?" JFK asked patiently, and Nitze reiterated that the Chiefs objected to a new order because "to their view, it compromises their standing instructions." Bundy and Rusk tried to act as go-betweens, suggesting that a personal message could be sent to the Chiefs explaining that the President wanted them to be sure everyone understood this particular paragraph. "It can surely be done," Bundy observed, "one way or the other."

But, Nitze then resolutely informed the President that the JCS had also made another point in their response—a startling point: "NATO strategic contact [a nuclear attack from the U.S.S.R.] requires the immediate execution of EDP in such events."

"What's EDP?" Kennedy asked candidly.

"The European Defense Plan," Nitze answered chillingly, "which is nuclear war." "Now that's why," the President barked, "we want to get on that, you see." But Nitze tried to explain, "No, they said the orders are that *nothing* can go without the presidential order."

The commander-in-chief's reservations about the military were obvious in his sharply focused reply. "But you see, what they don't know in Greece and Turkey—uh, Turkey and Italy—what we know. And therefore they don't realize there *is* a chance there will be a *spot reprisal*, and what we gotta do is make sure these fellows [at the Jupiter sites] *do* know, so that they don't fire 'em off and think the United

---

ever, as General Taylor conceded during the October 16 discussion about attacking the Cuban missiles, no first strike could ever be 100% effective.

[112]Rusk's remark is hardly surprising given the ignorance about the Turkish missiles displayed even by top defense officials at the first October 16 ExComm meeting. For a later recollection by Bundy about what Rusk knew, or didn't know, about the operability of the Jupiters, see Blight and Welch, *On the Brink*, 75.

States is under attack. I don't think," he asserted flatly, "we ought to accept the Chiefs' word on that one, Paul." "All right," Nitze mumbled grudgingly. Kennedy then struck a more conciliatory pose, "I understand why they did that. These fellows... they think that everybody knows as much as we know, and they *don't*." Rusk came to the President's defense, noting that in the event of a Soviet strike in Turkey, the Jupiter base personnel could erroneously conclude that "a nuclear war is already on."

President Kennedy's wariness suggests that he was mindful of the barely concealed contempt for his authority and judgment bubbling beneath the surface during his meeting with Joint Chiefs on October 19; he undoubtedly feared that the military authorities might "misunderstand" his orders.[113]

Nitze, despite President Kennedy's conciliatory tone, tried again to defend the JCS position, "But *surely* these fellows are *thoroughly* indoctrinated *not* to fire," he bristled, banging on the table, "and this is what McNamara and I went over . . . and they *really are* indoctrinated on this point." Kennedy cut him off with a temperate but firm order: "Well, let's do it again, Paul." The President's response was clear: *his* orders would be carried out, regardless of JCS rules and procedures.

"I've *got* your point, we'll do it again," Nitze answered, finally retreating. Some strained laughter broke out at the resolution of this "difference of opinion," and Bundy relieved the pressure by telling Nitze, in a tongue-in-cheek tone, "Send me the documents, and I will show them to a doubting master," likely glancing towards the President. The laughter, possibly including Nitze himself, briefly grew even louder.[114]

[113]Earlier that year, Kennedy had read a popular novel, *Seven Days in May*, by Fletcher Knebel and Charles Bailey, about a military coup against a president regarded as too weak by the leaders of the armed forces. "It's possible. It could happen in this country," JFK concluded ambivalently, "but the conditions would have to be so preposterous as to be virtually impossible. It won't happen on my watch, though." (Paul Fay, *McCall's* (August 1966), 107)

[114]JFK seemed to be hinting again that a Soviet strike against the Turkish Jupiters might be acceptable as an even exchange for an American attack on the missiles in Cuba. Within an hour, General Taylor sent an urgent message to the NATO commander which was to remain secret from the Turks and Italians: "Make certain that the Jupiters in Turkey and Italy will not be fired without specific authorization from the President. In the event of an attack, nuclear or non-nuclear . . . U.S. custodians are to destroy or make inoperable the weapons if any attempt is made to fire them." (May and Zelikow, *The Kennedy Tapes*, 223) Nitze did not mention this exchange with President Kennedy in his published memoirs. (Nitze, *Hiroshima to Glasnost*, 214–38)

Bundy returned to the crucial issue of maintaining NATO's solidarity. He stressed the need to reassure their European allies that the American response in Cuba was primarily aimed at protecting Berlin and reinforcing *European* security. "Those are good points," JFK affirmed. "I don't think we've thought enough about 'em in our communications to these heads of state." The President urged that all background briefings for ambassadors and diplomats should stress America's credibility on Berlin and the preservation of the strategic balance. The NATO allies must be made to feel that they had been fully informed and consulted, he reasoned, so that they didn't react to the blockade as a symptom of America's Cuban obsession. "I thought I'd make these points this afternoon," a more pacific Nitze announced, "when I meet with the military subcommittee just *before* your speech." "Fine," JFK replied. Bundy stressed giving the allies "assurance of *full* information and *full* consultation."

Suddenly, a note was handed to the President by press secretary Pierre Salinger, who had just entered the room. After they whispered together briefly, Kennedy revealed in an edgy voice that Soviet Foreign Minister Gromyko was going to make a major announcement in two hours upon his departure from the United States. A wave of concern swept across the room. "You want to get on the air quicker?" Bundy inquired. JFK recommended immediately announcing that his speech to the nation was set for 7:00 P.M.—thus diminishing the impact of any statement by Gromyko. "Well, why don't you announce *that*," he told Salinger, "so at least we're not going on the air after the Russians are." Salinger confirmed that the announcement could be made in 15–20 minutes. "Well, the quicker the better on *that*," JFK reiterated. "Yeah," the press secretary agreed. "Because," the President explained, "what we don't wanna do is have the Russians announce this thing." He also urged immediately confirming the evening meeting with the congressional leadership, "*Right now. Right now,* then."

JFK expressed concern that the Soviets would scoop him by declaring that they had shipped only defensive missiles to Cuba. "They're certainly gonna *defend* this," Nitze predicted, as someone chuckled nervously, "with *a great big* announcement *defending* these missiles." RFK suggested, if the Russians were going to announce it, the U.S. should put out a statement in an hour about the discovery of the missiles and also announce the presidential speech later that evening. JFK quickly agreed, "So it doesn't look like the Russians *first* announced this thing," and Nitze emphasized, "I think it's *awfully* important to get ahead of the Russians." Kennedy also asked Bundy to prepare such a statement "*right now*," saying simply that Soviet missile bases had been detected in Cuba and the President would discuss American responses at seven this evening. JFK then sparked some awkward laughter by irreverently joking, "What else do we have to worry about in Berlin?"

President Kennedy was especially concerned that the Soviets would say, "if we do anything about it [the missiles], that they're going to do such-and-such. That's what we've always been concerned about." Perhaps, he speculated, Gromyko's statement reflected Soviet uneasiness, "I think they think maybe we're gonna invade Cuba, because that's the way the buildup [in Florida] suggests."[115] "I think that would be bad," RFK interjected, "to have them say, 'Don't invade Cuba or we're gonna knock your block off' and then you go on television and announce—" JFK instinctively finished his brother's sentence, "the quarantine." The President was determined to have the administration make the first statement so that newspapers around the world would report that the U.S. had broken the story. "I think we ought to get to work on this. We don't have much time."

Salinger's report was a false alarm. Gromyko made a routine statement at the airport and never mentioned the missiles. As a result, there was no need to announce the discovery of the missiles before the President's speech, and the statement Bundy had been told to prepare was dropped. The ExComm discussion ended with a decision to reconvene for a final pre-announcement meeting at 3:00 that afternoon.

Military preparations moved forward rapidly in the next few hours. The Strategic Air Command implemented a massive alert of its B-52 nuclear bomber force and ordered B-47 nuclear bombers dispersed to airfields around the country. The JCS raised U.S. military forces around the world to a DEFCON 3 military alert. Pierre Salinger arranged for thirty minutes of network time for the President to speak to the nation on "a matter of highest national urgency." The President expected Khrushchev, at the very least, to blockade Berlin in response to the U.S. quarantine of Cuba. "Suppose Khrushchev says to me," he remarked to Ambassador Thompson, "'Well now, you've blockaded

---

[115]When Khrushchev learned about the President's speech, he and many in the Presidium did indeed assume that an invasion was imminent, "a feeling of impending doom hung in the air." (Fursenko and Naftali, *"One Hell of a Gamble,"* 240–41)

Cuba and I've blockaded Berlin. How do you like that?'" Thompson pulled no punches, "'It will be 1948 all over again.'" The Navy deployed 150 ships, 250 aircraft and 30,000 men to set up and enforce the quarantine around Cuba.[116]

Meanwhile, in Moscow, the Presidium hesitantly authorized General Issa A. Pliyev, commander of Soviet forces in Cuba, to protect his nearly 43,000 troops, missiles and other weapons by using Luna tactical nuclear weapons, without a direct order from Moscow, if required to blunt an American invasion. These missiles had a limited range (about 30 miles) and could not threaten the American mainland. They were designed instead for battlefield use, to destroy an invasion fleet or to wipe out forces landing on Cuban beaches. Each warhead, nonetheless, had about 1/7 the explosive power of the Hiroshima bomb—a big enough bang. The U.S., however, had no firm intelligence that tactical nuclear weapons were in Cuba. Khrushchev was also eager to prevent the capture of the strategic missiles by the Americans, but nonetheless refused to allow these far more dangerous weapons to be fired without specific approval from the Kremlin.[117]

Sometime that day, Colonel Oleg Penkovsky, a high-ranking Soviet military official who had been passing invaluable microfilm and other information about Soviet intelligence and rocket forces to the United States, was taken into custody by the KGB at his Moscow residence. He was never seen alive again, and documents released after the collapse of the U.S.S.R. confirm that he was executed.[118]

[116]Chang and Kornbluh, *Cuban Missile Crisis*, 377; Brugioni, *Eyeball to Eyeball*, 350–51, 371. The term "quarantine" was chosen, at least in part, to emphasize the limited purpose of the American action since a blockade could be technically construed as an act of war.

[117]Pliyev had been "rewarded" by Khrushchev with the Soviet military command in Cuba after crushing the anti-government demonstrations in Novocherkassk the previous June. (Zubok and Pleshakov, *Inside the Kremlin's Cold War*, 264); Khrushchev and defense chief Rodion Malinovsky did not actually sign the order to allow the use of the tactical nuclear weapons without authorization. The order was countermanded by October 29 and a decision was made by late November to withdraw these missiles from Cuba. (Fursenko and Naftali, *"One Hell of a Gamble,"* 210–12, 242–43, 276, 311–12)

[118]Penkovsky "did not learn, at least in time to tell us anything," about the missiles in Cuba (see remarks by Raymond Garthoff in Blight, *et al.*, *Cuba on the Brink*, 133–35; Chang, "The View from Washington and Nowhere," 149).

Monday, October 22, 3:00 P.M., Cabinet Room

Identified Participants: John Kennedy, George Anderson, George Ball, McGeorge Bundy, Henry Fowler, Roger Hilsman, Robert F. Kennedy, Curtis LeMay, John McCone, Edward McDermott, Robert McNamara, Dean Rusk, David Shoup, Theodore Sorensen, Maxwell Taylor, Llewellyn Thompson, Earle Wheeler.[119]

"Khrushchev will *not* take this without a response, maybe in Berlin or maybe here. But... I think we've done the best thing, at least as far as you can tell in advance."

President John F. Kennedy

The full National Security Council, including the Joint Chiefs, convened at 3:00 for their final preparatory meeting before the President's speech. They were joined, rather ominously, by Edward McDermott, director of the Office of Emergency Preparedness. Several minutes at the start of the discussion were not recorded—apparently because the President simply neglected to turn on the machine when the meeting began.

After brief discussion of a new message from British prime minister Harold Macmillan, a review of the political and legal advantages of securing OAS support for the blockade and the regular intelligence briefing by McCone, which included the disquieting news that a fleet of Soviet submarines would be in Cuban waters within a week, JFK launched into an uncharacteristically lengthy monologue. He stressed that everyone at the meeting would be expected to fully support the quarantine decision in order to assure domestic political unity. Every administration voice, Kennedy instructed, was to "sing one song in order to make clear that there was now no difference among his advisers as to the proper course to follow." He described the quarantine as "a reasonable consensus."[120]

The President's thoughts, as they did so often during that week, turned to the terrible and possibly irrevocable risks in *any* course of action, and he pessimistically reminded the NSC that if the wrong choice had indeed been made, we may not even have "the satisfaction of knowing what would have happened if we had acted differently."[121]

---

[119]Tape 33.1, POF, PRC, JFKL.

[120]Minutes of the 507th Meeting of the National Security Council, October 22, 1962, NSF, JFKL, 2–3.

[121]*Ibid.*; This observation is remarkably similar to JFK's reported "brass hats" remark to Dave Powers three days earlier.

After beginning a review of the reasons for his choice of a blockade, JFK belatedly turned on the tape recorder. The President seemed at ease with the quarantine decision and ready to make his case before the American people and the world, but nevertheless remained extremely unsure about how the situation would evolve over the next few days. The administration *had* to act, he declared almost defensively, to prevent a shift in the Latin American balance of power and to scotch the perception that Soviet advances were inevitable. "So we decided to do *something*, and then we start *here*." An invasion of Cuba might yet be necessary, he admitted. "Khrushchev will *not* take this without a response, maybe in Berlin or maybe here. But we have done, I think—the choices being one among second best—I think we've done the *best* thing," he added fatalistically, "at least as far as you can tell *in advance*." He stressed, however, that two dangerous matters remained "to be settled in the coming days. What are we gonna do when I... one of our U-2s is shot down, which we have to anticipate maybe in the next few days, over a SAM site? What will be our response *there*? Number One. And secondly, what will we do if the work *continues* on these sites, which we assume it *will*? . . . Do we intensify the blockade [and] . . . If they shoot down one of our U-2s, do we attack *that* SAM site or all the SAM sites?" But, he reminded his advisers, in the event that anyone should develop cold feet, "I don't think there was anybody *ever* who didn't think we shouldn't respond." His meaning was plain in spite of his grammar.

"As I've said from the beginning," he admitted, "the idea of a quick strike was *very* tempting and I really didn't give up on that until yesterday morning" because of the Pearl Harbor parallel and the fact that General Sweeney[122] had conceded that all the missiles could not be eliminated from the air, "The job can *only* be finished by an invasion. . . . [and] we are moving those forces which will be necessary in case, at the end of the week, it looks like that would be the only course left to us." Obviously aware of the military disadvantages of issuing a warning before the air strikes, the President tried to placate the Joint Chiefs, "I want to say this very clearly to the military that I recognize we increase your problems in any military action you have to take in Cuba by the warning we're now giving... giving. But I *did* want you to know that the reason we followed the course we have is because, while we would have been able to take out more planes and missiles without

---

[122]Walter C. Sweeney, head of the Air Force Tactical Air Command.

warning, as we *are* involved all around the world and *not* just in Cuba, I think the shock to the alliance might have been nearly fatal, particularly as it would have excused very drastic action by... by uh... Khrushchev."

Rusk, backing the President but evidently aiming his remarks at the JCS as well, cautioned that "if any of our colleagues think that this is, in any sense, a *weak* action, I think we can be quite sure that in a number of hours we'll have a *flaming* crisis on our hands. This is gonna go *very* far, and possibly *very* fast."

Robert Kennedy, with evident reluctance, broached the sensitive area of politics and public relations by asking the President how the administration would respond to inevitable charges that forceful action, including a blockade, should have been taken at least a month ago. The attorney general, with his eye always on the mid-term elections and the 1964 presidential campaign, was obviously concerned about potentially damaging press reactions after the President's speech that evening, possibly accusing the administration of incompetence or duplicity for not acting much sooner. JFK replied in detail: without hard evidence, he argued, which had not become available until October 16, it would have been very difficult to get OAS support[123] and NATO would have regarded risking Berlin as proof of "almost a fixation on the subject of Cuba, which up to quite recently most of us never... did not assume would be turned into an offensive base. . . . If we didn't get an OAS resolution," he explained, "it would have to be a declaration of war and a declaration of war on Cuba *at that point* would have placed us in an isolated position [since] the whole foreign policy of the United States since 1947 has been to develop and maintain alliances *in this hemisphere* as well as around the world." Kennedy reminded the ExComm, "And, of course, no one at that time was certain that Khrushchev would make such a *far-reaching* step, which is *wholly* a departure from Soviet foreign policy, *really*, since I would say the Berlin Blockade."

JFK also acknowledged that although there had been rumors from refugees, "Mr. Hilsman, who's in charge of that [intelligence and research at the State Department], says that most of them were ta... that they were all talking about these SAM sites, the air... ground-air missiles. Is that correct?" Hilsman, evidently unsure whether to be flat-

---

[123]Dean Rusk lobbied hard the next day at an urgent OAS meeting in Washington and received unanimous support for the quarantine.

tered or embarrassed by the President's remark, and likely irritated that RFK had again questioned the accuracy of the pre–October 16 intelligence reports, responded hesitantly, "Yes, sir. I..." and mumbled almost inaudibly, "I wouldn't say I was in charge." "What?" Kennedy pressed, and Hilsman repeated, "I wouldn't say that I was in *charge* of the whole thing." Obviously amused by Hilsman's discomfort, Kennedy responded, "Well, whoever," and specifically asked about the controversial refugee reports, sparking a soft ripple of laughter in the room.[124]

After first suggesting that McCone "probably would like to speak to it," Hilsman reviewed the surveillance since August 29, admitting that suspicions had increased after big crates, especially IL-28 crates, were spotted, but there had been no confirmation until October 14. But, the CIA chief surely increased Hilsman's uneasiness by cautioning his colleagues, "I think we have to be careful at this point. . . . I wouldn't be *too* categoric that we had no information" because "there were some 15 refugee reports" indicating "that *something* was going on"—which turned up in Senator Keating's speeches. McCone acknowledged, however, that there had been no "hard intelligence" from late August to mid-October. RFK agreed that "refugees' reports frequently proved inaccurate" and surveillance flights would not have "been able to tell *up* until the last ten days or two weeks." JFK pointedly reminded his colleagues that none of the Eastern European satellites had nuclear weapons on their territory and "this would be the *first* time the Soviet Union had moved these weapons outside their own" borders.[125] And, RFK stressed, Dobrynin, and later Gromyko, even in his conversation with the President just a few days before, had insisted "that this was not being done."

The President remained concerned that critics might ask why the administration had decided not to attack the missiles. Bundy recom-

[124]Some refugee reports about offensive missiles in Cuba, cited by Senator Keating, turned out to be "remarkably accurate." Hilsman obviously had mixed feelings about taking responsibility for the reliability of all the intelligence reports gathered from Cuban refugees. (For an up-to-date investigation of Keating's sources, see Holland, "A Luce Connection," 139–67)

[125]In fact, declassified Soviet documents reveal that the U.S.S.R. *had* briefly deployed nuclear weapons outside its own territory—in East Germany—in 1959. JFK and top intelligence officials in the administration appear to have been unaware of this earlier nuclear deployment. (Matthias Uhl and Vladimir I. Ivkin, "'Operation Atom': The Soviet Union's Stationing of Nuclear Missiles in the German Democratic Republic, 1959," *CWIHPB* *12/13* (Fall/Winter 2001), 299–306)

mended avoiding any reference to "the difficulty of hitting these targets" since air strikes might still be necessary in a few days. RFK advised sticking to "the Pearl Harbor thing," but Rusk suggested emphasizing the obligation to bring this threat before the OAS and the U.N. JFK noted, "It is a fact that even with the air strike . . . we couldn't perhaps get all the missiles that are in sight." Bundy retorted impatiently, "*Entirely true*, Mr. President. But I *don't* think the next few days is the time to talk about it." President Kennedy replied with unusual irritation, "Well, I know, but I want everybody to understand it, Mac, if you don't mind. The fact of the matter is there *are* missiles on the island which are not in sight!"

In addition, JFK noted that even though he had decided, at least for the moment, to avoid a "Pearl Harbor" by not bombing the missiles without warning, critics could still try to equate the Soviet missiles in Cuba and the U.S. missiles in Turkey and Italy, "which the Soviets put up with, which are operational and have been for two to three years."[126] President Kennedy also asked to see the State Department brief being prepared "on that matter. Could you get that? I'd like to take a look at it afterward." Rusk argued forcefully that his department's brief made clear that the cases were *not* comparable—the U.S. and NATO had decided in 1957 to deploy these missiles in Turkey and Italy *after* the U.S.S.R. had announced that they "were equipping their armed forces with nuclear... nuclear missiles. . . . [and] were insisting upon having hundreds of these weapons aimed at Europe and no... none of these weapons pointed the other way."

JFK emphatically agreed that the administration must make the case "for our ambassadors . . . [and] the American press and others" that the U.S. had no operational ICBMs at that time and therefore "the situation doesn't match." The President began reading from a prepared statement: "The Soviet move [in Cuba] was undertaken secretly, accompanied by false Soviet statements in public and private . . . [and was a] departure from the Soviet position that it has no need or desire to station strategic weapons off the Soviet territory. . . . Our bases abroad are by published agreement to help local people maintain their independence against a threat from abroad. Soviet history is exactly the opposite. Offensive missiles in Cuba have a very different psychological and political effect in this hemisphere than missiles in the U.S.S.R.

---

[126]The missiles in Turkey actually became operational during the Kennedy administration—between November 1961 and March 1962. (Nash, *The Other Missiles*, 103)

pointed *to* us." The document JFK was reading relied on familiar Cold War tenets, contending that if the U.S. had failed to act after the Soviet deployment in Cuba, "Communism and Castroism are gonna be spread through the hemisphere," creating a domino effect in the Americas, "as governments frightened by this new evidence of power have toppled. All this represents a provocative change in the delicate status quo both countries have maintained." He concluded that the Soviet-Cuban gambit was "a probing action" to test whether Khrushchev could get away with grabbing Berlin. The President recalled that Llewellyn Thompson had made this argument several days earlier, and the former ambassador quickly confirmed that Khrushchev "made it quite clear in my last talk with him that he was squirming" under the pressure not to back down over Berlin.

Rusk also urged the President to publicly state that the missiles in Cuba represented "a special threat" to the United States and the 41 allies all over the world dependent on American "nuclear support." He insisted that a deployment "of this magnitude is not something that we can brush aside simply *because* the Soviets have some other missiles that could also reach the United States." The missiles in Cuba "would *double* the known missile strength the Soviet Union has to reach this country."[127]

The President returned inexorably to Berlin, arguing that no matter what the U.S. did in Cuba, Gromyko had made clear last week that the Soviets were "getting ready to move on Berlin anyway." The quarantine was not a threat, he started reading again, because it affected only offensive weapons and did not stop food or medicine or threaten war. He cited, as a further example of U.S. restraint, "Even today the Soviets inspect our, at least stop our [truck] convoys going into Berlin." He stopped reading and asked, "People get out, don't they? They don't inspect the trucks." Bundy, rather disdainfully, retorted, "No, sir, the people do *not* get out and this troop inspection is a... is a complicated one. They have *ample* means of surveillance, but *inspection* is *not* the word we want to use." Another participant, however, confirmed that U.S. forces sometimes did get out of the trucks and let the Soviets "look in through the tailgates to the trucks." JFK seized on this apparent vindication in his wrangle with Bundy, "They *do* let them. Yeah."

[127]American intelligence had significantly overestimated the number of ICBMs in the U.S.S.R. The Cuban deployment was even more numerically significant than Rusk knew at the time. (Raymond L. Garthoff, *Intelligence Assessment and Policymaking: A Decision Point in the Kennedy Administration* (Washington, D. C.: Brookings, 1984), 30)

"But the central point here is," Rusk demanded, "that we're in Berlin by *right* as well as by the acknowledgment and agreement of the Soviet Union. They're bringing these things into Cuba contrary to the Rio Pact. There's just all the difference in the world between these two situations." The President was impressed by the logic of this argument and seemed confident that the administration could make a convincing case in the court of world public opinion that the blockade of Cuba was not comparable to the Soviet Berlin blockade in 1948: "we're permitting goods to move into Cuba at this point, food and all the rest. This is not a blockade in that sense. It's merely an attempt to prevent the shipment of weapons there." Khrushchev, Kennedy contended, was trying to force the U.S. to choose between attacking Cuba, "which would free his hand" in Berlin, "and/or appearing to be an irresolute ally—so it's time we chose where we begin on the road."

President Kennedy was determined to publicly defend the blockade as a reasonable and restrained response to a Soviet provocation. Despite recognizing that he might still have to order bombing, JFK did not want to hand the Soviets a propaganda plum by revealing that surprise air attacks had ever been considered, and he was quite willing to mislead the press and manage the news to preserve this cover story. For that reason, he tersely ordered his advisers not to mention that bombing the bases had even been discussed as an option. "So I think we oughta just scratch that from all our statements and conversations, and not ever indicate that that *was* a course of action open to us. *I can't say that strongly enough,*" he instructed. We don't want the world to know "that this was one of the alternatives that we considered this week. Now it's gonna be very difficult to keep it quiet, but I think we ought to because that won't... it may inhibit us in the future." RFK suggested explaining that bombing was rejected as a "Pearl Harbor kind of operation," but Rusk recommended saying simply that air attacks were not done, rather than not considered. JFK promptly agreed, "Well, I think that's fair enough."

General Taylor, however, raised a far more dicey public relations issue: "Mr. President, I should call attention to the fact we're starting moves now which are very... are overt, and will be seen and reported on and commented on." "Precautionary, every one of them!" Bundy muttered irritably. But, Taylor persisted, "And you'll be faced with the question, 'Are you preparing to invade?'" Rusk, somewhat naively, suggested telling the press that these "precautionary moves" could not be explained in detail: "it's not in the public interest to try to explain each one of the moves." "We don't want to look as if we got scared off from anything," Bundy counseled. JFK pointed out that it was neither strategically nor politically helpful to "have it hanging over us that we're preparing invasion." McNamara suggested stating simply that "you ordered us to be prepared for any eventuality," but Taylor objected that it's the business of the military "to have plans for any contingency." The President sought to cool the general's rhetoric, "By plans, I think we mean it in the more... not in the military sense but in the...," but trailed off without completing his sentence. JFK asked instead for a report on how troop movements had been publicized or censored, voluntarily or otherwise, during "the first days" of the Korean War.

As the meeting moved toward a conclusion, Rusk asked whether the President had considered extending "our stop and search program to aircraft, should nuclear weapons be sent to Cuba by air." JFK again moved to reign in the potential for escalation, "I don't think we ought to do it on the aircraft just yet" because if a Berlin crisis erupted, "we may have to rely on aircraft and I don't think *we* ought to initiate that." RFK asked about how to respond to questions from the press about the potential delivery of missiles to Cuba by air and Bundy recommended an intensive Defense Department study of this possibility. McNamara, however, advised "saying that we're prepared to quarantine movement of weapons by whatever means, *period*." If any planes flew from the U.S.S.R. to Cuba, "we'll have to watch this carefully and decide what to do at that time."

The secretary of state also pondered whether the press might ask if the President was planning to call up National Guard or Reserve units or declare a national emergency. Rusk urged saying, "'Not at this time, but that could change in an hour's time.'" Admiral Anderson also reported that call ups were under review on a day-to-day basis. The potential urgency of the situation was dramatically underscored when JFK questioned Treasury under secretary Henry Fowler about the impact of the crisis on "the balance of payments, gold and all the rest." Fowler urged clearly establishing who would decide "on such a question as the closing of the exchanges should any situation bordering on panic develop in the next day or two."

The administration had to clearly explain, Rusk also suggested, that the blockade "is not, from our point of view, an act of war." The President, in that context, asked whether ships from friendly nations, obviously not carrying strategic weapons, would be stopped at the blockade line "so that we get the precedent established in case we want to extend this to oil and petroleum and so on." Admiral Anderson replied by the book, "I think that we *should* stop and visit and search and play this thing straight," and Rusk strenuously concurred, "it has to be *effective*, and to make it *effective*, you stop all ships."

JFK ended the meeting by again demanding, despite his confidence that "security's been so well held in this group," complete public silence about all discussions of tactical, strategic or military options. Bundy proposed a standard reply to such inquiries, "'No orders have been given.'" "Thank you very much," JFK remarked as he turned off the tape recorder.

Just after the conclusion of the ExComm meeting, JFK, Rusk and G. Mennen Williams, assistant secretary of state for African affairs, met in the Oval Office with Ugandan prime minister Milton Obote and several members of his cabinet. The President, perhaps seeking a break from the tension, actively participated in a wide-ranging discussion of African economic development and resisted several attempts by Rusk to shorten the meeting. Later that evening, when Obote watched Kennedy's televised speech, he was astounded that the President had given so much time and attention to the discussion and had managed to appear entirely normal and composed.

The President met with his Cabinet at 4 P.M. McCone had offered to conduct a joint briefing with Lundahl, but the President, evidently irritable, rejected the idea: "No, it just might confuse the issues." Instead, he brusquely revealed that offensive missiles had been discovered in Cuba and that he would make an address to the nation at 7 P.M. Kennedy later seemed perplexed that much of the Cabinet had seemed dumbfounded by his announcement and asked no questions; their reaction, however, was not surprising since many of them had never been in the loop on military or national security matters. Secretary of Agriculture Orville Freeman, nonetheless, remained after the meeting and asked the President if any planning had been done on possible food shortages if the crisis stretched out over many weeks. Kennedy admitted that the issue had been ignored and Freeman promised to prepare plans to deal promptly with any food emergency.[128]

At 5 P.M., the President, Rusk, McNamara, Thompson, McCone, Lundahl and deputy CIA director Ray Cline met in the Cabinet Room

---

[128]Orville Freeman to Dino Brugioni, January 4, 1978, cited in Brugioni, *Eyeball to Eyeball*, 353–54.

with nearly twenty leaders of Congress of both parties. The congressional leadership had been summoned to Washington from all across the country since Congress was not in session; many had been pulled away from vacations or campaign appearances and flown to the Capital in military aircraft. There had been a great deal of speculation about Cuba in the press and most of these experienced Washington hands had obviously figured out that something major was about to happen. However, some of the congressional leaders resented that they had not been consulted earlier and were being informed of the President's decision barely two hours before his speech to the nation. JFK had never been an insider in the House and many of his Senate colleagues had dismissed him as an indifferent senator at best, a playboy at worst. Now, whether they liked it or not, he was the President of the United States. But that fact did not mean they would passively accept his decisions.

Monday, October 22, 5:00 P.M., Cabinet Room

Identified Participants: John F. Kennedy, Hale Boggs, Ray Cline, Everett Dirksen, J. William Fulbright, Charles Halleck, Bourke Hickenlooper, Hubert Humphrey, Lyndon Johnson, Thomas Kuchel, Arthur Lundahl, Michael Mansfield, John McCone, Robert McNamara, Dean Rusk, Richard Russell, Leverett Saltonstall, George Smathers, Llewellyn Thompson, Carl Vinson.[129]

"The people who are the best off are the people whose advice is not taken because *whatever* we do is *filled* with hazards."

President John F. Kennedy

The meeting began with intelligence briefings by McCone and Lundahl. The President, flanked by Rusk, McNamara and Thompson, sat patiently as material all too familiar to him was explained to the legislative leaders for the first time. JFK undoubtedly watched the faces of his congressional allies and opponents, wondering what they were thinking and whether they would support his decision. The CIA director, clearly reading from notes or a written report, referred to "this *unprecedented* Soviet move" and did not dodge the troubling admission that "Late in September, persistent reports came to us from refugee

[129]Tapes 33.2 & 33A.1, POF, PRC, JFKL. LBJ has not been listed as a participant in this meeting since he never spoke. However, his comments to JFK the following morning, discussed below, strongly suggest that he did attend.

sources from Cuba indicating that defensive deployment [of surface-to-air missiles] was only the *initial* phase and was to be followed by the delivery of offensive missiles." Unmistakable photographic proof of the construction of offensive sites, he explained, however, was not obtained until a U-2 flight on October 14, and construction was in fact continuing "in an urgent, highly secretive manner."

McCone piled on the grim details: 25 Soviet bloc ships were on their way to Cuba and 18 were already in Cuban ports; 24 MRBM missile launchers (with a range of 1,020 miles) and 12 IRBM launch pads (with a range of 2,200 miles) were under construction; four MRBM sites, containing 16 launchers, "are in full operational readiness as of October the 22nd." The Soviets had also installed 24 SAM bases, several cruise missile coastal defense sites and had delivered about 40 MiG 21 fighters and 20 IL-28 nuclear bombers with a range of 1,500 miles.[130]

On the most critical question, however, McCone acknowledged that only one, and possibly three, nuclear warhead storage sites had thus far been identified. He pointedly cautioned, however, that warheads could be concealed and "we are afraid *firm* evidence on this point may *never* become available from intelligence resources at our command. The warheads *could* be in Cuba, in concealment or temporary storage, without our discovering them. Nevertheless, since the medium-range and intermediate-range ballistic missiles are relatively ineffective weapons without nuclear warheads, we think it prudent to *assume* that nuclear weapons are now or shortly will be available in Cuba."

The congressional leaders sat in apparently stunned silence as McCone turned the briefing on surveillance photography over to Arthur Lundahl. "Mr. President, gentlemen," he began, "I would seek to very briefly summarize in graphic form the statistics which Mr. McCone has shown to you." Lundahl displayed U-2 photo boards, marked with red and black dots, triangles and arrows, identifying and locating several types of missile installations, twenty-one IL-28 bombers (most still in crates), thirty-nine MiG 21 fighters on Cuban airfields and the likely location for the storage of nuclear warheads—ominously "right next to an IRBM launching site." As he had done for the President on October 16, Lundahl stressed that the axis of several launching pads was 3-1-5,

---

[130]The actual combat radius of the IL-28s was under 750 miles—which McNamara clarified later in the meeting. McCone was referring to the total mileage on a round-trip from base to target.

"which brings you from this area straight up the middle part of the United States." The photos, he asserted, firmly supported the conclusion that the entire U.S., except for the Pacific Northwest, was vulnerable to the IRBMs. As Lundahl continued to pile on the evidence, several muted conversations broke out around the table.

Lundahl, with unmistakable pride in his work, raised his voice over these conversations and concluded: "We have dozens and dozens of other examples. But if I've made the point with you that the facts that have been drawn on this chart are backed up by photographic data, there's no doubt in our mind of our identification, I think I will have accomplished my point, Mr. President." The briefing had lasted some twenty minutes and had obviously persuaded the congressional leaders of the accuracy and gravity of the technical evidence. But, agreement on identifying the problem did not guarantee agreement on the President's proposed course of action. "Are there any questions?" JFK asked rather anticlimactically.

The leaders of Congress absorbed the data and asked a few preliminary questions about the range and mobility of the MRBMs and IRBMs: for example, Ray Cline of the CIA confirmed that the MRBM range was 1,020 nautical miles.[131] McCone, however, added a point with profound implications for any American military action in Cuba: "I have only one thing to add, Mr. President, and that is that from a variety of intelligence sources we have concluded that these bases, both the ground-to-air SAM sites as well as the missile sites, are manned by Soviets and, for the most part, put the Soviet guards to keep the Cubans out. We don't think there are very many Cubans on these bases."

Senator Richard B. Russell, Democrat of Georgia, the powerful conservative and segregationist chairman of the Senate Armed Services Committee, clearly disturbed by the briefing, initiated an exchange about technical details that probably impressed his congressional colleagues, the intelligence specialists and the President:

"Mr. McCone, one question. I'm sure you're monitoring this. Do you think they have their complex electronics installed yet?"

"We do yes," McCone responded, on the more advanced MRBMs.

"Well, they'd be ready to fire now?" Russell inquired.

"Yeah," McCone replied.

---

[131] A nautical mile is 6,080 feet but a statute mile is only 5,280 feet—thus 1,020 nautical miles are equivalent to 1,175 statute miles.

"And that's true," Russell interrupted, "as to the ground to... sur-face-to-air sites?"

"Yes," McCone replied, "On the surface-to-air we have... we have found that their... that their radars have been latching on to our U-2s the last couple of days, and while they have not fired a missile at us, we think that they will within a short time."

"*My God!*" Russell gasped.[132]

Senator Thomas Kuchel of California asked if the photos had been taken by a U-2. McCone replied affirmatively, but cautioned that the administration was simply referring in briefings to "military reconnaissance planes" without making any public reference to the U-2s. JFK added, "We're not using the precise numbers." Senator Bourke Hickenlooper of Iowa questioned when the missile sites would be capable of launching "an *extensive* attack against the United States," and McCone reiterated that 16 MRBM launchers were already operational, several more would be activated by the end of October and 8–12 IRBMs would be ready by December. Kuchel suggested that a nuclear launch from Cuba would be suicide. "*Yes*, it would be suicide," McCone observed matter-of-factly, "that's odd, because we could respond." But Rusk warned that such a response would inevitably become part of a "general nuclear exchange."

Reflecting the widely accepted belief in monolithic world communism, Hickenlooper asked if the Soviet move in Cuba was linked to the current "Chinese operation against India as a basic worldwide movement." McCone explained, "we have no information to that effect at all."[133] President Kennedy then turned to Ambassador Thompson, who "has had a lot of conversations with Khrushchev . . . to say something about his evaluation of his purposes." Thompson recalled that at their farewell talk last July, Khrushchev had indicated that "time's running out" on the Berlin problem—"he felt that he'd gone too far out on a limb to... to go back." The experienced diplomat categorically declared that the timing and purpose of the Cuban buildup was to pro-

---

[132]On September 20th, the Senate Foreign Relations and Armed Services Committees approved a joint resolution favoring the use of force to prevent Russian/Cuban aggression and subversion in the Western Hemisphere. "The leader of this effort was Senator Richard B. Russell, who regarded President Kennedy as weak and ineffectual in dealing with Cuba and the Russians" and hoped "to get the President off of his dead ass." (Brugioni, *Eyeball to Eyeball*, 152–53)

[133]Communist China had just launched a large-scale surprise military assault across the Indian border.

voke "a showdown on... on Berlin. In my view that's the... that's the main thing that he has in mind."

Rusk pushed the argument even further, emphasizing that the buildup in Cuba was "a *major* and *radical* move in Soviet policy and Soviet action." The U.S.S.R., Rusk pointed out (erroneously), had never placed missiles outside of their own territory, not even in the satellite states of Eastern Europe. Rusk noted that Soviet policy had become tougher over the past year, and labeled the Cuban gamble the most "reckless and hazardous" Soviet move since the Berlin blockade of 1948–49. Soviet policy-makers, he reasoned, had decided that the "peaceful-coexistence theme was not getting them very far" and the missiles in Cuba suggested the clear ascendancy of "the hard-line boys" in the Kremlin. Senator Russell's growing alarm was becoming apparent: "Mr. Secretary, do you see any other chance that it'll get any better if they keep on establishin' new bases and dividin' our space more and more," he pressed. "How... how can we gain by waiting since they're establishin' new bases?" "I'm not suggesting that things are getting any better," Rusk admitted rather defensively.

President Kennedy concluded the briefing with a somber but deliberately selective review of the options discussed over the past seven days of meetings, noting that intensive surveillance had been ordered immediately after the discovery of the missiles on the 14th and appealing to the Republicans in the room by revealing that he had sent McCone "to brief General Eisenhower." "If we invade Cuba," Kennedy explained, "we have a chance that these missiles will be fired—*on us.*" Khrushchev would likely seize Berlin and the unity of NATO would be shattered because "Europe will regard Berlin's loss . . . as having been the fault of the United States by acting in a precipitous way." He repeated, almost verbatim, his October 16 ExComm observation that the weapons in Cuba were five or six thousand miles from Europe, "So these missiles don't bother them and maybe we should think it should not bother us. So that whatever we do in regard to Cuba gives him a chance to do the same in regard to ah... ah Berlin." The President reasoned that "to not do anything" meant accepting the argument that since the U.S. had lived under the threat of Soviet missiles for years, the Cuban buildup merely "*adds* to our hazards but does not create a *new* military hazard" and the administration should instead "keep our eye on the main site, which would be Berlin. Our feeling, however, is that that would be a mistake."

President Kennedy, having carefully explained his thinking, finally announced his decision: "beginning tonight, we're going to blockade Cuba . . . under the Rio Treaty. We called for a meeting of the Rio Pact countries and hope to get a two-thirds vote for them to give the blockade legality." If the U.S. failed to get the vote, he admitted, the blockade against offensive weapons will be carried out illegally or with a declaration of war, "which is not as advantageous to us." Khrushchev's response, he conceded, was uncertain. "In order *not* to give Mr. Khrushchev the justification for imposing a *complete* blockade on Berlin, we're going to start with a blockade on the shipment of offensive weapons into Cuba, but stop all ships." If the situation deteriorated further, the blockade could be tightened to include POL. Plans for an invasion, he revealed, were still going forward. But, "if we invade Cuba, there's a chance these weapons will be fired at the United States." And, "if we attempt to strike them from the air, then we will not get 'em all because they're mobile. . . . and they can move 'em and set 'em up in another 3 days someplace else. . . . So after a good deal of a... searching, we decided this was the place to start." But, he candidly admitted, "I *don't* know what their response will be."

The President had generally observed the news censorship he had imposed at the end of the afternoon NSC meeting: he never mentioned the extensive discussions of bombing and the Pearl Harbor issue, except to briefly dismiss that option because the missiles could be moved. "If there's any strong disagreements with what at least we've set out to do," he concluded, "I want to hear it." He also predicted that the Soviet response "will be very strong" and asked the congressional leaders to remain in close contact over the coming days.

Rusk, perhaps anticipating congressional accusations that the President's decision was too weak, emphasized again that the blockade was only a first step and "a *brief* pause for the people on the other side to have another thought before we get into an *utterly* crashing crisis, because the prospects that are ahead of us at this moment are *very* serious." Since Khrushchev had surely underestimated the American response, Rusk continued, "a *brief* pause here is *very* important in order to give the Soviets a chance to pull back from the... from the brink here," before this becomes "a very grave matter indeed."

Senator Russell, plainly struggling to stay within the bounds of southern civility, suddenly lashed out: "Mr. President, I could not stay silent under these circumstances and live with myself. I... I... I think that our responsibilities to our people demand some stronger steps than that." The U.S., he maintained, would never be stronger or in a better position: "It seems to me that we're at the crossroads. We're either a first-class power or we're *not*." The Georgian tried subtly to hoist the President on his own petard: "You have warned these people time and again, in the most eloquent speeches I have read since Woodrow Wilson, as to what would happen if there was an offensive capability created in Cuba. They can't say they're not on notice." He rejected giving the Soviets "time to pause and think" because they would simply use it "to get better prepared." Khrushchev, he declared, had challenged "the announced foreign policy of the United States." "They can also," he warned, "blow Guantanamo off... off the map. And you have told 'em *not* to do this thing. They've *done* it. And I think that you... we should assemble as speedily as possible an adequate force and... and... and clean out that situation. The time's gonna come, Mr. President, when we're gonna have to take this gamble, in Berlin, in Korea and Washington, D.C. and Winder, Georgia for the... for the... for the nuclear war. I don't know whether Khrushchev will launch a nuclear war over Cuba or not. I *don't* believe he will! But I think that the more that we temporize, the more *surely* he *is* to convince *himself* that we *are* afraid to make any real movement and... and... and... and to really fight."

An obviously discomfited JFK suggested that Russell listen to McNamara's military analysis, but the senator cut in: "Pardon me. I... I... you had said if anybody disagrees, and I... I couldn't sit here feelin' as I do . . ." "I understand," Kennedy replied.

McNamara tried to scotch the senator's criticism by providing specifics on the operation and enforcement of the blockade—underscoring that any ship trying to penetrate the blockade would be disabled, seized or even sunk if necessary. He also summarized additional military moves already undertaken by the administration—air cover for U.S. merchant ships near Cuba, continued air surveillance of the island, a partial Strategic Air Command alert, reinforcing Guantanamo with 7,000 more men (and evacuating dependents), plus redeploying air defense forces to protect the southeastern coast of the United States.

Russell, nonetheless, became even more agitated: "Mr. President, I don't wanna make a nuisance of myself, but I... I... do... would like to complete my statement. I... my... my position is that these people have been warned." Khrushchev, he predicted, is "gonna start rattling his missiles, and making *firmer* and *firmer* and *firmer* statements about what he's gonna do about Cuba." Delaying an invasion, he contended, would give the MiGs a chance "to attack our shipping or to drop a few bombs around Miami or some other place" and when we do invade, "we'll lose a great many more men than we would *right now*."

"But Senator," JFK patiently explained, "we can't invade Cuba" because it would take several days to assemble and deploy the 90,000+ men required for an invasion. He acknowledged, however, "it may very well come to that before the end of the week." Russell insisted that an invasion of Cuba would present the Soviets with a *fait accompli* and make all-out war between the superpowers *less* likely, essentially the same argument made by General LeMay on October 19.

JFK, clearly becoming irritated, countered: "We *don't* have the forces to seize Cuba."

"Well, we can assemble 'em," Russell retorted sharply.

"So that's what we're doing now," Kennedy replied impatiently.

Russell would not relent: "This blockade is gonna... is gonna put them on the alert" and divide and weaken our forces, he sputtered, "around the... the... whole periphery of... of the free... free world."

House Minority Leader Charles Halleck recollected that before the discovery of the missiles, "We were told by somebody in the... in the Pentagon sittin' right over there it would take us *three months* to take Cuba. Am I right about that?" "I don't recall that," Russell muttered. McNamara attempted again, at JFK's urging, to defend the administration's covert planning for an invasion requiring 250,000 military personnel and over 100 merchant ships, to be carried out after just seven days of preparation. The ground assault, he revealed hesitantly, would be preceded by at least 2,000 bombing sorties. "I know," the defense chief told Halleck, "that I can count on you to keep it in confidence." "Bombing sorties with what kind of bombs?" Halleck asked; the defense chief, strikingly, seemed to leave *all* options open, "Initially, iron bombs."

Russell, obviously drawing on his Armed Services Committee expertise, criticized putting "these tired old B-49s, -47s," on 24-hour alert, complaining that these "nearly worn out" planes constituted the bulk of U.S. bomber forces. McNamara insisted that with available spare parts the bombers were prepared for an airborne alert, ironically proclaiming, "this opinion is shared by... by General LeMay. . . . It's been really remarkable," the defense secretary claimed, "that we have been able to do as much as we have without more speculation in the press." He also disclosed that the President had actually ordered the Pentagon nearly a year ago to prepare plans for invading Cuba: "We've reviewed them with the President over the past ten months on *five* different occasions. We're *well* prepared for an invasion, *as* well prepared as we could possibly be, facing the situation we do."[134]

President Kennedy, perhaps hoping to isolate Russell by appealing for support from the other congressional leaders, vividly and authoritatively laid out the stark choices on the table: "If we go into Cuba, we have to all realize that we are taking a chance that these missiles, which are ready to fire, won't be fired. So that's... is that really a gamble we should take? In any case, we're preparing to take it. Ah... well, I think, fact is, that that is *one hell* of a gamble."

He also made a rather disingenuous appeal for unity, since he had ignored the leaders of Congress up to the last possible moment, "I'm gonna have everybody in this room *be* here with us because we all have to decide this thing together." U.S. forces, JFK continued, would be in a position to invade "as quickly as we possibly can" and he pulled no punches, reading out loud from an intelligence report that the Soviets "do not expect this blockade to include Russian ships because this would mean war. . . . *So*, we may have the war by the next twenty-four hours." And, of course, "if the Soviet Union, as a reprisal, should grab Berlin in the morning, which they could do within a couple of hours, our war plan at that point has been to fire our nuclear weapons at *them*. So that these are all the matters which are... which we have to be thinkin' about. . . ."

The President's summation seemed to make Senator Russell even more combative: "Excuse me again, but do you see a time *ever* in the future when Berlin will *not* be hostage to this?" When JFK bluntly replied, "No," Russell declared brusquely that Berlin would remain a hostage in any case and sharply demanded that the President put up or shut up: "And if we're gonna back up on that, we might as well pull our horns in from Europe and save 15 to 25 billion dollars a year and just prepare to defend this continent. We've *got* to take a chance somewhere, sometime, if we're gonna re... retain our position as a great world power."

Russell even challenged the President's judgment of the military situation, recalling that "the last time we met here," presumably at a discussion of the possible deployment of missiles in Cuba, General Le-

---

[134]As discussed earlier, the U.S.S.R. and Cuba were also aware of these "contingency" invasion plans. (Talbott, ed., *Khrushchev: The Last Testament*, 510) McNamara's admission also provides striking confirmation of the documentary evidence subsequently unearthed by scholars. (see Hershberg, "Before 'The Missiles of October,'" 163–98)

May "said that he could get in under this radar and knock out *all* these installations. . . . he said it unequivocally. I talked to him about it later." The Georgia senator explained, however, that he thought the Navy and the Marines "could do a much better job on knocking 'em out with conventional weapons." "Now let me just answer that, senator," JFK shot back, likely irritated at having LeMay's name thrown at him. The President then broke his own embargo on revealing the details about the military options debated during the past week: he candidly reviewed the arguments against air strikes—the inability to destroy all the sites in an unannounced Pearl Harbor–type bombing attack and the risk of sparking a nuclear war if the Soviets retaliated in Turkey and the Jupiter missiles were launched against the U.S.S.R.

As a parting shot, Russell cited the President's pledge to act alone against the threat from Cuba even if the OAS refused to stand up with us:

"Now I understand," he remarked sarcastically, "that we're still waitin' while the secretary of state uh... tries to get *them* to... to agree to it."

"I'm not waitin'," Kennedy interjected sharply.

Russell finally backed off: "I'm through. Excuse me. I wouldn't have been honest with myself if I hadn't . . . So I hope you forgive me, but I... you asked for opinions . . ."

"Well, I forgive you," Kennedy broke in defensively, obviously trying to control his exasperation, "but it's a very difficult problem we're faced with. I'll just tell you that. It's a very difficult choice that we're facing together."

"*Oh, my God!* I know that," Russell exclaimed, not even letting the President finish. "Our authority and the world's destiny will hinge on this decision. But it's comin' someday, Mr. President. Will it ever be under more auspicious circumstances?" Citing Russia's preoccupation with the outbreak of war between Communist China and India, the Georgian declared, "I *don't* see how we gonna be better off next year, foolin' with the Organization of American States. I assume this blockade *will* be effective for a while 'til they make up their minds to try to force their way through."[135]

Kennedy pointedly ignored Russell's apocalyptic prophesy, but de-

---

[135]Senator Russell and General LeMay shared this view: "If there is to be war," LeMay had remarked, "there's no better time than the present. We are prepared and 'the bear' is not." (Brugioni, *Eyeball to Eyeball*, 377)

fended the administration's effort to get OAS backing for the blockade: "It's foolish to just kick the whole Rio Treaty out the window," he asserted. "Well, I don't wanna do that!" Russell protested. The President then reemphasized that the blockade would go forward legally with OAS support, or with a declaration of war or even illegally if the OAS refused, but the final judgment on an invasion would not be made until the military/diplomatic situation could be reassessed later in the week. "I understand the force of *your* arguments," JFK conceded, reminding Russell again "if we invade, we take the uh... risk, which we have to be conscious of, that these weapons will be fired."

The stress level in the room gradually diminished as several members of Congress asked about consultations with the NATO allies. Congressman Halleck, however, asked for clarification of a key point: "are we *absolutely* positive from these photos," he pressed the President, that the Soviet buildup, previously described as defensive, had now become offensive?

"Yes," JFK answered.

"We're sure of that?" Halleck repeated.

"That's correct," was the President's definitive reply.

McNamara assured Halleck, "you might question the missiles, but you can't question the IL-28s."

"What are they? What's an IL-28?" Halleck inquired.

Jet bombers, the defense secretary explained, "capable of carrying a 4,000-pound bomb load, 740 miles radius of action. . . . we haven't seen it [a missile site] with the warhead actually in place and you *might* possibly have some question in your mind about it. But you can't have *any* question in your mind about the IL-28 bombers. These without *any doubt whatsoever* are offensive weapons."

McCone, evidently irritated that his judgment about offensive missiles had been questioned, responded firmly: "I think the evidence that these are offensive weapons is... is conclusive, *except* for the fact that we *do not* have, *which I said*, positive knowledge that the warhead is actually there." Senator Russell came to McCone's defense, cautioning that the warheads would never be stored in an open or exposed place "where you could pick up the picture of it." In response to a question about whether the blockade would be interpreted by Russia as an act of war," JFK replied candidly, "They may or they may not or they may then put a blockade on Berlin. That would be... I don't think there is any doubt that they're gonna threaten us."

At that point, the meeting was interrupted as the President was handed a letter from British prime minister Macmillan, who had been briefed on the buildup and the blockade by U.S. ambassador David Bruce. Kennedy astutely chose to share the letter with the congressional leaders by reading it out loud: Macmillan pledged his support for the blockade, but urged the U.S. to prepare "the best legal case" for the United Nations Security Council debate. The prime minister speculated on possible Soviet responses in the Caribbean, in Turkey and "more likely in Berlin." But, he implored the President, Europeans had lived so long "in close proximity to the enemy's nuclear weapons of the most devastating kind that we have got accustomed to it. So European opinion will need attention." Finally, he cautioned, Khrushchev "will of course try to trade his Cuba position against his ambition in Berlin and elsewhere. This we must avoid at all costs, as it will endanger the unity of the Alliance." The letter must have been very gratifying to the President since he had repeatedly raised Macmillan's key concerns since the first day of the ExComm discussions.

There were, surprisingly, no comments on Macmillan's letter and the discussion quickly returned to the blockade and the President's speech. Massachusetts Republican Leverett Saltonstall suggested downplaying the illegality of a blockade launched without OAS support. The President assured his former senior Senate colleague, just as he had told Senator Russell minutes earlier, that the quarantine could be sanctioned by an OAS vote or by a declaration of war, but "we'll do it anyway"—perhaps with the assistance of some OAS ships if they endorsed it. Everett McKinley Dirksen, the sonorous GOP Senate Minority Leader, softly asked, "Mr. President, what will you cover in the speech?" JFK summarized the main points: the missile buildup, "the double-dealing of the Russian statements," this "basic change in Soviet strategy," the U.S. demand for removal of the missiles and "telling the Cubans that they've been sold out." But, he stressed, "I think it would be a *great mistake* to talk about invasion"—even though preparations were moving forward.

The President tried to placate his most vocal critic: "But, as I say," he began, "I appreciate the," pausing for several seconds to find the appropriate words, "the vigor and the strength of what Senator Russell feels and says." But the strategy failed: Russell renewed his attack, arguing again that delaying the invasion would allow Khrushchev to threaten war and stir up "a tremendous row in this hemisphere between the nations here." In that event, he added, calling into question the President's commitment to stay the course, "we'd be much more likely to have to abandon the venture completely, which I greatly feel we will before we're through."

Kennedy attempted a reply, "As I understand it, senator, your . . . ," but Russell cut him off with an uncompromising admonition: "You know, the right of self-defense is pretty elemental, and... and you relied on that in... in your... in that very *telling* statement you made. You relied on that, the right of self-defense, and that's what we'd be doin'."

Suddenly, another influential southern Democrat, Senator J. William Fulbright, weighed in against the President's chosen course of action.[136] An invasion, he insisted, was *less* risky: "I mean legally. I mean it's just between us and Cuba. I think a blockade is the... is the *worst* of the alternatives because if you're confronted with a Russian ship, you *are* actually confronting Russia." An invasion against Cuba "is not actually an affront to Russia. . . . They're [Cuba] not part of the Warsaw Pact."

The listener can almost feel JFK's incredulity about Fulbright's circuitous logic; the President tried again to raise the specter of the "immediate seizure of Berlin," but Fulbright persisted that it would be better to try for solution at the U.N. or invade Cuba: "A blockade seems to me the *worst* alternative." McNamara intervened to remind the Arkansas senator that McCone had already reported that the missile sites were occupied almost exclusively by Russians; an invasion would first require 2,000 air sorties directly against some 8,000 Soviet military personnel.[137]

"That's *quite* different," Fulbright maintained confidently; "they're in Cuba. And Cuba... Cuba still is supposed to be a sovereign country. It isn't a member of the Warsaw Pact. It's not even a satellite. . . . It's just a communist country."

[136]Kennedy had seriously considered asking Fulbright to serve as secretary of state, but decided against it because the Arkansas senator had signed the "Southern Manifesto" opposing the Supreme Court's unanimous 1954 ruling on school desegregation.

[137]JFK's estimate of the number of Soviet military personnel in Cuba highlights one of the most egregious and dangerous American intelligence failures of the missile crisis. General Anatoli I. Gribkov confirmed at the January 1992 Havana Conference that more than 42,000 Soviet troops had already been brought secretly to Cuba by the time of President Kennedy's October 22 speech. (Blight, *et al.*, *Cuba on the Brink*, 58–61) Sergo Mikoyan, personal secretary to his father, First Deputy Premier Anastas Mikoyan, actually floated the 42,000 figure at the 1987 Cambridge Conference. (Blight and Welch, *On the Brink*, 241, 382) JFK's estimate of 8,000 troops was consistent with the latest intelligence reports, although that number was revised to 12,000 to 16,000 by November 19. When U Thant visited Cuba in late October to try (unsuccessfully) to arrange for U.N. inspection of the removal of the missiles, he was told that only 5,000 Soviet troops were on the island. (Garthoff, *Reflections*, 18–20, 35–36)

Finally, his patience clearly strained, JFK asked, "What are you in favor of, Bill?"

"I'm in favor," Fulbright asserted, "on the basis of this information, of an invasion, and an all-out one, and as quickly as possible." Senator Russell must have been gratified, but remained silent.

The President objected, "you can't have a more confrontation than invasion of Cuba." But the senator pressed on: "They're *Cuban* sites. They're not *Russian* sites," and attacking Cuba was not the same as attacking Russia. "And you sink a Russian ship, this is a... is a *real* first shot. . . . But *firing* against Cuba is *not* the same as *firing* against Russia. I don't think a blockade is the... is the right way *at all*." He challenged the President to live up to his September 13 statement that the U.S. would do whatever must be done to protect its security in the event of an offensive buildup in Cuba. "An attack on a Russian ship," he reiterated, "is really an atta... an act of war against Russia. It is *not* an act of war against Russia to... to... to attack Cuba."

The President, clearly frustrated, reminded the Senate Foreign Relations Committee chairman of three key points: a blockade endorsed by the OAS would not be an act of war; the Soviet missiles in Cuba might be fired at the U.S. in response to an invasion; American forces would be directly attacking 8,000 Russians: "We are gonna have to shoot *them* up. And I think that it would be *foolish*," JFK challenged the former Rhodes Scholar, "to expect that the Russians would not regard that as a *far* more direct thrust . . . And I think that the inevitable result will be immediately the seizure of Berlin. Now, as I say, we may have to put up with all that, and uh... But uh... I think that if we're talkin' about nuclear war, then escalation ought to be at least with some degree of control." Of course, JFK acknowledged, it was offensive to the Russians to have their ships stopped, but "When you start talking about the invasion, it's infinitely *more* offensive."

"But *not* to the *Russians*, it seems to me," Fulbright persisted doggedly. "They have no... they have no right to say that you've had an attack on Russia. I don't see that they have." One of Fulbright's congressional colleagues objected, "Well, I can't quite agree, Bill."

"Well...," JFK muttered, in evident exasperation. "In the meanwhile," he confirmed, as he turned to arranging further contacts with the leaders of Congress, "we ought to be assembling all our forces." Senator Dirksen questioned McNamara about the availability of amphibious craft for a landing in Cuba, prompting the cantankerous Senator Russell, only days away from his 65th birthday, to grumble, "Would you speak a little louder, Everett? Some of us are getting old." McNamara assured the Illinois senator that amphibious craft were available and, after reviewing two alternative invasion plans, promised that either plan would lead to victory.

The President, as the tense meeting wound down, reemphasized that he was not sure that *any* strategy would lead to a peaceful resolution of the crisis: "It [the blockade] provides for the beginning of an escalation. I don't know where Khrushchev wants to take us," he admitted, especially in Berlin: "Let me just say that I said at the beginning that the person whose course of action is *not* adopted is the best off. . . . Some people would say, 'well, let's go in with an air strike.' You'd have those bombs [missiles] go off and blow up... up 15 cities in the United States. And they would have been *wrong*. . . . and you can *not* invade and have a worse situation and maybe encourage Khrushchev. You can invade and have those bombs go off and have him also seize Berlin. . . .The people who are the best off," he again reflected fatalistically, "are the people whose advice is not taken because *whatever* we do is *filled* with hazards."

"I'll say this to Senator Fulbright," Kennedy continued, expressively underscoring the predicament before them: "we don't know where we're gonna end up on this matter. Ambassador Thompson has felt *very* strongly that the Soviet Union would regard, will regard, the attack on these SAM sites and missile bases with the killing of four or five thousand Russians as a... as a greater provocation than the stopping of their ships. Now, who knows that? We've talked to Ambassador Bohlen; we've talked to Ambassador Thompson. We just tried to make good judgments about a matter on which everyone's uncertain. But at least that—at least it's the best advice we could get. So we *start* here, we don't know where he's gonna take us or where we're gonna take ourselves. . . . And I *quite* agree with Senator Russell, Khrushchev's gonna make the *strongest* statements, which we're gonna have to just ignore, about everything: if we stop one Russian ship, it means war! If we invade Cuba, it means war! There's no telling—I know all the threats are gonna be made."

"Now just wait, Mr. President," Senator Russell interjected again, "the nettle is gonna sting anyway..."

"That's correct," Kennedy acknowledged. "Now I just think at least we *start* here, then we see where we go. . . . I gotta go and make this speech."

Senator Hubert Humphrey of Minnesota, who had been one of JFK's principal rivals for the 1960 Democratic presidential nomination, inquired about a possible U.N.-sponsored conference with Khrushchev. The President explained that the U.S. was asking the U.N. "for withdrawal of these missiles," but suggested that the Jupiter missiles in Turkey and Italy could "complicate our posture to the world. . . . It's gonna make it more difficult."[138]

Finally, House Minority leader Halleck, a tough and partisan Republican, offered a surprising statement of support to the besieged commander-in-chief: "Mr. President, could I make just one . . . I didn't know what I was called in for. Happy to come. I'm glad you asked me. *I* don't have the background information to make these decisions. *You* do. And I've been glad to speak a piece or two here, but... uh... uh... whatever you decide to do . . ."

"Well, I appreciate that," the President replied gratefully.

"I guess that's it," Halleck concluded.[139]

John F. Kennedy switched off the tape recorder and headed for the Oval Office. He could not have failed to notice that all the congressional flak had come from southern Democrats. Sorensen recalled that the President emerged from the meeting "very disturbed" and muttered that "if they thought they could do the job better than he could, they could have it; it was no great joy to him." RFK also noticed the President's exasperation after the meeting. However, JFK soon cooled off, conceding that the tough stance by several congressional leaders, quite understandably, was much like the first responses by the ExComm on October 16. A few days later he told an aide, "The trouble is that, when you get a group of senators together, they are always dominated by the man who takes the boldest and strongest line. This is what hap-

[138]On the contrary, the Jupiter missiles in Turkey later provided an indispensable bargaining chip for resolving the crisis.

[139]Halleck reportedly pledged his support just before the meeting began, but, with an eye on the upcoming midterm elections, told the President that he wanted the record to show that he had been informed but not consulted. After the meeting, Halleck returned to his office and was quoted as telling an aide, "You remember my prediction a month ago? I said he'll pull the rug out from under the Republicans on the Cuba issue. Well, that's what he's done." (*Newsweek*, November 5, 1962) However, the tape reveals a very different side of Halleck; in this very private moment, not knowing he was being recorded, human empathy apparently outweighed politics. Halleck was plainly impressed by the terrible choices facing the President, and their parting exchange is one of the most unexpected and personal moments on the ExComm tapes.

pened the other day. After Russell spoke, no one wanted to take issue with him. When you talk to them individually, they are reasonable."[140]

At 6:00 P.M., Dean Rusk met with Soviet ambassador Dobrynin at the State Department and handed him an advance copy of the President's speech and a cover letter from JFK to Khrushchev; the letter was also wired to U.S. Ambassador Foy Kohler in Moscow for delivery to the Kremlin. Rusk warned Dobrynin that the U.S.S.R. had made a serious miscalculation and later recalled that Dobrynin aged "ten years in front of my eyes," confirming administration suspicions that he had been kept in the dark by his own government. Rusk told the stunned ambassador that the U.S. government had no intention of publishing the President's letter, but would inform Moscow if this decision had to be changed. Dobrynin reportedly looked sick as he left the State Department.[141]

The President's speech, which of course did not mention American covert action in Cuba, set off alarm bells in the Kremlin. Earlier in the day, as he awaited word from the White House, Khrushchev had grimly told his closest associates, "They can attack us, and we shall respond. This may end in a big war." Poised for an apparently imminent American attack on Cuba, he later recalled, "I slept on a couch in my office—and I kept my clothes on. I was ready for alarming news to come any moment and I wanted to be ready to react immediately." When the President walked out of the Oval Office after his talk, the American people and the world finally knew that the superpowers had been teetering on the edge of nuclear Armageddon for nearly a week. The "flaming crisis" prophesied by Dean Rusk was at hand.[142]

The American public reacted to the President's speech with genuine concern and some signs of panic. Food and emergency supplies rapidly disappeared from the shelves of supermarkets and hardware stores. Long lines were reported at gasoline stations and there was a sudden run on tires. People across America stood in silent, worried clumps around newsstands, grabbing papers as soon as they were thrown from

[140]Sorensen Oral History Interview, 59; Robert Kennedy, *Thirteen Days*, 43; Schlesinger, *A Thousand Days*, 812.

[141]For the State Department cable on Rusk's meeting with Dobrynin as well as JFK's letter and speech, see Chang and Kornbluh, *Cuban Missile Crisis*, 156–64, 378; *New York Times*, October 23, 1962.

[142]Fursenko and Naftali, *"One Hell of a Gamble,"* 241, 248; Talbott, ed., *Khrushchev Remembers*, 497.

delivery trucks and anxiously reading the latest headlines. At Phillips Academy in Andover, Massachusetts and at the Mount Hermon School in Northfield to the west, students received phone calls from their parents urging them to come home to be with their families—just in case.[143]

Ambassadors from the Organization of American States were briefed at the Department of State that evening by Edwin Martin and U. Alexis Johnson; Dean Rusk and Roger Hilsman then updated the rest of the diplomatic core. "I would not be candid and I would not be fair with you," Rusk admitted, "if I did not say that we are in as grave a crisis as mankind has been in."[144] *At one or two A.M., after another exhausting day, Dean Rusk and Harlan Cleveland, assistant secretary of state for international organization affairs, prepared to go home to get a few hours of sleep. Cleveland wished the secretary a good night and casually remarked, "I'll see you in the morning." Rusk replied, "I hope so." Cleveland later recalled that he had been so busy, that "the full enormity" of the situation "hadn't hit me until that moment." These sobering words, coming from the usually reticent and imperturbable Rusk, struck Cleveland as the emotional "equivalent of screaming."*[145]

American intelligence continued to monitor Soviet military activity throughout the night but failed to detect any imminent moves against Berlin or the Jupiter missile sites in Turkey. The President's speech had ended the secret phase of the crisis and low-altitude photographic missions would soon begin over Cuba. The low-level flights confirmed many new details about Soviet operations in Cuba and the President was amazed by the clarity and detail of the photos produced by these risky new missions.

Khrushchev's initial response to Kennedy's speech was angry and confrontational: he ordered Soviet ships approaching the blockade line "to ignore it and to hold course for the Cuban ports." Fortunately, with U.S. forces at DEFCON 3 and SAC bombers in the air 24 hours a day, loaded with nuclear weapons targeted for specific sites in the Soviet Union, deputy premier Anastas Mikoyan was able to modify the order, arranging for the ships to stop just before reaching the quarantine line, thus narrowly averting a potentially deadly naval clash be-

---

[143]Discussion with Edwin G. Quattlebaum III, Phillips Academy history faculty.
[144]Cited in Chang and Kornbluh, *Cuban Missile Crisis*, 379.
[145]Harlan Cleveland Oral History Interview, 1978, OHC JFKL, 34.

tween the superpowers. The Soviets nonetheless placed Warsaw Pact forces on full alert and cancelled all pending discharges from the Strategic Rocket Forces, air defense units and the submarine fleet.[146]

Early the next morning, the OAS began debating whether to endorse the naval quarantine, the United Nations Security Council prepared for an emergency afternoon session and President Kennedy and the Ex-Comm convened in the Cabinet Room. It was no longer necessary to meet in the Executive Mansion to maintain secrecy and throw the press off the scent; the remaining meetings were held in the Cabinet Room and, fortunately for the historical record, they were all recorded.

Tuesday, October 23, 10:00 A.M., Cabinet Room

Identified Participants: John F. Kennedy, George Ball, McGeorge Bundy, Roswell Gilpatric, Lyndon Johnson, U. Alexis Johnson, Robert Kennedy, Arthur Lundahl, John McCone, Robert McNamara, Dean Rusk, Theodore Sorensen, Maxwell Taylor, Llewellyn Thompson, Jerome Wiesner.[147]

"Well, my God! . . . I think it was *very* significant that we were here this morning. We've passed the *one* contingency: an immediate, sudden, irrational [nuclear] strike [by the U.S.S.R.]."

Secretary of State Dean Rusk

McCone, before JFK actually turned on the tape recorder, discussed important new evidence confirming that Soviet rather than Cuban personnel were in charge of the missile sites and that some 50% of the MiG fighters in Cuba were piloted by Russians. JFK hit the on switch just in time to catch the jarring sound of the Cabinet Room door being slammed shut. With McCone talking in the background, Robert Kennedy said softly to his brother, "Should I go now?" and JFK replied, "Yeah, you might as well get that over with now because I was thinking we'll probably need John McCone . . ."[148]

The CIA chief went on to review the aerial photographs taken over the previous twenty-four hours, revealing new Soviet efforts to extensively camouflage the missiles. "There's *one* panel that would interest

[146]Blight and Welch, *On the Brink*, 306; Chang and Kornbluh, *Cuban Missile Crisis*, 381, 383.

[147]Tapes 34.1, 34.1A, 34.2 & 35.1, POF, PRC, JFKL.

[148]The Kennedy brothers appear to have agreed in advance to reopen the issue of explaining publicly why the missile sites had not been discovered sooner. RFK had also raised this problem twice at the previous day's meetings.

you," he told the President, pointing out that three launchers at the most advanced MRBM site were no longer visible. "I'd like you to see those pictures."

Now that the crisis was out in the open, however, RFK, as intimated above, reopened the tricky political issue he had raised at earlier meetings—how to deal with inevitable Republican charges of duplicity or incompetence for not having responded much sooner in Cuba. He was concerned that the blockade would be perceived as too little, too late, and, in a worried tone of voice, suggested that the President might be accused of "closing the barn door after the horse is gone."

"I'm having Senator Keating's statements analyzed," JFK responded. "Actually, they're quite inaccurate." But, he nonetheless recommended that "somebody in a responsible position ought to take up this question" so that the administration can respond effectively. "I don't think it's realized [by the public and the press] how quickly these mobile bases can be set up and how quickly they can be moved." President Kennedy, eager to manage the news as effectively as possible, cautioned that reporters like Arthur Krock of the *New York Times* were already beginning to sniff around for additional information.[149]

McNamara reported that he had briefed 125 journalists the previous night, off the record, but recommended additional briefings for congressional leaders and reporters "who will be asking this kind of a question," and singled out Michigan Republican congressman Gerald Ford and "the Scotty Restons."[150] Vice President Johnson suggested that McCone should also brief Senators Russell and Fulbright, and, perhaps trying to ease JFK's exasperation from the previous evening, recounted, "I saw your speech with 'em last night and I think that the attitude was much *better* than was indicated here," particularly once you made clear that "you were gonna prevent the use of these missiles against us." Johnson subtly faulted the President for not explaining this point more carefully at the congressional briefing, "We didn't quite say that in the meetin' yesterday and they didn't get everything in the meetin' they got

[149]Arthur Krock, long-time confidant of Ambassador Joseph P. Kennedy, was instrumental in getting JFK's Harvard senior honors thesis revised and published as *Why England Slept* in 1940. But, by 1961, JFK was no longer particularly friendly with the conservative journalist.

[150]Ford was appointed late in 1963 to the Warren Commission investigating the assassination of President Kennedy. In 1973, he was named Vice President of the United States under the terms of the 25th Amendment and became President in 1974 after the resignation of Richard Nixon. James "Scotty" Reston was a respected *New York Times* journalist.

from your speech and McCone can give 'em a good deal more. I tried to give 'em a little bit myself later, after the speech." Johnson's words suggest that he did attend the October 22nd congressional briefing—although he never spoke. But, his use of "We" rather than "You" may have been calculated to soften his criticism of JFK for not making his case convincingly enough with the congressional leaders.[151]

The President was essentially orchestrating a public relations offensive to blunt any criticism from the House and Senate or the press and urged McCone to meet again with key members of Congress suggested by LBJ. He also asked McNamara about scheduling an on-the-record press conference later in the day and the defense secretary recommended waiting until after the signing of the quarantine proclamation. But, evidently put off by the hostile responses from Russell and Fulbright the previous evening, JFK added, "I don't think we oughta bring in too many [members of Congress]. They just feed on each other," and also asked whether there were "any members of the press who are of particular significance who John McCone oughta talk to."[152] He asked McCone to use his judgment but also offered to personally suggest "some of these *special* people that we think ought to get some *special* time today." McCone offered to call former President Eisenhower to "get permission from *him* to use *his* name in talking with these congressional people" and to get "his view of this thing as a soldier."

A consensus emerged that anyone speaking for the administration should stress the mobility of the missiles but avoid answering specific questions about what might be done about the sites already in Cuba or whether an invasion was planned. McNamara mentioned that during his press briefing the previous evening he had been pushed five times for these details but simply repeated the President's promise to take whatever action "is required to accomplish our objective." Ball agreed and Bundy contended, "It is of *great* importance, unless we get a *clear-cut* decision around *this* table to change," and he tapped the table for emphasis, "*we stay right with the President's speech,*" leaving open any and all diplomatic and military options. Two new Soviet statements,

[151]Senator George Smathers, however, definitely did attend and believed, "The President handled it masterfully." (Smathers Oral History, 12)

[152]Among the journalists targeted were Reston, Krock, Walter Lippmann, Stewart Alsop, Alfred Friendly of the *Washington Post*, columnist William S. White, Hanson Baldwin of the *New York Times* and *Washington Post* publisher Philip Graham. Several participants, including JFK, chuckled at the mention of Krock, and Kennedy teased McCone, "maybe you're a friend of his."

Bundy reported, were "just coming over the ticker" from Moscow, and the President asked if "my letter to Khrushchev," accompanying the speech, had been released to the public. Bundy responded testily, "*No sir*. We *told* Khrushchev that we would *not* do so." RFK advised, "I think probably you can get by with this for... this answer [about the missiles already in Cuba] for about 24 hours, but we're gonna have difficulty after that." Bundy disagreed, "In the broader sense, I don't think the country's reaction is that we've done too little."[153]

The President, evidently thinking about tightening the blockade, proposed, despite his negative view of their performance before the Bay of Pigs, a CIA analysis of "what the effects of a blockade of everything but food and medicine would be on Cuba, given their known supplies, and what it would do to the country's economy, and what the political effects would be in Cuba, as well as outside." "Do we want that," RFK queried, "on Berlin too?" JFK, always preoccupied with Berlin, quickly agreed that it would be valuable to know "what the effect would be of a blockade in Berlin *by them*." RFK murmured, "Of the same kind."

Arthur Lundahl, elaborating on McCone's earlier briefing, reviewed the previous day's photos which showed that several MRBM launchers were no longer visible, "And where they might have gone, we don't know at the present time." He speculated that they might be hidden in the trees or "They could have been moved quickly to another locale." The photos strengthened JFK's conviction that stressing the mobility of the missiles could help defuse charges that they should have been discovered earlier. McNamara reassured the President that he had already briefed the press on the differences between MRBMs and IRBMs and had explained that "the MRBMs are mobile and that we estimated that they could be *set up*, *torn down*, *moved* and *set up again* in a 6-day period. And *this* was why it was only this week that this information became available." "Let's get that on the record," Kennedy affirmed eagerly and the defense chief replied that he had a taped transcript of the briefing. McNamara also boasted that 25 sets of new U-2 photos had been processed in just one day in order to target the missiles in Cuba for air strikes; the President, evidently impressed, responded, "OK. Do you mind if I have these?"

Lundahl and McCone confirmed that photo reconnaissance now

---

[153] A Gallup poll on October 23 revealed that 84% of the American people supported the blockade and only 4% opposed it. However, 20% also believed the quarantine would bring on World War III. (David Detzer, *The Brink: Cuban Missile Crisis, 1962* (New York: Crowell, 1979), 192)

covered 97% of Cuba. McNamara stressed that the quarantine proclamation should be issued as soon as possible after OAS action[154] and
should be effective at dawn the next day [October 24] in order to intercept the first ship, the *Kimovsk,* which had hatches large enough to
carry these missiles.

JFK seemed skeptical: "Wouldn't you guess that anything that has a
missile on it would be turned around last night?" McNamara agreed,
but nevertheless reasoned that "we would like to have the first ship either turned around or stopped if found to have offensive weapons, one
or the other. . . . If they *don't* turn around and we... we search and
find offensive weapons on board, it's successful. What we wish to
avoid is intercepting one of the other ships that may *not* have offensive
weapons on it." The President repeated his assumption that any ship
carrying offensive weapons would likely be turned around. The defense
secretary also revealed that the seizure of ships would not be limited to
a specific zone, "We'll intercept any place where it appears that the
ship is moving toward Cuba," but he reaffirmed that the most unfortunate outcome would be to disable a ship that refused to stop and find
"it didn't have offensive weapons on it. That would be a poor way to
start." "A poor way to start," RFK repeated in the background.

Quite abruptly, the President, clearly still vexed about the prospect
raised earlier by RFK of politically damaging Monday morning quar-
terback attacks from the press, the Congress and the NATO allies *after*
a confrontation at sea, vehemently declared that the crisis could not
have been avoided: "There's no action we *ever* could have taken, unless
we'd invaded Cuba a year ago, to prevent them being there. . . . So
there's *no answer* to this unless you're gonna invade Cuba, *six* months
ago, or *a* year ago, or *two* years ago, or *three* years ago! That's... that's
the uh—and... and the *fact* of the matter is there wasn't *anybody* who
suggested an invasion of Cuba *at a time* when they *necessarily* could
have *stopped these things coming onto the island*!"

JFK, clearly on edge, again revealed his pragmatic, if not fatalistic,
realism: "So that... what *we* are doing is throwing down a card on the
table in a game which we don't know the ending of. . . . We recognize
that the missiles are already there. But we also recognize that there's
not a *damn thing* anybody could do about the missiles being there unless we invade Cuba at the time of the Bay of Pigs or a previous Cuban
invasion the year before. . . . Some of that you can't put on the record,

---

[154]The OAS debated and unanimously endorsed the quarantine later that day.

but it's a *very* legitimate point. There was no way we could *stop* this *happening*." [155]

JFK further remarked, with unmistakable annoyance, that the British press was also attacking the quarantine decision, "The *Manchester [Guardian]* and the whole lot of the British press are not even with us *today*." Bundy laughed while dryly observing, "Today we get the *Manchester Guardian*, Mr. President, we're wrong!" "Okay. Yeah. Okay," JFK replied, disdainfully amused.

This somewhat lighthearted moment evaporated quickly as Mc-Namara, rather officiously, yanked the discussion back to the serious business at hand. The defense secretary urged the President to sign an executive order extending the tours of duty of Navy and Marine personnel on active duty. "This will require or I think can best be done by an executive order signed by you. I have such an executive order here. I will leave it with Ted Sorensen to bring to your attention today. We *should* have it signed today and we will issue that." "Right," JFK murmured softly. Bundy also asked if international law specified "the amount of notice" required for implementing a blockade and Mc-Namara disclosed that Defense Department lawyers had concluded that a proclamation signed that night would become legally effective the following morning.

McNamara then brought up a far more dangerous issue—which the President had first raised at the afternoon meeting on the previous day—deciding on a U.S. response "to a U-2 accident" over Cuba—that is, to a U-2 either off course or shot down by a SAM missile. He explained that the Strategic Air Command was monitoring the U-2s "minute-by-minute" and would be required to immediately inform the Joint Chiefs of any deviation from course, "particularly if it's shot down." He reported confidently that this information would be available "*literally* 15 minutes after the incident." McNamara emphasized to the President that plans were in place, "if you decide to instruct them to do so," to have about 8 U.S. aircraft destroy the SAM site, "*if* that *is* your decision," within 2 hours, "so that we could announce *almost* simultaneously the loss of the U-2 and the destruction of the SAM site that allegedly destroyed it."

The President, initially hesitant about approving military action *before* a specific incident, asked about sending escort planes to "*assure*

[155]Kennedy was clearly hinting, quite defensively, that the Eisenhower administration, the year *before* the Bay of Pigs, had also failed to take preemptive action in Cuba.

the cause of the accident," so that he could be certain that it resulted from hostile action rather than mechanical failure, and also inquired about whether plans were in place to pick up downed pilots in the ocean around Cuba. McNamara assured JFK that air-sea rescue aircraft were ready. The President still seemed doubtful about whether "we wanna indicate that [decision to retaliate] in advance." But, at least for the moment, he put his doubts aside: "I suppose what we do is, when we take out that SAM site, we announce that if any U-2 is shot down, we'll take out *every* SAM site." "Exactly," McNamara affirmed. General Taylor, however, advised the President that it was "highly unlikely that we can *really* identify the... the guilty SAM site." "I understand," JFK replied, and Taylor concluded, "That doesn't really matter, I don't think, however."

JFK asked if there were any questions on this point. McCone inquired whether an attack on the SAMs would be ordered based on information received from the plane over Cuba or whether verification would have to be obtained after the plane returned to base. "Information received from the airplane," McNamara affirmed. Bundy observed that since the decision to strike the SAM site(s) had to be made within 15 minutes after confirmation that a U-2 had been shot down, it was impossible to be certain that the President would be available:

"Do you want to delegate that authority *now*," Bundy asked, "to the Secretary of Defense or do you want to... a... well what is your ...?"

The President, characteristically cautious, replied, "Well, what we want to do is, I will delegate to the Secretary of Defense on the *understanding* that the information would be *very clear*, that the *accident* that happened was not a malfunction."

Bundy interrupted: "That it was *in fact* a matter of military action."

"Action against us," Kennedy reaffirmed.

"Only if you're unavailable," McNamara summed up, "and only if it's clear."

JFK and the ExComm recognized, of course, that the quarantine was only a first step—and a risky one at that. If it failed, military action might still have to be ratcheted up, and the President asked if the resolution being debated by the OAS would also sanction additional surveillance and even an invasion. Alexis Johnson and George Ball read aloud from the OAS resolution, which called for "*all* measures, individually and collectively . . . to prevent missiles and bases in Cuba with offensive capability from ever becoming active threats to the peace and security of the Continent." They assured the President that the resolution was broad enough to encompass practically anything under consideration by the administration.

McNamara, in that context, declared that plans were moving forward for all possible military contingencies: the Navy and the JCS, for example, were considering rules of engagement if it became necessary to intercept Soviet aircraft heading to Cuba. On air strikes against the missile sites, the defense chief contended, "We *do* believe we should have warning the night before, in preparation for a dawn strike, however. In an emergency, it could be done with less warning, but we would recommend against it *except* in an emergency." For the most complex option, invading Cuba, McNamara reported that 20 military ships were available but it might be necessary to charter or requisition 60–70% of the merchant cargo vessels in U.S. East Coast ports to obtain the 134 ships required for an invasion; in addition, some 300 military transport aircraft would have to be ready when the air strikes began—a week before actually starting the invasion. Some concern was expressed that the need for so many American ships could hamstring the commercial shipping industry. McCone, who had been a successful shipbuilder during World War II, pointed out that the Northwest lumber business, dependent on American-flag ships, might be lost to the Canadians. He recommended using ships from friendly foreign nations, but Taylor countered that the risks would be too great in an invasion. McNamara acknowledged that the shipping issue was very complicated and that no final decision had been made on chartering or requisitioning ships. McCone also warned that the "effect on the economy . . . could be *very*, very serious." The President recommended looking into invoking national emergency powers to get around federal legislation requiring many exporters to use American ships.[156]

The discussion then came full circle, returning to concerns about the credibility of the photographic evidence which had dominated the beginning of the meeting. McNamara advised excluding POL from the initial contraband list, but urged implementing low-level reconnaissance later that day "to establish the details of these missiles and to obtain the evidence to prove to a layman the existence of missiles in Cuba." JFK seemed doubtful about the immediate need for low-level

[156]The 1928 Jones-White Act supported the U.S. merchant marine by restricting the use of foreign vessels for exports except in a national emergency.

missions unless the film was essential "for tactical reasons. I think we've proved it to the layman." Bundy, however, insisted that the photos themselves are "becoming of *great* importance in the international debate" and mentioned that Ambassador Stevenson had called to say that photographic proof could be critical at the U.N. McNamara recommended gathering the necessary evidence with SAC low-level missions today "across the entire area" at an altitude of about 200 feet. The President seemed genuinely surprised: "There *is* a question about whether these things really exist?" Bundy argued that merely showing the pictures to journalists and friends, "without leaving them in people's hands and not making them available for publication," was no longer adequate, and endorsed Stevenson's request to display the pictures at the upcoming Security Council meeting. The ambassador had been humiliated by using CIA-doctored photos during the Bay of Pigs debate at the United Nations and now insisted on irrefutable proof for the new American allegations.[157]

Bundy reported that there was support at the U.N. for identifying missile site locations by naming specific towns in Cuba. JFK objected to naming locations on the grounds that the missiles could be moved. He preferred waiting until an agreement was reached allowing U.N. inspectors to actually go to Cuba. "We'd give away quite a lot," he warned, and Bundy proposed naming only the fixed sites. McCone backed Bundy, citing skepticism in the European press, especially in Britain and France, and particularly a statement from the president of Mexico that "'*if* the evidence was conclusive, the attitude of Mexico towards Castro and Cuba would change.' And I think we ought to get the conclusive evidence and I think this is the way to do it." President Kennedy agreed.

After some additional discussion about the dangers involved in conducting low-level surveillance missions, such as going in under radar, and whether an additional (10th) missile complex had been discovered in Cuba, JFK asked about a possible call up of reserves. McNamara advised extending the tours of regular Navy and Marine personnel, but urged delaying a call up of naval reserves: "There is *not* need for that as yet. We'd like to postpone it. It's an action that's difficult to re-

[157]CIA officers, including Ray Cline, deputy director for intelligence, went to the U.N. on October 24 to brief Stevenson on the photos. The justifiably skeptical ambassador cautioned, "I hope you are in a position to prove beyond a shadow of a doubt that the missiles exist in Cuba." (Ray Cline to Dino Brugioni, April 3, 1978, cited in Brugioni, *Eyeball to Eyeball*, 395)

verse." On the other hand, he added, "The extension of tours that we will propose tonight *can* be reversed very easily." "The question is, though," JFK responded, clearly determined to keep all options open, "if we're leading up to an invasion, whether we're doing all the things that we would have to do?" "We... we believe so," the defense chief avowed, adding that "the Reserves would *not* be used in the invasion."

The President, rather unexpectedly, launched into an uncharacteristic attempt at military micro-management. Almost certainly recalling the destruction of American planes parked closely together on airfields during the Japanese attack on Pearl Harbor, JFK alerted General Taylor, "Everybody's lived in peace so long" down in Florida that planes might be lined up like sitting ducks on military airfields. "Obviously they'll take a reprisal. I would... I should think one of their planes would strafe *us*." Taylor acknowledged that the airfields were congested, but replied that air defenses were being reinforced and General LeMay was sending one of his most experienced officers to Florida to assess the situation. The former junior naval officer, now commander-in-chief, recommended photographing the Florida fields that afternoon to assess the dangers from a reprisal if a SAM site had to be hit in Cuba. The JCS chairman explained that airfield space was limited and JFK unexpectedly replied, "Well, for example, they're using the West Palm Beach airport, I wonder? That's a hell of a military airport. And it hasn't been used much." Taylor had to admit, "No sir, I don't know." "There's a lot of barracks there, too," JFK remarked, "You might check on that. West Palm is a pretty good field and it was a big base in the war and it isn't used much now."[158] "We have to figure that if we *do* execute this plan we just agreed on this morning," the President continued, to strike a SAM site if a U-2 is shot down, planes from Cuba could "strafe our fields and we don't want 'em to shoot up *100 planes*." Taylor, almost contritely, explained, "This is one of these... one of these rather humorous examples of our over-sophistication of our weapons. We have everything except to deal with simple aircraft coming in low."[159] President Kennedy was evidently amused and some

[158]General Taylor seems to have been surprised and discomfited by the President's remarkably specific knowledge of military sites in Florida. However, the Kennedy family had owned an estate in Palm Beach since 1933, and part of JFK's PT boat training had been in Jacksonville. He had also been assigned to a PT base in Miami after his service in the South Pacific.

[159]For an earlier discussion of possible low-level air raids from Cuba, first raised by General Taylor, see the 6:30 P.M. meeting on Tuesday, October 16.

muted laughter can be heard just before the tape suddenly cut off or was turned off.

As the new tape began (President Kennedy may have been out of the room for several minutes), the discussion had returned to selecting and displaying intelligence photos for the United Nations debate later that day. Ball reported that Stevenson wanted "a large map marked in color, showing *at least* some of the sites [and] . . . photographs showing locations and dates, and not merely anonymous photographs." Bundy, hopeful that new low-level flights would provide "*much more* interesting and effective evidence tomorrow," expressed doubts that the Soviets would dare to challenge the photographic evidence. "And I would *invite* them to challenge it," the President concluded sharply. McNamara, as an alternative, proposed using photos from the annual Moscow May Day military parade. "All right. I'll tell you what let's do," JFK finally instructed. "Let's let Mr. McCone and Mr. Ball settle exactly what they ought to give them [at the U.N.] then, and under what conditions." McNamara, Bundy and others can be heard affirming "Right," "I agree," and "Okay."

JFK also observed that "if... if the Russians respond with some actions which make an invasion desirable or inevitable," the U.S. must be ready to move quickly. Taylor suggested that "the real... real problem is the shipping problem" and President Kennedy again advised the use of emergency powers to allow exports utilizing foreign ships. On the quarantine itself, Ambassador Thompson pondered a delay in stopping Soviet ships until the OAS had approved the blockade—hopefully by the next day. "The *point* is that they're [the Soviets] *much* less apt to run a legal blockade than they are an illegal one. I think that you might want to keep that in mind."[160] The President agreed, "Well, we'll be in touch if we're not gonna get it. We just gotta tell the OAS to get to it."

Thompson also reported that the ambassadorial group would meet later that afternoon to consider how to respond to possible Soviet actions against Berlin, such as more rigorous inspection of U.S. truck convoys. "I think we ought to accept that," JFK quickly replied, instinctively resisting a military confrontation, "That's my quick reaction. . . . I don't think we're in very good shape to have a big fight

[160]Thompson had made a similar point at the October 18 morning meeting, advising President Kennedy that the U.S.S.R. was less likely to challenge a blockade legitimized by a formal declaration of war (which JFK rejected).

about whether they inspect our trucks." Taylor suggested taking a hard look at the situation and Thompson proposed suspending the truck convoys; but the President rejected getting into a "pattern where it's tough to begin 'em again. I would rather have 'em inspecting them."

The meeting ended with an agreement to reconvene at 6 P.M. when new information would likely be available from the latest reconnaissance missions, as well as from the OAS and ambassadorial group meetings that afternoon. JFK added a plea to "Try to keep these meetings as brief as possible." As some participants, apparently including the President, were leaving the room, several partially audible conversations continued: Bundy advised putting together a senior planning group to study long-range problems that had not been considered by ExComm. "Contingencies and reactions thereto," McNamara interjected; "That's it, that's it," Bundy concurred, declaring that Nitze might "be the man to beat" as the choice to chair this effort. There was also a conversation about whether to release to the press the reconnaissance photos to be shown at the U.N. debate; McCone insisted that the pictures could not be reproduced very clearly in newspapers.

Only a few participants remained in the room and Ball was placing a call to Ambassador Stevenson, when Dean Rusk, who had been attending the emergency meeting of the Organization of American States, suddenly returned. The secretary of state, noticeably excited, announced, "you might want to just hear this." Ball hung up as Rusk reported that with the possible exception of an abstention by Mexico on one paragraph, "we'll have the resolution, with a *large* majority, by shortly after three. . . . they're really runnin' around." Several Ex-Comm members exclaimed, "Oh, gee," "Wonderful," "Oh, God," and "Oh, terrific, terrific." Rusk mentioned that he had told several OAS delegates that the resolution was vital since there could be naval contact that afternoon. McNamara observed that the quarantine could therefore begin at dawn tomorrow. "Yeah, but don't tell *them* that," Rusk joked. "No," McNamara replied against a background of laughter.[161]

Rusk, becoming somewhat more subdued, admonished his enthusiastic colleagues, "Don't smile too soon here, boys," but a relieved Alexis Johnson exclaimed that if the OAS voted before the Security Council meeting, "Oh, that's gonna be a big help. Mmm. Pshewwwww. Our diplomacy is working." Rusk nonetheless soberly reflected: "Well, my

[161]The quarantine went into effect at 10:00 on the following morning, October 24.

God! Well, as a matter of fact, I said to someone . . . I don't know what John McCone thinks of this, but I think it was *very* significant that we were here this morning. We've passed the *one* contingency: an immediate, sudden, irrational [nuclear] strike [by the U.S.S.R.]."[162] "Yeah, yeah, yeah, yeah," Johnson murmured. Laughter followed when Rusk added, rather whimsically, "Further news from the U.N. is that when I say we're here, that they're here [the Soviets] either." Everyone understood, despite Rusk's tortured grammar, his relief that they had all lived to see another day. Ball added that the Soviets were delaying the U.N. meeting to prepare their own resolution. "Tell the Security Council," McNamara teased, "we would be happy to evacuate them to Seattle or someplace"—the only area in the continental United States believed to be just outside the range of the Soviet IRBMs in Cuba. Alexis Johnson exulted as the laugher subsided, "Oh gee, that's... that's... that's great. Oh, that's great news. That's terrific. We *really* caught them with their contingencies down."

Rusk soon left and several conversations continued among the few advisers still in the room: Bundy revealed that the President and Secretary Rusk had asked Nitze to head a special ExComm working group on Berlin. Ball and McCone conversed by telephone with Stevenson about the missile photos at the U.N. The CIA chief urged the ambassador to be wary of revealing too much, especially "about our means" of gathering this intelligence, and advised that if the photos were given to any foreign delegates they must also be given to the press. On the other hand, he worried that "they're totally unconvincing" when reproduced in a newspaper. McCone relayed to Stevenson Thompson's proposal to show the photos to non-Communist ambassadors in Stevenson's office instead of compromising U.S. security by releasing them "into the public domain, which we don't wanna do." He also promised to arrange for Lundahl to go to New York to help prepare the presentation.

After hanging up, Ball and McCone agreed to have deputy CIA director for intelligence Ray Cline join Lundahl at the U.N. "George," McCone quipped, "the question I have on my mind is, if it's this hard to start a blockade around Cuba, *how the hell* did we ever start World War II?" A burst of laughter followed. McCone then talked to Cline by phone, speaking over the shouts of children playing outside on the

[162]Rusk later recalled waking up the morning after JFK's speech and saying to himself, "'Well, I'm still here. This is very interesting.' That meant that the immediate response of the Soviet Union was not a missile strike." (Rusk Oral History, 134)

White House grounds, and arranged for Cline to go to the U.N., explaining that Stevenson had unknowingly displayed faked pictures at the time of the Bay of Pigs, "So he's kind of in trouble up there."

Finally, McCone questioned Jerome Wiesner, JFK's special assistant for science and technology, who had been waiting to discuss upgrading communications between the U.S. and Latin America, about so-called "black box" technology which might be used for detecting nuclear weapons on Soviet ships and even for eventually verifying the withdrawal of nuclear weapons from Cuba. McCone also asked Wiesner to explore establishing 24-hour-a-day radio communications between Washington and key sites in Latin America. Wiesner expressed some doubt about the need for a 24-hour system but they agreed to take up with the State Department precisely what would be required to upgrade the network and find the additional operators needed for establishing 24-hour communications capacity.

These fragmentary conversations soon ended and the tape, except for some background hiss, became silent before finally running out.

The President soon acted on several of the matters which had been discussed (after his departure) in the rump portion of the morning meeting by setting up ExComm subcommittees on Berlin (chaired by Paul Nitze), on advance planning and on emergency communications.

Dean Rusk's optimism was soon confirmed when the OAS unanimously endorsed the quarantine proclamation. By the time the United Nations Security Council convened at 4:00 P.M., the rhetoric had begun to heat up on all sides: Adlai Stevenson condemned the secret deployment of missiles in Cuba as proof of Soviet plans for world domination; the Cuban government denounced the blockade as violation of international law and an act of war; the Soviet U.N. ambassador, Valerian Zorin, mocked the U.S. charges as false and malicious and reiterated that only defensive weapons were being sent to Cuba.

Khrushchev's first written response to the President's speech arrived that afternoon. He insisted that the American ultimatum threatened to ignite a nuclear world war and contended that the weapons in Cuba were "destined exclusively for defensive purposes" and intended to prevent aggression—a proposition never taken seriously within the Kennedy administration. He also rejected the right of any nation to search ships in international waters and urged the President to "show prudence" and pull back from piratical and aggressive actions against

Cuba and the U.S.S.R. that could have "catastrophic consequences for world peace."[163]

Robert Kennedy's secret Soviet contact, Georgi Bolshakov, mean-while received somewhat more hopeful back channel signals from meetings, actually encouraged by RFK, with journalists Frank Holeman (who had facilitated the first Bolshakov-RFK meeting in 1961) and Charles Bartlett. The two Washington insiders reported that the Kennedy administration was open to the possibility of a negotiated settlement which would include trading the Soviet missiles in Cuba for the American missiles in Turkey and Italy. Bolshakov's superiors in Washington delayed relaying this potentially critical information to Moscow until October 24.[164]

Khrushchev, however, to his great relief, learned early on October 24 (Moscow time) that a ship carrying nuclear warheads to Cuba, the Aleksandrovsk, *had arrived without incident at the port of La Isabela only hours before the implementation of the blockade.*[165]

Tuesday, October 23, 6:00 P.M., Cabinet Room

Identified Participants: John F. Kennedy, George Ball, McGeorge Bundy, Roswell Gilpatric, Robert Kennedy, John McCone, Robert McNamara, Paul Nitze, Steuart Pittman, Dean Rusk, Theodore Sorensen, Maxwell Taylor, Llewellyn Thompson.[166]

"Now what do we do tomorrow morning when these eight vessels continue to sail on? We're all clear about how we handle it?"
    "Shoot the rudders off of 'em, don't you?"

President John F. Kennedy and
CIA Director, John McCone

The tape began with a cacophony of conversations as the participants entered the room and took their places around the table. Bundy began

---

[163]Nikita Khrushchev to John F. Kennedy, October 23, 1962, *FRUS, 1961–1963, VI, Kennedy-Khrushchev Exchanges,* Document #61.

[164]Fursenko and Naftali, *"One Hell of a Gamble,"* 248–52; Bolshakov had not been forewarned about the missiles by his own government.

[165]*Ibid.,* 255; the *Aleksandrovsk* later participated in the removal of nuclear warheads from Cuba. (Raymond L. Garthoff, "Documenting the Cuban Missile Crisis," *Diplomatic History* 24 (2000), 300–301)

[166]Tapes 35.2, 36.1, 36.1A, & 36.2, POF, PRC, JFKL. A Defense Department lawyer, Mr. McDonald, was also present early in the meeting.

the discussion with a review of the quarantine proclamation, which had already been examined by legal experts from the State and Defense departments, but had to be formally reviewed "in the President's presence before it is *in fact* sent on its way."

The President immediately questioned why the draft of the proclamation referred to the shipment of offensive weapons to Cuba by the so-called Sino-Soviet powers. "The 'Sino-Soviet'? Is that proper," he asked, "to put the Chinese in? Is that necessary and wise?" Rusk replied that the term "Sino-Soviet powers" had been used in the OAS resolution adopted earlier that afternoon even though the actual target was the U.S.S.R. Kennedy still seemed uncertain: "Some reason to put 'Sino' in there? What are the effects of this gonna be when you put them back in today? What are you going to do about that?" No one at the table questioned the concept of monolithic international communism or brought up the increasing hostility between Communist China and the U.S.S.R.

For the moment, the President dropped the issue, and the room remained silent for some 30 seconds as the participants read through the draft proclamation and discussed the exact time of implementation. JFK questioned whether it was necessary in public statements to list specific items being interdicted (such as "land-based surface-to-surface missiles") and the Defense Department lawyer in attendance explained that the proclamation was the official, legal notice saying "this is the contraband or this is the illegal thing."

After some additional discussion on the precise language and specific weapons to be named in the final proclamation, JFK argued for leaving out some items (such as motor torpedo boats), "We can stop 'em anyway, can't we?" McNamara, backed by RFK, explained that the Secretary of Defense could issue specific instructions, identifying any particular offensive weapon, at any time after the quarantine became effective. McNamara kidded his colleagues about having the last word and ignited a round of laughter when he quipped, "Yes, I will issue an order tonight that includes the original language." Bundy, on a more serious note, spelled out, "we delegate to the Secretary of Defense the breadth of the blockade."

McNamara, however, raised a particularly thorny question— whether to pursue and board a Soviet ship which was hailed, refused to stop, and turned and headed away from Cuba. "It's both a legal question and a practical question," he observed. "The legal foundation of such an act is confused. As a practical matter, I *don't* believe we should undertake such an operation." "Not right now," the President affirmed and McNamara added, "Not immediately. That's right. So... so my instruction to the Navy was, '*Don't* do it.'"

"That's right," the President quickly agreed, "cause they'd be grabbing stuff that might be heading home." RFK countered that it would be "a *hell* of an advantage" to seize a vessel believed to be carrying missiles in order to examine and get pictures of the weapons. He did concede, however, "Maybe you don't want to do it for the first 48 hours." JFK acknowledged that a suspicious vessel should be seized, but reasoned again that "they're not gonna choose *this* to have the test case on—they're gonna *turn that thing around.*" McNamara noted that the particular ship now under scrutiny was 1,800 miles away from Cuba and JFK pointed out doubtfully that we'd "have to grab it there." McNamara repeated President Kennedy's words—and literally laughed at the prospect of seizing a ship so far from Cuba. The President's preference was obvious from his dubious tone of voice: "Do we want to grab it if they turned it around—at 1,800 miles away?" The defense secretary advised keeping tabs on the ship during the night and delaying a final decision.

It would be "damn helpful," RFK persisted, to examine Soviet weapons and equipment, but McNamara cautioned that the initial U.S. objective should be "to *grab* a vessel *obviously* loaded with offensive weapons." He revealed that "our prime target at the moment is the *Kimovsk*," the location of which had yet to be pinpointed, but it probably could be intercepted the following morning much closer to Cuba. Rusk, uneasy about RFK's proposal, argued that it would be very difficult to distinguish a ship that was actually turning around from one "that is gonna play... play cats and mice with you." He preferred, "if they *do* seem to be turning around, give 'em a *chance* to turn around and get on... get on their way." McNamara, however, abruptly revised the position he had taken just minutes before, calling RFK's idea "an excellent suggestion, but not to apply the first day," and endorsed stopping a ship "*even* if it turns around and proceeds *indefinitely* away from Cuba, we would nonetheless *stop* it and *search* it because it very probably would have offensive weapons on board."

Rusk protested that the downside of seizing a ship that had reversed course far outweighed the advantages of photographing and examining the missiles. The diplomatic problem is, he patiently lectured the attorney general, "that from the Soviet point of view they're gonna be as sensitive as a *boil* because it's whether they think we're really trying to capture and seize and analyze and examine their missiles and their warheads and things. Now the purpose [of the blockade] is to keep 'em out of Cuba. This adds a... a *very* important element into it, you see." Any effort to confiscate Soviet technology, the secretary of state reasoned, would contravene the announced purpose of the blockade.

President Kennedy short-circuited this debate: in the next 24 hours, he cautioned, the Soviet ships could "refuse to haul to and we have to shoot at 'em, so that's really our problem tomorrow." The administration could decide later "whether we start grabbing 'em as they leave. So I think," he concluded bleakly, "we're gonna have all our troubles tomorrow morning." "I think so too," McNamara agreed.

Pointing to a historical parallel that might provide some guidance on Soviet strategy and intentions, JFK observed that the U.S.S.R. was now "faced with the same problem we were faced with in the Berlin blockade," deciding just how far to push the crisis. "We've given them as clear notice as they gave us," he recalled, "even in '47 or '8, we had an atomic monopoly, we didn't push it." He then added a chilling assessment of the risks of the naval quarantine that must have disconcerted his advisers: "Looks like they're *going* to."

Ball, however, introduced a point somewhat analogous to Rusk's appeal to limit the quarantine to just keeping these weapons out of Cuba. "I'd like to raise a question," Ball argued, "as to whether we shouldn't have *some* outer limit, however. It seems to me that the idea that we're picking up Soviet ships *anywhere*, just on the *prima facie* supposition that they're heading for Cuba is... is... tough... it'll get us into difficulties." "Don't... don't we have two problems?" McNamara countered. He rejected setting "outer limits in the proclamation" but acknowledged "the practical problem of how we apply this." The defense secretary underscored, for example, the necessity of avoiding an air attack from Cuba by operating outside the range of the IL-28s (about 740 miles) and the MiGs (about 450 miles). The *Kimovsk*, he reasoned, would be the best choice on the first day of the quarantine since it was far enough out to be safe from air attack and almost certainly carrying offensive weapons—"*if* we can find it and *if* we can stop it."

JFK was less confident and questioned McNamara about whether any ships carrying missiles might arrive in Cuba in the next few days and beat the blockade, but conceded realistically, "I suppose you can't pick 'em all up anyway." "All right," the President declared, sounding far more resigned than enthusiastic, "I'm gettin' all set to sign this thing [the quarantine proclamation]."

After dealing with a few "minor drafting" problems raised by Ted Sorensen, JFK rather abruptly came back to the question he had raised at the start of the meeting: whether the use of the term "Sino-Soviet powers" in the proclamation was unnecessarily confrontational, "What we're gonna do is *stop* the introduction of offensive military weapons into Cuba," he asserted. "Is it important whether we leave in or out the 'Sino-Soviets' anywhere?" Perhaps it would be less provocative, he suggested, to simply say "stop the introduction of weapons" instead of specifying the national origin of the weaponry: "Does it hit them *harder* to name them in a... in a way which may not be desirable? Is this more *challenging* than it needs to be?"

Bundy suggested the term "the Soviet power" as a possible substitute for "Sino-Soviet powers" and Rusk floated the cumbersome phrase, "extra-hemispheric powers of an offensive nuclear capability." But, the President finally agreed to put aside his objections and stick, as Rusk had noted, with the same language used in the OAS resolution; "we're gonna use the 'Sino-Soviet' text too," he conceded, and requested that press secretary Pierre Salinger announce a 7:00 P.M. signing of the proclamation.[167]

The discussion turned, once the details of the proclamation had been resolved, to the substance of the President's response to Khrushchev's latest message. Bundy circulated a draft letter and JFK asked, "What does Tommy think?" Ambassador Thompson speculated that the Soviets would be deciding tonight "what instructions *are* going to these ships" and perhaps another message might help them recognize that "there *is* an alternative to going ahead with *forcing* this thing which makes us *fire* on them, and therefore kicks off probably the reaction and the retaliation in Berlin." Thompson endorsed putting the ball in Khrushchev's court by responding to his most recent letter.

Rusk read aloud a proposed draft letter from the President to Khrushchev urging the Soviet leader to observe the quarantine and avoid gunfire at sea. The secretary of state concluded, however, that the first reports from U.S. intelligence were not encouraging: "We've had *no*

[167]The final title of Proclamation 3504, "Interdiction of the Delivery of Offensive Weapons to Cuba," did not specifically mention "Sino-Soviet powers," but that term did appear in the text of the proclamation. (*Public Papers of the Presidents: John F. Kennedy, 1962*, II (Washington, D.C.: United States Government Printing Office, 1963), 809–11)

indications," Rusk told the President, "of any Soviet instructions or re-actions or... in any way to pull away . . ." "None at all," McCone confirmed and Rusk reiterated, "Just the converse." McCone also reported that sources at the U.N. were speculating that Soviet ships had instructions to go through the blockade. Nitze countered that the Soviets might stop the ships in the hope of deterring either an attack on Cuba or an expansion of the blockade and, in effect, "*freeze* the status quo with the missiles there." Bundy reasoned that such a development was very unlikely, but possible and JFK replied, "Well, we can always come back and say that's unacceptable." The President again asked for Thompson's advice on sending the letter to Khrushchev. The former ambassador acknowledged that he did not feel strongly about it, but deduced that the President's message "could be helpful in their last-minute decision." JFK agreed, "OK. Well, let's send it then. Hell, I don't see that we're giving away much." The letter was soon dispatched to the U.S. Embassy in Moscow.

Rusk reported, in a sardonic tone, that the President's speech had stimulated a mob of 2,000 supporters of Lord Bertrand Russell's peace organization to storm the American Embassy in London—but ironically there had been no reports of disorder in Havana. On the other hand, McCone noted, "In Chile, the communist-dominated union is planning a nationwide strike."

The President, however, seemed more concerned about indications that the Soviets would challenge the blockade, "OK. *Now* what do we do tomorrow morning when this... these eight vessels continue to sail on? We're all clear about how we," he paused, "handle it?" Some strained laughter broke out just before JFK's last few words, spoken in a wryly humorous tone that likely reflected an awareness that no one in Washington or Moscow could predict or control the outcome of this potentially deadly confrontation. McCone advised matter-of-factly, "Shoot the rudders off of 'em, don't you?"

McNamara, apparently put off by the laughter, admonished, "Well, if you'd asked... this... this is a problem. We want to be *very* careful." He urged waiting until early in the morning before deciding precisely on the instructions to the Navy: "We *ought* to try to avoid shooting a ship... Soviet ship carrying wheat to Cuba or medicine . . . [and] *try* to pick a ship which *almost certainly* carried offensive weapons *as the first ship.*" "The only problem I see, Bob," the President interjected, repeating the point he had raised earlier in the meeting, "that's the one vessel I would think they would turn around."

McNamara countered that U.S. intelligence had yet to detect any course change by the ships approaching the quarantine line and Rusk prompted some laughter by joking, "Well that could well be the baby food ships," and suggesting that it would be advantageous to test the blockade "on any other kind of ship." "Moving outa Washington...," RFK teased. The defense secretary predicted that Khrushchev would likely instruct all ships, "'*Don't stop* under any circumstances,'" regardless of their cargo. "So the baby food ship comes up and we hail it and they'll think it odd when we shoot it," he exclaimed with an uncharacteristic burst of laughter. "We shoot three nurses!" Bundy joked.[168]

"That's still gonna happen," President Kennedy remarked grimly. The boarding of Soviet ships was not likely to be a laughing matter and could turn very serious, very quickly: "They're gonna keep going and we're gonna try to shoot this rudder off, or this boiler. Then we're gonna try to board it and they're gonna fire a gun and machine guns. And we're gonna have *one hell of a time* gettin' aboard that thing, getting control of it, because they're pretty tough, and I suppose they may be armed... or soldiers or marines aboard there. They certainly may have technicians who are military. So I would think that the *taking* of those ships is gonna be a *major* operation. We may have to *sink* it rather than just *take* it."

"Or they might give orders to blow it up," RFK speculated. "I think that's less likely," JFK asserted, "than having a real fight to try to board it, because they may have 5, 6 or 700 people aboard there with guns." McNamara reassured the President that most of the ships targeted for boarding were likely to have relatively small crews.

"What do we do now about a ship that *has been* disabled and it's *not* gonna sink?" Rusk pondered, "It just can't go anywhere." McNamara explained that a crippled ship would be towed to a U.S. prize port. "Well, then we take it to a back port," JFK retorted sarcastically, "and we find out that it's got baby food on it." McNamara, somewhat defensively, insisted that the ship would be inspected before being towed, but the President questioned whether "they'd let us aboard." "What if they don't?" Rusk remarked. "That's right," McNamara joked, "it's this baby food ship that worries me." "Did they sight a ship?" JFK asked. A bit of laughing can be heard as McNamara

[168]The references to baby food were likely connected to Castro's request for substantial amounts of baby food in the secret negotiations for the release of the Bay of Pigs prisoners.

replied, "No, I don't think they... a wheat ship or a *non*-offensive weapons ship." But the President teased, "I say those who considered the blockade course to be the easy way—I told them not to do it!" The discussion dissolved into an intense eruption of laughter and Bundy joked above the din, "We bad guys brought consensus today, everybody fell for it!"—reigniting the hilarity.

The laughter evaporated swiftly, however, as the President quickly returned to the serious dangers raised by the blockade, "Well, that's what I... that's what we're gonna have to do," he pronounced in an abruptly somber tone of voice. It was crucial, he insisted to provide "as detailed instructions as possible from those who are knowledgeable about the sea and know just how to proceed on this." JFK again floated an unsettling scenario: a Soviet ship is fired upon and disabled. The ship is drifting but refuses to allow U.S. personnel on board to inspect its cargo. "Then uh... then uh... I don't think we can probably get aboard," he cautioned again, without "a machine gun operation. . . . You have a real *fight* aboard there."

McNamara reiterated that the freighters had small crews and any firefight should be minor. After a moment of silence, during which someone was nervously tapping, possibly with a pencil, McCone sided with the President, "It won't be easy," and McNamara finally agreed. "It could be difficult," Rusk quipped, "It's a good reason to send this letter to Mr. Khrushchev, tell him to turn 'em around—not to challenge it." Some muted chuckles can be heard in the background.

President Kennedy, however, continued to stress the likelihood of an armed clash when boarding a Soviet ship and insisted again on explicit instructions for American naval forces. "First," he demanded, "we want to be sure that nobody on our boats have cameras." Rusk agreed, and McNamara disclosed that a specific order to that effect had gone out earlier in day.[169] Second, he wanted a clear decision on how to react if there was machine gun fire and the crew of a disabled ship resisted being boarded:

"Do we let them drift around?" JFK asked.

"I think, at that point, Mr. President," McNamara advised, "we have to leave it to the local commander," depending on the conditions at sea and whether a Russian submarine was in the vicinity.

[169]JFK did not explain his thinking on this point, but he certainly wanted to avoid any possibility that photos of a bloody clash on a Soviet ship might become public and further exacerbate the crisis.

"Well we don't want to tell him necessarily, 'go aboard there,'" JFK replied, pointedly ignoring the suggestion that the decision should be made by anyone other than the commander-in-chief. "If we disable it and they refuse to let us aboard, I would think he'd stay with it, and certainly for a day or so not board it—let it drift."

"I think we just have to say, Mr. President," General Taylor interjected, agreeing with McNamara, simply give them discretion "to use the minimum force required to cause—"

President Kennedy cut him off forcefully, "I think it misses the point. We... we... if he... if he disables the ship and they're 800 miles out and they refuse to let us aboard, I don't think we ought, he ought to be... feel that he has to board that thing in order to carry out our orders."

"Well he's... he's to keep ships going to Cuba," Taylor countered, "that's his... that's his basic mission now."

"*I think* at the *beginning* it would be better," the President concluded sharply, "if this situation happened, to let the boat lie there, disabled, for a day or so, not to try to board it and have a *real* machine gunning with 30–40 people killed on each side."

McNamara, however, raised a significant complication—it might be necessary to board and inspect a ship and either tow it or leave it there and get out of the area quickly because of the presence of Soviet submarines; he also cited Admiral Anderson's concern that a submarine might even "try to sink one of our *major* vessels, such as a carrier."

"I think," the defense secretary appealed to the President, "we're gonna have to allow the commander on the scene a certain amount of latitude . . ." McNamara also stressed that two American aircraft carriers, the *Enterprise* and the *Independence*, were in the area. JFK, tapping the table nervously, silently pondered the request for some ten seconds before observing, "Cause a submarine can really uh... they say these aircraft carriers could do a lot of damage." "All right," he finally agreed, but pointedly directed McNamara to personally review all instructions to naval forces on the quarantine line "having in... having in mind this conversation we've just had." "All right, I have," the defense chief assured the commander-in-chief, "and I'll do so again tonight, Mr. President." "All right," JFK concluded, "what's the next step?"

The discussion returned briefly to the potential impact of the blockade or a planned invasion of Cuba on U.S. coastal trade and shipping. But, JFK seemed far more concerned about the potential danger to U.S. merchant ships in or near the quarantine zone—speculating that the

Soviets or the Cuban might try to stop or even sink some of them, "I suppose that's what they *will* do." McNamara informed the President that merchant vessels sailing near Cuba were being warned about a possible attack by Castro's forces and given limited air cover, "we'd be prepared to *attack* their attackers. But I... this is a *real* possibility, we'd lose a merchant ship in and around Cuba, *quickly*." The President remained silent for nearly seven seconds before responding, in a particularly weary and strained tone of voice, "OK."

Shortly thereafter, the reel of tape appears to have run out. During the untaped break, JFK urged McNamara to "recommend appropriate arrangements for the continuation of U.S. Air Force General [Lauris] Norstad as Supreme NATO Commander during the crisis." The President had been impressed by a cable that day from Norstad, resisting the presumption that war was imminent and recommending "certain precautionary military measures . . . of a non-provocative and non-public nature" for U.S. forces in Europe.[170] When the recorded discussion resumed, unfortunately on a tape with very poor sound quality, Steuart Pittman, Assistant Secretary of Defense for Civil Defense, had begun briefing the President and the ExComm on U.S. domestic preparations for surviving a nuclear attack from Cuba.[171]

The President's mood had already seemed gloomy after McNamara's warning about the imminent loss of a merchant vessel, but that eventuality seemed trivial compared to the civil defense risks. Steuart Pittman reviewed the federal effort to focus the attention of local civil defense organizations on "the problems of nuclear warfare," including "training of police, firefighting, mass casualty care." Almost clinically, he discussed the threat to 92 million Americans living in 58 cities with populations greater than 100,000, in an arc of about 1,100 nautical miles from Cuba, in the event of a "relatively light nuclear attack." Efforts were also underway, he reported, to stock shelters with emergency supplies and to identify buildings which could provide protection

[170]McGeorge Bundy, Executive Committee Record of Action, October 23, 1962, 6:00 P.M., NSF, JFKL; John McCone: Notes on Executive Committee Meeting 23 October 1962, 6:00 P.M., in Mary S. McCauliffe, ed., *CIA Documents on the Cuban Missile Crisis, 1962* (Washington, D.C.: Central Intelligence Agency, 1992), 291.

[171]The JFKL Presidential Recordings Finding Aid dates Tape 36.1 at an unknown time on October 24. It appears instead to have been the conclusion of Tape 35.2 on the evening of October 23.

from a nuclear blast and exposure to radiation for "40 million people of the 92 million in this area."

"Let me just ask you this," JFK interjected (after whispering to someone, "OK, I'll be right there") "It seems to me the most likely problem we're gonna have in the next ten days is if we decide to invade Cuba, they may fire these weapons." The President took for granted that "people living out in the country, we can take care of them, to the extent that is possible, against radiation." He finally asked a disquieting question, "Can we, say before we invade, evacuate these cities?" Pittman bluntly replied, as JFK began to tap his knee nervously, that the President's assumption about protecting rural-area civilians against radiation was simply wrong: "Well, if we knew that it would... that there would be no nuclear response," Pittman explained, "it might make some sense. If there will be fallout, the only protection that exists *today* is in the cities, and there... there... there's little or no protection in the rural areas."

The President retreated to the hopeful supposition that "we're *not* gonna have an all-out nuclear exchange," but he nonetheless acknowledged that if an invasion of Cuba were launched, "there may be some bombs fired, 10 or 15," at the United States mainland. He pressed Pittman on whether civil defense might be able to reduce the risk to civilians with a 5, 6 or 7 day warning before American forces land in Cuba, "What is it we oughta *do* with the population of the affected areas *in case* the bombs go off? I just don't see," he noted with annoyance, "in your statement how you addressed yourself to that question effectively." The sound quality of the tape, suddenly, went from poor to essentially inaudible, making it impossible to hear Pittman's response to the President's blunt question.

More than ten minutes of tantalizingly inaudible conversations followed as the meeting began to break up, dealing in part with civil defense, Paul Nitze's new role as chair of an ExComm subcommittee on Berlin, and a suggestion by Bundy to "preempt Walt Rostow," chairman of the State Department Policy Planning Council, provide him "with an executive secretary from the White House staff and swing that into another subcommittee of this enterprise." Several participants agreed to hold a meeting at the State Department the following morning.

Just before 7:00 P.M. President Kennedy formally replied to Khrushchev's latest cable: "I am concerned that we both show prudence and

do nothing to allow events to make the situation more difficult to con-
trol than it already is. I hope that you will issue immediately the neces-
sary instructions to your ships to observe the terms of the quarantine
. . . which will go into effect at 1400 hours Greenwich time October
twenty-four."[172]

Minutes after 7:00 P.M. the President signed the quarantine proclamation in the Oval Office. After reading over the text one more time,
"He spread the four-page document in front of him. On the last page,
he wrote firmly and boldly his full signature, John Fitzgerald Kennedy—one of the few documents he signed thus, normally using only
his middle initial F." Then, as photographers snapped away intently, he
stuck the pen in his pocket, and, very conscious of the historical moment, declared, "I am going to keep this one."[173]

Tuesday, October 23, shortly after 7:00 P.M., Cabinet Room

Identified Participants: John F. Kennedy, McGeorge Bundy,
Robert Kennedy, Maxwell Taylor.[174]

"Well, it looks like it's gonna be *real mean*, doesn't it? But on the
other hand, there's really *no choice*."

President John F. Kennedy

After the signing, the President returned to the Cabinet Room, where
informal conversations continued, especially about possible NATO responses if the Soviets reacted to a U.S. attack in Cuba by blockading
West Berlin. Finally, all the participants had departed except JFK, RFK,
Taylor and Bundy. President Kennedy, clearly irritated, badgered the
attorney general about reports that Prime Minister Macmillan had
permitted a CIA briefing on classified U-2 surveillance photos to be
shown on British television without U.S. approval.[175] "Bobby," JFK asserted impatiently, "I don't wanna make it look like we're all fucked
up here"—by allowing the British to show the photos publicly but

[172]John F. Kennedy to Nikita Khrushchev, October 23, 1962, *FRUS, 1961–1963, VI, Kennedy-Khrushchev Exchanges*, Document #62.

[173]*New York Times*, October 24, 1962; Brugioni, *Eyeball to Eyeball*, 383.

[174]Tapes 36.1 & 36.2, POF, PRC, JFKL.

[175]Macmillan's decision may have resulted from a communication foul-up; but, he may also have been attempting to dampen anti-American suspicion in England by releasing the evidence.

denying access to the American press.[176] Robert Kennedy, always sensitive to JFK's political problems, suggested, "What about just saying we were planning to release them?" The President, eager to avoid antagonizing U.S. journalists, quickly agreed, "So why don't we get McCone and find out which of the pictures we *can* release—*here*."

The discussion quickly refocused on the President's principal preoccupation—Berlin. RFK, addressing his brother informally as "Jack," interrupted General Taylor's observations on the blockade to report that General Lucius Clay had offered to go to West Berlin as the President's representative in "an official/unofficial capacity." Clay had played a key role during the 1948–49 Berlin airlift and had become a symbol of American resolve to West Berliners. The retired general had also served as JFK's special representative to Berlin until earlier in 1962. "I guess the general agreement is," RFK continued, that it "would be bad to focus attention on Berlin right at the moment *by him going.*" The President revealed that he had phoned Clay earlier,[177] "just to have a chat," and Taylor confirmed that Clay had also called him just before 6:00 P.M. The President endorsed Bundy's suggestion to keep the general on standby in case the Soviets "squeezed" Berlin in the next 2–3 days.

Evelyn Lincoln interrupted with a message that Jacqueline Kennedy was on the phone. The President left the room to take the call and the informal gathering began to break up. As Taylor and Bundy prepared to leave, RFK teased about getting the general's advice about reviewing "our whole military strategy." Finally, he called after them and joked, "I have a feelin' I don't like to see you people go. You have all the answers!" After a bit more banter and laughter, and the sound of the door being slammed shut as JFK returned, the Kennedy brothers were alone in the Cabinet Room.

"*Oh, Christ!*" the obviously agitated President burst out, suddenly recalling that he was scheduled to attend a formal dinner that evening.[178] He was obviously not in the proper frame of mind for hours of social chit-chat.

---

[176]The language in the ExComm meetings was remarkably restrained and dispassionate. The President evidently felt comfortable using an "expletive" only when he was virtually or entirely alone with his younger brother.

[177]The conversation with General Clay was recorded on Dictabelt 32.1, POF, PRC, JFKL.

[178]The dinner, for royalty who had hosted Jacqueline Kennedy during her visit to India, had been arranged before the crisis.

But RFK quickly zeroed in on the real source of his older brother's irritability:

"How's it look?" he asked point blank.

"Well, it looks like it's gonna be real *mean*, doesn't it?" JFK exploded. "But on the other hand, there's really *no choice*. If they get this mean on this one—Jesus Christ! What are they gonna fuck up next?"

"No choice," RFK echoed.

"I don't *think* there *was* a choice," the President repeated.

RFK hastily added, "No, there wasn't any choice. I mean you woulda had a... you woulda been *impeached*."

"Well, that's what I think. I woulda been impeached," he agreed, after the mid-term elections, on the grounds of failure to live up to his public pledge to prevent an offensive military buildup in Cuba.

Robert Kennedy, eager to bolster his brother's self-assurance, contended that it was becoming clear to everyone that "you couldn't 'a done any less. The fact is," he went on, "you got all the South American countries and Central American countries to vote unanimously [for the OAS resolution] when they kicked us in the ass for *two* years, they vote *unanimously* for this, and then you get the reaction from the rest of the allies, you know, like David Ormsby-Gore[179] and everybody else, say that you *had* to do it." RFK seemed to be trying to reassure the President that if the crisis culminated in "the final failure" it would not be his fault: "You can't really... I mean, if it's gonna come, if you... it's gonna come, it's somethin' you couldn't have avoided."

The attorney general did, however, express regrets about not having maintained better communications with the Soviets and JFK asked about the ongoing contacts with Georgi Bolshakov. RFK had received reports about a Bolshakov luncheon meeting that day:

"What'd he say?" JFK probed.

"He said," RFK replied, "they're gonna go through" [the quarantine].

"The ships are goin' through?" JFK pressed.

RFK, with a derisive laugh, reported that Bolshakov had said "this is a defensive base for the Russians. It's got nothing to do with the Cubans."

JFK responded angrily: "Why are they lying then? Khrushchev's

---

[179]British ambassador to the United States and a friend of the Kennedys.

horseshit about the election![180] Anyway, it's a sickening thing that we were told, is that he's [Khrushchev] very mad about being revealed about this. *How* is that embarrassing in the election?"

RFK mentioned that the new Soviet ambassador, Anatoly Dobrynin, resented Bolshakov's influence in Washington and had recently advised the attorney general, "Don't pay any attention to Georgi."[181]

JFK pointedly mentioned that Soviet officials had consistently concealed the truth about the missiles in their discussions with RFK. The attorney general also recalled that he had relayed word to Bolshakov that the President had based his position "on a lot of these personal assurances because he thought that he could *believe* the ambassador and all the rest."

As this no-nonsense discussion gradually came to a close,[182] RFK emphasized that press reaction to the President's speech thus far "is pretty good." "Till tomorrow morning," JFK retorted pessimistically, and RFK agreed "it's gonna get unpleasant" after the blockade was implemented. But, he argued, it was "the luckiest thing in the world" that secrecy had been maintained until October 22. If public exposure had forced an earlier decision, almost certainly resulting in air strikes on the missiles, RFK pointed out, there would not have been time to line up OAS support and the situation "would've been awful tough." JFK agreed if the U.S. has started with air strikes and "had been over there shootin' up everything, then the Russians *really* would tense."

Instead, RFK reasoned, the quarantine would include the cooperation of the OAS and if shots had to be fired across the bow or a ship had to be disabled and boarded, "It's not just the United States doing it." As the tape ended, the Kennedy brothers speculated on a possible OAS role in actually boarding a Soviet ship. They did not have the slightest idea how things would actually turn out a few hours after sunrise the next morning.[183]

---

[180]The Kennedy administration had been repeatedly assured in September by senior officials that no provocative actions would be taken in Cuba before the fall elections; Bolshakov had personally delivered one of these deceptive messages.

[181]In early November, in a *Washington Post* column, Joseph Alsop exposed Bolshakov's effort to deceive the President. Dobrynin assumed that the Alsop piece had been instigated by RFK. (For Dobrynin's cables to Moscow, see "New Evidence on the Cuban Missile Crisis: More Documents from the Russian Archives," *CWIHPB 8–9* (Winter 1996–97), 270–343)

[182]The Kennedy brothers were clearly not thinking about the fact that their conversation was being taped.

[183]The Navy, however, had very detailed and specific plans in place for implementing the blockade (see Garthoff, *Reflections*, 67–69).

Fidel Castro spoke defiantly to the Cuban people that evening in a ninety-minute televised address. He denied the presence of Soviet offensive missiles in Cuba but reasserted the right of his nation to defend itself against American aggression. He also placed the Cuban military on the alarma de combate, *the highest level of alert, and ordered total mobilization.*

At the State Department, Edwin Martin expressed concern that Cuban exile groups might try to stage a military incident in order to force the President's hand in Cuba and recommended exploring an interim suspension of Operation Mongoose with the CIA and the ExComm. However, the President and his advisers never seriously focused on this issue and, although the White House and the CIA did finally halt Mongoose near the end of October, covert operations were not fully curtailed until early November.[184]

A few hours after the signing of the quarantine proclamation, either at the suggestion of the President or certainly with his full knowledge, RFK arranged to meet with Ambassador Dobrynin in his Soviet embassy office. The "obviously excited" attorney general denounced the deployment of missiles in Cuba as "hypocritical, misleading and false" and made no effort to hide his own and the President's fury over Soviet duplicity. Dobrynin cabled the Kremlin, quoting RFK's assertion, "The President felt himself deceived and deceived deliberately." The ambassador clearly wanted his superiors in Moscow to understand that the Kennedys' anger was personal as well as official. Nevertheless, Dobrynin told RFK that he had no personal knowledge of Soviet offensive missiles in Cuba and added ominously that he had not received any indication that Soviet ships heading for Cuba had been instructed to change course.[185]

RFK returned to the White House after 10:00 P.M. *to relay this unsettling information to the President, who was meeting privately with British ambassador David Ormsby-Gore after the evening dinner party. The ambassador suggested contracting the quarantine line around Cuba from* 800 *miles to* 500 *miles to delay a confrontation at sea and give the Soviets more time to reassess their plans. The President phoned McNamara to endorse this suggestion, but the record remains murky as*

---

[184]Fursenko and Naftali, *"One Hell of a Gamble,"* 287–88; Chang and Kornbluh, *Cuban Missile Crisis,* 380–81.

[185]Anatoly Dobrynin, October 24, 1962 Cable to Moscow, *CWIHPB* 5 (Spring 1995), 71–75; Robert Kennedy, *Thirteen Days,* 50–51.

to whether the Navy had ever regarded the 800 mile line as practical or enforceable.[186]

Soviet ships actually reacted with considerable caution. All the vessels carrying military equipment and missiles had slowed down, stopped or turned around before 10:00 A.M. on October 24 when the quarantine became effective—exactly as President Kennedy had predicted at the ExComm meetings. By later that evening, the National Security Agency informed the CIA that preliminary data suggested that Soviet missile-bearing ships had turned back toward their home ports.

At 9:00 A.M. that morning McNamara was briefed by the Navy on the movement of Soviet ships toward the quarantine line, but was not given the preliminary NSA information that some ships had reduced speed, come to a standstill or reversed course. At a press conference later that morning, the defense secretary openly speculated that the U.S.S.R. would directly challenge the blockade within twenty-four hours. Admiral Anderson later called McNamara at the White House to brief him on the latest data; when the defense chief learned that this information had been available before his morning press conference, outraged and embarrassed, he marched into the Navy Flag Plot room at the Pentagon (the control room for implementing the quarantine) "like a madman" and clashed angrily with several top officers, including Anderson himself.[187]

Early on the morning of October 24, Moscow time, William Knox, president of Westinghouse Electric International, visiting the U.S.S.R. on business, was summoned to the Kremlin by Khrushchev. The Soviet leader vented his anger for more than three hours, accusing the United States of aggression and piracy and threatening to sink an American naval vessel if Soviet ships were harassed at sea. Knox, precisely as Khrushchev had expected, immediately relayed a detailed account of the meeting to Washington. Khrushchev also released a letter to British peace activist Lord Bertrand Russell offering to meet with President Kennedy to resolve the crisis.[188]

Meanwhile, McNamara approved a first-ever JCS request to raise SAC bombers to DEFCON 2, the highest state of readiness short of war itself.

---

[186]*Ibid.*, 52; Chang and Kornbluh, *Cuban Missile Crisis*, 381.
[187]Brugioni, *Eyeball to Eyeball*, 399–400.
[188]William E. Knox Oral History Interview, 1977, OHC, JFKL.

Wednesday, October 24, 10:00 A.M., Cabinet Room

*Identified Participants: John F. Kennedy, George Ball, McGeorge
Bundy, Douglas Dillon, Roswell Gilpatric, U. Alexis Johnson,
Robert Kennedy, Arthur Lundahl, John McCone, General John A.
McDavid, Robert McNamara, Paul Nitze, Kenneth O'Donnell,
Dean Rusk, Maxwell Taylor, Jerome Wiesner.*[189]

"It seems to me we want to give that sh… ship a chance to turn
around. You don't wanna have it be… word goin' out from Moscow, 'Turn around,' and suddenly we sink their ship."

President John F. Kennedy

The President and his advisers gathered in the Cabinet Room at virtually the moment that the quarantine proclamation, signed fifteen hours
earlier, became legally operational.

McCone began the discussion with a good news–bad news briefing
on intelligence collected since the last ExComm meeting. Evidently
reading from a prepared report, his voice almost drowned out by intense background noise, he announced the good news first: the Soviets
were *not* moving "on a crash basis" to upgrade the combat readiness of
their forces and had thus far confined themselves to verbal attacks on
the quarantine. A great deal of bad news, however, soon followed: the
latest aerial surveillance had confirmed "continued rapid progress in
completion of the IRBMs and the MRBM sites." Even more ominously, he reported that a U-2 flight from the previous day had revealed that buildings believed to be for the storage of nuclear materials
were "being assembled with great rapidity."

McCone also confirmed that of the 22 ships heading for Cuba, three
had hatches large enough for carrying missiles. In addition, seven ships
had begun receiving urgent messages by 1:00 A.M. yesterday, Moscow
time, and "all ships, including the *Kimovsk*, were receiving urgent messages" by 2:30 A.M. this morning. And, "shortly afterwards," news arrived that "the Odessa control station notified all ships that hereafter
all orders would come from Moscow." He tempered this intriguing but
ambiguous development with news that although no Soviet aircraft appeared to be headed for Cuba, a Soviet submarine was trailing the *Kimovsk* and 3 or 4 Russian submarines were already in the Atlantic. The

[189]Tape 36.3, Parts 1 & 2, POF, PRC, JFKL.

U.S.S.R. was also preparing to deploy some long-range aircraft to their Arctic bases and had increased the state of readiness of Soviet Bloc military forces around Europe.

Dillon complained that Coast Guard and Treasury Department "black boxes" for detecting radioactivity on planes or ships had been delivered to the CIA, leaving a shortage at American ports. McCone and JFK, just as the severe background noise cleared up, briefly discussed ordering replacements. "Mr. President," McCone continued, "Mr. Lundahl has two or three [photo] boards of this low-level flight which I'd like to clarify here." "May I come around beside you, sir?" Lundahl asked. The President swiftly agreed and Lundahl can be heard gathering up and carrying his briefing materials over to the President's place at the table. Lundahl used a U-2 photo, which he called "one of the old favorites," to contrast with the details visible for the first time on photos from "the low-level flight which was consumated yesterday." He seemed especially intent on alerting the President to recent Soviet efforts to camouflage the missile sites. "If they were to get this ground cover down," JFK hypothesized after examining the new photos, "the thing would be awfully difficult to find." But Lundahl pointed out that camouflage "never was successful in World War II, sir. We always managed to get through the camouflage. It was successful best against high-level bombers who were trying to pick their aiming points." He assured the President that NPIC photo interpreters "use camouflage detection film and a lot of other things that hadn't been brought into the game yet there." He confidently predicted that his staff of photo analysts would find any camouflaged missile sites.

Lundahl was buoyed by the clear details of the launch pads and control bunkers in the new low-level photos and seemed tickled to tell the President, "I think you can see personnel walking around on the ground down there." He also displayed pictures of the ongoing construction of an IRBM site, and pointed out again, with evident satisfaction, "You can see the troops standing around." He also pointed out a probable nuclear storage bunker. Lundahl concluded by telling the President, "I think that that's all I have for you this morning." JFK's response, unfortunately inaudible but very likely a bit of sardonic humor expressing his feeling that this new intelligence was more than enough for one day, provoked some laughter around the table.

McCone suggested sending several of the "most convincing panels" to Ambassador Stevenson for the U.N. debate. But the President, surprisingly, seemed less impressed, commenting that the new photos were "not as... as dramatic as those earlier ones which had the actual missiles." McCone explained that Stevenson had "used those last night" and JFK replied, "Right."

The discussion promptly returned to the precarious military situation which could develop very quickly if the Cubans challenged the surveillance flights or Soviet ships resisted the quarantine. Rusk revealed that an intelligence intercept had indicated that Cuban forces had been instructed not to fire at surveillance aircraft except in self defense; at the same time, he read from a State Department analysis suggesting that in "Moscow, in spite of their threatened resistance to U.S. efforts to stop Soviet ships," Khrushchev's "public line seems designed to leave him with some option to back off if he chooses." Nonetheless, Rusk continued, it was probable that the Soviets would risk an incident at sea, "in the expectation that the resultant further rise in tension will stimulate pressures on the U.S. to end the quarantine." In short, they had not yet decided whether to seek a compromise "whereby the missiles can be withdrawn gracefully or whether to risk escalation and the countermeasures that the U.S. plans to make."

Bundy reminded the President that Jerome Wiesner, special assistant on science and technology, and an interdepartmental team were standing by to discuss improving telephone communications with Latin America. McNamara, however, insisted on first returning to a danger much closer to home: "Mr. President, first a question you raised yesterday about our own desire for security"—pointing to photos of U.S. aircraft parked closely together on military airfields in Florida. Taylor explained that the JCS was studying how to reduce the vulnerability of these planes to attack by Cuban MiG fighters without at the same time degrading their readiness to launch air strikes in 1–2 hours. But JFK pressed the defense team, "There's no way to disperse these planes any more?" If a U-2 is shot down and a SAM site is taken out, he remarked sardonically, it would be "terrific if 50 to 60 MiGs could come over and really shoot up a lot of the airstrips."

"We're making every preparation against that that we can," Taylor replied, but the commander-in-chief probed further: "How many fields are we using there?" Taylor responded, somewhat defensively, "Four *big* ones, but only two really in danger are Homestead and Key West— at least in *serious* danger. If the MiGs run out... if they come in low-level they can't reach the northern fields." McNamara recommended keeping "a substantially smaller alert force" ready to strike "a SAM site or a limited target in Cuba" on 1–2 hours of notice and "the great bulk of those aircraft would move *back* to their home fields" where they would still be ready for a major strike against Cuba with 12 hours notice, "But I think this is an acceptable reduction in lead time." The President seemed satisfied with these recommendations.

Everyone at the table, however, recognized that the imminent interception, boarding or disabling of a Soviet ship could trigger a chain of events that might *start* with a Cuban MiG attack on Florida, but quickly escalate to Russian military reprisals in Berlin, Turkey or elsewhere. McNamara revealed that two Soviet ships, the *Gagarin* and the *Kimovsk* would be approaching the quarantine barrier at midday. The *Gagarin* claimed to be carrying "technical material," McNamara explained, and a check of the records suggested that this was a typical way to conceal "an offensive-weapons carrying ship from the Soviet Union. . . . Both of these ships," he pronounced rather perfunctorily, "therefore, are... are good targets for our first intercept. Admiral Anderson plans to try to intercept one or both of them today."

But the greatest menace, the defense secretary quickly added, might actually be lurking beneath the waves: "There is a submarine very close, we believe, to each of them."

"Two submarines," the President muttered.

The defense chief did not try to minimize the risks: "The [Soviet] submarine will be at the barrier tonight . . . and therefore it should be 20 to 30 miles from these ships at the time of intercept. And hence it's a *very* dangerous situation. The Navy recognizes this, is fully prepared to meet it, undoubtedly will declare radio silence and therefore neither we nor the Soviets will know where our Navy ships are for much of today."

"Which one are they going to try to get on? Both of them?" the President asked.

"They are concentrating on the *Kimovsk*," McNamara replied, "but we'll try to get both." The *Kimovsk*, he added, had hatches large enough to accommodate missiles.

The President also wanted to know, "What kind of a ship is going to try to intercept? A destroyer?"

McNamara confirmed it would be a destroyer, but "the [aircraft carrier] *Essex*, with antisubmarine-equipped helicopters, will be in the vicinity, and those helicopters will attempt to divert the [Soviet] submarine from the intercept point."

McCone suddenly interrupted this increasingly bleak discussion with a dramatic announcement: "Mr. President, I have a note just handed me from . . . it says that we've just received information through A... ONI [Office of Naval Intelligence] that all six Soviet ships *currently* identified in *Cuban waters*—I don't know what that means—have either *stopped* or reversed course."

Someone at the table reacted with an audible, "Phew!" but Rusk amplified McCone's doubts, "Whadda' you mean? Whadda' you mean, 'Cuban waters'?" The CIA chief reiterated that he did not know at that moment. McNamara speculated that the note referred to ships in Cuban waters moving from Cuba to the Soviet Union and President Kennedy cut in to ask McCone, "Why don't we find out whether they're talking about the ships leaving Cuba or the ones coming in?" "I'll find out what this says," McCone promised. As he got up from his chair to leave the room, Rusk quipped, "Makes *some* difference," and some edgy laughter can be heard at the table as Bundy murmured, "It *sure* does."

The President, obviously unsure about the importance of McCone's message, quickly returned to the more immediate military contingencies: "*If* this submarine should sink our destroyer," he continued very deliberately and hesitantly, "then what is our... proposed... reply?" Alexis Johnson evaded the President's direct question and reported instead that he had sent a message to Moscow and to the Soviet embassy in Washington outlining the standard international procedures, presumably accepted by the Soviets, for identifying submarines at sea.

McNamara, however, made the rather startling announcement that he had set up a new procedure just yesterday: "We have depth charges that have such a small charge that they can be dropped and they can actually *hit the submarine* without *damaging* the submarine." "They're practice depth charges," General Taylor explained. "These are practice depth charges," McNamara repeated confidently. "We propose to use those as warning depth charges." The message to the Soviets referred to by Johnson, McNamara continued, explained that "when our forces come upon an unidentified submarine we will ask it to come to the surface for inspection by transmitting the following signals, using a depth charge of this type and *also* using certain sonar signals which they *may not* be able to... to accept and... and interpret. Therefore, it's the depth charge that is the... the warning notice and the instruction to surface."

Robert Kennedy, who *may* have read a transcript or listened to the tape of this meeting in preparing his posthumously published 1969 account of the crisis, claimed that the President was profoundly unsettled by McNamara's cold certainty that these anti-submarine weapons could be used harmlessly, and with such precision, that the U.S.S.R. would not be provoked into military retaliation. The attorney general vividly recalled that President Kennedy covered his mouth with his hand and clenched and unclenched his fist as "we stared at each other across the table. For a few fleeting seconds, it was almost as though no one else was there and he was no longer the President."[190]

Taylor reminded the defense chief that the sonar signal would be tried first, followed by the depth charge, and McNamara repeated his unpromising assumption that "The sonar signal very probably will not accomplish its purpose." Kenneth O'Donnell, presidential appointments secretary, asked, "What if he doesn't surface, then it would get hot?" and JFK finally asked, "If he [the submarine] doesn't surface or if he takes some action—takes some action to assist the merchant ship, are we just gonna attack him anyway?" Taylor interjected, "We're going to attack him because....," but the President cut him off, "At what point are we gonna attack him?" but immediately answered his own question: "I think we ought to wait on that today, cause we don't wanna have the first thing we attack is a Soviet submarine. I'd much rather have a merchant ship."

McNamara firmly, but respectfully, disagreed, "I think it would be *extremely* dangerous, Mr. President, to try to defer attack on this submarine in the situation we're in. We could *easily* lose an American ship by that means. The... the range of our sonar in relation to the range of his torpedo, and the inaccuracy, as you well know, of antisubmarine warfare is such that I don't have any... any great confidence that... that we can... can *push* him away from our ships and make the intercept securely."

The President must have been struck by the contradiction between McNamara's acknowledgment of the imprecision of submarine warfare as opposed to his confidence about using practice depth charges to harmlessly force a Soviet submarine to surface. The defense secretary warned that it would be especially dangerous to limit the discretion of the naval commander on the scene, "I... I looked into this in *great* detail last night," he pointedly told the President, "because of your interest in the question." The plan, he explained in response to a question

[190]Robert Kennedy, *Thirteen Days*, 53–54.

from Rusk, was to use anti-submarine helicopters, equipped with "weapons and devices that can damage the submarine. And the plan therefore is to put pressure on the submarine, *move* it out of the area by that pressure, by the pressure of potential destruction, and then make the intercept. But," the usually self-assured defense chief admitted, "this is *only* a plan and there... there are *many, many* uncertainties." "Yeah," Rusk conceded. "Okay," JFK yielded, despite his obvious doubts, "let's proceed."[191]

The quarantine, despite the fact that it was already in effect, was still *terra incognita* and many procedural questions, with potentially deadly consequences, had yet to be worked out. Rusk, for example, revisited a point he had disputed with the attorney general at the previous evening's meeting: he acknowledged that circumstances might change later, but insisted that the administration had "to be *quite* clear what the object of this present exercise is: it is to *stop* these weapons from going to Cuba. It is *not* to capture them for ourselves at this stage. It is *not* to do anything other than keep 'em from going to Cuba. I take it that uh... that we all understand the... the *present* purpose."

Bundy seemed uncertain and pressed Rusk on whether there was "*no* priority concern to capture the weapons" despite conceding, "This is an important point to get clear." The secretary of state repeated that the quarantine, at this stage, should be strictly limited to preventing the delivery of offensive weapons to Cuba. The President interjected, asking whether this was "a significant question, right now," and Bundy countered only if a ship was stopped and boarded. JFK agreed to return to this issue when and if a ship were actually seized.

[191]In a recent book published in Russia but not yet translated into English, *Kubinskaya Samba Kvarteta Fokstrotov*, "Cuban Samba of the Foxtrot Quartet," journalist Alexander Mozgovoi has revealed that one of four diesel Soviet submarines submerged in Cuban waters was encircled by the U.S. Navy and came under hours of attack from "signaling depth charges" that exploded right next to the vessel—presumably practice depth charges. The grenade-like explosions felt like "sledgehammers on a metal barrel," the temperature in the submarine rose to over 122 degrees and some crewmen lost consciousness. The irate captain, unable to surface for communications with the Soviet defense ministry but determined to make the Americans pay a heavy price, ordered the arming of a nuclear-tipped torpedo. Fortunately, he reconsidered and instead surfaced at night in an area illuminated by searchlights from U.S. ships. In a slightly different version, discussed at the October 2002 Havana conference, the captain actually gave the order to fire because he believed that World War III had already started—but was finally persuaded to wait by another officer. (*Boston Globe*, June 22, 2002; also see Fursenko and Naftali, *"One Hell of a Gamble,"* 247; Press Release, October 2002 Havana Conference, October 11, 2002; *Boston Sunday Globe*, October 20, 2002)

Robert Kennedy, who had remained strangely silent on the very point he had contested with Rusk less than 15 hours earlier, unexpectedly introduced an issue with pivotal implications for the outcome of the quarantine:

"I *presume* that somebody on the destroyer speaks Russian."

McNamara replied quietly: "We've asked about that Bobby and I don't have any answers."

"The Navy," Bundy observed, "undertook to make arrangements on that several days ago."

"They *have* Russian-speaking personnel with these ships," Gilpatric asserted, "but whether this specific ship has one or not, I just don't know."

"I'm looking into that Ros, excuse me," McNamara answered almost inaudibly.

"May we get this, as a matter of procedure, at the... at the quickest possible point," the President instructed, "that you can get a Russian-speaking person on every one of these ships?"

"Yes, Mr. President," McNamara responded.

"That is being done," Bundy affirmed.

"That's being done," McNamara reaffirmed.

This discussion of a likely clash at sea brought the President's attention back to his most persistent preoccupation: a potential showdown in Berlin. "Depending of course on the word [on the track of Soviet ships] Mr. McCone gives back," JFK speculated darkly, "I would think that if we have this confrontation and we sink this ship, then we would assume there would be a blockade then and possibly one of the responses in Berlin, which would be complete, in which they would say, that there's no movement in or out of Berlin—a blockade. Then we would be faced with ordering in air [support] in there, which is probably gonna be shot down, which is ah.... What is then our situation? What do we do then?"

Paul Nitze responded with a tough scenario for military escalation, reminiscent of his October 22 wrangle with the President over the European Defense Plan and the potential risk of accidentally firing the Jupiter missiles in Turkey at the U.S.S.R.: "Of course, what we do then," Nitze declared self-confidently, is "we try to shoot down *their* planes and keep the air corridor [to Berlin] open." If, he calculated, "they're going to put in *overpowering* air force in the air corridor" then NATO will have to decide whether to attack the SAM sites and "the bases from which the planes come ... then regroup and produce more force before we go further."[192]

McCone's abrupt return to the meeting aborted this potentially intriguing exchange between Nitze and the President. "Whadda ya have, John?" JFK asked glumly. The CIA director reported that the six ships in question, the *Poltava*,[193] the *Gagarin*, the *Kimovsk*, the *Dolmatovo*, the *Moscow Festival* and the *Metallurg Kursk*, had indeed been inbound for Cuba and reiterated that the Office of Naval Intelligence had concluded that Moscow had "either stopped them or reversed direction." The President asked whether this report applied to all Russian ships or just selected ones and McCone indicated "this apparently is a selected bunch because there's 24 of them." McNamara suggested that the ships in question might be those closest to the quarantine barrier and JFK interposed firmly: "Well, let's just say... wait a minute... now what if this is... if this report is accurate, then we're not gonna do anything about these ships close in to Cuba." Bundy appeared to agree, "The ships further in, we would not wish to stop, would we?"[194]

President Kennedy, sounding recharged for the first time in days, reasoned that if all the ships within a certain distance from Cuba had turned around, that would mean that the Soviets were not picking out only those carrying offensive weapons: "Now we won't ... we're not planning to grab any of those, are we?" McNamara confirmed that there were no plans "to grab any ship that is not proceeding toward Cuba." Rusk speculated that this Soviet move "possibly could fit" a remark allegedly made by the Cuban U.N. ambassador to his Brazilian counterpart that Castro might accept U.N. inspection if the U.S. delayed the blockade for a day or so. McCone groaned skeptically, "Oh, come on!" and Rusk conceded that this report was probably unreliable.

RFK inquired about whether this new information was being given to the Navy and Rusk backed him up, "Yeah, we better be sure the

[192]Gilpatric later recalled that Nitze "had a very strong emotional bias for military action." (Gilpatric Oral History, 55)

[193]The CIA reported that the *Poltava* "has one hatch of sufficient size to accommodate objects up to 80 feet long." (Central Intelligence Agency, Soviet Bloc Shipping to Cuba, October 23, 1962, NSF, JFKL)

[194]May and Zelikow, *The Kennedy Tapes*, 358, claim that Bundy appears to laugh in the background shortly thereafter and speculate that Rusk had just made his now famous remark, "We are eyeball to eyeball, and I think the other fellow just blinked." They could be right, but I have unable to detect any laughter by Bundy, or anyone else, at this point on the Kennedy Library tape.

Navy knows that they're not supposed to pursue these ships." "They understand that," McNamara avowed. Several ExComm members later recalled that after this surprising turn of events they felt for the first time that the crisis might possibly have reached a turning point; but it was far too early to pin too much hope on such a meager and unconfirmed scrap of evidence. "But everyone looked like a different person," Robert Kennedy recalled. "For a moment the world had stood still, and now it was going around again."[195]

Jerome Wiesner, joined by several military and civilian communications specialists, was finally invited in to report on communications problems with Latin America.[196] He contended that telephone, telegraph and teletype connections with Central and South American nations were far less adequate than those with Europe. He was particularly concerned about the inability to encrypt many circuits and the fact that many embassy lines were not manned around the clock.

Wiesner had been speaking for nearly 6 minutes when he suddenly became rather hesitant, paused and finally stopped. McNamara had begun whispering to the President about new information dealing with Soviet ships heading for Cuba. Some of the President's remarks can be faintly heard: "We oughta check first," he told McNamara, "How do we find out if the [six] ships are simultaneously turning? ... We oughta' maybe wait an hour." After whispering for more than a minute with the defense secretary, JFK asked Taylor, "What does the Navy say about this report?" The JCS chief confirmed that "three ships are *definitely* turning back," including the *Poltava*, which he admitted "we're most interested in," and "others are showing indications which indicate they *may be* turning back." Admiral Anderson, he added, was sending planes and patrols into the area to provide verification.

After pausing for some six seconds, the President made his position clear to everyone in the room—a confrontation at sea was to be averted if at all possible: "It seems to me," he stated firmly, "we want to give that sh... ship a chance to turn around. You don't wanna have it be... word goin' out from Moscow, 'Turn around,' and suddenly we sink their ship." He urged immediate contact with the aircraft carrier *Essex* to "tell them to wait an hour and see whether that ship continues

[195]Robert F. Kennedy, *Thirteen Days*, 55.
[196]Wiesner had attended at least part of the morning ExComm session on October 23, but had not been able to discuss communications until after the President had left the Cabinet Room.

on its course in view of this other intelligence. Wouldn't that be your judgment? We have to move *quickly*," he urged, "because they're gonna intercept between 10:30 and 11:00."[197] McNamara corroborated that the *Kimovsk* was about 500 miles from Cuba and could be intercepted at any moment. McCone pointed out to the President that the matter just discussed in the presence of Wiesner's communications team had "the highest classification and therefore must *not* go out of this room." "Yes," JFK replied rather casually, "I'm... I'm *sure* they know."

At the President's prompting, Wiesner finally resumed his report on communications: he stressed that the existing communications system with Latin America was "satisfactory for normal peacetime circumstances" but would never resemble the command and control network required in an emergency. General John A. McDavid, director of communications-electronics for the Air Force, then outlined a Defense Department plan to establish instantaneous communication from the Panama Canal to eight nations of Latin America.

McNamara called the plan "a magnificent opportunity to break down a diplomatic block which has existed for years," but seemed worried about successfully negotiating agreements with Latin American nations. Rusk urged President Kennedy "to conclude *now* that the *great* United States of America can't face a series of crises without adequate communications," and urged especially that the plan should not get bogged down in the "picayune problems of the budget." McCone was equally enthusiastic about establishing a national communications facility capable of serving the entire federal government.

Despite the stark possibility that a naval clash with the U.S.S.R. might be occurring at that very moment, the ExComm, just as JFK switched off the tape recorder, was focused on getting congressional appropriations for a new communications network with Latin America! Before the meeting broke up completely, however, the President returned to the potential connection between the crisis in Cuba and the future of Berlin and also directed that the United States Information Agency should be represented at subsequent ExComm meetings.[198]

[197]The meeting had begun at about 10:00 A.M. and JFK made this remark some 30 minutes into the tape—just inside the anticipated window for interception.

[198]McGeorge Bundy, Executive Committee Record of Action, October 24, 1962, NSF, JFKL. The United States Information Agency (USIA) was founded in 1953 to promote the Cold War foreign policy of the United States.

At midday, George Ball sent a cable to Raymond Hare, U.S. Ambassador to Turkey, and Thomas Finletter, U.S. Ambassador to NATO, alerting them that it might be necessary to negotiate a deal with the U.S.S.R. involving the removal of the Soviet missiles in Cuba and "the dismantling and removal" of the Jupiter missiles from Turkey. At the United Nations in New York, acting U.N. secretary general U Thant sent private appeals to both President Kennedy and Premier Khrushchev, "at the request of more than forty non-aligned states," urging a 2–3 week cooling off period in which the shipment of offensive weapons to Cuba would be halted and the naval blockade would be suspended.[199]

That afternoon, a team including Ray Cline and several military intelligence officers carried examples of aerial photography to New York and briefed Adlai Stevenson in his U.N. office. Stevenson, skeptical about the photos after his embarrassing experience during the U.N. Bay of Pigs debate in 1961, eventually got their permission to show the pictures to a group of U.N. ambassadors.

After 4:00 P.M., President Kennedy kept a scheduled meeting with Portugal's foreign minister, Alberto Nogueira, and ambassador to the United States, Pedro Pereira. About an hour later, several ExComm members (including RFK) met without the President to review evidence from the first day of the blockade and concluded that the Soviets had indeed decided to avoid the seizure of a ship carrying missiles. George Ball, who had clearly paid close attention to JFK's words at the meeting that morning, recommended new orders for the naval vessels on the quarantine line since it appeared extremely unlikely that a ship carrying contraband would actually try to pass through the blockade. The President later agreed that this was "a good course of action" and a blunt directive was issued: "Do not board or stop. Keep under surveillance. Make continuous reports." At the same time, the Defense Department publicly acknowledged that "some of the Soviet Bloc vessels proceeding toward Cuba appear to have altered their course."[200]

[199]Chang and Kornbluh, *Cuban Missile Crisis*, 382–83.

[200]Brugioni, *Eyeball to Eyeball*, 400; Chang and Kornbluh, *Cuban Missile Crisis*, 383; Garthoff, *Reflections*, 68–70.

Wednesday, October 24, about 4:30 P.M., Oval Office

Identified Participants: John F. Kennedy, McGeorge Bundy, Robert McNamara, Paul Nitze, Kenneth O'Donnell, Dean Rusk.[201]

"the *irony* will be that the Russians led us into a trap."

President John F. Kennedy.

Shortly before heading for the ExComm meeting with the congressional leadership scheduled in the Cabinet Room at 5:00 P.M., the President briefly switched on the tape recorder during an informal conversation with several advisers, apparently in the Oval Office. The audible portion of this tape fragment lasts for just a few minutes.

The tape sputtered on for a few seconds as JFK exclaimed, "the risk will be with us for three...," but then sheared off into silence. The sound suddenly resumed about twenty seconds later as Bundy recommended that the administration "get in touch with the Soviets and get their view on the generation of this crisis and why we've reacted."

Paul Nitze reminded the President of the skepticism of the NATO allies, "They're worried about the *conviction* which they can give as to these things [the missiles] *really* being there [in Cuba]." "Well, that London picture that was in this morning's [*Washington*] *Post*," the President pointed out, "is the *best* one that captures that."[202]

Nitze also suggested that the allies were "worried about this camouflage point. They say, 'Why didn't the Russians camouflage?' Well, this demonstrates that the Russians *did* do their best to camouflage them. Using these pictures, I think, could be *very* helpful."

"It means they *are* now camouflaged," JFK observed. "They are now camouflaged," Nitze repeated, "That's right."

"Well I think that they're gonna... the *irony* will be that the Russians led us into a trap," the President declared.

Bundy interrupted to ask the President for clearance to release the photos—presumably of the camouflaged sites, "The Russians have been very resistant to let us say what *is a fact.* . . . the Russians *did* camou-

---

[201]Tape 37.1, POF, PRC, JFKL.

[202]The photos had been released to the American press by the United States Embassy in London after the Macmillan government had permitted photos from a CIA briefing to be shown on British television (see the beginning of Tape 36.2 on the evening of October 23rd).

flage these things by their standard practice, *very carefully*. They proceeded by night, our agents' reports now indicate—our refugee reports. They have *never* been good at overhead camouflage," he asserted, nearly shouting, "It's just *doctrinally backwards* they are! If we can *break* this out of intelligence and *use* it to back our aim, it would help,"—especially with the European allies. JFK approved making additional photos available to the press and, just after McNamara asked, "Mr. President, could Secretary Rusk and I talk to you?" the gathering began to break up. There were a few additional discernible remarks: for example, someone asserted, "Furthermore, the Russians are *so* crafty."

The Oval Office door had been opened by that point because Evelyn Lincoln's voice plus typing and ringing phones can be heard in the background. Kenneth O'Donnell came in after several minutes and told McNamara, "Bob, General [Lyman] Lemnitzer is calling periodically. He's very anxious to see the President." McNamara cracked, "Yeah, I would say it's on the line... he's snapped," prompting O'Donnell to retort, "Why the hell does he keep fucking with us again?"[203] Some laughter followed as the remaining participants chatted, largely inaudibly, in small groups for several minutes before leaving for the 5:00 P.M. meeting in the Cabinet Room with the congressional leadership. Miscellaneous office noises continued until the recording faded out.

Forty-eight hours had passed since the President had met with the leaders of Congress just before his speech to the nation on Monday evening. In the interim, the crisis over the missiles in Cuba had become public and the naval quarantine had been implemented. President Kennedy must have wondered if this meeting with his former congressional colleagues would be any less difficult.

[203]This exchange is *extremely difficult to hear* but it seems to indicate that the September 1961 SIOP briefing may indeed have soured the relationship between the then–JCS chairman and the President. The McNamara and O'Donnell comments suggest that Lemnitzer was pressing for a meeting with JFK—presumably to push for immediate military action

**Wednesday, October 24, just after 5:00 P.M.,
Cabinet Room**

*Identified Participants: John F. Kennedy, McGeorge Bundy,
Everett Dirksen, J. William Fulbright, Bourke Hickenlooper,
Hubert Humphrey, Thomas Kuchel, Robert Lovett, Michael
Mansfield, John McCone, Robert McNamara, Dean Rusk,
Richard Russell, George Smathers, Carl Vinson.*[204]

"Our best judgment is that they are... they are... scratching their
brains *very hard* at the present time, deciding just exactly how they
want to play this, what they want to do about it."

Secretary of State Dean Rusk

President Kennedy switched on the tape recorder after McCone's intelligence briefing as Rusk reviewed the international diplomatic scene.
The secretary of state observed that despite remarks as "bitter and as
violent as ever" by Soviet U.N. ambassador Zorin, the Soviets seemed
"to go to some *pains* to keep the finger on the *Cuban*-U.S. aspects of
the matter rather than the U.S.S.R.-U.S. aspects of the matter." He also
noted that the state-controlled press in the Soviet Union, perhaps trying
to avoid "war scares there," had apparently not revealed the presence
of the Cuban missiles to their own people. "We *do* think," he cautioned, "that there are... although the situation is highly critical and
dangerous, that it is not *frozen* in any inevitable way at this point."

Rusk promised that the administration would continue to watch Soviet reactions very closely "to see what is likely to happen" but admitted "I *don't* think I can give a *definitive* view *today* as to what the *real*
attitude of the Soviet Union is on this matter. Our best judgment," he
added rather colorfully, "is that they are... they are... scratching their
brains *very hard* at the present time, deciding just exactly how they
want to play this, what they want to do about it." Finally, he read
from Khrushchev's telegram to British peace activist Bertrand Russell,
"The Soviet Union will take no rash actions" despite the "unjustified
actions of the United States" and "will do everything which depends on
us [Rusk's emphasis] to prevent the launching of a war. . . . In other
words," he concluded, "I think that we *can* report that there is no *confirmed, frozen* Soviet reaction to the situation, as yet."

At the President's suggestion, McNamara summarized the details of

[204]Tapes 37.1 & 37.2, POF, PRC, JFKL.

the quarantine and emphasized, "There have been *no* intercepts today and none were necessary." He also reported that Navy and Marine tours of duty had been indefinitely extended, and in response to question from several senators, explained that cruisers or destroyers, aided by anti-submarine carriers, would be used for the intercepts. He admitted that it was very difficult to pinpoint the exact location of Russian ships en route to Cuba, "We can't say exactly. There's a tremendous expanse of ocean that we are endeavoring to... to watch—roughly from the Azores to Bermuda." Finally, McNamara conceded that he did not know when a confrontation at sea would take place and had no firm information on whether Soviet ships had been instructed to change course.

Secretary Rusk, probably unintentionally, reignited tensions from the Monday evening meeting with the congressional leaders by hesitantly suggesting, "Mr. President, I... if I may, I'd like to urge that we... we not make any [public] reference to ships of special interest to the United States because this would be information the Soviets might find useful." Senate majority leader Mike Mansfield eagerly jumped in: "Mr. President, as long as the secretary's brought up the question of withholding information, I was deeply disturbed to read this morning's [*New York*] *Herald Tribune*, a story by Rowland Evans, which *I think* ought to be discussed here." The article, Mansfield subsequently explained, provided details about the President's October 22 session with the leaders of Congress, specifically mentioned Senator Richard Russell and claimed that President Kennedy had "made up his mind" to invade Cuba in just a few days. Mansfield quickly put Russell on the hot seat: "Dick, I don't know whether you saw this or not?"

The Georgia senator claimed, rather self-protectively, "I haven't seen it but I heard about it. . . . I refused to talk to Mr. Evans," he claimed. "He tried to call me late yesterday afternoon." The senator read from a statement issued by his office affirming that the only "voice to speak for the United States is the President and I'm supportin' the program he's announced." Russell vigorously denied leaking the story, "I don't know *who's* released it. I know *I* haven't."

Mansfield seemed reluctant to let his colleague off the hook, but Russell continued to insist, "Well, it... it didn't quote from me, but it... it treated me very broadly and I may say, correctly." The senator, perhaps to divert attention from this awkward incident, suddenly put on an impressive display of southern charm: "But inasmuch as I've been such a devil's advocate, Mr. President, and have been at times highly critical of the State Department, I *would* like to take this opportunity to heartily congratulate the secretary of state on what I regard as a *magnificent* triumph in the Organization of American States on yesterday—and rather lost sight of in all of the momentous march of events. But I... I thought it was a... a tremendous job." Another senator joined in the praise and Russell quipped, "I never would have believed it could've been done. I hope, Mr. Secretary, that that'll take the edge off somethin' I might have said to you earlier."[205]

As laughter followed, Rusk, especially gratified by support from the influential senator from his home state of Georgia, thanked the senators, "The two of you are very generous in attributing all of that to me, but I *would* like to say that our Latin American friends" deserve praise for facing up to the deployment of offensive missiles in Cuba as "a matter of the *utmost* importance, and they came forward, as they *had* to do." The strategy worked; the apparent leaks in the Rowland Evans article, whether or not Russell was responsible, were never discussed again.

Senator Russell's more accommodating manner suggested, in contrast to the first congressional meeting, that since the President's blockade decision had been announced and implemented, the leaders of Congress would put aside their personal misgivings, at least for the moment, and publicly support the commander-in-chief. The tone of the questions, this time around, seemed more informational than confrontational. If the blockade were to fail, however, the President certainly realized that there would be ample opportunity for political "I told you so's" at the expense of the administration and the Democratic party in the mid-term elections, less than two weeks away.

Republican Senators Everett Dirksen and Leverett Saltonstall guardedly questioned Rusk about a peace initiative apparently involving former U.S. ambassador to the U.N., James Wadsworth. The secretary confirmed that Acting Secretary General U Thant would soon call for a 2-week moratorium on arms shipments to Cuba and a suspension of the quarantine. Rusk made clear that he was not impressed, since the proposal made only "vague references to verification and *no* reference to the *actual* missiles in Cuba itself," and confided that efforts were

---

[205]At the October 22 congressional meeting, an angry Russell had accused the President of delaying military action in Cuba to seek OAS support and then waiting timidly "while the secretary of state tries to get them to agree to it."

underway to get U Thant to withhold his statement. Dirksen also asked whether Khrushchev might propose a summit conference:

JFK retorted dismissively, "He had to say that. The Secretary can read that."

"That was *no* direct invitation to you," Dirksen concluded after Rusk read aloud from Khrushchev's statement.

"No," JFK mumbled.

"Do you want any comment on a summit meeting?" Dirksen asked.

"I think it'd be useless," Kennedy declared.

"I would too," Dirksen affirmed, "*Absolutely* useless."

Senator Hubert Humphrey pressed the President on whether there had been any official contacts with the U.S.S.R. JFK mentioned his exchange of official letters with Khrushchev, but candidly emphasized that the situation was very fluid: the Soviets might turn back some ships carrying weapons; or they might choose a ship "for a test case, either to have us sink it, or disable it, and have a fight about it"; or they might "submit to the quarantine those ships which are obviously not carrying any of these offensive weapons." JFK expressed the hope that this uncertainty could be resolved in the next 24 hours: "Until we know that, we don't... we don't know much," he admitted rather glumly. "When we know that, then we'll know where... at least we'll have some indications where we're going."

Senators Fulbright and Russell, the President's principal antagonists only 48 hours before, inquired whether the Soviets might try to deliver missiles to Cuba by plane. JFK defended the decision to initially stop only ships "because the only way you can stop a plane is to shoot it down" and, he suggested, "with *our* problem in Berlin," that would be a very dangerous step. McNamara also pointed out that the Soviets, unlike the U.S., did not have enough large commercial planes to deliver missiles, although they could fly in warheads. He did not rule out the possibility that they might decide to "use their bombers for that purpose."[206]

Senator Saltonstall, however, inadvertently created an awkward moment for the President's defense team by inquiring about the presence of Soviet submarines in Cuban waters. McNamara replied hesi-

[206]In an effort to forestall the delivery of nuclear weapons by plane, JFK worked out agreements with the governments of Guinea and Senegal to deny the Soviets the landing rights required for completing the long flight from the U.S.S.R. to Cuba. (Philip M. Kaiser, *Journeying Far and Wide: A Political and Diplomatic Memoir* (New York: Macmillan, 1993), 197–99)

tantly, "Ah..." and paused before continuing, "I want to answer that, but I want to say that our knowledge of submarines, Soviet Union submarines, in the Atlantic is the *most highly classified* information we have in the Department." Saltonstall tried to back off gracefully, "Well, if you prefer not to answer it, don't do it. I...." The normally articulate defense chief suddenly became tongue-tied, "Well... I... I... think... I'd better," until he was bailed out, ironically, by Senator Russell. The chairman of the Senate Armed Services Committee urged McNamara to keep this sensitive information off the table "in view of what happened here after the Monday's conference."[207] Some self-conscious throat-clearing can be heard in the background as Rusk whispered generalities about "a large number" of Soviet submarines but, like McNamara, resisted giving any specifics to the congressional leaders.

Senator Dirksen deftly changed the subject—inquiring if the administration was surprised by the slow pace of the Soviet response to the quarantine. Rusk deferred to the expertise of Ambassador Thompson, "my chief adviser on this sort of thing," but seemed eager to answer the question directly this time: "Their timing was, as we look back on it now, was terrific: Khrushchev could come to the U.N. in late November, prepared to lay on a real fracas over Berlin in a direct talk with the President. And he wanted to have all this [the missile bases] in his pocket when he had that talk. And our impression *so far* is that we have not caught them with a lot of contingency plans all laid on and ready to go—that this has upset their timing somewhat."[208]

Representative Carl Vinson of Georgia, chairman of the House Armed Services Committee, asked McCone for the latest CIA estimate of the number of Soviet MiG-21s in Cuba. McCone admitted that "Our original estimate was...was *one*, which we saw, and then 12 *possible* because of the crates that we... which we suspected to be MiG-21s. The next *real* hard information we had was when we saw 39, which I believe was on the 17th of October." Vinson also pressed McCone about the nationality of the MiG pilots: "Do we have any monitoring that would indicate, by pilot chatter or otherwise, whether these are bein' flown by Cubans or just Russians?" "About half of

[207]This remark is clearly related to the alleged leaks in the Rowland Evans article discussed earlier. Perhaps Russell hoped that his tough stance on keeping this information secure would help insulate him from Mansfield's earlier charge.

[208]For a discussion of Khrushchev's failure to plan for the premature discovery of the missiles, see Sergei Khrushchev, *Nikita Khrushchev*, 502, 559–62.

them were by... by Russians," McCone calculated; "*one*, we suspect was by a Czech, the balance by Cubans."

The presence of Soviet pilots surely raised the military stakes. If MiG-21s from Cuba strafed or bombed airports in Florida, a possibility already discussed at several earlier meetings, some of the pilots were likely to be Russians. And, Russian attacks on American soil could easily spark public demands for nuclear retaliation. McCone also confirmed another ominous point raised at the first congressional meeting: the missile sites were manned exclusively by Soviet personnel. If the United States bombed the missile sites or invaded Cuba, hundreds if not thousands of Russians would be killed or wounded. McCone was able to provide one scrap of potentially good news when Dirksen asked whether the Red Chinese been brought in, "Not to our knowledge," the CIA director replied. "We have *no* information one way or the other on that, senator."[209]

The questions began to peter out after a few more exchanges, for example, about whether non-Russian foreign vessels would be stopped under the quarantine, the chance of pressure from Khrushchev for a summit meeting and whether Soviet ships would actually try to go through the blockade. McNamara reported that the quarantine would "apply to all ships equally" and Rusk noted that several friendly nations were voluntarily turning their ships back. On the possibility of a summit, however, the President became more cagey: only minutes before he had dismissed a high-level conference as "useless." But, when pressed again by Senator Bourke Hickenlooper, he denied that a formal request had been received and seemed ready to keep all options open, "Well, why don't we wait if the message comes through. But there's no such message as yet. . . . And I think, until we see... do receive one and see what the... it says . . ." Hickenlooper also asked whether Soviet ships were still heading toward Cuba. "Some seem to be. Some may not be," JFK admitted. "But I don't think we'll know for 12 hours." The Iowa Republican cited radio reports that Khrushchev had ordered his ships to resist the blockade. "Now if that happens," he asked bluntly, "then we're in it, aren't we?" JFK remained evasive, "Well, we'll have to wait and see, Senator. I think in the next 24 hours we can tell what our problems are gonna be on the quarantine itself."

Finally, the President, evidently encouraged by the constructive tone

---

[209]Dirksen's question obviously reflected the conventional wisdom about monolithic world communism.

of the meeting, explored how to keep in touch with the leaders of Congress:

"Now Everett,[210] what's your judgment about a—I don't think we have much until we know a little more about the quarantine—about [meeting again with] the leadership?"

"I think 24 hours," Dirksen replied.

Kennedy agreed, "Well, I think we ought to know whether they're gonna stop, or whether we have to sink one and what, so that we'd probably know more about it then I would think by morning."

"Some members are anxious, of course, to get home," Dirksen observed, since the mid-term election campaign was in full swing.

JFK suggested that "we could break up now with the understanding that we can always get you back here before any major action is taken. . . . In any case we ought to meet on Monday" [October 29] or sooner if required.

"Well, would you like to set a Monday meeting?" Dirksen suggested.

"Why don't we set *definitely* a Monday meeting, with the understanding we're on an 8-hour standby basis for return."

Dirksen seemed satisfied, "Everybody can let Bob [presumably McNamara] know at what telephone he can *always* be reached."

In order to avoid the appearance of "relaxing our effort," the President agreed to Rusk's suggestion to announce that there would be another meeting with the leaders of Congress shortly, and that they were on 8-hour standby for recall to Washington.

Senator Humphrey asked McNamara for a clarification of "military equipment and associated materials" covered by the blockade. But, Senator Russell, reverting to the tougher stance he had taken forty-eight hours before, criticized the exclusion of conventional weapons and cited a report that 5,000 rifles had just been sent to Cuba. The defense chief explained that rifles were excluded because they were not directly associated with the missile systems and reiterated that the terms of the quarantine could always be tightened in response to new circumstances.

Senator Fulbright, perhaps emboldened by Russell's argument, signaled that he was still well disposed toward an invasion:

[210]JFK campaigned for Dirksen's Democratic opponent that fall, but genuinely liked the Illinois senator and was not concerned about his reelection. (O'Donnell and Powers, *Johnny, We Hardly*, 314–15)

"It's *still* my understanding that in 7 to 10 days *you will be ready* to take ac... *definite* action *if* conditions warrant it?

"We are prepared to do so," McNamara confirmed, "if conditions warrant."

"You'll be... you *will* be prepared?" Fulbright reiterated.

"Yes," McNamara repeated, "that is correct."

The President, however, in response to another question about the rifles sent to Cuba, repeated that they were not covered because in "the first collision with the Soviets" the emphasis was consciously on offensive missiles "for political reasons . . . because this puts us in a much stronger position around the world." But, he revealed, "if they *accept* the quarantine, we will *not* permit these rifles to go through."

The issue of keeping the ExComm deliberations secret, first raised by Senator Mansfield early in the meeting, suddenly resurfaced. Another participant argued forcefully that no one should comment on the meetings "in any shape, form or fashion. That it will... that any... any release will come from the White House. We won't even tell 'em where somebody sat! I remember one time a commentator called me and wanted to know which side of President Eisenhower was the secretary of state on. I said I'm *not* going to comment and he slammed the receiver in my ear. But it seems to me that we ought to make it, the secrecy, *absolute* and just say we... there is no comment. I'm saying that because otherwise the finger of suspicion points at *every person* who is here."

The President, however, did not seem overly concerned: "I must say that we've had just about I suppose 8 or 10 meetings since I've been here and I think the security's been awfully good. So if we can keep it up, I think we'd make our meetings much more productive." Rusk, in an effort to illustrate the need for total secrecy, explained "If I were quoted as saying that there are elements of caution in the Soviet attitude, the Soviet government would *certainly* take steps to prove they're unwarranted." Senator Thomas Kuchel of California asked if the administration would "require a personal disavowal" from each meeting participant and the President replied supportively, "I don't think so. I think we can probably do without it."

After final clarification that the congressional leaders would remain on eight-hour alert for another meeting, Senator Hickenlooper asked how to respond to wires arriving at his office "to the effect that: 'Why isn't this referred to the United Nations?'" and Rusk offered to provide answers to that question. The session broke up into a cacophony of small conversations as the participants slowly left the Cabinet Room. The President switched off the tape recorder and headed for the Oval Office.

Wednesday, October 24, 6:00 P.M., Oval Office

Identified Participants: John F. Kennedy, McGeorge Bundy, Robert Lovett, John McCone, Robert McNamara.[211]

"If in fact... that if they put the screws on Berlin in the way that Gromyko said they were going to, then we are... I know that we were bound to invade Cuba under those conditions."

President John F. Kennedy

Shortly thereafter, the President turned on the taping device as he chatted informally in the Oval Office with a small number of advisers who had just attended the latest meeting with the congressional leadership. Former defense secretary Robert Lovett did not seem surprised to learn that Senator Fulbright had privately informed the President that "he's convinced *himself*" that the blockade is "the *proper* course of action"[212] or that "Senator Russell seems to be a little more belligerent or prepared for further... further action." He also mentioned having tried personally to respond to Russell's concerns. "It seems to me," Lovett advised the President, who had already come to essentially the same conclusion, "that the... that the wis... that the *basic* wisdom here is to regard Cuba *really* as an extension of Berlin, and to consider the Berlin reaction as the one in which this Cuban affair was, at least in part, aimed. Therefore we have to *avoid* in the case of Cuba, a *diversion* of attention, and troops, involvement there, at this stage."

The primary benefit of the quarantine, Lovett emphasized, was to expose "the *intentions* of the Russians." He predicted that the Soviets would "stay off balance for a couple of days while they make up their *own* minds what their intentions are." Lovett, like JFK, was also suspicious of JCS overconfidence, especially the "congenital habit of *overstating* the *ease* as well as the *results* of an air strike." The views of the 67-year-old Lovett dovetailed closely with those expressed repeatedly at the ExComm meetings by the 45-year-old commander-in-chief: "I don't think there's any such thing as one of these quick and easy, san-

---

[211]Tape 37.3, POF, PRC, JFKL.

[212]Fulbright had explained his position in a brief discussion with the President just before the 5:00 P.M. congressional meeting.

itary movements," Lovett counseled. "There's no such thing as a *small* military action, I don't think. Now the moment we start *anything* in this field, we have to be prepared to do *everything*." (Someone, probably Bundy, muttered, "Exactly.") Lovett urged the President to resist the pressure to act prematurely and to wait until Soviet intentions had become clear: "I don't think the decision can be made now, but has to be made in the light of what happens within these next few days," especially if the Soviets accelerated the buildup in Cuba.

"There seems to be some disposition on [West German chancellor Konrad] Adenauer's part," JFK observed, "and I think you might even say Macmillan . . . ," but trailed off inconclusively.

Bundy, however, obviously assuming he understood Kennedy's thinking, confirmed that "David [Ormsby-Gore] said he shares that estimate of Macmillan."[213]

"That what?" JFK inquired, "That he'd look with equanimity upon invasion?"

"Well," Bundy clarified, "that he thinks you mustn't have a half-finished job."[214]

"Look," Lovett asserted, "when do you tell whether it's half-finished?"

Bundy replied, "That's *quite* right. I could agree with that."

McCone also conceded that there was no such thing as a small military action but remained worried that the U.S. might be trapped if the Russians "don't try to penetrate" the blockade but completed the construction of the missile sites: "And we have no way of telling well...

[213]Bundy told JFK that Macmillan was skeptical about an "exchange of military bases" (presumably Cuba and Turkey) because "It would look like a rather cynical exchange and a weak ending to the U.S. beginning." The prime minister instead proposed a Kennedy-Khrushchev discussion of Cuba in the context of a "general disarmament program." Ambassador Ormsby-Gore, on the other hand, urged JFK to tell Macmillan that "the US cannot stand down its blockade without progress toward the removal of the missiles." (McGeorge Bundy to John F. Kennedy, October 24, 1962, NSF, JFKL)

[214]At this point in the crisis, Macmillan was still on the fence about endorsing U Thant's moratorium proposal vs. supporting the blockade or even a U.S. invasion. Indeed, in a phone conversation with JFK minutes after the meeting ended, Macmillan criticized U Thant's plan "because it looks sensible and yet it's very bad" and dismissed it as "a very dangerous message." And, when JFK reported that the U.S. was mobilizing "so that, if we decide to invade, we will be in a position to do [so] within a few more days," Macmillan replied, "I am glad to hear that." (British notes on Macmillan-Kennedy phone conversation, October 24, 1962, in May & Zelikow, *The Kennedy Tapes*, 387–88) However, the next morning, Macmillan reacted to mounting criticism in England by sending a message to JFK endorsing U.N. inspection and a suspension of the blockade if the Soviets halted work on the sites—leaving the existing missiles intact.

how the... what the further status of warheads is." He pointedly warned, "this might happen," since "the pictures that we saw here today, which were taken yesterday," had confirmed that work on the sites was continuing; but he promised, "We'll take some more tomorrow or the next day."

McNamara, however, interrupted McCone to voice a more upbeat view, "Mr. President, I thought of Cuba as *our* hostage. I think it's just as much *our* hostage as Berlin is a *Soviet* hostage.[215] I think if we can remain *cool* and *calm* here, we've *really* got the screws on 'em. They're being restricted from what the world will think is their right." But, for the President, Berlin always remained a risky wild card: "If in fact... that if they put the screws on Berlin in the way that Gromyko said they were going to, then we are... I know that we were bound to invade Cuba under those conditions." But, when Lovett interjected, "we can also put the screws on Cuba," the President acknowledged, "They've committed their prestige much more heavily now—much more than I have in Berlin." "Exactly," Lovett and McNamara affirmed. "Well," JFK cracked, "I think then we've got their neck [in Cuba] just like we've got it [our neck] there [in Berlin]."

President Kennedy acknowledged that McCone's concern, that work might continue on the missile sites despite a successful blockade, would have to be considered carefully in the next 24 hours. The United States could be faced with 50 or 60 missiles in November instead of the current 30. "Under what conditions," JFK speculated, "would the Russians *fire* them? They might be more reluctant to fire them," he noted with a touch of ironic *realpolitik*, "if they've already grabbed Berlin than they would be if we suddenly go in, *there*. But anyway these are the... that's what we gotta make a judgment on."

As the conversation began to break up, the President read aloud the full text of U Thant's proposal for a joint voluntary suspension of Soviet arms shipments and the U.S. quarantine, a scenario he suspected was more likely to help create rather than prevent the hazardous situation just envisaged. JFK also noted that he had "walked through this" plan with Stevenson and had made clear that there would have to be an immediate guarantee of no further arms shipments to Cuba. McCone insisted that any agreement, in addition to cutting off the delivery of

---

[215]Some advisers worried that President Kennedy was "imprisoned by Berlin, that's all he thinks about." (Hugh Sidey, *John F. Kennedy, President* (New York: Athenaeum, 1963), 218)

weapons, had to include a halt to work on the missile sites and assurances that no missiles would be placed on launchers—to be verified, as Lovett pointed out, by on-site U.N. observers. JFK agreed, but cautioned, "We ought to welcome his [U Thant's] efforts," and Bundy confirmed, "Oh yes, that's... that's the first sentence."

After a few desultory exchanges about briefing several influential newspaper editors and journalists, including David Lawrence, publisher of *U.S. News and World Report*, Walter Stone, editor of the Scripps-Howard newspapers, Arthur Krock and Henry Luce, the meeting ended and the tape machine finally stopped recording.

McNamara returned to the Navy Flag Plot room, probably later that evening, for an update on Soviet ships approaching the quarantine line. The defense secretary later recalled asking Admiral Anderson:

"'When the ship reaches the line, how are you going to stop it?'

'We'll hail it,' he said.

'In what language—English or Russian?,' I asked.

'How the hell do I know?' he said, clearly a little agitated by my line of questioning.

I followed up by asking, 'What will you do if they don't understand?'

'I suppose we'll use flags,' he replied.

'Well, what if they don't stop?' I asked

'We'll send a shot across the bow,' he said.

'Then what, if that doesn't work?'

'Then we'll fire into the rudder,' he replied, by now clearly very annoyed."

McNamara finally exploded: "'You're not going to fire a single shot at anything without my express permission, is that clear?'"

Anderson contemptuously replied that the Navy had been running blockades successfully since John Paul Jones.

McNamara responded angrily, "'this was not a blockade but a means of communication between Kennedy and Khrushchev'" and ordered Anderson not to use force without the defense secretary's permission—which first required direct consultation with the President.

"'Was that understood?'" McNamara demanded.

Anderson's "tight-lipped response was 'Yes.'"

McNamara also demanded "that he be fully informed minute by minute during an interception so that he could consult with the President, and then the President and he would issue the Navy pertinent fur-

ther instruction. He then turned on his heels and departed." The defense chief was deeply shaken by this experience: "'That's the end of Anderson,'" he told Gilpatric on the way back the Pentagon, "'He won't be reappointed. . . . As far as I'm concerned, he's lost my confidence.'" McNamara kept his word—Anderson was not reappointed when his term as Chief of Naval Operations expired in June 1963.[216]

General Taylor, contrary to the rest of the Joint Chiefs, shared McNamara's perspective on the purpose of the quarantine: "President Kennedy, very rightly in my judgment, wanted to know where every ship was every morning and to find out just what instructions went to every ship's captain. This appeared to my naval colleagues as being unpardonable intervention in the execution of purely military movements. The argument I made, and I believe correctly, was that this was not really a military situation, but a political situation; it just happened that the power being used by the Government were military toys. . . . This was political chess and those ships were involved in that kind of game and very properly directed by the master player, the President of the United States."[217]

At 10 P.M., *Soviet Army military intelligence operatives at the embassy in Washington intercepted a JCS order, broadcast in the clear, to place the Strategic Air Command on DEFCON 2 nuclear alert: "In fifteen years of intercepting U.S. military messages, the Soviet military intelligence service may never have seen anything like this." A few hours later,* New York Herald Tribune *journalists Robert Donovan and Warren Rogers were talking openly at a National Press Club bar about an imminent U.S. invasion of Cuba. Their discussion was overheard by a bartender and repeated to another customer—suspected KGB agent Anatoly Gorsky. The agent relayed the information to the embassy, which arranged to have a junior embassy officer waiting in the parking lot when Rogers left the bar. The official asked the journalist if "Kennedy means what he says?" Rogers replied, "You're damn right, he does. . . . He will do what he says he will do." An embassy first secretary arranged to have lunch with Rogers that day to confirm this report that*

[216]Blight & Welch, *On the Brink*, 63–64; Nitze, *Hiroshima to Glasnost*, 230–31; Gilpatric Oral History, 61. Significant differences in perspective obviously remained between advocates of a "hard" (military) blockade vs. a "soft" (political/diplomatic) blockade.

[217]Taylor Oral History, 57–58; Alexis Johnson also recalled the resentment of Anderson and the Navy about "having in effect their destroyers controlled from the Cabinet Room of the White House." (Johnson Oral History, 44) "Advances in the technology of communications made it possible for political leaders in the basement of the White House to talk directly with commanders of destroyers stationed along the quarantine line." (Allison and Zelikow, *Essence of Decision*, 231)

Kennedy was ready to attack Cuba "to finish with Castro." This information, believed to be accurate, was relayed to Moscow and made its
way to Khrushchev himself.[218]

A new message from Khrushchev, probably written before the Rogers story reached the Kremlin, soon arrived at the State Department
and was available for the President within an hour; the letter was
tough, emotional, repetitive and not very encouraging. Khrushchev denounced the quarantine as an unacceptable ultimatum. "I cannot agree
to this," he declared, "and I think that in your own heart you recognize
that I am correct." The Soviet premier refused to order ships bound for
Cuba to observe the quarantine—which he defined as "the folly of de-
generate imperialism [and] . . . an act of aggression which pushes mankind toward the abyss of a world nuclear-missile war." Khrushchev
warned that the U.S.S.R. would not relinquish the freedom to use international waters: "Mr. President, if you coolly weigh the situation
which has developed, not giving way to passions, you will understand
that the Soviet Union cannot fail to reject the arbitrary demands of the
United States. . . . try to put yourself in our place and consider how the
United States would react to these conditions." He concluded with a
transparent threat: "We will then be forced on our part to take the
measures we consider necessary and adequate in order to protect our
rights. We have everything necessary to do so."[219]

Less than three hours later, JFK's response was on its way to Moscow through the Soviet embassy in Washington. "I regret very much,"
the President began, "that you still do not appear to understand what it
is that has moved us in this matter." He went on to review "the most
explicit assurances from your Government and its representative, both
publicly and privately, that no offensive weapons were being sent to
Cuba." JFK then expressed shock "that all these public assurances were
false." He reminded the Soviet premier that "it was not I who issued
the first challenge in this case" and urged Khrushchev "to take the necessary action to permit a restoration of the earlier situation."[220]

[218]Fursenko and Naftali, "One Hell of a Gamble," 257–61.
[219]Nikita Khrushchev to John F. Kennedy, October 24, 1962, in Chang and Kornbluh,
Cuban Missile Crisis, 173–74. Khrushchev referred once to U.S. naval forces "blockading"
Cuba, but otherwise used the term "quarantine." He apparently chose not to exacerbate
the crisis by calling attention to the fact that a blockade could be interpreted as an act of
war under international law.
[220]John F. Kennedy to Nikita Khrushchev, October 25, 1962, in Chang and Kornbluh,
Cuban Missile Crisis, 183.

Meanwhile, tough words were not the only things moving relentlessly toward a confrontation. The transport of military equipment and thousands of ground combat troops to Florida by train continued around the clock. At night, the work proceeded under floodlights. More than 6,000 vehicles and thousands of tons of weapons and supplies were loaded onto nearly 40 trains, each hauling as many as 150 cars. The massive buildup was openly reported by local press and television stations. The Defense Department released voluntary guidelines urging prudence in reporting these activities, but the administration did not regret that news of the buildup would surely reach the Soviet Union.

In Moscow, after receiving Kennedy's reply, Khrushchev, unbeknownst to anyone in Washington, had begun to prepare for a calculated retreat from the nuclear abyss. "Moscow would have to find another way to protect Fidel Castro" by offering to remove the missiles in exchange for an American pledge not to invade Cuba and by ultimately allowing U.N. inspection of the missile sites. After the Presidium approved this new initiative, Khrushchev announced, "'Comrades, let's go to the Bolshoi Theater this evening. Our own people as well as foreign eyes will notice, and perhaps it will calm them down.'" He later acknowledged, however, "We were trying to disguise our own anxiety, which was intense."[221]

Thursday, October 25, 10:00 A.M., Cabinet Room

Identified Participants: John F. Kennedy, George Ball, McGeorge Bundy, Douglas Dillon, Roswell Gilpatric, U. Alexis Johnson, Robert Kennedy, John McCone, Robert McNamara, Paul Nitze, Dean Rusk, Maxwell Taylor, Llewellyn Thompson, Donald Wilson.[222]

"This is *not* the *appropriate* time to *blow up* a ship. ... So let's think a little more about it."

President John F. Kennedy

As the ExComm reconvened, 24 hours after the quarantine had been activated, the overriding uncertainty remained: would the Soviets challenge the U.S. Navy, as threatened in Khrushchev's latest letter, or would they choose to defer or avoid hostilities at sea? President Ken-

---

[221]Fursenko and Naftali, *"One Hell of a Gamble,"* 259–60; Talbott, ed., *Khrushchev Remembers,* 497.

[222]Tapes 37.4, 38.1 & 38.2A, POF, PRC, JFKL.

nedy switched on the tape recorder as he conversed with Donald Wilson, acting director of the U.S. Information Agency, about Cuban attempts to jam Voice of America broadcasts and Castro's public denial that Soviet offensive missiles were on Cuban soil. JFK seemed irritated that the Cuban regime had "left out evidently, in what... whatever broadcast they had of my speech, our charge about the missiles" and suggested finding out whether foreign embassies in Cuba had determined "whether it's generally accepted [by the Cuban people] that there are missiles and whether the dropping of pictures of missiles in there ultimately would have any effect." Wilson seemed attracted to the idea, "I believe the dropping of... of pictures would be *very good*," but the notion was shelved for the moment because of concerns about the risks to U.S. aircraft.

McCone read his standard intelligence briefing, beginning with the disquieting news that there had been no change detected in "the scope or pace or the construction of the IRBMs and MRBM missiles sites in Cuba." Although "Cuban armed forces continue their alert ... [and] known and suspected dissidents are being rounded up," there were no signs, as yet, of any "*crash* procedure and measures to increase the readiness of the Soviet armed forces." Some units were on alert, but there had been no significant redeployments. He confirmed the "widely known turnaround" of Soviet ships bound for Cuba and noted that several Latin American nations were preparing to offer military personnel for the quarantine and "there is generally little adverse reaction in that hemisphere." The CIA chief also revealed that Sir Kenneth Strong, chairman of the British Joint Intelligence Committee, had examined the photos in Washington and, despite initial skepticism, "became thoroughly convinced," and informed his government that "the evidence presented was compelling and he felt the situation was *most* provocative. I think this is a very useful thing that by coincidence he happened to be here." The latest low-level photos, McCone claimed, were even "more valuable than was... than was first thought."

McCone also reported on "another almost forgotten subject that we... gave us a great deal of concern," the ongoing negotiations to free the Bay of Pigs prisoners in exchange for Castro's extensive list of medicine, plasma, baby food (27% of the list) and other supplies. Finally, he revealed that "there's great worry *in* Havana, great anxiety among the people. They're mounting aircraft... anti-aircraft guns on the roofs of buildings. Their military are in a high state of alert." The President, intrigued by this information in terms of a potential invasion of Cuba, asked if it might be possible to get an up-to-date analysis, "about the state of morale of the people there and their viewpoint about all of this." He was especially interested in whether the Cuban people knew about the missile sites, "their reaction to it and their support of the regime." McCone promised to "go into it carefully. We have a… quite a number sources."

The attention of the ExComm quickly shifted to the unpredictable overnight situation at the quarantine line. McNamara reviewed the steps by which the Soviet tanker *Bucharest* had been intercepted by a U.S. destroyer at 7:15 A.M. that morning. Since the tanker was not carrying offensive weapons and Khrushchev, despite his harsh words, appeared to be maneuvering to avoid a clash at sea, the *Bucharest* was permitted to pass through the blockade after identifying itself and its point of origin (the Black Sea), destination (Havana) and cargo (petroleum products). However, the defense secretary revealed that the *Bucharest* remained under surveillance and could be boarded later in the day. "I believe," he stressed, "we should establish a pattern of boarding as a quarantine technique and do it *immediately*." The President responded, "Have we got any other ships we can board now?" McNamara explained that there were many non-Soviet ships, but turned to the tanker *Grozny* when JFK asked about potential Soviet vessels. The *Grozny* may have "deviated from its established course and then resumed course during the night. And it appears to be moving now towards Cuba. It's of *great* interest to us," McNamara made clear, because it's probably carrying "missile fuel tanks on deck" and should reach the blockade barrier at about 8:00 P.M. Friday evening [October 26].

McNamara also revealed some particularly intriguing information, "There is *much* evidence that the Soviets have instructed the Cubans to act very cautiously. . . . It appears that they've given instructions to Cuban MiGs *not* to fire on U.S. aircraft. And more than that, it appears that in a separate instruction, they gave orders to Cuban MiGs *not* to take off from the airfields." Equally noteworthy, he added, the Soviets were camouflaging the SAM sites, "thereby reducing their readiness because they have to pull these covers off in order to fire effectively." The defense chief urged the President to exploit this military opportunity by setting up a pattern of low-level surveillance flights that would seem to the Cubans and the Soviets consistent with, and therefore indistinguishable from, flight patterns which could later be used to initiate air attacks. This low-level surveillance, he therefore concluded, could be conducted "with *very* little risk of... of an incident that we did not wish to incite ourselves."

JFK, apparently puzzled by McNamara's reasoning, inquired about the benefits of this pattern of low-level surveillance and the defense secretary listed three advantages: it would provide new, useful and low-risk intelligence; it would "establish a pattern of operation that is consistent with an *attack* and cannot be differentiated from an *attack*, and therefore reduces the warning of an *attack*, and *may* make it possible to attack with lesser forces because we reduced the warning . . . an *extremely* important point we can discuss later." It would also demonstrate to the public and the world that the U.S. and the OAS are "*not only* interested in stopping the flow of offensive weapons to Cuba but also *definitely* have as our objective the removal of the weapons that are there." This low-level surveillance was crucial, he contended, because "the Soviets are camouflaging their sites. There is *tremendous* evidence of this. You can see the camouflage nets drying on the ground. It's been raining and it's wet and they're drying them out. They're under instructions to camouflage *immediately* and they've camouflaged not *just* the weapons, but various buildings, trucks, all kinds of things."

"It's all gray to me," JFK quipped sarcastically, "this whole Russian thing . . . ahh . . . someday!" Some laughter can be heard as he continued, "Why they didn't camouflage it before? Why they do it now and at what point they thought we were gonna find it out? I don't see this. This whole reference is the most...," but unfortunately he trailed off indistinctly.[223]

"It... it's... it's an *amazing* thing," McNamara replied, "but *now* I think we're beginning to read their minds," he laughed softly, "*much more clearly* than... than was true... 72 hours ago."

"Maybe their minds are clearer," Bundy interjected.

McNamara repeated his recommendation to take advantage of Soviet efforts to camouflage "everything in sight" by publicly announcing the start of low-level surveillance, "to go in and... and check on what's going on," with about 8 aircraft in a pattern that would mask a subsequent air attack on the missile sites, the IL-28s, the MiG airfields, the Komar boats (missile-bearing patrol craft) and SAM sites; he quickly added, at Gilpatric's suggestion, the nuclear storage areas, "which they

---

[223]For a discussion of conflicting Soviet organizational goals in Cuba, "to be ready for action and to conceal its activity" with camouflage, see Allison and Zelikow, *Essence of Decision*, 212–14.

are working on with great speed and effort. . . . And I think it will establish a pattern of operations *consistent* with an attack, and therefore it will *camouflage* an attack." "Why do we even bother to announce it?" JFK asked, "Why don't we just do it?" McCone pointed out that the President had specifically mentioned continuing surveillance in his October 22 speech. McNamara agreed to defer discussion on making an announcement but argued that the eight required aircraft should initially be unarmed—although he seemed open to arming later flights.

Taylor also endorsed the proposal, "This low level is very desirable, Mr. President." The defense chief asked for permission to order the flights immediately and JFK replied, "Alright." Rusk also endorsed the President's proposal to "do it without an announcement" and McNamara finally agreed. Taylor left the meeting to convey the order for these immediate unannounced low-level surveillance flights to the JCS.

The defense secretary, evidently encouraged by securing the President's approval for low-level reconnaissance missions which could mask plans for later air strikes, further pressed his rather Machiavellian scheme to destroy the missiles with low-risk attacks by *"very* few aircraft." If low-level photos, which could be interpreted in 3–4 hours, confirmed that *"every single missile site* is 8 hours from launch . . . then we have *very* little risk of going in within that eight-hour period" with the Cubans and Soviets thrown off guard by previous low-level surveillance missions flown in exactly the same pattern. A further advantage could also be gained in the diplomatic/political sphere: if *"all* the Cuban forces, to the best of our knowledge, are under orders not to attack," McNamara explained, the United States should push the U.N. Security Council plan for neutral inspection of the missile sites. The result, he suggested, would almost certainly be a veto by the U.S.S.R. The U.S. would then have the rationale for quickly converting these unarmed low-level reconnaissance missions into surprise air attacks, capable of striking the missile bases within the crucial 4–8 hour window needed to prepare the missiles for launch—with almost no risk of retaliation.

Robert Kennedy promptly punctured McNamara's confidence by raising the troubling possibility that these "instructions of the non-firing and the non-offensive action might be based on the expectation or the wish that we fire the first shot and then they'll all be loosed." McNamara had to reluctantly admit, *"Possibly*, Bobby, I don't know." Perhaps, RFK suggested, "maybe we would want to do this in the next 48 hours," but McNamara guardedly recommended taking only those steps at this moment "that'll give us the *option* to do it if we later *choose* to." The U.S. could act once these low-level flights had begun and the Security Council veto was cast, McNamara explained, "Then we don't have to do anything more today." RFK agreed.

The President returned to the political and diplomatic options for enforcing the quarantine: "whether the political... whether the political situation at the U.N. and everyplace else is such that we want to let this *Bucharest* pass today without making the inspection. That's *really* the question: What is the political effect of our letting that pass? Are we better off to make this issue come to a head *today*, or is there some advantage in putting it off till tomorrow?" Rusk did not see any reason for stopping the *Bucharest* a second time, "We've already passed it through." But, McNamara objected, "We haven't *passed* it! We just hailed it, it replied and we're... we're shadowing it." JFK asked about the advantages of putting off searching a Soviet ship for 24 hours and McNamara explained that boarding and searching could safely be put off for as much as 48 hours. "From my point of view," Rusk reasoned, "a tanker is not the *best* example," since POL was not on the contraband list and there was no suspicious cargo visible on deck, and "there's not much room for them under... beneath deck."

The President was of the same mind: "Alright, because obviously if that had contained a missile they woulda' turned it around." The reason not to board the *Bucharest*, JFK maintained, was pragmatic: "we wanted to *give* sufficient grace to the Soviet Union to get these instructions clear or for the U.N. to have a chance to operate. That seems to be the best grounds to put it on if we decide this isn't our... our a... our best... our *first* case. . . . At this point, in view of U Thant's appeal, we let this go." After some additional debate about which ship to board, Sorensen contended "if it's important to board a Russian ship, and it seems to me it is," a tanker might provide the "*best* chance" because "They'll *never* let you board a ship that *really* has something serious on it." President Kennedy reasoned, "Quite obviously they don't want us to grab anything. I think the *whole problem* is to make a judgment of Khrushchev's message to me last night combined with—in which he said they're *not* gonna do it [allow ships to be searched]. They're gonna take action if we *do*—combined with what is happening at the U.N. and so on." Unless additional time might "make it more likely that we're gonna get something out of either the U.N. or Khrushchev," he concluded, adopting Senator Russell's earlier metaphor, "then I suppose you have to grasp the nettle."

Rephrasing the argument he had just been making as a question, JFK asked: "What impression do they get over there [in the Kremlin] that we... we let this one [the *Bucharest*] go?" McNamara replied simply that this ship was a tanker and was not carrying weapons, "They told us it was carrying only POL. That was not on our list and we let it go through." RFK asked if the *Grozny* could be picked up the next day since the *Bucharest* had been allowed to pass and the defense secretary quickly replied, "Yes." "Now what's the advantage of let uh... letting this one [the *Bucharest*] pass?" the obviously uncertain President asked yet again. McNamara recapitulated, "The only advantage is avoiding a *shooting* incident over a ship that is... appears to the public to be an obvious example of a ship *not* carrying prohibited weapons." "This is the point. This is not a very good... a very good test case," Rusk interjected, and McNamara advised, "I don't think we've weakened this forceful position that'll lead to removal of the missile sites by letting the *Bucharest* go through." Bundy asked for Thompson's view, "I think this is the course to follow," the former ambassador advised, since the Soviets would surely turn the *Grozny* around if the *Bucharest* were boarded.

McNamara recommended announcing that the *Bucharest* had not been stopped because it didn't have a deck load and its hatches were too small to be carrying missiles, but RFK proposed a more politically subtle explanation: "I suppose you could say that obviously, at the present time, the Russians are observing the quarantine. They've sent all their other ships back." McNamara and Bundy suggested an additional step—the Navy should be instructed not to intercept tankers at this time, without making any public announcement of that internal decision. JFK observed that this strategy would give the administration more time and Rusk added that it would avoid provoking an incident at sea during the current U.N. discussions.

"I think," RFK insisted, "we have to face up to the fact that we're gonna have to intercept a ship that doesn't have... that doesn't have contraband." McNamara conceded that if all ships delivering missiles were turned back a vessel like the *Grozny*, carrying a deck load, would have to be seized. The President nonetheless recognized the political advantage in his brother's proposal to announce that the quarantine was being observed: "as Bobby said, the quarantine *to a degree* is already successful because . . . How many ships have turned back?" McNamara, Bundy and others responded, "Fourteen." "Fourteen ships," JFK continued, "have *turned back* as a result of the quarantine." But, he also cautioned, almost using RFK's exact words, "that we've got to face up to the fact that we're gonna have to grab a Russian ship and that he [Khrushchev] says he's not gonna permit it. Now, the question is whether it's better to have that happen today or tomorrow." Bundy expressed the hope that in the next 48 hours, U Thant might convince the U.S.S.R. to avoid challenging the quarantine, "It's not likely, but it's conceivable." "In that case," JFK decided halfheartedly, "we might as well wait."

The President, nonetheless, had no illusions about avoiding an eventual naval confrontation. Despite the unusual circumstances surrounding the passage of the *Bucharest* through the blockade, the seizure of a Soviet ship seemed inevitable in the next day or two. RFK remarked that the situation at the quarantine line had yet to come to a head and JFK concluded, "I think we oughta have a ship available to grab, depending on what happens tomorrow afternoon, this other ship [the *Grozny*]." McNamara concurred: "I think you should instruct them, Mr. President, to be prepared to intercept tomorrow during daylight— if it's at all possible to develop a practical plan to do so." "And no matter where it might be," RFK added, which elicited McNamara's full agreement.

McCone, on a somewhat more hopeful note, cited a CIA report indicating that many Soviet ships had turned around in the vicinity of the Mediterranean, "pretty far *east*, which is *quite* significant, I think," suggesting that they were not simply waiting for a day or two to regroup in a convoy and challenge the quarantine. Ball agreed that this early course change indicated that the Soviets did not expect the blockade to be lifted any time soon. But, Nitze countered with a much bleaker assessment, "The other... the other explanation might be that they're counting on *taking* forceful action against the first one we intercept." "That's right," JFK muttered almost inaudibly. Bundy cautioned, however, "There's nothing, Mr. President—I've just checked the language in your speech—which requires you to *stop* any ship, simply, '*If* found to contain cargoes of offensive weapons, it will be turned back.'" JFK murmured, "Yeah," as Bundy concluded, "The way in which we find this [contraband] is our business." Interestingly, no one responded directly to Bundy's intriguing observation.

McNamara, instead, recommended adding missile fuel to the list of prohibited items and RFK asked if the *Bucharest* was carrying missile fuel. "We're almost sure," the defense chief replied, that the answer was 'no' "because the missile fuel would not be in *these* tankers. It would be on... on deck load." The discussion continued, in progressively more minute detail, as the ExComm tried to predict and prepare for virtually any contingency that might develop on the high seas. Ball, for example, asked if these ships carried "Kerosene missile fuel" and McNamara replied, "No, fuming nitric acid." "There's a lot of interest in what's happening to these ships," JFK pointed out; but, the fact that no ships had been stopped was bound to come out, making it increasingly difficult to just sit around for 24 hours waiting for the *Grozny*. McNamara again proposed saying simply that all ships were being hailed and those like the tanker *Bucharest*, obviously not carrying prohibited materials, were allowed through. "It's *extremely unusual* for tankers to carry deck cargo," he pointed out. "This is why the *Grozny* is *so* extraordinary."

There was no hard evidence, however, other than Khrushchev's latest letter and the presence of Soviet submarines in the Atlantic, that the Russians might actually try to run the blockade. Don Wilson wondered "if we should give out information that they [Soviet ships] *have indeed* turned back," and JFK agreed that once the answer to "what's happened to Russian ships" was clear, "I would think that the Pentag... the Defense Department could announce about these—I think it's pretty well out, isn't it?" On the other hand, the fact that 14 ships appeared to have turned around, raised hopes that the Soviet leader was rethinking his official hard-line stance. Rusk advised being very careful about giving the general impression that most ships had turned back because if the Navy grabbed one, "it will put the bee on us for being . . ." "Warmongers," the President muttered, finishing Rusk's sentence. "Well, we're caught with one crowd *or* the other," Bundy observed cynically.

JFK tried to be realistic—ruminating that it was politically risky to make too much of the ships that had evidently reversed direction, "I don't... don't want a sense of euphoria passing around," he counseled. "That message of Khrushchev is much tougher than that." McCone advised the President to stick with the statement from the previous evening, "They've altered their course and we don't know the significance of it." But McNamara disagreed, arguing that the administration should avoid public speculation on "what the Soviet ships are doing" and simply confine all statements to the day's quarantine activities.

Once a ship was stopped in a day or so and the Soviet response was clear, JFK proposed, POL would have to be put on the contraband list because work on the missile sites was continuing. McNamara advised adding aviation gas as well since the IL-28s were still being assembled.

As soon as that was done, the President made clear, all tankers would be seized, "We first wanna get the test case to be a better one than a tanker," JFK added, "is that the argument?" and McNamara confirmed, "Yes, I think so, Mr. President." RFK worried that the *Grozny* might also turn back, leading Bundy to quip, "Damned few trains on the Long Island Railroad."

The strained laughter that followed lasted only a few seconds since McNamara replied, "I would *seriously* think in a case like . . . the idea you had Bobby, that you go out there and if it turns around, you board it anyhow." "My God," RFK replied testily, it would be better to grab a ship like the *Kimovsk*, believed to be carrying missiles, even if it had turned around. "I suppose that's too late," he conceded, "isn't it?" Rusk admonished, if "it has radioed Moscow that it has turned around and it's still boarded, *that's bad*," but Nitze suggested that the *Grozny* would probably reverse course as soon as the announcement on missile fuel was made public. RFK agreed that an official statement "might scare 'em off." "But they'd let you wait until Lent," he wisecracked, provoking another touch of laughter. McNamara reaffirmed that missile fuel should be added to the contraband list sometime that day, but Rusk reiterated, "Isn't our *purpose* to turn it around without shooting, if we *can*?" RFK nonetheless persisted, "The point is that we may eventually have to intercept a ship, and... and... and we'd like to intercept a ship that had something rather than a lot of baby food for children." Nitze concluded, "I think Dean is right," if the ships indeed turn around, "that's fine," but those that reach the blockade must be inspected. "Otherwise *they're* deciding," Bundy declared, "what... what meets our proclamation."

Ball, echoing Rusk's doubts, urged restraint: "I think personally it would be a *great* mistake to intercept a ship if it were in the process of turning around because this puts us in *no* position, it seems to me, no defensible position." The President restated that the key issue in the next 24 hours was "whether we ought to let this tanker [the *Bucharest*] go through. . . . We're not gonna grab any other tankers today. . . . We've got *some* credit on our side, which is the 14 ships that *may* have turned around. And we've got the question of whether this procedure is a little *flat*. . . . Is there a political advantage," he conjectured, "in stretching this thing out? That's *really* the question. Are we gonna get anything out of the U.N. or Khrushchev?"

At that point, Bundy interrupted and proposed turning to Ambassador Stevenson's draft of a reply to U Thant's proposal for a moratorium on the delivery of missiles to Cuba and a suspension of the quarantine. JFK, perhaps eager to change the subject, swiftly agreed, "OK. Why don't we do that." Rusk can be heard rustling through his papers and then read Stevenson's proposed draft message aloud. The secretary of state emphasized the key American conditions for any suspension of the quarantine: the U.N. would guarantee that "no offensive armament reaches Cuba during the 2 or 3 week period mentioned in your message" and that "the nations of this hemisphere can be assured of the suspension of work on the establishment of missiles and other offensive weapons in Cuba. During these preliminary talks the present quarantine measures would of course continue. The United States therefore accepts your proposal for preliminary talks on the basis described and hopes the U.S.S.R. will do the same."

The President listened quietly but his skepticism surfaced immediately: the quarantine could only be lifted, he remarked, "If the U.N. can give, which they *can't* give, but... adequate guarantees against the introduction of offensive material during this period. . . . Well they *can't* do that, but at least," he observed, with an eye again on the politics of the situation, "it doesn't make us look quite as negative." Irritated by what seemed like naïve meddling by U Thant, JFK seemed eager to fix the blame for the probable failure of this U.N. peace plan, "I'd rather stick the cat on his back." Ball insisted again that the quarantine must be kept in place during these preliminary U.N. talks, despite pressure from U Thant to lift it "right away," and the President responded sharply, "Well we *can't* take the quarantine off until he offers a substitute and he hasn't offered a substitute."

Bundy boldly suggested addressing that issue right off the bat in the statement to the U.N.: "Why don't we say that in sentence one? There's no *pain* in that. That's an *absolutely fundamental* proposition with us. The quarantine is *there* to prevent the introduction of offensive weapons." He then summarized the emerging consensus: the quarantine could only be lifted if three conditions were met: a halt in the delivery of offensive weapons to Cuba, cessation of construction of the missile sites and reliable inspection and verification. "And," Rusk added, "U.N. observers to ensure that offensive weapons are not operational." McNamara, however, urged his colleagues to remember that stopping the delivery of missiles had always been taken for granted, but "the quarantine to us is a form of pressure to assure *the removal* of those weapons." There should be no loophole, he demanded, allowing the lifting of the quarantine before "effective steps have been taken" to guarantee the withdrawal of the missiles already in Cuba.

Rusk attempted to clarify the U.N. moratorium proposal: 2–3 weeks of preliminary talks with the quarantine in place, followed by a U.N. quarantine and U.N. observers to verify that work had ceased and the missiles were inoperable, and finally, "getting the weapons out of there." But the flak from his colleagues was immediate: Bundy worried whether "when you *get* into a *haggle* of this kind the status quo doesn't come to have a momentum of its own." McNamara admitted that he had never believed these weapons would be removed from Cuba "without the application of substantial force." He quickly explained, however, in words similar to the argument he had made at the evening meeting on October 16, that "force" could be economic or military— noting that Cuba was already experiencing rising insurance rates and would soon face a loss of foreign trade. But, he advised against removing the quarantine, even with U.N. inspection, "*unless* they agreed to take the weapons out." Bundy affirmed that the critical issue was moving the status quo forward toward the goal of removing the weapons already in Cuba and McNamara added, "This is my point, exactly."

After Rusk reread the last line of the proposed draft, the President remained unconvinced, "We're not gonna get anyplace with this thing because they can't guarantee... there's no way they can accept with American ships preventing weapons coming in. In addition, the Cubans aren't gonna take this too well." At the President's prompting, Rusk again read aloud the revised version of the message to U Thant—which was later clarified and shortened in discussions with Stevenson to emphasize the necessity of removing the weapons from Cuba. The letter was finally dispatched to New York that afternoon.

The secretary of state shifted the focus of the meeting to another diplomatic initiative, which he called "a very interesting possibility"—a Brazilian proposal to declare Latin America a nuclear-free zone. The President immediately seemed cool to the idea, asking for clarification on whether they meant "nuclear-free" or "missile-free" and pointing out that the U.S. had proof of missiles in Cuba but no verification of nuclear warheads. Rusk replied that the plan called for making Latin America nuclear-free and suggested that the idea might be applicable to Africa as well: "I just wanted to mention this possibility," Rusk explained, "because this could create an *enormous* pressure in the [U.N.

General] Assembly and around the world, and I think on the Soviet Union, on the presence of these weapons in ah... in Cuba."

President Kennedy, evidently uninterested, simply changed the subject, "OK. What else we got?" Bundy advised taking a moment to review the October 23 exchange of letters between Khrushchev and the President, and, at JFK's suggestion, he read aloud pertinent paragraphs from the Soviet leader's message—after first mocking Khrushchev's statements "about our immorality, and that the quarantine's no good, and the OAS is no good and their people will follow the norms of combat." Ambassador Thompson commented bleakly that Khrushchev's letter "indicated preparation *for* resistance by force, that is, forcing us to take forcible action." Bundy then read portions of JFK's reply and the President muttered almost despondently, "And there we are."

Nitze speculated that Khrushchev was actually maneuvering to "not let his ships be put in a position where they can be held captive, boarded and searched" and Bundy conjectured that "we *may* be moving into a... some kind of a de facto, unclarified quarantine." The prospect of a protracted and inconclusive status quo in Cuba alarmed McNamara. He asked the President to consider several possible developments in the next 24 hours: a) the U.N. fails to take effective action b) there is no Soviet ship to intercept or the only ship available is not carrying prohibited weapons, c) work continues on the missile sites. In that case, he asked point blank, "What do we do?" Ball promptly declared, "I think we escalate to the uh...," but the President cut in, "Well, we first stop a Soviet ship, uh... uh... someplace, and have this out on what they're gonna do."

McNamara warily pointed out that the choices might be more complicated: the Soviets might decide to permit the inspection of a ship that was not carrying offensive weapons. In short, they might comply for the time being with the prohibition on shipping offensive materials to Cuba while they continued the construction of the missile sites. "Now what do we do under these circumstances?" The defense chief did not wait for an answer, but instead endorsed Ball's inference about escalating the quarantine. Bundy, in response, recommended convening "a meeting of this committee *without* the President" for an examination of the specifics of all the possible choices open to the U.S.—that way the procedural options could be sorted out without bothering JFK with the minutiae. Kennedy asked if adding POL to the quarantine would be "the obvious escalation," but McNamara instead urged including aviation gas or jet fuel because of the continuing assembly of the IL-28 bombers.

"That's not much of an escalation," McNamara nonetheless admitted, "because there aren't any tankers immediately within our grasp here. . . . It would seem to me that the timing is important. We don't want to allow any particular period of time to go by that starts to freeze the situation. We want to continue to move toward this ultimate objective of removing the missiles." Bundy requested a general consensus around the table on this point, and tried to pin down "especially the President's own view. I... I share that view, *very much*, that a... that a plateau here is the most dangerous thing." Several participants expressed agreement but Rusk seemed unsure and President Kennedy asked: "What is the difficulty if they continue the work, our timing POL, because it doesn't have any particular relationship to the work being continued?" McNamara reasoned that adding POL would appear to be "a provocative move, Mr. President, unless it's related directly to one of these offensive weapons." Taylor advised that prohibiting IL-28 fuel was "not much of an escalation," and McNamara agreed, instead recommending the drafting of a more effective "program of escalation that we might put into effect in the next 24 to 48 hours."

JFK, evidently impressed by McNamara's logic, reopened the possibility of having U.S. destroyers, protected by air cover, intercept the *Bucharest* in the morning before it made landfall in Cuba. But Bundy, citing Rusk's "eyeball to eyeball" remark, suggested that it would be damaging to appear to have waffled for 24 hours over seizing the *Bucharest* and recommended that it would be better "to take her now or to let her go." "I... I agree with Mac, Mr. President," McNamara affirmed. "I *don't* think the *Bucharest* is a very useful case... case for us to... gamble." The President pointed out that "the only important thing" was the fact that the *Bucharest* had been the first ship to cross the barrier, but Bundy underscored firmly that "there is a *real* case to be made, which has perhaps not been presented as strongly this morning as it... as it *could* be, for *doing* it and *getting* it done," so that the United States retained the initiative in determining the effectiveness of the quarantine. Rusk remained unconvinced and the President stressed that "the object is *not* to stop offensive weapons because the offensive weapons are already there, as much as it is to have a showdown with the Russians of one... one kind or another." Rusk and McNamara repeated that a tanker did not provide "much of an excuse for a show-down" and could actually "weaken our position for the *next* step."

Bundy, rather intrepidly, ratcheted up the pressure by admonishing the commander-in-chief, "It is *important* for you to know, Mr. President, that... that there is a *good*, substantial argument and a lot of people in the argument on the other side, *all* of whom will fall in with whatever decision you make." He suggested, however, that Nitze "would feel much differently" and the hard-hitting assistant defense secretary promptly took the cue,[224] urging the President to ignore the distinctions between ships and fully enforce "the *principle* of a blockade. . . . You've *declared* a quarantine, which has certain implied rules. Why don't you just go ahead and carry out those rules indiscriminately, against everybody, not selecting ships or the types of ships. But just go ahead and *do* that. I think that would be the easiest in the end." "That's correct," Bundy affirmed. Rusk, however, again urged restraint, citing "what the effect is on... if the present Soviet conduct about turning back ships continues . . . because in the circumstances, it's already escalated *very*, *very* fast."

The President's response, at this potentially critical turning point, was disjointed, agitated and ungrammatical, but his intent was inescapable: he decided again to delay a military confrontation: "Alright, well, in any case, I'll tell you what let's do," he began. He then stammered out a series of sentence fragments, his thoughts often outpacing his words, which tumbled out in rapid-fire stream of consciousness: "Let's wait until... we gotta... let's come back this afternoon and take this ship. I don't... I think we can always... your point about, we didn't act, so, 'eyeball to eyeball'. . . We coulda said, 'no, we're waiting for Khrushchev, we're waiting for U Thant'..."

His next sentence, however, was unmistakably clear, "We don't want to precipitate an incident with major new..."

"I was thinking about it tomorrow morning, Mr. President," Bundy interjected.

"OK, well," Kennedy continued, "we still have then another 6 or 7 hours [to stop the *Bucharest*]. I think the only argument's for *not* taking it. I think we could grab us one of these things anytime. I don't think it makes a hell of a lot of difference what ship it is... but a... whether it's a tanker... I would think the only argument would be that, with U Thant and the U.N. asking us for a...."

---

[224]Bundy likely either knew in advance or certainly suspected what Nitze would say.

"We've given them a letter," Bundy assured the President.

"This is *not* the *appropriate* time to *blow up* a ship," President Kennedy directed, "so that ah... maybe that a... and since I wrote back to Khrushchev we could justify postponing our action to our 5 this afternoon [meeting], if that's the way. So let's think a little more about it."

"Right," Bundy assented.

Robert Kennedy amplified one of his brother's last points, "Can you take a tanker without blowing it up, Bob?" and McNamara replied confidently, "Yes." After Bundy and Rusk briefly referred to the timing of the next U.N. Security Council meeting (at 4:00 that afternoon), RFK endorsed Bundy's earlier proposal, "Can we have a meeting of our group without the uh... President?" As Bundy answered, "We can," the reel of tape either ran out or the President switched off the tape recorder.

That afternoon, responding to pressure from Ambassador Stevenson, U Thant sent a second message to Khrushchev and Kennedy; he urged the Premier to keep Russian ships away from the quarantine line and advised the President "to do everything possible to avoid a direct confrontation with Soviet ships in the next few days."[225] *Meanwhile the Pentagon announced that some 12 Soviet ships had reversed course short of the quarantine perimeter and acknowledged that the Bucharest had been hailed and questioned but allowed to continue toward Cuba.*

A few hours later the United Nations Security Council convened in New York. Soviet U.N. ambassador Valerian Zorin, apparently without instructions from Moscow and unaware of Khrushchev's missile deployment in Cuba, defiantly denied that the U.S.S.R. had placed offensive nuclear weapons ninety miles from the American mainland. He ridiculed Ambassador Stevenson's "so-called evidence" and demanded to know why President Kennedy had not shown these "incontrovertible facts" to Foreign Minister Gromyko during their October 18 meeting at the White House. The reason, Zorin declared, was obvious: "Because no such facts exist." President Kennedy, after watching the televised U.N. session, authorized Stevenson to stick it to Zorin by confronting him with the aerial photos during the Security Council debate.[226]

[225]U Thant to Nikita Khrushchev, October 25, 1962, in Chang and Kornbluh, *Cuban Missile Crisis*, 384.

[226]*New York Times*, October 26, 1962.

The ExComm resumed its discussions at around 5:00 P.M., but President Kennedy, apparently watching the televised U.N. debate, joined the meeting somewhat late. The intelligence briefing revealed that Soviet technicians were working intently to complete the construction of the missile sites and the assembly of the IL-28 bombers. McNamara, picking up where he had left off during the morning meeting, discussed alternatives for turning up the heat on the blockade so that the precariously evolving situation would not become frozen in place. Rusk too warned that "the missiles in Cuba were becoming operational and the IL-28s would soon be dangerous."[227] When the President entered the Cabinet Room and turned on the tape recorder, McNamara was discussing a ship that was steadily approaching the blockade line.

Thursday, October 25, after 5:00 P.M., Cabinet Room

Identified Participants: John F. Kennedy, George Ball, McGeorge Bundy, Douglas Dillon, Robert Kennedy, John McCone, Robert McNamara, Paul Nitze, Walt Rostow, Dean Rusk, Theodore Sorensen, Maxwell Taylor, Llewellyn Thompson.[228]

"I think if the work continues, we either have to do this air business and the... *or* we have to put POL on because we... we got to bring counter pressure because otherwise the work's going on and *we're not really doin' anything else.*"

President John F. Kennedy

McNamara reported that an East German passenger ship, the *Völkerfreundschaft*, carrying about 1,500 industrial workers, including 550 Czech technicians and 25 East German students, was being tailed by the destroyer U.S.S. *Pierce* and would reach the quarantine barrier that day. "The question is, should we ask it to halt and submit to inspection? If it did *not* halt, should we pass it without *forcing* it to halt, or should we *force* it to halt. . . . If we use [naval] fire and we damage the ship, with 1,500 people on board" and do not find prohibited materials, McNamara counseled the President, it would weaken the American

---

[227]McGeorge Bundy, Executive Committee Record of Action, October 25, 1962, 5:00 P.M., Meeting No. 5, NSF, JFKL; Bromley Smith, Summary Record of NSC Executive Committee Meeting No. 5, October 25, 1962, NSF, JFKL.

[228]Tapes 38.2 & 38.2A, POF, PRC, JFKL.

position. "I should recommend to this group and to you that we *not* ask this ship to stop."

The President, mindful of the political risks raised by McNamara, expressed concern that the U.S. could not unilaterally observe U Thant's request to avoid a military incident at sea if Khrushchev refused to keep his ships away from the quarantine line. Bundy pointed out, somewhat smugly, that U Thant's message applied only to Soviet vessels and the ship in question was East German. Ted Sorensen cleverly interjected that this ambiguity presented an opportunity to demonstrate that the American response was "*not* a soft one at all." The United States, he suggested, could have it both ways by stopping a ship and at the same time avoid challenging "the prestige of the Soviets—directly." He also asked skeptically, "How do you tell a missile technician from an agricultural technician?"

The discussion about whether to stop the *Völkerfreundschaft* exposed the persistent uncertainty about how to proceed in this unprecedented situation. "What do we *gain* by stopping it?" McNamara asked, "I can see *some* possible loss." Bundy, however, renewing his argument from the morning meeting, emphasized the danger to American credibility in simply revealing to "the [Soviet] *bloc* that you're *not* stopping." The President argued that the decision depended on Khrushchev's response to U Thant's message: specifically, whether he kept his ships out of the area, or rejected the offer or failed to respond. "Then," JFK reasoned, "we have to pick up some ship tomorrow, after the shoe drops."

The President revealed lingering doubts, however, by immediately asking McNamara, "What do you think, Bob?" The defense secretary again asserted forcefully that risking loss of life on a passenger ship would demonstrate to the world that "we'd acted irresponsibly" and "would be absurd." JFK appreciated the political wisdom in McNamara's position, acknowledging that "the only reason for picking *this* ship up is we gotta prove sooner or later that the blockade works." The defense chief offered an alternative discussed at the morning meeting: intercepting the *Grozny*, "a Soviet tanker with a deck cargo," which might reach the blockade line tomorrow afternoon. "Right, I remember that," JFK interjected. "And I would *strongly* recommend," McNamara continued, "we do just that." The President seemed receptive—since focusing on the *Grozny* would give Khrushchev at least another day to respond to U Thant's message.

Robert Kennedy, evidently arriving late, tried to "give another side of it." He argued that increased surveillance of Cuba and the planned tightening of the blockade had already proven "that we're not backing off at all from it." But, if these two tankers [the *Grozny* and the *Bucharest*] were allowed through and the Russians turned their other ships around, even if McNamara later announced that tankers would no longer be allowed through, there might not be another ship available for at least 3 or 4 days. Reaffirming persistent concerns about being trapped in a stalemate, the attorney general focused again on the key issue unresolved by the quarantine: "they're continuing their buildup" in Cuba. In short, "rather than have the confrontation with the Russians at sea," he suggested impassively, "that it might be better to have a... knock out their missile base as the *first step*." Echoing his firm stance at the early ExComm meetings, RFK nimbly sidestepped the issue of an American Pearl Harbor by proposing to warn Soviet personnel "to get out of that vicinity in 10 minutes and then we go through and knock [off] the base." The administration, he reasoned, could quickly demonstrate "that we're not backing off and that we're still being tough with Cuba. That's really the point we have to make."

No one at the table openly backed RFK's scheme, although Dillon hinted that it seemed logical to confine any actual military confrontation to Cuba itself. Rusk's reaction was measured and restrained but implicitly critical, "When you *really* step back and look at it for a second, on... based on any *real* suspicious information that *we* have, the blocka... the quarantine is now *fully* effective." Several voices can be heard affirming, "That's right" or "That's correct." "If you wanted to really wait," RFK added, the effectiveness of the blockade provided an excuse, "without losing face." McNamara interposed that a confrontation with the Cubans or the Soviets could be postponed for 48 hours, but at the same time "we could appear to be forceful" by increasing aerial surveillance over Cuba during the day and using flares to check on work done overnight. "These two actions I think in themselves will convince both our public and the world that we *are* maintaining an adequate... a forceful position"—which was all the more necessary, he added, because a pilot earlier that day had sighted "additional IL-28s out of the crates."

JFK appeared to be leaning toward letting the East German passenger ship through the quarantine and delaying a decision on the *Grozny* until Khrushchev replied to U Thant. If the Soviet leader "announces all the ships [heading to Cuba] are being suspended," the President declared, "that's *that* point." But, he predicted, "I don't think he will, probably." If surveillance confirmed that work on the missile bases and assembly of the IL-28s was continuing, RFK observed—but JFK finished his thought—we can put POL on the contraband list. And jet bomber fuel as well, McNamara advised.

RFK, rather elliptically, urged the President to let the *Grozny*, like the *Bucharest*, through the blockade. "Then what do you do?" the President asked. RFK argued that even though no Russian ships would be coming along for 4 or 5 days, the administration could then announce, since most ships had turned back, that the quarantine had been successful. "And then what do we do?" JFK inquired again, before answering his own question, "Then we need to decide about this air strike again, *or* we then put POL on the thing or..." McNamara assured the President, "We have a lot of harassing actions—" "*Exactly*," RFK interrupted—"we could carry out, and incidents we can provoke if we'd wish to."

Four days earlier the President had decided that a quick air strike was too risky because all the missiles could not be destroyed. Now, apparently in response to his brother's suggestion, JFK had resurrected the air attack option as a response to a possible stalemate at sea which could give the Russians time to finish the missile sites. RFK returned to his most persistent theme: "The only weakness, in... in my judgment, is the idea to the Russians that you know... backing off and that we're weak..." He nonetheless conceded, "If you did some of these *other* things quickly . . . It's a *hell* of a thing, really, when you think of it, that 15 ships have turned back. And I don't think we really have any apologies to make." Sorensen suggested letting the *Grozny* go through but stopping the East German ship. RFK replied that he was unsure, but seemed impressed by McNamara's point about risking the safety of the 1,500 passengers.

Rusk, somewhat diffidently, explained, "Mr. President, since I recommended a blockade, I haven't been very helpful about applying it in particular instances." But, he reiterated that seizing either a tanker or a passenger ship was not the best way to initiate a confrontation and urged the President to choose as "our *first* case" a ship with highly suspicious deck cargo "or a blind ship" with unidentified dry cargo. If the Navy fired on, disabled or sank a ship carrying 1,500 people, Rusk warned, "I think we're just in a *hell* of a shape." "I assume we don't have to sink it," Sorensen remarked.

Walt W. Rostow, chairman of the State Department Policy Planning

Council, spoke for the first time, advising that short of going directly into Cuba, adding POL to the quarantine would have a prompt and serious impact on the Cuban economy: "The POL thing is *very* serious for them" because of "a 100% reliance on it and a *very* short supply" and a cut off would grind their economy to a halt. McCone dissented, insisting that the impact would not be felt for months and RFK agreed, "Yes, I don't think we can rely on it." Rostow cited the German experience in World War II and Ball recalled that "the German Air Force fell apart" because of shortages after their fuel production facilities were bombed. Rostow claimed to have several studies backing his stand on a POL cut-off, but several participants insisted that a Defense Department study had actually reached the opposite conclusion.

The President finally cut through the increasingly circular discussion and enunciated a set of decisions for handling the next 48 hours of the quarantine: given the U Thant initiative, which held out a least "a chance of *easing* this," he ruled out intercepting the East German passenger ship, "if you try to disable it, you're apt to sink it. There are no guarantees when you try to shoot a rudder off, because you either sink it or have it catch fire." That danger, plus the slight hope from the ongoing U.N. negotiations, dictated waiting, "We don't want to sink that ship tomorrow. So I think we can let that one go." He also decided to give Khrushchev more time to respond to U Thant before making a judgment on seizing the *Grozny*, "We've got *two* days." Finally, the President again edged closer to RFK's tougher stance, "I think if the work continues, we either have to do this air business and the... *or* we have to put POL on because we... we got to begin to bring counter pressure because otherwise the work's going on and *we're not really doin' anything else*." RFK, evidently heartened by the President's renewed determination, added, "And we've got to show them that we mean it."

As the meeting began to break up, there was some discussion about taking steps to prevent the Cubans from confusing night reconnaissance flares with a bombing attack. McNamara suggested giving a "warning ahead of time" and a few people chuckled in the background when someone advised being "sure these missiles aren't on their launchers" when starting the night missions. JFK questioned Rostow again on the value of cutting off Cuba's supply of POL. "It's... it's... it's a *very* strong act sir," Rostow maintained. "The clock begins to tick. On the other hand, it still gives them time to negotiate." The President repeated his judgment to defer a decision on the *Grozny*; but, on the East German passenger ship, he declared again, "Let's let that go."

Finally, President Kennedy turned to Ambassador Thompson, "What do you think, Tommy?" "Oh, I think that's... I think you've really considered it right," Thompson replied, but he echoed RFK's uneasiness about maintaining a tough position, "I'm a little troubled by Khrushchev's *strong* letter of yesterday" and want to be sure that we "show him that we're not backing away because of a threat. On the other hand, he *is* backing away and that tips the balance." RFK agreed, "he *definitely* has," but remained cynical. "We retreat an inch and he says, 'six feet to go.'" Thompson also cited a talk he had with the Yugoslav ambassador after a recent diplomatic briefing: "He *volunteered*, without my bringing it up, but he said, 'I just want to tell you one thing. I don't agree with your analysts on your papers, that Khrushchev thinks you're afraid to act or are weak.'" The Yugoslav diplomat recalled several private conversations with Khrushchev and assured Thompson, "he said he *doesn't* think this."

JFK conjectured that it was impossible to pin down Khrushchev's motives in Cuba: explanations ranged from "frustration over Berlin" to a test of American resolve. "In other words," the President reflected philosophically, "you can take your choice on these." Thompson replied, "Yeah," just as the recording stopped.

Sometime after President Kennedy had left the Cabinet Room, the tape machine suddenly started recording again. There may have been a technical glitch, a delay in switching to the backup recorder, or the tape may simply have run out and been replaced. It is also at least possible that JFK turned it off but RFK, sitting near the President's chair during these rump conversations, turned it back on.

This tantalizing segment, about ten minutes in length, picked up bits and pieces of background chit chat among several ExComm members still in the room. Robert Kennedy and McNamara, for example, both fully conversant on covert activities coordinated by the Special Group (Augmented),[229] can be heard exploring the possibility of using Operation Mongoose Cuban operatives, instead of U.S. military forces, to sabotage and destroy the missile sites or perhaps even to facilitate an American invasion of Cuba. Another fragmentary exchange dealt with

[229]RFK chaired the Special Group (Augmented) and Roswell Gilpatric represented Secretary of Defense McNamara. The other regular members were McGeorge Bundy (White House), U. Alexis Johnson (State Department), John McCone (CIA) and Maxwell Taylor (JCS).

carrying out surveillance missions and air strikes against the SAM sites, the MRBMs, the IRBMs and the nuclear storage facilities—when the recording machine seems to have been abruptly turned off.

The U.N. Security Council meeting continued into the evening and Adlai Stevenson prepared to respond to Ambassador Zorin's scornful charge that the United States had trumped up the evidence of offensive missiles in Cuba. Millions of Americans, including the President, viewed the televised debate. Stevenson calmly asked, "if I heard you correctly say that they do not exist or that we haven't proved they exist." When Zorin refused to budge, Stevenson angrily pushed aside his notes: "All right, sir, let me ask you one simple question. Do you, Ambassador Zorin, deny that the U.S.S.R. has placed or is placing medium- and intermediate-range missiles and missile sites in Cuba? Yes or no—don't wait for the translation—yes or no." When Zorin contemptuously responded that he was not in an American courtroom, Stevenson countered firmly, "You are in the courtroom of world opinion right now and you can answer yes or no. You have denied that they exist— and I want to know if I have understood you correctly." Zorin replied that he would respond in due course and Stevenson shot back, "I am prepared to wait for my answer until hell freezes over, if that is your decision." The Security Council delegates burst into laughter.

Stevenson then displayed the photo boards prepared by the CIA, and Zorin, recalling the doctored pictures shown during the Bay of Pigs invasion, responded, "One who has lied once will not be believed a second time." Stevenson irately challenged the Soviet Union to "ask their Cuban colleagues to permit a U.N. team to go to these sites. If so, Mr. Zorin, I can assure you that we can direct them to the proper places very quickly." Ambassador Stevenson concluded: "We know the facts, and so do you, sir, and we are ready to talk about them. Our job here is not to score debating points. Our job, Mr. Zorin, is to save the peace. And if you are ready to try, we are." The response to Stevenson's presentation, in the White House and the entire nation, was enthusiastic. The debate represented the twice-defeated presidential candidate's finest hour and his standing in public opinion surveys spiked to an all-time high.[230]

[230]Robert Kennedy, Thirteen Days, 57–59; Stevenson's enhanced standing did not last. An article by journalists with close Kennedy connections soon charged that the U.N. ambassador had advocated "a Munich" during the ExComm meetings. (Stewart Alsop and Charles Bartlett, "In Time of Crisis," Saturday Evening Post, December 8, 1962, 16–20)

Late that evening JFK responded to U Thant's message, conceding that during preliminary discussions at the U.N. the United States would make every effort to prevent a clash at sea as long as Soviet ships avoided the quarantine zone. By the next morning, Khrushchev replied that, for the moment, he had ordered Soviet ships to stay away from the illegally deployed American naval vessels in Cuban waters. Meanwhile, Castro delivered another passionate harangue denouncing U.S. surveillance and pledging never to submit to American aggression.

Secretary McNamara, during the ExComm intelligence briefing the previous evening, had identified the Marucla, a Soviet-chartered Lebanese freighter, as an ideal choice for boarding but reported that it might be reversing course. Early the following morning, however, the destroyers Pierce and Kennedy confirmed that the vessel had remained on course and they had hailed and boarded the Marucla just after sunrise on Friday, October 26.[231] The Greek crew cooperated fully with the inspection, which lasted nearly three hours, and the Marucla was permitted to proceed toward Cuba. No one had expected that stopping a Soviet-chartered ship would be so uneventful.

By that morning, however, JFK and his advisers had nonetheless become convinced that the crisis had reached a dangerous impasse. The President and several others had acknowledged at the previous day's meetings that the missiles already in Cuba would not be affected by the quarantine, making additional political or military steps inevitable. Indeed, an early morning CIA report had confirmed that construction of the MRBM and IRBM sites was "proceeding without interruption."[232] The massive movement of troops and supplies to southern Florida continued as well, and the press was reporting that an invasion of Cuba was imminent.

RFK, or even JFK himself, may have been the source of this damaging and inaccurate story. (Bernstein, "Reconsidering the Missile Crisis," 102, 128)

[231]The U.S.S. Kennedy was named for the President's older brother, Joseph P. Kennedy, Jr., killed in a plane explosion near Calais in 1944. The assignment of the U.S.S. Kennedy to be one of the first ships to test the quarantine was apparently a surprise to JFK. (Robert Kennedy, Thirteen Days, 63)

[232]Chang and Kornbluh, Cuban Missile Crisis, 385.

Friday, October 26, 10:00 A.M., Cabinet Room

Identified Participants: John F. Kennedy, George Ball, McGeorge Bundy, Douglas Dillon, Roswell Gilpatric, Robert Kennedy, John McCloy, John McCone, Robert McNamara, Paul Nitze, Dean Rusk, Adlai Stevenson, Maxwell Taylor, Llewellyn Thompson, Donald Wilson.[233]

"The only thing that I'm saying is that we're not gonna get 'em out with the quarantine. ... We're either gonna trade 'em out or we're gonna have to go in and get 'em out—ourselves."

President John F. Kennedy

During the routine ExComm intelligence briefing, McCone reported that the arrival of the *Bucharest* in Havana during the night had set off boisterous celebrations. He also reconfirmed that Soviet forces in the U.S.S.R. and eastern bloc countries remained on high alert but no significant redeployments had begun. When the President subsequently switched on the tape recorder, McCone was discussing ongoing pressure, particularly from RFK, to expand the activities of Operation Mongoose to deal with this urgent situation in Cuba—efforts which had become bogged down in turf wars between the CIA, Mongoose operations chief Edward Lansdale and the Pentagon.

Bundy advised, "Mr. President, my suggestion is that we should reconstitute Mongoose as a subcommittee of this committee in the appropriate way, and I think we can work that out this afternoon." McCone endorsed the idea, specifically reminding the President "it's a matter *you* called me about last night." JFK confirmed that he had phoned McCone about organizing "a crash program" to create a new civil government for Cuba in the event of an American invasion. The President was clearly operating on the assumption that *all* military options discussed since October 16 remained on the table if the blockade failed to compel the withdrawal of the missiles from Cuba.

Bundy stressed that "These are *very* important matters" and suggested making "part of the discussion at the Mongoose meeting this afternoon . . . the paramilitary, the civil government, the correlated activities to the main show that we need to reorganize." JFK pointed out that someone at State, CIA, and Defense should be in charge of these plans. "Post-Castro Cuba," Bundy reminded his colleagues, "is the

[233]Tapes 39.1 & 39.1A, POF, PRC, JFKL.

most complex landscape," and McCone reiterated that this subject would be taken up at the afternoon Mongoose meeting. President Kennedy suggested utilizing any CIA analyses of the Cuban community in greater Miami to identify doctors and other professionals "who would be *useful* if we have an invasion of Cuba."

McCone also endorsed more effective use of "the Lansdale organization, the Mongoose organization" in Cuba and asked about whether the U.S. Navy ship monitoring high frequency communications from 10–12 miles off Cuba might be able to risk moving in closer to the coastline. McNamara, however, instead suggested moving the ship 20–30 miles out, at least temporarily, to reduce the chance of a "loss of security if its personnel were captured." Bundy turned to some administrative matters, briefly discussing committees that were being set up to deal with Berlin, advance planning and communications and also mentioning ongoing concerns about accelerating civil defense preparations without creating "a crash or panicked atmosphere," and preventing leaks to the press. He repeated that "this organization of the Lansdale enterprise" would be up for discussion at the Mongoose meeting later that afternoon.[234]

The discussion then returned to the status of the quarantine and McNamara revealed that Navy personnel were, at that very moment, on board the Soviet-chartered Lebanese freighter *Marucla*—chosen because "it was a non bloc ship" which could be stopped and boarded "with the least possible chance of violence." He reported that the crew had cooperated with the boarding party and the cargo was being inspected. "It won't be held long," he assumed, and urged public release of this information. President Kennedy seemed apprehensive about publicly explaining this particular interception: "Now the only question that I've got is how do we justify I mean... we have to... stopping *this* ship and then letting the East German one go forward?" McNamara and others explained that the *Marucla* was a general cargo ship, but JFK remained uneasy, "Will we have to announce that we let the other one through?" McNamara counseled, "Oh, I *don't* believe we should announce it" and Bundy asserted, "We have tried to lick that" by stressing that this passenger ship is not currently a target. "In any case," McNamara concluded, "it's been successful" and he urged that for maximum effect "a good story should be put out immediately."

[234]For a succinct summary of JFK's knowledge of Operation Mongoose, see Fursenko and Naftali, *"One Hell of a Gamble,"* 156–58, 217–19.

The defense chief also reported that there were no bloc or non-bloc ships "within easy range of the quarantine ships" except for the *Grozny*, which was expected to "reach the barrier tomorrow night at 11 P.M. . . . So there's *very* little quarantine activity with respect to Soviet ships that we can anticipate in the next few days." However, he also revealed surveillance had confirmed that work on assembling the IL-28 bombers in Cuba "has continued at an accelerated pace." Therefore, he told the President, "acting under *your* authority, I am adding to the prohibited list bomber fuel and the materials from which it is manufactured." JFK, clearly discomfited, replied hesitantly that he would rather add POL because it was directly related to the missiles rather than the bombers: "the missiles are the more *dramatic* offensive weapons. There's gonna be such bombers everyplace. So is there some way that we could talk... tie it into the construction of these missile sites rather than just the bombers?" McNamara suggested including both bomber fuel and related petroleum products, and Bundy pushed the President to decide, "The larger question is whether... whether you want at the end to have the bombers there. If you want to get them out, this is as good a time as any to tie them into..." But JFK persisted, "I would rather tie as much as we could to the missiles... to the missiles."[235]

"Can't we do them both?" McNamara urged again, and the President endorsed announcing that the U.S. was restricting the delivery of fuel that contributed to the construction of the missile sites as well as aviation fuel for the IL-28 bombers; but, he reemphasized, "I think the *missiles* are the *dramatic* one. Bombers—hell, or they might say, 'we can destroy all *your* bombers every place.'" Rusk recommended a 24-hour delay in adding POL in order to give the U Thant talks a chance. Bundy, however, expressed concern about "*not* losing the momentum" and McNamara affirmed, "That's right. That's right." General Taylor, in an anguished *cri de coeur*, exclaimed, "Mr. President, should we announce every day—that when we have that evidence of... that the work has continued, that a need exists to hit back—with mounting indignation in our voices?" "Yes," McCone muttered in the background, "this is an awfully important point," and Bundy tried again to nail down a

[235]President Kennedy had decided, six days earlier, that any air attacks would be limited to the missiles and "repeated his view that the U.S. would have to live with the threat arising out of the stationing in Cuba of Soviet bombers." (Minutes of the 505th Meeting of the National Security Council, October 20, 1962, 8) In the post–October 28 discussions, however, he would take a much harder line on removing the bombers.

consensus that blockading POL would be, after further discussion of the U Thant initiative, "the next step on the line of pressure."

At the 5:00 P.M. meeting the previous day, Robert Kennedy had reintroduced the idea of demonstrating American toughness by bombing the missile sites "as the *first step*," in order to avert the danger that work on the bases might continue during a stalemate in U.N. negotiations. Now, on the eleventh day of the meetings, those who doubted that tightening the quarantine alone could neutralize the threat from the bases already under construction in Cuba picked up important support. The soft-spoken Treasury secretary, Douglas Dillon, elaborating on a brief reply he had made the previous evening in response to RFK's latest air strike suggestion, exposed the ExComm's lingering doubts about the wisdom of merely tightening the blockade, "If we follow this track," Dillon cautioned, "we'll be sort of caught up in events not of our own control. We will *have to* stop a Soviet ship with what appears to be peaceful cargo on it. We will run into Soviet reactions around the world which could be similar—I mean they might shoot at an American ship."

This decision, Dillon predicted, could easily make the situation worse: "We might wind up in some sort of a... sort of a naval encounter all around the world with the Soviet Union which would have *nothing* to do with the buildup of the missile bases in... in Cuba. The end result of that would be we either go on to a possible general war or pressures get so extreme that we have to stop, both sides, doing this sort of thing. Meanwhile the missiles continue in Cuba." Escalating the quarantine, Dillon insisted, put all the emphasis on a U.S.-U.S.S.R. encounter at sea but did not stop the work in Cuba. Instead, he recommended downplaying the seizure of a Soviet ship and, as RFK had suggested, if the work continued, redirecting the confrontation toward Cuba "by preparing for air action to hit these bases," thus putting pressure on the U.N. "to get inspectors in there to stop this thing."

Bundy and McNamara pushed Dillon's argument aside: "I'm not *sure*," Bundy came back, that the distinction between tracks is "as sharp as you make it." "Nor... nor am I," McNamara added, "I don't believe they're alternative courses." And, since no one, not even RFK, openly endorsed Dillon's position, McNamara pushed again for announcing "that it is our policy to continue surveillance—*day and night*." He proposed sending in 8–10 aircraft that day, followed by 4 that night using roughly 10 flares to illuminate each target. The flares would be thrown out of the planes at about 5,000 feet and become operational at around 2,000 feet, allowing the pilots "to determine the extent to which development of the offensive weapon systems is continuing." Rusk again urged delaying nighttime reconnaissance "until we've had a crack at the... at the U Thant discussions" but also expressed concern that the flares might be provocative because they had been used in the past as preparation for night bombing raids, "we're not sure what the interpretation of the other side would be."

McNamara insisted that the Cubans could be warned in advance about the flares and the President, at least initially, did not see anything wrong with announcing both day and night surveillance. Ambassador Stevenson, who had come to Washington after his public confrontation with Zorin the previous day, recommended continuing surveillance without announcing it at all, but Bundy thought a statement was important and Rusk again contended that otherwise "they might think there's something *big* behind it." "Well, what we're tryin' to do," JFK explained, "is to build up this case that they're continuing the work because sooner or later we're gonna have to do somethin' about *that*. So that's all we're tryin' to do—*here*." But, after further discussion of whether an announcement was necessary, the President reversed himself and backed Rusk on delaying the night flights: "Why don't we wait on this surveillance until we get the [results of] political talks [at the U.N.]." On the daytime flights, however, he instructed, "Just get them goin'. We can announce it later."

Rusk took a moment to praise Stevenson's performance at the U.N. the previous night: "He put [Soviet ambassador] Zorin in the position where Zorin made himself ridiculous. And this kind of attitude throughout the U.N. is very helpful." He then reintroduced a collateral issue, first discussed at the start of the morning meeting on October 25—continuing "the constant barrage of the Cubans" by dropping photos or leaflets over the island. Perhaps indulging in some wishful thinking, the nation's top diplomat declared, "One of the possible *outs* here is to produce such pressures there *in Cuba* as to cause something to crack on the island." The President inquired about when the leaflets had been dropped and deputy USIA director Donald Wilson revealed that the materials were ready and waiting for a presidential order and a surprised JFK commented, "Oh, they're *not* dropped yet." Kennedy endorsed releasing the leaflets 15 minutes ahead of time "if we have decided to do an air strike," but cautioned, "We don't want to get 'em so used to leaflets dropping that they don't bother to read them when the key moment comes." As someone, probably Bundy, chuckled, JFK suggested that leaflets would be useful over "Havana, Santiago and a few other places" rather than over the missile sites; "just do it once if we're gonna do it." Bundy responded wryly, "There's no need telling the people on the missile sites that there are missiles in Cuba."

Wilson, however, complained about the technical quality of the missile base photographs available for printing on the leaflets. The President suggested using the picture that had appeared on the front page of the *Washington Post*, but Wilson reiterated that "it doesn't come up too well" and requested a photo used by Ambassador Stevenson at the U.N. the previous evening. "But Donny, there *are* some special restrictions on some of these pictures," Bundy pointed out, "that I think the President sees. But if everything is waived, you get the one you like best." JFK quickly confirmed that Wilson could use any picture "among those that have been, one place or another, released"— including at the U.N.

John McCloy urged Wilson to use the well-publicized May Day parade picture "of the *big* bomb going through Red Square."[236] He recognized that it "isn't the same bomb, the same missile that we have down there [in Cuba] . . . This looks as... it's half a city block long. I'd stick that in there, because that made them raise their eyebrows—at least there's nothing defensive about *this*." He also proposed that the leaflets should stress the argument that Castro himself was exposing the Cuban people to risk and possible disaster. The President assured Wilson that he could have any of the released pictures "and do it whatever way you think best."[237]

Returning to the delicate negotiations set to resume later that morning in New York for a U.N.-sponsored moratorium on the delivery of weapons to Cuba and a suspension of the quarantine, Rusk, in one of his most forceful monologues, defined the "minimum requirements before any further talks can... can... can go forward." He insisted that there must be no further delivery of offensive weapons to Cuba and that the Soviets must halt the construction of missile sites and bombers and render all missiles and warheads already on Cuban soil inoperable. The only way to assure that these conditions were met, Rusk warned, and "we have to insist upon that *very hard*," would be

[236]McCloy, a special adviser to JFK on disarmament and a Republican, had been brought back from Europe to help toughen Stevenson's performance at the United Nations and had flown to D.C. with the ambassador for this meeting.

[237]The leaflets were ready to be released by the weekend, but unanticipated developments made them superfluous by early on Sunday morning, October 28.

to require that U.N. inspectors from neutral nations take over the sites; but, he predicted, Cuba and the U.S.S.R. would strenuously resist outside inspection and "what will happen is that the Soviets will go down into the role of... the path of talking, talking indefinitely, while the missile sites come into full operation, including those in the intermediate range. And then we are *nowhere*."

An effective inspection effort, Rusk stressed, would require a minimum of 300 personnel "drawn from countries that have a capacity, a technical capacity, to know what they're looking at and what ah... what measures have to be taken to insure inoperability." He listed, as examples, Sweden, Switzerland and Austria and left the door open for a limited number of nations like Brazil, and "countries of that sort. Perhaps Canada. We can't have *Burmese* or *Cambodians* going in there . . . in the face of three regiments of Soviet missile technicians and being led down the garden path on the operational problem." The secretary of state had evidently forgotten that acting U.N. Secretary General U Thant, responsible for initiating these negotiations, was Burmese.

In addition, Rusk insisted that the American quarantine must remain in place until the U.N. could set up an effective alternative means for verifying the cargo of incoming ships at Cuban ports. "But we would have to keep our force in the immediate *background* to move promptly *if* the U.N. arrangements are not... are not trustworthy." Any final agreement, he reiterated, "*must* include no further arms shipments, no continued buildup and a *defanging* of the sites that are already there." Dillon, undoubtedly sensing an opening to repeat his argument for bombing the missile sites, quickly commented that if the Soviets and Cubans consistently refused to accept these conditions, "that gives you your excuse to take further action." Nitze contended, as an alternative, that since U.N. inspectors could not arrive at the sites for some time, the Soviets could demonstrate inoperability by separating the missiles from the erectors and fuel trucks and moving them "into an open field, where we could get *a view* of them." McCone agreed, insisting that the sites must actually be dismantled, otherwise, "'*inoperable*,' that could be just having a switch turned off or something."

McCloy dissented on a key point in Rusk's presentation: maintaining that the inoperability of the sites had to be the first rather than the last priority. He warned darkly that the Soviet buildup in Cuba "was for a sinister purpose" and probably timed for "an adventure in some other area." It would be a great mistake to suspend the quarantine because it could never be reintroduced with OAS support "once we let it drop," and because "there's a growing momentum of opinion" in the country slowly crystallizing behind it. Rusk agreed that U Thant must understand that "the quarantine is related to the presence of the missiles, ("Right," McCloy murmured in the background) the missile sites, and *not just* to the shipment of new... additional arms." The President acknowledged, "even if the quarantine's 100% effective, it isn't any good because the missile sites go on being constructed. So this is only a *first step.*" "And have a pistol at your hip by tomorrow," McCloy interjected theatrically.

Rusk also expressed the hope that "the actual *removal* of these things from Cuba is something to be worked out in the 2 to 3 weeks" of negotiations after the standstill called for by the U.N., but JFK cut him off: "Obviously, we can't expect them to remove them, but ah... at this point, without a long negotiation," and he conjectured, "you won't get 'em ever out but ah... unless you take 'em out. But at least for the purposes of negotiation...," JFK conceded, the United States had to exhaust every chance for a political settlement in the event that force was eventually unavoidable.

The President asked for Ambassador Stevenson's thoughts, but Rusk interrupted to reintroduce another potential diplomatic strategy for increasing political pressure on the U.S.S.R.: encouraging Brazil and Mexico to take the lead in declaring Latin America an atom-free zone. Rusk had floated this proposal 24 hours earlier without arousing much interest—especially from the President. He argued again, "unless the Defense Department sees some *utterly* far-reaching objections to it," that a plan to bar the shipment of nuclear weapons to Latin America in peacetime seemed feasible—although he recognized complications about the U.S. storing nuclear weapons in the Canal Zone and the "use of Latin American airfields for transit in peacetime." McNamara commented, "We need to study and consider this possibility," adding that "The Chiefs are *very* cool toward it for a variety of reasons that General Taylor can outline." But, again breaking ranks with the military officials under his authority, McNamara revealed, "I'm inclined to favor it."

Buoyed by McNamara's support, Rusk further elaborated on his reasoning: if the United States could get a large percentage of the U.N. to support an atom-free Latin America, "you *may* give the other side an occasion for pulling back, because they've been supporting nuclear-free zones for years. And they may find in this a face-saving formula ..." On the other hand, a Soviet rejection would be on the record for all the world to see "before any ah... any ah... forcible action has to be taken." General Taylor, speaking for the JCS, argued that the nuclear-free zone plan would divert the U.N.'s attention, "while we should be bearing down on the removal of the missiles." Rusk acknowledged the political complexities in the proposal, especially the possibility of U.N. pressure to apply the atom-free zone concept to Africa, but reiterated that "the other side *possibly* could accept this. And if they turn it down ... our necessities are much clearer to everybody." McNamara, however, qualified his support, endorsing Taylor's concern that the administration must not permit itself "to be maneuvered into a position in which *this* is *the* approach we take in order to achieve the elimination of the missiles from Cuba. And with that single qualification, which is *an extremely important qualification*, I would *strongly* favor that." Sorensen also seemed skeptical about U.N. action, instead raising Edwin Martin's suggestion that if the OAS passed a resolution declaring Cuba's possession of nuclear weapons to be a violation of the Rio Pact, it would strengthen the U.S. position in the U.N. or provide "greater grounds for an attack on them."

President Kennedy, however, put his finger on a key issue: "Isn't it part of the Brazilian initiative," he asked, "that we, the OAS, the U.N. or somebody else would guarantee Cuba? I thought the proposal was that they would remove these weapons if we would guarantee the territorial integrity of Cuba." "Very much so," Bundy confirmed. The President reasoned realistically, "Well, obviously we're gonna have to pay a price. We're not gonna get these missiles out of there without either fighting them to get 'em out or..." Rusk interrupted to insist that the U.N. Charter and the Rio Pact had already affirmed the territorial integrity of Cuba. But, President Kennedy concluded pragmatically, "if that's one of the prices that has to be paid to get these out of there, then we commit ourselves not to invade Cuba."

Rusk turned to yet another long-shot diplomatic initiative, reading aloud the draft of a State Department cable to the Brazilian government—intended to be delivered to Castro by the Brazilian ambassador in Havana. The message identified only two "nonnegotiable" issues between Castro and the U.S.—Cuba's political and military ties to the Soviet Union and support for political subversion in Latin America. The draft concluded with a proposal roughly parallel to the understanding which would ultimately be accepted by the U.S. and the U.S.S.R. on October 28: "If Castro tries to rationalize the presence of these missiles as due to Cuban fear of U.S. invasion," the Brazilian ambassador would reply "that he is confident that the OAS would not accept an invasion of Cuba once the missiles were removed and that the U.S. would not risk upsetting hemispheric solidarity by invading a Cuba so clearly committed to a peaceful course." Rusk bluntly admitted that this concluding offer, "was the seduction, as far as Castro is concerned."

The President objected to language in the draft cable suggesting that the Soviets were angling to betray Cuba for concessions from U.S. allies—a strategy Rusk had first suggested on October 16. "I mean that's pretty clumsy. I don't think the... I don't think that there's enough evidence to indicate *that*. So I think probably that our stating it would be regarded as rather insulting." Rusk explained that this argument would actually be made by the Brazilian ambassador and JFK dropped his objections, "Well, if the Brazilians want to say it, it's alright," and he agreed to send the cable. Rusk restated JFK's earlier point that if the Cubans agree to "*get rid* of these offensive weapons then, I assume, that it is *not* our purpose to invade Cuba."

Paul Nitze, however, was far less sanguine about trusting either the Cubans or the Soviets. "Isn't the question here *when* they're gonna get rid of them?" He raised the specter of "long drawn-out negotiations" and insisted that "we've *got* to make clear" that there is a deadline. Bundy quickly agreed that "the inspectors have to be there" and Dillon pressed for a 24-hour time limit. Rusk worried that if "you pass the 24th hour without having taken the action, then you've undermined the whole message." Dillon conceded "Well, you might say perhaps, 'not more than a few days,'" and Stevenson recommended insisting on removal with "great urgency."

McCone also objected to Rusk's proposal: "One thing I don't like about this, and that is that it sort of insulates Castro from further actions. And ah... long before these missiles were there, his link with the Soviet Union and the use of Cuba as a base of operations to communize all of Latin America *was a matter of great concern to us*. Now what this *does* is... is more or less leaves him in that position. The missiles aren't there, but still this situation that has worried us so much for the last 2 or 3 years goes on." In short, McCone believed Rusk's plan would allow the removal of the missiles to undermine the key American objective: "to have the Cuban people take over Cuba and... and take it away from Castro. This does *not* involve a... a... a *break* between Castro and the Soviet Union."

Rusk held his ground, insisting that the message "would repeat the

President's statement that... that the military-political connection with Moscow is not negotiable, as well as the ah... the actions aimed at other Latin American countries. Now," he wished out loud, "*if Castro* were, through some miracle, to get his militia together and turn on the Soviets on these missiles, then this problem is solved, John." "Yeah," McCone replied very skeptically, "that's a big 'if' though." Rusk acknowledged "It's a *very big* 'if,' but that's the... it's on that *off* chance and that's the purpose of this operation, *if possible*, you see." RFK amplified McCone's skepticism by pressing the secretary of state on whether the U.S. would support an uprising in Cuba and what the response would be if "other weapons are sent in there and they export them to Venezuela or Columbia"—after the missiles were withdrawn. Rusk replied firmly that the OAS had sanctioned a response in that eventuality, but conceded that even this message to Castro "does not give assurances against any kind of rascality."

Evidently concerned by the lack of precision in this discussion, Bundy urged President Kennedy not to be distracted by secondary issues: "Mr. President," he declared forcefully, "I believe myself that *all* of these things need to be measured in terms of the very *simple, basic, structural* purpose of this whole enterprise: *to get these missiles out.* Now Castro *is* a problem. If we can bring Castro down in the process, *dandy.* If we can turn him on other people, dandy. But if we can get the missiles out..." The President broke in sharply, if somewhat opaquely: "I wouldn't worry yet. If we can get the missiles out we can take care of having Castro hung out. If they do somethin' in Berlin then we can always say, 'well this changes the... then our commitments.' So I think we ought to concentrate on the missiles right now."

Ambassador Thompson, reflecting on the likely Soviet reaction to U.N. inspections in Cuba, cautioned, "In my opinion, the Soviets will find it *far* easier to remove these weapons or to move them to port for a removal than they would to accept inspections, I think. Putting Soviet technicians under U.N. people would... I think they would resist." The President finally put an end to the increasingly repetitive discussion: "We gotta get moving," he declared, and authorized sending the message to Castro via the Brazilians "after one more look at it, Mr. Secretary. Let's send this off. It won't matter," he declared with a transparent lack of enthusiasm. "It won't get any place. But let's send it. But I think for now we've gotta put in 'the greatest urgency' because time's running out for us." JFK reemphasized his overriding concern about work continuing on the missile bases while these conversations went on, "which we're verifying every day, during these negotiations. We have to keep saying that to U Thant, the Brazilians. We can't screw around for two weeks" and allow the Soviets to finish the missile sites.[238]

At that point, President Kennedy, in all probability inadvertently, initiated one of the most acrimonious exchanges of the ExComm meetings when he turned to Adlai Stevenson and asked for the second time, "Governor, do you want to talk a little and give us your thoughts?"[239] The U.N. ambassador surely sensed that the ExComm was stacked against him: Bundy, Dillon, McCloy and McCone were Republicans; RFK had worked in Stevenson's 1956 presidential campaign, but after becoming convinced that the Illinois governor was weak and indecisive had actually voted for Eisenhower; JFK himself never forgave Stevenson's quixotic effort to pull off a third presidential nomination at the 1960 Democratic convention. The distrust and antagonism in the room directed toward Stevenson was almost palpable.

The U.N. ambassador, notwithstanding, intrepidly launched into an explanation and defense of the U Thant moratorium plan, "I think it's well for you all to bear in mind that the concept of this proposal is a *standstill*. That is to say, no one was to take *further* action for . . . 2 or 3 weeks while we negotiated a final settlement." He then made a curious distinction—"one of the objectives of the final negotiations" would be to make the weapons inoperable. But "I would be *very much* troubled by the a... trying to get that included" in the initial few days of negotiations "because it includes something that is *not* a standstill. It includes a *reverse*... reversal of the a... of something that has already taken place." But, he added circuitously, "I think it would be *quite proper* to include in our original demands ah... ah... that the weapons be *kept* inoperable." Stevenson had carefully sidestepped the crucial problem of whether the missiles were *already* operable—a factor already of great concern to the ExComm.

"Would the work on the sites be ceased?" the President asked skeptically. "Work on the sites, of course," Stevenson replied. "Now the three points that we've talked about are suspending the—" Bundy in-

---

[238]Khrushchev agreed to remove the missiles before the Brazilian message could be delivered to Castro.

[239]Stevenson had served as governor of Illinois from 1949 to 1953—his only elective office.

terrupted, barely concealing his patronizing scorn, "Excuse me. You're gonna have to be clear. Are we talking now about the first 2 days or about the first 2 weeks?" Stevenson diffidently explained that 2–3 weeks of negotiations toward a final settlement would proceed only after nailing down three objectives in the first two days: "*no ships* go to Cuba carrying arms," "no further construction on the bases and how that's to be policed," the U.S. "would then suspend our quarantine."

Rusk jumped on a glaring ambiguity in Stevenson's argument: "The work on the bases *stops*—includes the inoperability of the missiles."

"Well, that could *not* help," Stevenson added softly. "I think it would be quite proper to... to *attempt* to include that, to *keep* them inoperable rather than to say that they should be *rendered* inoperable, because that requires possibly—"

"*Keep* them inoperable then," Rusk interjected.

"Well, when did they... when did they become inoperable?" McNamara bristled, "They're operable now."

"*Insure* that they *are* inoperable!" Bundy demanded stridently.

"Well that's... you see this...," Stevenson replied hesitantly, "I'm trying to make clear to you that this was a *standstill*. There would be *no more* construction, *no more* quarantine, *no more* arms shipments. Now when you say, 'make them *inoperable*,' that's *not* a standstill."

"You can *insure* that they *are* inoperable," Bundy contended, "and that leaves open whether it's a standstill."

"No," Stevenson protested.

"If they turn out to be operable," Rusk continued, "then that would be something wholly different."

Stevenson stuck to his guns: "But I don't think in the ah... that there should be any misunderstanding about what was intended here, which was a *standstill* and *only* a standstill."

The besieged U.N. ambassador, despite a chorus of skeptical comments from around the table, pushed on to review the long-term goals for the 2–3 weeks of U.N.-sponsored negotiations. The Soviets, he calculated, would dismantle the bases and withdraw these weapons from the hemisphere, but "what *they* will want in return is, I anticipate, a new guarantee of the territorial integrity of Cuba. Indeed," he argued audaciously, "that's... that's what they said these weapons were for—to defend the territorial integrity of Cuba" against an American invasion—an argument that had been conspicuously missing from the ExComm discussions. Stevenson then dropped the other shoe: "It is *possible* that the price that might be asked of us in the long-term negotiation, 2-week negotiation, might include dismantling *bases of ours*, such as Italy and Turkey, that we have talked about." As a final point, the U.N. ambassador agreed that long-term talks might include an effort to get Cuba to agree to a Latin American nuclear-free zone and to curb subversion in the hemisphere.[240]

McCloy had remained silent during Stevenson's presentation but he finally lashed out: "I don't believe... I don't agree with that, Mr. President. I feel *very* strongly about it. And I think that the... the real *crux* of this matter is the fact that he's got these pointed, for all you know, *right now* at our... at our hearts. And this is gonna produce... I think it *may* produce, a situation when we get to [a crisis in] Berlin after the [mid-term] elections that changes the entire balance of world power. It puts us under a very great handicap to carry out our obligations to our... not only to our Western European allies, but to the... to the hemisphere. And I think that we've got the momentum now. . . . That *threat must be removed* before we can drop the quarantine." If the quarantine were suspended, he concluded for the second time in the meeting, "we're never gonna be able to put it in effect again and I feel that we *must say*," as he rapped the table for emphasis, "that *the quarantine goes on until we are satisfied that these are inoperable.*"[241] Stevenson must have been especially discomfited at being openly criticized before the ExComm by his U.N. negotiating "assistant." The administration had publicly explained McCloy's assignment to the U.N. as an effort to add a bi-partisan Republican voice to the negotiations. In fact, McCloy was sent to New York because of concern that Stevenson was not tough enough to deal with the Soviets—a view confirmed for many in the room by this exchange.

The President promptly intervened to say that the quarantine itself would not remove the weapons already in Cuba in any case: "So you've only got two ways of removing the weapons." One way, he emphasized, coming strikingly close to Stevenson's position on the Jupiter missiles, "is to negotiate them out, or in other words, trade them out.[242]

[240]Paul Nitze later recalled: "I was outraged by his [Stevenson's] attempt at total appeasement." (Nitze, *Hiroshima to Glasnost*, 227)

[241]This speaker has been identified as John McCone in the Harvard Press and Norton editions of ExComm transcripts. The author, however, has carefully matched and compared the voices of McCloy and McCone and has concluded that this is indeed John McCloy. Also, earlier in the meeting, McCloy had made exactly the same point about being unable to reintroduce the quarantine after it had been suspended.

[242]Stevenson had first suggested such an arrangement in a note to the President early on October 17 and repeated it at the unrecorded 2:30 P.M. meeting on October 20—after it

And the other is to go in and take them out. I don't see any other way you're going to get the weapons out..." McCloy insisted on inspections to see "at what stage they are." Dillon muttered, "That's right," before McCloy continued emotionally, "Look, this is the security of the United States! I... I believe the strategic situation has *greatly* changed with the presence of these weapons in Cuba." "That's right," Kennedy acknowledged: "The only thing that I'm saying is that we're not gonna get them out with the quarantine. I'm not saying we should lift the quarantine," he hedged, "or what we should do about the quarantine. But we have to all now realize that we're not gonna get 'em out. We're either gonna trade 'em out or we're gonna have to go in and get 'em out—ourselves. I don't know of any other way to do it."

Bundy eagerly pointed out that the first 2 days of the U.N. proposal Stevenson had outlined "*does* involve a dropping of the quarantine without what I would recall... call adequate momentum. Very far from it!" Rusk, however, seemed somewhat more confident in U.N. monitoring: "Mr. President, I *do* think that if you had U.N. people at these sites and they were required to report in to their center every hour," any negative change "would immediately cause *us* to send planes over to take a look" and allow time to act "if they were actually raising one of these things on its launcher."

JFK endorsed McCloy's contention that once the U.S. quarantine "is substituted for the... by a U.N. group, the point is you don't... we'll never get the quarantine back in again." But, he repeated that the quarantine would not compel the U.S.S.R. to remove the missiles anyway: "Why should the Soviets take these things out? I don't see why they should... The Soviets are not gonna take 'em out." Dillon mumbled in agreement, "They're not gonna take them out. That's why we're going to have to..."

McNamara interrupted, admitting to being confused about the precise details of the U.N. plan for Cuba. Stevenson tried again to explain that U.N. inspectors would have to confirm that the shipment of weapons and construction of the sites had ceased before the U.S. would have to lift the quarantine. "And we'd have U.N. inspectors down there," McNamara asked, "to do that?" Stevenson replied affirmatively and suggested that the ExComm should begin at once to discuss recruiting

had already been raised by McNamara. President Kennedy had floated the idea twice at the morning discussion on October 18.

these inspectors. "Well on that point," McCloy interposed, "I think it's… it seems to me pretty clear though, as the secretary said, that we can't expect a bunch of *Burmese* to go down there and take the security of the United States in its hands. *I* think we've got to insist upon having our *own* people down there. These… the Soviets are already there. Their technicians…" The President suggested that daily overflights could provide assurances, but Bundy disagreed, "Not really, Mr. President. If we're talking about inoperability, we have to *be* there." McCloy also reiterated, "You have to have *technicians*. You have to have somebody that *knows what these things mean*."

"The only thing is," the President repeated again, "as I say, it isn't as if what we're now doing is gonna get 'em out of there." "No sir, but we *are* on a *course* which we intend to get them out of there," Bundy replied firmly, "and if we adopt a course at the U.N. which presumes that they might *stay there*, we've had it." Kennedy patiently repeated that Stevenson's proposal assumed that "we give this thing the time to try to negotiate 'em out of there. Now we… we're not gonna be able to negotiate 'em out of there. But otherwise I don't see that we're going to get 'em out of there unless we go in and get them out." Rusk predicted that "a major back down" by the Soviets was extremely unlikely. But McCone remained suspicious of the U.N. plan because the Soviets could arm the missiles in barely 8 hours: "they could put these things on their stands and… and we'd be looking at them." Stevenson pointed out that "the quarantine isn't going to prevent that" and McCone insisted that "if we detect any such move" during the 2-day preliminary talks or the 2 weeks of extended negotiations "we can take such action as necessary." The U.N. ambassador conceded that "if there's any violation of the standstill" during the two-week negotiations for a final settlement, "it serves them right, all bets are off. We're back to status quo."

Nitze broke long his silence to endorse McCloy and McCone's tough stand. "Disassembly," he argued, separating the missiles from the erectors and removing the wings from the IL-28s, "would really give you some secure… security during the period while these negotiations go on." "This isn't a *standstill* until you've got that," McCloy nearly shouted. Demanding such a guarantee, Nitze and McCloy argued vigorously, was not a violation of the standstill, but Stevenson countered that these details belonged in the long-term negotiations. "No!" Nitze objected, buttressed by several other "No's." "During the negotiations they disassemble, so we're not negotiating under the threat. In your speech," he reminded the President, "you said we wouldn't negotiate under threat." "Have we seen a missile *on* a launcher?" Rusk asked. A chorus of voices responded, "Right next to it."

Since the Soviets were still denying that their weapons were even in Cuba, Bundy declared, "I don't see *any* reason why we can't take an *extremely forward* position on this on the diplomatic track. We *all know* that if we don't get satisfaction on the diplomatic track, it's going to get worse." Negotiating for the status quo, he contended, clearly aiming his remarks at Stevenson, "is *not* in our interest." McCone tried to pressure Stevenson on the Soviet denial, "I think it would be very appropriate for you to invite the Cuban [U.N.] ambassador and Mr. Zorin to get in an airplane with you and fly down and look at 'em." Stevenson explained that "we asked him if he would agree to send a... a U.N. inspection force down there to determine the existence of the missiles if he had... if there was any question about it and of course he didn't pick up that offer." "I just don't see," Dillon demanded, "how you can negotiate for 2 *weeks* with these things sitting on... right next to the launchers. (Someone further from the concealed microphone interjected, "And the IRBMs are becoming operational.") It's just got to be made inoperable or you're going back on our statement that we wouldn't negotiate under threat." Stevenson then asked to be excused to take a call from his United Nations aide Charles Yost. "OK, sure thing," JFK replied. "Why don't you go in my office."[243]

McCloy returned to the issue of finding "sophisticated people" for this crucial inspection mission to Cuba and demanded a U.S. role in nominating them. Dillon suggested the British; McCloy agreed to the British and mentioned the French; JFK referred to the Canadians. "I want somebody," McCloy repeated, "that *knows* something about this business." Robert Kennedy objected, "I can't *believe* that they'd allow a lot of foreigners runnin' around their missiles." Dillon and RFK

---

[243]The phone conversation was recorded: Stevenson grumbled to Yost about being pressured to add the inoperability of the missiles to the standstill proposal. (Dictabelt 38.1, Cassette K, POF, PRC, JFKL) Stevenson must have experienced mixed emotions as he talked alone in the Oval Office—possibly from the President's desk. There is abundant evidence of the less than cordial feelings between JFK and his U.N. ambassador and it must have been very difficult for the twice-defeated presidential candidate to sit in the office he clearly felt *he* deserved to occupy.

warned that missiles could easily be separated from the erectors and be moved or hidden in the woods and Taylor admitted, "We can make 'em account for the one's we've actually seen but those we've never seen, we have no control." The President observed with unusual bluntness, "Governor Stevenson has this proposal for dealing with the missiles, which nobody's very much interested in. [Stevenson was still on the phone in the Oval Office.] But the point is that the blockade is not going to accomplish the job either, so we've got to have some *other* alternatives to accomplish what Governor Stevenson suggests may or may not be accomplished by negotiations." The blockade, he predicted, "is going to bring the confrontation [he mispronounced it as "confrontration"] closer, which may or may not be desirable . . . What other devices are we gonna use to get 'em out of there?"

Rusk urged the President to resist pressure to relax the quarantine until arms shipments and the buildup of missile sites and bomber facilities had ceased and the weapons had been rendered inoperable. McNamara argued that "you could define that as separating the missiles from the sites" and Bundy reemphasized Rusk's final point, again revealing his disdain for Stevenson, "But it's the *inoperable* that's obvious—it's very important that the Governor must get that clearly in his head." "Then we have a double choice, Mr. President," Bundy concluded, unless we choose to "do nothing. One is to expand the blockade and the other is to remove the missiles by force." "Right. OK," JFK replied, "It seems to me this should provide some direction for the Governor this afternoon [at the U.N.]. Then he'll come back and tell us that they won't agree to this and then we continue with the blockade." Bundy also urged the President to mention the importance of bipartisan representation in the U.N. negotiations—the cover story for assigning McCloy to the U.N.

"During any negotiation, Mr. President," Taylor demanded again, "shouldn't we be raising the noise level of our indignation over this?" President Kennedy agreed with the general, asking McNamara whether the most recent photos corroborated that work was continuing on the missile sites. "They *do* indeed," McNamara replied, "I have the evidence here." JFK pronounced flatly, "and we can't *accept* that." Tomorrow, the President declared, would be the time to decide whether to expand the blockade by adding POL "or if we're gonna decide to go the other route, the force route."

Taylor proposed increasing the pressure by starting night photography of Havana and Bundy suggested to the President, "with your permission," convening an ExComm working group to meet in the State Department and consider the next steps in turning up the quarantine. Rusk cautioned that it was still essential "to explore the political thing, to be sure that the Soviets have *turned down* these three conditions before we put on the night... the night photography." "Well, that's fair enough," JFK quickly agreed. "I wouldn't do it in... in the *middle* of the night." He also instructed that a statement should be issued by the White House declaring that work was going forward on the sites, in part to avoid the public impression that the Defense or State Departments were actually calling the shots. Bundy seconded the idea, noting "There *is* stuff on the wires that... that the Soviets are saying the U.S. military have taken over at this point." Kennedy asked Gilpatric and Bundy to carefully draw up a statement to highlight "the severity with which we judge this. . . . We've perfected the blockade but the... that's only half the job." POL, he conjectured, would have to be added.

As the meeting drew to a close, Donald Wilson asked whether the President had made a decision on dropping propaganda leaflets over Cuba, suggesting "this may be a time to stir up things." "All right," JFK decided, "we're gonna drop them." He also proposed, specifically recalling Dillon's misgivings about emphasizing the U.S.-U.S.S.R. confrontation at sea rather than focusing on eliminating the threat from Cuba with air strikes, "a presentation tomorrow by the Defense Department on air... an air action again . . . In some ways that's more advantageous than it was even a week ago. I'd like to have us take a look now at whether that can even *be* an option."

President Kennedy was becoming less confident that the Soviet Union had actually "blinked" by diverting ships carrying offensive weapons away from Cuba. He was coming under increasing pressure in the ExComm to view this move at sea as a tactical decision which did not alter the strategic fact, confirmed by the latest aerial photography, that work on the missile sites already in Cuba was moving forward rapidly. JFK, as a result, seemed to be leaning toward breaking the logjam over U.N. negotiations by turning up the heat on the Soviet Union—perhaps by bombing the missile sites after all. The ExComm hard-liners, as a direct consequence of the evolving diplomatic stalemate, appeared poised to potentially gain the upper hand.

The meeting dissolved into random conversations and several participants chatted about an upcoming planning session at the State Department. JFK soon switched off the tape recorder.

In the early afternoon, ABC News State Department correspondent John Scali met with Soviet embassy public affairs counselor Aleksandr Fomin [his real name was Feklisov] at a Washington restaurant. Fomin, the KGB Chief of Station in Washington, had met with Scali several times in the past, but he had initiated this meeting with a great sense of alarm. "War seems about to break out," Fomin announced, urging Scali to contact his "high-level friends" about a possible deal to end the crisis. The U.S.S.R., Fomin proposed, might agree to remove the missiles from Cuba, verified by United Nations inspectors, in return for an American commitment not to invade Cuba. The excited journalist soon reported the discussion to Roger Hilsman and Dean Rusk at the State Department. The secretary of state, like Scali, assumed that Fomin was acting on instructions from the Kremlin and perhaps from Khrushchev himself. Rusk agreed that there were real possibilities in Fomin's scheme, and, after getting approval from the White House, wrote a brief response by hand on a sheet of yellow lined paper. Rusk asked Scali to relay the message to Fomin, but urged him to make clear that time was running out.[244]

At the State Department, the ExComm subcommittee created that morning at Bundy's suggestion reviewed several options for air strikes against the missile sites and the IL-28 nuclear bombers. General Taylor and the JCS, consistent with the position they had taken for more than a week, urged the President to order more extensive air strikes against the SAM sites, Cuban airfields, and other targets. Meanwhile, President Kennedy authorized the State Department to move forward urgently on plans to occupy Cuba and establish a civil government in the wake of an American invasion. McNamara advised the President that Defense Department studies suggested there would be heavy American casualties in any invasion of Cuba.

Later that day, National Photographic Interpretation Center analysis of the most recent U-2 and low-level reconnaissance photographs confirmed that Soviet technicians in Cuba were working at top speed

[244]The Scali-Fomin meetings have become part of the lore of the missile crisis and have been featured in several film dramatizations. However, documents available since the fall of the Soviet Union have revealed that Fomin was almost certainly not speaking for Khrushchev or the Soviet embassy. (Blight and Welch, *On the Brink*, 336–37; Chang, "The View from Washington and Nowhere," 144–45; Garthoff, "Documenting the Cuban Missile Crisis," 299) Nonetheless, "there is reason to believe that the documents do not tell the full story" and "speculation [continues] about the possibility of a special KGB operation." (Aleksandr Fursenko and Timothy Naftali, "Soviet Intelligence and the Cuban Missile Crisis," in Blight and Welch, *Intelligence and the Cuban Missile Crisis*, 80–83)

to complete construction and achieve full operational status at both the MRBM and IRBM sites. In addition, support equipment used to prepare the missiles for firing had been moved into position very close to the launchers. Arthur Lundahl and his photo interpreters also discovered that the Russians were turning increasingly to the use of foliage and canvas netting in an effort to camouflage their activities. Some of the work appeared to have been done after dark.

There were also disquieting indications that the U.S.S.R. might also be deploying tactical nuclear weapons in Cuba. If Soviet military personnel in Cuba had chosen to fire even one of these weapons in response to an American invasion, and it is now known that the Presidium had decided that the choice could be made on the scene in Cuba, the pressure on President Kennedy for nuclear retaliation against Cuba and/or the Soviet Union would have been all but irresistible. During these critical thirteen days, however, the Kennedy administration never confirmed the presence of Soviet tactical nuclear weapons in Cuba and was of course unaware of the Presidium's instructions. American officials "saw no sense in the island's defenders employing battlefield atomic weapons and thereby risking escalation"—just as they had discounted the probability of Soviet deployment of long-range missiles in Cuba before October 14. Lundahl, alarmed by this new intelligence, contacted McCone and a private meeting with the President was hastily arranged. Lundahl was convinced that the crisis was entering a new and dangerous phase and realized that the latest photography would likely have a profound impact on the ExComm deliberations. He was determined to avoid hyperbole and to dispassionately present the evidence to the commander-in-chief.[245]

[245]Fursenko and Naftali, *"One Hell of a Gamble,"* 242–43; Gribkov, "View from Moscow and Havana," 3–5, 27–28; William Y. Smith, "The View from Washington," in Gribkov and Smith, *Operation ANADYR,* 141; *Public Papers of the Presidents: John F. Kennedy, 1962, II,* 812; Chang and Kornbluh, *Cuban Missile Crisis,* 385–86.

Friday, October 26, around 12:00 noon, Oval Office

Identified Participants: John F. Kennedy, Arthur Lundahl, John McCone.[246]

"I'm getting more concerned *all* the time. . . . They've got a substantial number of these so they could start at dark and have missiles pointing at us the following morning."

CIA director John McCone

The President turned on the tape recorder sometime after McCone had begun the briefing. JFK was fascinated by this nuts-and-bolts discussion and examined the photographs very closely. He was particularly interested in the recent Soviet efforts to camouflage the missiles, "Now look, if we hadn't ah... isn't this peculiar... if we hadn't ah... gotten those early pictures," he remarked eagerly, "we might'a missed these. Wonder why they *didn't* put that cover over it?" "I don't know. I don't know," McCone admitted. President Kennedy also seemed genuinely angry, remarking scornfully about the Soviet Union, "They always think *they're* so smart though..." As McCone pointed out missiles stands, shelter tents and the missiles themselves, it was obvious that the President was still a novice after ten days of examining these photos, "Those are missiles?" he asked and McCone replied patiently, "Yeah."

JFK was especially critical of the press for questioning the accuracy of the evidence, "Did you see the *New York*... the *London Times*," he asked contemptuously, "which said we'd misread the pictures?" McCone reported that he had debriefed Kenneth Strong "on that yesterday."[247] "Yes, and he knows this," the President added sardonically. "He actually said, 'I guess they're missile sites,' but what we said were missiles were actually ground to air [SAM sites]." JFK also seemed particularly intrigued by the fact that "you don't see any people, do ya?" and McCone agreed "I don't see any people here." "What... what would be a good question, it seems to me, for the future," Kennedy added, "is to find out what our pilots see themselves compared to what the pictures show." "Well," McCone replied, "they don't see very much." "Don't they?" the President nevertheless continued, "If we're gonna do an air strike, whether these fellows can pick this up themselves going at that speed."

[246]Tape 40, POF, PRC, JFKL.
[247]McCone was referring to Sir Kenneth Strong, chairman of the British Joint Intelligence Committee, who happened to be in Washington at the time.

McCone continued the briefing by pointing out specific features of an entire missile complex, "You see, here's the... the missile erector. Here's a cable that goes over here to a power source . . . and then there's the missiles stored over in the missile building." McCone did provide some hopeful news, "*I've* concluded it isn't possible to... to... to *really* hide these things as we have sometimes thought. They're mobile, but they're not quite as mobile as a tractor-trailer. Furthermore, they're *big*." "Is this all there is to this thing? This could be fired now?" JFK asked.[248] "No. No, this can't be fired," the CIA chief explained. But, in order to answer the President's questions more fully, McCone went to the Oval Office door and shouted to Lundahl, who was waiting with the remaining pictures, "Bring all of 'em in, Art."

The CIA chief also informed the President of the views of the "military people that are seconded to the agency [CIA]... We conclude that... we feel there's a *higher* probability of immobilizing these missiles, *all of them*, with a strike than I think we have... our thinking has tended in the last few days. Now it won't be *final* because we don't see *all* the missiles for which there are launchers and SAM sites. Therefore there's *some* that haven't been moved into position and also a few to be repaired." JFK, obviously thinking again about Berlin, responded with a striking question, "Have we got a mobile missile that's transportable by plane that has in range, a 1,000 miles?" Lundahl initially responded, "I don't believe so, sir," but immediately corrected himself, "I would take that back," citing a recent statement by McNamara "which was news to me." "We could," JFK continued, "if we ever had to, fly, say 15, into Berlin if we wanted to?" McCone was firm, "I think so, yes," specifically mentioning the shorter range Pershing I missiles stationed in West Germany.

McCone asked Lundahl, who can be heard setting up the photo easels, to display some specific pictures, "What I'm anxious to see, Art, and to have the President see, is one or two of those pictures . . . the low-level pictures which show how extensive this complex is." Lundahl was obviously gratified when the President recognized a site from the

[248]Zelikow and May point out that Robert Kennedy included an accurate quote from McCone's briefing in *Thirteen Days* (despite erroneously placing it in the morning Ex-Comm meeting) and conclude that he was present at this discussion in the Oval Office. If RFK attended, he was uncharacteristically silent. This voice is clearly JFK's. Since transcripts of several meetings were turned over to RFK's secretary in 1963 (although this tape is not listed), RFK may have read a transcript sometime before 1968. (Zelikow, *et al.*, eds., *John F. Kennedy: The Great Crises*, v. 3, 325; Naftali, "Origins 'Thirteen Days,'" 23–24)

previous U-2 photographs, "Is this one of the places that we had earlier pictures which show the degree of accuracy?" "Yes, sir," Lundahl responded. McCone specifically identified a picture of missiles and technical support equipment "we released for the ah... for use in the pamphlet" to be dropped over Cuba. "Well, we've got 'em lined up," Kennedy observed, "haven't we?" and McCone answered "Yeah, yeah." "Can one bullet do much to that?" JFK asked. "Well," McCone explained, "if a fella went across there with bullet punctures, it would. It invariably wreaks hell with it."[249] "Would it blow or is it just...?" the President inquired, and Lundahl asserted, "It would be fuming red nitric acid, sir, very heavily lined trucks, so if they're opened up, they might make some *real* trouble for those who are trying to contain it." JFK wondered if the Soviets "may hide *these* pretty quickly" and McCone confirmed, "Well, we have evidence that they are."

McCone mentioned that additional reconnaissance flights had been sent out that day and pointed out further photographic details of Soviet efforts to camouflage the sites. Lundahl noted that the ground was so wet from recent rainfall that "they have to lay their cables above ground on little stanchions. And they have to put catwalks around it. There's all kinds of water in there. . . . Here's some of their advanced equipment, sir." McCone interjected, "Now this is an interesting— they're equipped..."[250]

President Kennedy asked about the difficulty of a ground attack on the tactical equipment evidently just mentioned by McCone—"But you couldn't shoot *these* up much?" and McCone admitted, "No, you couldn't shoot them up." McCone continued to point out details of missiles, launchers and related equipment and JFK, obviously thinking again about Soviet casualties in a possible air attack, asked how many people were assigned to guard these missile sites. McCone estimated "as many as 500 personnel on-site with 300 additional Soviet guards."

As Lundahl noisily gathered his materials and prepared to leave, JFK asked, "What conclusions does this lead you to, John?" McCone talked briefly with Lundahl and called out, "Thanks very much, Art," but his delayed reply to the President was tough and direct, "I'm getting more

[249]This exchange evidently relates to discussions about the possibility that Operation Mongoose Cuban operatives could attack the missile sites on the ground—an option JFK had even considered in August before the actual discovery of the missiles. (*FRUS: Cuba, 1961–1962*, X, 954)

[250]A classified portion of this statement may have touched on the still-unconfirmed presence of Soviet FROG tactical nuclear weapons in Cuba.

concerned *all the time* . . . I think that they've got a *substantial* number of these so they could start at dark and have missiles pointing at us the following morning. For that reason, I'm growing increasingly concerned about following a political route which... unless the... the initial and *immediate* step is to insure that these missiles are immobilized by the *physical separation* of the missile, which is on a truck and trailer, from the launcher." "Well, now the only problem is... I agree, that that's what we want," JFK maintained. "The alternative course is we could do the air strike or an invasion. We still are gonna face the fact that if we invade, by the time we *get* to these sites after a very bloody fight, then we'll have... they'll be pointing at us. So it still comes down to a question of whether they're gonna fire the missiles." "That's correct. That's correct," McCone conceded grimly.

The President, sounding quite pessimistic, reiterated that diplomacy alone was not likely to be successful in getting the missiles out, nor would "a combination of an air strike and probably invasion" eliminate "the prospect that they might be fired." The CIA director had no easy answers for the commander-in-chief, contending that an invasion was going to be "a much more *serious* undertaking than most people realize." The Russians and Cubans, he observed, have "a *hell* of a lot of equipment . . . very lethal stuff they've got there. Rocket launchers, self-propelled gun carriers, half-tracks . . . [will] give an invading force a *pretty bad* time. It would be no... be no cinch by any manner or means."

JFK asked whether American air control over Cuba would make it possible to "chew those up," but McCone swept aside that upbeat premise as well; "It's *damn* hard to knock out these field pieces." The CIA chief recalled World War II and Korea, "where you had complete air [supremacy]," President Kennedy interjected, and McCone repeated, "where you had *complete* air and go and pound hell out of these gun sites... *they're still there.*"

The President inquired about who was in charge of invasion planning at the Pentagon; McCone mentioned Earl Wheeler, Army Chief of Staff, and George Anderson, Chief of Naval Operations. "What about the air strike?" JFK persisted. The CIA director, assuming that the President was asking who was responsible for air strike preparations, replied, "I don't know who has that." JFK retorted somewhat impatiently, "No, but I meant... what about the... What course of action does this lead you to?" McCone unhesitatingly answered, "Well, this would lead me... this would lead me to moving quickly on an air strike." President Kennedy had apparently heard enough and abruptly turned off the tape recorder.

The President, as the October 26 meetings reveal, was again leaning towards military action along the lines that had first been debated at the early ExComm sessions. The overriding concern was to quickly eliminate the missiles in Cuba before they could be fired. After the McCone-Lundahl briefing, JFK and Bundy worked out a public statement emphasizing that "there is no evidence to date indicating that there is any intention to dismantle or discontinue work on these missile sites. On the contrary, the Soviets are rapidly continuing their construction of missile support and launch facilities and serious attempts are underway to camouflage their efforts." Operation Mongoose discussions also resumed that afternoon in the Pentagon, with emphasis on sending Cuban sabotage squads to attack the missile sites. But, disagreements between General Taylor, Secretary McNamara and RFK led to a delay in implementing the plan. Finally, the meeting turned to setting up a civil government in Cuba after an invasion had presumably toppled Castro.[251]

The U.N. moratorium plan, JFK finally decided, was not acceptable to the United States without an immediate agreement on several key points. Stevenson met with U Thant that afternoon and reported the stringent American conditions: if the U.S.S.R. suspended arms shipments, ceased construction of the missile bases and immobilized the missiles within 48 hours, the United States would, after compliance had been independently verified, lift the quarantine. The secretary general was very gloomy about a deal; the Soviets, and certainly the Cubans, he predicted, would never allow outside inspectors into Cuba.

The President nonetheless followed through on the ExComm agreement to make an attempt at back channel diplomatic contacts with Castro. U. Alexis Johnson, deputy under secretary of state for political affairs, drafted the final cable discussed earlier by ExComm, heavily influenced by Rusk's thinking, to be delivered to Castro by the Brazilian ambassador to Cuba. It admonished the Cuban leader that the missiles represented a great danger to the survival of Cuba itself and stressed that the U.S.S.R. was concerned only with its own interests, had already turned its ships around and was making secret diplomatic ap-

[251]David L. Larson, *The Cuban Crisis of 1962: Selected Documents, Chronology and Bibliography* (Lanham, Maryland: University Press of America, 1986), 171–72.

proaches to America's allies, "for exchanges of their positions in Cuba for concessions by NATO countries in other parts of the world. Thus you are not only being used for purposes of no interest to any Cuban, but deserted and threatened by betrayal." The message concluded with "the seduction" mentioned by Rusk at the meeting that morning, an assurance that the U.S. would be unlikely to invade Cuba if the missiles were removed.[252]

Just after 5:00 P.M., the President met with Braj Kumar Nehru, Indian ambassador to the United States, for a discussion of Communist China's recent attack on India. JFK's preoccupation with the U.S.S.R. inevitably spilled over into the discussion; "I say this as an anti-communist now, to an anti-communist," Kennedy declared, we should not allow Khrushchev to get away with pacifying the Chinese and at the same time portraying himself "as a real friend of India, which he isn't." Right now, he noted, Russia and China have been drawn closer "together because the Chinese are involved in a war and the Russians," he concluded grimly, "are involved nearly in a war." We ought to get tougher with the Russians, the President demanded, certainly thinking of the hard choices he would have to make in the next few hours or days.

As JFK was concluding his meeting with the Indian ambassador, shortly after 6:00 P.M., a new message from Khrushchev began arriving at the State Department from the U.S. embassy in Moscow. The four-part letter, received over three hours, was lengthy, emotional and personal. The copy delivered to the American embassy had actually included Khrushchev's handwritten notations, and officials at the State Department and the White House assumed that the letter was a direct private appeal by the Soviet leader to the President of the United States—perhaps sent without the approval of the Presidium. However, recently declassified documents confirm that Khrushchev had consulted the Central Committee as well as the Presidium before sending the message to President Kennedy. This shift in Soviet strategy "had already been approved."[253]

Khrushchev appeared to be offering an olive branch, but his Marxist belief system remained firmly in place. "Everyone needs peace: both capitalists, if they have not lost their reason, and, still more, commu-

[252]U. Alexis Johnson to McGeorge Bundy, draft cable, October 26, 1962, NSF, JFKL; Chang and Kornbluh, *Cuban Missile Crisis,* 386.

[253]Fursenko and Naftali, *"One Hell of a Gamble,"* 263.

nists, people who know how to value not only their own lives, but, more than anything, the lives of the peoples."[254] *The Soviet leader argued passionately that the weapons in Cuba were defensive (to deter an American invasion) rather than offensive (to threaten the United States). On the other hand, he no longer denied their presence: "The weapons which were necessary for the defense of Cuba are already there." The knot of nuclear war could be untied, he proposed, if the Soviet Union ceased sending armaments to Cuba and the United States pledged not to invade. "Then the necessity for the presence of our military specialists in Cuba would disappear." Khrushchev's language was elliptical, especially on verification, but his meaning seemed clear: the missiles would be removed if the United States agreed not to invade Cuba.*[255]

At 7:35 P.M., before Khrushchev's entire letter had even been received, John Scali met again with Alexsandr Fomin and relayed a message from Rusk, "I have reason to believe that the [United States government] sees real possibilities and supposes that the representatives of the two governments in New York could work this matter out with U Thant and with each other. My impression is, however, that time is very urgent." Fomin rushed off to communicate with the "highest Soviet sources." President Kennedy and the ExComm, for the remainder of the crisis, continued to act on the assumption that Fomin's offer and Khrushchev's message were "really a single package." In fact, Fomin's initial report did not arrive in Moscow until well after Khrushchev's impassioned letter had been written and delivered to the U.S. embassy. Meanwhile, the FBI reported that the Soviets were burning documents at their Washington embassy and their U.N. headquarters on Long Island. Ambassador Dobrynin, however, at the 1989 Moscow conference, vigorously denied that any records were destroyed.[256]

Several of JFK's ExComm advisers, including RFK and Sorensen, examined the new message late that evening and detected a faint ray of hope, especially since they took for granted a connection between

[254]Americans, it would appear, were not the only Cold War protagonists driven by ideological tunnel vision and self-serving myths.

[255]Nikita Khrushchev to John F. Kennedy, October 26, 1962, in Larson, *The Cuban Crisis*, 175–80.

[256]Roger Hilsman, *To Move a Nation: The Politics of Foreign Policy in the Administration of John F. Kennedy* (Garden City, New York: Doubleday, 1967), 219; Garthoff, *Reflections*, 80–81; Chang and Kornbluh, *Cuban Missile Crisis*, 386; Robert Kennedy, *Thirteen Days*, 70; Blight and Welch, *On the Brink*, 344.

Khrushchev's letter and Fomin's contacts with Scali. General Taylor and the JCS, however, rejected the message as a transparent attempt to stall for time while the missile sites were rushed to completion. General LeMay was characteristically blunt, ridiculing the argument that the missiles were defensive as "a lot of bullshit" and declaring that Khrushchev must believe "we are a bunch of dumb shits, if we swallow that syrup."[257]

In Cuba, Castro received new intelligence that American air strikes and an invasion were only 2–3 days away—in fact these military options remained active at the ExComm meetings and the buildup in Florida was rapidly moving forward. Khrushchev meanwhile approved a plan to defend Soviet installations in Cuba against an American military assault. Castro arrived at the Havana apartment of Soviet ambassador Aleksandr Alekseev in the early morning hours, contending that the odds were 20 to 1 that the Americans would attack within three days.[258] *He nervously dictated to Alekseev, in Spanish, draft after draft (a total of ten) of an emotional letter to Khrushchev. Castro told the ambassador "the situation is developing in such a way that it's either we or they. If we want to avoid receiving the first strike, if an attack is inevitable, then wipe them off the face of the earth." He admonished Khrushchev: "the Soviet Union must never allow the circumstances in which the imperialists could launch the first nuclear strike against it." Alekseev reported to the Kremlin, "At the beginning I could not understand what he meant by his complicated phrases." But the ambassador finally asked, "Do you wish to say that we should be the first to launch a nuclear strike on the enemy?" Castro replied, "No," but nonetheless argued against permitting the Americans to act first, "deciding that Cuba should be wiped off the face of the earth." Castro seemed to be writing "a last testament—a farewell." Alekseev translated the message into Russian and urgently cabled Moscow. "Not a trace seemed to be left," Sergei Khrushchev later wrote, "of the Soviet ambassador's former friendship with Fidel."*[259]

[257]Brugioni, *Eyeball to Eyeball*, 448.

[258]Alekseev, "who had worked for many years in Havana, ostensibly as a TASS correspondent," had been chosen as ambassador by Khrushchev and Gromyko. (Gribkov, "View from Moscow and Havana," 13)

[259]Fursenko and Naftali, *"One Hell of a Gamble,"* 272–73; Sergei Khrushchev, *Nikita Khrushchev*, 628, 642; Blight and Welch, *On the Brink*, 342–44; Blight, *et al.*, *Cuba on the Brink*, 481–82. Castro later wrote angrily to Khrushchev denying that he had advocated a nuclear strike on the U.S., "because that would be more than incorrect, it would be immoral and insane." Nonetheless, Castro reiterated that the use of nuclear weapons "was

Late that Friday evening, according to Anatoly Dobrynin's personal account at the 1989 missile crisis conference in Moscow, President Kennedy, without informing the ExComm, may have dispatched RFK to meet again with the Soviet ambassador in his embassy office. Dobrynin later recalled defending the deployment in Cuba as a quid pro quo for the American missiles in Turkey, but RFK then suggested that the Jupiter missiles might be included in a settlement and left the room to call his brother at the White House. He soon returned to report that the President was willing to arrange a deal on the missiles in Turkey. The ambassador consequently brought up the American threats to invade Cuba. RFK left the office again to phone the White House and came back with news that the President was, if the missiles were removed, ready to offer assurances that the U.S. would not attack Cuba. Dobrynin, however, never mentioned this alleged Friday, October 26 meeting in his memoirs, published six years after the Moscow conference, and instead specifically links this breakthrough on the Cuba–Turkey missile deal to his well-documented October 27 meeting with RFK (discussed below).[260]

It seems likely that Dobrynin simply made an error at the 1989 Moscow gathering. Nevertheless, although no Soviet documents have surfaced confirming an October 26 meeting, the present author discovered that the White House telephone logs do verify that two calls from the attorney general were received by the President at 4:15 and 4:32 that afternoon. The time elapsed between these two calls (17 minutes) seems to fit quite well into Dobrynin's account of his Friday meeting with Robert Kennedy. Unfortunately, the telephone logs do not record the place of origin of incoming calls. RFK's desk diary, on the other hand, does not mention a meeting with Dobrynin. Sergei Khrushchev, nonetheless, has concluded in correspondence with the author that the telephone logs provide strong circumstantial evidence that the encounter did take place after all. But, he believes that this meeting occurred several hours earlier than originally claimed by Dobrynin and a few

---

unavoidable if Cuba was to be saved." (Fursenko and Naftali, "One Hell of a Gamble," 292)

[260]"This account of the [10/27] meeting is based on my contemporary report in our archives, which was written immediately afterward and is to be regarded as authoritative." (Anatoly Dobrynin, In Confidence: Moscow's Ambassador to America's Six Cold War Presidents (New York: Random House, 1995), 78–91) For Dobrynin's telegram to the Soviet Foreign Ministry, October 27, 1962, see Richard N. Lebow and Janice G. Stein, We All Lost the Cold War (Princeton, New Jersey: Princeton University Press, 1994), 523–26.

*hours before the White House had received Nikita Khrushchev's entire
message offering to remove the missiles in Cuba in exchange for an
American non-invasion pledge. The historical jury is still out.*[261]

Saturday, October 27, 10:00 A.M., Cabinet Room

*Identified Participants: John F. Kennedy, George Ball, McGeorge
Bundy, Douglas Dillon, Lyndon Johnson, U. Alexis Johnson, Robert
Kennedy, John McCone, Robert McNamara, Paul Nitze, Dean Rusk,
Pierre Salinger, Theodore Sorensen, Maxwell Taylor, Llewellyn
Thompson.*[262]

"I think you're gonna have it very difficult to explain why we are
going to take hostile military action in Cuba, against these sites . . .
when he's saying, 'If you get *yours* out of Turkey, we'll get *ours* out
of Cuba.' I think we've got a very tough one here."

President John F. Kennedy

The President again turned on the tape recorder after McCone's intelligence briefing. The CIA director's latest data was extremely ominous:
NPIC photo analysts had discovered that most of the MRBM sites were
now completely operational and could launch their missiles in six to
eight hours. In addition, the Soviets were installing anti-aircraft artil-
lery at the MRBM complexes—substantially increasing the danger to
American pilots if the President ordered air assaults. Also, there was
still no firm indication, despite Khrushchev's statement to U Thant,
that Soviet ships approaching the quarantine line had actually changed
course. On the other hand, there was also no evidence of a significant
redeployment of the Soviet armed forces worldwide.[263] McNamara reported that the *Grozny* was only 600 miles from Cuba and steadily approaching the blockade line.

As the recording began, the President was just agreeing to George
Ball's proposal to alert U Thant on the precise location of the quarantine line so that if the Soviets chose to avoid a confrontation, they
could be advised on precisely when and where to safely turn their ships

[261]For Dobrynin's 1989 account, from the Moscow conference transcript, see Blight and
Welch, *On the Brink*, 337–38; see also Garthoff, *Reflections*, 87–88; Chang and Kornbluh,
Cuban Missile Crisis, 386–87; President's Telephone Memorandum, October 26, 1962,
POF, JFKL; Robert Kennedy, Attorney General Papers, Desk Diaries, 1962, JFKL. Sergei
Khrushchev to Sheldon M. Stern, October 2, 2001.
[262]Tapes 40.1, 40.2 & 40.3, POF, PRC, JFKL.
[263]McAulliffe, ed., *CIA Documents on the Cuban Missile Crisis*, 328.

around. McNamara assured the President that the Defense Department would be in position to send the message in an hour and JFK directed, "OK. Put it out. Send it over to him." The defense chief asserted, and McCone agreed, that the *Grozny* was unlikely to be carrying prohibited materials; but, McNamara nevertheless acknowledged the mounting pressure to take *some* action, "But I think we ought to... I think we ought to *stop it*, anyhow, and use force if necessary." He also recommended using about eight planes for two extensive low-level surveillance missions of the missile sites later that day. The President urged interrogating the pilots to "to see what they saw," despite McCone's assertion the previous evening that they couldn't see very much. JFK even asked again, "Will they take one turn around there to see how much they can pick up," and Taylor explained that each pilot would have discretion to make that decision during the mission.

Suddenly, JFK interrupted the discussion to read aloud a United Press and Associated Press statement just handed to him: "Premier Khrushchev told President Kennedy in a message today he would withdraw offensive weapons from Cuba if the United States withdrew its rockets from Turkey." The President and the ExComm were clearly startled and puzzled by this report.

"Hmm... he didn't," Bundy recalled.

Reuters said the same thing, Sorensen noted, adding, "He didn't really say that, did he?"

"No, no," Bundy insisted.

"He may be putting out another letter," JFK immediately speculated.

"Pierre!" JFK called abruptly, echoed at once by Bundy. As the press secretary entered, JFK asked, "That wasn't in the [Friday] letter we received, was it?"

"No," Bundy interjected, just as Salinger replied: "I read it pretty carefully and it didn't read that way to me either."

"Is he putting," JFK asked, "supposed to be putting out a letter he's written me or putting out a statement?"

"Putting out a letter he wrote to you," Salinger presumed.

"Well," the President concluded, "let's just sit tight on it."

Bundy asked, "Is it a different statement?" and Rusk asked an aide to check the news ticker to see whether this new message might actually be the same one that Khrushchev had sent on Friday evening.

President Kennedy had certainly been seriously contemplating some form of missile exchange—which he had mentioned several times since the third day of the ExComm meetings. After Stevenson had audaciously endorsed a missile trade on October 26, in the face of open hostility from most ExComm participants, JFK had reiterated that the United States might have no choice but to "negotiate them out, in other words, trade them out." And, by the evening of Saturday, October 27, the President would begin to distance himself from the larger group and confer privately with his brother and a limited number of advisers on this persistently divisive issue. Indeed, whether or not the October 26 meeting between RFK and Dobrynin actually did take place, President Kennedy had all but made up his mind, notwithstanding ExComm opposition, to accept some arrangement involving the Turkish missiles if it became inescapable as the price for averting "the final failure."[264]

McNamara returned to plans for escalating air surveillance over Cuba. JFK asked about the advantage of another mission and McNamara explained, "It creates a pattern of *increasing* intensity of surveillance, Mr. President. We believe we should do this." JFK replied, "OK," and the defense chief requested specific authorization for two daytime and one night mission of 8 planes each since "there appears increasing evidence that they're working night and day on these sites." Bundy sought more explicit confirmation: "The night [mission] is laid on but not finally authorized?" and JFK replied, "You don't have to come back to me. If you want to do it then it's alright." Bundy proposed making a public announcement, but Rusk raised an objection, "I *really* think we ought to have a talk about the political part of this thing, because if we put on this thing [night surveillance] after two days on the basis of withdrawal of these missiles—" JFK interjected revealingly, "From Turkey?" and Rusk retorted, "No, not from Turkey, from Cuba. The Turkish thing hasn't been injected into this conversation in New York [at the U.N.] and it wasn't in the letter last night." Rusk finally articulated the emerging realization in the Cabinet Room about Khrushchev's latest maneuver, "This appears to be something *quite* new."

"This is what worries me about the whole deal," McNamara cautioned. "If you go through that [Friday] letter, to a layman it looks to be fulla' holes," and, joined by Bundy, he urged the President to "keep the heat on" by approving day and night reconnaissance missions and specifically announcing the night mission. But, McNamara and Bundy

[264]Blight and Welch, *On the Brink*, 338.

seem to have jointly sensed JFK's uncertainty—since he waited some six seconds to reply—and they each asked if he preferred to hold off the night mission: "Do you want to hold it?" Bundy inquired. "We can hold it, Mr. President," McNamara confirmed. "All right," the President instructed, "I tell you what let's do. I... I think we ought to go ahead if they want it, so that it's all right with me." But, he conspicuously and instantly qualified his own decision and opted for a delay after all, "I think we might have one more conversation about it, however, (McNamara interjected, "All right, sir.") about 6:00 o'clock, just in case during the day we get something that's important." The defense chief, in an unusually reassuring tone of voice, declared, "Plenty of time. We'll keep it on alert," and, along with Bundy, agreed to draft an announcement about night reconnaissance but to hold it until formal authorization by the President later that afternoon. Lyndon Johnson asked if night missions would require using flares and McNamara replied, "Yes, it does, Mr. Vice President."

Rusk, moments before, had asserted that Khrushchev's reported proposal to swap the missiles in Turkey and Cuba had not been in his Friday letter and seemed to be "something *quite* new." But, President Kennedy had been probing this option with the ExComm for more than a week. This time around, faced with Khrushchev's politically shrewd public announcement, he resumed the effort, "I want to ah... getting to this... in case this *is* an accurate statement," he asked, "where are we with our conversations with the Turks about the withdrawal of these...?" Nitze responded firmly, "The Turks... the Turks say that this is *absolutely* anathema" and view it "as a matter of prestige and politics." Ball reported that NATO contacts had indicated that removing the missiles from Italy "would be relatively easy" but "Turkey creates more of a problem" and might require substituting Polaris-equipped submarines if the Jupiters were dismantled. The situation was further complicated, Ball observed, by the fact that the Jupiter deployment had been a NATO decision.[265] Nitze continued to push a hard

[265]Ambassador Raymond Hare, October 26, 1962 Cable to the State Department, quoted in Chang and Kornbluh, *Cuban Missile Crisis*, 386; Finletter resisted the trade because he felt it could weaken American credibility and because the Turks resented losing the prestige and shared authority symbolized by the physical presence of the missiles. The Turks, as cited earlier, actually first took control of a launch site during the missile crisis—on October 22. (Finletter to Rusk, October 25, 1962, *FRUS, 1961–1963*, XVI: *Eastern Europe; Cyprus; Greece; Turkey* (Washington, D.C.: United States Government Printing Office, 1996), 730–33; Nash, *The Other Missiles*, 103)

line, urging the President "to say that we're prepared *only* to discuss *Cuba* at this time," but "we'd be prepared to discuss *anything*" after the Cuban issue is settled.

JFK understood the real world of "prestige and politics" as well as anyone in the room, but he was also mindful of the horrific potential of a reckless or misguided decision at this critical juncture: "Well, I don't think we can" discuss only Cuba, he told Nitze rather awkwardly, "if this is an *accurate* [report], then this is the whole deal, we'll just have to wait. I don't think we can take the position..."

Bundy argued that if Khrushchev had changed his terms and backed away from the "purely Cuban context" of last night's letter, the President should not soften his resolve: "There's nothing... no... nothing wrong with our posture in sticking to that line."

JFK persisted, "let's wait and let's assume that this is... that this is an accurate report of what he's *now* proposing this morning. Well maybe they changed it overnight."

"But he... he... he... I don't... I... I still think," Bundy continued hesitantly, "he's in a difficult position to change it overnight, having sent *you* a personal communication on the other line."

"Well now, let's say he *has* changed it," JFK snapped, "and this is his latest position."

"Well, I... I would answer back," Bundy insisted testily, "saying that 'I would prefer to deal with you're a... you know... with your interesting proposals of last night.'" Someone egged Bundy on, whispering, "Go for it!"

President Kennedy's reply, however, represents a fundamental turning point in the ExComm discussions—leaving no doubt about his evolving position: "Well now, that's... that's what we oughta be thinkin' about. We're gonna be in... in an *insupportable* position on this matter if this becomes his [Khrushchev's] proposal. In the first place, we last year tried to get the missiles out of there because they're not militarily useful, number one. Number two, it's gonna—to any man at the United Nations or any other *rational* man, it will look like a very fair trade."

"I don't think so," Nitze countered firmly, as someone muttered "No, no, no" in the background, insisting that there would be support in the U.N. for saying, "'Deal with this Cuban thing. We'll talk about other things later.' But I think everybody else is worried that *they'll* be *included* in this great big trade if it goes beyond Cuba."

Rusk and Bundy speculated that the allies would support the Cuba-first position but conceded that the neutral nations would likely be more sympathetic to a Cuba-Turkey deal. Rusk was about to explain his point when Salinger interrupted to hand the President some "entirely new stuff, Mr. Secretary," from a news ticker. JFK rapidly read the latest news flash aloud, confirming the earlier hints about Khrushchev's new public effort to link the missile bases in Cuba and Turkey. President Kennedy was certainly not surprised, "Now we've known this has been... might be coming for a week. I... we can't ah... we're gonna get hung up here now," he warned. "*This* is their proposal."

The President, suddenly sounding quite annoyed, grumbled, "How much negotiation have we had with the Turks this week? Who's done it?"

"We haven't talked with the Turks," Rusk explained. "The Turks have talked with us."

"Where have they talked with us?" JFK demanded.

"In NATO," Rusk replied.

"Yeah, but have we *gone* to the Turkish government before this came out this week? I've talked about it now for a week," the President protested. "Have we got any conversations *in Turkey* with the Turks?"

Rusk explained that Ambassadors Finletter and Hare had been consulted, but repeated, "We've not actually talked with the Turks."

Ball tried to clarify that approaching the Turks on withdrawing the Jupiter missiles "would be an *extremely* unsettling business."

"Well," JFK came back firmly, "*this* is unsettling *now* George, because he's got us in a pretty good spot here. Because most people will regard this as not an *unreasonable* proposal. I'll just tell you *that*."

"But, what '*most* people,' Mr. President?" Bundy asked skeptically.

The President shot back: "I think you're gonna have it very difficult to explain why we are going to take hostile military action in Cuba, against these sites . . . when he's saying, 'If you get *yours* out of Turkey, we'll get *ours* out of Cuba.' I think you've got a very tough one here."

"I don't see why we pick *that track*," Bundy argued, "when he's offered us the other track in the last 24 hours."

JFK repeated impatiently before Bundy had even finished, "Well he's *now* offered us a new one!"

"You think the public one is serious when he has a private one that's in...?" Taylor asked rather incredulously.

"*Yes!*" the President declared stubbornly, "I think we have to assume that this is their *new* and *latest* position, and it's a *public* one."

Ball cleverly suggested pulling the rug out from under Khrushchev by releasing his October 26 letter and Bundy endorsed the idea, "I think it has a good deal of virtue."

"Yeah, but I think we have to," the President countered, only partially suppressing an exasperated laugh, "be now thinking about what our position's gonna be on *this* one, because this is the one that's *before* us and *before* the world."

Sorensen speculated that "practically everyone here would favor the private [Friday] proposal."

"We're *not* being offered a choice," Rusk remarked realistically. "We *may not* be offered a choice."

JFK pointed out that Khrushchev's private Friday offer also had "serious disadvantages . . . which is this guarantee of Cuba [against invasion]. But in any case," he repeated yet again, "this is *now* his official one. We can release his other one, and it's different, but this is the one that the Soviet government obviously is going on."

Despite nearly unanimous ExComm opposition, President Kennedy remained steadfast on taking Khrushchev's public offer seriously. The limited objective of removing Soviet missiles from Cuba, in his mind, did not justify risking nuclear war merely to keep the Jupiter missiles in Turkey—a gamble which would reasonably be regarded as reckless or worse by most of the world. JFK's stance calls to mind his thoughts from the South Pacific in 1943. "The people deciding the whys and wherefores had better make mighty sure that all this effort is headed for some definite goal, and that when we reach that goal we may say that it was worth it, for if it isn't, the whole thing will turn to ashes, and we will face great trouble in the years to come...."[266]

Nitze tried to shake the President's determination by suggesting that the Soviets might be pursuing both a private track with Cuba and a public track with the U.S. "to confuse the public scene and divide us with additional pressures."

JFK readily admitted, "It's possible."

"I think, personally," General Taylor cut in, perhaps backing away from his earlier doubts about the importance of the new public message, "that statement's one that the Soviets take seriously."

But, the opponents of the trade refused to roll over and play the role of "yes men." Rusk argued that NATO-Warsaw Pact arms represented a separate problem, "They've got hundreds of missiles looking down

[266]John F. Kennedy to Inga Arvad, September 26, 1943, NHRM, MHS.

the throat of every NATO country. . . . The Cuba thing is a Western Hemisphere problem, an intrusion into the Western Hemisphere." Nitze also insisted, "I think we ought to handle these [Cuba and Turkey] as much as we can on a separate basis" and Bundy chimed in, "Absolutely." "I'd handle this thing," Nitze advised, "so that we continue on the *real* track," getting the missiles out of Cuba. Bundy was even more direct, "if we *accept* the notion of the trade at this stage, our position will come apart very fast."

The President's dissatisfaction bubbled over again, "Well, I'd just like to know how much we've *done* about it, because, as I say, we talked about it..." Bundy replied rather condescendingly, "We decided *not* to, Mr. President. We decided *not* to play this directly with the Turks." Ball warned that any discussions with the Turks "would be *all over* Western Europe," and would inevitably leak to the Soviet Union and seriously undermine American credibility. "If we had talked to the Turks," Bundy lectured, "it would *already* be clear that we were trying to sell our allies for our interests. That would be the view in all of NATO. Now it's *irrational* and it's *crazy*, but it's a *terribly powerful fact*." Ambassador Thompson went even further, urging the President to instruct Stevenson at the U.N. to "immediately say we will not discuss this ques... the Turkish bases." "The problem is *Cuba*," Bundy repeated, "The Turks are not a threat to the peace."

President Kennedy brushed aside Thompson's proposal, "rather than saying *that*, until we get time to think about it," he instructed that Stevenson try to get clarification at the U.N. of this new and "entirely different" [Soviet] proposal: "As I say," he reiterated, "you're going to find a lot of people thinking this is rather a reasonable position." "That's true," Bundy admitted, and JFK cautioned, "Let's not kid ourselves." The President again read aloud briefly from the news ticker account of Khrushchev's public statement, but Rusk repeated that Turkey was a NATO–Warsaw Pact problem—entirely unrelated to Cuba. Kennedy did concede Nitze's point that the Soviets had made their latest proposal public "to cause *maximum* tension and embarrassment. . . . He has put it out in a way in which the Turks are bound to say that they won't agree to this. And therefore we're at mercy of these others. They're not American proposals."

At least for the next few hours, until Soviet intentions had been spelled out and "we have gotten our position a little clearer," the President concluded "we ought to go with this last night's business" and not get bogged down about Turkey until Khrushchev's new offer has been officially received. "OK," Bundy responded, and Rusk added, "There's nothing coming in *yet* on our tickers." JFK read aloud from the draft of Stevenson's U.N. message and urged getting a public statement ready which referred to "*last night's*" letter and reiterated the demand that work on the bases must be stopped "while we can have a chance to discuss these matters. I don't know," he remarked, rather disingenuously *if* the secret RFK-Dobrynin meeting did take place the previous evening, "what we're gonna say on the Turkish matter." Ambassador Thompson speculated that Khrushchev may have mistakenly concluded that Austrian foreign minister Bruno Kreisky's October 25 proposal for a Cuba-Turkey missile trade "was inspired by *us*." McCone remarked that he would not be surprised if "the Russians got Kreisky to do it."[267]

President Kennedy chatted briefly with Rusk before temporarily leaving the meeting. Dillon can soon be heard muttering, "The United States *cannot* accept a... a Turkey-Cuba trade at this point." "No, not with Berlin coming up," Rusk agreed. The remaining participants reviewed several diplomatic documents for a few minutes before Robert Kennedy cut in, "Can I throw out some ideas?" The attorney general outlined several key points for the U.S. negotiating stance. First, the issue of the Cuban missile bases "must be resolved within the next few days. This can't wait" because "the work is continuing despite our protests . . . so therefore it's got to be resolved—*and quickly*." Second, the quarantine is "an action by all of Latin America countries plus the United States." Third, this situation "has *nothing* to do with the security of the countries of Europe, which *do* have their own problems." Nonetheless, he added, "*We* would obviously consider negotiating the giving up of bases in Turkey if we can assure the Turks and the other European countries for whom these bases were placed" that their own security will be protected. "This will entail inspection as we anticipate that there will be some inspection in Cuba and in the United States at the time that the Cuban... that these bases are withdrawn from Cuba and we give assurances that we are not going to invade... Something along those lines."

The low-key, informal conversations that continued with the President still out of the room, despite RFK's nominal effort to "stand in"

[267]Austria did not regain its independence after World War II until the Soviet Union agreed to join Britain, France and the U.S. in a 1955 peace treaty. Austria declared its neutrality and remained almost equally divided between East and West in the Cold War.

for his brother, exposed the depth and persistence of ExComm hostility to a Cuba-Turkey missile trade. Ball reported that Stevenson had called to say there was no disposition among the U.S. delegation to the U.N. to get Turkey involved at all, "that they want to keep it strictly separate—keep the Turkey business out." Rusk seemed equally determined, "I think that we... we must insist with U Thant that *U Thant* not fall for this." RFK still had doubts as well, "I don't see how we can ask the Turks to give up their defense," he contended, unless the Soviet Union was also going to give up their weapons aimed at Turkey—and, McNamara added, "agree not to invade Turkey" and permit inspections to prove that they're keeping their word. RFK declared that the United States would welcome such a move by the Russians and "finally feel that this is a *major* breakthrough and we would be glad to discuss that." But, he concluded, the first order of business was the removal of the threat to the U.S. and Latin America posed by the missiles in Cuba. Dillon seemed willing to go along with RFK's suggestion if the parties involved "accept the same inspections. Reverse the risks. While we're fooling around it puts it right back on them." Gilpatric cautioned that these proposals should be checked first with the President.

McNamara tried to sort out some confusion over the timing of recent messages from the Kremlin, "Khrushchev's statement to U Thant is *absolutely* contradictory to his [October 26] statement to the President. Now the question is, which came first? I thought the reply to U Thant came first. . . . We ought to mention this in the reply." Thompson pointed out that the message to JFK had been delivered to the Moscow embassy in Russian and had to be translated. McNamara suggested getting official confirmation of the delivery time of Khrushchev's letter to the President. "I think," Rusk conjectured "that message to U... to U Thant was *later* than that long letter sent last night to us." Thompson reminded his colleagues that the delivery time of diplomatic messages would be recorded but "you can never be sure" when they were actually sent.

A brief discussion followed about whether to release Khrushchev's October 26 letter—Ball seemed reluctant to make public a secret message between heads of state for the first time and Thompson asserted, with Bundy's backing, "I would *not* release this." Paul Nitze, however, escalated ExComm resistance to the Turkish trade:

"Attack this Turkish thing *hard*," Nitze demanded. "It seems to me that's the thing to do with that Turkish..."

"In what way?" Bundy interjected.

"Say we're not gonna *do* that," Nitze insisted.

"Yeah, I agree," Bundy replied, "That *has* to be said."

"It's an *entirely* separate situation," Nitze continued. "It's *not* a threat."

"You see this as a diversionary tactic," Taylor asserted.

"And then direct attention *back*," Bundy maintained, "to the fact that the Cuban matter remains urgent. The buildup is continuing. Ships have *not yet* obeyed the instructions on which Mr. Khrushchev gave assurances to U Thant." Gilpatric, McNamara and Bundy quietly agreed that the U.S. should instead be pushing demands for halting construction on the bases, followed by the inoperability and removal of the missiles.[268]

Rusk, at this juncture, was handed copies of the new public message from Khrushchev just received on a White House foreign broadcast news ticker. Shortly after Rusk began to read and summarize Khrushchev's latest statement, the President seems to have quietly returned to his seat in the Cabinet Room.[269] Two key lines read by Rusk confirmed that the Soviet leader had indeed made a high stakes public offer: "I propose that we agree to remove from Cuba the means which you consider aggressive. Your representatives will then remove analogous means from Turkey."

McNamara reacted incredulously, "Dean, how... how do you interpret the addition of still another condition over and above the letter that came in last night? We had one *deal* in the letter, now we've got a different deal."

"And in *public*," General Taylor asserted.

Rusk tried to decipher the new, tougher Soviet position: "I suppose the boys... the boys in Moscow decided this [earlier proposal] was too much of a setback for 'em."

"How can we negotiate," McNamara repeated, "with somebody who changes his deal before we even get a chance to reply and *announces publicly* the deal before we receive it?"

"I think he must... there must have been an overruling in Moscow," Bundy speculated.

Rusk guessed that the personal and emotional Friday night letter must have been sent out "without clearance," and a consensus quickly developed that, "The Politburo intended *this one*."

---

[268]Nitze, Bundy and Taylor, some of the most vocal ExComm opponents of the Turkish missile trade, had been among those most receptive to plans discussed the previous year for a nuclear first-strike against the U.S.S.R. (Kaplan, "JFK's First-Strike Plan," 81–86)

[269]Bundy, in the background, can be heard saying, "Thank you, Mr. President."

"You see, it *completely changes* the character of the deal we're likely to be able to make, and... and also, therefore, our action in the interim." McNamara observed, "So *my* point is we oughta *really* keep the pressure on them in this type of situation."

"*This* should be knocked down publicly," Bundy demanded, by separating out the Turkish issue and focusing attention on Cuba: "*Privately* we say to Khrushchev: '*Look*, your public statement has been... is a very *dangerous* one because it makes *impossible* immediate discussion of your *private* proposals and requires us to proceed urgently with the things that we have in mind. You'd *better* get straightened out!'" McCone, backed by several others, affirmed, "This is exactly right!" Bundy still opposed releasing Khrushchev's October 26 letter, but proposed instead making a subtle threat: "We say we are reluctant to release this letter which displayed the inconsistency in your position, but we don't have very much time."

"Our point Bobby is," McNamara tried to explain to the attorney general, "he's changed the deal." But RFK questioned the wisdom of publicly exposing Khrushchev's flip-flop: "What is the advantage? I don't know when... which... where you are 24 hours from now. So we win *that* argument. . . . but the fact [remains], that *he's* gonna have a ploy public... publicly that's gonna look rather satisfactory, as the President says. How are we going to *have him* do anything but take the ball away from us publicly if we don't agree. . . . We can have an exchange with him and say, 'You've double-crossed us and you've... and we don't know which deal to accept'. . . . In the meantime, he's got all the play throughout the world." McNamara had a very direct response, "Just turn it down publicly," but RFK replied, "Yeah, but I think that's *awful tough*." McCone also pointed out that a public rejection would, in any case, require referring to the content of Khrushchev's October 26 letter.

Robert Kennedy, evidently thinking out loud, asked again for consideration of the somewhat convoluted mutual inspection proposal he had briefly floated earlier in the meeting: the United States would suggest to Khrushchev that they combine the removal and inspection of the Cuban missile bases with an American non-invasion pledge and U.N. inspections in the U.S. "to ensure that we're not getting ready to invade. Now this is one of the things U Thant said." As to the missiles in Turkey, RFK suggested telling Khrushchev "we think that's *excellent* that you brought that up," and proposed linking the withdrawal of the Turkish Jupiter missiles to a Soviet guarantee to stand down its bases for invading Turkey, backed up by inspection of both Turkey and the Soviet Union. "I think it's *too* complicated, Bobby," Bundy protested, but RFK snapped, "Well, *I* don't think it is!"

The President had already argued vigorously that Khrushchev's public offer had probably made removal of the Turkish missiles unavoidable and his immediate concern, despite the nearly unanimous resistance of the ExComm, was to prevent the Turks from constricting his options. "Wait just a... it seems to me," JFK cut in, breaking his silence for the first time since rejoining the meeting, "the *first* thing we oughta try to do is not let the Turks issue some statement which is wholly unacceptable." He reiterated that work on the missile sites had to stop today, "before we talk about *anything*. At least then we're in a defensible position." The President contended again that the Turks did not realize that if the U.S. took military action in Cuba, the Soviets could retaliate against the Jupiter missiles—exposing Turkey to great danger. "We gotta have a talk with the Turks because I think they've got to understand the *peril* that they're going to move into next week if we take some action in Cuba. I think the chances are that he'll [Khrushchev] take some action in Turkey. They oughta *understand* that. And in fact they [the U.S.S.R.] may even come out and say that once the Turks turn us down. . . . So I think the Turks ought to *think* a little about it and we oughta' try to get them *not* to respond to this 'til we've had a chance to consider what action we'll take. Now, how long would it take to get in touch with the Turks?"

Ball, supported by Rusk, predicted that it would be "awfully hard" to keep the Turks from publicly rejecting the withdrawal of the Jupiters and Bundy defended the right of the Turkish government to say that NATO military arrangements have nothing to do with Cuba. "It seems to me," Bundy declared firmly, joined by Taylor, "it's important that they *should*. If anyone pulls them in it will be us and they *can't* be expected to do *that*." "No, but ah... we want to give 'em... we want to give 'em some guidance," the President contended firmly. "These are *American* missiles not *Turkish* missiles. They're under *American* control not *Turkish* control." McNamara explained, however, "The missiles belong to Turkey and they're manned by Turks, but the warheads are in U.S. custody." "And they're committed to NATO," Taylor proclaimed, which McNamara repeated verbatim. "In other words," JFK observed reluctantly, "we couldn't withdraw the missiles anyway, could we? They belong to the Turks. All we could withdraw is the warheads?" McNamara clarified that even the warheads could only be released by the President in accordance with NATO nuclear policy procedures.

President Kennedy was thrown off stride by this procedural complication but remained determined to prevent the Turks from closing the door on a critical U.S. option and urged acting quickly to restrain the Turks "until we've had a chance to think a little more about it." He proposed that the U.S. should acknowledge receiving "several publicly and privately *different* proposals, or *differing* proposals, from the Soviet Union. They *all* are complicated matters and involve some discussion to get their *true meaning*. We *cannot* permit ourselves to be *impaled* on a long negotiating hook while the work goes on on these bases. I therefore suggest [in response to U Thant's negotiation initiative] that work... that the United Nations *immediately*, with the cooperation of the Soviet Union, take steps to provide for cessation of the work, and then we can talk about *all* these matters, which are *very* complicated."

Bundy, nonetheless, would not relent on the Turkish bases and urged the President to say, "the current threat to peace is *not* in Turkey—it is in *Cuba*. There's no pain in saying that even if you're going to make a trade later on." The immediate threat is in Cuba, he repeated, tapping the table for emphasis, "and that is what has got to stop." "That being so," JFK acknowledged, "until we find out what is *really* being suggested and what can *really* be discussed, we *have* to get something on *work*. Their weakness is... the work's going on." "That's right," Bundy admitted. But, the President reaffirmed, "There isn't any doubt—let's not kid ourselves. They've got a God... they've got a *very good* proposal, which is the reason they've made it public with an announcement."

Bundy tried to explain that an informal consensus had emerged while the President was out of the room. "I don't know whether Tommy agrees," but we have concluded that the Friday evening message was written personally by Khrushchev but the Saturday morning public message resulted from "his own hard-nosed people overruling him, this public one... that they... they didn't like what he said to you last night." "Nor would I," Bundy added colorfully, "if I were a Soviet hardnose." Ambassador Thompson reiterated that the Soviets might have interpreted the Kreisky speech as "*our* underground way of suggesting this."

JFK remained convinced that the Soviets had deliberately chosen to make the offer public and Bundy and Thompson agreed that a public proposal was more likely to build up pressure on the United States. President Kennedy, nevertheless, underscored again that the public offer could not be disregarded and bluntly acknowledged that Khrushchev had been politically astute: "the fact that work is going on is the one *defensible* public position we've got. They've got a very good prod and this one is gonna be *very tough*, I think, for us. It's gonna be tough in England, I'm sure, as well as other places on the continent." U.S. action in Cuba, he insisted, would give the U.S.S.R. "not a blank check but a pretty good check to take action in... in Berlin on the grounds that we are *wholly* unreasonable. Most think... people will think this is a rather even trade and we ought to take *advantage* of it." It would be very difficult, as a result, for the U.S. "to move with world support" against Cuba. "This is a pretty good play of his. That being so, I think what we're... the only quite... thing we've got him on is the fact that while they put forward *varying* proposals in *short* periods of time, *all* of which are complicated, under that shield this work goes on. Until we can get someone... an agreement on the cessation of work, how can we *possibly* negotiate with proposals coming as fast as the wires will carry them?" "And the ships are still moving," Bundy exclaimed, "in spite of his assurances to U Thant."

Rapid-fire criticism of the President's position on Turkey continued. Dillon pointed out "what might be a *very* dangerous sentence" in Khrushchev's public message which "I've been afraid of all along on the Cuban trade." The reference to American bases surrounding the U.S.S.R., Dillon suggested, could be interpreted to apply to installations in countries other than Turkey. "That was propaganda," the President responded, "the *direct* trade is suggested with Turkey." Thompson, in the same vein, speculated that the phrase, "'the means which you consider aggressive,'" could be intended to include planes and technicians as well as the Turkish missiles. Bundy worried that Khrushchev might demand a missile-for-missile Turkish-Cuban trade "which wouldn't be good enough from our point of view" because there are many more missiles in Cuba than in Turkey. "Why we could talk for three weeks on that message, couldn't we?" JFK remarked. "But the problem is to get these... work on their bases stopped. That's, in my opinion, *our* defensible position."

McNamara shot back: "It isn't enough to stop work on a base that's already operable." JFK did not reply directly, but Nitze pushed the President even harder by insisting that emphasizing the differences between Khrushchev's last two messages "looks to the public as though *we're* confused." JFK repeated his concern that Khrushchev might "hang us up in negotiations on different proposals while the work goes on." "That looks like a rationalization of our *own* confusion," Nitze rejoined. "I think we've got to take a *firmer* line than that." Bundy pronounced confidently, "*I myself* would send back word by [Aleksandr] Fomin, for example, that last night's stuff was pretty good. This is *impossible* at this stage of the game and that time is getting very short. . . . But I think it's very important to get *them* to get the message that they... if they want to stop something further in Cuba they have to do better than *this* public statement." JFK had listened patiently but sidetracked this increasingly contentious discussion by asking to have a call placed to Ambassador Stevenson at the U.N.

The President, while waiting for the connection to New York, asked how many Soviet IRBMs "may be facing Turkey." "I don't know offhand," Taylor acknowledged, but Nitze replied, "I would guess it is at the order of at least 100 . . . [and] we have 15 Jupiters" in Turkey. But, McNamara added, "we have a lot of planes with nuclear weapons [in Turkey]. Those are the 'analogous weapons' he's [Khrushchev's] speaking of here [in the public message]." Evelyn Lincoln soon interrupted to inform the President that Ambassador Stevenson was on the line. The tape, of course, picked up only JFK's part of the conversation—while several ExComm members whispered together in the background. President Kennedy, on the phone for several minutes, asked principally for Stevenson's judgment on the disparity between Khrushchev's last two messages and finally asserted, "What we gotta do is get them to agree to stop work while we talk about all these proposals."

After hanging up, perhaps prompted by something Stevenson had said, JFK exclaimed with a mischievous chuckle, "What about our putting something in about Berlin? . . . I mean... just to try to put some sand in *his* gears for a few minutes." "In what way?" Bundy inquired—sounding somewhat perplexed. The President, evidently thinking of comparable Russian demands for non-invasion guarantees for Cuba, responded in an unusually patronizing tone of voice, "*Well, satisfactory guarantees for Berlin!*" But, he promptly conceded, "which he's not gonna give. I'm just tryin' to think of what the public problem is about this... because everybody's gonna think this [the Turkish swap] is *very* reasonable."

Dillon, possibly rethinking the Turkish option, told the President "you're quite right" to view Khrushchev's offer in terms of Berlin and "the overall European context." He predicted that the Germans as well as the Turks would be taking "a *very* strong position" on this issue in the next few hours. JFK pressed the ExComm again on initiating contacts with the Turkish government, "Who has talk... who has talked to the Turks? Did Finletter talk to them?" Alexis Johnson answered, "No," and Rusk mentioned that the Turkish prime minister "talked on his own, yesterday, to ah... to ah [Ambassador] Hare." "I would say," Dillon speculated, "that the Turkish proposal opens the way to a *major* discussion of relaxed tensions in Europe, including Berlin." Nitze strenuously objected, "Oh, no, no, no, no, no, no! ... If you mention that, you've lost the Germans." "That's right," McCone affirmed. "Right then and there," Nitze pronounced.

The recording suddenly cut off—probably because the automatically activated backup recorder ran out of tape and, apparently, no one was on standby to put in a new reel.[270]

Alexis Johnson reported, according to the written meeting notes, that the government of Turkey, as expected, had released a statement to the press denouncing the Russian scheme to remove the Jupiter missiles. In addition, the ExComm received a Soviet announcement indicating that the base proposal, as Dillon had warned, might involve "not merely Turkey but all of NATO." RFK, clearly still ambivalent about his brother's stance on a missile trade, asserted "that we make doubly clear that Turkish NATO missiles were one problem and that Cuba was an entirely separate problem." Roswell Gilpatric agreed, stating "that it was crucial for us to stand on the position that we will not negotiate with the Russians while the Soviet missile threat is growing in Cuba."[271]

The President, however, did not retreat, recalling that the United States had considered removing the Jupiter missiles from Turkey more than a year ago "because they had become obsolete. . . . But we are now in a position of risking war in Cuba and in Berlin over missiles in Turkey which are of little military value. From the political point of

---

[270]Robert Bouck, nonetheless, claimed that the President "was using it [the tape recorder] so much at the time of the missile crisis that I stayed down there day and night for several days in order to change the tapes." (Bouck Oral History, 10)

[271]Bromley Smith, Summary of NSC Executive Committee Meeting No. 7, October 27, 1962, NSF, JFKL, 4.

*view, it would be hard to get support on an air strike against Cuba be-
cause many would think that we would make a good trade if we offered to take the missiles out of Turkey in the event the Russians would
agree to remove the missiles from Cuba. We are in a bad position if we
appear to be attacking Cuba for the purpose of keeping useless missiles
in Turkey." The Turks, he insisted, must be informed of "the great
danger in which they will live during the next week and we have to
face up to the possibility of some kind of a trade over missiles."[272] JFK
then left the meeting, just before noon, to meet with a delegation of
state governors.*

*RFK expressed concern about the possible deterioration of the U.S.
position if talks with the Soviets dragged on for weeks or even months
and the Cubans refused to allow inspections to verify that the missiles
were inoperable—but, he added with obvious interest, "we could then
decide to attack the bases by air."[273] Several ExComm members agreed
to meet at the State Department without the President at 2:30 that afternoon before reconvening in the Cabinet Room with President Kennedy at 4:00 P.M.*

*JFK, in the meantime, greeted the Civil Defense Committee of the
Governor's Conference cordially, but several participants later recalled
that he seemed "unusually somber and harried." Some of the governors
felt that the President had not been tough enough with Khrushchev.
California's Edmund Brown, a Democrat, asked bluntly, "Mr. President, many people wonder why you changed your mind about the Bay
of Pigs and aborted the attack. Will you change your mind again?" "I
chose the quarantine," Kennedy retorted, "because I wondered if our
people are ready for the bomb."[274] Shortly afterwards, McNamara informed the President that the JCS, after reviewing the latest intelligence, had again demanded extensive air strikes followed by a full-
scale invasion.*

*After the morning ExComm meeting, a report arrived that a U-2
from a Strategic Air Command base in Alaska, supposedly on a "rou-*

---

[272]*Ibid.*, 5.

[273]*Ibid.*

[274]Governor Brown's indecision over backing JFK for the 1960 presidential nomination
had infuriated the Kennedy camp. Brown, a Catholic, had ambitions to be the vice presidential candidate and knew that Kennedy could never choose a Catholic running mate;
Governor Elmer Anderson to Dino A. Brugioni, March 23, 1978, cited in Brugioni, *Eyeball
to Eyeball*, 453–57.

tine air sampling mission," had accidentally strayed into Soviet air space as a result of a navigational error. Soviet MiGs scrambled for an interception, but may have actually "dawdled" in order to allow the U-2 to safely cross the frontier. No shots were fired and the spy plane returned to its base escorted by F-102 fighters equipped with nuclear air-to-air missiles. McNamara, according to some accounts, was absolutely terrified when he learned about the incident and shrieked, "This means war with the Soviet Union." But the President, with classic gallows humor, is reported to have joked, "There is always some son-of-a-bitch who doesn't get the word."[275]

Just before leaving for the 2:30 meeting, McNamara learned that the morning U-2 flight over Cuba was more than 30 minutes overdue. The small group, meeting at the State Department, focused on eliminating the missile bases. RFK recommended allowing Soviet tankers to pass through the quarantine line: "if we attack a Soviet tanker, the balloon would go up." Instead, RFK again urged full preparation for air attacks on Cuba by Monday or Tuesday. McNamara reintroduced a familiar ExComm issue, suggesting that the Cubans should be notified before launching the air strikes. As the group was about to leave for the full ExComm meeting with the President at 4:00 P.M., McNamara learned that the U-2 was still missing and that low-level reconnaissance flights had been fired on over Cuba.[276]

Meanwhile, Castro's cable from Havana, which would not be declassified for nearly three decades, reached the Kremlin in Moscow on Saturday. "It became clear to us that Fidel totally failed to understand our purpose," Khrushchev later wrote. "We had installed the missiles not for the purpose of attacking the United States, but to keep the United States from attacking Cuba." The Soviet leader was horrified by

[275]Hilsman, *To Move a Nation*, 221; Sergei Khrushchev, *Nikita Khrushchev*, 605; David Detzer, *The Brink*, 281; Chang and Kornbluh, *Cuban Missile Crisis*, 388. Several other incidents could have led to Soviet miscalculation during the crisis: the dropping of "light depth charges on a submerged Soviet sub," discussed earlier, the launching of a U.S. test ICBM, "stationed near armed ICBMs," without the knowledge of top American leaders and a false early warning radar report of a missile launched from Cuba toward the U.S. (Bernstein, "Commentary: Reconsidering Khrushchev's Gambit," 238); Allison and Zelikow, *Essence of Decision*, 239; Scott Sagan, *The Limits of Safety: Organizations, Accidents and Nuclear Weapons* (Princeton, New Jersey: Princeton University Press, 1995), 135–37.

[276]Bromley Smith, Summary of NSC Executive Committee Meeting No. 7, October 27, 1962, NSF, JFKL, 5; Chang and Kornbluh, *Cuban Missile Crisis*, 389.

Castro's apocalyptic tone and interpreted the message as a call for a preemptive nuclear first strike against the United States. "Is he proposing that we start a nuclear war?" he asked his son Sergei. "This is insane. We deployed missiles there to prevent an attack on the island, to save Cuba and defend socialism. And now not only is he preparing to die himself, he wants to drag us with him." Perhaps Castro's cable had reminded Khrushchev, and Ambassador Alekseev as well, of Adolf Hitler's last testament in his Berlin bunker. In his message to President Kennedy the previous evening, before *receiving Castro's cable, Khrushchev had already been thinking about government and military officials in Washington, Moscow or Havana who might be tempted to deliberately unleash a nuclear war: "Only lunatics or suicides, who themselves want to perish and to destroy the whole world before they die, could do this."*[277]

Khrushchev, like JFK, was determined to hold back the dogs of war and decided to discount these reports from Havana. "In your cable of October 27," Khrushchev later replied to his Cuban ally, "you proposed that we be the first to carry out a nuclear strike against the territory of the enemy. You, of course, realize where that would have led. Rather than a simple strike, it would have been the start of a thermonuclear world war. Dear Comrade Fidel Castro, I consider this proposal of yours incorrect, although I understand your motivation. We have lived through the most serious moment when a nuclear world war could have broken out. Obviously, in that case, the United States would have sustained huge losses, but the Soviet Union and the whole socialist camp would have also suffered greatly. . . . Cuba would have been burned in the fire of war. . . . We struggle against imperialism, not in order to die, but to . . . achieve the victory of communism." Castro's demand for a nuclear first strike "may well have influenced Khrushchev's decision to proceed with a settlement with the United States."[278]

[277]Jerrold L. Schechter, ed. and trans., Nikita Khrushchev, *Khrushchev Remembers: The Glasnost Tapes* (Boston: Little, Brown, 1990), 177; Sergei Khrushchev, *Nikita Khrushchev*, 625; Castro, at the 1992 Havana conference, claimed that his cable had been mistranslated and had merely stated that if Cuba were invaded, the U.S.S.R. would have to defend itself with nuclear weapons. (Chang and Kornbluh, *Cuban Missile Crisis*, 387); Nikita Khrushchev to John F. Kennedy, October 26, 1962, in Larson, ed., *The Cuban Crisis*, 175–80.

[278]Nikita Khrushchev to Fidel Castro, October 30, 1962, in Blight, *et al.*, *Cuba on the Brink*, 485–88; Domínguez, "The @#$%& Missile Crisis," 313.

Saturday, October 27, 4:00 P.M., Cabinet Room

Identified Participants: John F. Kennedy, George Ball, McGeorge Bundy, Douglas Dillon, Roswell Gilpatric, Alexis Johnson, Lyndon Johnson, Robert Kennedy, John McCone, Robert McNamara, Paul Nitze, Dean Rusk, Theodore Sorensen, Maxwell Taylor, Llewellyn Thompson, Donald Wilson.[279]

"I just tell you, I think we're better off to get those missiles out of Turkey and out of Cuba because I think the way of getting 'em *out* of Turkey and *out* of Cuba is gonna be *very, very* difficult and *very* bloody, one place or another."

President John F. Kennedy

President Kennedy switched on the tape recorder as McNamara and Taylor were explaining that low-level reconnaissance flights over Cuba had been forced to turn back from their targets because of apparent ground fire. Rusk advised, "Mr. President, we're gonna have to make a decision later today as to what we do about *that*—the air surveillance," but JFK promptly urged restraint, "Well, we better wait 'til we hear more about *why* they aborted it." McNamara recommended issuing a statement justifying night reconnaissance, "whether we decide to carry it out tonight or not." JFK advised emphasizing that the OAS resolution provided legal backing for carrying out night surveillance flights.

USIA acting director Donald Wilson proposed running Voice of America radio announcements in Spanish every 5 to 10 minutes "telling [the Cuban] people that the ah... the light in the sky, the explosion [of flares for night photos] is harmless."

"I think we'd better wait," the President finally decided. "I don't know whether tonight's the night to do it."

Taylor agreed on the need to "evaluate the technique before we let them go."

"Yeah, I think we'd better wait on that," JFK repeated.

"We could report it," once this night reconnaissance decision is made public, Wilson observed. "There would be no harm in that 'cause that's very low-key."

The President reaffirmed, "Bob, I think we'd better wait till we find out what happened to these planes before we put this out about tonight."

McNamara explained that one mission had been aborted because of

[279]Tapes 41, 41A & 42, POF, PRC, JFKL.

mechanical failure and another recalled for unknown reasons. "What time do you want to put this out?" JFK asked. "Right now?"

"I think we oughta put it out now," McNamara pressed. "We don't have to *do* it tonight. This simply says that night surveillance is required. . . . I don't see we're committed to it."

"Yeah, I don't think you'd better go every five minutes with it [on Voice of America] though," JFK observed.

"Oh, no! I wouldn't," Bundy agreed.

"What he—what he was gonna do," RFK added reassuringly, "the night that you *do* it, he [Wilson] was gonna *tell* people in more *detail* about it."

"Okay," JFK finally yielded, and Wilson left the meeting to implement the decision and be sure "that nobody does anything wrong on this one."

The conversation then returned to drafting the precise language of the President's response to Khrushchev's contradictory letters of October 26 and 27. The discussion centered initially on establishing a connection between any U.S. assurances against invading Cuba (or supporting other forces planning an invasion) and demands for an equivalent commitment from the Cubans not to support military aggression or subversion in Latin America.[280] Robert Kennedy insisted on linking the two points: "I mean, all bets are *off* on this, I would think," he declared, if Cuba supplied arms to Latin American insurgents.

The President objected to the "put the bets off" wording and lectured his brother, "I don't think we can use *this* language." "Well," RFK explained, "this is *just* assurances." JFK instead proposed dangling the possibility of the Turkish missile deal mentioned in Khrushchev's new letter. He recommended new wording: "'As I was preparing this letter, which was prepared in response to your private letter of last night, I learned of your [new message].'" But, the real crisis is in Cuba and "'When we get *action* there [a cessation of work], I shall *certainly* be ready to discuss the matters you mentioned in your *public* message.' You see," he explained, "that's more forthcoming" than totally rejecting his public message. But, he added bleakly, "This isn't gonna be successful. We might as well realize *that*."

President Kennedy, at that point, essentially took charge of the dis-

---

[280]Khrushchev had asked for assurances that "the USA itself would not participate in an attack on Cuba and would restrain others from actions of this sort." (Nikita Khrushchev to John F. Kennedy, October 26, 1962, in Larson, ed., *The Cuban Crisis*, 175–80)

cussion: if the U.S. rebuffed Khrushchev's message on Turkey, he reasoned, "then where are we gonna be? Tomorrow he'll come back and
say the United States has *rejected* this proposal he's made." The cessation of work issue, he repeated, is "the only place *we've got him*. So I
think we oughta be able to say that the matter of Turkey and so on, in
fact *all* these matters oughta be... can be discussed if he'll cease work.
Otherwise he's going to announce that we've rejected his proposal."
He paused dramatically for some six seconds before reiterating darkly,
"And then where are we?" "We're *alright*," he continued after another
pause, "if he would cease work and dismantle the missiles. Then we
could talk for another two weeks. . . . Unless we *want* him to announce
that we've rejected it [the Turkish swap], I don't think we ought to
leave it [the letter] this vague. I think we ought to say that, if we're
gonna discuss this, then we're gonna have a cessation of work, and
we're not gonna get a cessation of work prob'ly, and therefore the burden's on *him*. That's our only, it seems to me, defense against the appeal of his ah... trade. I think we... our message oughta be that we're
glad to discuss this [Turkey] and other matters but we've gotta get a
cessation of work." "And the dismantling of the bases that are already
there," RFK added pointedly.

Ball revealed that Soviet U.N. ambassador Zorin had told U Thant
that Khrushchev's confidential October 26 letter had been "designed to
reduce tension but so as far as *he* was concerned," the public October
27 message, just as the President had persistently argued, "contained
the substantive proposal." JFK proposed putting pressure on U Thant
that afternoon by affirming that the United States would consider the
NATO-related matters suggested in Khrushchev's latest public letter, in
consultation with the NATO allies, *if* the secretary general could obtain assurances "which can be impl... ah... inspected, that they will
cease the work, and then we'll discuss these matters. Then I think we're
on a much better ground. . . . Now look, we oughta make it a *formal*
request, I think, George." Ball quickly agreed and JFK decisively dictated specific wording for the message to U Thant, "'If we're going to
discuss *these* [issues with the NATO counties] we must have *some* assurances which can be *verified* that the Soviet Union and the... will
cease work on the missiles and that the missiles which are presently
there have been made inoperable. Would the secretary general get from
the Soviet Union these assurances? In that case, the United States
would be prepared to discuss any proposals of the Soviet Union.'"

"Is there a shorthand expert around here?" Rusk quipped, producing a brief spurt of laughter at the table.[281] The letter was further reworded while Ball phoned U Thant's office, apparently to begin making arrangements for the delivery of the President's nearly completed statement. JFK asked Sorensen to write out the draft and added, "I'd like to have a written message which could be released if necessary." RFK, apparently persuaded that the reference to consultation with NATO would reassure the Turkish government, advised, "Jack, it would be well to get that out pretty quickly . . . so that the Turkey thing isn't a big story." The President agreed, "Yeah, that's right. That's why we wanna get it out tomorrow morning."

Bundy reported that he had talked to Charles Bohlen in Paris. The new ambassador felt that the "the knockdown of the Turkey-Cuba" link had been well received in France and Rusk reacted by candidly expressing hope for "a revolt in NATO" against removing the Jupiter missiles from Turkey. Bundy also revealed, despite the President's determined arguments in favor of the Turkish option, that he had instructed NATO ambassador Finletter to tell the alliance's permanent representatives that the U.S. opposed involving Turkey in a Cuban settlement. But, Finletter was authorized to listen to their points of view if they felt that the American decision exposed them to an "unusual hazard." JFK did not comment.

At that moment, General Taylor received an update on one of the most perilous issues pending that day: reports that low-level reconnaissance planes had been fired on over Cuba that afternoon. The JCS chairman reported that eight planes, flying in pairs, had taken off and one had developed mechanical problems "so the *pair* turned back." The remaining six approached Cuba in three flight plans. "One in flight plan was fired on, so following instructions to avoid it, turned back, leaving four planes who presumably have completed the mission." Rusk immediately got to the point, "fired on by what?" and Taylor replied, "Presumably low-level ack-ack—that's the only thing that could fire." He added that the pilots should be back on base by 6:00 P.M. Everyone in the room understood the grim implications—the first shots of the Cuban missile crisis had almost certainly been fired.

The President, clearly troubled by this development, asked if this was the night intended for starting night reconnaissance missions. He

---

[281]Gilpatric also privately suggested dictating a press release to Evelyn Lincoln, but JFK snapped, "For God's sake, don't give it to her, she can't take dictation." (Gilpatric Oral History, 58–59)

still seemed reluctant to actually give the order: "Just have it ready," he counseled after some further discussion, "I just think we might have one more conversation about the details of this firing on." "Do you want to hold it up, Mr. President?" Gilpatric asked. "Yeah, I think you gotta do that now until I talk to... I just want to have a talk with the Secretary a little more about it before we put it [the statement] out. We may wanna do something else."

Rusk, quite matter-of-factly, then brought up the even more alarming report that a U-2 had apparently strayed into Soviet air space near Alaska. There appears to be more to this episode than first meets the ear: the secretary of state proposed a step-by-step scenario as a public explanation for the incident, but his mannered language and cadence strongly indicate that he was reading from a prepared text. His calculating tone, especially his reference to a possible "advantage" in presenting this particular explanation, also hints that he might have been proposing a cover story rather than actually providing a straight presentation of the facts for the President—a striking example of a potentially crucial historical clue that can only be gleaned from *listening* to the tapes. "Now they will probably be making a big blast out of that in the next day or so," Rusk warned. "The question would be would there be any advantage in our saying that [begins reading] 'an Alaska-based U-2 flight engaged in routine air sampling operations in an area... assigned to an area normally a 100 miles from the Soviet Union had an instrument failure and went off course. Efforts by ground stations and our aircraft to recall it to its course did not succeed in time to prevent it from overflying a portion of the Soviet Union.' [stops reading] Now, whether we should leave the...."[282]

President Kennedy interrupted, arguing for toughing it out without an official explanation: "I think we're better off *not* to do it if we can

[282]At the 1987 missile crisis conference in Hawk's Cay, Florida, Professor Scott Sagan questioned whether this U-2 flight was part of the Strategic Integrated Operational Plan for nuclear war: "'What about the U-2 which strayed into Siberian air space on the 27th and which was reported to be on an air-sampling mission? Why wasn't that mission turned off?' McNamara brusquely replied, 'We just didn't know it was up there collecting air samples. . . . There are some things you can't foresee, and you can't process all the relevant information at once.' It was clear that McNamara considered it a question with an obvious answer, and equally clear that McNamara's answer left Sagan entirely unsatisfied." (Blight and Welch, *On the Brink*, 62–63, 126) Sagan later discovered that the U.S. planes escorting the U-2 out of Soviet airspace had been "armed with low-yield nuclear air-to-air defense missiles"—to be fired at the pilot's discretion. (Scott Sagan, *Moving Targets: Nuclear Strategy and National Sec*urity (Princeton, New Jersey: Princeton University Press, 1989), 147; Chang, "The View from Washington and Nowhere," 148)

get away with not having some leak. But I... because I think... last time we did it because of this... to maintain our credibility with Khrushchev." Bundy countered, "We didn't do it even then until he commented to us, last time." Well, very close," JFK pressed. "Didn't we uh...?" Bundy persisted, "No, sir." "Well, we acknowledged it," JFK finally declared.[283] "I don't feel there's any advantage now. It just makes... it gives him a story tomorrow and it makes it look like we're maybe the offenders. I don't see the advantage of it."[284]

McNamara then jolted the meeting yet again: he recommended that the incident involving the "stray" U-2 should not be announced because confirmation had also just been received that the plane fired on during the afternoon low-level reconnaissance mission over Cuba had been "hit by a 37-millimeter shell. It's coming back. It's all right, but it simply indicates that there's *quite a change* in the character of... of the orders given to the Cuban defenders." Just 48 hours before, McNamara had reported that the Russians had instructed the Cubans to act very cautiously and not fire on U.S. aircraft. In this complex new state of affairs, he advised against confusing the issue with a White House announcement about the U-2. The President immediately agreed, "Let's let it go."

Rusk returned to the draft of the proposed letter from the President to Khrushchev about the U.N. negotiating proposals. JFK, instead of commenting directly on these new and threatening military developments, raised two questions: "One *is*, do we want to have these conversations go on, on Turkey and these other matters, while we get to a sort of a standstill in Cuba? Or, do we want to say that we *won't* talk about Turkey and these other matters until they've settled the Cuban crisis. I think it's two different questions." He quickly provided his own answer: "Now that they've taken a public position, *obviously* they're not gonna settle the Cuban question until they get some conversation on Cuba. That being true, I think the best position now with him and publicly is to say 'we're glad to discuss this matter' [Turkey]

[283]The references are to President Eisenhower's clumsy statements following the shooting down of a U-2 over the U.S.S.R. in May 1960.

[284]Khrushchev's message the next day took the U-2 "air sampling" incident *very* seriously: "One asks, Mr. President, how should we regard this? . . . Your aircraft violates our frontier and at times as anxious as those which we are now experiencing when everything has been placed in a state of combat readiness. For an intruding American aircraft can easily be taken for a bomber with nuclear weapons, and this could push us toward a fatal step." (Nikita Khrushchev to John F. Kennedy, October 28, 1962, in Chang and Kornbluh, *Cuban Missile Crisis*, 238)

. . . [once] they have ceased their work in Cuba." JFK emphasized that a more flexible stance "puts *us* in a *much* stronger world position because *most* people will think his offer is rather reasonable. So I think we ought to put our emphasis, *right now*, on the fact that we want an indication from him in the next 24 hours that he's gonna stand still and disarm these weapons. Then we'll say, that under *those* conditions, we'll be *glad* to discuss these matters. But I think that if we *don't* say that, he's gonna say that we *rejected* his offer and therefore he's gonna have public opinion with *him*. So I think our only *hope* to escape from that is to say that... we should *insist* that he should *stand still*. Now, we don't think he'll do *that* and therefore we're in *much* better shape to put our case on *that*, than rather that Turkey's irrelevant."

The President then read out loud the draft message to be forwarded to U Thant, and repeated, "I think that's the best position for us." He asked candidly, "Does anybody object to that?" One voice, probably McCone, can be heard faintly saying, "No, that's fine," but that was *definitely not* the dominant view in the room. JFK requested that Stevenson pass the message to U Thant "right away and ask for an answer, don't you think, George?" but Ball objected, "Well the only question I'd like to raise about that is that that *really* injects Turkey as a... as a quid pro quo for a..." "That's my worry about it," Bundy chimed in. "*No! With negotiations!*" JFK replied testily. The problem, he repeated calmly, was to keep all viable options open: "The point is that we're not in a position today to make the trade. That's number one. And we won't be... if the trade *may be* made in 3–4 days, I don't know. We have to wait and see what the Turks say. We don't wanna be... we don't want the Soviet Union or the United Nations to be able to say that the United States *rejected it*. So I think we're *better off* to stick on the question of the *freeze*," he concluded impatiently, "and *then* we'll discuss it. I don't think... I don't think we..."

Bundy cut the President off with a stinging dissent: "There are two different audiences here, Mr. President, there *really* are. And I think if we *sound* as if we wanted to make this trade to our NATO people and to all the people who are tied to us by *alliance*, we are in *real trouble*." The national security adviser unflinchingly admonished the commander-in-chief, "I... I think that we'll... we'll *all* join in doing this if this is the decision. But I think we... we *should* tell you that that's the *universal* assessment of everyone in the government that's connected with these alliance problems." He repeated that Ambassadors Finletter and Hare felt strongly that if the United States appeared to be trading the defense of Turkey for the elimination of the threat from Cuba, "we just *have* to face a *radical* decline in the effectiveness" of NATO.

President Kennedy, addressing Bundy as "Mac," nonetheless repeated firmly, "this trade has *appeal*. Now, if we *reject* it out of hand, and then have to take military action against Cuba, then we'll *also* face a decline" in NATO and a loss of support around the world. He conceded that it was worth trying "to word it so that we don't harm NATO. But the thing that I think *everybody* would agree to is that while these matters, which are complicated, *are* discussed, there should be a cessation of work. Then I think we can *hold* general support for that. If they won't agree to *that*, the Soviet Union, then *we* retain some initiative. That's my response." The President had effectively decided, notwithstanding Bundy's likely exaggerated claim of "universal" opposition within the administration, that the door had to be left open to negotiations on the Jupiter missiles in Turkey.

Sorensen recommended linking the language of the U.N. draft to previously announced American disarmament proposals and McNamara, along with McCone, suggested emphasizing NATO and the free world rather than just Turkey. JFK expressed interest in the latter idea, but soon left the room to take a call from NATO supreme commander General Lauris Norstad. In the President's stead, RFK argued that the public would surely learn about Khrushchev's new offer on the radio today, "And people are gonna think it's quite reasonable. . . . Well, therefore we can't—the fact is that we just can't out of hand *reject* this . . . and after 24 hours we go and make a *bombing* attack, we're going to be in tough shape." The attorney general, however, added his own rather calculating caveat—"But on the other hand, if we offer them something that they're not gonna accept anyway," such as placing U.N. personnel on the missile sites, "then we're in much better shape throughout the world to go ahead and take whatever [military] steps are necessary." But, the President's purpose, RFK underscored, was to "take the initiative away" from the U.S.S.R.

Another version of the draft letter to Khrushchev was cobbled together during several more minutes of give and take on U.S. preconditions for negotiations with the Soviet Union. The same repetitive ideas continued to churn around the table, such as consulting with the NATO allies on any changes in defense arrangements and demanding that the Soviets cease work on the missile bases, render the offensive weapons inoperable and provide for reliable international verification. McNamara claimed again that these issues went "beyond Turkey" and might also require negotiations about U.S. bases in Italy and the United Kingdom, "and a number of other complicated issues relating to a number of countries." Including the Warsaw Pact, Rusk pointed out. "But my point is," McNamara stressed, "we're trying to get it away from the Turkish bases. It involves the *entire* defense of NATO." Sorensen indicated that Khrushchev had not mentioned bases other than those in Turkey and the defense chief, backed by Dillon, replied forcefully, "Oh, he *certainly* did. *Yes,* he did." Bundy also reiterated, "*Yes, he did.*" After several more moments of multiple dissonant conversations, during which McNamara ruminated about "the unilateral disarming of the Turkish Jupiters, changed to the Polaris, preliminary to an invasion of Cuba," Rusk finally exclaimed, "I wonder if... I wonder if this would get us one inch farther," and then read aloud from his updated draft of the message to Khrushchev.

Bundy, Sorensen and Ball reacted to Rusk's reading of the draft by expressing concern about apparent inconsistencies in several White House statements, but the defense chief defended President Kennedy's political strategy in his absence, "I think the President's feeling, Dean, was he wanted to indicate he was willing to negotiate on, in a sense, Turkish bases, but *only* after we have these assurances." RFK added that the President "would be willing to discuss the Turkish bases or... or anything that they *want* to discuss," and McNamara repeated, "the point was he [JFK] wanted to appear *reasonable.* He didn't want to appear to turn down a proposal which some people in the world would think was a reasonable proposal." McNamara nonetheless surmised, "He wanted to turn it down. He wanted to *defer* consideration of it, but do it with a good excuse, which was that they hadn't *yet* given us this assurance [on cessation of work and inoperability]."

RFK, still torn between his own combative instincts and his fierce loyalty to the President, reopened an earlier debate, "Tommy brings up the point" about whether Khrushchev's Saturday message "blows the whole" proposal in the Friday letter and Bundy asked, "How do you mean, Tommy?" Ambassador Thompson, ExComm's acknowledged "authority" on the Soviet Union, readily took the cue: explaining that Khrushchev's Friday evening letter: "made this proposal that... you see the whole problem's raised by our threat to Cuba and we're prepared to remove that threat [with a non-invasion pledge]. This point [about

Turkey in the second letter] undercuts that effort *entirely*. The minute we start talking about this, that's...."

Bundy eagerly pursued Thompson's point, "The minute we start talking about what?"

U.S. willingness, Thompson explained, "to discuss this question of the [Turkish] bases with only a freeze in Cuba."

"Yeah," Bundy quickly agreed, but he also asked about Ball's earlier report of a remark by Zorin at the U.N. that morning. Dillon reminded his colleagues that the Soviet ambassador in New York had apparently claimed that the October 26 message "wasn't the real Soviet position."

"For one or two reasons," Thompson deduced, "they've changed their minds on this. One was that they may have picked up this Kreisky thing and thought they could *get* more. The other was Khrushchev may have been overruled. In *either* case, we've gotta *change* that, which means we have to take a tough line—because this wobbling, I think..."

Rusk urged giving U Thant some more time "to work on the original [Friday] track if possible," but Dillon noted pessimistically, "Well the way this situation's going in Cuba with this fellow being shot at [on the reconnaissance mission], we haven't got but one more day." "That's right," Bundy and McNamara agreed, and Nitze warned, "The real question is whether our target is Khrushchev or whether it's the U.N." Bundy observed bluntly, "Turkey and Cuba is *not* workable for us except in the context of our doing a violent thing. And if we've done a violent thing," the usually self-assured national security adviser admitted, "we none of us know *where* to go. The one chance of avoiding that is to impress Khrushchev and get him back where he was last night [before the public proposal about Turkey]." Alexis Johnson concurred, "We have to operate on Khrushchev's public warning using a carrot and a stick" and Thompson, clearly on the same page, implicitly criticized the President's interest in "changing our whole policy for a public relations aspect," unless, he warned, a definite decision had already been made "that we're going in" to Cuba.

The secretary of state returned to working out the final wording of President Kennedy's letter to Khrushchev. Vice President Lyndon Johnson, who had attended several sessions but had rarely spoken up, particularly when JFK was present, unexpectedly urged breaking the impasse over Khrushchev's last two letters by simply informing the Soviet leader that the United States would be willing to discuss issues involving the security of NATO "as soon as the present Soviet-created threat [in Cuba] has ended." "There it is! That's the proposal to 'em," LBJ asserted, "sayin' we *can* and *will* just as soon as you get rid of these bases and make 'em..."

"Well, I see no reason," Bundy cut the Vice President off, "why a private message to the chairman shouldn't be a touch more forthcoming," and suggested instead telling Khrushchev, "'We understand your sensitivity on this matter but right now we can't get *at this* until we get past the Cuba problem.'" RFK reminded his colleagues, "Well, I think here what Bob [McNamara] said is what concerns the President." The Soviet offer, to the man in the street, "is *very* reasonable, and we just turned it down. And people are gonna start thinkin about the... the two things—Turkey and the Uni... and Cuba. And we just turned it down, now suddenly we drop the bomb on Cuba."[285] "We didn't turn it down," LBJ responded with obvious irritation. "This says we'll *continue* [talking about Turkey]," he insisted, rapping the table for emphasis, "soon as you stop the work."

Just as Sorensen was trying again to get agreement on final language for the messages to U Thant and Khrushchev, President Kennedy rejoined the meeting. "We really cut it up while you've been out of the room," RFK quipped, and several people chuckled as JFK replied, "Is this the new draft, Ted? I want to read it." Thompson, however, undaunted in his opposition to the Turkish option, admonished the President, "you're gonna end up with Soviet control of Cuba and so on..." Bundy boldly put his own spin on the planned reply to Khrushchev, "The justification for *this* message is that we expect it to be turned down, expect to be acting [militarily] tomorrow or the next day. That's... that's what it's for and it's *not* good unless that's what happens." Several voices can be heard affirming, "That's right."

Rusk, however, was far less certain whether the Turkish scheme in Khrushchev's latest letter was intended as "a *real* sticking point up to the point of shooting with them" or merely "an attempt at the last minute to try to get something *more* after they had indicated last night they will settle for something *less*." RFK advocated asking U Thant to find out if the Soviet U.N. delegate would agree that during discussions of the proposals of the last 36 hours, "work will stop on the missile bases and the missiles remain inoperative under United Nations supervision." At the same time, Bundy proposed "holding him [Khrushchev]

[285]RFK almost certainly did not mean "the bomb," that is, a nuclear weapon.

to last night while we do this." Several voices affirmed, "Yes," as Bundy concluded, "That's the pattern that would make sense to me." After several more minutes of mixed and overlapping discussions, the brief draft message to U Thant was nearly completed. But, Rusk noted, some revisions would be required to ensure consistency in the messages to the U.N. and to Khrushchev.

In the context of the rapidly evolving military and diplomatic situation, Bundy also pressed McNamara, "What's your military plan?" The defense chief explained unflinchingly, "the military plan now is *very* clear. A limited strike is out"—because reconnaissance aircraft had been fired on. "So the military plan now is... is *basically* invasion, because we've set a large strike to lead to an invasion. We might *try* a large strike without starting the invasion ... so we have time to cancel invasion plans. But they should be put on. We should start the strike, call up the reserves. We need the air units for the invasion in any case." But, McNamara cautioned, the administration had to first try to "minimize the Soviet response against NATO" after a U.S. attack on Cuba and also had to decide "how we're gonna respond" to Soviet reprisals against NATO. He again proposed the idea he had raised tentatively earlier in the meeting—alerting the U.S.S.R., *before* an air attack in Cuba, that the Jupiter missiles in Turkey had been rendered inoperable. "Now, on *that* basis," he reasoned, "I *don't* believe the Soviets would strike Turkey. They might take other actions, but I don't think they'd take *that* action."

Rusk, however, verbalized the threat everyone had been thinking about since the first ExComm meeting, the Soviets "might then aim their action at Berlin." McNamara readily acknowledged, "They might." The defense secretary was clear about the military plan but far from sure that it should actually be carried out, "I'm not prepared to state... *at this moment* to recommend air attacks on Cuba. I'm just saying that I think we must now begin to look at it more realistically than we have before." Thompson seemed skeptical about McNamara's assumption that the Jupiters could be replaced by submarine-launched Polaris missiles in only 24 hours, but the defense secretary remained convinced, "Oh yes, we can. . . . We say we've had a Polaris in the Mediterranean, we're deploying immediately to key places off the coast of Turkey at x time." Ball too was not persuaded: "There *is* a dilemma in this... that formula and that is that if you advertise the Polaris *publicly* as a substitute, then from the point of view of the Soviet Union they've achieved nothing by getting rid of the Jupiters."

"Well, they haven't *achieved* anything," McNamara retorted, "but they *sure have less* of a basis for striking Turkey when it...."

"That's right," Ball conceded, "yes, you minimize Turkey as a target."

"What I would hate... What I would try to avoid," McNamara avowed, "if we *could*, is an *immediate* Soviet military response to a U.S. attack on Cuba."

"Well," Thompson pointed out, "we have... he has no clear reply."

"That's right," McNamara acknowledged.

Refocusing the discussion on the nearly completed message to U Thant, JFK asked, "Do you release that or we just send it?" The wording was finalized after a bit more tinkering and JFK repeated, "Now what about releasing this? Do we... we give it to him and then we put it out?" RFK urged, "It should get out in the next hour though." Rusk suggested getting the message to the U.N. by phone and then releasing it. "Right. Very good," the President declared. Ball recommended calling Stevenson right away and JFK instructed, "we'll put it out at 6:00, tell him."

Despite the stubborn ExComm maneuvering against a Cuba-Turkey missile trade, especially during his brief absence from the meeting, President Kennedy quickly moved to put the Turkish option back on the fast track. He reported that General Norstad, in their phone conversation, had recommended convening "the NATO Council tomorrow morning so we can present this [the Cuba-Turkey trade] to them so that they all have a piece of it. Otherwise, no matter what we do—If we don't take it we're gonna be blamed; if we do take it we're gonna be blamed." "I think," JFK observed pragmatically, "he's very right." The NATO allies, the President asserted, have to understand the precise consequences of rejecting this proposed deal, "Otherwise, it's too easy to say, 'well, let's not take it then.' " The President instructed that Ambassador Finletter call a NATO Council meeting the next morning.

RFK made no effort to conceal his persistent doubts: the NATO Council meeting, he muttered, "blows the possibility of this other one, of course, doesn't it?"

"What?" the President asked.

"It blows the possibility in your first letter," RFK reiterated.

"Of what?" JFK repeated impatiently.

"Of getting an acceptance of the proposal that goes up in your letter now . . . I think that if they understand you're having a meeting in NATO on this..."

"That's the *disadvantage* of the Council meeting," Bundy agreed.

But Dillon insisted that it was "perfectly obvious" that the NATO Council would be interested in meeting about any Soviet proposal involving Turkey.

"I don't think there's any pain in the meeting," Bundy finally affirmed. "Why don't we get the meeting called?"

"The *advantage* of the meeting," the President reiterated, "*is* that if we *reject* it [the Turkey deal], they've participated in it. And, if we *accept* it, they've participated in it."

Robert Kennedy set off yet another round of dissent on the Turkish issue: "The other possibility is if you wait 24 hours ("What?" JFK interrupted) and see if they accept this other thing"—the positive reply to Khrushchev's October 26 offer. But, the attorney general trailed off and admitted pessimistically, "But they won't... they're not gonna accept it, yeah."

"You mean that... if the work's ceasing?" the somewhat puzzled President responded.

"Well no," RFK tried hesitantly to clarify, "the proposal..."

"The trade of last night [removal of the missiles for a non-invasion pledge]," Bundy explained, trying to clarify RFK's line of reasoning.

Ball also urged sticking to the Friday night offer: "*If* this [public message linking Turkey and Cuba] was simply a kind of fishing expedition in Moscow to see if they *could* get beyond what... what he'd put in his last night's letter, they may get the impression that they *can't do it.*"

"That's what I think," Bundy declared.

Rusk also proposed, given the letter just dispatched to U Thant, new language in JFK's message to Khrushchev in order to deal consistently with the Turkish issue: "As I was preparing this letter," he read, "I learned of your broadcast message today. That message raises problems affecting many countries and complicated issues not related to Cuba or the Western Hemisphere. The United States would be glad to discuss these matters with you and other governments concerned. The immediate crisis is in Cuba and it is there that very prompt action is necessary. With that behind us, we can make progress on other and wider issues."

President Kennedy recognized at once that Rusk's proposed language did *not* reflect his persistent stance on a possible Turkey-Cuba missile trade—his advisers appeared to be trying a rather transparent end run around his position. JFK's pique about these stalling tactics had begun to intensify:

"Well, isn't that really rejecting their proposal of this morning?" JFK quickly countered.

"I don't think so," Bundy replied, "It's rejecting..."

"I wouldn't think so," Rusk agreed.

"It's rejecting the *immediate* tie-in [on Turkey]," Dillon argued, "But we've *got* to do that."

"We're *not* rejecting the tie-in," President Kennedy responded firmly. "If we go reject it, I think we ought to have all of NATO rejecting it. What *we* want to insist on now is a cessation of work, etc., while we *discuss* it. Then we *may* reject it, but NATO ought to reject it because I think the reprisal's gonna be on all NATO. . . . It's just a question of timing, isn't it?"

If the NATO Council meets in the morning, Ball predicted, "I think you're gonna get a *flat* rejection of this [Turkey deal], which then ties our hands." He also reported that the NATO ambassadors to the U.N., that afternoon, "took a *very* strong line against any discussion of this."

"I don't think," the President replied stubbornly, "the *alternative* has been explained to them." They don't realize, he reiterated yet again, that if the U.S. takes military action in Cuba, Soviet reprisals will be against NATO. "I'd like to have them have *that* [information] before they reject it."

Dillon predicted that the NATO Council would "say, '*Don't trade,*' but they'd also say, '*Don't* do anything in Cuba!'—which," he added pensively, "may well be right."

McNamara, evidently viewing this latest bottleneck over linking Turkey and Cuba as another chance to press the strategy he had recommended earlier in the meeting, again urged the President to "take certain action with respect to the Jupiters in Turkey and Italy *before* we act in Cuba." The defense chief contended again that limited air strikes were no longer practicable "when they're shooting at our reconnaissance aircraft," which limited U.S. options to 500 sortie air attacks on the SAM sites and the MiG airfields followed by "an invasion in about 7 days." If that happens, he continued, "the Soviets are *very* likely to... to feel forced to reply with military action someplace, *particularly* if these missiles, Jupiter missiles, are *still* in Turkey." But, he reasoned, if the Jupiters in Turkey and Italy were defused and replaced with Polaris submarines "stationed off the shores of those nations to carry the same targets the Jupiters were directed to," the Soviets would have no excuse to attack Turkey and Italy, "the full defense of NATO" would remain intact and the United States would be "in a *much* better [political] position to present this whole thing to NATO."

What would the reaction be, Ball pressed McNamara, if the Soviets replied that "they were going to maintain three atomic [missile-carrying] submarines off the United States coast?" The defense secretary, almost casually, confirmed that three Soviet submarines had *already* been detected off the U.S. coast in the last 48 hours, "as far as we know, they don't carry missiles, but that's just happenstance."[286]

This disquieting exchange prompted President Kennedy to point out again, "The Turks won't take 'em out, will they? . . . except if we *took* 'em out [of Turkey], we'd get the trade the Russians have offered us. If we take 'em out, they'll take 'em out [of Cuba]." McNamara repeated that the Jupiters would have to be replaced with Polaris missiles, but Bundy remained adamant about the political fallout: "It's one thing to stand them down, Mr. President, in political terms. It's one thing to stand them down as a favor to the Turks, while we hit Cuba; it's quite another thing to trade them out, I think."

McNamara continued to insist that if the Jupiters were defused either unilaterally or bilaterally with the Turks, the U.S. could tell the Soviet Union, "The threat [from Turkey] is *gone*. You don't have to worry about that," and could then try instead to get Khrushchev back to his Friday proposal to remove the Cuban missiles in return for a non-invasion pledge. But Bundy and Dillon remained unconvinced, predicting that the Soviets would inevitably demand the removal of missiles from Italy and England as well. RFK advised that since the U.S.S.R. had already received an American offer at the U.N., the U.S. would have to move soon against Cuba if work continued on the missile sites. On the other hand, if they discontinued construction of the bases, but still demanded a Turkey-Cuba trade, NATO would have to consider it, "We haven't lost anything and they've discontinued the work on the bases." But, he again came down against convening a NATO Council meeting the next morning because it would signal U.S.

---

[286]In April 2001, retired Admiral Vitaly Agafonov revealed that Soviet submarines sent to the blockade line around Cuba each carried a nuclear-tipped torpedo. This chilling disclosure led Robert McNamara to conclude that the danger of nuclear war was far greater than anyone on the U.S. side had realized at the time: "they had torpedoes with nuclear warheads aimed at our ships—including the USS Joseph P. Kennedy." ("Cuban Missile Crisis: Soviet Subs Were Armed With Nukes," *Newsweek*, May 14, 2001, 6) Soviet nuclear torpedoes were capable of destroying an aircraft carrier. (Fursenko and Naftali, *"One Hell of a Gamble,"* 242)

abandonment of Khrushchev's October 26 offer. He recommended instead keeping the pressure on so "We don't look like we're weakening on the whole Turkey complex. I mean, I don't see that you're losing anything by not having the meeting tomorrow morning, except to perhaps—I admit you're *risking* something because some of the allies are gonna say *you're outa your mind* or..."

The President recapitulated impatiently: "You see, they [NATO] haven't had the alternatives presented to them. They'll say, 'Well, God! We don't want to trade 'em off!' They don't realize that in 2 or 3 days we may have a military strike which would bring perhaps the seizure of Berlin or a strike on Turkey. And then they'll say, 'By God! We should have taken it!' " JFK therefore decided that a NATO Council meeting was crucial for either Sunday or Monday morning.

The discussion continued to bog down over the same issues, uncertainties and doubts. If neither U Thant nor Khrushchev responded favorably to the President's new message by morning, McNamara queried, "Is it important to strike tomorrow? Or do we have some more time?" He concluded that if military action was necessary within 24 hours, "there ought to be a NATO meeting tomorrow morning." RFK, however, contemplated an even more convoluted scenario: if Khrushchev agreed to discontinue work on the bases and make the missiles inoperative, but also offered to "work out with you United Nations supervision. That could take three weeks to just work *that* problem out with them, couldn't it?" "Easily," McNamara muttered in agreement. In that event, the defense secretary recommended continuing air surveillance and the blockade until U.N. observers arrived in Cuba, "That's an *excellent* course of action, which I don't believe he's going to accept. The probability is, he *won't* say he'll stop work on the bases. And we're faced with a decision tomorrow of what to do." In that case, RFK added, the U.S. would be in much better shape in terms of world opinion.

Thompson once again recommended a tougher response—releasing all of Khrushchev's correspondence including Friday evening's private letter: "He broke *his* [Saturday] proposal [publicly] before you got it, and I'd do the same thing. Then you've got to fasten the world focus back on Cuba and Latin America and the fact that we're prepared not to invade [if the missiles are removed]. And this makes it, I think, much *tougher* for him to go ahead..." President Kennedy passed over Thompson's suggestion without comment and instead criticized the reports of "tough talk" from NATO ambassadors at the U.N. and at

NATO headquarters in Paris rejecting any connection between Cuba and Turkey. "They don't have a... they don't realize that... what's coming up." But Rusk, more in tune with Bundy and Thompson, persisted, "Mr. President, if NATO seems *solid* on this [rejecting the Cuba-Turkey linkage], this... this has a chance of shaking Khrushchev off this point."

Ball came up with still another strategy, putting the Kremlin in a bind by having U Thant release both Khrushchev's private Friday letter and the affirmative U.S. reply—without mentioning Turkey at all. The U.S. could say, Bundy added, "Why thank you, yes," and then Khrushchev "is in a difficult position." Taylor asked how much Ambassador Finletter would be allowed to tell the NATO allies about the military options being considered for dealing with Cuba. President Kennedy restated the position he had taken repeatedly: the public offer of a Cuba-Turkey deal had put the United States and NATO in a very tough position. "Well," the President surmised, "I think that he'd [Finletter] *probably* just say that the work's going on. 'If you're *not* going to take these... if they're *not* interested in this deal, then I think we're gonna have to do *something*.' I don't know if he has to say what it *is*, but the escalation's gonna go *on*. We think this is *very* likely that there'll be some reprisal against *possibly*, Turkey, and *possibly*, against Berlin. They [NATO] should be *aware* of that. What we *don't* want," JFK emphasized starkly, "is sort of a *cheap* turn-down by them without realizing that the turndown puts *us* in the position of then having to do something. What we're gonna be in the... faced with *is*, because we wouldn't take the missiles out of Turkey, we're gonna either have to *invade* or have a *massive* strike on Cuba which may *lose Berlin*! That's what concerns me!"

Rusk proposed another option with perhaps an outside chance of acceptance by both sides, that "the missiles in Cuba and the missiles in Turkey be turned over to the U.N. for destruction. And that the... the nuclear defense of NATO, including Turkey, is provided by other means—an actual disarmament step." But Thompson quickly dismissed the idea: "The Soviets don't want to let anybody get out there and see what their technology is." The President preferred more practical steps, "I think we'd a... the *real* problem is what we do with the Turks *first*."

McNamara swiftly returned to his earlier scheme for neutralizing the threat to Turkey and NATO: "Well, what I'd say... what I'd say to the Turks, 'Look here, we're gonna have to invade Cuba. You're in *mortal danger*. We want to *reduce* your danger while at the same time maintaining your defense. We propose that you defuse those missiles tonight. We're putting Polaris submarines along your coast. We'll cover the same targets that your Jupiter missiles did, and we'll announce this to the world before we invade Cuba and *thereby* reduce the pressure on the Soviet Union to attack you, *Turkey*, as a response to *our* invasion of Cuba.' Now this is what I would say to the Turks."

Forty-eight hours earlier, when the defense secretary had suggested that the missile sites might be vulnerable to air attacks because the Cubans had been instructed not to fire on U.S. planes, RFK had questioned whether the Soviets and Cubans were maneuvering to have the U.S. fire the first shots to justify launching their missiles; McNamara could only acknowledge, "Possibly, Bobby, I don't know." This time, RFK exposed a significant gap in McNamara's reasoning on neutralizing Turkey with Polaris missiles: "Now they [the Turks] say, 'And what if the Soviet Union attacks us anyway? Will you use the missiles on the nuclear submarines?'" The defense chief conceded that before attacking Cuba a decision had to be made on how to respond "to Soviet military pressure on NATO. And," he admitted candidly, "I'm not prepared to answer that question." The President pointed out yet again, "Aren't the Soviets gonna take their missiles out if we take 'em out of ah... Turkey? If they don't, they're in an *impossible* position." McNamara cautioned that details would have to be worked out with the Turks first, "then we announce it to the world" and tell Khrushchev that the U.S. accepts his earlier offer to withdraw the missiles for a non-invasion pledge. "Now the question," JFK added doubtfully, "is whether we can get the *Turks* to do it." "Well," McNamara reasoned, "*I* think it would be important to them."

Taylor, however, admonished the President, "You're *deeply* in trouble with NATO by [choosing] this bilateral kind of approach." Bundy, still hostile to a Turkish deal, suggested instead turning up the heat by expanding the blockade to include POL, and Rusk recommended "shaking Khrushchev off this position of this morning" by calling up additional military units, declaring a state of national emergency and initiating some mobilization both at home and in NATO. Bundy also brought up Sorensen's observation that Khrushchev's Friday night message, "is not *categorical* about taking the missiles out. It says the *specialists* would go out." "Yeah, that's right," McNamara remarked, "It's a very loose..." The President, as a counterpoint to these suggestions, pushed again for responding instead to Khrushchev's latest proposal for a missile trade, "Well this morning's [message] is more precise, isn't it? More precise."

Thompson, whose experience in the Soviet Union carried great weight in the ExComm, was clearly becoming more and more disturbed by the drift of the President's thinking, "Mr. President, if we go on the basis of a trade, which I gather is somewhat in your mind, we end up, it seems to me, with the Soviets *still* in Cuba with planes and technicians and so on. Even though the missiles are *out*, that would *surely* be unacceptable and put you in a worse position."

President Kennedy replied with practical and determined logic: "But our... our technicians and planes and guarantees would still exist for Turkey. I'm just thinking about what... what we're gonna have to do in a day or so, which is 500 sorties in 7 days and possibly an invasion, *all* because we wouldn't take missiles out of Turkey." Perhaps calling to mind his own wartime experience, JFK continued, "And I... I... we all know how quickly the... everybody's courage goes when the blood starts to flow and that's what's gonna happen in NATO. When they start these things and they grab Berlin, everybody's gonna say, 'Well, that was a pretty good proposition.' Let's not kid ourselves," he repeated for the third time, "that we've got a... That's the difficulty. *Today* it sounds great to reject it, but it's *not* going to after we *do* something!"

No one in the room could have doubts any longer about the President's attitude toward Khrushchev's public Cuba-Turkey offer. Nitze nonetheless argued "I think that there are alternatives," such as carrying out the 500 air sorties and planning for a Soviet attack somewhere other than in Turkey or making "the blockade total and *live* with the missiles [already in Cuba]." He also reminded JFK that the Soviets and the Cubans would not tolerate the reconnaissance flights indefinitely and planes would be shot down over Cuba. But, as in the case of the President's blockade decision days before, the ExComm advisers inevitably began to fall into line behind the commander-in-chief. JFK repeated his concern about NATO taking "a hard position" against the Turkish deal without understanding the risks to their own security, and Nitze even reported that he and Rusk had already talked to the British, French and West Germans about "how *serious* this was... [and] about the *alternatives* they face." President Kennedy wondered whether the NATO Council meeting should be called by Ambassador Finletter or NATO secretary general Dirk Stikker and Bundy replied, "Finletter can get the meeting called. His own advice is against having them in a group, but he may not be as shrewd as [General] Norstad about it."

The President also respected Norstad's judgment and selectively cited the general's views to back up his own position on a missile trade: "Norstad just feels that no matter *what* we do, it's going to be... We've gotta have NATO have a hand on this thing or otherwise we'll find no matter if we take *no* action or if we take *action*, they're all gonna be saying we should have done the reverse and we've gotta get them in on some of this." If the Turks are not receptive to the idea of replacing the Jupiters with Polaris missiles, he continued, "then we ought to go to the general NATO meeting because the NATO meeting may put enough pressure on them. I just tell you," he lectured, "I think we're better off to get those missiles out of Turkey and out of Cuba because I think the way of getting 'em *out* of Turkey and *out* of Cuba is gonna be *very*, *very* difficult and *very* bloody, one place or another."

Nitze and Dillon predicted that the Turks would never agree to remove the Jupiter missiles except under pressure from NATO. Bundy, however, finally seemed to be coming to terms with the President's determination, "Well I'm not sure of Turkey. Let's speculate with this, Mr. President. If you have that conviction and you are yourself *sure* that... that this is the way we want to... the *best way out*, then I would say that an immediate personal telegram of acceptance [of Khrushchev's Cuba-Turkey swap] was the best thing to do." JFK objected, however, on political grounds, "What I think we'd have to do is get *the Turks* to agree. . . . [rather than] accepting it over their opposition and over NATO opposition. . . . I'd rather go the total blockade route," he argued warily, "which is a *lesser* step than this military action. What I'd *like* to do is have the Turks and NATO *equally* feel that this is the *wiser* move."

Sorensen pressed the President to delay replying to Khrushchev's public missile trade offer for 24 or 48 hours and instead respond privately to his Friday evening letter: "There's always *a chance* that he'll accept *that*. . . . We meanwhile won't have broken up NATO over something that never would have come to NATO." In response, Rusk read Ambassador Stevenson's proposed draft of a letter from JFK to Khrushchev, stressing that *after* work on the bases had ceased and the missiles had been rendered inoperable, opening the way to their eventual removal and U.S. guarantees of Cuban independence, NATO defense issues could be open for negotiation.

After some additional discussion of the Stevenson draft, President

Kennedy, becoming clearly exasperated, snapped, "The point of the matter is Khrushchev's gonna come back and refer to his thing this morning on Turkey. And then we're gonna be screwing around for another 48 hours. I think what we've *got* to do is say that we've got to make the *key* of this letter the cessation of work. *That* we're all in agreement on! There's *no question* about that! Then the question of whether Turkey's in or just Cuba. Otherwise he'll come back and say, 'Well we're glad to settle the Cuban matter. What is your opinion of our proposal about Turkey?' So then we're on to Monday afternoon, and the work goes on, and we haven't had a chance to specifically get his good faith on the cessation of work. We haven't got an answer to *that* question. So I think that we ought to make *that* the key question—it's the cessation of work. Then if we get the cessation of work we can settle the Cuban question and do other things. Otherwise he can hang us up for *three days* while he goes on with the work." "For three weeks!" Dillon muttered irritably. Rusk, however, persisted that Stevenson and U Thant still hoped to work out an agreement at the U.N. without bringing Turkey into the discussion at all.

JFK continued to press for two objectives—halting work on the sites and making the missiles inoperable—as the key demands for the White House letter to Khrushchev. "Let's start with *our* letter . . . because otherwise we'll never get an answer. We're gonna take the *cease work* and try to get inoperable. . . . It's got to be finessed, . . . we have to finesse him." Nonetheless, President Kennedy had no illusions about the Soviet leader's response to U.S. requests to first settle Cuba, "which he *isn't* gonna give us. He's *now* moved on to the *Turkish* thing. So we're just gonna get a letter *back* saying, 'Well, he'd be glad to settle Turkey when we settle... settle Cuba when we settle Turkey.' So I think we *have to* make the *crucial* point in this letter, without opening up Turkey, is the question will he—at least in the next 24 hours while we discuss *all* these matters—will he agree with me to stop the work on the bases . . . because he either has to say yes or no to it. If he says no to *that*, then we're... at least we have some indication." "*Then*," JFK continued, after some additional tinkering with the wording of the message, only after "U.N. verification of this action [stopping the work], we would get into discussion of *all* these matters [including Turkey]." In the end, in response to continuing questions about implementing U.N. verification, guarding against the possibility that the missiles could be hidden under trees and assuring that the Cubans would not continue to fire on reconnaissance planes, JFK concluded realistically,

"Well, let's see what he comes *back with* here. I mean... I don't think he's gonna get enough for this. But I mean let's make it as *reasonable as possible*."

Rusk remained hopeful about utilizing Stevenson's draft letter to Khrushchev, "What Adlai says about what to do about Turkey and other problems is pretty good." The President reacted very strongly after reading quickly through the draft, "The only thing is, you see, what he's [Stevenson] saying is that they've gotta get the weapons out of Cuba before we'll discuss the general détente [including Turkey]. Now we're not gonna be able to *effect* that. He's [Khrushchev] not gonna agree to that." Rusk proposed some further revisions of the letter but the President declared emphatically: "It seems to me what we oughta... *be reasonable*. We're *not* gonna get these weapons out of Cuba, probably, anyway, but I mean, by negotiation. We're gonna have to take our weapons out of Turkey. I don't think there's any doubt he's not gonna... now that he made that public." JFK turned to Thompson, "Tommy, he's not gonna take 'em out of Cuba if we don't...," but the former ambassador dissented again:

"No, I... I don't agree, Mr. President," Thompson replied. "I think there's still a chance that this... we can get that line going."

"You think he'll back down?" JFK asked doubtfully.

"Well," Thompson reasoned, "he's already got this other proposal which he put forward [on Friday]."

"Yeah," the President observed skeptically, "now this other public one, it seems to me, has become their public position, isn't it?"[287]

"This is maybe just pressure on us," Thompson speculated. "The important thing for Khrushchev, it seems to me, is to be able to say, 'I saved Cuba. I stopped an invasion.' And he can get away with this if he wants to, and he's had a go at this Turkish thing, and that we'll discuss later."

After briefly discussing further amending the letter to Khrushchev to emphasize the importance of rapid progress toward cessation of work

[287]Khrushchev apparently made the Friday offer because of intelligence predicting an imminent American invasion of Cuba. He hoped to head off the invasion first and deal later with the Jupiters in Turkey. Only hours later he received reports that the invasion scare was erroneous and sent another message introducing a Turkish missile withdrawal, "pride and arrogance again took the upper hand over prudence: he could not look weak in the eyes of his subordinates." In the end, he retreated because of his conviction that JFK was "too weak" to prevent the hawks and the military from attacking Cuba. Vassily Kuznetsov later declared, "Khrushchev shit [in] his pants." (Zubok and Pleshakov, *Inside the Kremlin's Cold War*, 266–67)

and the inoperability of the missiles "under reasonable standards," JFK remarked, "I mean, I wanna just come back to that. Cause that's... Otherwise," he reflected, abruptly becoming very pensive, "time ticks away on us." "In other words, Mr. President," Sorensen summarized, "*your* position is that *once* he meets this condition of the... halting work and the inoperability, you're *then* prepared to go ahead on either the *specific* Cuban track or what we call a *general* détente track?" The President responded carefully, but nevertheless distanced himself from Thompson's opposition to linking Turkey and Cuba: "That *is* a substantive question because it really depends on whether we believe that we can get a deal on just the Cuban [issue] or whether we have to agree to his position of tying it [Turkey to Cuba]. Now Tommy doesn't think we do. I think that having made it public, how can he take these missiles out of Cuba if we just do nothing about Turkey?"

Bundy, backed by several others, suggested as an alternative, "You give him something else" and Ball urged offering a promise "that when all this is over there can be a larger... larger discussion." Thompson speculated again that Khrushchev might still accept the Friday missile removal/non-invasion deal since he could still say that the U.S. threat to Cuba had started the crisis and he had removed that threat.

"He must be a little shaken up," Robert Kennedy pointed out, "or he wouldn't have sent the [removal for non-invasion] message to you in the first place."

"That's *last night*," JFK snapped impatiently.

"Yeah," RFK added, "but it's *certainly* conceivable that you could get him *back* to that. I don't think that we should abandon it."

JFK finally agreed that there was no harm in trying. "Well, I think Adlai's letter is all right then [on dealing with Cuba first and Turkey later]." "All right," he finally conceded, "Let's send *this*." But, he cautioned that two key questions remained unresolved: the timing of a NATO Council meeting and "what are we gonna do about the Turks." JFK also left open the option of delaying a Sunday NATO meeting if there had been no reply from Khrushchev.

Bundy endorsed releasing Khrushchev's Friday letter and someone mentioned that Stevenson had also suggested releasing the President's letter to put pressure on the Soviets. "Well, the only thing is," RFK complained, "we're proposing in here the abandonment... you know that's gonna raise *some* points."

"What? What?" the President interjected testily, "What are we proposing?"

"The abandonment of Cuba [to the Communists]," RFK asserted.

"No," Ball objected, "we're just promising not to invade."

"Not to invade," Sorensen repeated, "You've changed that language."

"If we're gonna put that [letter] out," JFK suggested, "let's take *another* look at it." Sorensen remarked, "Add it...," sparking a burst of laughter around the table. RFK asked his brother, rather hesitantly, "think it'd be worthwhile talking to...?" "Who?" JFK replied, and RFK responded, "Eisenhower." JFK's reply, unfortunately inaudible, prompted yet another round of laughter.

President Kennedy respected Eisenhower's military expertise, but the principal reason for consulting his predecessor, as discussed earlier, was political—to prevent or blunt criticism of the administration's handling of the crisis by the highly respected former general and president. JFK had certainly not forgotten that reports of an Eisenhower speech, flailing the President for allowing the construction of the Berlin Wall and "threatening foreign bases," had appeared in the press on the very morning of the first ExComm meeting.[288] Eisenhower's public support significantly diminished the likelihood of strident Republican attacks on the President—at least for the moment. Although the ExComm meetings were not, in fact, dominated by political considerations, it would be naïve to assume that the President was not concerned about the impact of the crisis on the upcoming Congressional elections and his own reelection campaign in 1964.

JFK seemed very doubtful about the political wisdom of suggestions to release his new letter to Khrushchev. Bundy argued that making the letter public "puts some heat on" Khrushchev to put out his Friday letter and Alexis Johnson reported that Stevenson had also suggested releasing the letter "in order to get this back on the Cuba track, and away from... and the focus away from *his* letter of this morning about Turkey." President Kennedy, in response, revealed significant political anxiety about publicly disclosing a U.S. guarantee of Cuban independence: "No, we don't wanna put it out until we *know* whether there's any chance of acceptance. There's gonna be *a hell of a fight* about that part [the public commitment not to invade Cuba]. I don't mind takin' it on if we're gonna get somewhere. I don't wanna take on the fight if we're not even gonna get it."

Responding almost cheerfully to a request for another reading of the

[288]*New York Times*, October 16, 1962.

draft presidential letter to Khrushchev, JFK exclaimed, "Oh, here we go." "Will everyone listen?" Rusk pronounced as he began to read, "'I have read your letter of October 26 with great care and find in it the indication of a willingness on your part to seek a calm solution to the problem.'" President Kennedy proposed substituting "'your statement of your desire,' because," he observed coldly, "we don't really find a 'willingness.'" "What's the rest of that?" RFK remarked acerbically, "I thought that was almost too nice." "Well, we changed it a little," JFK acknowledged. Rusk resumed reading, "'I note and welcome indications in your second [Saturday] letter, which you've made public, that you would like to work toward a more general arrangement as regards *other armaments*.'" The President objected again: "Now wait a sec... now that second letter is the one on Turkey. 'I note and welcome.' 'I note your *second* letter,' I don't think we ought to '*welcome*' it," he added rather irritably. JFK also agreed to Rusk's suggestion to delete a direct reference to Turkey, "Why don't we make *that* more general?. . . Why don't we just say 'other countries'? Let's leave Turkey out." McCone pointed out that Khrushchev was talking specifically about Turkey and JFK replied, "We have to ah... keep it vague, unfortunately or fortunately, because we haven't cleared it with Turkey or NATO. So I suppose we have to *fudge it* somewhat. But I agree with you; he's just talkin' about Turkey."

After Rusk read the revised message yet again, however, RFK renewed his push for trying a positive response to Khrushchev's secret Friday evening proposal, "Send this letter and say you're accepting *his* offer. He's *made* an offer and you're *in fact* accepting it. And you state... I think that letter [Stevenson's draft] sounds slightly defensive about the fact—'God, don't bring in Turkey now. We want to settle [Cuba first].'. . . He made an offer last night. This letter [the JFK/ExComm draft] *accepts* that offer."

"Well, in any case," JFK observed, "the two letters are a... more or less... there's no policy difference, is there?"[289]

"Well *I* think that this [likely Stevenson's draft] has an *entirely* different quality," RFK grumbled.

"*Oh God*, let...," the exasperated President exclaimed irritably, before suggesting reconciling the language in the two letters by substitut-

---

[289]Scholars, as well as general readers, may find the references to these two draft letters somewhat confusing. Even McGeorge Bundy, after listening to this tape, told the author that he was sometimes uncertain which letter was being discussed.

ing "'would undertake to give assurances regarding peace in the Caribbean'" for "'to give assurances with respect to [Cuba's] territorial integrity and political independence.'"

"No," Sorensen objected, "I thought we'd said we'd follow 'not to invade Cuba' though, that's the language he asked for in that letter."

"That's correct," JFK admitted. "But I don't think if we're gonna make this public *at this point*, 'til we know what we're gonna get, we don't wanna get into that [political] fight."

"You gotta give him *something*," Bundy insisted.

"What?" the President replied brusquely.

"You've gotta give him *something*," Bundy repeated, "to get him back on this [Friday] track."

"On *this* track, yeah," Rusk muttered in the background.

JFK contended that Stevenson "likes his draft so much better. He's gonna have to conduct it [the U.N. discussions]. I don't think that there's a substantive difference about it [the two drafts], do you?"

"Well I think there is!" RFK griped yet again.

"Why?" JFK asked.

RFK pointed once more to the "*rather* defensive" language in the Stevenson version which seemed to say, "please don't get into ah... ah... the discussions of NATO or Turkey because we wanna talk about... about Cuba." The President's letter to Khrushchev, he claimed, is more direct, stating "'*You* made an offer to us [on Friday evening] and we *accept* it. And you've also made a *second* offer, which has to do with NATO, and we'll be glad to discuss that at a later time.' The other... first letter, of Adlai, I don't think says anything . . . except we don't like what you said." A consensus had gradually begun to form around the notion of responding favorably to Khrushchev's Friday offer and deferring or ignoring his latest proposal involving Turkey. Sorensen suggested using parts of Stevenson's letter to amend the last part of the President's letter along the lines proposed by RFK.

The Turkish proposal, the attorney general persisted, "has really thrown us off" and "I think we just say, 'He made an offer. We accept the offer, and it's silly bringing up NATO at this time.'" "What is the reason Adlai's unhappy about our first letter?" JFK inquired; he was told that the U.N. ambassador thought the letter "sounds too much like an ultimatum—that it's making demands." RFK finally tried to break the logjam over the wording of the two messages, "Why do we bother you with it, Mr. President?" the attorney general told his increasingly impatient brother. "Why don't you let us work it out?"

"I think we oughta move. I don't... there's no question of bothering me," JFK replied. "I just think somebody... we're gonna have to decide which letter we send."

"Why don't we try to work it out for you without you being able to pick these all open," RFK quipped, and a wave of laughter rolled across the room.[290]

"Yeah, but then you have to worry about ol' Adlai," JFK came back quickly, "so you might as well work it out with him." The room rocked with laughter again.

"Actually, I think Bobby's formula is a good one," Sorensen observed, "we say, 'we are accepting your offer of your letter last night and therefore there's *no need* to talk about these other things.'" The President, after Rusk again read aloud the revised message to Khrushchev, seemed willing to go along with this scheme on the slim chance that Khrushchev would at least agree to a cessation of work, but he clearly remained unconvinced and unenthusiastic, "As I say, they're not gonna... he's not gonna [accept] now [after his public offer on Turkey]. Tommy [Thompson] isn't so sure. But anyway, we can *try* this thing, but he's gonna come back on Turkey.[291] But the only thing is, I don't want him... That's why we've gotta emph... *end* with saying, *whatever* we're gonna do, that we've got to get a cessation of the work." Bundy jumped on the bandwagon as well, "That's right, Mr. President. I think that Bobby's notion of a *concrete* acceptance on our part of how we read last night's telegram is *very* important."

General Taylor, however, injected a significant dissent, reporting that the JCS had met that afternoon and recommended that "the big [bombing] strike, that is, Oplan 312," should begin no later than *Monday* morning, the 29th, "unless there is irrefutable evidence in the meantime that offensive weapons are being dismantled and rendered inoperable"—followed by "the invasion plan [Oplan 316] seven days

[290]The listener is inevitably struck by the special empathy between the Kennedy brothers. It is difficult to imagine any other ExComm member making this remark. The President had been clearly irritated several times during the meeting by RFK's resistance to the Turkish deal and objections to the Stevenson letter; but, despite his impatience, JFK instinctively turned to his younger brother for the critical evening mission to Ambassador Dobrynin.

[291]JFK's willingness to try this scheme—accepting Khrushchev's Friday offer and evading his public Saturday message—has been celebrated in the missile crisis literature as the "Trollope Ploy," a reference to a plot device by nineteenth-century British novelist Anthony Trollope in which a woman decides to interpret a man's casual romantic interest as an impending offer of marriage. For a detailed discussion of this decision, see the Conclusion.

later." "Well," RFK teased, "*I'm surprised!*" and laughter again briefly punctured the unrelenting pressure in the Cabinet Room.[292]

As the laughter subsided, Taylor emphasized, "I think the Monday morning invasion, however, is something to think about. It does... it *does* look now from a military point of view..." The President interrupted, "What are the reasons why?" The general replied, "They [the JCS] just feel that the longer we wait now..."[293] "I know, OK. But there's no...? Right. OK," JFK responded perfunctorily, but Dillon observed impatiently, "Well, also we're getting *shot at* as we go in for our surveillance."

The President abruptly broke off the discussion of an invasion and arranged to have the revised letter cleared with Stevenson: "Bobby, you want to go out now and get this letter set with Adlai." He then immediately returned to the issue he had been accentuating throughout the meeting—"Now the next question is the Turkish one and NATO. We've got Secretary McNamara's proposal [to defuse the Jupiters in Turkey and replace them with Polaris missiles] and... Did we ever send that message to [Ambassador] Hare [in Turkey]?" "No," Bundy replied, reporting that a long message from Hare had arrived: "he'll do his *damnedest*, but it's *very* difficult" to convince the Turks to give up the Jupiters.

In the wake of Taylor's report on the most recent JCS demand for bombing and invading Cuba, JFK seemed even more determined to facilitate the removal of the Jupiter missiles from Turkey as quickly as possible. He made clear once again that the decision, in his mind, was not *whether* but *how* to implement a deal on Turkey: "Well, now we have the question of a choice between the *bilateral* arrangements with Turkey, in which we more or less *do* it [defuse the Jupiters and substitute Polaris missiles as recommended by McNamara] *or* whether we go through NATO and let NATO put the pressure on and also explain to the Turks what's gonna happen to them."

Dillon, supported by Bundy, worried that all the missiles in Turkey could never be disarmed in time for carrying out air strikes by Monday morning (October 29), but McNamara suggested that the time could be shortened if the President sent a message to the Turkish prime minister

[292]Oplan (Operations Plan) 312 and 316 had been approved weeks before the discovery of the missiles (see Hershberg, "Before 'The Missiles of October,'" 185–86); RFK actually had great respect for the JCS chairman and even named one of his sons Matthew Maxwell Taylor Kennedy, in January 1965.

[293]The JCS had made the same argument at the October 19 meeting with the President.

stating, "'This is the *problem* and this is the way I think it ought to be *solved*, and I'm prepared to do it *tonight*. And I *need* an answer from you within 6 hours or 8 hours or something like that.' That's... that's one way to do this." The defense secretary also recounted that he had spoken recently to [Giulio] Andreotti about the Jupiters in Italy. The President asked openly, "Who's Andreotti?" McNamara and Bundy simultaneously identified Andreotti as the defense minister of Italy, and McNamara reported his counterpart's belief that, "the Italians would be *happy* to get rid of them if we want them out of there." Bundy observed that the difference in attitude on the Jupiters reflected in reports from the American ambassadors in Italy and Turkey "is between night and day" and McNamara predicted that "we can get Italy to go along with us, *I* think . . . and this will put some additional pressure on Turkey."

Despite recognizing the potential political perils from a bilateral deal with Turkey, President Kennedy appeared ready, nonetheless, to move ahead, either bilaterally or through NATO. "Not having had it *explained* to NATO what's gonna be the effects of *continuing* the [deployment of the Jupiter] missiles, it's going to look like ah... we're ah... caving in," he admitted. But, "To get it *done*, probably you have to do it bilaterally, to take all the political effects of the cave-in of NATO. Or do we want to have a meeting in the morning of NATO and say, 'If we *don't* do it, here's the *problem*.'" McNamara recommended taking both steps simultaneously, but Bundy countered that "the disadvantage of having a NATO meeting and going to the Turks tonight and tomorrow is that you don't give this [Friday] track a fair run, that you just tried out on [Khrushchev]." The President did not respond directly—he obviously had no real confidence in the ultimate effectiveness of that supposedly brilliant diplomatic slight of hand.

McNamara, however, reminded his colleagues that crucial military decisions also had to be made "while these discussions go on on the deal of last night. We have *intense* ground fire against our... our..." [low-level reconnaissance flights]. A decision would have to be made by tomorrow morning to either discontinue the missions or send them in with adequate protection. Taylor, strikingly, tried to downplay the Cuban ground fire. "I wouldn't say that. I wouldn't say 'intense' here." McNamara mentioned that he had asked Gilpatric "to talk to Curt LeMay" and the JCS chairman objected, "No, I would not. Flak came up in front of the flight and they... and they veered... they veered away." "What about the *hit*?" Bundy exclaimed, but Taylor replied,

"That has not been confirmed." McNamara, nonetheless, pressed on, insisting that the planes had been fired on and a decision would have to be made by tomorrow morning. "I think we have basically two alternatives. Either we decide not to send them in *at all* or we decide to send them in with *proper* cover. If we send them in with proper cover and they're attacked, we must attack back, either the SAMs and/or MiG aircraft that come against them or the ground fire that comes up."

"We have *another* problem tomorrow," the defense chief divulged: the *Grozny* was entering the quarantine zone despite Khrushchev's claim that he had ordered his ships to avoid the blockade sector—which had been specifically and publicly identified at the U.N. "If a Russian ship moves into the zone after he said that publicly, we have *two* choices: stop it and board it or don't."

"*Stop it,*" Bundy murmured firmly.

"Now when you... when you put the *two* of these together," McNamara reasoned, "the question of... of *stopping* surveillance and *not* stopping the ship, it seems to me we're *too weak.*"

"Yeah," Bundy and a colleague, probably McCone, affirmed.

"I'd say we *must* continue *surveillance,*" Taylor demanded. "That's *far* more important than the ships."

"Well, what... my main point is," McNamara continued, "I *don't* think at this particular point we should... should show a... a *weakness* to Khrushchev. And I think we would show a weakness if we... if we failed on *both* of these actions."

"And we mustn't fail on surveillance," Taylor insisted again. "We *can't* give up 24 hours at *this* stage."

"I... I fully agree, Max," McNamara emphasized. "I was just trying to lay out the problem. Therefore, I would recommend that tomorrow we carry on surveillance but that we defer the decision as late as possible in the day to give a little more time. Because if we... if we go in with surveillance, we *have* to put a cover on, and if we start shooting back, we've *escalated substantially.*" "The cover isn't much good," the President replied doubtfully, "because you've got antiaircraft guns. You've got somebody up there at 10,000 feet and actually they can't give much more cover. What you'd really, it seems to me, *have* is a justification for more *elaborate* [military] action, wouldn't you? And do... do we want to worry about whether we're gonna shoot up that one gun [firing at a U.S. plane], or do we wanna just use this as a reason for doing a lot of other...?" "Shooting up the SAMs," McNamara interjected, completing JFK's thought.

Taylor argued that the crucial issue was "to assure effective reconnaissance—whatever that ah… implies." In the interim, however, the President recommended caution, "I would think we ought to just take a chance on reconnaissance tomorrow without the cover, because I don't think the cover's really gonna do you much good. You can't protect… well hide it from ground fire." However, if there was no answer from U Thant, he added, air attacks might be necessary by Monday morning, but "I'm *not* convinced yet of the invasion, because I think that's a much…" Taylor cut in to back the commander-in-chief, "I… I *agree* with that. My *personal* view is that we be made more ready to go on Monday [with bombing] but then also *ready* to invade, but make no advance decisions."

"Whadda ya think?" the President asked McNamara, reiterating "I don't think your cover's gonna do much good." The defense chief responded, "I *don't* think we should stop the surveillance tomorrow. That's… that's point number one. Point number two is that if we *do* carry on a surveillance tomorrow and they *fire* on us…" "Now that's a signal then," JFK concluded grimly, "Then we know…" In that event, McNamara proposed, "we're either going to *return* that fire, *tomorrow*, in a limited fashion against the things that fired against us or against their air defenses. *Or*, alternatively, if we *don't* return the fire tomorrow, we ought to go in the next day with the recommended [full air strike] sorties. One or the other!" "That's right," the President affirmed, "I'm more inclined to take the more general response and a… However, why don't we wait. Let's be *prepared* for either one tomorrow. Let's wait and see if they fire on us tomorrow, in the meanwhile we've got this message to U Thant…" Dillon pointed out that if the planes were attacked, "then we *do* need to have the general response. There's no time to do what you're talking about with Turkey unless we do that." "*Do* the reconnaissance tomorrow," the President instructed, without worrying too much about the air cover. "If we get fired on then we'd meet here and we'd decide whether we do a *much more general* [bombing strike]. I *announce* that we've been fired on, *announce* that work is going ahead, *announce* that we haven't gotten an answer from the Soviets. Then we decide whether we're gonna do a much more general one, than just shooting up some gun down on the ground."

At that moment, on the knife's edge of a critical military decision, President Kennedy was clearly leaning toward ordering comprehensive air strikes if low-level reconnaissance planes came under attack again over Cuba. But ironically, Dillon, a persistent doubter on the Turkey initiative, redirected the discussion to the President's ace in the hole, "Yes, but what about moving ahead with this Turkish...?" "Well that's what I want to come to now," JFK readily affirmed. "Now let's get on to the Turkish thing."

Nitze advised that it would be very difficult to get instructions to a NATO Council meeting in Paris by early on Sunday morning, but the President countered, "We can get them to Finletter in six, seven or eight hours, nine hours." Thompson, evidently recognizing the President's determination on the Turkish deal, endorsed alerting the Turkish and Italian prime ministers that if surveillance planes were fired on again the U.S. could be compelled to use force in Cuba which in turn could result in Soviet attacks on the Jupiter missiles, "We are *therefore* considering whether or not it would be in *your* interest for us to *remove* these . . . and we *may* be having to take this up in NATO." "We oughta send that to the Turks," JFK vigorously agreed, "cause it's *their* neck. And, of course, they're liable to say, 'Well, we can *take it*.' So we've gotta have it look to the *general* interest as well as theirs, and a more *effective* defense for you. Now they're not gonna want to *do* it," the President reasserted, "but we may just decide we *have* to do it in *our* interest." Of course, JFK acknowledged, it would be far better politically to have NATO endorse taking the Jupiters out:

"I don't think we would *get* that, Mr. President," Bundy predicted. "I don't think we should expect..."

"Once you start explaining it to 'em," JFK inquired skeptically, "what's gonna happen?"

"I doubt," Bundy persisted, "if the [NATO] Council will recommend that we stand down Turkish missiles."

"Even with an offer of a Polaris?" Ball declared.

"Who would oppose it other than the Turks?" Thompson wondered.

"Those missiles kind of make us a hostage," McCone observed.

Rusk explained that the Turks had already rejected [in 1961] substituting Polaris for the Jupiters; "the Turkish reaction was, 'Well, the missiles are *here* and as long as they're here, you're here.'"

JFK acknowledged, "Most of the NATO members aren't going to be very happy about it because it's inevitable, I think it's *Berlin* that's gonna be..."

"Here's one way to put it," McNamara proposed: the British have accepted the need to replace the obsolescent Thor missile and the Turks and Italians have to understand that the Jupiter is even more obsolete.

But JFK was far less sanguine, "they'll say that this is because the United [States wants] . . . to make a trade, if we did it. I don't see how we can put it to 'em without the trade. What we *want*, obviously, is the *Turks* to suggest it, but they're pretty *tough* and they probably figure that ah... that their security is better with them in than it is with them out."

Several participants seconded the President's assessment of the Turkish position, but McNamara suddenly seemed irritated by this hard-line Turkish position, "Well, I... I don't see *that*." Someone muttered, "We have about 17,000 people there," and McNamara exclaimed, "We have our air squadrons there with nuclear weapons!" "We want... in other words, Bob," President Kennedy asked, "do we want to send a message to our ambassadors to begin this *track*, who would then just send a message to the NATO to begin to explain to them what the facts of life are today? They don't know what's coming up. It's not gonna be so *happy*." The President also made an astute political calculation: "if the Turks say no to us," he reasoned, it would be much better if all of NATO said no as well, since "what *always* happens, a few days later when the trouble comes," is that they then say "that we should have asked them and they would have told us to get 'em out." Kennedy wanted, in short, to deny the NATO allies the chance to claim, with 20/20 hindsight, that they would have advised a course of action which he believed they would have actually rejected. RFK recommended delaying the NATO Council meeting until Monday, "By then we'd know what we would want to do. I don't think we *really* know exactly what we want to do." "Well we oughta... just it seems to me," JFK replied, "begin a negotiation with the Turks now, shouldn't we?" "I think," RFK counseled "somebody perhaps should go over."

"Now I think it's *very* difficult to negotiate with the Turks" (JFK interposed, "Alone?"), Bundy objected yet again, "as long as we think there's anything in last night's track. Now I think that's what's dividing us at the moment." Bundy explained again that Ambassador Hare had not talked directly to the Turks and Ball declared, "He had specific instructions *not* to talk to the Turks." "Are the Turks *more* likely to take them out," the President persisted, "if we have a bilateral or a NATO decision?" "I think NATO," Rusk replied. "NATO," Dillon agreed, "as part of an overall decision." "That's the way they were put in, weren't they," McCone confirmed, "It was through NATO." "What is the *rush* about this?" RFK asked impatiently—except for deciding on the timing of an air strike?

The protracted, repetitive and often vigorous debate over diplomatic options for dealing with the Turkish Jupiters abruptly became almost academic and perhaps even irrelevant. In an instant, the earlier alarm bells about a U-2 allegedly straying into Soviet air space or ground fire on a reconnaissance flight over Cuba seemed comparatively trivial. Some two hours into the meeting, at about 6:00 P.M., a message arrived that propelled the missile crisis to a new threshold of extreme danger. President Kennedy's reaction can be heard first in the background, "Yeah... the U-2," just as McNamara made the startling announcement: "The U-2 was shot down."

"The U-2 shot down?" JFK asked almost incredulously.

"Yes," McNamara confirmed, "it was found shot down."

"Was the pilot killed?" RFK asked.

"This was shot down over Banes, which is right near a U-2 site," the distressed Taylor announced mistakenly, "in eastern Cuba."

McNamara and Bundy instantly corrected him, "A SAM site."

"The pilot's body is in the plane," Taylor continued. "Apparently this was the... the SAM site that had actually had the active [missile guiding] Fruitcake... Fruitcake radar. So it all ties in in a very plausible manner."[294]

"Well now, this *is*," President Kennedy observed unemotionally, "much of an escalation by *them*, isn't it?"

"Yes, exactly!" McNamara acknowledged.

The defense chief, almost certainly thinking of the potential risks from an immediate military response, recommended prudence—air attacks on Cuba could still be deferred for 4–5 days, he explained, "but *only* if we continue our surveillance and... and fire against anything that fires against a surveillance aircraft, and *only* if we maintain a tight blockade in this interim period." That way, he reasoned, there would still be "time to go to NATO" for a possible agreement on the missiles in Turkey. The President, in light of Khrushchev's Friday message and reports of earlier instructions to forces in Cuba to fire only if attacked,[295] groped for an ex-

[294]Air Force Major Rudolf Anderson was the only known fatality of the Cuban missile crisis.

[295]"Khrushchev had apparently never given explicit orders not to open fire" on U.S. aircraft. (Chang, "The View from Washington and Nowhere," 145)

planation for the apparent "change in orders" that led to the use of flak and the firing of a SAM missile, "How do we...?" "How do we interpret this?" McNamara bleakly finished JFK's thought, "I don't know how to interpret it." RFK made an indistinct reference to John Scali, but Taylor explained, "They feel they must *respond* now 'cause the whole world knows where we're flying."

The initial shock in the room soon gave way to a rising sense of anger:

"I raise the question of retaliation against this SAM site," Taylor declared, adding that the specific site which downed the U-2 could probably be identified.

"How can we send a U-2 fellow over there tomorrow," the President acknowledged, "unless we take out *all* the SAM sites?"

"This is *exactly* correct," McNamara declared. "I don't think we can."

"Can they see the pilot?" JFK questioned

"Yes, sir," Taylor confirmed.

"And it's on the ground?" Rusk asked.

"The wreckage's on the ground," Taylor added, "and the pilot's dead."

"It's in the water, isn't it?" McNamara asked.

"I didn't get the water part of it," Taylor replied grimly.

"I wonder if *this* shouldn't cause a more stark, *violent* protest," McCone contended firmly, "right directly following up your letter right to Khrushchev. Here's an... here's an action they've taken against... against us, a new order in defiance of... of... of public statements he made."

"*They've* fired the first shot," Nitze pointed out stridently.

"If there's any continuation of this," McCone demanded, "we got to take those SAM sites *out of there.*"

"We should retaliate *against* the SAM site," Taylor demanded, "and announce that if any of 'em have any other planes fired on we will come back and attack it." He also reminded the President that a military response to shooting down a U-2 with a SAM had been agreed to days ago.

"You can go against one [SAM], can you?" Bundy probed. "Now? Tonight?"

"No. It's too late [in the day]," McNamara explained, wondering aloud whether "given the [new] situation," air attacks should be deferred until Wednesday or Thursday.

Taylor insisted that reconnaissance "will be very dangerous, I would say, Mr. Secretary, unless we can recon... reconnoiter... reconnoiter each day."

McNamara agreed emphatically, "And if we're gonna reconnais... carry out surveillance *each day*, we must be prepared to *fire each day*."

"That's correct," Taylor affirmed.

"We can't very well send a U-2 over there," President Kennedy reiterated, "can we *now*, and have a guy killed again *tomorrow*?"

"We certainly wouldn't... shouldn't do it," Taylor urged, "until we *retaliate* and say that if they fire again on one of our planes that we will come back with great force."

"I think you've just *gotta* take out that SAM site," Nitze asserted, "or you can't maintain surveillance."

President Kennedy and the ExComm seemed more unsettled and uncertain than they had been since the initial discovery of the missiles. JFK observed that even if the specific SAM site responsible for shooting down the U-2 were destroyed, subsequent reconnaissance planes would still be vulnerable to attack from the other sites. McNamara declared that after the first site was destroyed, more SAMs and the MiG aircraft could be taken out tomorrow if there were additional SAM launches. "Will we want to announce tonight that this U-2 was shot down?" JFK queried. "I think we should," McNamara recommended. Gilpatric reminded the President that the Defense Department had already issued a statement about planned counteraction. "Do we want to announce we're gonna take counteraction," JFK continued, "or just take it tomorrow morning?" "Just take it," Gilpatric advised and Ball urged announcing the reprisals *after* they had been carried out. "I understand Havana's announced it," Taylor maintained, "that's where we..." The President was quick to see a political advantage, "Well, I think we ought to announce it because it throws off Khrushchev's protestations about this."

Several participants seemed troubled about announcing that the U-2 had been shot down and the pilot killed based solely on a report from Havana—obviously concerned that the claim might be propaganda. "We haven't confirmed that, have we?" the President acknowledged, almost stifling a sardonic laugh. "There are so goddamn many [rumors and reports]... We could stay here all day with these... ("problems," someone else, probably Sorensen, finished his sentence). Well now, let's say *if* the... *if* we're sure the U-2's been shot down, it seems to me we've gotta announce it or it's gonna dribble out. Havana's announced it anyway. We ought to announce it." Bundy cautioned, "We don't know that yet, Mr. President" "Then we oughta *not* say anything," JFK replied, "don't you think, and just take the reprisal without making any announcement? We don't wanna announce we're gonna take a reprisal against *that* SAM site tomorrow, or would that make our reprisal more difficult?" McNamara claimed that an announcement certainly would make retaliation more risky.

"I think that we oughta... that we oughta announce," the President finally instructed, "that a... that a... and that action's being taken—action will be taken to protect our a... our aircraft." "*Exactly*," McNamara agreed, "Then we oughta go in at dawn and take out that SAM site. And we oughta send a surveillance aircraft in tomorrow in the regular flights early in the morning, and we oughta be prepared to take out more SAM sites and knock out the... aircraft." "Well, what we wanna do then," the President summarized, "is get this announcement written. Ros [Gilpatric], why don't you write this out, plus this thing about what we're gonna do." But, JFK then added a striking coda, "Then we'll go back to what we're gonna do about the Turks and NATO." Obviously, the President had not given up on the Turkish missile trade as the most promising way out of this rapidly escalating predicament.[296]

McNamara again urged revealing that a U-2 had already been shot down in order to explain publicly why surveillance planes would henceforth be protected by fighter aircraft—an action the President had explicitly discouraged earlier in the meeting. RFK also suggested adding POL to the quarantine, but McNamara advised waiting until after the air strike against the SAM site. Taylor confirmed that the plane was actually on the ground and not in the water, and Bundy urged, "let's put it out then because otherwise *they* will put it out." The President, however, appeared hesitant about making a public announcement about the U-2 without confirmation, "Except we don't know. It's overdue anyway, isn't it? So we can assume it." "It's hours overdue now," Taylor confirmed. "Do we want to say it was shot down?" the President asked. "We don't know whether it... Did they say it should be shot down—the Cubans?" President Kennedy finally instructed Gilpatric and Taylor to prepare an announcement to cover all contingencies,

[296]In fact, JFK had already instructed Gilpatric to draft a plan for withdrawing the Jupiters from Turkey and Italy if Khrushchev agreed to stop work on the missile sites in Cuba. (Gilpatric Oral History, 52)

"It may be... we don't know if it was shot down." McCone conceded, "We don't *know* it."

A prompt public statement should be made about the U-2, Mc-Namara asserted, "because the probabilities are that it *was* shot down and we want an *excuse* to go in tomorrow and shoot up that SAM site and send in our..." Dillon observed, somewhat sarcastically, "If the... if the plane's on the ground there, it *was* shot down. I mean... it didn't just come down and land," but McNamara countered "it might have had a mechanical failure, possibly." "The only thing that troubles us," JFK pointed out, "is the *other* plane was shot at [with ack-ack]." "That's right, exactly," McNamara affirmed.

"That's why I'd like to find out," President Kennedy remarked, "whether Havana says they *did* shoot it down." Bundy reasserted his belief that no confirmation had yet been received from Havana. Gilpatric, however, put his finger on a critical question: "We *assume* these SAM sites are manned by Soviets. That's the significant part of it *if* the SAM fired." McNamara conceded, "This is a *change* of pattern. Now *why* it's a change of pattern, I don't know." "I think the important thing to find out," Gilpatric stressed, "is, if we *possibly* can, whether this is a SAM site." "There's *no way* to find out," McNamara conceded. "What we know *is* that *that particular* SAM is the one that had the Fruitset [*sic*] radar, which is required for control of the... of the missiles, and it was in operation, we believe, at the *same time* that the U-2 was over. We checked it this morning."[297] "This is a *very different* thing," Gilpatric cautioned. "You could have an undisciplined antiaircraft... Cuban antiaircraft outfit fire [at low-level surveillance planes]. But to have a *SAM* site, with a *Russian* crew, fire is *not*... not any accident."

After some further speculation on the cause of the U-2 crash and the fate of the pilot, the President left the Cabinet Room and the meeting temporarily recessed. Multiple voices can be partially heard in several informal conversations as the table was cleared and the room cleaned up. In addition, with the door open, Evelyn Lincoln's voice can be picked up in the background. Some of the informal chatter dealt with interpreting the motives behind Khrushchev's conflicting messages and deciphering coded communications. JFK returned after about 10 minutes and the meeting resumed.

[297]McNamara inadvertently said "Fruitset" radar instead of "Fruitcake" radar.

The President reported yet another troubling development—Castro had just announced that any plane violating Cuban air space would be fired on. He nonetheless puckishly invited Ball, "George, come up and sit here now, you're another civilian," and chuckled as Taylor quipped, "Come on into General Taylor's lap." But JFK promptly returned to the serious business at hand: "Let's talk a little more about the Turks, how we're gonna handle that. NATO and the Turks, that's the *one* matter we haven't settled today." Dillon volunteered that Castro's statement and the downed U-2 would make it very difficult to wait 4–5 days before attacking the missiles sites. But JFK, nervously tapping on the table, insisted on calling the NATO Council meeting and sending instructions to Ambassador Hare about promptly beginning a conversation with the Turks. "We need to explain to them what's happening over here. Otherwise, we're gonna be carrying *a hell of a bag.*"

Dillon warned that domestic American political pressure for reprisals would intensify in the wake of the U-2 loss, but the President decided to proceed quickly on removing the missiles from Turkey rather than speed up the bombing of Cuba: "Therefore, we gotta move. That's why I think we gotta have a NATO meeting *tomorrow.* . . . I'm just *afraid* of what's gonna happen in NATO... to Europe when we get into this thing more and more, and I think they oughta feel that they were part of it. Even if we don't do anything about the Turks, they ought to feel that they know what the... What do you think?"

McNamara and Ball recommended that the U.S. prepare a clear message for both the NATO Council meeting and for U.S. ambassadors in the capitals of the relevant governments because the permanent representatives to NATO lacked instructions and would be reluctant to initiate anything. The President asked if a night reconnaissance mission had been scheduled for that night. McNamara replied "No, we're not," and JFK observed, with a touch of irony, "Of course, it would be relatively easy if we wanted to get NATO to *reject* this" deal on the Turkish missiles, "But I think that isn't necessarily what we *want* right now, is it?" The defense secretary speculated that once the American position was firmly decided, "I think we can *force* 'em [NATO] and I think we can *do* it in such a way that the aftereffects will not... not be too severe. But I think we've *got* to decide ahead of time what it is we want to do, and what I would suggest we decide is, we want those missiles taken out of Turkey. And we simply say that we believe this is, as *I do* believe, in the interests of the alliance, and that we will replace those missiles with other fire."

"But they... they're gonna say is," the President predicted realistically, "that we're definitely seeking a trade with the Russians, aren't they? But what do I... that's alright isn't it?"

"But I... I would say," McNamara suggested, "'We... we may have to attack Cuba. If we *attack* Cuba, they're holding Turkey as a hostage and they're likely to... to *attack* Turkey.'"

"'To free our hands in Cuba,'" Bundy proposed, apparently coming to terms with the President's determination to seek a deal involving Turkey, "'we *must* get these missiles out of Turkey,' is what we say."

"Yeah," McNamara agreed, "without... without endangering *you*, the alliance. This... this is the *theme* we're gonna put it on."

Ball added that the NATO allies must understand that the missiles in Cuba are a threat "to the retaliatory power of the United States, which is the *central* defense of the whole free world, including *yourselves*."

"I would put out this," the defense secretary stressed, 'We're *not* trading *Turkish* missiles for *Cuban* missiles.'"

"No, no," Bundy affirmed.

"*Not a bit*," McNamara exclaimed. "We're *relieving* the alliance of a *threat* that is presently upon them."[298]

The President again predicted that the NATO meeting delegates would say, "'Well now, do you have a deal with the Russians if we take 'em out of Turkey?'" Bundy underscored, "It will be *seen* as a trade by a great many people, Mr. President. There's *no doubt* about that. We've looked that one in the eye. If we don't buy that, then it seems to me, Bob [McNamara] has the best way of dealing with it." JFK replied that the best result would be to have the Turks themselves offer the withdrawal, but McNamara concluded there was insufficient time to work out the details, especially since the Turks "are a *terribly* stubborn people to talk to on this kind of point." But, as the President had hinted when discussing the inevitable NATO perception that this *was* a trade—"that's alright isn't it"—the point was to get the deal done and argue about details later when the threat of nuclear war had passed. Of course, domestic political considerations were another matter entirely,

---

[298]McNamara, although he had advocated defusing the Jupiter missiles to discourage a Soviet attack on Turkey, continued to resist a "direct" trade. Nonetheless, when JFK was out of the room earlier in the meeting, McNamara had defended the President's "reasonable" inclination to "defer" rather than "turn down" Khrushchev's Cuba-Turkey proposal. Ball, on the other hand, actually reversed course on the Turkish missiles after word arrived that a U-2 had been shot down over Cuba.

and the ultimate agreement to remove the Turkish missiles remained secret for nearly a quarter-century.

RFK and Sorensen, who had been out of the room for several minutes completing JFK's letter to Khrushchev, returned to the Cabinet Room with the revised and final draft—essentially accepting the offer made in Khrushchev's private October 26 message. JFK tersely approved the letter, in which he clearly had limited confidence, before resuming the discussion of the Turkish missile withdrawal. McNamara suggested drafting a message to the NATO governments explaining that the President had decided to withdraw the missiles "because of the *danger* to NATO of this situation and because we can *relieve* that danger without in any way reducing the defense of NATO." "Let's be clear," Bundy pointed out, "We *can't* withdraw the missiles and therefore the action we take is that the President has ordered inoperability." "Yes," McNamara agreed, "they're defused." JFK still persisted, "Well, I'd say we'd withdraw the warheads, wouldn't we?"

But, the President again dismissed any illusions about actually concealing American motives: Turkey and NATO will conclude "that this is on the cheap for them, they'll say the United States is... is... is pulling out in order to try to make a deal on Cuba. I mean, no matter whether we say it's to protect Turkey or not, that's the way they're gonna think about it." That possibility didn't appear to bother the President because he knew, and he assumed NATO knew, that the claim to be protecting Turkey was essentially a diplomatic cover story.

The defense chief, however, continued to resist the idea of a direct trade, "We can say, 'We're in a position where we believe we're gonna have to attack Cuba. If we attack Cuba, there's a great likelihood that the Soviets will attack the missiles in Turkey.'" "Or... and Italy. Throw in Italy," the President interjected. The United States, McNamara continued, is willing to defuse the Jupiter missiles and substitute Polaris submarines, "'*before we attack Cuba*, thereby increasing your safety if you wish us to do so.' I would put it on *that* basis. If they don't take it, that's *their*... decision." "And if they don't take it," the President asserted, "we feel you [Turkey] should recognize this danger or accept that danger." JFK urged getting the proposal ready for a NATO meeting tomorrow, but Bundy dissented, "No, I... I would *not* do it tomorrow, Mr. President, myself." President Kennedy simply disregarded Bundy's objection, "I think we oughta get moving on it. The fact is, time's running out. I think we have tomorrow afternoon. You see, it's already midnight there." McNamara agreed to send the message to the NATO governments that evening in preparation for a meeting by late tomorrow and JFK repeated, "I want the meeting tomorrow because any... time's running out on that."

"I must say this is *very* difficult," Ball objected, "because we *can't* be in a position where we render these things [Turkish Jupiters] inoperable or take them out and *don't* get a Cuban deal, then we don't have anything except freedom of action."

"Well... well, that's... that's quite a bit," McNamara retorted.

"Well, such as what... what?" Bundy inquired.

"I mean if we," Ball explained, "all we're doing on this maneuver is, we are achieving what is the equivalent to the price... to... to Khrushchev's price [for removing the Cuban missiles]."

Dillon disagreed, "Well, but the only time we... we'd say that we've rendered them inoperable is when we've determined that we're gonna attack in Cuba."

"*This* is the point," McNamara exclaimed, "if we attack in Cuba..."

"We don't say *this* publicly," Dillon cut in, "before we've attacked. We... we say this just... this is few hours before we attack, and then we attack."

"Let's draft the message," McNamara asserted

President Kennedy, however, was clearly thinking of the Turkish missile trade, not in terms of McNamara's politically cunning diplomatic/public relations scheme to make an attack on Cuba seem less risky for NATO, but rather as a bold stroke to resolve the crisis entirely without using military force at all.

At this juncture, JFK again left the Cabinet Room and the meeting again became less structured and far more spontaneous. Vice President Lyndon Johnson, normally assertive, domineering and charismatic, had often seemed oddly passive and reticent in President Kennedy's presence. Johnson had spoken briefly earlier in the meeting—also when JFK had left the room. Now, with the President gone again, Johnson began to speak out—repeatedly, colorfully and articulately. The Vice President had a significant impact on the ExComm discussions for the first time, and unexpectedly, continued to speak his mind even after the President rejoined the meeting some 45 minutes later.[299]

[299]For compelling insights into the JFK-LBJ relationship, by a journalist who worked for

LBJ immediately exposed the chasm between the McNamara and JFK approaches to a Turkish missile withdrawal—and seemed to be siding with the President: "What you're... what you're sayin is you're willing to give 'em up, as McNamara proposes. Why not trade?" Ball promptly endorsed Johnson's common sense view, "And then save a few hundred thousand lives." McNamara, however, vigorously tried to defend his position with four propositions:

First: "We *must* be in a position to attack *quickly*. We've been *fired on* today! We're gonna send surveillance aircraft in tomorrow. Those are gonna be fired on *without question*. We're gonna respond. You *can't* do this very long. We're gonna lose airplanes. We'll be shooting up Cuba bit by bit, but we're gonna lose airplanes every day. You just *can't* maintain this position very long. So we must be prepared to *attack* Cuba ("That's right," Dillon interjected)—*quickly*."

Second: "*When* we attack Cuba, we are going to *have* to attack with an *all-out* attack, and that means 500 sorties at a minimum the first day, and it means sorties every day thereafter, and I *personally* believe that this is *almost certain* to lead to an invasion." "Unless you get a ceasefire around the world," Dillon muttered. "Or a general war," Bundy warned.

Third: "*If* we do this, if the Sov... and leave those missiles in Turkey, the Soviet Union *may*, and I think probably *will*, attack the Turkish missiles."

Fourth: "*If* the Soviet Union attacks the Turkish missiles, we *must* respond." "That's right," Dillon chimed in. "We *cannot* allow a Soviet attack," McNamara contended, "on the... on the Sov... on the Jupiter missiles in Turkey without a military response by NATO." "Somewhere," Dillon interposed again. McNamara clearly appreciated the Treasury secretary's backing: "Somewhere, that's right." Ball, however, still seemed uncertain, but pressed McNamara to continue, "Go ahead. Go down the track, because I think that this... Frankly, I don't, I don't..." "Now, the *minimum* military response by NATO," the defense chief resumed, "to a Soviet attack on the Turkish Jupiter missiles would be a response with conventional weapons by NATO forces in Turkey. That is to say, Turkish and U.S. aircraft *against* Soviet warships and/or naval bases in the Black Sea area. Now that... that to me is the *absolute* minimum. And I would say that it is *damn dangerous*

Senator, Vice President and later President Johnson, see George Reedy, *Lyndon B. Johnson: A Memoir* (Kansas City, Missouri: Andrews McMeel, 1982).

to... to have had a Soviet attack on Turkey and a NATO response on the Soviet Union. This is *extremely* dangerous. Now I'm not sure we can avoid anything like that *if* we attack Cuba. But I think we should make *every effort*," he rapped the table for emphasis, "to avoid it. And one way to avoid it is to *defuse* the Turkish missiles *before* we attack Cuba. Now this... this is the sequence of thought."

McNamara must have been taken aback by the eruption of critical and almost shouted responses. McCone backed LBJ's position on the swap: "I don't see why don't you make the trade then!" Ball again challenged McNamara' logic, arguing irritably that defusing the Turkish missiles could be pointless since it "may mean a reprisal *elsewhere* . . . in Berlin or somewhere else. Then you're in a position where you've gotten rid of your missiles *for nothing*." "Well, wait a minute now," McNamara replied, "I didn't say it saves you from a reprisal. I simply said it reduces the chances of military action against Turkey." "Well, what... what good does that do you," Ball countered testily, if it leads to "action against Berlin or somewhere else." "I'm not... I'm not *at all* certain," the defense secretary responded, that the Soviets would attack in Berlin or elsewhere if there were no longer active Jupiters in Turkey. "Oh, I am," Taylor grumbled.

"Bob," LBJ asked sharply, "if you're willin' to give up your missiles in Turkey, think you oughta give these, why don't ya *say that* to him [Khrushchev] and say we're tradin'." ("Make the trade!" someone, probably Ball, cut in shouting, "Make the trade then!") before LBJ concluded, "Save all the invasion, lives, everything else." "We've sat down over in the State Department," McCone asserted impatiently, "day and night and we've talked about this, and we'd say we'd be *delighted* to trade those missiles in Turkey for the thing in Cuba." "I said," McNamara protested, "I thought it was the realistic solution to the problem." "Sure," McCone continued, "What we were afraid of was he'd never offer this, but what he'd want to do is trade something on *Berlin*."

"I'm not opposed to it *now*," McNamara tried to explain above the din of opposition. "All I'm suggesting is *don't* push us into a position where we *haven't* traded it, and we *are* forced to attack Cuba and the missiles *remain* in Turkey. That's all I'm suggesting. Let's avoid that position, and we're fast moving into that." Bundy's reply was particularly intriguing in the context of his adamant opposition to a Turkish swap, "We were going to *let* him have his strike in Turkey is the way I understood it last week. At one point at least, that was the way we thought about it." "That's right," McNamara replied, "that was one alternative."[300] Ball, however, returning to McCone's theme, countered, "Actually, what *we* were thinking last week was that what he [Khrushchev] was doing, was gonna trade this against Berlin—or nothing. We thought that if we could trade it out for Turkey this would be an *easy* trade and a *very* advantageous deal. Now we've... we've... now we've made that offer to him." "And it doesn't look so good," Bundy interjected. Now, ironically, Ball continued, "And... and we don't want it. And we're... were talking about a course of action which involves military action with *enormous* casualties and a *great*, grave risk of escalation." McNamara tried to placate Ball by suggesting, "Why don't we look at *two* courses of action?"

Ball, who had shifted ground on the Turkish deal by almost 180 degrees since the U-2 was shot down, remained adamant, "Well, I would *far* rather, if we're gonna get the *damn* missiles out of Turkey *anyway*, say... 'if *this* is a matter of *real* concern to you [Khrushchev] to have these on your borders, *all right*, we'll get rid of 'em. You get rid of 'em in Turkey...,'" he quickly corrected himself, "'in... in Cuba.'" The Jupiters were obsolete anyway, he stressed, and the Polaris missiles in the Mediterranean would provide an even greater deterrent for NATO. Bundy interrupted, "I'm sorry, George, I missed your statement" and Ball repeated, "I'd say, '*Sure*, we'll accept your offer. If this is a matter of *grave* concern to you and you equate these things [the missiles in Cuba and Turkey], which *we* don't, but if *you* do, OK, we can... we can work... work it out.'" "And what's left of NATO?" Bundy griped. "*I don't think* NATO is going to be wrecked," Ball retorted sharply. "And if NATO isn't any better than that, it isn't that *good* to us."[301]

---

[300]It is problematic to pin down the "one point" recalled by Bundy and McNamara. At the morning meeting on October 18, JFK had mused about how the crisis might have worked out in reverse if Khrushchev had warned the U.S. against putting missiles in Turkey and then destroyed them after they were deployed. "There's some advantages to that if it's all over," without additional escalation. Soon after he wondered if a limited U.S. action might lead to a limited Soviet response: "I feel that there's a difference in our action and therefore in their response, between our knocking out these missiles and planes and knocking out... and invading Cuba." He seemed to be suggesting that a reprisal against the Jupiters in Turkey would be much less serious, and perhaps acceptable, compared to a Soviet invasion of Turkey. This point may help explain the President's insistence, at the unrecorded 2:30 meeting on October 20 and the noon meeting on October 22, on new instructions to the JCS to prevent the firing of the Turkish Jupiters without presidential authorization—even if they were attacked.

[301]Ball had warned on October 18 that it would be unwise to stop allied ships in the

"What happens to the missiles in Cuba over the next three weeks," Dillon objected, "while this is going on?" "No," Ball explained impatiently, "you do this . . . on the basis of an *immediate* trade" and continue surveillance over Cuba. McNamara recommended writing two messages to cover the contingencies *he* thought most suitable: one assuming that a trade of Turkish and Cuban missiles was unacceptable to the Soviets or the U.S. and an attack on Cuba was imminent and the other calling for defusing the Jupiters in Turkey before a U.S. attack on Cuba. He did not propose a message accepting a direct trade. "I'd like to see *both* of these messages written," Bundy declared. The defense secretary agreed that the letters should be drafted—each potentially intended for the Turks, the leaders of the NATO governments and the North Atlantic Council.

The meeting had already been going on for several grueling hours. "Do people want dinner downstairs," Bundy asked, "or they want trays or they want to wait?" "Well, let's wait. You don't have to worry," McNamara muttered almost inaudibly, "eating is the *least* of my worries." His dismal tone momentarily exposed the depths of exhaustion, insecurity and anxiety which these men had endured virtually around the clock since the morning of October 16.[302]

But, the defense secretary quickly returned to the inescapable issues on the table and announced that Taylor and the JCS were working out a low-level surveillance plan for tomorrow, "But we're just gonna get shot up, *sure as hell*. There's just no *question* about it. Then we're gonna have to go in and shoot," and after two, three or possibly four days of air action "we're gonna lose planes." He also reported that four of the day's eight reconnaissance flights had been fired on and had

---

blockade and JFK retorted, "I don't think anybody who gets excited because their ships are stopped under these conditions—they're not very much help to us anyway." Their differences vis à vis the allies had clearly narrowed by October 27.

[302]"No one at the sessions spoke of his own fatigue," Barton Bernstein has written, "the future of his family if war came, or the destruction of America. Nor did they ever introduce moral or ethical standards to win a point or rebut an argument. They operated as tacticians and concealed whatever personal fears they felt. They knew—without any need for repeated reminders—that the decisions the president made could be truly momentous." ("Reconsidering the Missile Crisis," 84) Denial was a potent psychological survival mechanism for men who respected toughness and were embarrassed by doubts and fears. But, the moral arguments against a Pearl Harbor–like strike on Cuba, the concern about killing Russians, the discussion about protecting civilians from radiation, and JFK's explicit warning to the JCS about 80–100 million U.S. casualties ("you're talkin' about the destruction of a country!"), suggest that human and ethical considerations lurked just beneath the surface of these "tactical" discussions.

to abort their missions. "You know," McCone exclaimed in response, "it seems to me we're missing a bet here. I think that we ought to take this occasion to send directly to Khrushchev, by *fast wire*, the most *violent* protest, and demand that he... that he... that he stop this business and stop it *right* away, or we're gonna take those SAM sites out *immediately*. That's what I'd tell him." But, the tough-minded CIA chief again sided with the President on using the Jupiters to effect a quick resolution to the crisis, "And I'd trade these Turkish things out *right now*. I wouldn't even talk to *anybody* about it. . . . And I'd make that *part* of the message." Perhaps, he added, Khrushchev might be persuaded to accept the Turkish trade if we "Tell him we're gonna conduct surveillance as announced by the President, and *one shot* and in we come. He can expect it. If he wants to sit down and talk about this thing, he can call off his gunfire and do it right away."

McNamara complained that even if the trade offer was made, Khrushchev might delay or refuse to accept it—then "nothing happens and we're losing airplanes." Dillon agreed, "Well, I mean, this is what John said." "Lemme go back a second," the usually businesslike defense secretary burst out, his stress and frustration finally erupting, "When I read that message of last night this morning, I thought, *my God!* I'd never sell... I'd never base a... a transaction on *that* contract. Hell, that's *no* offer! There's not a *damn* thing in it that's an offer! You read that message carefully—he *didn't* propose to take the missiles out. Not once that... there isn't a *single* word in it that proposes to take the missiles out. It's twelve pages of...," Dillon interrupted to finish his sentence, "fluff," and McNamara repeated, "of fluff." McCone, however, echoing an earlier JFK remark, pointed out that "his message this morning wasn't that way—his public message." McNamara repeated that he was referring to the Friday message, "The last night message was 12 pages of fluff. That's *no* contract. You couldn't *sign* that and say we know what we signed," before he exploded again, "And *before*," he slapped his hands for emphasis, "we got the *damned thing* read, the whole deal changed, *completely* changed!"

The defense chief concluded, as a result, "nothing's gonna be signed quickly" and urged continued preparation for an all-out attack on Cuba, but at the same time deciding how long an attack could be safely postponed and pursuing diplomatic options, such as McCone's suggestion to send a tough new letter to Khrushchev "to try to negotiate a deal." The CIA director, however, insisted that he was not actually recommending negotiating a deal, "I'd send him a *threatening* letter.

I'd say, 'You've made public an offer; we'll accept that offer. But, you shot down a plane today before we even had a chance to send you a letter, despite the fact that *you* knew that we were sending *unarmed* planes on a public, announced surveillance.'" If these unarmed reconnaissance planes were fired on again, McCone demanded, Khrushchev had to be told that the U.S. would immediately take out the SAM sites. "But what I'd do," McNamara countered, "is disassociate that from the Turkish missiles, John." McCone disagreed sharply, "No, I wouldn't, because then the pressure gets back at you. You get another proposal. You'll have Berlin thrown in it tomorrow." "Oh, I think that's possible." McNamara conceded. "That's why *I* think we have to be prepared for an attack," and he urged the prompt drafting of the messages discussed earlier in the meeting to be rushed to the NATO capitals. Dillon also asked McCone to write his proposed letter to Khrushchev and the rump ExComm meeting broke up into several smaller clusters of conversation.

For more than half an hour, only tantalizing fragments of these conversations are partially audible in the background. Vice President Johnson, for example, can be heard asking if the shooting down of the U-2 had been made public, "Is that on the wire?" RFK replied somberly, "Well the fact that it's ah... it's been ah... lost, is on the wire." LBJ speculated soon after about the likelihood of a Turkish missile deal, "Why, if you were prime minister of Turkey, say that we're gonna hit Cuba, but he's got this big fuse here and it's all advertised. He's got a big red light on each one of these Jupiters. We want to take 'em out. We're gonna give you more protection than ever, with Polaris, with less advertising. And it's gonna make it less likely you'll get hit. Why wouldn't he buy that?" "I'm not sure," Nitze replied, "*why* he wouldn't buy it. I a... but the whole proposition hasn't been made to him, as far as I know." Johnson answered his own question, "No, but I say, suppose you were prime minister? What would you do about it? Wouldn't you rather have Polaris in there? I think the reason he wouldn't buy it would be a fear that that meant that we were through and we wouldn't come [to Turkey's defense]."

The Vice President continued to reflect rather casually, eventually insinuating that the administration had been retreating or backing down "gradually from the President's speech" and that the American people were becoming more insecure. As proof, he claimed that Soviet "ships are comin' through" the blockade. Robert Kennedy reacted angrily, "No! The ships aren't coming through. They all turned back...

90% of them." But Johnson stuck to his guns, "I don't think . . . at this moment, that it looks like we're as strong as we were on the day of the President's announcement." This exchange, providing only a tantalizing hint of the bitter enmity between Bobby Kennedy and LBJ, petered out and the attorney general apparently left the Cabinet Room.

Johnson laughed at times with several ExComm colleagues, and, although much of the fragmentary conversation is inaudible, he can be heard contending again that the public was becoming disenchanted with the administration's lack of resolve: "I don't say it's *wise*. I just say that's the temperature—it's 101 degrees." Several minutes later, after chatting about the U Thant negotiating proposals, the Khrushchev and Kennedy messages, the shooting down of the U-2 and the need to continue surveillance until confirmation that work on the bases had stopped, LBJ responded flamboyantly to Dillon's inquiry about whether an announcement was imminent "that we might do night surveillance." The Vice President chuckled softly and declared, "No, I don't... hope it hasn't. Hah, hah. I've been afraid of those damned flares [lighting for night reconnaissance] ever since they mentioned them." He pointed out that unarmed, low-level reconnaissance planes had already been forced to turn back because of ground fire. "Imagine some crazy Russian captain . . . the damn thing [the night flare] goes '*blooey*' and lights up the skies. He might just pull a trigger. ("Right," Rusk murmured in the background.)[303] Looks like we're playin' Fourth of July over there or somethin'. I'm scared of that, and I don't see... I don't see what you get with that photograph . . . You know they're workin at night and you can see 'em workin' at night. Now what do you do? Psychologically you scare 'em [the Russians and the Cubans], well, hell, it's always like the fellow tellin' me in Congress, 'Go on and put the monkey on his back.' Every time I tried to put a monkey on somebody else's back, *I got one*. If you're gonna try and psychologically scare them with a flare, you're liable to get your bottom shot at."[304]

The conversation soon turned to drafting three messages: McNamara's scheme to the Turks to substitute Polaris for the Jupiters before

[303]Rusk had raised a similar point on Friday morning—warning that flares had been used in preparation for night bombing raids in the past and could be misinterpreted by Cuban and Soviet ground personnel.

[304]Dillon, JFK and LBJ used the words "afraid" or "scared" during the decisive October 27 meetings. Marshall Carter had been the first to verbalize this entirely reasonable reaction on October 16.

an attack on Cuba; Ball's move to accept Khrushchev's offer of a straightforward trade and McCone's ultimatum to the Soviet leader accepting the trade but demanding the inoperability of the missiles and an immediate end to attacks on surveillance aircraft. After Dillon read a draft of the McCone-inspired ultimatum, Rusk asked Johnson whether he thought the U.S. would soon be forced to act. "I think you're at that point," the Vice President replied. "I think you're gonna have a *big* problem right here, internally, in a few more hours in this country" because the public would soon demand more action, "'Where have you been? What are you doin'? The President made a fine speech. What else have you done?'" He repeated his claim, disputed earlier by RFK, that some ships were going through the blockade, "There's a *great* feeling of insecurity," he cautioned, spreading across the nation. Rusk inquired about Johnson's views on the national reaction to "accepting the Turkish aspect," but the Vice President admitted candidly, "I don't know."

LBJ, still thinking out loud, hypothesized about telling the Turkish prime minister directly, "'Now you've got these Jupiters and they're lighted up there. The searchlight's on 'em and everybody knows about 'em. They're not worth a damn. And we'll take that old T-Model out, we'll give you Polaris, a much better job.'" He wondered, however, whether the Jupiter missiles provided the Turks with a physical sense of assurance of American support. Rusk pointed out incredulously, "We've got 17,000 *men* there!" and Johnson countered, "We've got 20,000 men there." LBJ contemplated whether the Turks might eventually agree that they were in less danger with Polaris after the U.S. hit Cuba and Dillon suggested that they might be persuaded by "the message that's being drafted." Johnson, however, paused to reflect gloomily, "I think governments are all old, and tired and sick..." "Who, the Turks?" Dillon replied, obviously puzzled by the remark.

Perhaps, Johnson urged Rusk, partially echoing McNamara's "defusing" argument, the U.S. should "try to *sell* 'em on that" by having Ambassador Hare tell the Turkish prime minister, "You're more *likely* to get hit *this* way [with the Jupiters] than you are the other way [with Polaris]. Isn't that true, Tommy?" Ambassador Thompson, however, remained skeptical about the trade, "The trouble with all this is that unless we're *absolutely* decided we're going to hit Cuba, bomb them, then this would leave us in a *very* weak position." Even if the Soviets removed the missiles, "they'll leave their technicians in Cuba, their bombing planes in Cuba, and we're in a *hell* of a mess." The only justification for pressuring Turkey, Thompson concluded, "is if they know you're gonna bomb [Cuba]." LBJ seemed to agree, pointing out "the weakness of the whole thing is," that if the U.S. gave up Turkey after the Soviets shot down one plane, Moscow might expect the surrender of Berlin if they shot down another plane. "You know, a... a *mad* dog, he tastes a little blood, he...."

"I think they've been put off [their October 26 offer] by the Lippmann piece," Thompson conjectured, "encouraged to think that we *really* are prepared to swap Turkey for Cuba."[305] He warned that Khrushchev had "gotten onto the idea that he can get a lot more. His [new] proposal was that whatever you... you want out of Cuba, you take out of Turkey." Dillon was of the same opinion, predicting that the Soviets would now expect an overall quid pro quo—trading missiles, planes and technicians in both Turkey and Cuba. "That's why I think," Thompson advised, "any suggestion that we're going to accept this," short of "an irrevocable decision that we're going to take these out by *bombing* [Cuba], is... is *very* dangerous. . . . I *can't* believe it's necessary, when you know the night before he was willing to take this other line." "So what happened?" LBJ inquired. "Did somebody *force* him to up his ante? Or did he try to just say, 'Well, maybe they'll give up more. Let's try it and I can always come back to my original position.'"

Khrushchev might have been overruled, Thompson hypothesized again, or he and his colleagues had been "deceived by the Lippmann piece" or believed that the U.S. was behind the similar scheme floated by Austrian foreign minister Kreisky, suggesting "that we were willing to make the trade." Dillon pointed out that Khrushchev had made the Cuba-Turkey offer *after* the publication of Lippmann's article and Thompson also noted that Lippmann had a close relationship with Mac" [presumably Bundy]. Thompson indicated that Khrushchev might now be thinking, "'These boys are beginning to give way. Let's push harder.' I think they'll change their minds," he added, "when we

---

[305]Walter Lippmann's piece proposing a Cuba-Turkey missile deal appeared in the *Washington Post* on October 25. Soviet archival evidence has confirmed that Khrushchev *had* indeed read the article. Lippmann later met with Ambassador Dobrynin and confirmed that although JFK had not urged him to write the piece, he had talked with officials in the Arms Control and Disarmament Agency, "possibly with John McCloy himself." (Fursenko and Naftali, *"One Hell of a Gamble,"* 275, 393–94) For a discussion of Ambassador Thompson's belief that Lippmann's article helped to explain "the shift in Soviet demands," see Nash, *The Other Missiles*, 132–37.

take… we take any forceful action, stopping their ship, or… or taking out a SAM site that ends up killing the Russians—somewhere." Dillon wondered whether Khrushchev should be warned that if reconnaissance planes were attacked again, the U.S. would take out all the SAM sites, or whether it would be better to go in and take out the site which actually fired the missile without giving any warning. "I'm inclined," Thompson replied, "to take one out" and LBJ quipped, "You war hawks oughta get together," laughing alone and self-consciously at his own joke. Johnson asked whether Khrushchev had received Lippmann's article after he sent the Friday letter but before sending the Saturday message. Thompson replied, "No," but nevertheless suggested that after "wobbling around" in the October 26 letter, Khrushchev had finally decided on a tougher line.

McCone finally read aloud the draft of his proposed "threatening" letter from JFK to Khrushchev. On the one hand, he asserted that firing on unarmed reconnaissance planes and shooting down a U-2 was a "*shocking* further provocation on your part" and declared that military action would be taken to protect them in the event of new attacks. But, he left open the door to negotiations on each of Khrushchev's three recent messages, "*All* are worthy of serious consideration and discussion," but nonetheless demanded an immediate cessation of work "on your offensive bases in Cuba," steps to make the missiles inoperable and progress toward their verified removal.[306] Dillon immediately noticed that the letter did not include a specific reference to removing the Jupiters from Turkey, but McCone explained that a deal on Turkey was implicitly included in the offer to talk about *all* of Khrushchev's proposals.

"The Cubans are beginning to realize that something serious is up," Rusk observed, and gunfire over Cuba was likely to begin again very soon. LBJ expressed surprise that the Cubans had allowed U.S. planes to fly over their territory for so many days before firing on them. "Except I've been concerned," the Vice President added, "at how gleeful our people have been for the last couple of days in the papers. . . . And I don't think that's *good* for us." He stressed that Khrushchev was "behind the eight ball a little bit and he's got to get a little blood—and he's *got* it." Johnson explained that since a U-2 had been shot down and "we're lettin' this ship go through and that ship's goin' through and we've had a hell of a talk, they wanna know what we gonna be

[306]McCone included Khrushchev's Friday message to U Thant as well as the Friday and Saturday letters to President Kennedy.

doin'. I guess," he observed skeptically, "it'll be done tomorrow. I guess we'll be doin' somethin' tomorrow. Put the blanket [reconnaissance] down. I imagine they'll shoot, we'll shoot and that's..." Thompson softly agreed, "That's your main concern."

Rusk also made an apparent reference to covert plans, never actually carried out, to land "a ship loaded with the Cubans" [exiles] to gather intelligence. LBJ suggested that the Russians were also "doin' it, but you can't give 'em hell" and Dillon cautioned that "The Russians are doing it, but we never kill their Russians."

Thompson, however, promptly returned to his adamant opposition to any deal involving Turkey that might, in his view, weaken the U.S. diplomatic position, "You can see that we have two conflicting things here: one is to prepare for an attack on Cuba, and the other is to get a peaceful solution along the lines which he proposed [on Friday]. And the purposes are conflicting. If you want to get him to accept this thing that he put in his letter last night, then you shouldn't give *any* indication that we're ready to... to talk about the Turkish thing." Thompson further underscored the point: "They've [the Soviets] done two things: they've upped... they've upped the price and they've escalated the...," LBJ cut in firmly, "the action," and the former ambassador repeated, "the action." "And I think," Thompson concluded, "to mention this, as McCone does [in his new draft letter to Khrushchev], that we can discuss this other thing [Turkey] . . . is bad for the perspective of Khrushchev. I think it's a further sign of weakness . . . to indicate willingness just to talk about this thing which he put up which *was*, I think, comparatively unacceptable to us. This is missile for missile, and technicians for technicians and planes for planes." "Therefore, he's *really* sayin'," the Vice President remarked sarcastically, "'I'm gonna re... I'm gonna *dismantle* the foreign policy of the United States for the last fifteen years in order to get you... get these missiles out of Cuba.'" LBJ paused dramatically for some ten seconds—before explicitly rebuking President Kennedy's stance on a Cuba-Turkey deal, "Then we say we're glad, and we appreciate it and we want to discuss it with you." Moments before Johnson had seemed to back the trade, but he plainly still had doubts.

If JFK's latest letter to Khrushchev were released, Thompson reasoned, "that offsets a lot of things, things that worried the President, about the public posture. . . . He's put this forward [the Friday proposal], then suddenly he's shifted. The public will *realize* that he's suddenly stepped up the ante," and LBJ observed that the downing of a

U-2 "is not gonna make the folks too anxious to trade anyway." Dillon endorsed essentially releasing JFK's letter by sending it to *both* the Kremlin and the U.N. and someone else pointed out that releasing the President's letter would, in point of fact, make the contents of Khrushchev's Friday letter public, since the President had instructed press secretary Pierre Salinger to respond to questions about Khrushchev's October 26 message by saying, "'You can draw your own conclusions from the letter President Kennedy wrote.'" Dillon, however, seemed uneasy about actually publicizing Khrushchev's Friday letter since such a move could disrupt or shut down a potentially useful private channel of communication with the Soviets.

The rump discussion briefly turned to resuming reconnaissance over Cuba and carrying out the administration's announced intention to take out the SAM site that had brought down the U-2. "You just ask yourself" LBJ asserted, "what made the greatest impression on you today, whether it was his [Khrushchev's] letter last night, or whether it was his letter this morning, or whether it's about that U-2 boy's downing."

"U-2 boy," Dillon immediately echoed.

"That's *exactly* what did it," the Vice President affirmed. "That's when everybody's color changed a little bit and sure as hell that's what's gonna make the impression on *him* [Khrushchev]—not all these signals that each one of us write. He's expert at that palaver."

President Kennedy returned to the Cabinet Room at about 7:30 after an absence of just over three-quarters of an hour. During the time away from the meeting he had approved the final version of the letter to Khrushchev after last-minute revisions by RFK and Sorensen. He did not reveal to the full ExComm that before rejoining the discussion he had arranged to have Robert Kennedy meet with Anatoly Dobrynin in the Attorney General's office at the Justice Department (at about 8:00 P.M.) to orally explain the details of the President's new message to Khrushchev. About ten minutes later, at the conclusion of this extended meeting, JFK invited eight members of ExComm to the Oval Office for a discussion of RFK's imminent appointment with the Soviet ambassador.

The President apologized for the excessive length of the meeting and immediately reopened discussion of the pending messages to Turkey and the NATO countries. Bundy boldly pointed out that before instructions could be sent to Ambassador Finletter, "we have *really* to agree on the *track*, you see, Mr. President, and I think that there's a *very* substantial difference between us." "Let's see what the difference is," JFK replied patiently, "then we can think about that. What is the difference?" Bundy seemed reluctant to make the case, "Well, I haven't been in as much of the discussion as some others, Mr. President, to back them up at this stage."[307]

Thompson, however, jumped into the breach, methodically reviewing the arguments he had made during the President's absence: "I think we *clearly* have a choice here," he declared, "that either we go on the line that we've... we've decided to attack Cuba and therefore are set to prepare the ground for that or we try to get Khrushchev back on the... on a peaceful solution, in which case we shouldn't give *any* indication that we're going to accept anything on... on Turkey because the Turkish proposal is, I should *think*, *clearly* unacceptable. It's missile for missile, plane for plane, technician for technician, and it leaves, if... if it worked out, it would leave the Russians installed in Cuba." The Soviets, he warned, have "upped the price and they've upped the action. And I think we have to bring him back [to the Friday proposal] by upping our action and by getting him back to this other thing without any mention of the Turkish business." The ambassador shrewdly appealed to the President's political instincts by predicting that if Khrushchev's October 26 offer was revealed by releasing the President's response, it would diminish any need to discuss Turkey. "It seems to me the public will be pretty solid on that, and that we ought to keep the heat on him and get him back on a line which he obviously was on the night before." The Friday message, Thompson deduced, seemed "almost incoherent and showed that they were *quite* worried" and the Lippmann article and the Kreisky speech "has made him think they can get more and they backed away from it."

President Kennedy had repeatedly emphasized that Khrushchev had moved beyond his Friday proposal by making the Turkish offer public, but he nonetheless asked about the timing of the Kreisky and Lippmann proposals. Thompson explained that Kreisky's remarks had appeared in a public speech and Bundy and Sorensen noted that Lippmann's article had been in the *Washington Post* two days before. The President moved again to conciliate the opponents of a Turkish deal by agreeing that "*first* we oughta *try* to go the first route which

---

[307]Bundy had apparently been out of the room during much of the rump discussion between LBJ, Thompson, Dillon, Rusk and McCone.

you suggest and get him back [to the Friday offer]. That's what our letter's doing." But, at the same time, he revealed his lack of confidence in that strategy by insisting on keeping the other option open: "Then it seems to me we *oughta* have a discussion with NATO about these Turkish missiles . . . [and] an up-to-date briefing about where we're going."

Vice President Johnson continued his active participation in the discussion, notwithstanding JFK's presence. He summarized the alternatives proposed by McNamara (substituting Polaris for the Jupiters before attacking Cuba), by Ball (a direct trade of the Turkish and Cuban missiles), and by McCone (an ultimatum on ending attacks on the reconnaissance planes—"'You shot down our man there and we're not gonna *take* any more of this'"—sweetened by a willingness to trade the Jupiters in Turkey). "Putting the bee on Cuba on that one," Rusk observed colorfully. "Mr. President," the secretary of state continued, using Thompson's argument as well as his words, "I think that the... the trouble with Ball's track" is that it might compel the U.S. to match "plane for plane, man for man, missile for missile." "Who said this?" JFK asked. "Ball's track," Rusk replied, "would just get us *completely* out of Turkey *in every respect or* leave the Soviets *very much* in Cuba. It's the track of last night we want to get him back to. I think if we step up our actions tomorrow against Cuba, not against... necessarily against the Soviet Union..." "Well," JFK replied, "we're gonna call up some Air Reserves tonight." Dillon declared, "instead of an ultimatum and a lot of talk," about any new attacks on unarmed U.S. planes, take out a SAM site immediately, "Don't say anything. Just *do* that."

JFK, still wary of military overreaction, reopened the question of confirming the fate of the U-2. "But we don't know whether that plane was shot down yet, do we?" He was advised that there was no firm evidence "on our side" that it was shot down, but Havana radio had announced that the plane had been destroyed by antiaircraft fire. "Oh, I'm sorry. I didn't know that yet. . . . I'm not sure that Secretary McNamara knows that," the President admitted. Thompson seized the chance to apply even more pressure, "I also think that we ought to—if that Soviet ship [*Grozny*] comes in with... within this [quarantine] line, we ought to stop it."

After a brief run-through on the *Grozny*'s cargo, JFK again shifted the discussion back to the Turkish issue. "In his message this morning on Turkey, didn't he say if we took out the missiles in Turkey, he'd take out the missiles in Cuba?" Thompson read from Khrushchev's message—"We agree to remove from Cuba those means which you regard as offensive means . . . [if the U.S.] will remove its similar means from Turkey"—but the former ambassador contended once again that the offer was a trap: "That's why I think it's *very* dangerous to indicate any... any tentative play on this thing. He's *really* got us there. As the Secretary [Rusk] says, it's either/or if we get along this path. We either get out of Turkey completely, or we leave the Soviets [technicians and bombers] in Cuba and have only missiles out."

Ball contended that the U.S. could make a counterproposal and Bundy suggested offering to take everything out of *both* Turkey and Cuba. But Dillon—as Bundy perhaps counted on—emphatically disagreed, "You can't do that!" President Kennedy, once again, cut through the determined ExComm opposition to make his views unmistakably plain, "We can't very well invade Cuba, with all its toil and blood there's gonna be, when we could have gotten 'em [the missiles in Cuba] out by making a deal on the same missiles on Turkey. If that's part of the record, but ah... then you don't have a very good war." He paused for some six seconds before concluding, "But other than that, it's really a question now of what we... what to say to NATO." Khrushchev's public offer, from JFK's perspective, had made a deal on the Turkish missiles politically inescapable.

Vice President Johnson, in the most dramatic challenge to the President's judgment since the stinging attacks by General LeMay and Senators Russell and Fulbright during the first week of meetings, flatly disagreed: "It doesn't mean just ah... missiles... missiles. He's gonna... he's gonna... he takes his missiles out of Cuba, takes his men out of Cuba and takes his planes out of Cuba—why then your whole foreign policy is gone. You take everything out of Turkey—twenty thousand men, all *your* technicians, and all *your* planes, and all *your* missiles— and... and crumble."

"How else are we gonna get those missiles out of there then?" JFK replied impassively, again refusing to make a direct response to tough criticism, "That's the problem."

"Well, *last* night he was prepared," Rusk reminded JFK, "to trade them for a promise not to invade."

"That's right, now he's got something completely new," the President pointed out yet again.

"*Somebody* told him to try to get a little more," Johnson cut in.

McCone suggested sending Khrushchev "a pretty tough message" and JFK countered, "Well, I've already sent him one."

"Well, this is a thoughtful one," McCone teased, referring to his own "threatening" draft letter—which led to a brief spurt of laughter before the President quickly read through the draft.

The stressful and draining meeting had finally run out of steam after almost four hours. The strain of the discussions, after nearly two weeks, was clearly taking a toll "on people's stamina and composure."[308] The President suggested reconvening in the Cabinet Room at 9:00 P.M.—urging "everybody get a bite to eat then let's come back" to decide whether to send McCone's letter, "to see about what we do about this trade" and "see about our two messages to the U.N., and, I mean, this Turkish thing." The ExComm discussion finally dissolved into several miscellaneous conversations and gradually came to an end.

Decades later, McNamara remembered his anguish about how Khrushchev might respond to the President's latest message: "I remember the sunset. We left at about the time the sun was setting in October, and I, at least, was so uncertain as to whether the Soviets would accept replying to the first instead of the second [Khrushchev message]. . . that I wondered if I'd ever see another sunset like that."[309]

After the ExComm had dispersed, Ball, Bundy, Gilpatric, RFK, McNamara, Rusk, Sorensen and Thompson met with President Kennedy, at his invitation, in the Oval Office. "The best available evidence indicates that the president was the dominant person at that small session. He called the meeting, selected the participants, and excluded about another eight men." JFK revealed that his brother was about to hand deliver the new letter for Khrushchev to Dobrynin in a potentially decisive private meeting at the Justice Department and requested advice on what the attorney general should tell the ambassador. The group quickly agreed that RFK should warn Dobrynin that military ac-

---

[308]Gilpatric Oral History, 58–59; Rusk, nonetheless, insisted that nervousness and fatigue at the meetings never deteriorated into panic or despair. He believed that JFK's "great control . . . gave leadership to ExComm in a way that stabilized the attitudes and the emotions of ExComm members." (Rusk Oral History, 128)

[309]McNamara's recollection is cited in Bernstein, "Reconsidering the Missile Crisis," 94. In fact, the meeting ended at about 7:45, well after the late-October sunset. Perhaps McNamara had been watching the sun going down through the Cabinet Room windows during the second half of the meeting or he may have later conflated this occasion with a different evening. In any event, the anecdote no doubt accurately reflects his state of mind at the time.

tion against Cuba was imminent if the missiles were not removed. However, consistent with the decision to respond first to Khrushchev's Friday proposal, RFK was also authorized to state that the United States was prepared to make a commitment not to invade Cuba if the missiles were promptly withdrawn.[310]

But, more importantly, the President continued to press for a deal on the Turkish missiles. Finally, Dean Rusk, mindful of JFK's persistence and determination, suggested that RFK should advise the ambassador that although a public quid pro quo for the missiles in Turkey was unacceptable, the President was prepared to remove them once the Cuban crisis was resolved. "The proposal was quickly supported by the rest of us," Bundy wrote decades later, "and approved by the president. It was also agreed that knowledge of this assurance would be held among those present and no one else. Concerned as we all were by the [political] cost of a public bargain struck under pressure at the apparent expense of the Turks, and aware as we were from the day's discussion that for some, even in our closest councils, even this unilateral private assurance[311] *might appear to betray an ally, we agreed without hesitation that no one not in the room was to be informed of this additional message. Robert Kennedy was instructed to make plain to Dobrynin that the same secrecy must be observed on the other side, and that any Soviet reference to our assurance would simply make it null and void." This informal statement of intent, limited to the Jupiter missiles, also satisfied Thompson's concerns about trapping the U.S. in a binding agreement to remove all missiles, technicians and planes from Turkey. "The fact of a private deal undoubtedly met the objections of some of the serious opponents of a public deal. But the central fact was," Barton Bernstein has concluded, "that the president made clear that he cared deeply about this issue, he chose the policy, and nobody would resist him. They were the president's men, and he was the president."*[312]

Sometime later that evening, after facilitating the RFK-Dobrynin meeting, and this time without the knowledge of virtually the entire

---

[310]Bernstein, "Understanding Decisionmaking," 160. Unfortunately, this small, brief but critical discussion was not taped. JFK included Bundy and Thompson, the most vocal opponents of the Turkish trade in this meeting, but excluded McCone—who had defended it. Perhaps he hoped that personal loyalty to the commander-in-chief would bring these key dissenters on board—at least publicly.

[311]Sorensen later preferred to describe this arrangement as a private deal.

[312]McGeorge Bundy, *Danger and Survival*, 432–33; see also Robert Kennedy to Dean Rusk, October 30, 1962, POF, JFKL; Bernstein, "Understanding Decisionmaking," 161.

ExComm, President Kennedy participated in another attempt to head off imminent military action in Cuba. JFK had almost no confidence in the "Trollope Ploy"—aimed at maneuvering Khrushchev back to his Friday night proposal. Instead, he worked secretly with Dean Rusk, apparently at the Secretary's suggestion, to cobble together a fall-back plan. Rusk phoned former deputy U.N. secretary general Andrew Cordier at Columbia University and asked him to assist in implementing an emergency back channel strategy by which U Thant would announce a neutral United Nations plan through which the U.S. and the U.S.S.R. would mutually agree to remove their missiles from both Turkey and Cuba. The Secretary General would make the public request only after receiving private word from Rusk that negotiations had stalled or failed. JFK was prepared to gamble that if the United States publicly accepted this allegedly neutral plan, despite the domestic political risks, it would be very difficult, if not irrational, for the Soviets to reject it. Khrushchev's unexpected decision the following morning made the Cordier gambit moot and Rusk did not reveal this closely held contingency plan for over twenty-five years.[313]

Meanwhile, also at the urging of Dean Rusk, John Scali arranged to meet again with Aleksandr Fomin late that afternoon. The ABC newsman demanded an explanation of Khrushchev's switch from the October 26 missile removal–non-invasion pledge offer to his public missile swap proposal. Fomin tried to blame the change on inadequate communications, but Scali exploded, calling Khrushchev's new message "a stinking double cross" and warned that an invasion of Cuba was imminent. Fomin insisted that a new message from the Kremlin was due shortly and pleaded with Scali to persuade U.S. officials that the Soviet Union was serious about reaching a settlement. Scali, despite his belief that the change in Khrushchev's terms suggested Soviet treachery, agreed to convey a message about their latest meeting to the ExComm.[314]

[313]Dean Rusk, as told to Richard Rusk, *As I Saw It* (New York: W.W. Norton, 1990), 240–41; James G. Blight, Joseph S. Nye, Jr., and David A. Welch, "The Cuban Missile Crisis Revisited," *Foreign Affairs* 66 (Fall 1987), 178–79; Bernstein, "Reconsidering the Missile Crisis," 100–101, 127; Chang and Kornbluh, *Cuban Missile Crisis*, 391. For discussion of an earlier and also unused "Cordier ploy" to call for "a U.N. commission to monitor the status of the missiles in Cuba and Turkey," see Garthoff, "Documenting the Cuban Missile Crisis," 298.

[314]Chang and Kornbluh, *Cuban Missile Crisis*, 389–90. Scali had obviously been informed of the contents of Khrushchev's secret Friday letter.

The President was also informed that Soviet ships were continuing on course toward Cuba and Adlai Stevenson reported that Soviet U.N. Ambassador Zorin had refused to accept information from the United States pinpointing the precise location of the quarantine line. In addition, Fidel Castro rejected U Thant's appeal to suspend work on the missile sites during U.N.-sponsored negotiations unless the U.S. first lifted the quarantine. Castro did, however, invite the acting secretary general to Cuba for urgent talks on resolving the crisis.

Declassified Soviet sources have confirmed that the launch of the SAM missile against the U-2 was ordered by local air defense officers without permission from General Pliyev in Cuba or from the Soviet air command headquarters in Moscow. "Castro's joy was indescribable," but Khrushchev was furious and ordered that no firings take place without his direct order: "No independent initiatives. Everything is hanging by a thread as it is."[315]

When General LeMay received word that the U-2 had apparently been lost, he ordered F-100 air-to-surface rocket-carrying fighters readied for an attack on the Cuban SAM sites. "The White House, realizing that there was a standing order for the immediate destruction of a firing SAM site," ordered LeMay "not to launch the aircraft until he received direct orders from the president." The Air Force chief of staff hung up in disgust. "He chickened out again. How in hell do you get men to risk their lives when the SAMs are not attacked?" An aide offered to wait for the President's call, but LeMay contemptuously predicted, "It will never come!" The Strategic Air Command, nonetheless, had already been placed on full nuclear alert. Nearly 1,600 U.S. Air Force bombers and just over 275 missiles (177 ICBMs and 100 Polaris) were armed and ready if the President should decide to order a nuclear attack on the U.S.S.R.[316]

RFK returned to the White House at about 8:45 P.M. after telling Dobrynin that continuing work on the missile sites, ground fire at U.S. reconnaissance planes and the shooting down of a U-2 were extremely serious developments and time was running out. The attorney general had reiterated the President's willingness to renounce invading Cuba, suggested that the removal of the Jupiters from Turkey was possible,

[315]Allyn, *et al.*, "Essence of Revision," 160–61; Sergei Khrushchev, *Nikita Khrushchev*, 609.

[316]Brugioni, *Eyeball to Eyeball*, 463–64; Fursenko and Naftali, *"One Hell of a Gamble,"* 258.

but not as a written quid pro quo, and specifically assured Dobrynin that the withdrawal could be carried out in 4–5 months. RFK was nonetheless convinced, he later said, that the chances for a peaceful settlement were at best "a hope, not an expectation." Determined to avoid creating a paper trail of his "informal" arrangement with Dobrynin about the Turkish missiles, Robert Kennedy went so far a few days later as to falsify his memo to Rusk about the meeting by actually crossing out a reference to this top secret understanding.[317] Only about half of the ExComm knew about RFK's secret mission on the evening of October 27. The remaining half were never formally told. President Kennedy's letter and Dobrynin's personal account of his meeting with RFK were in Khrushchev's hands in Moscow by the early morning hours of Sunday, October 28.

Saturday, October 27, 9:00 P.M., Cabinet Room

Identified Participants: John F. Kennedy, George Ball, McGeorge Bundy, Douglas Dillon, Roswell Gilpatric, Robert Kennedy, John McCone, Robert McNamara, Dean Rusk, Theodore Sorensen, Maxwell Taylor, Llewellyn Thompson.[318]

"And then we need to have two things ready, a government for Cuba, because we're gonna need one after we go in with 500 aircraft. And secondly, some plans for how to respond to the Soviet Union in Europe, cause *sure as hell* they're gonna do *something* there."

Secretary of Defense Robert McNamara

The President switched on the tape recorder during Rusk's update on the diplomatic situation. Khrushchev, he reported, had made a public speech on the crisis earlier in the day. "He's got to worry a *great deal* about how far he wants to push this thing," the secretary of state observed. "He's *on* a bad footing on his relations with the United States, his relations with *you*, the *actual* strategic situation." Rusk urged the

---

[317]Robert Kennedy, *Thirteen Days*, 80–84. For recently declassified documents on the Dobrynin-RFK discussions, see Jim Hershberg, "Anatomy of a Controversy: Anatoly F. Dobrynin's Meeting With Robert F. Kennedy, Saturday, 27 October 1962," *CWIHPB* 5 (Spring 1995), 75, 77–80; the Jupiters were withdrawn from Turkey in April 1963. For an account of RFK's "blatant falsification of the historical record," and a copy of his deceptive October 30 memo to Rusk, see Jim Hershberg, "More on Bobby and the Cuban Missile Crisis," *CWIHPB* 8–9 (Winter 1996–97), 274, 344–47.

[318]Tape 42, POF, PRC, JFKL.

President, by tomorrow, "to take certain steps to build up the pressure. We have a... enforced surveillance. We shoot at anybody who gets in our way. We see whether U Thant produces any result tonight or during the morning. We intercept that Soviet ship [the *Grozny*]. We consider tomorrow afternoon putting POL on the blockade." He also advised keeping the American military focus on Cuba, "keep the monkey on *Cuba's* back with this regard. If we *do* have to enforce our right to overfly and to have a look," Rusk declared, in words somewhat reminiscent of Senator Fulbright's position on October 22, "the accidental fact that some Russian technicians may be around at the time we have to shoot, since they've already fired the first shot, is something that is regrettable but it's *not* something that we can make a very public issue out of. We're... we're enforcing this with respect to *Cuba,* not the Soviet Union, this surveillance business." Dillon once again asked about taking action against the SAM that brought down the U-2 and JFK replied, "We don't know if it did yet, Doug."

"Would you like the discussion of the surveillance problem?" Taylor asked, and JFK replied, "Yes." "I went back this morning and talked this over with the Chiefs," Taylor reported, and the latest intelligence indicated that low-level flights near the SAM sites and some missile bases were "becoming difficult" because of ack-ack fire. "There was a lot of firing today, wasn't there?" the President commented redundantly. Taylor confirmed, "Quite... quite a bit. The planes have turned back, got over usually the first of the missile sites and then, at the second, turned back and cut out. So we have *some* photography." The Chiefs, he explained, were not ready "to go back with... with *armed* reconnaissance," but instead recommended about six flights tomorrow around sites not believed to have antiaircraft flak in order to verify that work on the missile complexes "is *still* going ahead, and also prove we're *still* on the job. But we're approaching the point, I think, Mr. President, where low-level reconnaissance will... will... will be entirely impossible." Sending in medium- or high-level missions, he added, would require knocking out perhaps ten SAM sites, if not "the whole works." But, he repeated, "low-level reconnaissance *probably* is on its way out, and I think we'll learn it at the end of tomorrow." McNamara added that the U-2 mission planned for Sunday was "just *too* dangerous," but urged the President to continue low-level reconnaissance with fighter escorts and, if the planes were fired on again, to launch an "attack on the attackers." "We don't think," Taylor dissented, "that fighter escort on the low level will help tomorrow." "*If* our planes are fired on tomorrow," McNamara counseled again, "we ought to fire back."[319]

President Kennedy instead endorsed waiting until Sunday afternoon for a possible breakthrough if U Thant went to Cuba. But, he declared, if the planes were attacked again and the Soviets failed to respond diplomatically, the administration should make a public statement about the firing and "then go in [on Monday] and take out *all* the SAM sites." He specifically rejected firing at a single 20 millimeter antiaircraft gun on the ground, "We just hazard our planes and the people on the ground have the advantage. On the other hand, I don't want... I don't think we do any good to begin to sort of *half* do it. . . . If they fire on us," he summarized, tell the pilots "to come on out, then if we don't get some satisfaction from the Russians or U Thant or Cuba tomorrow night, figure that Monday we're gonna do somethin' about the SAM sites."

Despite these tough words, JFK had, in effect, stepped back from his explicit October 23 commitment to order *immediate* air strikes against any SAM site that fired on a U-2 or against all the SAM sites (or to delegate that decision to McNamara if the commander-in-chief was briefly unavailable). The 36–48 hour delay, as it fortuitously turned out, made it much less politically awkward for Khrushchev to announce on Sunday morning (Washington time) that he had chosen to withdraw Soviet missiles from Cuba. The President's decision actually reached the Pentagon (discussed above) just in time to head off a retaliatory air strike on the SAM site believed responsible for knocking Major Anderson's U-2 out of the sky.[320]

"What do you think?" JFK again asked McNamara. The defense chief urged keeping "*some* kind of pressure on tonight and tomorrow night that indicates we're firm. Now if we call up these air squadrons tonight, I think that settles that," and the President replied, "That's right. We're gonna do that, aren't we?" McNamara revealed that he had prepared a written statement calling up "24 air reserve squadrons, roughly 300 troop carrier transports, which are required for an invasion. And this would... would both be a preparatory move and also a *strong* indication [to Cuba and the U.S.S.R.] of what lies ahead." Sev-

---

[319]JFK, at the 4:00 P.M. meeting, had already questioned the value of fighter escort cover for the surveillance planes.

[320]Garthoff, *Reflections*, 98–99.

eral voices can be heard in the background affirming, "That's right," and JFK readily agreed, "I think we oughta do that." But, although he endorsed calling up the air reserve squadrons, he also recommended waiting until tomorrow on dealing with the need for ships, "Because the air is the focus of interest right now and what we're tryin' to do is get a settlement of this."[321] McNamara then read aloud the statement to be released to the press about calling up Air Force Reserves and providing fighter escorts in response to the ground fire against low-level surveillance planes. Gilpatric and Taylor, likely recalling the President's earlier objections, advised deleting the reference to providing fighter escorts for the surveillance planes.

JFK also asked whether fighter planes would be called up later with the troop carriers. "Just the troop carriers," McNamara explained. "We have... we *could* call up some fighters. But they're just cats and dogs, Mr. President. It isn't worth it." Rusk questioned whether calling up some fighter planes would be useful from "the public point of view" and have some "effect on Khrushchev," but Taylor pointed to the danger from the SAM sites. "Dean, it isn't worthwhile," the defense secretary concluded, and Rusk backed off, "I just wanted to be sure." Finally, McNamara returned to the Pentagon and released the statement at a press conference just before 9:30 P.M.

After some informal conversation in the background, during which McCone speculated about the delivery of JFK's latest message to Khrushchev, "[U.S. Ambassador Foy] Kohler would be at his doorstep at twelve o'clock tomorrow noon, which would be four o'clock in the morning our time," attention quickly shifted to the imminent arrival of the *Grozny* at the quarantine line. Robert Kennedy, perhaps shaken by his just-completed private meeting with Dobrynin, took a remarkably restrained position, suggesting it might be wise to let the *Grozny* through since "if they [the Soviets] fired and the complication really comes from them," the U.S. could end up "firing on a Russian ship" or by Monday, "we're gonna perhaps fire on all of Cuba. Whether this ship gets in or not is not really gonna count in the big picture." "Hell, we oughta wait and see tomorrow," JFK agreed; if the ship, contrary to Khrushchev's October 26 assurances to U Thant about avoiding a confrontation at sea, actually challenged the quarantine, then "no ships come through beginning

[321]Later that evening President Kennedy instructed the Secretary of the Air Force to activate the 24 Air Force reserve units totaling some 14,200 men. (Chang and Kornbluh, *Cuban Missile Crisis*, 390)

the next morning." Sorensen, however, backed by Bundy, pointed out that those assurances were given to U Thant and the U.N. rather than JFK or the U.S. The President, in response, proposed getting Stevenson to inform U Thant, who could in turn alert Ambassador Zorin on the approach of the *Grozny*. "After all, the assurance was to U Thant not to me that they were gonna keep 'em out of there and the U.N., for the record, is clearer."

The JCS, Taylor announced, had concluded that "there's no great... there's *no* need for reconnaissance tomorrow" except to verify that work on the sites was continuing; but, at the same time, he declared "it would be a mistake to *back away* our alternatives... back away at this time." "That's right. I agree," the President replied, quickly adding, "if they're firing tomorrow, that's gonna be it. We're gonna announce that." McNamara returned to the meeting after his brief press conference and endorsed notifying Stevenson and the U.N. about the location of the *Grozny*. RFK, however, again urged "just a minute's discussion" about whether it was advisable to intercept a ship at this moment. The President insisted that the U.N. should be given the *Grozny's* latitude and longitude and told when it would be reaching the quarantine zone. "We don't need to say what we're gonna do about it, but we ought to say this [ship] is approaching and we'd like to have him [U Thant] know about it." RFK and McNamara noted that a decision on U.S. action against the *Grozny* could be safely delayed until around noon on Sunday.

There was no reason to be defensive about this delay, Rusk insisted, since the administration had already moved forward on seven important steps that day, in order "to see whether we're building up the pressures on Khrushchev to get back to a pact [the Friday offer] that we can live with." These actions included: the White House statement on Khrushchev's public message; clarifying the quarantine intercept zone; announcing enforced surveillance; responding to Khrushchev's October 26 message and U Thant's initiative; calling up air reserve squadrons; and warning U Thant on the approach of the *Grozny*. Rusk, with obvious satisfaction, pointed out that these steps were quite significant for only one day, but "tomorrow we'll need to be sure that the pressures [on Khrushchev] continue to build up." JFK declared that once the U.S. announced that Khrushchev's promise to avoid the quarantine zone had been broken, the pressure on the Soviets could be tightened by adding POL to the contraband list and by stopping all ships.

Responding to an inquiry from Rusk, McNamara revealed that the call up of 14,000 air reservists constituted only a small portion of the recent congressional authorization to mobilize 150,000 reserves. Taylor reminded the President about the importance of calling up the ships required for invading Cuba, but JFK repeated that he would prefer to wait at least a day to take that action and also accepted McNamara's advice to postpone calling up the National Guard.

Turning again to the planned Sunday morning meeting of the North Atlantic Council and the pending messages to NATO and Turkey, President Kennedy read aloud a private letter he had received from General Lauris Norstad. The supreme NATO commander advised that Ambassador Finletter should be "brief, factual, . . . cool and skeptical" at the NAC [North Atlantic Council] meeting and should initially avoid suggesting that the President had taken a "firm and final position" on a Turkish missile trade. But, the general also revealed a political sophistication which evidently appealed to the President. Norstad felt that it was essential to get the views of the NATO allies on the record, "In any event, it should help to avoid a situation in which you *can* be wrong *whatever* you do and your allies can be *right* and *wise* regardless of developments"—exactly the point Kennedy himself had made at the earlier ExComm meetings. Norstad nonetheless concluded pragmatically that a NATO Council meeting "will not, I fear, substantially relieve you of the burden of making a difficult decision." The general listed a series of propositions for the President: he rejected equating the missiles in Cuba with the missiles in Turkey; he questioned the wisdom of treating Turkey as a satellite; he warned that although a missile trade might provide "short-term relief, would such action be taken as a sign of weakness?" and he predicted that a missile deal would undermine NATO's confidence in American resolve. He finally urged the President to reject Khrushchev's proposal and to instruct Ambassador Finletter "to indicate this as the general direction of U.S. thinking."

After drafts of the instructions to Finletter were distributed, Rusk questioned "whether it is necessary for the United States to give *its first choice* ("That's right," McCone muttered) at the time that we *first* discuss this problem with NAC." But, Rusk acknowledged, the Council must be consulted and informed that the U.S. might have to take action in Cuba that would create dangers for NATO. The U.S., he summarized, had three alternatives: keeping the Cuban situation entirely distinct from Turkey and rejecting any effort to compromise NATO's defenses; offering McNamara's plan to replace the Jupiters with Polaris;

accepting Ball's recommendation to make a straight trade. "If we were asked," Rusk concluded, "for an *especial* preference, *of course* the preference is one—that we go ahead with this Cuban business without *regard* to bargaining with NATO—but that *NATO* must understand the nature of the risks that are involved for NATO."

The President had argued indefatigably that Khrushchev's public offer could not be rejected and he recommended exerting subtle pressure on NATO: "Well, if you're gonna *really* present it to 'em that way," [indicating that the U.S. preferred to separate Cuba from Turkey], "you wouldn't want it to state a... a position, I don't think, Mr. Secretary, would you, because they'll feel compelled then to agree with that; it sounds sort of *strong* and *firm* and *clear*." The real question, he continued, is whether "we're sure that's the direction we want to *steer* them. I think we can *steer* them in that direction. It's initially the *easiest* position, but I... I... I think we ought to be sure that that's what we *want* to do." Overt pressure might even be counterproductive: "It seems to me though, Mr. Secretary, even if we *want* them to end up that way, we don't want it to look like that's where we *urged* them and therefore they have accepted, some reluctantly, some eagerly, the United States' opinion. Then this goes bad, which it may well, and they say, 'Well, we followed you and you bitched it up.'" In short, President Kennedy wanted to be sure that the allies consulted at the Sunday NAC meeting fully understood the probable military consequences, for them, of rejecting the Turkey-Cuba trade.[322] The NATO allies had to be told, "'This is it! This situation's getting *worse* and we're gonna have to take some action.'" And, if we reject the Cuba-Turkey connection, "then we want everybody to understand that... what we think may be the alternative cause *we're* gonna have to move." The specific hard choices, he felt, could be discussed if necessary at another NAC meeting on Monday morning.

Dillon endorsed the view that the U.S. ought to make clear "that we aren't pushing them *either* way," and Rusk expressed a hope that some members of the NATO Council "may come up with an idea that would unlock this *damn* thing, something that we haven't thought of." He added, with little conviction, "It's *just* possible." But the President reiterated, "with the introduction of Turkey . . . [and] the way it's escalating, they [the U.S.S.R.] *may* hit Turkey or *may* hit Berlin and we

---

[322]Neither Rusk nor JFK, of course, mentioned the secret arrangement agreed upon in the Oval Office just before RFK's private meeting with Dobrynin.

want them [NATO]... if they want to get off, then *now* is the time to speak up."

Recognizing the lingering uncertainty and division in the ExComm over the Turkish missiles, McNamara asked bluntly, "Mr. President, do we believe that we will be able to settle Cuba more easily with or without the Jupiters in Turkey? I think we ought to decide this point, before we—open a door to NATO—to make up our own minds." RFK cut in, rather irritably, before JFK could answer: "Can't we wait? Isn't it possible to get through tomorrow at three or four o'clock without even getting into the NATO, with the Turkey business?" The attorney general, always concerned about exposing weakness, predicted that "if they [the Soviets] find us playin' around and figuring on Turkey, and accept we're willing to make some deal; if I were they, I'd *push* on that, and then I'd *push* on [the Jupiters in] Italy."

Instead, RFK urged yet again, trying to get Khrushchev back to his October 26 offer by waiting another 18–24 hours and remaining "*hard* and tough on this. We call up these planes tonight and then we wait and we find out if U Thant's successful." But, even the hawkish attorney general, undoubtedly mindful of the secret understanding on the Turkish missiles reached by the small group in the Oval Office earlier that evening as well as his own discussion with Dobrynin shortly thereafter, acknowledged that if U Thant is "not successful and the whole thing looks like it's collapsing and we're gonna have to go in there," then we go to the NATO allies with the Turkish proposal despite our preference to keep the issue "completely in the Western Hemisphere." And explain to them, Bundy added, that "we had an obligation to consult with you" about the Soviets "raising this irrelevancy [the Cuba-Turkey missile swap]." "And one day [delaying air strikes until Tuesday], I can't believe," RFK insisted, "it's gonna make that much difference."

RFK strongly recommended that Finletter should remain noncommittal at the NATO Council meeting, which he assumed would be seriously divided, and simply inform the allies that a U-2 had probably been shot down, air squadrons had been called up and ships might soon be mobilized as well and also disclose the messages relayed through John Scali and others. Most importantly, he concluded that Finletter should emphasize that "'the President is *very* reasonable.'" But, if the Russians rejected the U.S. acceptance of their Friday message and still insisted on their latest offer involving Turkey, NATO must be given an opportunity to make a decision affecting their own security.

The attorney general, despite his secret offer to Dobrynin, still seemed to be anticipating, if not hoping, that Khrushchev might say "nyet" and NATO, in response, would decide, "We want to hold fast, and then on Tuesday we go into" Cuba.

JFK asked Bundy and Sorensen to draw up instructions for Finletter "based on what Bobby said," directing the ambassador to "take the temperature" in NATO without overtly pressuring the allies to adopt any position. Rusk observed hopefully, "I think Finletter ought to have, or has, some ideas about... about the alternatives." President Kennedy's position, however, on the Turkish missile withdrawal remained far less ambivalent than RFK's—the European allies must be prepared, he stressed again, "for a *disaster* to NATO later in the week in Berlin or someplace. You ought to be *saying* to them that if... the reason we're consulting with them is that the situation's deteriorating [in Cuba] and *if we take action* we think there *will* be reprisals..." RFK suggested sending "somebody that's been involved in these discussions" to the NAC gathering to "explain all of this," but Bundy pointed out that the meeting was only seven hours away. "Is it?" the surprised President replied.

Sorensen wondered if the NATO Council should take up "the military question. Have... ask them to examine how valuable *are* the Jupiters." McNamara strenuously resisted opening that discussion, "they may split up, and you may have chaos." No one at the table could doubt what President Kennedy thought NATO should do—in its own best interests. At the same time, he decided that instructions to U.S. ambassadors to the NATO countries should regard any discussions of the Jupiters as "for your eyes" only in order to avoid leaks which might compromise ongoing negotiations with the Russians about Khrushchev's conflicting messages. Bundy agreed that the message "should *not* be related to the Soviet proposal but *to* the [diplomatic/military] situation."

President Kennedy and his advisers, regardless of their significant differences over removing the Turkish missiles, recognized that events could quickly reach a flashpoint at the quarantine line or in the air over Cuba within hours. McCone, for that reason, tried to redirect attention to his proposed tough note to Khrushchev "on this provocation"—shooting down the U-2. A consensus quickly developed for continuing the reconnaissance flights without additional announcements. "We've got enough messages right now, John," the President gently told the CIA director. "I think that he [Khrushchev] knows about the plane.

We've announced it." Sorensen was more blunt, "I think in some ways it's a sign of weakness if we just keep responding in messages." President Kennedy agreed, "I think we shouldn't send him one again," concluding instead that the more immediate danger was whether the Soviets would turn the *Grozny* around before it reached the quarantine line. He also recommended, after some initial uncertainty, sending letters to the leaders of Britain, France and West Germany, "because it involves Berlin, more or less giving the resume of what the situation is." JFK was especially concerned about de Gaulle's reaction, because "his view is *key* in this."

"What about the Turks now?" JFK asked again. "What do we gotta say to [Ambassador] Hare?" The President seemed uneasy about relaying precise instructions to the ambassador in Turkey. "It seems to me that on Hare, if we don't wanna try to get the Russians off the Turkish trade then we probably don't wanna do anything with Hare for 24 hours 'til we get some sort of an answer [from Khrushchev]." However, undoubtedly realizing that not everyone in the room knew about the confidential consensus reached in the Oval Office between the last two meetings to "unofficially" offer withdrawal of the Jupiters from Turkey, and that only Rusk knew about the secret Andrew Cordier initiative, JFK became cagey and ambiguous. "Let's give him [Hare] an explanation of what we're tryin' to do. We're tryin' to get it *back* on the original proposition of last night and a... because we don't wanna get into this trade. If we're *unsuccessful*, then we... it's *possible* that we may have to get *back* onto the Jupiter thing. If we *do*, then we would of course want it to come from the Turks themselves and NATO, rather than just the United States. We're *hopeful*, however," JFK observed somewhat disingenuously, having already acted secretly to conditionally accept Khrushchev's public proposal on Turkey, "that that won't come. If it does, his judgment on the... how should it be handled with the Turks, if we're... if we're prepared to do the Polaris and others, does he think this thing [the trade] can be made? We'll be in touch with him in 24 hours when we find out if we are successful in putting the Russians back on the original track. It seems to me that's about what we want to say to Hare today."

At that point, people began gathering their papers and getting up from the table as the discussion started to break up. The President decided after all to only send messages to de Gaulle and Adenauer since he had already written to Macmillan that evening. McNamara, however, insisted that a decision on tomorrow's low-level reconnaissance missions had to be made soon. "We'll do that by tomorrow morning," JFK replied, "*or* when they *say* they've shot down our U-2. If they *say* they shot it down... then that raises..." But McNamara exhorted the President, "This time... this time we would make it *perfectly* clear if they attack our aircraft, we're going in after some of their MiGs." "Yeah, but we *won't* do the ground thing," against the SAMs and the antiaircraft batteries, JFK cautioned. "I think we oughta save that for a *real* operation which under this schedule you wouldn't do until Tuesday morning, because we'll have to go back to NATO again Monday in which we say the situation is getting worse and so on and so forth and give them their *last* chance"—to avoid an attack by removing the Jupiters.

The defense secretary also raised another difficult subject—preparing an interim civil government for Cuba "in case we *do* shoot up Cuba." The President asked if anyone was working on that problem and McNamara mentioned a task force, suggesting, "we ought to take the time tomorrow to talk about that." RFK, referring to the President's September 30 decision to send federal troops and marshals to Oxford, Mississippi to put down a riot sparked by the attempted enrollment of James Meredith, a black Air Force veteran, at the University of Mississippi, quipped that the Army might soon be going from Mississippi to Cuba. After some mixed laughter and conversation, the President joked, "Well, I just wanted to go to Boston," and soon left the Cabinet Room.

A few ExComm members remained during the following exchange:

"How you doing, Bob?" RFK teased the defense chief.

"Well," McNamara joked, "how about yourself?"

"All right," RFK replied.

"Got any doubts?" McNamara asked.

"No," RFK responded, "I think we're doin' the only thing we can do, and so on, you know."

"I think the one thing, Bobby," McNamara added, "we must *surely* do is before... before we attack them, you've gotta be *damned sure they* [the U.S.S.R.] *understand it's coming*. In other words, you need to *really* escalate this."

"Yeah," RFK murmured.

"And then we need to have two things ready," McNamara observed, "a government for Cuba, because we're gonna need one after we go in with 500 aircraft. And secondly, some plans for how to respond to the Soviet Union in Europe, cause *sure as hell* they're gonna do *something* there."

Dillon suggested that even "the smallest thing" the Soviets might try in Europe could aggravate tensions. But, McNamara vividly advised restraint:

"*I* would suggest *a half* an eye for an eye."

"That's right," Dillon agreed.

"If it isn't too serious an attack," McNamara added as a qualification.

"Yeah, that would do it," Dillon muttered.

"I'd like to take Cuba back," RFK interposed wistfully. "That would be nice."

"Yeah," McCone asserted, "and I'd take Cuba away from Castro."

Several participants then joked about "all of [Operation] Mongoose," and someone wise-cracked, amidst laughter, "Yeah, how are they gonna partition that [Cuba]?" Someone else teased, "Well, suppose they make Bobby mayor of Havana?" provoking even more laughter.

"...that's something you're going to get undone tomorrow," Dillon quipped.

The tape recorder, which probably ran out of tape, suddenly cut off—ending one of the toughest days of the Cuban missile crisis and one of the most riveting documents in American history. Several members of ExComm spent restless or sleepless nights in their offices.

The instructions to Ambassador Finletter and NATO, exhaustively debated at the last two ExComm meetings, were cabled just after midnight. The message warned that "the situation as we see it is increasingly serious and time is growing shorter" and concluded that military action might be necessary "within a very short time . . . to remove this growing threat to the Hemisphere."

Just after 6:00 A.M., the CIA provided solid evidence to back up this pessimistic forecast—Soviet technicians had rushed all twenty-four MRBM sites to operational status. The Soviets also knew that the Strategic Air Command had already targeted nearly six dozen Russian cities for nuclear attack. "The situation was fraught with dangers of slipping out of control."[323]

[323]Chang and Kornbluh, *Cuban Missile Crisis*, 391; Garthoff, *Reflections*, 96.

*By early on Sunday morning October 28, Moscow time, Khrushch-
ev, "in complete control of the Soviet leadership" had made up his
mind without pressure from Kremlin hardliners: the danger was simply
too great. "Anyone with an ounce of sense," Khrushchev later wrote,
"can see I'm telling the truth. It would have been preposterous for us
to unleash a war against the United States from Cuba. Cuba was
11,000 kilometers from the Soviet Union. Our sea and air communications with Cuba were so precarious that an attack against the US was
unthinkable." "Remove them," the Soviet leader ordered, "as soon as
possible. Before something terrible happens." He promptly sent an order to General Pliyev, "Allow no one near the missiles. Obey no orders
to launch and under no circumstances install the warheads." In addition, the previous week's authorization to use tactical nuclear weapons
without a direct order from Moscow was reversed. Khrushchev, in the
presence of his son, Sergei, in effect told his foreign minister, "'Comrade Gromyko, we don't have the right to take risks. Once the president announces there will be an invasion, he won't be able to reverse
himself. We have to let Kennedy know that we want to help him.' Father hesitated at the word 'help' but after a moment's silence repeated
firmly, 'Yes, help. We now have a common cause, to save the world
from those pushing us toward war.'" He instructed Gromyko to direct
Ambassador Dobrynin to contact Robert Kennedy at once and tell him
that a reply to the President's message would arrive shortly, "Emphasize that the answer is a positive one."*[324]

*The Kremlin had received a report from the Soviet embassy in
Washington that President Kennedy had scheduled a television address
on Sunday afternoon—in all probability, they assumed, to announce an
invasion of Cuba. In fact, the broadcast was simply a repeat of JFK's
October 22 blockade speech. Soviet leaders, however, had little understanding of a free media and assumed that the telecast of a presidential
speech had originated at the highest levels in Washington. Khrushchev
decided, as a result, not to risk sending his message through the cumbersome and unreliable channels for transmitting diplomatic messages
between national leaders, but instead, to broadcast it immediately over
Moscow radio. "This was an unusual, perhaps unprecedented, step in
international practice, but an effective one. The answer would be on
the President's desk in just a few minutes. It was widely known that*

---

[324]Fursenko and Naftali, *"One Hell of a Gamble,"* 273, 276–77; Talbott, ed., *Khrushchev: The Last Testament,* 511; Sergei Khrushchev, *Nikita Khrushchev,* 626–30.

American radio intercept services were very efficient and very fast."[325]
*At around noon in Moscow, the Soviet government alerted the United
States embassy that an official diplomatic message was imminent.*

*In Washington, President Kennedy was preparing to attend 10
o'clock Mass at St. Stephen's Church when intelligence sources reported that the Grozny had come to a complete stop in the water before reaching the quarantine line. John McCone had gone to Mass an
hour earlier after hearing on his car radio that the Kremlin would
shortly make a significant announcement; he later joked that it seemed
like the most interminable Mass he had ever sat through. JFK reacted
to Khrushchev's message with surprise, relief and some skepticism. The
Soviets, after all, had systematically deceived the United States about
putting the missiles in Cuba and Gromyko had personally lied to the
President on October 18. It seemed entirely possible that the announcement might be a trick.*

*The Joint Chiefs remained extremely suspicious, warning the Presi-
dent that the announcement was an effort "to delay direct action by
the United States while preparing the ground for diplomatic blackmail." They also urged JFK to order sweeping air strikes in Cuba in 24
hours, followed by an invasion, unless irrefutable evidence proved that
the missile sites were being dismantled. General Taylor dissented, but
agreed to transmit the recommendation to the Secretary of Defense. "I
can assure you," the JCS chairman later remembered, "that if I was
classified as a hawk in the arena of the Executive Committee, I was
definitely viewed as a dove in the arena of the Joint Chiefs of Staff."
Admiral Anderson moaned, "We have been had." General LeMay denounced the agreement as "the greatest defeat in our history" and
banged the table demanding, "We should invade today!" McNamara
later recalled that JFK was so stunned by LeMay's outburst that he
could only stutter in response. The President later remarked, "The first
advice I'm going to give my successor is to watch the generals and to
avoid feeling that because they were military men their opinions on
military matters were worth a damn."*[326]

[325]Sergei Khrushchev to Sheldon M. Stern, October 2, 2001; Zubok and Pleshakov, *Inside the Kremlin's Cold War*, 267; Sergei Khrushchev, *Nikita Khrushchev*, xiv.

[326]May and Zelikow, *The Kennedy Tapes*, 635; Chang and Kornbluh, *Cuban Missile
Crisis*, 392; Taylor Oral History, 57; Beschloss, *The Crisis Years*, 544; Benjamin Bradlee,
Conversations With Kennedy (New York: W.W. Norton, 1975), 122; President Kennedy
"never felt closer to Khrushchev than when he imagined him having to cope with a Curtis
LeMay of his own." (Freedman, *Kennedy's Wars*, 208)

By the time JFK returned from St. Stephen's a groundswell of elation had overwhelmed the White House. Nuclear war had apparently been averted. One participant described the mood as "a miasma of self-congratulation."[327] *McCone, however, reminded his colleagues that many issues remained unresolved—such as inspection and verification, the presence of MiG fighters and IL-28 nuclear bombers, defined as "offensive" weapons by the United States, and the precise terms of the American non-invasion pledge.*

Sunday, October 28, about 11:00 A.M., Cabinet Room

Identified Participants: John F. Kennedy, McGeorge Bundy, Robert Kennedy, John McCone, Robert McNamara, Dean Rusk, Maxwell Taylor. Additional members of ExComm likely attended as well.[328]

"Now in this situation, I mean, there's some... there's some gratification for everyone's line of action, except 'do nothing.'"

Secretary of State Dean Rusk

Before the meeting began, the President and the ExComm read the full text of Khrushchev's message offering to withdraw the missiles in Cuba under U.N. supervision. JFK turned on the tape recorder as Dean Rusk commended the President and the ExComm for a job well done. He recalled President Kennedy's sardonic remark at an earlier meeting "that whichever line of action you adopt, those who were in favor of it were gonna regret it" because there were really no satisfactory choices. "Now in this situation, I mean, there's some... there's some gratification," he continued, "for everyone's line of action, except [advocates of] 'do nothing.'" The secretary of state concluded that those who favored invading Cuba had backed the course that "turned out to be the major quid pro quo for getting these weapons out of Cuba." But, just as he mentioned those who supported air strikes, the tape suddenly cut off.[329]

---

[327]Brugioni, *Eyeball to Eyeball*, 489.

[328]Tapes 43.0A & 43.1, POF, PRC, JFKL.

[329]Philip Zelikow, *et al.*, eds., *John F. Kennedy: The Great Crises*, speculate, "At this point, perhaps finding the self-congratulation tiresome after hearing only a few seconds of it, President Kennedy switched off the tape recorder. He left it off for the rest of the meeting." (v. 3, 518) This explanation seems unconvincing since JFK wanted these tapes for writing his memoirs and had every reason to preserve these remarks—even if he later decided to ignore them or perhaps poke fun at them. Allan Goodrich, senior audiovisual ar-

"Bundy interrupted to say that everyone knew who were hawks and who were doves, but that today was the doves' day." McNamara reported that *"we would not have to face a decision on halting a Bloc ship today"* because the Grozny *"was lying dead in the water outside the quarantine zone and no other Bloc ships, if they continued toward Cuba, would be reaching the barrier."* Rusk and McNamara recommended, and the President agreed, *"that no air reconnaissance missions be flown today."*[330]

JFK, obviously concerned about potential Soviet treachery, *"asked what we would substitute for our air surveillance of Cuba."* McNamara suggested U.N. or joint U.S.-U.N. surveillance *"in a neutral plane, flown by Brazilians or Canadians."* The President insisted that *"every effort be made to get the U.N. to fly reconnaissance missions Monday"* and he authorized *"the release to U.N. officials of classified information on Soviet armaments in Cuba,"* including photographs and refugee reports, *"to facilitate the inspection task which we expected the U.N. to promptly undertake."* He also *"suggested that we tell the U.N. they must carry out reconnaissance or else we will."*[331]

JFK also approved a public statement *"welcoming the Soviet decision to withdraw offensive weapons from Cuba."* Rusk reported that Vasily Kuznetsov, first deputy minister of foreign affairs, was coming to New York to conduct the negotiations. The President cautioned all those talking to the press *"to be reserved in all comment"* in order to strengthen Khrushchev's position against sniping by Soviet hawks or his Cuban allies. *"Although we welcome Khrushchev's reply,"* JFK advised, *"we are under no illusions nor can we reach any general conclusions about how the Russians will act in the future in areas other than Cuba. Khrushchev's decision has yet to be implemented and many serious problems will be encountered in the withdrawal of Soviet weapons from Cuba."* He specifically mentioned the problem of communist subversion in Latin America and directed that Ambassador Stevenson should raise this question with U.N. officials.[332]

---

chivist at the Kennedy Library, believes that JFK could have accidentally hit the on/off switch while drumming his fingers under the table—a nervous habit often observed by his colleagues. (Conversation with Allan Goodrich, September 27, 2001) The content of the rest of the meeting was fortunately preserved in two sets of written notes.

[330]Bromley Smith, Summary Record of NSC Executive Committee Meeting No. 10, October 28, 1962, 11:10 AM, NSF, JFKL, 1; McGeorge Bundy, NSC Executive Committee Record of Action, October 28, 1962, 11:00 AM, Meeting No. 10, NSF, JFKL, 1.

[331]Smith, *Ibid.*; Bundy, *Ibid.*

[332]Smith, *Ibid.*, 1, 2; Bundy, *Ibid.*

Finally, President Kennedy urged a private approach to Khrushchev on removing the IL-28 bombers but cautioned that the U.S. "should not get hung up on this issue." General Taylor recommended that "our objective should be the status quo ante." JFK agreed "but added that he did not want to get into a position where we would appear to be going back on our part of the deal. The IL-28 bombers were less important than the strategic missiles." He also directed that a formal reply to Khrushchev be drafted immediately. The President approved the message later in the day and it was released to the press at 4:35 P.M.[333]

Around noon, shortly after the ExComm meeting ended, JFK phoned former Presidents Dwight Eisenhower, Harry Truman and Herbert Hoover—and deliberately misinformed his three predecessors. He accurately reported that Khrushchev had privately suggested on Friday withdrawing the Cuban missiles in exchange for an American promise not to invade Cuba, but then sent a public message early on Saturday offering to remove the missiles if the U.S. pulled its Jupiters out of Turkey. But, President Kennedy informed Eisenhower, "we couldn't get into that [Turkey] deal," told Hoover that Khrushchev had gone back "to their more reasonable [Friday] position" and assured Truman, "we rejected that. Then they came back with and accepted the earlier proposal." Eisenhower, who had dealt personally with Khrushchev, seemed skeptical and asked if the Soviets had tried to attach any other conditions. "No," Kennedy replied disingenuously, "except that we're not gonna invade Cuba." Ike was concerned that Khrushchev might try to extract an American commitment that "one day could be very embarrassing." But, the former President, knowing only half the truth, concluded, "this is a very, I think, conciliatory move he's made."[334] *Such deceptions shaped the administration's cover story and inevitably helped to generate the "Trollope Ploy" myth. The full story of the secret Turkish missile arrangement would not become public until long after the deaths of these four presidents.*

Castro heard the news of Khrushchev's decision over the radio in Havana. The Cuban leader flew into a rage over not being consulted, cursing the Soviet leader as a "son of a bitch, bastard, asshole." Castro spoke at the University of Havana several days later and publicly ridiculed Khrushchev for lacking the "cojones" (balls) for a final showdown with American imperialism. He also demanded an end to the

[333]Smith, *Ibid.*, 2; Bundy, *Ibid.*
[334]Cassette L, Side 1, Dictabelts 41.2, 41.3 & 41.4, POF, PRC, JFKL.

Sunday, October 28   389

U.S. economic embargo against Cuba, the cessation of aerial reconnaissance, a halt to exile attacks and the withdrawal of American forces from the Guantanamo naval base.[335]

Soviet personnel in Cuba received instructions within hours to start dismantling the missile bases and the work reportedly began by 5:00 P.M. on Sunday. A cable from the Kremlin received at the Soviet embassy in Havana contended that the U.S.S.R. had chosen to avoid a "global conflagration" but would not abandon "its international duty to defend . . . the Cuban revolution." Later that evening, John Scali met again with Aleksandr Fomin, who told the ABC reporter, "I am under instructions to thank you. The information you provided Chairman Khrushchev was most helpful to him in making up his mind quickly. And that includes your explosion of Saturday."[336]

President Kennedy, after scheduling a 10:00 o'clock ExComm meeting for Monday morning, October 29, left the White House to join his wife and children at their private retreat, Glen Ora, in the Virginia countryside. He had reportedly written just five words on the pad left on his desk, "Berlin, Berlin, Berlin, Berlin, Berlin."[337]

Radio Moscow praised Khrushchev for frustrating the Pentagon and saving world peace by securing American guarantees against invading Cuba.[338] Kuznetsov met on Monday morning with U Thant at U.N. headquarters in New York to finalize details on dismantling the bases and removing the missiles from Cuba. The Soviet envoy agreed to report directly to the Security Council "which would then authorize a U.N. team to visit Cuba for 'on-site' inspection." Meanwhile, an interdepartmental task force met at the Defense Department to begin planning for the prompt withdrawal of the Jupiter missiles from Turkey. In Moscow, the Presidium voted to send Anastas Mikoyan, first deputy chairman of the Council of Ministers, to Havana to negotiate with Castro about Cuba's part in implementing the settlement—particularly in setting up on-site inspection and verification by the United Nations.[339]

[335]Blight, et al., Cuba on the Brink, 23; Fursenko and Naftali, "One Hell of a Gamble," 288–89; Chang and Kornbluh, Cuban Missile Crisis, 392.

[336]Chang and Kornbluh, 392–93.

[337]Brugioni, Eyeball to Eyeball, 491.

[338]Ambassador Thompson had remarked at the October 27th 4:00 P.M. meeting that Khrushchev would be able to say, "I saved Cuba. I stopped an invasion."

[339]Chang and Kornbluh, Cuban Missile Crisis, 393; Garthoff, Reflections, 99. For an account of Mikoyan's mission as documented in Soviet archives, see Fursenko and Naftali, "One Hell of a Gamble," 290–315.

Monday, October 29, about 10:00 A.M., Cabinet Room

Identified Participants: John F. Kennedy, McGeorge Bundy, Marshall Carter, Joseph Charyk, Douglas Dillon, Roswell Gilpatric, John McCone, Robert McNamara, Paul Nitze, Dean Rusk, Maxwell Taylor, Llewellyn Thompson.[340]

"This photography will tell us much more than *his* words. He doesn't know *what the hell to look for*, any more than *I would*."

President John F. Kennedy

McCone's intelligence briefing began with a report that the Soviets might be continuing work on the Cuban missile bases—underscoring continued uncertainty, apprehension and suspicion by the President and the ExComm. Barely 24 hours after Khrushchev's surprise Sunday morning announcement, no one could really be sure that the crisis was irrevocably moving toward a peaceful resolution. As the tape began, the CIA director, reading from a prepared text, provided new information about deteriorating relations between Communist China and the Soviet Union, "The Chinese Communists sent a note to the Cuban ambassador in Peiping implying that the U.S.S.R. was an untrustworthy ally" because Moscow had been refusing to give China technical information on the production of nuclear arms since 1959. "This is a year earlier than the previous estimates." He also discussed the ongoing Sino-Indian War, the testing of nuclear missiles in the U.S.S.R. and Brazilian diplomatic contacts with Castro.

At that point, President Kennedy returned to the subject of Cuba, reading his announcement establishing a Coordinating Committee "to give full time and attention to the matters involved in the conclusion of the Cuban crisis."[341] Rusk raised the critical issues of resuming aerial surveillance, which had been suspended on Sunday, and effectively maintaining the quarantine. He advised deferring a final decision on surveillance until "we get some reading out on whether Kuznetsov is throwing in some *major* monkey wrenches into this thing" during his meeting with U Thant later in the morning. "I *do* think we need surveillance today," he counseled, but urged waiting to decide "how many, what kind, where, after we find out . . . what Kuznetsov is up

[340]Tape 43.2, POF, PRC, JFKL.

[341]The committee, John McCloy (chair), George Ball and Roswell Gilpatric, acted under the supervision of Dean Rusk, Robert McNamara and Adlai Stevenson, who reported to the President.

to," especially since the CIA had concluded, contrary to McCone's earlier assertion, "that there does not appear to be much danger that the Soviets will attempt to delay implementation of the final dismantling of sites."

President Kennedy acknowledged the importance of conducting surveillance Monday or Tuesday, but seemed more concerned about "the longer-range problem." He recommended that the coordinating committee meet right away to determine, "How are we gonna maintain a satisfactory degree of knowledge about Cuba? We can't rely on the U.N. to do it." McNamara agreed that this was "a *very* difficult problem," and asked for comments from Joseph Charyk, under secretary of the Air Force, who had discussed this issue with U Thant and his military adviser, Indian General Indar Jit Rikhye. Charyk revealed that the U.S. had offered to make available to the U.N., by that morning, an RC-130 camera-equipped aircraft "which *is* painted white with the U.N. insignia." Rikhye seemed willing to use an American plane but had "*grave* concern as to the use of an American air crew." In any case, he had been unable to finalize arrangements for qualified crews from Canada, South Africa or Indonesia to conduct U.N. observer flights later that day. "Rikhye's nationality is what?" JFK asked. "Indian," Charyk replied. In addition, he reported that U Thant should be in Cuba within 24 hours and U.N. observers would be flown "to the sites to observe the actual status of the dismantling operation." Rikhye had also told Charyk that with U.N. observers on the scene, "it was incomprehensible that the Soviets would fail to comply with their commitment to dismantle" and insisted that it would be "*most* unfortunate" if the U.S. conducted surveillance flights while U Thant was in Cuba.

JFK raised a very pertinent issue, "How long is the Secretary General gonna be there?" Tuesday and Wednesday, Charyk replied. The Air Force undersecretary also revealed that Rikhye had suggested "a voluntary suspension of the blockade on Tuesday, simultaneous with the arrival of the Secretary General," during which U.S. ships would remain in place and report suspicious ships to U.N. inspectors stationed at Cuban ports. The U.N. personnel would check the "ships with which we were primarily concerned" for prohibited items and then report back on the results of the inspections. Rikhye also urged keeping Kuznetsov informed on all U.S. decisions relating to reconnaissance and the quarantine.

The conditions and limitations proposed by United Nations officials quickly exposed the depths of distrust of the Soviet Union and the U.N. by the President and his advisers. McNamara urged Kennedy to send out surveillance missions late that afternoon, after notifying Kuznetsov and the Cuban U.N. ambassador, and to direct the new Coordinating Committee "to work out detailed plans for continuing reconnaissance." On the quarantine, Rusk was even more blunt, "Mr. President, I *do* think that we have to keep emphasizing that the measures that we've been... that we have taken are to continue into effect until U.N. machinery can effectively replace them." "Exactly," McNamara affirmed. "Because if we give up *that* point," Rusk warned, "we may be subject to a *massive* trick here." JFK and McNamara agreed that the statement to Kuznetsov should make clear that U.S. ships would remain on station and continue to challenge vessels as required.

Kennedy also objected to any long-range surveillance plan which excluded Americans, at least as observers, from the missions, "This is one of those things the [Coordinating] Committee ought to do. We ought to be *very hard*," he contended, "that there's gonna be an American on that plane." The President endorsed "weekly flights or twice-weekly flights for an *indefinite* period, with an Amer... at least an American aboard who has to know how to operate the camera"—with a copy of the film later going to the United States. "That would be one of the conditions." The President also observed that aerial reconnaissance was "the least obtrusive . . . to the sovereignty of Cuba because any... one way or another it's gonna be inspected," and he predicted that "they'll probably insist that a Cuban may be on this plane." McNamara noted that Rikhye would be happy to have a Cuban and a Russian on board; Ball, McCone and several others cautioned that in any case aerial surveillance could only be a supplement to effective ground inspection.

The conversation then turned to several other unresolved military/diplomatic issues. First: JFK anticipated that reporters would ask Pierre Salinger about the status of the quarantine, "I think we ought to say, 'Our ships are on station,' and... and leave it just at that... just try to leave it that ambiguous, I would think, for the next 24 hours." Rusk and JFK finally agreed on saying that ships remained on station pending United Nations arrangements. Second: the President asked McNamara if the Saturday call up of 24 Air Reserve squadrons should be reversed and the defense secretary insisted that no change should be made at that time. Third: JFK, rather irritably, urged the Coordinating Committee to refuse to accept the exclusion of Americans from the group traveling to Cuba with U Thant, "We said we'll let a Russian go, but let's have an American in there. If we *can't* get an American, then we shouldn't have a Russian." Fourth: McNamara raised the problem of continuing Cuban "covert aggression" in Latin America. The President mentioned that he had discussed language on curbing subversion with Ambassador Stevenson, but concluded gloomily, "if they begin to continue what they did in Venezuela, we're gonna be doing things."[342] Rusk quickly agreed, "If these fellows cause trouble, we'd have to cause trouble there." "Why doesn't Ros and George [Gilpatric and Ball] leave right now" to join Stevenson at the U.N., the President urged. "The quicker you get up there the better, I think."[343]

"We have prepared," Taylor also reported, "to go to observe *all* the offensive weapons sites that we've been looking at," and the President asked whether surveillance would be carried out by a high-level U-2. Taylor explained that low-level flights were preferable. Rusk speculated that U-2 flights would be less politically provocative and better suited technically to discover "if they're building... if they're digging a hole nearby to bury some of these *damn things* before the U.N. gets there." McNamara acknowledged the political risks from low-level missions but sided with Taylor, who argued that U-2s would not be effective because of cloud cover, and instead recommended 6–8 low-level missions to get adequately detailed pictures. "There isn't any doubt that it's a hazard," President Kennedy acknowledged, "not to the planes so much as politically a hazard." He again questioned, "What is the advantage of it?" Taylor reiterated that new photographs were the only way to test "the bona fides of the... of the Soviet government," since photography from Friday into Saturday had revealed work on the sites going on "just as intensively." "Well that would be natural though, wouldn't it?" JFK reasoned. He nevertheless agreed that the U.S. had to determine whether the Soviet pattern of work had changed from Sunday to Monday. "From Saturday until Monday afternoon," McNamara insisted, reminding the President that there had been no missions on Sunday. Taylor, evidently doubtful about the reliability of

[342]Venezuelan communists, just two days earlier, had responded to an appeal from Castro by bombing power stations owned by U.S. oil companies and destroying or damaging one-sixth of Venezuela's oil refining capacity. (Garthoff, *Reflections*, 89; May and Zelikow, *The Kennedy Tapes*, 638–39). The Cubans, in the event of a U.S. invasion, were preparing for guerrilla warfare: "the United States would suffer retribution within its own borders. Cuba would bring war and destruction to American homes and to American interests and citizens abroad." (Amuchastegui, "Cuban Intelligence and the October Crisis," 98–99)

[343]Gilpatric and Ball did not actually leave for about 10 more minutes.

U.N. ground observers, asserted that low-level flights, rather than a mere supplement to on-site inspections, would actually "have to be the backbone of our surveillance."

"Have we got a longer-range plan," JFK probed again, "on how we can survey this place through other means?" Paul Nitze jumped in to urge a tough stance on surveillance until the U.N. took over. "You could exploit the thing that U Thant said to Cuba: after all, 'you don't have to... you Cubans don't have to fear photographs, the way you fear... should fear a bomb.'" Nitze urged the President to resume reconnaissance today, "This is why I have... I have a hesitation about saying we're gonna do this *pending* U.N. substitution. Therefore, I think we ought to *attack* the general *principle* of the *propriety* of surveillance." JFK asked if Khrushchev had specifically mentioned halting low-flying reconnaissance in his October 28 message, but Rusk, backed by Nitze, countered, "He expressed a wish on that. But he didn't make it a condition, you see, just a wish."

"If it would help any," Taylor suggested, "we could offer to have U.N. observers be with us while we process the film," but JFK doubted that they would want to get involved. Rusk warned, quite presciently as it turned out, "U Thant has two big hurdles to get over to bring this thing [inspection] home: one is Kuznetsov and the other is Castro. And he's gonna have, I think, more trouble with Castro perhaps than Kuznetsov. And a... so we've got to think a little bit about that." Nitze suggested informing the Soviets and the Cubans privately about the flights without making any public announcement. "And save their face?" Dillon asked; "And save their face," Nitze agreed, "and it will give us more flexibility in how to work this thing out."

"That may be a good... I... I agree with you about that," JFK interposed. He added, however, that Kuznetsov would have to be informed in advance since the decision might otherwise appear to be a reversal of Sunday's announcement suspending surveillance. "We don't wanna *bitch* this thing up, just to... to do a... just to do a flight." "Vis-à-vis Castro," Dillon observed, "it might be helpful to do this." But, the mention of the wild card represented by Castro prompted President Kennedy to ask again about the dangers to low-level flights, "He [Castro] fires at our plane. Now what do we do then?" McNamara countered that firing was much more likely to come from the "Soviet antiaircraft batteries around the missile sites." "Well, tell me again now General," the President persisted, "tell me why they [low-level flights] are so important?" "To find out," General Taylor declared, "whether the Soviets *really* mean what they told you in the letter—whether they stopped work." JFK replied uncertainly, "Well, they haven't been able to do much yet."

Ambassador Thompson also defended the flights as the only way to confirm that the Soviets were keeping their word on dismantling the sites. "We want to *see* that," Taylor murmured in the background. "U Thant's guess," McNamara explained, "was that by Wednesday, when his inspectors arrive at the sites, there will be no missiles available to be inspected. I think he's probably right. And if that's *true* we should *certainly* see a lot of *change* between Saturday and today."

JFK, obviously mindful of Taylor's concern about the competence of U.N. ground observers, asked the general if he thought U Thant could really judge "whether there's any dismantling because he... he won't have sophisticated enough people with him." The JCS chief again insisted that "the air photograph" was indispensable and the President bluntly declared, "This photography will tell us much more than *his* words. He doesn't know *what the hell* to look for any more than *I would*. Unless we know that there are technical people on this mission in whom we have confidence, we really need that photographed at our own lens." "You'd need an army," McNamara began, but Gilpatric finished the sentence, "to cover all of the sites, to take all of the pictures." McNamara, rather skeptically, noted that U Thant's "total U.N. force," flying to Cuba in a small Caravel aircraft, could be no more than 10–15 people. "Well," the President replied, "I think that you [Gilpatric] and George [Ball] on the way up [to the U.N.] ought to be thinking about what it is that we do with the limitations of U Thant" and this whole U.N. operation.

The meeting broke up into multiple conversations as several participants tried to arrange transportation to return to their offices. President Kennedy, no longer at his regular seat, asked if U Thant could provide "some assurances on the photographs" by Wednesday. He seemed genuinely worried that Khrushchev's offer to withdraw the missiles might still unravel. "We're not sure *ourselves* that we can get the photography *today*. So they're going ahead with the work. Well then, that means the whole deal *blows*. Whether it blows today or Wednesday, we're gonna be faced with the same problem, generally."

McNamara attempted to summarize three key points about the continuing surveillance problems: First, he declared, "I *don't* believe there'll be U.N. reconnaissance flights. I think it's almost *impossible* the way they're working and talking." Second, he maintained that "we

need to show our people that we're properly protecting their interests."
Third, he admitted that it would be useful, but not essential, to know
what had happened on the missile bases between Saturday and Monday. Rusk was somewhat more upbeat, citing encouraging political
signs such as the tension between China and the U.S.S.R. mentioned
earlier by McCone, "So, I'm not... I'm not discouraged *yet* about the
possible... this may be for real." "I think they're gonna *dismantle* these
things now," JFK contended. The Soviets might hide some mobile missiles in the woods, but "There's no *logic* to their going *ahead* now with
the construction with U Thant arrives Tuesday and Wednesday to be
broadcast. I think what we'll find is a cessation of work."

On the other hand, finding a way to resolve the long-range surveillance problem, the President repeated, "*That* is *essential*! *Today's* mission, in my opinion, is *not* as important. It's the *this week's* mission
that is important. . . . So I think that U Thant has to give us the assurances that he is going to have, this week, photographic reconnaissance,
or we're gonna do it ourselves." "Mr. President," McNamara warned
again, "*I* don't think we're gonna have U.N. reconnaissance capabili-
ties develop without *tremendous* pressure from us. . . . they're not...
they're not *at all* interested and they're *particularly* not interested in
doing it in any *practical* way." In that case, JFK finally declared, let's
tell the U.N., "We're gonna do this reconnaissance today, and we're
gonna desist depending on... *pending* the setting up by the U.N. And if
they *don't* do it, then we're gonna have to continue the surveillance."
McNamara added, "I don't think we'll *ever* get them to do it." The
President recommended first telling U Thant and Kuznetsov that we are
"doing this in order to give *our own* people . . . and others, including
the OAS," assurances that are verifiable. The U.N. and the Soviets have
to be told, the President stressed, "'Either we're gonna do it or the
U.N.'s gonna do it.' If the U.N. does the procedure, we'll withdraw."
As they were about to leave the Cabinet Room, the President instructed
that today's low-level reconnaissance mission should be laid on. "We
ought to get it [the notification] to U Thant before he leaves."

After some brief background chatter, during which one participant
shouted over the din, "I've got my car," the tape machine was turned
off.

*The President returned to the Oval Office, joined at about 12:30 by
several members of the Joint Chiefs of Staff, for a briefing about ongoing plans for a possible invasion of Cuba. Khrushchev's public com-*

mitment to dismantle the Cuban bases and withdraw the missiles, made only 24 hours earlier, had yet to be backed up by any hard evidence that work on the sites had actually ceased. President Kennedy and his advisers continued to discuss all military options because they could not be certain that the Sunday morning announcement from Moscow would actually turn out to be the decisive turning point in the crisis. And, in fact, weeks of difficult negotiations were just beginning on several critical issues: inspection and verification of the dismantling of the missile sites, the disposition of the IL-28 nuclear bombers, the precise terms of a U.S. pledge not to invade Cuba and Soviet efforts to pin down the secret "understanding" on withdrawing the Turkish missiles.

Monday, October 29, about 12:30 P.M., Oval Office

Identified Participants: John F. Kennedy, George Anderson, David Shoup.[344]

"We just have to assume that we're gonna be back with Cuba in a... 2 or 3 months if they start to build up their conventional forces."

President John F. Kennedy

President Kennedy turned on the tape recorder during an exchange apparently touching on the possible use of any Soviet tactical nuclear weapons in Cuba if the United States invaded. General David Shoup reported that air surveillance photos were being analyzed carefully, but admitted that "we *really* don't know how much they've got [in Cuba]. Then we'd have to *find* out, which can be done, and it's done at a price. . . . you *take* 'em out, *every* airplane, and then you can take that place, *absolutely*." He nonetheless raised an unsettling question, "Now, what they would do with the nuclear weapons if they had 'em?" and offered his own answer, "I don't... I don't know. I think they'd *shoot* 'em. Then the question is: are we at nuclear war?"

"Now what if they didn't use their nuclear weap[ons]?" JFK ruminated, but instead used "those armored vehicles, self-propelled, and all the rest." The President, revealing a grasp of the historic anti-American sentiment that transcended Cuba's internal political divisions, something he had failed to do during the planning of the Bay of Pigs operation, expressed concern that American invasion forces might get

[344]Tape 43.3, POF, PRC, JFKL.

bogged down in Cuba, "probably the younger Cubans *are* loyal to Castro and have enough nationalist spirit, even ones that don't like Castro, so that we would certainly run into a *hard-core* situation with a lot of guerrilla [resistance]. . . .You think that... your judgment is that it's... it's *not* a major military effort, or is it?"

"It would be a *major* military effort, *yes sir*," Shoup replied firmly, but he remained confident that since Cuban tanks and troops were "confined to one longitudinal highway," U.S. intelligence "can get pictures of what they're doing" at night using flares and inflict significant damage on military forces moving anywhere in the country. JFK asked if Cuban armored vehicles could be taken out by airplanes without using nuclear weapons, pointing out that "there's one picture where they're all in a row," and was assured by Admiral George Anderson that by using "250-pound low-flying bombs which we carry *a lot of* on our planes, well, we'd... we'd really make a shambles of it." But, he did express concern about whether "all of these missiles and weapons" had actually been located and whether the Cubans and Soviets had plans to demolish port facilities and airfields to impede an American invasion. Shoup also suggested that ports and beaches might be mined. "Well, we just have to watch," President Kennedy concluded, "and if they continue this conventional buildup into Cuba, then we just have to draw conclusions from *that*. So I think we just stay *on* it."

The President recalled, very scornfully, that the Russians had secretly shipped their missiles to Cuba despite assurances to RFK and Rusk from Ambassador Dobrynin, who "is regarded *very well* in Russia. . . . He's around telling both the attorney general, he told Rusk that they would never send *missiles* there. That was 2 *weeks ago*. So now he's liquidated as a source, cause nobody believes *him* anymore, and the chances are he probably *didn't know*! He looked so *shocked* that day, when Rusk showed him, he still wouldn't believe it. So it's probable they didn't even tell *him*." JFK concluded pessimistically that the Russians could not be trusted, "When you're dealing under those conditions, where there's *no* basis [for trust]... We just have to assume that we're gonna be back with Cuba in a... 2 or 3 months if they start to build up their conventional forces. Then I think you're gonna have to say this is a breach of the spirit of the..."[345]

As the briefing started to break up, President Kennedy and Admiral

---

[345]JFK obviously did not think the same way about the continuing covert actions against Cuba.

Anderson chatted amiably about college football before JFK remarked, "I see you're on the cover of *Time*, admiral." "Sir," Anderson replied, "I haven't read the article yet, but..." "I'm sure they'll be kinder to you," Kennedy observed sarcastically, "than they are yet to me." The conversation then drifted back to football, but JFK remarked, "I imagine the Air Force must be a little mad, aren't they?"—referring to the division of responsibility for aerial photography between the Air Force and the Joint Chiefs' photo-reconnaissance office. But Anderson replied, "No, actually our cooperation has been splendid." "So they did a good job on those photographs," Kennedy observed. "Oh, yeah," Anderson responded. "We had decided Saturday night to begin this air-strike on Tuesday," the President noted somewhat abruptly, "and it may have been one of the reasons why the Russians finally did this."

Kennedy, Anderson and Shoup, at that point some distance from the microphone, conversed briefly about practical limitations on the use of nuclear weapons. JFK noted that "we have them in those places where we *can't* use them," but Shoup observed, "the 64-dollar question" is whether the Soviets might even now use the tactical nuclear weapons in Cuba "because they would deal bloody hell with Guantanamo." JFK seemed skeptical, "But my guess is... everybody sort of figures that, *in extremis*, that everybody would use nuclear weapons. Using... the decision to use any kind of a nuclear weapon, even the tactical ones, presents *such a risk* of it getting out of control *so quickly* that there's..."

"But Cuba's so small compared to the world," Shoup observed. "If that joker [Castro] ever had... had the control now," but the Soviets are "tellin' him that they have the keys, like we've got the keys."

"I'm sure they do... to Cuba," JFK agreed.

"The Russians say [to the U.S.]," Shoup continued, "'We have the keys; you have the keys. You trust us; we trust you.'"

"*No*," JFK responded firmly, "we don't *trust* each other. But we figure that they're never gonna give 'em to the Cubans anymore than we'd give them to, you know, *the Turks*. Because we know that... I don't think anybody wants that weapon to escape from their control. It's just too..."[346]

The President also mused about using the Cuban crisis as an oppor-

---

[346]As cited earlier, JFK seemed unaware that "the first [Jupiter] launch position was transferred to the Turks . . . in the middle of the Cuban Missile Crisis." "Kennedy could have ordered the U.S.-owned and -controlled warheads home, thus disarming the IRBMs," but this step would have violated "the formal bilateral deployment agreement and was in any case politically infeasible." (Nash, *The Other Missiles*, 103, 111)

tunity for progress on the Berlin issue, "Berlin really is a *paralyzing*" problem, he declared in frustration. "*That's right!*" Anderson cut in. "Because everything you want to do, you say, 'Oh, well, it will screw us in Berlin.' And I think if we can ever get any kind of a decent deal in Berlin... it's just the *worst* place for us to let them *always...*" "I *certainly* agree," Anderson reiterated. "It *really* gives them the *initiative* all the time," JFK continued, "it always makes us look like it divides the Allies." He even pointed out that the status quo did not serve the long-range interests of the 2 million West Berliners, "They could be blocked off on any day and they'll never get out of there." He recalled that "Rusk told me the other day" that George Marshall, during World War II, had predicted that Berlin would "become an *impossible* situation over the years. . . . So that's what I think what we oughta do now while we've got some initiative here." "Well, it's nice of you to receive us now," Anderson finally remarked. The President expressed his appreciation and thanked the JCS for doing "a good job." "Well, we're *always* available," Anderson quipped, and JFK chuckled, "Good."

After the military brass left the Oval Office, the President can briefly be heard writing at his desk. A few advisers came by, probably including Sorensen, and the conversation turned to possible press speculation about the talks continuing at the United Nations. Despite having sent John McCloy to New York to look over Stevenson's shoulder in the negotiations with Kuznetsov, JFK insisted, "Now have we got it all clear about the... I mean Adlai's... Adlai's in charge up there [at the U.N.] There's no problem about this thing. Adlai's in charge of the U.N. delegation. I'll get to McCloy this afternoon and make it... I just want to be sure that there's no press. . . . I don't want the... you know... let the Republicans have a piece of this," the President warned, "just ten days before [the mid-term] election." There won't be a political problem, he repeated emphatically, as police or ambulance sirens wailed in the street outside, "providing we don't make it *look* like it's a problem." JFK again offered to call McCloy himself and asked Sorensen to call Clayton [Fritchey, Stevenson's press spokesman] "because Adlai's difficult to talk to. . . . I named McCloy to *assist* Adlai. What he's *now* doing is working on the technical details of the problems under Adlai's direction. . . . Adlai's in charge. He's working under Adlai's supervision. But you've got to have a defense man . . . some guy who's *just doing this*. . . . But we want *U Thant* to know that Adlai is our voice. So I think that that's the general line." "Yeah, I'll see to that," Sorensen promised.

Dean Rusk came in soon after Sorensen left and the President can be heard suggesting, "What we're gonna do is... I'm gonna decorate that widow some time"—a reference to the wife of Major Rudolph Anderson, the U-2 pilot killed over Cuba. After a brief exchange about verification of the dismantling of the missile bases in Cuba, the conversation turned to smoothing the progress of the secret understanding on removing the Jupiter missiles from Turkey. The President unexpectedly became quite incensed and abruptly chewed out the secretary of state, "Now listen, we gotta get the policy. Now I gotta tell you this in private. When the Soviets came in, I told them [the State and Defense Departments] on *Sunday*, and have notes to *show it*, about this Turkish thing, and if they were gonna come in on that they ought to be reviewing it." When the Soviets made the Turkish proposal on Saturday, he continued, "there was *nothing* done, really. There was a wire sent to Hare asking his opinion about it and one sent to Finletter, but we were *not* really prepared to know what we were gonna *say* and we weren't prepared if we have negotiations with the Turks in case this would really prove to be desirable . . . so that we *could* do it if we wanted to do it. Now it seemed to me that it was *obvious* that was coming along, and as I say in my notes," notes from a conversation last Saturday "which shows that I *asked* them to review this, particularly asked *Nitze*, because it's a NATO commitment."[347]

The President respected his advisers and welcomed the fact that they had strong views of their own. He was distressed, however, because resistance to the Turkish trade, which had been determined and persistent at the ExComm meetings, had evidently been accompanied by bureaucratic foot-dragging and even obstruction by high-ranking officials. "Now it seems to me," he demanded, "that some way or other the State Department ought to be about *a week ahead*, not be drawing plans up for *six months ahead*." Rusk mentioned that "we had a plan out there and we had it passed to you," but tried to explain that he did not know what "George Ball and others" did with it. "We had it [the Soviet offer on Turkey] for 24 hours," Kennedy continued irritably, "and *now* we're trying to figure out how... whether we turn it down and nobody had any idea *really* what the Turks would go for and all the rest. I'm just thinking, what if this's gonna be our problem next

[347]JFK's repeated references to trying corroborate these claims with written notes provide striking insight into his decision to secretly record White House meetings and phone calls.

week?" Rusk, rather diffidently, referred to some State Department policy papers, but JFK retorted sharply, "Well *I'd like* to *get* them." The administration's top diplomat tried to speak again, but the President cut him off angrily, "I never get your stuff! *You* talk to Mac [Bundy] *now*," he ordered, "and have somebody over in the White House that's responsible for liaison with you, so I can see some of these things." He calmed down quickly, however, explaining in a much more composed tone of voice, "Can you get 'em to me more? In other words, what we don't wanna do more is get *too* far ahead in our planning."

President Kennedy had been all but imperturbable for two intensely stressful weeks. But, with the most dangerous phase of the crisis apparently over, his frustration about possibly calculated delays in preparing a coherent response to Khrushchev's October 27 message had finally overcome his self-control. Rusk, almost certainly startled by the President's sudden and uncharacteristic outburst, left the Oval Office.

Bundy and Sorensen dropped by with something for Kennedy to sign and the former asked, "You think we'd go tomorrow...?" JFK responded wearily, "Not tonight, Mac," mentioning "a little" obligation for that evening or night. "Could you decide on that one?" Bundy pressed, and JFK promised a decision. A few minutes later, the President talked with his secretary, Evelyn Lincoln, about whether she had anything for him to sign and asked, "Did you see [if] Arthur Schlesinger's here yet?" and "How is the museum group? Are they happy?" before pushing a button on the phone console and telling an aide:

"I want to get a President's commemorative for the Executive Committee of the National Security... of the National Security Council who've been involved in these... this matter. What I thought of is something that would have," he hesitated momentarily, "the month of October on it and the 10 days have a line drawn around the calendar days; yeah, it would just be a calendar."

"Yeah. Yeah. In other words, you see, in other words just like a page out of a calendar. . . . How could you get that so it wouldn't be too expensive? You want to get at that? It's about 12 [days], about 12. . . . a line drawn around it. . . . It's the 29th actually today so it would be the 28th. . . . Thank you. Okay." [348]

A few seconds later, the President switched off the tape recorder.

---

[348] The subsequent association of the missile crisis with "thirteen days" did not really become indelible until the publication of RFK's book in 1969.

Each commemorative silver calendar, with highlighted engraving of the 13 days from October 16 to 28, was inscribed with the initials of the President and those of the individual recipient and prepared by Tiffany's for over two dozen ExComm advisers—as well as for Jacqueline Kennedy and presidential aides David Powers and Kenneth O'Donnell for their behind-the-scenes support.

Epilogue: The November Post-Crisis

"We don't plan to invade Cuba. *But*, we're ready to give that in a more formal way when they meet *their* commitments."

President John F. Kennedy

JFK's decision to create commemorative calendars, engraved through October 28, suggests that even if the Sunday morning agreement had yet to be nailed down, he remained hopeful that the superpowers had turned the corner in resolving this dangerous nuclear standoff in Cuba. However, the private understanding between the Kremlin and the White House began to fray almost immediately—largely because of resistance and obstruction from Castro. The Cuban missile crisis was not *really* over after all.

Ambassador Dobrynin delivered a letter from Khrushchev to Robert Kennedy on October 29. The message explicitly identified the terms of the agreement reached on that fateful weekend: Soviet withdrawal, in Khrushchev's words, of "those weapons you describe as offensive," on-site verification by United Nations inspectors, a United States pledge not to invade Cuba, plus an American commitment to remove the Jupiter missiles from Turkey. After consulting with the President, RFK met Dobrynin again the next day. The attorney general returned the letter and, in line with the confidential strategy adopted in the Oval Office on the early evening of October 27, refused to formalize the secret understanding about the Turkish missiles in writing. RFK even admitted, according to Dobrynin, that he could not "risk getting involved in the transmission of this sort of letter, since who knows where and when such letters can surface or be somehow published—not now, but in the future—and any changes in the course of events are possible. The appearance of such a document could cause irreparable harm to my political career in the future. This is why we request that you take this letter back." Dobrynin chose not to press the matter any further.

Meanwhile, State Department analysts advised the President that the

IL-28 bombers should also be classified as "offensive weapons" that must be withdrawn. U Thant arrived in Cuba on October 30 and found Castro in an "impossible and intractable mood." The Cuban leader railed bitterly about Soviet betrayal and "declared categorically that there could be no inspection of any kind by any outside agency on Cuban soil."[349] JFK ordered continuation of the quarantine and the resumption of U-2 and low-level reconnaissance flights despite threats from Castro that Cuban forces would fire on American aircraft.

At the same time, negotiations at the U.N. between Ambassador Stevenson (assisted by John McCloy) and Ambassador Zorin (assisted by Vasily Kuznetsov) bogged down over whether the IL-28 bombers should be defined as offensive weapons. JFK, in the early ExComm meetings, had argued that the U.S. would have to learn to live with the presence of Soviet bombers in Cuba. But, in the altered political climate in the wake of Khrushchev's unanticipated retreat, and with the mid-term elections barely a week away, he gradually hardened his position.

Khrushchev's principal deputy, Anastas Mikoyan, arrived in Havana in early November to try to persuade Castro to accept outside verification of the dismantling of the missile sites and removal of the nuclear bombers. Castro "grudgingly" met Mikoyan's plane, but then refused to confer with him for almost a week before finally presenting his own list of tough demands, including suspension of the American economic blockade, an end to U.S.-sponsored sabotage and illegal overflights and the return of the Guantanamo naval base. Castro told Khrushchev's emissary, "we oppose this inspection," insisting that Cuba had "the right to defend our dignity." Mikoyan remained in Cuba for twenty-two days and needed more than two weeks just to convince Castro to give up the IL-28s. But the Cuban leader would not budge on outside verification. The refusal of the Kennedy administration to make direct contact with Castro "placed the entire burden of coping with Cuba on the Soviet government, which, in effect, was being asked to serve as a U.S. ally in the handling of relations with Cuba."[350]

[349]Chang and Kornbluh, *Cuban Missile Crisis*, 394; Adlai Stevenson to Dean Rusk, November 1, 1962, in Chang and Kornbluh, *Cuban Missile Crisis*, 259.

[350]Brenner, "Thirteen Months," 202; Garthoff, *Reflections*, 99–102, 109; Domínguez, "The @#$%& Missile Crisis," 307; Castro's list of demands was ignored by the Americans *and* the Soviets. In essence, Khrushchev decided it would be easier to negotiate with the Americans rather than the Cubans. In 1968, Castro delivered a scathing speech, kept secret for decades, denouncing Soviet betrayal in 1962. The speech was so bitter that it could

Tensions between the Soviets and their Cuban allies bubbled over at a November 7th Soviet embassy dinner marking the 45th anniversary of the Bolshevik Revolution. The Soviets clumsily neglected to offer a toast to Fidel Castro and a Cuban military intelligence official shocked his hosts by proposing "a joint toast to Fidel and Stalin." Khrushchev was livid when informed of this "offensive" effort to toast "that which we condemn." He was becoming increasingly alarmed that Castro's intransigence, especially on verification, threatened to nullify the entire October 28 agreement, especially the American pledge not to invade Cuba.[351]

By the end of the first week of the post-crisis, the President had already concluded that even if the missiles were removed, the continued presence of the IL-28 bombers, the failure to implement ground inspection and the likelihood of continued Cuban support for political and economic subversion in Latin America had thrown into question any formal U.S. non-invasion pledge. JFK pressed McNamara to be prepared for "an unforeseen turn of events in Cuba that offered a worthwhile opportunity for exploitation by the United States . . . [to launch] an airborne assault in the vicinity of Havana by two airborne divisions, followed as quickly as possible by an amphibious assault by the 2d Marine Division/Wing Team over beaches to the east of Havana." Two days later, on November 7, JFK endorsed McNamara's contention that aerial surveillance was the only effective method for confirming that offensive weapons were not being reintroduced into Cuba. The President contended "that'd be a pretty cheap price" if the Cubans agreed "to let us look at the abandoned sites." In that case, McNamara concluded emphatically, seconded by Dillon, the only remaining issue would be the IL-28s, "and the assurances against reentry, Mr. President." "With this election now over," JFK candidly admitted, "we ought to just play it...," "Cool for a while," Bundy interjected." "Well, no," the President replied revealingly, "*very straight*, say what is pleasing and what is not. We don't have to... we're not being... this constant thing of somebody gouging us. I don't... I think we'll have a little *time* now."[352]

---

have led to a rupture of relations between Cuba and the U.S.S.R. See Philip Brenner and James G. Blight, "Cuba 1962: The Crisis and Cuban-Soviet Relations: Fidel Castro's Secret 1968 Speech," *CWIHPB* 5 (Spring 1995), 1, 81–89 and James G. Blight and Philip Brenner, *Sad and Luminous Days: Cuba's Secret Struggle with the Superpowers After the Missile Crisis* (Lanham, Maryland: Rowman and Littlefield, 2002).

[351]Fursenko and Naftali, *"One Hell of a Gamble,"* 295, 296–97.

[352]John F. Kennedy to Robert McNamara, *FRUS: Cuban Missile Crisis and After-*

President Kennedy then posed a rhetorical question, "Whadda we want?" and immediately answered it himself, "We wanna get the IL-28s out there and we want assurance they don't come in, then we probably wouldn't invade," unless, he explained, there was a major appeal from the Cuban people or the Soviets reintroduced offensive weapons. "Then we would invade. Otherwise our commitment ought to stay. We don't plan to invade Cuba. *But,* we're ready to give that in a more formal way when they meet *their* commitments."[353]

JFK also speculated about using the quarantine as a lever to pressure other free world nations to put "the squeeze voluntarily" on Castro to agree to the removal of the nuclear bombers. If the U.S. strictly enforced the quarantine, the President argued, it would cause those countries "a lot of grief because we're gonna have to stop Russian ships and have a direct encounter over the IL-28 matter." He added, somewhat hopefully, "I think that under those conditions they should be willing to *join us.*" "I think," Rusk added, as Bundy chuckled, "they would go to great lengths to avoid that situation."[354]

On November 8, the Defense Department announced that all known Soviet missile bases in Cuba had been dismantled, but, on the same day, a sabotage team carried out an attack on a Cuban factory—despite the suspension of Operation Mongoose on October 30. The President continued to insist, however, that success or failure on removal of the IL-28s would determine the U.S. posture "at the U.N. and nationally and internationally," on whether to stand by the non-invasion pledge. "I don't think we'd look very good to say, 'Well, we withdraw our commitment that we won't invade,' because most people... that one's gonna be the more difficult position to sustain at the U.N. certainly and . . . [in] this hemisphere." JFK was determined not to appear to have been painted into a corner, "since we failed to get what we wanted, we're settling for less. . . . I think that it's gonna be *damned* important" to make clear to the international community that the withdrawal of the IL-28s would determine the viability of the American non-invasion pledge.[355] In an effort to break the impasse, Robert Kennedy invited Georgi Bolshakov to his home on November 9

math, 1961–1963, XI, Document #150; Tape 53a, November 7, 1962, POF, PRC, JFKL.

[353]Tape 53a, November 7, 1962.

[354]Tape 54, November 8, 1962, POF, PRC, JFKL.

[355]Brenner, "Thirteen Months," 203; Tape 55, November 9, 1962, POF, PRC, JFKL.

and later explained that the administration could not resolve the Cuban crisis without "the rapid removal of the IL-28s."[356]

President Kennedy and the NSC were particularly concerned about persistent rumors that the Soviets had left missiles behind in Cuba—perhaps concealed in caves. McNamara essentially dismissed these reports, but acknowledged that "plenty of people in this country will think they *would* and *that's* our problem." Nitze estimated a 10% chance of deception but the defense chief contended that the likelihood of Soviet treachery "was far less than that, a 1/10 of 1% chance" and joked that 30% of the public and 80% of the Congress would believe these rumors. Laughter erupted, however, when Rusk quipped that Phoumi Nosavan, the anti-communist Laotian general was going to visit Moscow: "So if Phoumi can go to Moscow, surely Castro can come to Washington."[357]

Ambassador Stevenson informed the President on November 12 that the U.N. negotiations with Zorin and Kuznetsov on the IL-28s had deadlocked. Nevertheless, even if Khrushchev refused to remove the bombers, the President worried that enforcing the full quarantine would be very risky politically, since, with the missiles out of Cuba, the U.S. would no longer command unified support in Latin America or Europe. Instead, he proposed putting the screws on Khrushchev through "our refusal to give the assurances on invasion and the continued surveillance [of Cuba]. . . . I think we're probably in maybe better shape to do *that* than we are to put back a... a really... the kind of a quarantine which we never *really* enforced, which was to stop everybody and search 'em. Now are we ready to do that if we get an unsatisfactory answer to this [on the IL-28s]? Because my *guess* is that he'll either *accept* this or we'll get an answer back which says we'll get 'em out within a reasonable period of time. He'll never give us *flat* no." That evening, RFK informed Dobrynin that the U.S. expected the bombers to be withdrawn in about 30 days, and suggested that a Soviet promise "to remove the bombers according to a definite schedule" could be sufficient to allow the lifting of the quarantine.[358]

In Havana, also on November 12, Mikoyan again pressed Castro to accept the removal of the bombers—which Mikoyan described as mili-

[356]Fursenko and Naftali, *"One Hell of a Gamble,"* 299–300.
[357]Tape 55, November 9, 1962.
[358]Tape 56, November 12, 1962, POF, PRC, JFKL; Fursenko and Naftali, *"One Hell of a Gamble,"* 303.

tarily insignificant. Khrushchev's envoy promised his Cuban allies that this concession would be the last from the Soviet side and argued that the Americans would not lift the blockade unless the IL-28s were withdrawn. Two days later, Khrushchev wrote to JFK, "I can assure the President that those planes will be removed from Cuba with all the equipment and flying personnel. It can be done in 2–3 months."[359]

Castro, however, again vowed that his government would not permit U.S. reconnaissance planes to violate Cuban sovereignty, emotionally telling Mikoyan that "we will open fire on all American military planes" in a few days—and the order would stand regardless of Soviet objections. Mikoyan complained to Khrushchev that the Cubans were too emotional and "bitter feelings often overcome reason." The furious and frustrated Soviet leader declared, "Either they cooperate or we will recall our personnel." Khrushchev felt that the American non-invasion pledge constituted a major step to assure the survival of the Cuban revolution, which had been the Kremlin's principal goal from the outset, and demanded that Castro "must show more flexibility."[360]

JFK, on November 16, repeated his concern that "cranking on the quarantine to get the IL-28s out is not particularly satisfactory" and Bundy provoked general laughter by drolly interjecting, "There are two people to whom it's *wholly* unsatisfactory, Mr. President, you and the Chairman [Khrushchev]." "That's right. That's right," JFK repeated.[361] The President was determined, however, not to let Khrushchev off the hook. Even if the missiles were withdrawn and the quarantine were lifted, he insisted "that we're gonna maintain close surveillance and that our [non] invasion commitment is a... and any other commitments are... we're not... we're not gonna give those commitments *until* he gets the IL-28s *out*. Then when we continue our flyover, when they shoot at us and we shoot back and he [Khrushchev] gets the kind of escalation which he can't *like very much* because it's... And in addition . . . any other negotiation which he may want more to go on in Berlin or anything else are held up because of our public charge that he did not *fulfill* his agreement." The U.S. would continue to dangle the non-invasion pledge over Khrushchev's head but, at the same time, "we would not have to bring on the direct encounter [at sea] again."

[359]*Ibid.*, 302; Nikita Khrushchev to John F. Kennedy, November 14, 1962, *FRUS: The Cuban Missile Crisis and its Aftermath, XI*, Document #176.

[360]Fursenko and Naftali, *"One Hell of a Gamble,"* 304–7.

[361]Tape 58, November 16, 1962, POF, PRC, JFKL.

Meanwhile, amphibious landing exercises were carried out in North Carolina and the JCS reported that 100,000 Army troops, 40,000 Marines, nearly 15,000 paratroopers, as well as 550 combat aircraft and 180 ships, were poised to invade Cuba.[362]

"We're *not* going to invade Cuba," JFK continued nonetheless to insist. "What we want from the Russians is the withdrawal of their military presence... conventional, or certainly a great lessening of it. That's a... it isn't just taking out the IL-28s." The ultimate goal is to guarantee "that Cuba is not an armed camp [and then] we would not *invade* Cuba." But, at the same time, he was determined to leave *all* military options open, especially if Castro continued to support political subversion in Latin America. "Now let's just see," Kennedy pondered, "the conditions under which we'd invade. We'd invade Cuba only if a civil war broke out, *really*. We'd invade Cuba only if a military threat came to us, or if they were carrying out their threat against their neighbor. Now, that's *quite* obvious. Then we'd invade Cuba probably only if there was a real outbreak of civil war where our presence might be a *decisive* factor. I don't think *otherwise* we're planning... we're gonna find the condition in the next two or three years where we're gonna be able to justifiably, *in our interests*, taken around the world, of *invading* Cuba."[363]

Most importantly, JFK conceded, "We'd like to get him [Castro] out. But I don't think we're probably gonna be able to get Castro *out of there* by an invasion by the United States forces. So we don't wanna tie our hands too much cause these other conditions might arise." Nevertheless, regardless of his ambivalence about invading Cuba, the President neither abandoned or even cut back on covert operations against Castro and the Cuban economy over the coming months.[364]

On November 18, Stevenson told the President that the Soviet negotiators at the U.N. remained obdurate on the IL-28s. John McCloy tried to break the logjam by informing Kuznetsov that the President would overlook the on-site inspection issue, in spite of lingering official and public suspicions that missiles might be concealed in Cuban caves, and would "guarantee the noninvasion of Cuba from other Latin American countries" if the bombers were withdrawn: "That would be

---

[362]*Ibid.*; Chang and Kornbluh, *Cuban Missile Crisis*, 401.

[363]Tape 59, November 16, 1962, POF, PRC, JFKL.

[364]*Ibid.*; see Stephen G. Rabe, *The Most Dangerous Area in the World: John F. Kennedy Confronts Communist Revolution in Latin America* (Chapel Hill, North Carolina: University of North Carolina Press, 1999).

a deal." But, JFK nonetheless pessimistically notified the leaders of England, France and West Germany that Khrushchev was unlikely to back down again.[365]

On November 19, however, Castro finally gave in to intense diplomatic pressure from the Kremlin and advised U Thant that he would not stand in the way of the withdrawal of the IL-28s. A formal letter from Khrushchev, agreeing to pull the nuclear bombers out of Cuba, was delivered to JFK by Bolshakov on November 20. "Well," Khrushchev told his adversary in Washington, "I think, this answer of mine gives you not bad material for your statement at your press conference." JFK soon instructed McNamara to lift the quarantine.[366]

Hours before the President's scheduled November 20 statement to the nation, RFK, McCone and several other National Security Council members urged JFK to resist giving any public assurances that the U.S. would not invade Cuba. With the quarantine removed, they reasoned, the noninvasion promise was the only remaining lever for putting pressure on Khrushchev. President Kennedy seemed uneasy, "Now how do we prevent this from looking too much like we're welching on it as well?" The attorney general, notwithstanding his personal negotiations with Dobrynin, continued to take a hard line, insisting that "we didn't say we're gonna give formal assurances. . . . I don't think that we owe anything as far as Khrushchev is concerned; nor does he expect it at the moment." RFK did concede, "maybe we wanna throw this in as a piece of cake." JFK continued to wonder, however, whether a noninvasion promise would make it politically less difficult for Khrushchev to withdraw his conventional forces from Cuba.[367]

In the end, JFK toughened his stance. Despite announcing at his 6:00 P.M. press conference that the Soviets would withdraw the IL-28s within 30 days, he added that since on-site inspection and verification had not been implemented, the preconditions for the U.S. noninvasion pledge had not been met. He did affirm, however, that if offensive weapons were kept out of Cuba, and Castro ended "the export of aggressive Communist purposes, there will be peace in the Caribbean."

[365]Fursenko and Naftali, *"One Hell of a Gamble,"* 307–8; Chang and Kornbluh, *Cuban Missile Crisis*, 402.

[366]Fursenko and Naftali, *"One Hell of a Gamble,"* 309–10; "By November 19 our military posture for operations against Cuba was at a peak and continued in that state until November 21, when the President officially lifted the quarantine." (Nitze, *Hiroshima to Glasnost*, 229)

[367]Tape 63A, November 20, 1962, POF, PRC, JFKL.

Khrushchev seemed satisfied, telling Mikoyan, "Evidently, Kennedy himself is not an extremist."[368]

Over the next few months, Khrushchev worked behind the scenes to repair damaged Soviet relations with Cuba and invited Castro to visit the U.S.S.R. in the spring of 1963. Castro's travel plans were kept secret because Khrushchev believed "there was a real possibility of an 'accidental' attack on the plane carrying Fidel over the ocean. It was well known that one of the aims of the 'Mongoose' operation was his physical elimination." Castro's trip was not announced publicly until after his plane had landed safely in the U.S.S.R.[369]

Historians continue to wrestle with a murky question: in the wake of the allegedly sobering lessons of the missile crisis, did President Kennedy, after November 1962, adopt "a dual-track policy toward Castro of ideological antagonism and accommodation"—including rethinking plans to get rid of the Cuban leader?[370] Operation Mongoose, for example, was terminated at the beginning of 1963. In the spring, after anti-Castro exiles attacked Soviet vessels and personnel in Cuba, JFK instructed them to suspend operations against Soviet interests. Jose Miro Cardona, the zealous head of the Cuban Revolutionary Council, resigned in protest. In May, journalist Lisa Howard interviewed Castro in Havana and later reported to the CIA on "possible [Cuban] interest in rapprochement with the United States." JFK agreed in September to explore contacts with Castro's government, through intermediary William Attwood, former Ambassador to Guinea. The President also met privately with French journalist Jean Daniel, just before the reporter's November trip to Cuba. Kennedy acknowledged America's share of culpability for the suffering caused by Batista and expressed sympathy for a revolutionary and collectivist Cuba free from external Soviet control. Castro, after later talking to Daniel, seemed receptive to pursuing a secret dialogue with the U.S.[371]

[368]*Public Papers of the Presidents: John F. Kennedy, 1962 II,* 830–38; Fursenko and Naftali, *"One Hell of a Gamble,"* 309–10.

[369]Sergei Khrushchev, *Nikita Khrushchev,* 658; Fursenko and Naftali, *"One Hell of a Gamble,"* 327–30.

[370]Stephen G. Rabe, "After the Missiles of October: John F. Kennedy and Cuba, November 1962 to November 1963," *Presidential Studies Quarterly* 30 (December 2000), 716, 724. Also see Thomas G. Paterson, "Fixation with Cuba: The Bay of Pigs, Missile Crisis, and Covert War against Fidel Castro," in Paterson, ed., *Kennedy's Quest for Victory,* 123–55.

[371]The Daniel contact appears to have been initiated by Cuban intelligence in New York and Paris, with "severe restrictions placed on who had access to [this] information . . . Cu-

On balance, however, these tentative and ad hoc steps do not out-weigh the remaining evidence. On December 29, 1962, before some 40,000 Cuban exiles in Miami's Orange Bowl, JFK paid tribute to the recently released Bay of Pigs prisoners and pledged that their brigade flag would fly over a "free Havana." The Cubans chanted, "Guerra! Guerra!" Only a month later, President Kennedy reconstituted covert operations under a new Interdepartmental Cuban Coordinating Committee. He also continued to press forward with "contingency invasion plans," personally approved sabotage against Cuban shipping and in-frastructure and supported economic warfare "to tighten the noose around the Cuban economy." Contrary to private assurances to Khru-shchev, JFK even authorized "inciting Cubans" to assault Soviet mili-tary forces in Cuba "provided every precaution is taken to prevent at-tribution." Thirteen major CIA covert operations against Cuba were approved for just the last few months of 1963, "including the sabotage of an electric power plant, a sugar mill and an oil refinery." Attempts to kill Castro continued as well. U.S.-Soviet relations did moderate in the year after the settlement of the missile crisis, but there was no com-parable thaw in U.S.-Cuban relations.[372]

---

ban intelligence considered the signals Kennedy gave in response to these overtures highly positive. Castro was very enthusiastic, and became convinced that a settlement was possi-ble. . . ." But, "this hopeful period" ended on November 22. (Amuchastegui, "Cuban Intel-ligence and the October Crisis," 107); FRUS: Cuba, 1961–1962, X, 738–46; Schlesinger, A Thousand Days, 998–1000; Peter Kornbluh, ed., "Kennedy and Castro: The Secret Quest for Accommodation," National Security Archive Electronic Briefing Book No. 17, August 16, 1999; Rabe, "After the Missiles of October," 723–24.

[372]O'Donnell and Powers, Johnny, We Hardly Knew Ye, 276–77; FRUS: Cuban Missile Crisis and Aftermath, XI, Document #376; Rabe, "After the Missiles of October," 717–21, 725; Brenner, "Thirteen Months," 205–7; Garthoff, "Documenting the Cuban Missile Cri-sis," 302–3.

Conclusion

Listening and Learning:
Insights from the JFK ExComm Tapes

The objective of this book has been to provide a new avenue of access to the often neglected core event of the Cuban missile crisis: the secret ExComm meetings. Historians regularly quote from notes or transcripts of these discussions, but, until now, no one has written a comprehensive and interpretive narrative account of this gripping and unique primary source.[1] All that has been available in-depth on the actual conversations are two editions of published transcripts (see Appendix). However, transcripts alone, no matter how accurate, simply cannot capture the full human dimension of these meetings.

Some historians, of course, completed their work before all the October 16–28 recordings, the most indispensable recently declassified American resource on the missile crisis, were finally opened by early 1997. Marc Trachtenberg, for example, working with the incomplete and frequently inaccurate 1983 transcript prepared principally by McGeorge Bundy, understandably downplayed the view that the Cuban decision to fire on low-level U.S. reconnaissance planes had nearly pushed the superpowers into war. "It is clear from the transcript of the October 27 ExComm meetings that the American response to these attacks was not to order a counterescalation. Cuban antiaircraft fire was

---

[1] For example, Alexander Fursenko and Timothy Naftali, in their invaluable study of the missile crisis based largely on declassified Soviet sources linguistically inaccessible to most Western scholars, devote only 17 pages to the ExComm meetings (*"One Hell of a Gamble,"* 222–39).

instead leading the United States to pull back." Trachtenberg cites General Taylor's remark that low-level surveillance will soon become "entirely impossible" and concludes, "When one studies these events at this level of detail, one does not detect a process of escalation spiraling out of control. Toughness was not met by countertoughness, but by accommodation."[2]

The complete tape, on the contrary, makes clear that Taylor was actually arguing that although low-flying reconnaissance might soon become impossible, medium and high-level missions could still be launched if at least ten SAM sites or "the whole works" were knocked out. McNamara was even more combative, urging the President to continue the low-level surveillance missions with fighter escorts and if the planes were fired on again, to "attack the attackers." JFK decided instead to wait until Sunday afternoon for a possible breakthrough if U Thant traveled to Cuba. But, if that initiative failed and the Soviets did not respond diplomatically, he recommended making a public statement about the antiaircraft fire and "then go in [on Monday] and take out *all* the SAM sites."[3]

The essence of this exchange, as captured on the tape, reveals that Taylor and McNamara were ready to unleash American air power against Cuba without delay. President Kennedy, although similarly pessimistic about diplomatic progress through U Thant or Khrushchev and very uncertain about how the military situation would eventually play out, was nonetheless disposed to put off escalation for perhaps a day or so—just in case. Toughness, the tape demonstrates, was not really met by accommodation, but rather by JFK's fatalistic but fortuitous decision to at least try to delay countertoughness.

Philip Nash, in his authoritative exploration of the Jupiter missiles in Turkey and Italy, also written before the release of the recordings, claimed that "Neither Robert Kennedy nor Llewellyn Thompson opposed a trade outright at the afternoon meeting [on October 27]," and also insisted that "the claim by [Paul] Nitze and others" that a majority of ExComm opposed a Turkish missile deal "is almost certainly untrue

[2]Marc Trachtenberg, "Commentary: New Light on the Cuban Missile Crisis," *Diplomatic History* 14 (spring 1990), 243.

[3]On the other hand, as discussed in the narrative, JFK, in effect, had backed away from his October 23 decision to immediately attack one or all the SAM sites if U.S. planes were fired on again—fortunately making it far easier for Khrushchev to retreat the following morning.

and definitely unsubstantiated by the evidence." The definitive primary sources, the October 27 ExComm tapes, incontrovertibly uphold Nitze's view.[4]

Lawrence Freedman's important study, actually published several years *after* the tapes became available, also depended on the second-hand accounts in minutes and transcripts. He noted, for example, that the tension of the October 27 meetings "comes through in both the records of the meetings and the transcripts, during which the participants sound [?] fatigued and nervous."[5] There is simply no substitute for documenting this observation by *listening* to these conversations. McNamara's response to Bundy's suggestion to break for dinner during the protracted late afternoon meeting on "Black Saturday" is a particularly arresting case in point. The defense secretary's tone communicates his mental, emotional and physical exhaustion as no transcript possibly could: "Well, let's wait. You don't have to worry," he groaned wearily, "eating is the *least* of my worries." His words alone can never fully communicate the bleakness and anxiety captured by his voice.

This ExComm narrative, derived directly from the tapes, fine tunes the inner history of the missile crisis by underscoring the human, political and intellectual dynamic between JFK and his advisors. In the process, this account fills an important gap in the historical literature, and, although never intended as a reinterpretation of the missile crisis as a whole, requires reconsidering many conventional assumptions about the ExComm discussions—and, by extension, rethinking the broader crisis itself. For example: Dean Rusk, contrary to Arthur Schlesinger, Jr.'s claims, emerges as an articulate, outspoken and influential participant; Robert Kennedy is snared by the contradiction between his aggressive and often contradictory posture on the tapes and his written account in *Thirteen Days*; Llewellyn Thompson comes into clear focus as a virtually unwavering ally of the hard-liners.

But, most importantly, the narrative approach provides special insight into the off-the-record depth and color of President Kennedy's handling of these secret meetings. JFK's leadership style rarely comes across in paper records (or even in his speeches—notwithstanding the frequent flashes of wit and intelligence). So much that cannot be captured, even in the most accurate transcripts, is there on the tapes for

[4]Nitze, *Hiroshima to Glasnost*, 219–20; Nash, *The Other Missiles*, 136, 147.
[5]Freedman, *Kennedy's Wars*, 210.

the listener with a discerning ear: the nuances of his voice and temperament, his impatience, his Cold War assumptions and convictions, his doubts, his blind spots, his political instincts, his quick mind, his dispassionate self-control, his persistence, his caution, his skepticism about military solutions to political problems, and his ironic sense of humor.

Kennedy's management of the ExComm discussions was subtle and understated, but remarkably effective. JFK virtually never lost his temper, at least, Dean Rusk might add, not during the high point of the crisis, and remained all but imperturbable in the face of sometimes severe criticism from the Joint Chiefs, the ExComm or the leaders of Congress. He was never arrogant or egotistical, never put anyone down harshly and barely raised his voice even when obviously irritated or angry—except in the Rusk incident on October 29. Even when Kennedy chastised Rusk, however, he specifically pointed out that his criticism was being leveled in private. JFK was always willing to let people have their say, regardless of whether he agreed with their position, confident that in the end the constitutional authority to decide remained entirely in his hands.[6]

The views of ExComm members, of course, shifted, evolved and even reversed direction in response to the changing diplomatic, political and military situation, their own beliefs and values and the arguments of their colleagues. In addition, their willingness to express critical points of view was often directly affected by whether or not JFK was present. The character of the discussions, as described in the narrative, changed dramatically when the President left the room. The reluctance

[6]During World War II, never more precariously than in 1940 when a Nazi invasion seemed inevitable, Prime Minister Winston Churchill and the war cabinet lived and worked in cramped quarters beneath the streets of London. In a stressful situation comparable to the missile crisis, Churchill, in contrast to JFK's unruffled leadership, repeatedly tried to get his way with strident outbursts of temper. But, when faced with serious opposition from the cabinet and the military, he always gave in. "When I thump the table and push my face towards him, what does he do?" Churchill later wrote of clashes with General Alan Brooke. "Thumps the table harder and glares back." Brooke, not surprisingly, later called Churchill "the most difficult man to work with." Although these dissimilarities in leadership can be explained in part by vastly different personalities, Kennedy had a potent advantage. Churchill, as prime minister and head of a cabinet responsible to Parliament, lacked the unambiguous constitutional authority of a president and commander-in-chief directly elected by the people. Kennedy and the ExComm knew precisely where the buck stopped. (M. R. D. Foot, "How on Earth Did We Win?," *The Times* 2, May 17, 2001, 2–4)

of Vice President Lyndon Johnson to speak up in JFK's presence, which persisted until the final hours of the October 27 meetings, is a particularly striking example. Some participants, in any case, were nearly always diffident and reflective; some were tough and assertive; some were eager to lead, despite the enormous stakes involved; others were content to follow and say very little.

The author has made a determined effort to capture as much of the nuance of the missile crisis meetings as a written narrative can possibly convey; but, only the tapes themselves can fully portray the human reality of these discussions. Imagine, for example, if it suddenly became possible to *hear* a recording of the actual Gettysburg Address. Our understanding of Lincoln's words, meaning and intent would certainly be changed by exposure to the unique power of the spoken word—especially when heard in its original historical context. It is hard to imagine that anyone would *first* choose to read the speech if the option to actually hear the original presentation existed as well.

The ExComm conversations, of course, were not consciously crafted public oratory. Yet, some revelations from the tapes can never be gleaned from the dry and impassive lines of a transcript—no matter how accurate. Only a narrative can expose, for example, the abrupt change in JFK's mood on the first day of meetings, "Last month I said we weren't going to [accept offensive Soviet missiles in Cuba]," he began with a note of ironic humor in his voice, "and last month I should have said we're... well, that we don't care. But when we said we're *not* going to and then they go ahead and do it, and then we do nothing," he observed very darkly, "then... I would think that our... risks *increase*."

And, similarly, only the tapes or a narrative can adequately convey the undercurrent of friction that developed between President Kennedy and McGeorge Bundy at the ExComm meetings. "Mac," as his colleagues called him, had a well-deserved reputation for brilliance—and abrasiveness.[7] He correctly assumed that JFK did not wish to be surrounded by ciphers. He spoke his mind freely and seemed to genuinely enjoy the intellectual challenge of these high-stakes discussions. When a colleague suggested on the first day that the U.S. could simply declare

---

[7]"Bundy possessed dazzling clarity and speed of mind—Kennedy told friends that, next to David Ormsby Gore, Bundy was the brightest man he had ever known—as well as great distinction of manner and unlimited self-confidence." (Schlesinger, *A Thousand Days*, 208–9)

that the Russian missiles are "entirely Cuban" if it became necessary to invade the island, Bundy, clearly relishing the power game, observed, "Ah well, what we say for political purposes and what we think are not identical here." Bundy, however, sometimes seemed to forget that *he* was not the President and his self-centered tone and repeated admonitions about what "I myself" would do, frequently strained JFK's patience.

Bundy first wrangled openly with the President on the third day of the ExComm meetings. He insisted, contrary to JFK's emphatically stated position, that the quarantine of Cuba must include a formal declaration of war in order to legitimize stopping and searching vessels belonging to U.S. allies. JFK retorted sharply, "I don't think anybody who gets excited because their ships are stopped under these conditions—they're not very much help to us anyway." Bundy, however, soon put the President on the spot again, contending that "your whole posture" must demonstrate that Khrushchev's move in Cuba was unacceptable. He audaciously predicted that with or without a declaration of war, "You will, in fact, get into the invasion before you're through... either way." Only minutes later, after the President had left the meeting, although Robert Kennedy remained, Bundy responded to a colleague's contention that JFK's decision to impose a unilateral blockade without a declaration of war was the worst possible choice, "You *must* declare, I think... I think the President did not fully grasp that."

Bundy collided with JFK again on October 22. The President had reiterated the disquieting fact, acknowledged days before by General Taylor, that all the missile bases could not be destroyed by air strikes. Bundy reacted rather condescendingly, "*Entirely true*, Mr. President. But I *don't* think the next few days is the time to talk about it." JFK responded with unmistakable annoyance, "Well, I know, but I want everybody to understand it, Mac, if you don't mind!"

A few minutes later, the President contended that since the naval quarantine covered only offensive weapons, but excluded food and medicine, it should be explained publicly as a limited first step. He claimed, as further evidence of American restraint, "Even today the Soviets inspect our [truck] convoys going into Berlin. People get out, don't they?" Bundy replied testily, "No, sir, the people do *not* get out and this troop inspection is a... is a complicated one. They have *ample* means of surveillance, but *inspection* is *not* the word we want to use."

A colleague, however, pointed out that U.S. forces did sometimes get out of the trucks and allow the Soviets to inspect them by looking through the tailgates. JFK seized on this vindication in his sparring match with Bundy, "They *do* let them. Yeah." These sharp-edged exchanges continued on the following day when the President asked whether the cover letter to Khrushchev sent to Moscow with his televised speech had been released to the public. Bundy replied curtly, "*No sir. We told* Khrushchev that we would *not* do so."

JFK and Bundy were at odds again two days later over whether to challenge the Soviet tanker *Bucharest* at sea. The President, with support from McNamara and Rusk, leaned toward letting it through the blockade, but Bundy declared "there is a *real* case to be made, which has perhaps not been presented as strongly this morning as it... as it *could* be, for *doing* it and *getting* it done." Bundy pumped up the pressure by lecturing the commander-in-chief, "It is *important* for you to know, Mr. President, that... that there is a *good*, substantial argument and a lot of people in the argument on the other side, *all* of whom will fall in with whatever decision you make." But, he shrewdly asked for Nitze's view and the tough assistant defense secretary called for full enforcement of the blockade "against everybody, not selecting ships or the types of ships." "That's correct," Bundy affirmed. The President, however, finally decided "We don't want to precipitate an incident," and allowed the *Bucharest* through the quarantine.

On the pivotal day of the crisis, Saturday October 27, the tension between Kennedy and Bundy intensified. The morning ExComm meeting was roiled by news that Khrushchev had offered publicly to trade missiles in Cuba and Turkey, apparently backing away from his earlier proposal to withdraw them in exchange for an American non-invasion pledge. Bundy insisted on sticking to the Kremlin's previous scheme. "Well maybe they changed it overnight," JFK countered. "But he... he... he... I don't... I... I still think," Bundy responded hesitantly, "he's in a difficult position to change it overnight, having sent *you* a personal communication on the other line." "Well now, let's say he *has* changed it," JFK snapped, "and this is his latest position." "Well, I... I would answer back," Bundy contended, "saying that 'I would prefer to deal with your a... you know... with your interesting proposals of last night.'" Someone in the background egged Bundy on, whispering, "Go for it!"

JFK, later in the meeting, stressed again that "most people will regard this [trade] as not an *unreasonable* proposal. I'll just tell you *that*." Bundy replied quite disdainfully, "But, what '*most* people,' Mr. President?" Kennedy shot back that it would be impossible to justify attacking Cuba after Khrushchev had said, 'If you get *yours* out of Turkey, we'll get *ours* out of Cuba.' I think you've got a very tough one here." "I don't see why we pick *that track*," Bundy repeated, "when he's offered us the other track in the last 24 hours." JFK reiterated with obvious annoyance, "Well he's *now* offered us a new one!" Bundy instead suggested trapping Khrushchev by releasing his private Friday withdrawal/non-invasion letter. "Yeah, but I think we have to," the President responded, only partially suppressing a derisive laugh, "be now thinking about what our position's gonna be on *this* one, because this is the one that's *before* us and *before* the world." "If we *accept* the notion of the trade at this stage," Bundy later admonished, "our position will come apart very fast."

Toward the end of the morning meeting, after talking on the phone with Adlai Stevenson at the U.N. about the draft of a new message to Khrushchev, the President suggested, almost whimsically, "What about our putting something in about Berlin? ... I mean... just to try to put some sand in *his* gears for a few minutes." "In what way?" Bundy asked somewhat obtusely. JFK, obviously thinking of Russian demands for a non-invasion guarantee for Cuba, snapped sarcastically, "*Well, satisfactory guarantees for Berlin!*"

President Kennedy continued to argue strenuously for the Turkish option at the nearly four-hour meeting that began in the late afternoon. Bundy finally cut him off with a piercing dissent: "if we *sound* as if we wanted to make this trade to our NATO people and to all the people who are tied to us by *alliance*, we are in *real trouble*. I think that we'll... we'll *all* join in doing this if this is the decision. But I think we... we *should* tell you that that's the *universal* assessment of everyone in the government that's connected with these alliance problems"—that the linkage to Turkey and NATO must be rejected. "The justification for *this* message," he continued, "is that we expect it to be turned down, expect to be acting [militarily] tomorrow or the next day. That's... that's what it's for and it's *not* good unless that's what happens." Several voices can be heard affirming, "That's right"—undoubtedly creating an uncomfortable moment for the President.

Later in the discussion, President Kennedy urged bringing Khrushchev's public Turkish proposal before a meeting of the NATO Council the following morning. "No, I... I would *not* do it tomorrow,"

Bundy declared rather abrasively, "Mr. President, myself." This time, JFK simply ignored Bundy's objection and changed the subject. Later in the meeting, when the President returned after a 45 minute absence and promptly reopened the discussion of Turkey and NATO, Bundy intrepidly pointed out again, "we have *really* to agree on the *track*, you see, Mr. President, and I think that there's a *very* substantial difference between us." JFK expressed a willingness to discuss these differences—notwithstanding the fact that he had already made up his mind.

The cumulative strain between President Kennedy and Bundy is unmistakable when *listening* to their pointed exchanges. Of course, Bundy, to his credit, was conscientiously doing his job as national security adviser. But, the drama of this steady intensification of personal friction can easily be swamped in a sea of minutiae when simply read in a transcript. Their words lose much of their impact without *hearing* their tone and nuance. Short of listening to the tapes in full, a daunting prospect for even the most experienced listener, only a narrative can capture the flavor and mood of these exchanges and fully document the depth and intensity, for example, of the ExComm hostility to a Turkish deal—a definitive illustration of why this book was necessary. Bundy's later claim that he sometimes "chose the role of 'devil's advocate' to focus the dialogue in meetings" simply fails to convincingly account for the compelling evidence on the tapes.[8]

Of course, a thorough hearing of the tapes can also uncover insights well beyond those of tone and mood. Was Secretary Rusk, for example, merely reviewing the facts or proposing a cover story about the U-2 that "strayed" into Soviet air space on an air-sampling mission near Alaska? The so-called "Trollope Ploy," however, provides the most striking case in point. Historians and missile crisis participants, largely as a result of Robert Kennedy's *Thirteen Days*, have often overestimated the importance of this celebrated scheme (the decision to respond to Khrushchev's secret Friday offer while "ignoring" his public Saturday proposal) in resolving the crisis. Indeed, this ExComm tactic, initially attributed to RFK alone, has become a fixture in the legend and lore of the missile crisis. At least in part, RFK overstated the significance of this clever diplomatic maneuver simply because the U.S.-Soviet understanding on withdrawing the Turkish missiles was still secret when his book was written and remained secret for decades afterwards.[9]

[8]Bernstein, "Understanding Decisionmaking," 157.
[9]Ted Sorensen, at the 1989 Moscow missile crisis conference, revealed that he had

In fact, listening to the October 27 meeting tapes suggests that scholars and ExComm members have read far too much cunning and coherence into the discussion of this thorny issue. Bundy was actually the first to float the partially formed idea of ignoring rumors of a new Khrushchev offer on the Turkish missiles by responding instead to his "interesting proposals" of Friday night. Soon after, JFK himself contemplated sticking with "last night's business," at least until Khrushchev's new message had actually arrived in Washington. Eventually, nearly the entire ExComm tenaciously endorsed the Friday track in order to thwart what they regarded as a Soviet ploy to divide NATO and squeeze additional concessions out of the United States.

President Kennedy, as the tapes document, stubbornly and persistently contended that Khrushchev's Saturday offer could not be ignored precisely because it had been made public. If the Soviets agreed to stop work on the missile sites and render the missiles inoperable, he reasoned, it would be politically and diplomatically counterproductive to exclude the Turkish missiles from discussions of an overall settlement. In fact, JFK's eventual message to Khrushchev did *not* really "ignore" the Saturday proposal on Turkey, but deliberately left the door open to settling broader international issues once the immediate danger in Cuba had been neutralized. The "Trollope Ploy," in that sense, is basically a myth. JFK ultimately offered the Kremlin a calculated blend of Khrushchev's October 26 and 27 proposals: the removal of the Soviet missiles from Cuba, an American non-invasion pledge (contingent on U.N. inspection), a willingness to talk later about NATO-related issues *and* a secret commitment to withdraw the Jupiters from Turkey.

In addition, the continuing importance of the ExComm discussions in helping the President to make up his mind, even in the final hours of the crisis, can only be fully grasped by either listening to the tapes or reading a narrative that captures the nuances in voices, tone and words—*when heard together*. Some scholars, especially before the tapes were available, concluded that JFK actually made up his mind on the blockade (in the first week) and on the Turkish missile trade (in the second week) essentially on his own or in private consultation with a few select advisers. The ExComm, they maintained, was "largely irrelevant to the President's decision-making at the height of the crisis" and had

---

deleted the Turkish-Cuban missile trade from RFK's posthumously published *Thirteen Days*.

become a mere forum for building consensus or gathering information.[10]

This view has persisted even since the release of the tapes: "However chaotic the process of policy formulation, there is no question that Ex-Comm did shift opinions and help the president ensure that all points of view were exposed and a consensus forged around his preferred option. It did not, however, provide the setting for many of the key decisions." The final ExComm discussion had become "a kind of charade"—deliberately obscuring the President's more selective and confidential decisions.[11]

There can be no question, after listening painstakingly to these recordings, that the often rough give-and-take with the ExComm played a decisive role in continuing to shape JFK's perceptions and decisions. The President, for example, surely did not miss the implications of Taylor's almost casual assertion that using nuclear weapons in Cuba would not necessarily provoke a nuclear response from the Soviet Union; or McNamara's confident assurances about using practice depth charges to "harmlessly" force Soviet submarines to surface; or Bundy's self-important claim that everyone in the government involved in alliance problems would be hostile to a Cuba-Turkey missile trade; or Nitze's inflexibility over amending JCS procedures to prevent the firing of the Turkish Jupiter missiles and advocacy of shooting down Soviet planes in the Berlin air corridor. In several of these cases, not to mention the taut exchanges with General LeMay and Senators Russell and Fulbright, JFK barely managed to conceal his sardonic disdain in the face of inflexibility, doctrinaire thinking and lack of imagination.

Even in the final days and hours of the crisis, the ExComm had an enormous emotional and psychological impact on President Kennedy's commitment to averting nuclear war. Every major option was discussed, frequently in exhaustive and exhausting detail—providing both the context and an indispensable sounding board for the President in

[10]See, for example, Elizabeth Cohn, "President Kennedy's Decision to Impose a Blockade in the Cuban Missile Crisis: Building Consensus in the ExComm After the Decision," in Nathan, ed., *Cuban Missile Crisis Revisited*, 226–31; Blight, *et al.*, "Essence of Revision," 159; David A. Welch and James G. Blight, "The Eleventh Hour of the Cuban Missile Crisis: An Introduction to the ExComm Transcripts," *International Security* 12 (1987–88), 15–16.

[11]Freedman, *Kennedy's Wars*, 171; Bernstein, "Reconsidering the Missile Crisis," 126.

making his final decisions. Bureaucratic interests and organizational thinking, that is, "where one sits," may provide "significant clues" about the positions taken, that is, "where one stands," at the ExComm meetings. But, the persistent uncertainty, stress and shifting of opinions at these meetings, Barton Bernstein suggests, indicates that "beliefs, proclivities, and perceptions," not to mention "personality or background" and "concerns about war" were likely far more significant. "There is serious reason to doubt whether generalizations from that crisis period would fit more normal times and situations. . . . The missile crisis embodied an important uniqueness: [because of] the concentrated period, and the sense of peril and possible disaster." President Kennedy, whose first reaction to the U-2 photos was, "He can't do that to me," turned out to be the most determined "'dove-like' person" in the critical October 27 meetings—suggesting the decisive importance of listening to the original discussions, or reading a narrative, in order to develop a more multifaceted "understanding of that chief executive, of how he viewed the world, and perhaps even of why he viewed it that way."[12]

Robert Kennedy tirelessly pressed his brother not to give up on Khrushchev's Friday proposal and JFK, although skeptical and reluctant, finally agreed to try this scheme despite repeatedly predicting that the Soviet leader would inevitably "come back" to his public offer on the Turkish missiles. The President had no illusions about forcing Khrushchev to settle for the terms in his earlier message and appears to have assented to this stratagem largely to placate unyielding ExComm opposition. In fact, as revealed by RFK's meeting with Dobrynin and other steps taken later that day and kept secret from much of the ExComm, JFK was determined not to allow this reasonable chance to avert nuclear catastrophe slip away. As he had reminded the gung-ho Joint Chiefs on October 19, an attack on Cuba could prompt the firing of these nuclear missiles against American cities and result in 80–100 million casualties—"you're talkin about the destruction of a country."

Indeed, President Kennedy's inclination to pursue the Turkish option actually seems to have hardened in response to the dogged intractability of his advisers. The tapes indicate that the ExComm continued to have a major impact, especially during the final meetings, simply by repeatedly and all but unanimously *opposing* JFK's preferred course of

---

[12]Bernstein, "Understanding Decisionmaking," 140–42, 157, 159, 163; Allison and Zelikow, *Essence of Decision*, 307.

action. It is a serious mistake, in that sense, to underestimate the importance of these discussions in prodding the President to implement this potential settlement—while there was still time.

As a historian trained in the turbulent 1960s and influenced by New Left historiography, I took for granted that John F. Kennedy had been a tough and relentless Cold Warrior. And, as discussed earlier, JFK and the Kennedy administration bear significant responsibility for precipitating the missile crisis in the first place. However, when I first listened to the tapes in the early 1980s, JFK's prudence and independence was a considerable surprise. No listener can doubt that the ExComm understood that the decisions would be made by the commander-in-chief alone.

The President consistently dug in his heels in the face of pressure to bomb the missile sites or invade Cuba—as a first step. He also repeatedly acted to prevent, postpone, or at least question the advisability of potentially provocative measures—such as mining international waters around Cuba; extending the quarantine to Soviet aircraft flying to Cuba; resisting Russian efforts to inspect U.S. truck convoys entering Berlin; using needlessly belligerent language in an official proclamation; deleting the word "miscalculate" from a presidential letter because Khrushchev had misinterpreted this concept when translated into Russian during the Vienna summit; seizing a Soviet ship that had reversed course; risking an armed clash if the crew of a disabled ship resisted boarding; enforcing the quarantine by attacking a Soviet submarine; arming U.S. reconnaissance planes and returning Cuban ground fire; initiating night surveillance using flares; or immediately assaulting the SAM sites if a U-2 was shot down. JFK repeatedly tried to rise above the Cold War rhetoric he had exploited from the 1960 campaign through his October 22 speech announcing the discovery of Soviet missiles in Cuba. And, as these recordings conclusively prove, he succeeded to a remarkable degree—although not without some "help" from Khrushchev *and* some genuine luck.

History is not a neatly cut jigsaw puzzle. Pieces of historical evidence do not have to fit together tidily or logically within fixed and predetermined borders. Indeed, despite the best efforts of historians, they do not have to fit together at all. History defines its own parameters and historical figures, unlike the precut pieces of a jigsaw puzzle, often defy our assumptions and expectations. Contradictions and inconsistencies, in short, are the rule rather than the exception in human affairs.

The evidence from the missile crisis tapes is anomalous and even surprising but no less true: JFK often stood virtually alone against war-like counsel from the ExComm, the JCS and Congress during those historic thirteen days. Nonetheless, he never abandoned his commitment, even *after* the Cuban missile crisis, to undermine the Cuban revolution and get rid of Fidel Castro. It was one thing, however, for President Kennedy to support efforts to overthrow or even eliminate the Cuban leader, but quite another for him to recklessly risk unleashing "the final failure."[13]

[13]On November 18, 1963, JFK told the Inter-American Press Association that the United States would not allow a communist regime "to subvert and destroy the process of democratic development" in Latin America. (*Public Papers of the Presidents: John F. Kennedy, 1963, III* (Washington, D.C.: United States Government Printing Office, 1964), 872–77) Some historians would likely dismiss this rhetoric as self-serving Cold War posturing. But, at the same time, they romanticize Castro's "support for revolutions in the hemisphere" and "the legitimacy of a radical revolution in the United States sphere of influence" (Paterson, "Fixation with Cuba," 154–55), idealize Castro's refusal to "renounce his commitment to revolution" (Rabe, "After the Missiles of October," 724), and claim that the U.S. represents a "counter-revolutionary tradition" (Paterson, "John F. Kennedy's Quest," 12). American democracy *has* repeatedly failed to live up to its professed principles at home and abroad, but, the fact remains that the historian's craft itself has always been one of the first fatalities of these "radical" and "revolutionary" regimes.

Appendix

The Published Cuban Missile Crisis Transcripts: Rounds One, Two and Beyond

An explanation is in order as to why I have not relied on the two published editions of ExComm tape transcripts. I worked extensively with these recordings as Kennedy Library historian, as discussed above, before they were declassified or transcribed and learned to rely on my own ears, experience and knowledge in handling these irreplaceable primary sources. And, of course, a book of this kind could only be based on direct research from the tapes.

In addition, I eventually discovered that the published transcripts were simply not as consistently reliable as they could and should have been. Initially I was delighted, but surprised, to learn in the fall of 1997 that the Harvard University Press was about to publish complete transcripts, edited by the prominent historians Ernest R. May and Philip D. Zelikow, of the nearly twenty-two hours of audio tapes of the meetings of the Executive Committee of the National Security Council recorded during the legendary 13 days of the Cuban missile crisis.[1] My surprise was based on the fact that the bulk of these tapes, more than 17 hours, had not been declassified until late 1996 and early 1997. As the first professional historian ever to listen to all of these recordings, I knew that many of the tapes were technically flawed and that producing accurate transcripts required substantial time and patience as well as knowledge and skill. But, there was every reason to have complete confidence in the editors, and I enthusiastically participated with them in a program about the new transcripts before a packed house at the Ken-

[1] *The Kennedy Tapes: Inside the White House During the Cuban Missile Crisis.*

nedy Library in late 1997. Over the next few years the book was widely and favorably reviewed. In my own work, especially with secondary school history teachers, I strongly applauded the new transcripts and recommended the book as one of the great historical primary source contributions of our time.

Early in 2000, however, I was shocked and dismayed to discover that the transcripts were repeatedly and seriously inaccurate, often misrepresenting and even reversing the intent of the speakers and significantly distorting the historical record. I subsequently published two articles explaining these findings.[2] Zelikow and May eventually acknowledged that the original draft transcripts prepared by court reporters "did not work out well" and that the results of special noise reduction techniques "were disappointing."[3] However, the editors assured readers late in 2000,

> we have kept going back over the missile crisis tapes repeatedly during the past three years, recently aided by new colleagues and new technology. A three-volume reference set with transcriptions of all Kennedy tapes from July 30 to October 28, 1962, will be published by W.W. Norton early in 2001, the products of the Presidential Recordings Project at the University of Virginia's Miller Center of Public Affairs. The Norton volumes will have accompanying CD-ROMs that include the audiotapes, synchronized with the transcripts. So anyone will now be able to judge the adequacy of the work for themselves (and perhaps gain a measure of empathy for the task).[4]

Zelikow and May also maintained that "we think few [readers of *The Kennedy Tapes*] will find the many amendments in our retranscriptions to be very important."[5] This claim is puzzling since a good part of the 2001 Norton-Miller Center edition is significantly different, indeed sometimes unrecognizable, when compared to the original 1997 version. But the key issue for readers today, of course, is the accuracy and reliability of the new edition.

The 2001 Cuban missile crisis transcripts total about 600 pages, some 35% of the new Miller Center edition.[6] The 3 volume set includes

[2]"What JFK Really Said," 122–28, and "The 1997 Published Transcripts of the JFK Cuban Missile Crisis Tapes," 586–93.

[3]Zelikow and May, "Source Material: Controversy: The Kennedy Tapes: Past and Future," *Presidential Studies Quarterly 30* (2000), 794.

[4]*Ibid.*, 793.

[5]*Ibid.*

[6]Volume 2, edited by Timothy Naftali, director of the Presidential Recordings Project, Miller Center of Public Affairs, University of Virginia, and Philip Zelikow, director of the Miller Center, includes the missile crisis transcripts from October 16 to 21. Volume 3, ed-

a CD-ROM containing all the written transcripts, all the sound recordings and remarkable graphics—a technical tour-de-force. Unfortunately, the CD-ROM is marred by poor audio reproduction and faulty
visual synchronization. This result is not surprising given the huge
amount of data compression needed to fit so much audio and graphic
material on one disc. It is unlikely that any reader will now be able "to
judge the adequacy of the work for themselves" using this CD-ROM
alone.

I have relied instead on the Kennedy Library cassettes (dubbed unal-
tered onto compact discs). These now declassified recordings, which I
used during my 23 years as Kennedy Library historian, were reproduced from the actual 1962 reel-to-reel master tapes made in the White
House and have not been altered by audio compression or sound fil-
tering of any kind—not even by Dolby noise reduction. The editors of
the Norton edition, on the other hand, explained that they worked
from professional quality Digital Audio Tapes, "not the less expensive
analog cassettes ordinarily sold to the public by presidential libraries,"
and certainly not from the Norton edition CD-ROM, to produce these
new published transcripts.[7]

In my two earlier analyses of the 1997 missile crisis transcripts, I
first checked the tape of the October 18 morning meeting after failing
to find in the transcript JFK's electrifying description of nuclear war as
"the final failure." This time around, I concentrated on a different section—several hours from the crucial, dramatic and generally audible afternoon and evening meetings on Saturday, October 27—which included the shooting down of an American U-2 spy plane over Cuba and
JFK's support for Nikita Khrushchev's offer to "trade" U.S. missiles in
Turkey for Soviet missiles in Cuba. In addition, I again spot-checked all
the other missile crisis transcripts.

The Random House Dictionary defines a transcript as "an exact
copy or reproduction, especially one having an official status." The editors were evidently determined to measure up to this definition, but
nonetheless acknowledged: "Although the Miller Center volumes are
intended to be authoritative reference works, they will always be subject to minor amendments."[8] The editors also explained their decision

---

ited by Zelikow and Harvard historian Ernest May, includes the transcripts from October
22 to 28.

[7]Philip Zelikow and Ernest May, "The Presidential Recordings Project," in *The Presidential Recordings: John F. Kennedy: The Great Crises*, V. 2, p. xv.

[8]Zelikow and May, "The Presidential Recordings Project," xv.

to make subjective editorial judgments in order to produce transcripts with the highest possible standards of fluency and clarity:

> In the effort to be exhaustive, sometimes there is a temptation to overtranscribe, catching every fragmentary utterance however unclear or peripheral. But the result on the page can add too much intrusive static, making the substance less understandable now than it was to listeners at the time. Obviously, what to include and omit, balancing coherence and comprehension against the completeness of the record, also requires subjective judgment. The object is to give the reader or user the truest possible sense of the actual dialogue as the participants themselves could have understood it (had they been paying attention).[9]

The Miller Center–Norton missile crisis transcripts are a significant improvement over the 1997 version. The number of "unclear" passages has been sharply reduced and overall accuracy has been substantially improved. Nevertheless, I regret that many troubling errors remain in the new version. My latest investigation turned up persistent and significant inaccuracies in the 50+ pages checked carefully in the new transcripts of the afternoon and evening October 27 tapes. A spot check of the remaining transcripts produced similar results.

These errors matter profoundly. No scholar would question the value of recovering passages still transcribed as "[unclear]" or catching important remarks that have been left completely out of the transcripts. But, it is also crucial for readers to understand that mistranscribing even a single word can significantly distort the intent of the speaker and alter the historian's understanding of the event itself. The transcripts in the 1997 volume have already been quoted in historical articles, monographs, surveys and biographies, in teacher training materials and workshops and even in Hollywood films. There is a real danger that inaccuracies, such as those detailed below in the 2001 edition, will also become part of the accepted historical record simply because few scholars are willing to invest the time and effort required to listen to the tapes.

The following is *a representative sample* of errors in three (sometimes overlapping) categories: 1) remarks transcribed as "[unclear]" which are, in fact, discernable 2) words, phrases, sentences or speakers missing altogether from the transcripts 3) mistranscriptions which alter the substance or interpretation of the historical record. Of course, many examples in categories 1 and 2 also affect historical interpretation.

[9]Zelikow and May, "The Presidential Recordings Project," xv–xvi.

1) Remarks Transcribed as "[unclear]":

Miller Center–Norton Edition, Volume 2, p. 404: [henceforth *MCNE, 2, 404*]: Rusk: "decide that this is the time to eliminate the Cuban problem by action [unclear] the island." [highlighting added]

Author's Transcription: [henceforth AT]: Rusk: "decide that this is the time to eliminate the Cuban problem by **actually moving into the island.**"

MCNE, 2, 443: Martin: "you've got to move immediately, or you're going to have a [unclear] in *this* country."

AT: Martin: "you've got to move immediately, or the... you're going to have a **ton of instability** in *this* country."

MCNE, 2, 534: Thompson: "I think Khrushchev will deny that these are Soviet bases. [Unclear.]"

AT: Thompson: "I think that Khrushchev will deny that these are Soviet bases. **But naturally, we take exception to that.**"

MCNE, 3, 50: JFK: "...appearing to be an irresolute ally. [Unclear.]"

AT: JFK: "...appearing to be an irresolute ally—**so it's time we chose where we begin on the road.**"

MCNE, 3, 109: Lundahl: "They could have been [unclear] to another locale."

AT: Lundahl: "They could have been **moved quickly** to another locale."

MCNE, 3, 126: JFK: "Well, we'll be in touch if we're not going to get it. [Unclear.]"

AT: JFK: "Well, we'll be in touch if we're not gonna get it. **We just gotta tell the OAS to get to it.**"

MCNE, 3, 159: JFK: "Is this more challenging that if we [unclear]?"

AT: JFK: "Is this more *challenging* **than it needs to be?**"

MCNE, 3, 171: JFK: "What is it that we ought to do with the population of the affected areas, in case some bombs go off? I just don't see [unclear] how you can [unclear] effectively."

AT: JFK: "What is it we oughta *do* with the population of the affected areas *in case* the bombs go off? I just don't see **in your statement** how you **addressed yourself to that question** effectively."

MCNE, 3, 188: Rusk: "Moscow, in spite of their threatened resistance to U.S. [unclear], has [unclear]."

AT: Rusk: "Moscow, in spite of their threatened resistance to U.S **efforts to stop Soviet ships....**"

MCNE, 3, 188: McNamara: "Mr. President, first [unclear] yesterday about our own [unclear]."

AT: McNamara: "Mr. President, first **a question you raised** yesterday about our own **desire for security.**"

MCNE, 3, 211: Mansfield: "...**particularly when you saw this** [unclear]."

AT: Mansfield (speaking to Senator Richard Russell): "**Dick, I don't know whether you saw this or not.**"

MCNE, 3, 212: Rusk: "[Unclear] said to me, but...."
AT: Rusk: "**The two of you are very generous in attributing all of that to me, but....**"

MCNE, 3, 223: JFK: "What, that he would [unclear] on invasion?"
AT: JFK: "**That** what, that he'd **look with equanimity upon** invasion?"

MCNE, 3, 240: JFK: "[Unclear] explain to me this whole Russian thing someday."
AT: JFK: "**It's all gray** to me, this whole Russian thing... **ahh...** someday."

MCNE, 3, 244: JFK: "All right, it's obvious [unclear] **and that's a re-straining factor. We wouldn't** turn it around."
AT: JFK: "All right, because obviously **if that had contained a missile they woulda turned it around.**"

MCNE, 3, 246: JFK: "Quite obviously **the most** [unclear]."
AT: JFK: "Quite obviously **they don't want us to grab anything.**"

MCNE, 3, 260: JFK: "...there's no way they can [unclear] with American ships **to prevent these** weapons coming in, in addition to [unclear]."
AT: JFK: "...there's no way they can **accept** with American ships **preventing weapons** coming in. **In addition, the Cubans aren't gonna take this too well.**"

MCNE, 3, 265: JFK: "Well, we first stop a Soviet ship someplace and have [unclear] what they're going to do."
AT: JFK: "Well, we first stop a Soviet ship, uh... uh... someplace, and **have this out** on what they're gonna do."

MCNE, 3, 268: JFK: "I think the only arguments for not taking it [unclear]. I don't think it makes a hell of a lot of difference...."
AT: JFK: "I think the only argument's for *not* taking it. **I think we could grab us one of these things anytime.** I don't think it makes a hell of a lot of difference...."

MCNE, 3, 279: Thompson: "On the other hand, he *is* backing away and that [unclear]."
AT: Thompson: "On the other hand, he *is* backing away and that **tips the balance.**"

MCNE, 3, 294: JFK: "'We can **just** [unclear] your bombers every-place.'"

AT: JFK: "'We can **destroy all** *your* bombers everyplace.'"

MCNE, 3, 320: JFK: "I'd like to have us take a look now at whether that can even be [unclear]."

AT: JFK: "I'd like to have us take a look now at whether that can even *be* **an option.**"

MCNE, 3, 368: Dillon: "[Unclear] **just** cannot accept a Turkey-Cuba trade at this point."

AT: Dillon: "**The United States** *cannot* accept a... a Turkey-Cuba trade at this point."

MCNE, 3, 370: Dillon: "[Unclear]. It puts it right back on them."

AT: Dillon: "**Reverse the risks. While we're fooling around** it puts it right back on them."

MCNE, 3, 377: McNamara: "...our action in the interim, in [unclear] has got to really keep the pressure on them, in this [unclear] situation."

AT: McNamara: "...our action in the interim. **So** *my* **point is we oughta** *really* **keep the pressure on them in this type of** situation."

MCNE, 3, 393: Bundy: "And the bases [unclear] that are already there."

AT: **RFK:** "And the bases **dismantled** that are already there."

MCNE, 3, 427: JFK: "I don't think he's going to get [unclear] **to** this."

AT: JFK: "I don't think he's gonna get **enough for** this."

MCNE, 3, 432: JFK: "It seems to me.... I don't believe [unclear] general."

AT: JFK: "It seems to me... **why don't we make that more** general?"

MCNE, 3, 443: JFK: "Most of the NATO members aren't going to be very happy about it because the [unclear] **problem is** [going to be] Berlin **is suddenly** [unclear]."

AT: JFK: "Most of the NATO members aren't going to be very happy about it because **it's inevitable, I think it's** *Berlin* **that's gonna be...."**

MCNE, 3, 491: Taylor: "I went back **to them** [unclear] and talked this over with the Chiefs."

AT: Taylor: "I went back **this morning** and talked this over with the Chiefs."

MCNE, 3, 504: Rusk: "I think Finletter ought to have [unclear] **of the house** some ideas about..."

AT: Rusk: "I think Finletter ought to have, **or has,** some ideas about...."

2) Missing Words, Phrases, Sentences or Speakers:

MCNE, 3, 51: Taylor: "Mr. President, I should call attention to the fact we're starting moves now which are overt, and will be seen and reported on and commented on. So that movement of armor, for example, to the East Coast.

AT: Taylor: "Mr. President, I should call attention to the fact we're starting moves now which are very... are overt, and will be seen and reported on and commented on."

Bundy: **"Precautionary, every one of them!"**

Taylor: "So that... movements of armor, for example, to the East Coast."

MCNE, 3, 130: Rusk: "you just might want to . . . ."

AT: Rusk: "you might want to **just hear this.**"

MCNE, 3, 166: Rusk: "It's a good reason to send this letter to Mr. Khrushchev and tell him to turn them around."

AT: Rusk: "It's a good reason to send this letter to Mr. Khrushchev, tell him to turn 'em around—**not to challenge it.**"

MCNE, 3, 187: Lundahl: "...use camouflage detection and a lot of other things."

AT: Lundahl: "use camouflage detection **film** and a lot of other things."

MCNE, 3, 191: McNamara: "There is a submarine very close, we believe, to each of them."

AT: McNamara: "There is a submarine very close, we believe, to each of them."

JFK: "Two submarines."

MCNE, 3, 197: Rusk: [reports a possible remark by a Cuban U.N. diplomat] "if we would hold off on the blockade for a day or so or until the Security Council votes."

AT: Rusk: "if we would hold off on the blockade for a day or so...."

McCone interjects, "Oh, come on!"

Rusk continues, "or until the Security Council votes."

MCNE, 3, 223: JFK: "They've committed their prestige much more heavily—"

AT: JFK: "They've committed their prestige much more heavily—**now much more than I have in Berlin.**"

MCNE, 3, 240: Bundy: "Maybe their minds..."

AT: Bundy: "Maybe their minds **are clearer.**"

MCNE, 3, 326: JFK: "Could one bullet do that? Would it blow or is it just..."

Lundahl: "**Assuming** red nitric acid, sir, very heavily lined trucks...."

AT: JFK: "**Can** one bullet do **much** to that?"

McCone: "**Well, if a fella went across there with bullet punctures, it would. It invariably wreaks hell with it.**"

JFK: "Would it blow or is it just...?"

Lundahl: "**It would be fuming** red nitric acid, sir, very heavily lined trucks...."

MCNE, 3, 371: Nitze: "It's an entirely separate situation. It's not a threat. This is a diversionary tactic."

AT: Nitze: "It's an *entirely* separate situation. It's *not* a threat."

Taylor: "**You see this as** a diversionary tactic."

MCNE, 3, 376: McNamara: "We had one deal in the letter; now we've got a different deal. And why shouldn't we say...."

AT: McNamara: "We had one *deal* in the letter, now we've got a different *deal*."

Taylor: "**And in** *public*...."

McNamara: "**And in...** yeah. And why shouldn't we say...."

MCNE, 3, 380: JFK: "They've got a very good proposal, which is the reason they've made it public—"

AT: JFK: "They've got **a God...** they've got a very good proposal, which is the reason they've made it public—**with an announcement....**"

MCNE, 3, 415: Dillon: "they'd say: 'Don't trade.' But they'd also say, 'Don't do anything in Cuba.'"

AT: Dillon: "they'd say, 'Don't trade,' but they'd also say, 'Don't do anything in Cuba'—**which may well be right.**"

MCNE, 3, 435: Bundy: "You've got to give him something to get him back on this track."

AT: Bundy: "You've gotta give him *something* to get him back on this track."

Rusk: "**On** *this* **track, yeah.**"

MCNE, 3, 441: JFK: "or do we want to just use this as a reason for doing a lot of other shooting at the SAMs?"

AT: JFK: "or do we wanna just use this as a reason for doing a lot of other....?"

McNamara: "**Shooting up the SAMs.**"

MCNE, 3, 452: JFK: "**Gentlemen,** come up and sit here now. **Gentlemen.**"

AT: JFK: "**George,** come up and sit here now, **you're another civilian.**"

Taylor: "**Come on into General Taylor's lap.**"

MCNE, 3, 454: JFK: "But they're going to say is we're seeking the trade with the Russians, aren't they?"

AT: JFK: "But they... they're gonna say is that we're **definitely** seeking a trade with the Russians, aren't they? **But what do I... that's alright isn't it?**"

MCNE, 3, 456: JFK: "I think we ought to get moving on it. I think we have until tomorrow afternoon."

AT: JFK: "I think we oughta get moving on it. **The fact is, time's running out.** I think we have tomorrow afternoon."

MCNE, 3, 462: McNamara: "It's 12 pages of fluff."
AT: McNamara: "It's 12 pages of...."
Dillon: "fluff"
McNamara: "of fluff."

MCNE, 3, 501: McNamara: "before we—open the door to NATO."
AT: McNamara: "before we—open a door to NATO—**to make up our own minds.**"

3) Mistranscriptions Which Alter the Historical Record:

MCNE, 2, 523: Rusk: "I think the American people will willingly undertake great danger and, if necessary, great suffering, if they have a deep feeling that we've done everything that was reasonably possible to determine whether this **trip** was necessary."

AT: Rusk: "I think the American people will willingly undertake great danger and, if necessary, great sacrifice, if they have a *deep* feeling that we've done everything that was reasonably possible to determine whether this **risk** was necessary."

MCNE, 2, 598: Wheeler: "If we **smear** Castro, Khrushchev **smears** Willy Brandt [in Berlin]."

AT: Wheeler: "If we **sneer at** Castro, Khrushchev **sneers at** Willy Brandt."

MCNE, 3, 78: JFK: "If we go into Cuba we have to all realize that we are taking a chance that these missiles, which are ready to fire, won't be fired. **So that's a gamble we should take.**"

AT: JFK: "If we go into Cuba we have to all realize that we are taking a chance that these missiles, which are ready to fire, won't be fired. So that's... **is that really a gamble we should take?**"

MCNE, 3, 207: JFK: "Well, I think that the **argument** will be that the Russians led us into a trap."

AT: JFK: "Well I think that they're gonna... the *irony* will be that the Russians led us into a trap."

MCNE, 3, 215: McCone: "The next real **target** we had was when we saw...."

AT: McCone: "The next *real* **hard information** we had was when we saw...."

MCNE, 3, 252: **Unidentified: "Have you ever seen** missile fuel?"
McNamara: "No. **[unclear mentions of "nitric acid."]**"
AT: **Ball: "Kerosene** missile fuel?"
McNamara: "No, **fuming** nitric acid."

MCNE, 3, 292: McNamara: "I don't believe we **have announced** it."
AT: McNamara: "Oh, I *don't* believe we **should announce** it."

MCNE, 3, 299: Bundy: "Donny, there are some special restrictions on some of these pictures. **But I think the President's good decision is that** everything is waived, **and** you get the one you like best."
AT: Bundy: "**But Donny, there** *are* some special restrictions on some of these pictures **that I think the President sees. If** everything is waived, you get the one you like best."

MCNE, 3, 329: McCone: "It's very **evil** stuff they've got there."
AT: McCone: "It's very **lethal** stuff they've got there."

MCNE, 3, 361: Nitze: "**Hare** says that this is absolutely anathema...."
AT: Nitze: "**The Turks... the Turks** say this is absolutely anathema...."

MCNE, 3, 376: Rusk: "**And most important, what if Moscow decides this is** too much of a setback for them?"
AT: Rusk: "**I suppose the boys... the boys in Moscow decided this was** too much of a setback for 'em."

MCNE, 3, 380: JFK: "In other words, we couldn't **destroy** the missiles anyway, could we? They belong to the Turks. All we can **destroy** is the warheads."
AT: JFK: "In other words, we couldn't **withdraw** the missiles anyway, could we? They belong to the Turks. All we could **withdraw** is the warheads?"

MCNE, 3, 382: Bundy: "I myself would send back word by **phone**...."
AT: Bundy: "I myself would send back word by [Aleksandr] **Fomin**...."

MCNE, 3, 405: Thompson: "That means we have to take **this other** line. **If he starts this wobbly**...."
AT: Thompson: "which means we have to take **a tough** line—**because this wobbling I think**...."

MCNE, 3, 426: JFK: "He's now moved on to the Turkish thing; so we're just going to get a letter back saying: 'Well, **we'll** be glad to settle Cuba when we've settled Turkey.'"
AT: JFK: "He's *now* moved on to the *Turkish* thing. So we're just

gonna get a letter *back* saying, 'Well, **he'd** be glad to settle **Turkey when we settle.**... settle Cuba when we settle Turkey.'"

MCNE, 3, 437: JFK: "But anyway, we can try this thing. But he's going to come back, **I'm certain.**"

AT: JFK: "But anyway, we can *try* this thing, but he's gonna come back **on Turkey.**"

MCNE, 3, 439: McNamara: "We have intense ground fire against our **air.**"

Taylor: "I wouldn't **worry.** I wouldn't **pay any attention.**"

AT: McNamara: "We have *intense* ground fire against our... **our...**"

Taylor: "I wouldn't **say that.** I wouldn't **say 'intense' here.**"

MCNE, 3, 470: Thompson: "I think they've been put **up** by the Lippmann piece. **It occurs to me** that we really **aren't** prepared to talk Turkey for Cuba."

AT: Thompson: "I think they've been put **off** by the Lippmann piece— **encouraged to think** that we *really* are prepared to **swap** Turkey for Cuba."

MCNE, 3, 475: Thompson: "One is to prepare for an attack on Cuba, and the other is to get a peaceful solution along the lines which **we have** proposed."

AT: Thompson: "One is to prepare for an attack on Cuba, and the other is to get a peaceful solution along the lines which **he proposed.**"

MCNE, 3, 482: JFK: "We'll see about what we do about **our plane.**"

AT: JFK: "We'll see about what we do about **this trade.**"

MCNE, 3, 492: McNamara: "I would say only that we ought to keep some kind of pressure on tonight and tomorrow night that indicates we're firm. Now if we call **off** these air **strikes** tonight, I think that settles that—"

JFK: "I [unclear] **want to** do that, I think—"

AT: McNamara: "I would say only that we ought to keep *some* kind of pressure on tonight and tomorrow night that indicates we're firm. Now if we call **up** these air **squadrons** tonight, I think that settles that.[10]

JFK: "**That's right.** We're **gonna** do that, **aren't we?**"

MCNE, 3, 497: Rusk: "We need just to see whether **they are building** up the pressures on Khrushchev **with an impact that we can live with.**"

AT: Rusk: "We need to see whether **we're building** up the pressures on Khrushchev **to get back to a pact we can live with.**"

---

[10]The editors also mistranscribed this important line in the 1997 edition. But, ironically, the 1983 McGeorge Bundy transcript, which they accurately describe as "a rough transcript," got it right. (May and Zelikow, *The Kennedy Tapes*, xii, 612; Bundy October 27 Transcript, JFK Library, 1983, 70)

MCNE, 3, 505: JFK: "I think that he knows about the plane. **He's** announced it."

AT: JFK: "I think that he knows about the plane. **We've** announced it."

MCNE, 3, 508: "They say they shot down our U-2. They say they shot it down."

AT: JFK: "**We'll do that by tomorrow morning** *or* **when** they *say* they've shot down our U-2. If they *say* they shot it down... **then that raises....**"

MCNE, 3, 510: McNamara: "Yeah, I would suggest **to have** an eye for an eye."

Unidentified: "Yeah. That's right. It isn't too serious."

AT: McNamara: "I would suggest **a half** an eye for an eye."

Dillon: "That's right."

McNamara: "**If** it isn't too serious **an attack.**"

Readers must understand that mistakes are inevitable in any transcriptions—including my own. But, scholars and general readers must decide for themselves if the instances cited above can be reasonably dismissed as mere "minor amendments," or the result of "a temptation to overtranscribe," and, most importantly, whether they undermine the integrity and reliability of this invaluable document. There is a profound historical difference between JFK warning the leaders of Congress that nuclear missiles could be launched from Cuba if the U.S. attacked the Soviet bases, "So that's... is that really a gamble we should take?" as opposed to saying, "So that's a gamble we should take"; or JFK discussing whether to "withdraw" or "destroy" missiles or warheads in Turkey; or Bundy urging contacting Moscow "by Fomin" or "by phone"; or McNamara advising restraint, "a half an eye for an eye," rather than "to have an eye for an eye" in the event of Soviet military reprisals.

The fact remains, notwithstanding entirely justifiable "empathy for the task," that these new transcriptions, in the words of the editors, are the work of "trained professional historians," and "every transcript has benefited from at least four listeners," using "the team method," "a special kind of 'peer review'" and "the best technology that the project can afford." "The volume editors remain accountable for checking the quality and accuracy of all the work in their volume, knitting together the whole. All of this work is then reviewed by the general editors" of all three volumes—Professors Zelikow and May. Nonetheless, many troubling slip-ups have somehow eluded this elaborate Miller Center review process—far more than could be included in this Appendix. Some errors are particularly disconcerting because they make no sense

in the context of the discussions and for that reason alone should have
been flagged during the editing process.[11]

This continuing process of constructive criticism and revision will
hopefully prompt other scholars to contribute to this ongoing effort to
improve the accessibility and utility of these unique and incomparable
presidential records. The Miller Center has taken a potential step in
that direction by initiating a new Website, WhiteHouseTapes.org, to
"encourage corrections, suggestions, and updates from the wider community of those interested in the presidential recordings"—with full at-
tribution. They have my best wishes for success as they move forward
on this project since, despite our ongoing disagreements, we are equally
committed to the integrity of the historical record.

[11]Zelikow and May, "The Presidential Recordings Project," xiv–xv; the author can
identify many additional examples for interested scholars.

Bibliography

Archives:

John F. Kennedy Library, Boston, Massachusetts [JFKL]
John F. Kennedy Personal Papers [PP]
John F. Kennedy Presidential Papers, 1961–63:
  National Security Files [NSF]
  Oral History Collection [OHC]
  President's Office Files [POF]
  Presidential Recordings Collection [PRC]
Massachusetts Historical Society, Boston, Massachusetts [MHS]
Nigel Hamilton Research Materials [NHRM]

Printed and Electronic Documentary Sources:

Chang, Laurence, and Peter Kornbluh, eds. *The Cuban Missile Crisis, 1962: A National Security Archive Document Reader.* New York: The New Press, 1998.

Claflin, Edward B., ed. *JFK Wants to Know: Memos from the President's Office, 1961–1963.* New York: Morrow, 1991.

Cold War International History Project Bulletin 1–13 [CWIHPB], Woodrow Wilson International Center for Scholars, 1992–2001: World Wide Web: (http://cwihp.si.edu/default/htm)

Foreign Relations of the United States, [FRUS] Vols. V–XVI. Washington, D.C.: United States Government Printing Office, 1994-1998. Also available on the World Wide Web:state.gov/r/pa/ho/frus/kennedyjf/

Larson, David L. *The Cuban Crisis of 1962: Selected Documents, Chronology and Bibliography.* Lanham, Maryland: University Press of America, 1986.

McCauliffe, Mary S., ed. *CIA Documents on the Cuban Missile Crisis, 1962.* Washington, D.C.: Central Intelligence Agency, 1992.

Public Papers of the Presidents: John F. Kennedy, 1961–1963. Washington, D.C.: United States Government Printing Office, 1962–64.

Secondary Sources:

Abel, Elie. *The Missile Crisis*. Philadelphia: Lippincott, 1966.

Acheson, Dean. Oral History Interview, 1964. OHC, JFKL.

Allison, Graham T. *Essence of Decision: Explaining the Cuban Missile Crisis.* Boston: Little, Brown, 1971.

Allison, Graham, and Philip Zelikow. *Essence of Decision: Explaining the Cuban Missile Crisis.* Second Edition. New York: Addison Wesley Longman, 1999.

Allyn, Bruce J., James G. Blight and David A. Welch, eds. *Back to the Brink: Proceedings of the Moscow Conference on the Cuban Missile Crisis, January 27–29, 1989.* Lanham, Maryland: University Press of America, 1991.

Allyn, Bruce J., James G. Blight, and David A. Welch. "Essence of Revision: Moscow, Havana and the Cuban Missile Crisis." *International Security 14* (Winter 1989–90), 136–72.

Amuchastegui, Domingo. "Cuban Intelligence and the October Crisis." In James G. Blight and David A. Welch, eds., *Intelligence and the Cuban Missile Crisis.* London: Frank Cass, 1998, 88–119.

Ball, George. *The Past Has Another Pattern: Memoirs.* New York: W. W. Norton, 1982.

Baron, Samuel H. *Bloody Sunday in the Soviet Union: Novocherkassk, 1962.* Stanford, CA: Stanford University Press, 2001.

Békés, Csaba. "New Findings on the 1956 Hungarian Revolution." *CWIHPB* 2 (Fall 1992), 1–3.

Bernstein, Barton J. "Commentary: Reconsidering Khrushchev's Gambit— Defending the Soviet Union and Cuba." *Diplomatic History 14* (Spring 1990), 231–39.

Bernstein, Barton J. "Reconsidering the Missile Crisis: Dealing with the Problems of the American Jupiters in Turkey." In James A. Nathan, ed., *The Cuban Missile Crisis Revisited.* New York: St. Martin's, 1992, 55–130.

Bernstein, Barton J. "Understanding Decisionmaking: U.S. Foreign Policy and the Cuban Missile Crisis." *International Security 25* (Summer 2000), 134–64.

Beschloss, Michael R. *The Crisis Years: Kennedy and Khrushchev, 1960–1963.* New York: Harper Collins, 1991.

Bird, Kai. *The Chairman: John J. McCloy and the Making of the American Establishment.* New York: Simon and Schuster, 1992.

Bird, Kai. *The Color of Truth: McGeorge Bundy and William Bundy: Brothers in Arms.* New York: Simon and Schuster, 1998.

Bissel, Richard. Oral History Interview, 1967. OHC, JFKL.

Blight, James G. *The Shattered Crystal Ball: Fear and Learning in the Cuban Missile Crisis.* Savage, Maryland: Rowman and Littlefield, 1990.

Blight, James G., Bruce J. Allyn, and David A. Welch. *Cuba on the Brink:*

Castro, The Missile Crisis and the Soviet Collapse. New York: Pantheon, 1993.

Blight, James G., and Philip Brenner. *Sad and Luminous Days: Cuba's Secret Struggle with the Superpowers after the Missile Crisis.* Lanham, Maryland: Rowman and Littlefield, 2002.

Blight, James G., and Peter Kornbluh, eds. *Politics of Illusion: The Bay of Pigs Invasion Reexamined.* Boulder, Colorado: Lynne Rienner, 1998.

Blight, James G and David A. Welch. "The Cuban Missile Crisis and Intelligence Performance." In James G. Blight and David A. Welch, eds., *Intelligence and the Cuban Missile Crisis.* London: Frank Cass, 1998, 173–217.

Blight, James G., Joseph S. Nye, Jr., and David A. Welch." The Cuban Missile Crisis Revisited." *Foreign Affairs 66* (Fall 1987), 170–88.

Blight, James G., and David A. Welch, eds. *Intelligence and the Cuban Missile Crisis.* London: Frank Cass, 1998.

Blight, James G., and David A. Welch. *On the Brink: Americans and Soviets Examine the Cuban Missile Crisis.* New York: Noonday Press, 1989.

Blight, James G., and David A. Welch, "What Can Intelligence Tell Us About the Cuban Missile Crisis, and What Can the Cuban Missile Crisis Tell Us About Intelligence?" In James G. Blight and David A. Welch, eds., *Intelligence and the Cuban Missile Crisis.* London: Frank Cass, 1998, 1–17.

Bohlen, Charles E. *Witness to History, 1929–1969.* New York: W. W. Norton, 1973.

Bohlen, Charles. Oral History Interview, 1964. OHC, JFKL.

Bouck, Robert. Oral History Interview, 1976. OHC, JFKL.

Bowles, Chester. Oral History Interviews, 1965, 1970. OHC, JFKL.

Bradlee, Benjamin. *Conversations With Kennedy.* New York: W. W. Norton, 1975.

Branch, Taylor, and George Crile III. "The Kennedy Vendetta: How the CIA Waged a Silent War Against Cuba." *Harper's Magazine 251* (August 1975), 49–63.

Brenner, Philip. "Thirteen Months: Cuba's Perspective on the Missile Crisis." In James A. Nathan, ed., *The Cuban Missile Crisis Revisited.* New York: St. Martin's, 1992, 187–219.

Brinkley, Douglas. *Dean Acheson: The Cold War Years.* New Haven: Yale University Press, 1992.

Brugioni, Dino. *Eyeball to Eyeball: The Inside Story of the Cuban Missile Crisis,* edited by Robert F. McCort. New York: Random House, 1991.

Bundy, McGeorge. *Danger and Survival: Choices About the Bomb in the First Fifty Years.* New York: Random House, 1998.

Caldwell, Dan. *The Cuban Missile Crisis Affair and the American Style of Crisis Management.* Santa Monica, California: Rand Corporation, 1989.

Chace, James. *Acheson: The Secretary of State Who Created the American World.* New York: Random House, 1998.

Chang, Laurence. "The View from Washington and the View from Nowhere:

Cuban Missile Crisis Historiography and the Epistemology of Decision Making," In James A. Nathan, ed., *The Cuban Missile Crisis Revisited.* New York: St. Martin's, 1992, 131–60.

Charyk, Joseph. Oral History Interview, 1968. OHC, JFKL.

Chayes, Abram. *The Cuban Missile Crisis.* New York: Oxford University Press, 1974.

Chayes, Abram. Oral History Interview, 1964. OHC, JFKL.

Cleveland, Harlan. Oral History Interview, 1978. OHC, JFKL.

Cohn, Elizabeth. "President Kennedy's Decision to Impose a Blockade in the Cuban Missile Crisis: Building Consensus in the ExComm After the Decision." In James A. Nathan, ed., *The Cuban Missile Crisis Revisited.* New York: St. Martin's, 1992, 219–38.

Courtois, Stephanie, *et al. The Black Book of Communism: Crimes, Terror, Repression.* Cambridge, Mass.: Harvard University Press, 1999.

Dallek, Robert. "Tales of the Tapes." *Reviews in American History* 26 (1998), 333–38.

Detzer, David. *The Brink: Cuban Missile Crisis, 1962.* New York: Crowell, 1979.

Dillon, C. Douglas. Oral History Interview, 1964. OHC, JFKL.

Divine, Robert A., ed. *The Cuban Missile Crisis.* New York: M. Wiener, 1988.

Dobrynin, Anatoly. *In Confidence: Moscow's Ambassador to America's Six Cold War Presidents.* New York: Random House, 1995.

Domínguez, Jorge E. "The @#$%& Missile Crisis: (Or, What Was Cuban about U.S. Decisions During the Cuban Missile Crisis?)." *Diplomatic History* 24 (Spring 2000), 305–15.

Fawcett, Stephanie. "The JFK White House Recordings." Unpublished paper presented to the Society for Historians of American Foreign Relations, 1997.

Foot, M. R. D. "How On Earth Did We Win?" *The Times* 2 (May 17, 2001), 2–4.

Freedman, Lawrence. *Kennedy's Wars: Berlin, Cuba, Laos and Vietnam.* New York: Oxford University Press, 2000.

Fursenko, Aleksandr, and Timothy Naftali. "Soviet Intelligence and the Cuban Missile Crisis." In James G. Blight and David A. Welch, eds., *Intelligence and the Cuban Missile Crisis.* London: Frank Cass, 1998, 64–87.

Fursenko, Aleksandr, and Timothy Naftali. *"One Hell of a Gamble": Khrushchev, Castro and Kennedy, 1958–1964.* New York: W. W. Norton, 1997.

Gaddis, John Lewis. *We Now Know: Rethinking Cold War History.* New York: Oxford. University Press, 1997.

Gaddis, John Lewis. *The Long Peace: Inquiries into the History of the Cold War.* New York: Oxford University Press, 1987.

Garthoff, Raymond L. "Berlin, 1961: The Record Corrected." *Foreign Policy* 84 (Fall 1991), 142–56.

Garthoff, Raymond L. "The Cuban Missile Crisis: An Overview." In James A. Nathan, ed., *The Cuban Missile Crisis Revisited*. New York: St. Martin's, 1992, 41–54.

Garthoff, Raymond L. "Documenting the Cuban Missile Crisis." *Diplomatic History* 24 (Spring 2000), 297–303.

Garthoff, Raymond L. *Intelligence Assessment and Policymaking: A Decision Point in the Kennedy Administration*. Washington, D. C.: Brookings, 1984.

Garthoff, Raymond L. "New Evidence on the Cuban Missile Crisis: Khrushchev, Nuclear Weapons, and the Cuban Missile Crisis." *CWIHPB 11* (Winter 1998), 251–62.

Garthoff, Raymond L. *Reflections on the Cuban Missile Crisis*. Rev. ed. Washington, D.C.: Brookings, 1989.

Garthoff, Raymond L. "US Intelligence in the Cuban Missile Crisis." In James G. Blight and David A. Welch, eds., *Intelligence and the Cuban Missile Crisis*. London: Frank Cass, 1998, 18–63.

George, Alexander. "The Cuban Missile Crisis." In Alexander George, ed., *Avoiding War: Problems of Crisis Management*. Boulder, Colo.: Westview Press, 1991, 222–68.

Gilpatric, Roswell. Oral History Interview, 1970. OHC, JFKL.

Goodwin, Richard. *Remembering America: A Voice from the Sixties*. Boston: Little, Brown, 1988.

Gordon, Lincoln. Oral History Interview, 1964. OHC, JFKL.

Gribkov, Anatoli I. "The View from Moscow and Havana." In Anatoli I. Gribkov and William Y. Smith, *Operation ANADYR: U.S. and Soviet Generals Recount the Cuban Missile Crisis*. Chicago: Edition Q, 1994, 3–76.

Hamilton, Nigel. *JFK: Reckless Youth*. New York: Random House, 1992.

Harlech, Lord (William David Ormsby-Gore). Oral History Interview, 1964. OHC, JFKL.

Haynes, John Earl, and Harvey Klehr. *Venona: Decoding Soviet Espionage in America*. New Haven: Yale University Press, 1999.

Hershberg, James G. "Before 'The Missiles of October': Did Kennedy Plan a Military Strike Against Cuba?" *Diplomatic History* 14 (Spring 1990), 163–98; also in different form in James G. Blight and David A. Welch, eds., *Intelligence and the Cuban Missile Crisis*. London: Frank Cass, 1998, 237–80.

Hershberg, Jim. "More On Bobby and the Cuban Missile Crisis." *CWIHPB* 8–9 (Winter 1996–97), 274–77.

Hilsman, Roger. *The Cuban Missile Crisis: The Struggle Over Policy*. Westport, Conn.: Praeger, 1996.

Hilsman, Roger. Oral History Interview, 1970. OHC, JFKL.

Hilsman, Roger. *To Move a Nation: The Politics of Foreign Policy in the Administration of John F. Kennedy*. Garden City, New York: Doubleday, 1967.

Holland, Max. "A Luce Connection: Senator Keating, William Pawley, and the Cuban Missile Crisis." *Journal of Cold War Studies I* (Fall 1999), 139–67.

Hurwitch, Robert A. Oral History Interview, 1964. OHC, JFKL.

Isaacson, Walter, and Evan Thomas. *The Wise Men.* New York: Simon and Schuster, 1986.

Johnson, U. Alexis. Oral History Interview, 1964. OHC, JFKL.

Kaplan, Fred. "JFK's First-Strike Plan." *Atlantic Monthly* 288 (October 2001), 81–86.

Kaplan, Fred. "Kennedy Legacy Shines..." *Boston Globe.* January 13, 2001.

Kaplan, Fred. *The Wizards of Armageddon.* Stanford, California: Stanford University Press, 1991.

Kaysen, Carl. Oral History Interview, 1966. OHC, JFKL.

Kennan, George F. *Memoirs: 1950–1963.* Boston: Little, Brown, 1967.

Kennedy, Robert F. Oral History Interview, 1964, 1965, 1967. OHC, JFKL.

Kennedy, Robert F. *Thirteen Days: A Memoir of the Cuban Missile Crisis.* New York: W. W. Norton, 1999 edition.

Khrushchev, Sergei. *Nikita Khrushchev and the Creation of a Superpower.* University Park, Pennsylvania: Pennsylvania State University Press, 2000.

Klehr, Harvey, John Earl Haynes, and Kyrill M. Anderson. *The Soviet World of American Communism.* New Haven, Conn: Yale University Press, 1998.

Kornbluh, Peter, ed. "Kennedy and Castro: The Secret Quest for Accommodation." National Security Archive Electronic Briefing Book No. 17.

Kramer, Mark. "New Evidence on Soviet Decision-Making and the 1956 Polish and Hungarian Crises." *CWIHPB 8–9* (Winter 1996–97), 358–84.

Lansdale, Edward G. Oral History Interview, 1970. OHC, JFKL.

Lebow, Richard N., and Janice G. Stein. *We All Lost the Cold War.* Princeton, New Jersey: Princeton University Press, 1994.

Lovett, Robert. Oral History Interview, 1964. OHC, JFKL.

Mastny, Vojtech. *The Cold War and Soviet Insecurity.* New York: Oxford University Press, 1997.

May, Ernest R., and Philip D. Zelikow. "Camelot Confidential." *Diplomatic History* 22 (Fall 1998), 642–53.

May, Ernest R., and Philip D. Zelikow. *The Kennedy Tapes: Inside the White House During the Cuban Missile Crisis.* Cambridge, Mass.: Harvard University Press, 1997.

Mayers, David. "JFK's Ambassadors and the Cold War." *Diplomacy & Statecraft 11* (November 2000), 183–211.

Naftali, Timothy. "Introduction: Five Hundred Days," in Timothy Naftali, ed., *The Presidential Recordings: John F. Kennedy: The Great Crises, Volume 1.* New York: W. W. Norton, 2001, xli–liv.

Naftali, Timothy. "The Origins of 'Thirteen Days.'" *Miller Center Report 15* (Summer 1999), 23–24.

Nash, Philip. *The Other Missiles of October: Eisenhower, Kennedy and the*

Jupiters, 1957–1963. Chapel Hill, North Carolina: University of North Carolina Press, 1997.

Nathan, James A., ed. *The Cuban Missile Crisis Revisited.* New York: St. Martin's, 1992.

Nitze, Paul H. (with Ann M. Smith and Steven L. Reardon). *From Hiroshima to Glasnost: At The Center of Decision: A Memoir.* New York: Grove Weidenfeld, 1989.

O'Donnell, Kenneth, and David Powers, with Joe McCarthy. *Johnny We Hardly Knew Ye: Memories of John Fitzgerald Kennedy.* Boston: Little, Brown, 1970.

Parmet, Herbert S. *Jack: The Struggles of John F. Kennedy.* New York: Doubleday, 1980.

Paterson, Thomas G. "Fixation with Cuba: The Bay of Pigs, Missile Crisis, and Covert War Against Fidel Castro." In Thomas G. Paterson, ed., *Kennedy's Quest for Victory: American Foreign Policy, 1961–1963.* New York: Oxford University Press, 1989, 123–55.

Paterson, Thomas G. "John F. Kennedy's Quest for Victory and Global Crisis." In Thomas G. Paterson, ed., *Kennedy's Quest for Victory: American Foreign Policy, 1961–1963.* New York: Oxford University Press, 1989, 3–23.

Paterson, Thomas G., ed. *Kennedy's Quest for Victory: American Foreign Policy, 1961–1963.* New York: Oxford University Press, 1989.

Paterson, Thomas G. "When Fear Ruled: Rethinking the Cuban Missile Crisis." *New England Journal of History 52* (Fall 1995), 12–37.

Perret, Geoffrey. *Jack: A Life Like No Other.* New York: Random House, 2001.

Powaski, Ronald E. *The Entangling Alliance: The United States and European Security, 1950–1993.* Westport, Conn.: Greenwood, 1994.

Rabe, Stephen G. "Controlling Revolutions: Latin America, the Alliance for Progress, and Cold War Anti-Communism." In Thomas G. Paterson, ed., *Kennedy's Quest for Victory: American Foreign Policy, 1961–1963.* New York: Oxford University Press, 1989, 105–22.

Rabe, Stephen G. "After the Missiles of October: John F. Kennedy and Cuba, November 1962 to November 1963." *Presidential Studies Quarterly 30* (December 2000), 714–26.

Rabe, Stephen G. *The Most Dangerous Area in the World: John F. Kennedy Confronts Communist Revolution in Latin America.* Chapel Hill, North Carolina: University of North Carolina Press, 1999.

Reedy, George. *Lyndon B. Johnson: A Memoir.* Kansas City, Missouri: Andrews McMeel, 1982.

Reeves, Richard. *President Kennedy: Profile of Power.* New York: Simon and Schuster, 1993.

Rostow, Walt W. Oral History Interview, 1964. OHC, JFKL.

Rusk, Dean, as told to Richard Rusk. *As I Saw It.* New York: W. W. Norton, 1990.

Rusk, Dean. Oral History Interview, 1970. OHC, JFKL.

Sagan, Scott. *Moving Targets: Nuclear Strategy and National Security.* Princeton, New Jersey: Princeton University Press, 1989.

Sagan, Scott. *The Limits of Safety: Organizations, Accidents and Nuclear Weapons.* Princeton, New Jersey: Princeton University Press, 1995.

Salinger, Pierre. *With Kennedy.* Garden City, New York: Doubleday, 1966.

Salinger, Pierre. *John F. Kennedy: Commander in Chief.* New York: Penguin, 1997.

Scali, John. Oral History Interview, 1982. OHC, JFKL.

Schechter, Jerrold, ed. and trans. *Khrushchev Remembers: The Glasnost Tapes.* Boston: Little, Brown, 1990.

Schefter, James. *The Race.* New York: Doubleday, 1999.

Schlesinger, Arthur M., Jr. *A Thousand Days: John F. Kennedy in the White House.* Boston: Houghton Mifflin, 1965.

Schlesinger, Arthur M., Jr. *Robert Kennedy and His Times.* Boston: Houghton Mifflin, 1978.

Schoenbaum, Thomas J. *Waging Peace and War: Dean Rusk in the Truman, Kennedy and Johnson Years.* New York: Simon and Schuster, 1988.

Shoup, David M. Oral History Interview, 1967. OHC, JFKL.

Sidey, Hugh. *John F. Kennedy, President.* New York: Atheneum, 1964.

Sidey, Hugh. Introduction to *Prelude to Leadership: The European Diary of John F. Kennedy—Summer 1945.* Washington, D.C.: Regnery, 1995, xv–xlv.

Smathers, George. Oral History Interview, 1964. OHC JFKL.

Smith, William Y. "The View from Washington." In Anatoli I. Gribkov and William Y. Smith, *Operation ANAYDR: U.S. and Soviet Generals Recount the Cuban Missile Crisis.* Chicago: Edition Q, 1994, 79–159.

Sorensen, Theodore C. *Kennedy.* New York: Harper and Row, 1965.

Sorensen, Theodore. Oral History Interview, 1964. OHC, JFKL.

Steel, Ronald. *Walter Lippmann and the American Century.* Boston: Little, Brown, 1980.

Stern, Sheldon M. "What JFK Really Said." *Atlantic Monthly 285* (May 2000), 122–28.

Stern, Sheldon M. "Response to Zelikow and May." *Presidential Studies Quarterly 30* (December 2000), 797–99.

Stern, Sheldon M. "Source Material: The 1997 Published Transcripts of the JFK Cuban Missile Crisis Tapes: Too Good to be True?" *Presidential Studies Quarterly 30* (September 2000), 586–93.

Stern, Sheldon M. "The JFK Tapes: Round Two." *Reviews in American History 30* (December 2002), 680–88.

Sweig, Julia. *Inside the Cuban Revolution: Fidel Castro and the Urban Underground.* Cambridge, Mass.: Harvard University Press, 2002.

Talbott, Strobe, ed. and trans. *Khrushchev Remembers.* Boston: Little, Brown, 1970.

Talbott, Strobe, ed. and trans. *Khrushchev Remembers: The Last Testament.* Boston: Little, Brown, 1974.

Taylor, Maxwell. Oral History Interview, 1964. OHC, JFKL.

Thomas, Evan. *Robert Kennedy: His Life.* New York: Simon and Schuster, 2000.

Thompson, Llewellyn. Oral History Interview, 1964, 1966. OHC, JFKL.

Thompson, Robert Smith. *The Missiles of October: The Declassified Story of John F. Kennedy and the Cuban Missile Crisis.* New York: Simon & Schuster, 1992.

Uhl, Matthias, and Vladimir I. Ivkin. "'Operation Atom': The Soviet Union's Stationing of Nuclear Missiles in the German Democratic Republic, 1959." *CWIHPB 12/13* (Fall/Winter 2001), 299–307.

Utz, Curtis. *Cordon of Steel: The U.S. Navy and the Cuban Missile Crisis.* Washington, D.C.: Naval Historical Society, 1993.

Weathersby, Kathryn. "New Findings on the Korean War." *CWIHPB 3* (Fall 1993), 1, 14–18.

Weinstein, Allen, and Alexander Vassiliev. *The Haunted Wood: Soviet Espionage in America—The Stalin Era.* New York: Random House, 1999.

Welch, David A., ed. "Proceedings of the Hawk's Cay Conference on the Cuban Missile Crisis." Cambridge, Mass.: Center for Science and International Affairs, 1989.

Welch, David A. and James G. Blight. "The Eleventh Hour of the Cuban Missile Crisis: An Introduction to the ExComm Transcripts." *International Security 12* (Winter 1987–88), 5–29.

White, Mark J. *Missiles in Cuba: Kennedy, Khrushchev, Castro and the 1962 Crisis.* Chicago: Ivan R. Dee, 1997.

White, Mark J. *The Cuban Missile Crisis.* London: Macmillan, 1996.

Wilson, Donald M. Oral History Interview, 1964, 1972. OHC, JFKL.

Zelikow, Philip. "American Policy and Cuba, 1961–1963." *Diplomatic History 24* (Spring 2000), 323–26.

Zelikow, Philip D., and Ernest R. May. "Source Material: Controversy: The Kennedy Tapes: Past and Future." *Presidential Studies Quarterly 30* (December 2000), 791–96.

Zelikow, Philip, Timothy Naftali, and Ernest May, eds. *The Presidential Recordings: John F. Kennedy: Volumes 1–3, The Great Crises.* New York: W. W. Norton, 2001.

Zubok, Vladislav, and Constantine Pleshakov. *Inside the Kremlin's Cold War: From Stalin to Khrushchev.* Cambridge, Mass.: Harvard University Press, 1996.

Index

In this index an "f" after a number indicates a separate reference on the next page, and an "ff" indicates separate references on the next two pages. A continuous discussion over two or more pages is indicated by a span of page numbers, e.g., "57–59." *Passim* is used for a cluster of references in close but not consecutive sequence. References indexed directly from the ExComm meetings include dates as well as page numbers, e.g., "Kennedy, John F., preliminary decision to strike missile sites (10/16), 75."